Flat Pattern Cutting and Modelling for Fashion

Third Edition

Also published by Stanley Thornes (Publishers) Ltd:

Martin Shoben and Patrick Taylor, *Grading for the Fashion Industry*, Second Edition
(ISBN 0 7487 0423 X)

Flat Pattern Cutting and Modelling for Fashion

Third Edition

Helen Stanley, ACFI, MCSD
Lecturer in Fashion
London College of Fashion
and
The American College in London

Stanley Thornes (Publishers) Ltd

© Helen Stanley 1972, 1982, 1983, 1991

All rights reserved. No part of this publication may be reproduced or transmitted in any form or by any means, electronic or mechanical, including photocopy, recording, or any information storage and retrieval system, without permission in writing from the publisher or under licence from the Copyright Licensing Agency Limited. Further details of such licences (for reprographic reproduction) may be obtained from the Copyright Licensing Agency Limited, of 33–4 Alfred Place, London WC1E 7DP.

First published as *Modelling and Flat Cutting for Fashion – from Design to Pattern* in 1972, reprinted 1975, 1977, 1981.

Second edition published as *Modelling and Flat Cutting for Fashion 1* in 1983, reprinted 1986 (Hutchinson Education).

Modelling and Flat Cutting for Fashion 2 and *Modelling and Flat Cutting for Fashion 3* first published in 1982 (Hutchinson Education).

Third edition, combining all 3 volumes, published in 1991 by:
Stanley Thornes (Publishers) Ltd
Old Station Drive
Leckhampton
CHELTENHAM GL53 0DN
UK

British Library Cataloguing in Publication Data

Stanley, Helen
  Flat Pattern Cutting and Modelling for Fashion – 3rd ed.
  1. Women's Clothing. Making Patterns. Cutting & design
  I. Title
  646.4072

ISBN 0-7487-0427-2

Typeset by Tek Art Ltd, Addiscombe, Croydon, Surrey
Printed and bound in Great Britain at The Bath Press, Avon

Contents

Preface   vii
Abbreviations   viii
Introduction   1
    One-fifth scale blocks
    Metric size chart
    Imperial size chart
    Equipment

1 Drafting the basic blocks   10
    The waist block
    The dress skirt block
    The tailored skirt block
    The basic sleeve block
    The trouser block

2 Waist bodice and darts   18
    Preparing the dress form for modelling
    Modelling the front waist block
    Modelling the back waist block
    Modelling the bodice darts
    Modelling the hip blocks or dress foundation
    Moving darts by the slashing method
    Block development
    Principles of pivoting
    Making the card block or foundation pattern

3 Bodice styling   38
    Gathers, yokes and pleats
    Button closings and facings
    Blouse and shirt developments

4 Strapless bodices and vertical seams   50
    Comparison of measurements
    Bust formation influence on seam placement
    Princess lines
    Jackets

5 Necklines and collars   60
    Bateau and round neckline
    Square and V-necklines
    Raised necklines
    The basic hood
    Necklines of sleeveless bodices
    Flat collars
    Roll collars
    Revers collars
    Stand collars
    Flat cutting of collars
    Roll collars cut flat
    Three shirt collars
    Adding collar stands
    Basic collars and different necklines
    Grown-on wing collar cut flat
    Tuxedo collar
    Jabots and other neck finishes

6 Modelling in the garment fabric   79
    Developing the design
    Cutting on the bias

7 Sleeves   84
    Set-in sleeve cut flat
    The shirt sleeve
    The Bishop sleeve
    Sleeves gathered at crown
    Raglan sleeves
    Position of the shoulder seam
    Centralising the bodice and sleeve blocks
    Kimono block development
    Dolman sleeve
    Modelling of basic sleeves
    The kimono sleeve

8 Skirts   106
    Skirts
    Preparing the form
    Modelling the straight two-piece skirt
    Gathered tiered skirt
    Long skirt with godets
    Modelling the flared skirt
    Gored skirts
    Skirt with front seaming and gathers
    Skirt with yoke feature and gathers – modelled
    Wrap-over skirt with side pleats
    Half circle skirt – modelled
    Full circle skirt – cut flat
    Quarter circle skirt – cut flat
    Straight skirts

9 Cowl drapery   124
    Cowl necklines
    Underarm cowl
    Cowl drapery in sleeves
    Cowl skirts

10 Wedding dresses   136
    Trains
    Wedding dress 1
    Wedding dress 2
    Wedding dress 3
    Underskirts
    Full length veil

11 Trousers 151
Trouser silhouettes
Trouser development
Constructing the trouser block
Trouser block adaptations
Fitting the trouser block
Jeans
Bloomers
Tracksuit trousers
Jodhpur trousers
Jumpsuit
Dungarees
Ski-suit
Culottes
The dress foundation or hip block

12 The jacket block and two-piece sleeve 176
Jacket block development
Blazer jacket with side body
Two-piece sleeve for a jacket

13 Lingerie 182
Slips and cami-knickers
Camisoles, teddies and cropped t-shirt tops
Lingerie panties
Briefs, panties and trunks
Cami-knickers based on the panties block
Basic slip – cut flat
Basic cami-knickers
Princess line slip
Cami-knickers – princess line variation
Basic bra-slip
Cami-knickers – bra variation
Brassieres
Nightdress
Pyjamas with bias piping

14 Maternity wear 204
Method of padding a dress form
Development of the maternity dress block: 1
Development of the maternity dress block: 2
Pleated sleeves for the maternity dress
Maternity smock
Soft collar
Sleeve for maternity smock
Raglan style maternity smock
Waisted maternity garments
Maternity skirt with cascade drapery
Development of the basic maternity skirt cut flat
Basic maternity trousers

15 The technique of good fitting 220
The basic principles of fitting
Fashion and fabrics
Fitting in the wholesale sample room
Fitting for couture and retail dressmaking
Fitting a ready-made garment
The fitting of bodices
The fitting of sleeves
The fitting of skirts

Index 229

Preface

This one-volume edition, revised and with a large amount of new material added, has been compiled from my previous three volumes: *Flat Pattern Cutting and Modelling for Fashion.* By popular demand, particularly from the American College in London, I have added drafting instructions for the basic waist and hip blocks, skirt blocks, sleeve and trouser blocks in addition to the ready-made fifth scale blocks which are presented again in this volume.

Draping or modelling? The first term is used in the USA, the second in the UK, with apologies to my many enthusiastic readers in the United States, I have decided to continue to use the term 'modelling', except when fabric is 'draped' as in cowl drapery. So please, just read 'draping' whenever the term 'modelling' is used in this book.

The programme of work employs both flat pattern cutting and modelling methods and is presented in the familiar form of self-contained 'lessons' with text and diagrams closely related. This feature has proved advantageous to teachers and instructors when preparing course and lesson material and also to students of fashion and clothing following BA and MA degree courses, college diplomas, the BTEC National and Higher National Diploma courses in Clothing and Fashion Design. This volume should continue to be popular with CGLI and GCSE and A–level courses and also with pattern cutters and designers working on their own, in the theatre and television or in industry, and with many lay designers and home dressmakers.

Metric measurements, with imperial values in brackets, are used throughout the book to facilitate the change to the metric system and for the benefit of American readers.

I should like to thank Katherine Baird BA, ALA, chief librarian and Barbara Smith BA, ALA and also Diane Mansbridge, BA, ALA and the whole library staff of the London College of Fashion for their assistance during research.

I should like to express further thanks to Mr Joseph H. Houghton, Director of Education and Vice President and Mr Louis W. Randall, former Director of Education and Vice President, to Marie Aja-Herrera, Program Director and Valerie Johnston, former Program Director of The American College in London for their support and interest.

My acknowledgements and grateful thanks are due to Winant, Towers Ltd, who kindly gave me permission to reproduce the illustrations on pages 82, 135, 136, 137, 160, 165 from *English Women's Clothing in the Present Century* by C. Willet Cunnington, Faber & Faber, 1956. I would like to thank Joanne Murray for the figure drawing of the dartless drop-shoulder shirt on page 48.

I am especially grateful to Mary James, Stephanie Richards and Tania Hackett, my editors, for their invaluable advice and guidance during the preparation for press.

Helen Stanley, 1991

Abbreviations

F = Front
B = Back
N – W = Nape to waist
CB = Centre back
CF = Centre front
cm = centimetre
mm = millimetre
m = metre
in = inches
approx. = approximately
BP = Break point
trueing = Improving roughly drawn lines

Introduction

Figure 1

Modern students of dress design and pattern making have one fervent wish: to translate their designs as speedily as possible into finished garments. In their restlessness they are supported by the fashion industry with its large turnover of styles.

The young designer's approach to pattern making is a three dimensional one, the approach of a sculptor to his creation. With an illustration or sketch before him he can work directly on the dress form, modelling and pinning the various sections together on the dress form to achieve the desired effect. He will note seam lines and dart positions, ascertain position and relationship of pockets, buckles and buttons to design and fabric; indicate in pencil stripes, checks and other prominent patterns on the modelling fabric and assess trimmings until satisfied with the 'final look'.

This book upholds the designer's approach. It aims at overcoming the difficulties beginners have in understanding the subject of pattern cutting with all those measurements, fractions and scales. It establishes the fundamental principles of pattern making, beginning with modelling and draping on the dress form. When confidence increases, and with a greater knowledge of the anatomy of the human figure, flat pattern cutting methods are introduced. With practice both methods are used side by side. Indeed, leading designers employ a synthesis of both methods.

When comparing modern dress forms with those of the Edwardian period, it will be noted how much the fashion silhouette has changed (**Figure 1a and b**). Less obvious are the slight changes made every year to provide the designer with a more fashionable silhouette and with, perhaps, new shoulder and side seam placements. Readers are advised to observe current fashion silhouettes and basic seam changes and make small adjustments to their dress forms, e.g. moving seam lines or padding certain parts of the form before modelling. The new lines are then transferred to the basic blocks for further use.

The scheme of work is presented on the principle of beginning each chapter with the most basic pattern developments and gradually leading up to the more complex constructions, often referring to previously covered diagrams and instructions. Immediate use can be made of newly acquired knowledge.

The large quantity of styles produced in the fashion industry, influenced by sociological, ethnic and ergonomic factors, not forgetting periodic fashion changes, demands from today's designer and pattern cutter a greater degree of versatility; a knowledge of pattern making of **bridalwear, bias-cut garments, cowl drapery and boned bodices,** of **jacket development,** various **trouser constructions, lingerie, beachwear and maternitywear.** In view of students' interest in small private businesses, I have included a comprehensive section on the **Technique of Fitting** approached from a different angle than hitherto. I have tried to satisfy those needs in this book.

Important styles, such as cascade drapery, circular sleeve flounce and two-piece sleeve, are incorporated in chapters on maternitywear, wedding dresses and jacket block development. These styles can be extracted and used in the designs of other garments. A glance at the index will help to select the required item.

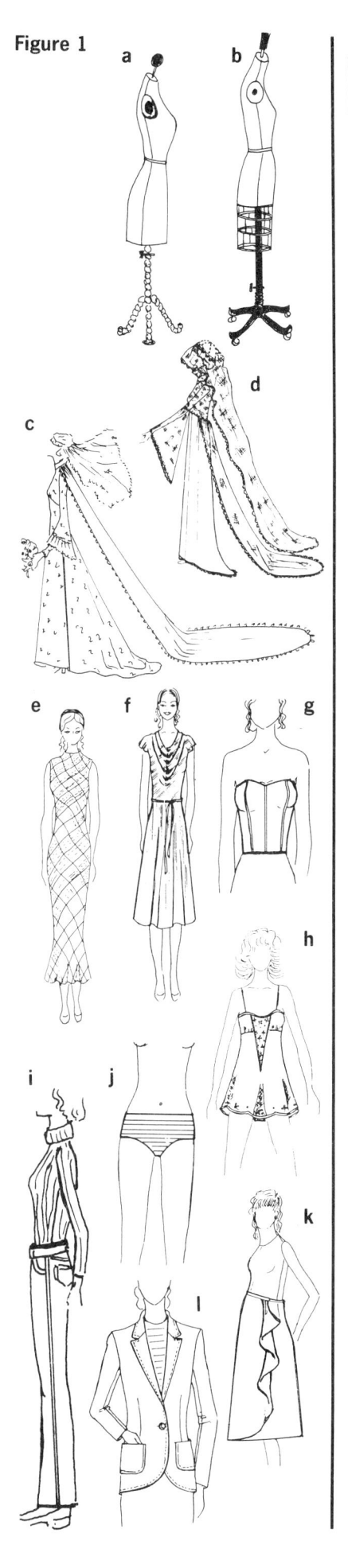

One-fifth scale blocks

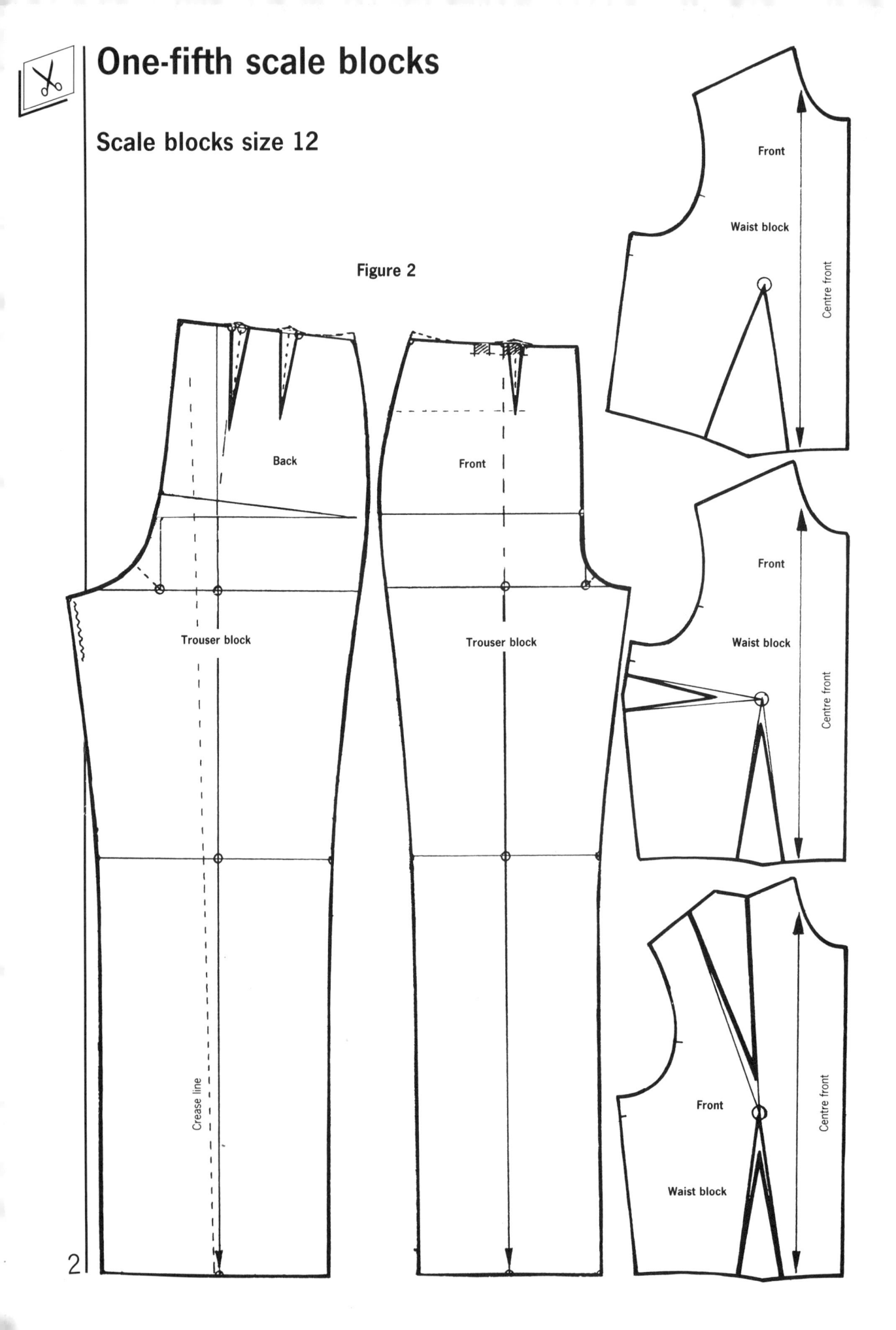

Scale blocks size 12

Figure 2

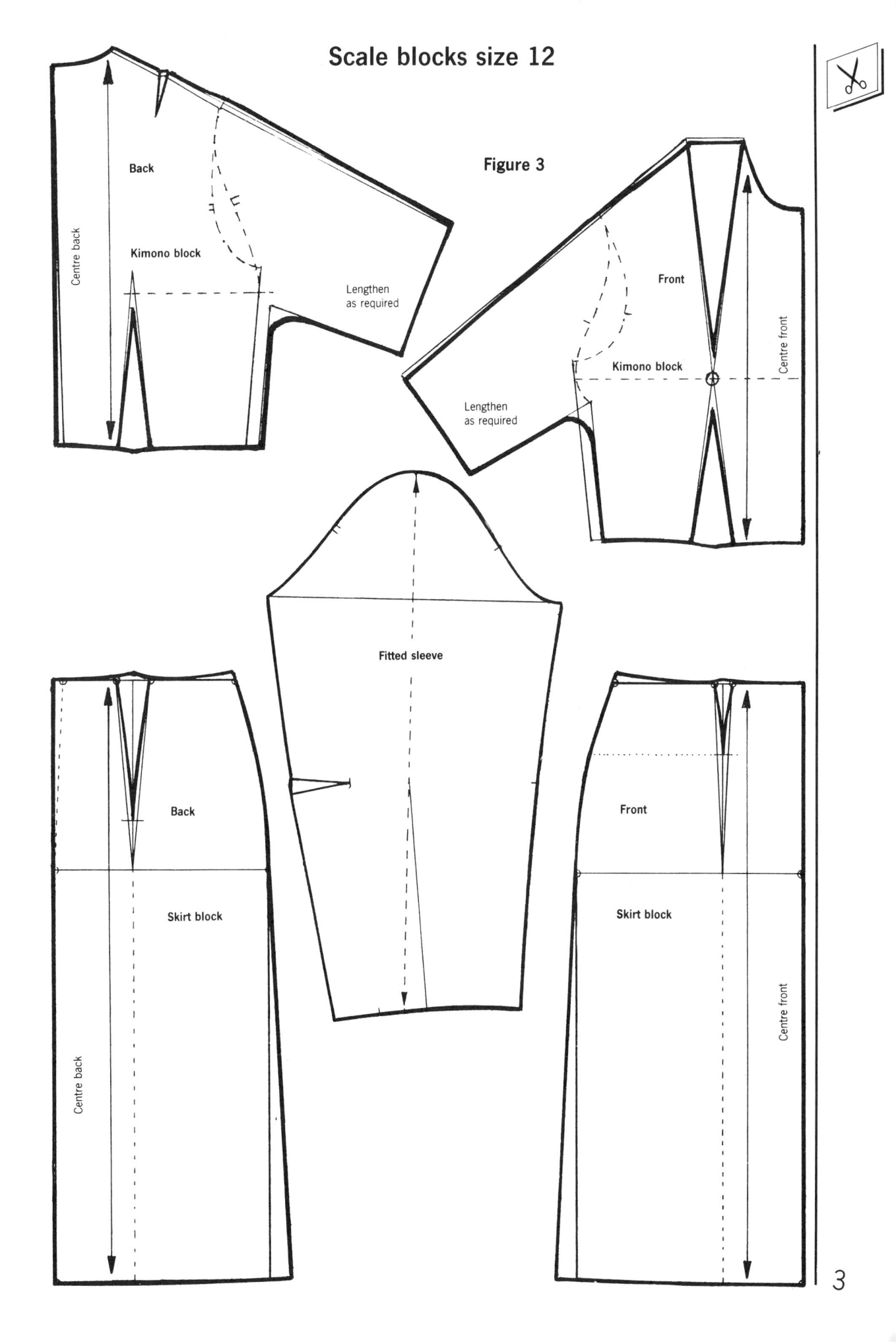

Scale blocks size 12

Figure 3

Scale blocks size 12

Figure 4

Scale blocks size 12

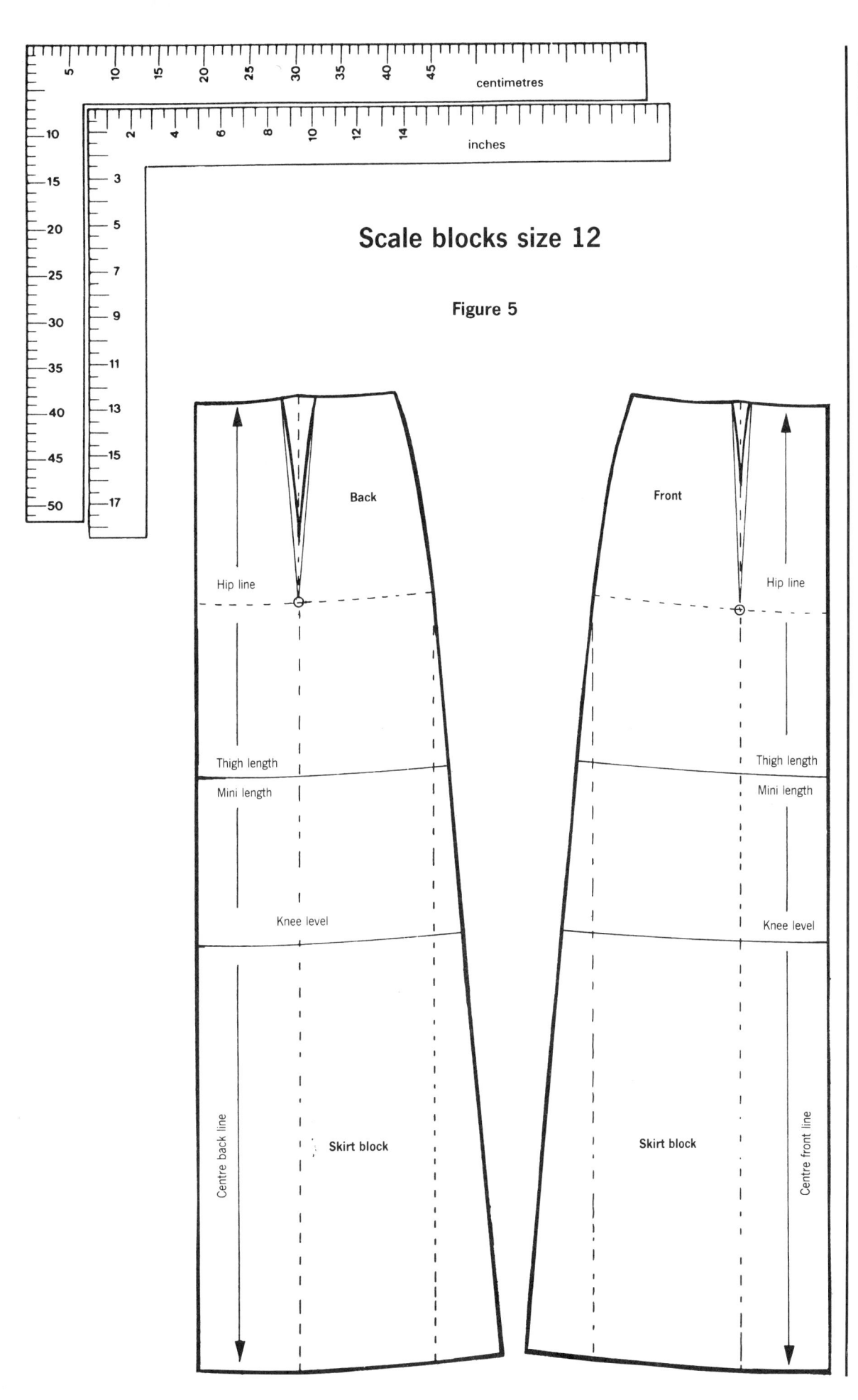

Figure 5

Metric size chart

Based on the average figure of average height of 164–169 cm

Size	38	40	42	44	46
To fit	10	12	14	16	18
Bust from	82 to 86	86–90	90–94	95–99	100–104
Hips from	87 to 91	91–95	95–99	100-104	105–109

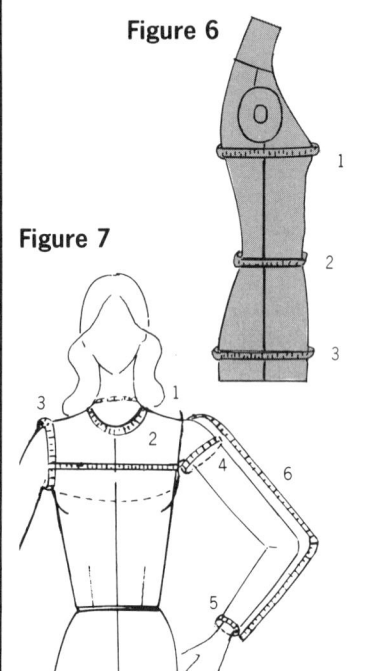

Figure 6

Figure 7

Finished measurements (Figure 6)

		10	12	14	16	18
1	Bust	92	97	102	107	112
2	Waist	66	71	76	81	86
3	Hips (20 cm down from waist)	96.5	101.5	106.5	111.5	116.5

Front and arm measurement (Figure 7)

		10	12	14	16	18
1	Neck girth	37	37.6	38.2	39.4	40.6
2	Across chest (4 cm up from bust line)	34.5	35.5	36.5	37.5	38.5
3	Armhole circumference	41	42	43	44.5	46
4	Upper arm girth taken at armhole point	33	34.2	35.5	37	38
5	Wrist	18.5	19	19.5	20.5	21
6	Sleeve length	57.2	57.2	58.4	59	59.7

Figure 8

Back measurements, length and trouser measurements (Figures 8 and 9)

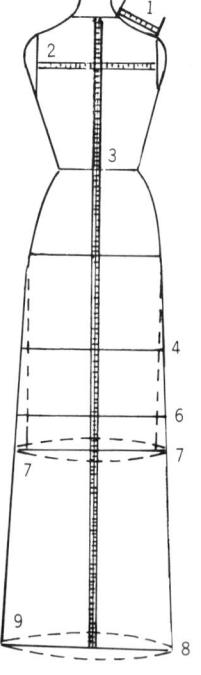

		10	12	14	16	18
1	Shoulder length	12	12.5	13	13.6	14.2
2	Across back (11 cm from nape)	34.5	35.5	37	38	39.5
3	Nape to waist	40	40.5	41.2	41.8	42.5
4a	Body rise from waist	27.5	28	28.5	29	29.5
4	Thigh (miniskirt) level (according to height) 39 cm from waist					
5	Thigh level (half hip to knee) approximately 39 cm from waist					
5	Thigh girth (according to style) from 55–63 cm					
6	Knee level 56–61 cm from waist					
6a	Knee girth (according to style) 40–49–60 cm					
	Skirt length covering knee from waist 65 cm average					
7	Hem circumference (straight skirt)	92	97	102	107	112
8	Full length (according to height) 100–109 cm					
9	Hem circumference slight 'A'-line	126	130	134	138	142
10	Outside leg (according to height)	103	104	104	104.5	104.5
11	Trouser bottom circumference 32–44–60 cm according to style					

Figure 9

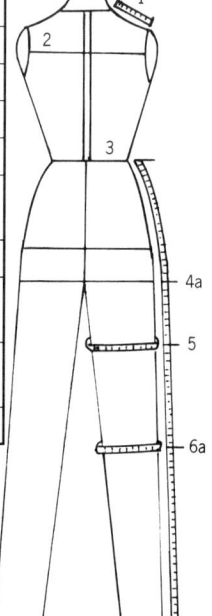

Seam allowances

1.5 to 2.5 cm
Side seams
Sleeve seams
Shoulder seams

1 to 1.5 cm
Armhole/sleeve head
Waist
Panel and style lines

0.5 cm to 0.6 cm
Neckline
Collars
Facings

Imperial size chart
Based on the average figure of average height of 5 ft 4–6 in

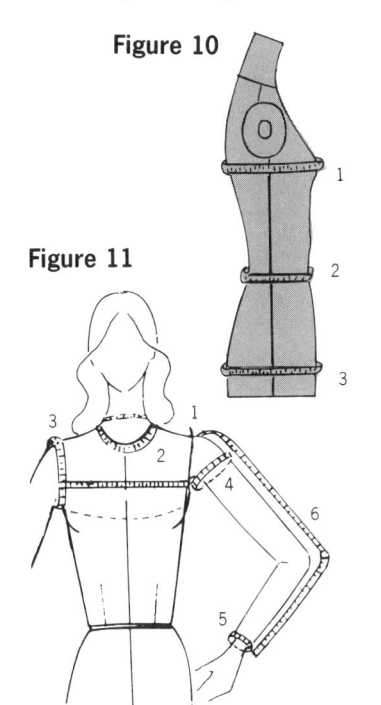

Size	10	12	14	16	18
To fit					
Bust	32	34	36	38	40
Hips	34	36	38	40	42

Figure 10

Figure 11

Finished measurements (Figure 10)

		10	12	14	16	18
1	Bust	36	38	40	42	44
2	Waist	26	28	30	32	34
3	Hips (8 in down from waist)	38	40	42	44	46

Front and arm measurement (Figure 11)

1	Neck girth	14½	14¾	15	15½	16
2	Across chest (1½ in up from bust line)	13⅝	14	14⅜	14¾	15⅛
3	Armhole circumference	16	16½	17	17½	18
4	Upper arm girth taken at armhole point	13	13½	14	14¾	15½
5	Wrist	7¼	7½	7¾	8	8¼
6	Sleeve length	22½	22½	23	23¼	23½

Back measurements, length and trouser measurements (Figures 12 and 13)

Figure 12

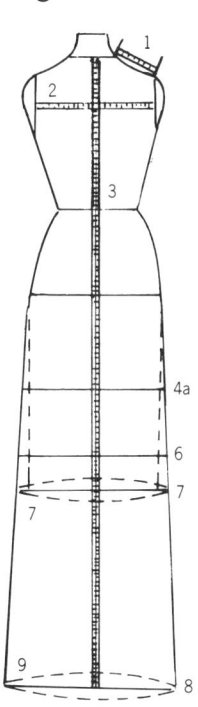

		10	12	14	16	18
1	Shoulder length	4¾	4⅞	5½	5⅜	5⅝
2	Across back (4¼ in from nape)	13½	14	14½	15	15½
3	Nape to waist	15¾	16	16¼	16½	16¾
4	Body rise from waist	10¾	11	11¼	11½	11¾
4a	Thigh (miniskirt) level (according to height) 15½ in from waist					
5	Thigh level (half hip to knee) approximately 15½ in from waist					
5	Thigh girth (according to style) from 21½–25 in					
6	Knee level 22–24 in from waist					
6a	Knee girth (according to style) 15½–19¼–23½ in					
	Skirt length covering knee (from waist) 25½ in average					
7	Hem circumference (straight skirt)	36	38	40	42	44
8	Full length (according to height) 39½–43 in					
9	Hem circumference slight 'A'-line	49½	51	52½	54¼	55¾
10	Outside leg (according to height)	40½	41	41	41⅛	41⅛
11	Trouser bottom circumference 12½–17¼–23½ in according to style					

Figure 13

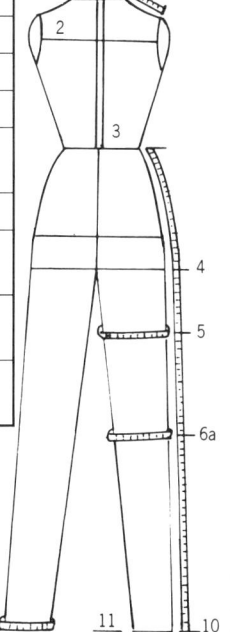

Seam allowances

⅝ to 1 in	½ in	¼ in
Side seams	Armhole/sleeve head	Neckline
Sleeve seams	Waist	Collars
Shoulder seams	Panel and style lines	Facings

7

The dress form

Figure 14 A dress form of the right size and proportions is an utmost necessity for the dress designer. The most suitable form is covered with good quality canvas; it should be fitted to a flat base or solid castors and it should be adjustable in height. A form with collapsible shoulders is well worth the extra cost: it is often difficult to slip a fitted dress over the rigid shoulders of a standard dress form.

Size and measurements must be considered carefully; the dress form represents the size of a fitted finished garment and not the body measurements of the person for whom the dress is intended, i.e. dress form measurements are 'finished measurements' and are standard body measurements plus an allowance for ease (see size charts on **pages 6 and 7**). Size charts in this book are based on the recommended British Standard Sizing Code, but other size charts are also in use. It is advised to consider dress forms of more than one manufacturer before finally purchasing one nearest the required measurements.

A size 14 (continental size 44) dress form is a good average size to work on. Its measurements are small enough to fit a slim woman and it can be padded to fit a larger size. If purchasing dress forms for a workroom, three different sizes are preferable to one form that is adjustable to different sizes. Couture houses are known to pad their forms to the sizes of individual customers. When designing for yourself, a dress form in a size nearest your own measurements is best.

Figure 14

Large cutting table

This must be comfortable to work on in a standing position. A wooden surface is good provided tracing wheel or other marks are not objected to. Formica, or any other very hard surface, is not suitable.

Large set square and metre and/or yard stick

Figure 15 These are essential for drafting accurately at right angles and at 45°. The perspex kind with incised lines for grading, marking seam allowances, etc. is very good, but there are also long arm aluminium set squares which are helpful when squaring longer lines. Made of metal, plastic or wood, the metre or yard stick is essential.

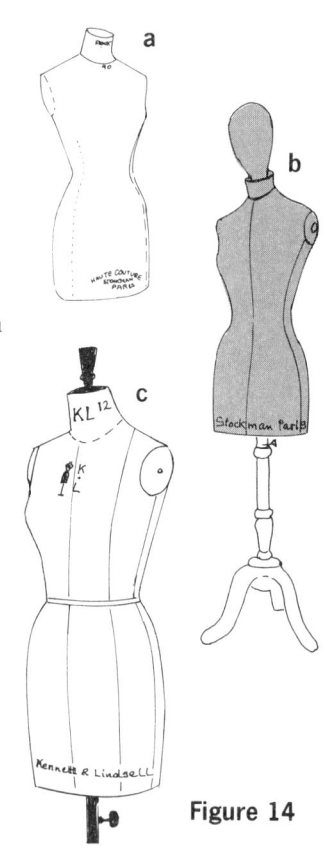

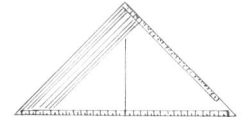

Figure 15 A set square

Aluminium vary curve

Figure 16 This is extremely useful for curving armholes and necklines and slightly curved lines.

Figure 16 Vary curve

Perspex ruler and tape measure

Figure 17 The ruler should be about 45 cm (18 in) long. Both the ruler and the tape measure should have imperial and metric markings.

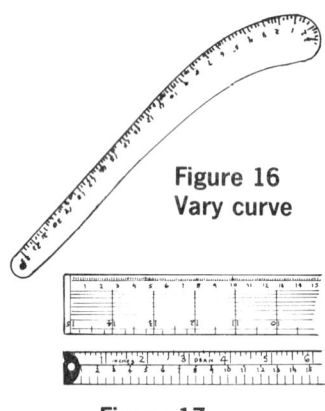

Figure 17 Measuring tools

Cutting shears

Figure 18 These should have long blades and must be sharp and easy to handle.

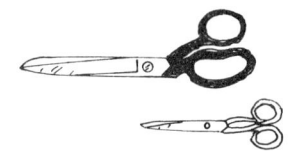

Figure 18 Cutting shears

Pins and pin cushion

Pins are indispensable for modelling on the dress form and for assembling garment sections for sewing. They are made in sizes from 2.5–4.5 cm (1–1¾ in).

Tracing wheel

Figure 19 This is an essential tool and should be of a strong metal construction with a wooden handle.

Figure 19 Tracing wheel

Pattern paper

Figure 20 The choice of pattern paper is very much a matter of individual preference. Some pattern cutters draft on plain white paper, others prefer white 'spotted' lay paper. Its dot and cross markings at 2.5 cm (1 in) intervals, printed at right angles to the edge of the paper, automatically provide the grain line for the pattern. It is possible to use it for modelling blocks and simply styled garments. Its main use in industry is for lay-planning and marker-making.

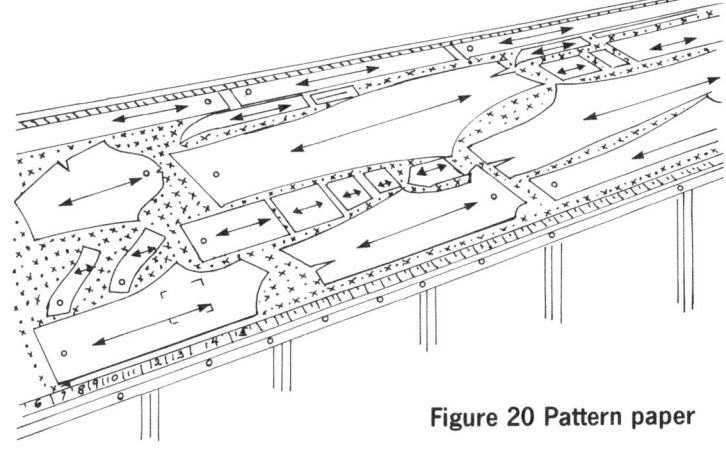

Figure 20 Pattern paper

Pattern card

Two weights are recommended. A heavy card (or a more durable, coloured plastic board) is produced in different colours for basic blocks of various sizes, e.g. green for size 10, blue for size 12, red for size 14, etc. Use a lighter weight card for completed and tested sample patterns which are named, numbered and dated with fabric requirements and sketch of the garment attached. The patterns are then punched and hung on a specially designed pattern rack (see page viii).

Tissue paper, muslin, two weights of unbleached calico (cotton), fine vilene

Select the modelling material that most resembles the weight of your garment fabric, e.g. fine muslin for soft voiles and silks and heavier calicoes for woollen suits. Cheap jersey fabrics and small remnants are also good media for modelling.

Pencils, felt-tipped pens, tailor's chalk

Soft pencils for sketching, very soft pencils, or sometimes felt-tipped pens, for marking style and fitting lines while modelling on the dress form and a hard pencil for pattern drafting are important tools. Held between thumb and forefinger, squares of graphite or tailor's chalk are ideal for drawing armholes and necklines. One or two coloured pencils, felt-tipped pens and coloured tailor's chalk are useful for correcting fitting lines and to distinguish a new line from an old, discarded one. Tailor's chalk is also used for marking onto cloth.

Figure 21
A scriber

Figure 22
Notchers

Other tools

- **Weights** – Hold card blocks in place while outlining; they also hold down slashed pattern sections in the process of development and pattern pieces on cloth prior to marking.
- **Scriber/stiletto (Figure 21)** for marking dart points, etc.
- **Pattern notcher (Figure 22)** for marking seam allowances, balance marks, dart positions and other data.
- **Fifth scale set square/French curve (Figure 23).**
- **Pattern cutting books.**
- **Fashion magazines.**
- **Sketch pads and note books.**

Figure 23
Scale set square and French curve

1 Drafting the basic blocks
The waist block*

Size 12 – All ease and tolerance allowances are included. Finished measurements in centimetres and inches.
Cut a rectangle of pattern paper 48 cm (19 in) long by 56 cm (22 in) wide.
Fold in half widthwise and crease. This crease is the first step (the central tree) in the construction of your waist block.

Central tree (Figure 1.1a)

1	0–1	Equals nape to waist measurement Draw perpendicular line in previously made crease Square to left from 0, square to left and right from 1	40.5 cm (16 in)
2	0–2	Armhole depth; square to left and right	22.5 cm (8⅞ in)
3	0–3	Across back level; halfway between 0–2	10.8 cm (4⅜ in)
4	0–4	Shoulder level; square to left with short line	4.0 cm (1½ in)

Back (Figure 1.1b)

5	2–5	Quarter bust measurement minus 1.25 cm (½ in) Square up and down; mark intersections 5^1, 5^2 and 5^3. This is **centre back** line	23.0 cm (9 in)
6	5–6 6–6^1	Half back neck width Back neck/shoulder point; square up; curve 5–6^1 for back neckline	6.7 cm (2⅝ in) 1.5 cm (⅝ in)
7	6^1–7	Shoulder length plus 1.0 cm (⅜ in) touching shoulder level line	13.5 cm (5¼ in)
8	5^1–8 7–8–2 9–9^1	Half across back measurement. Square down to 9 Draw back armhole Waist dart position Halfway 5–9; square down to 9^2	17.8 cm (7 in)
		The shoulder dart is optional and is omitted when it is intended to 'ease' the back shoulder seam into the front shoulder seam. Drafting instructions for dart: mark dart position in centre of shoulder; mark 6.3 cm (2½ in) on armhole line down from shoulder point; square out 6.3 cm (2½ in); connect with previously marked shoulder point. This obtains a dart angle parallel to armhole line. The dart is 5–6 cm (2–2½ in) long and 1.0 cm (⅜ in) deep.	

Front (Figure 1.1c)

	2–10	Quarter bust measurement 24.25 cm (9½ in) plus 1.25 cm (½ in); square up and then down to 10^1	25.5 cm (10 in)
	10–10^2	Equals 5–5^2 22.5 cm (8⅞ in) plus 2 cm (¾ in) connect to 10^1 This is **centre front** line. Square to left	24.5 cm (9⅝ in)
9	10^2–10^3	Neck base and shoulder level line; square to left	7.5 cm (3 in)
10	10–10^4	Chest level line – from bust line up; square to left	4.0 cm (1½ in)
	10^2–11	Front neck width, equals 5^2–6 minus 0.2 cm (⅛ in)	6.5 cm (2½ in)
11	11–11^1 11–11^2 11^3 11^3–11^4 11^5 11–11^4–11^1 11–10^3 11^1–12	Dart width Centre of 11–11^1 square down to waistline Intersection with armhole depth line True bust line position – **bust point** Intersection with waist line Draw dart Draw neckline Shoulder length, touching horizontal line	7.0 cm (2¾ in) 3.5 cm (1⅜ in) 2.5 cm (1 in) 12.5 cm (4⅞ in)
12	10^4–12^1	Half across chest (omit dart when measuring); square up a short distance and down	18.4 cm (7¼ in)
	13 12–12^1–2 2–2^1	Squared down from 12^1 Draw front armhole True bust level – draw dotted line	2.5 cm (1 in)
13		Waist suppression is determined by the waist measurement and by the degree of close-fitting that is required	
	10^1–10^5	Lowered waistline; connect as shown	1.2 cm (½ in)

*For hip block/dress foundation, see page 176.

1 Drafting the basic blocks

In order of drafting:

		10		12		14		16	
		cm	in	cm	in	cm	in	cm	in
1	Nape to waist	40.0	15¾	40.5	16	41.5	16¼	42	16½
2	Armhole depth	21.5	8½	22.5	8⅞	23.5	9¼	24.5	9⅞
3	Back width level	10.0	4	10.8	4¼	11.1	4⅜	11.4	4½
4	Shoulder level	3.7	1½	4.0	1½	4.0	1⅝	4.0	1⅝
5	Bust	92.0	36	97.0	38	102.0	40	107.0	42
6	Half back neck width	6.5	2⅝	6.7	2⅝	7.0	2¾	7.5	3
7	Shoulder length	12.0	4¾	12.5	4⅞	13.0	5⅛	13.6	5⅜
8	Across back measurement	34.5	13½	35.5	14	37	14½	38.0	15
9	Front neck level	7.5	3	7.5	3	7.5	3	7.5	3
10	Chest level	4.0	1½	4.0	1½	4.0	1½	4.0	1½
11	Dart width	6.5	2½	7.0	2¾	7.5	3	8.0	3⅛
12	Across chest measurement	35.5	14	36.8	14½	38.1	15	39.5	15½
13	Waist (for this draft)	66.0	26	68.5	27	71.0	29	74.0	30¾

Figure 1.1a The Central Tree

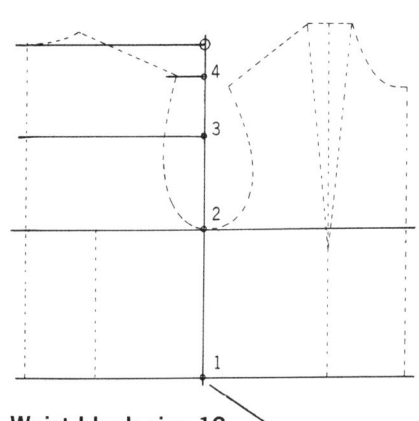

Trace blocks on to new paper. Add seam allowances; cut out; pin darts and seams together. True all lines, particularly armholes at shoulder and side seam underarm position and also at waist line. Pin dress form or person with same measurements. Observe the fit and make any adjustments if required. Move the front shoulder dart to other positions by either the slashing or the pivoting method (Figure 1.2).

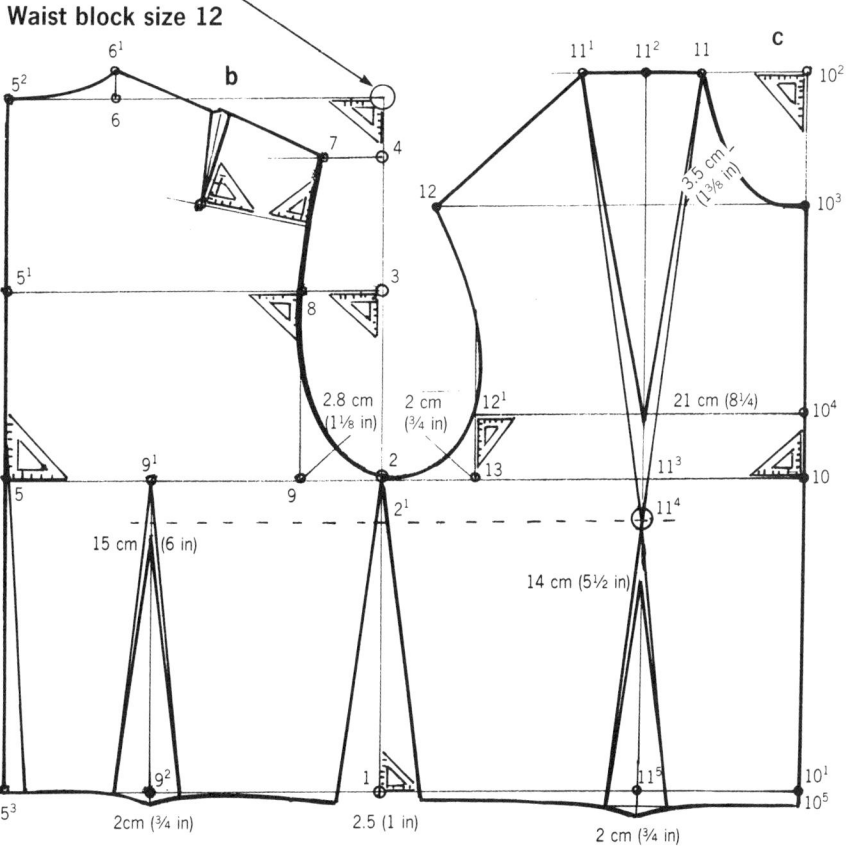

Figure 1.2 Other waist blocks

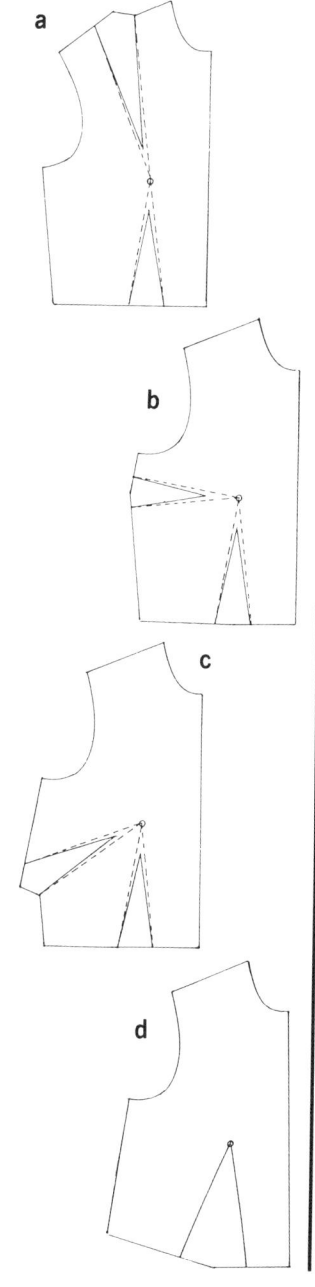

Waist block size 12

The dress skirt block

1 Drafting the basic blocks

Size 12

Ease and tolerance allowances are included in the measurements. Cut a rectangle of pattern paper 69 cm (29 in) long by 56 cm (22 in) wide as waist block.

1	**Figure 1.3** 0–1	**The central tree** Equals skirt length measurement, this line represents the side seam line Square out at 0 to left and right; name waist line Square out at 1 to left and right; name hem line	65.0 cm (25½ in)
	0–2	Equals hip level measurement Square to left and right; name hip line The distance from the waist to the largest part of the hips can vary from 18–24 cm (7–9½ in) according to height and figure	20.0 cm (8 in)
2	**Figure 1.4** 2–2^1	The front skirt, here, is wider by 2.5 cm (1 in) across waist, hips and hemline than the back skirt and corresponds with **the waist bodice (Figure 1.2)** Equals half front hip measurement Square up and down to meet waist and hem lines; name centre front. Mark 0^1 and 1^1	25.5 cm (10 in)
	2–2^2	Equals half back hip measurement Square up and down to meet waist and hem lines; name centre back, Mark 0^2 and 1^2	24.0 cm (9½ in)
3	2^2–2^3	Deduct half waist measurement from half hip measurement: 49.5–34.3 cm = 15.2 cm (19½–13½ in = 6 in) This is the amount by which the hip measurement is reduced by darting to fit the waist closely and comfortably. The position of the darts and the shaped side seams must correspond with those of the waist bodice Represents centre position of back waist dart Square up to meet waist line. Mark point 0^3	9.0 cm (3½ in)
	2^1–2^4	Represents centre position of front waist dart Square up to meet waist line. Mark point 0^4	9.0 cm (3½ in)
4	**Figure 1.5** 0^3	On waist line, take out 2 cm (¾ in) each side of back dart centre line; connect to hip line Foreshorten to 15 cm (6 in)	
	0^4	Take out 1 cm (⅜ in) each side of front dart centre line; connect to hip line Foreshorten to 7.5 cm (3 in)	
	0	Take out 4 cm (1½ in) to left and to the right of centre side seam line (central tree) This is the side seam waist shaping. Curve to 1.5 cm (⅝ in) measurement Connect to straight side seam line	
	0^2–0^5	Location for centre back seam if required	1.25 cm (½ in)
		This draft produces a straight skirt which, when worn, appears to narrow at hemline, sometimes demanded by fashion. The skirt appears straight however, when a small amount of stride allowance is added each side of side seam line	2.5 cm (1 in)
5	**Figure 1.6**	Cut out back and front skirt, but leave 3 cm (1¼ in) paper above waist line. Pin darts and join side seams. Blend waistline. Trace through folded darts	
	Figure 1.7	The new waistline should appear as shown when darts are unfolded. Complete dress skirt block	

Finished measurements include all tolerances

Skirt length	65.0 cm	25½ in
Waist to hip level	20.0 cm	8 in
Hips	99.0 cm	39 in
Waist	68.5 cm	27 in

Figure 1.5

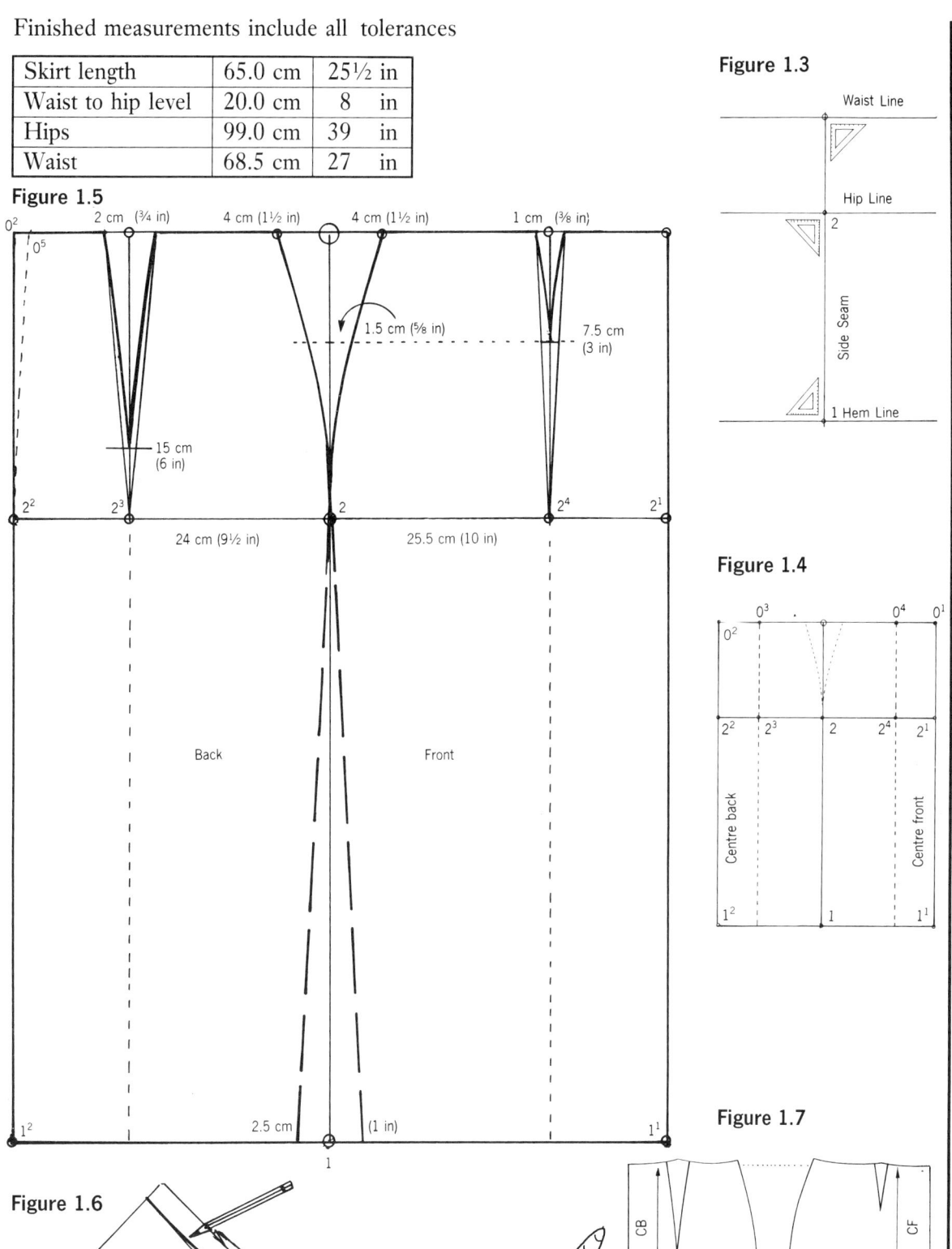

2 cm (¾ in) 4 cm (1½ in) 4 cm (1½ in) 1 cm (⅜ in)

1.5 cm (⅝ in)   7.5 cm (3 in)

15 cm (6 in)

24 cm (9½ in)   25.5 cm (10 in)

Back   Front

2.5 cm (1 in)

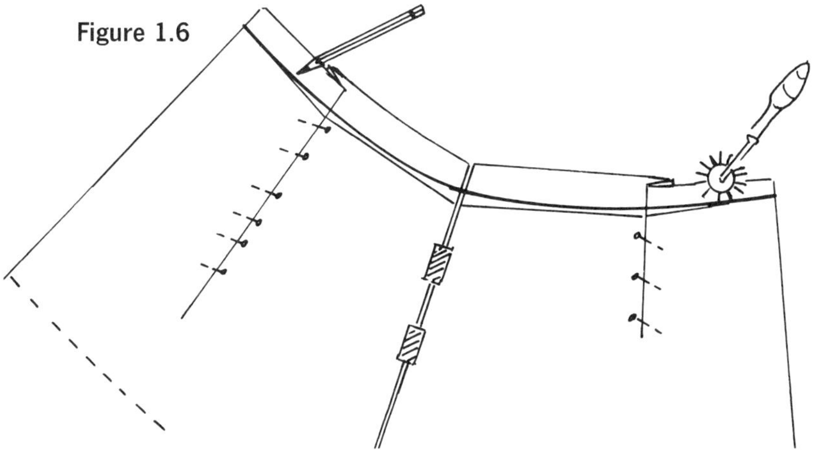

Figure 1.3

Waist Line
Hip Line
Side Seam
Hem Line

Figure 1.4

Centre back   Centre front

Figure 1.6

Figure 1.7

CB   Dress skirt back Size 12   Dress skirt front Size 12   CF

2.5 cm (1 in)

1 Drafting the basic blocks

13

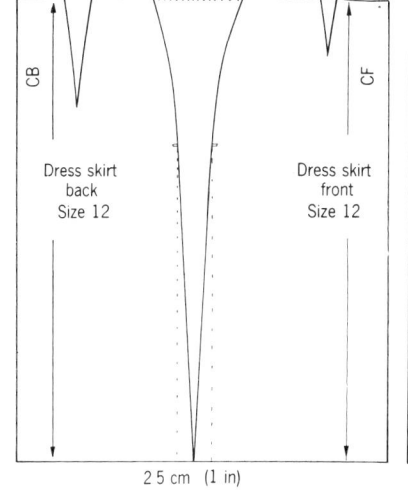

The tailored skirt block

1 Drafting the basic blocks

Figure 1.8

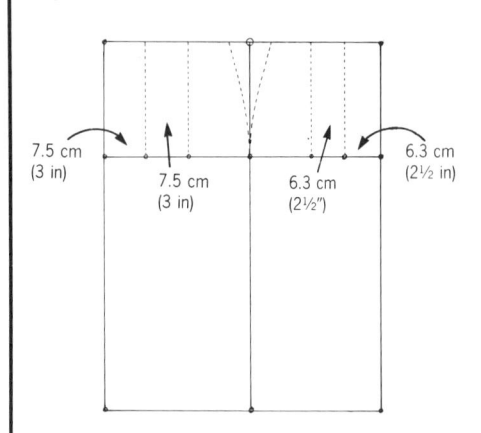

Finished measurements include all tolerances

Skirt length	65.0 cm	25½ in
Waist to hip level	20.0 cm	8 in
Hips	101.5 cm	40 in
Waist	68.5 cm	27 in

Figure 1.9

The basic construction of this block is the same as for the dress skirt block in Figure 1.5, except here the back skirt is wider by 5 cm (2 in) than the front skirt.

Take out two darts on the back waist line and two darts on the front waist line as shown.

A stride allowance of 4 cm (1½ in) is added each side of the centre side seam line.

Blend waistline as for dress skirt block (Figure 1.6). Also blend hemline by joining lower side seams.

Complete tailored skirt block by placing balance mark, grain lines and cutting instructions as Figure 1.7.

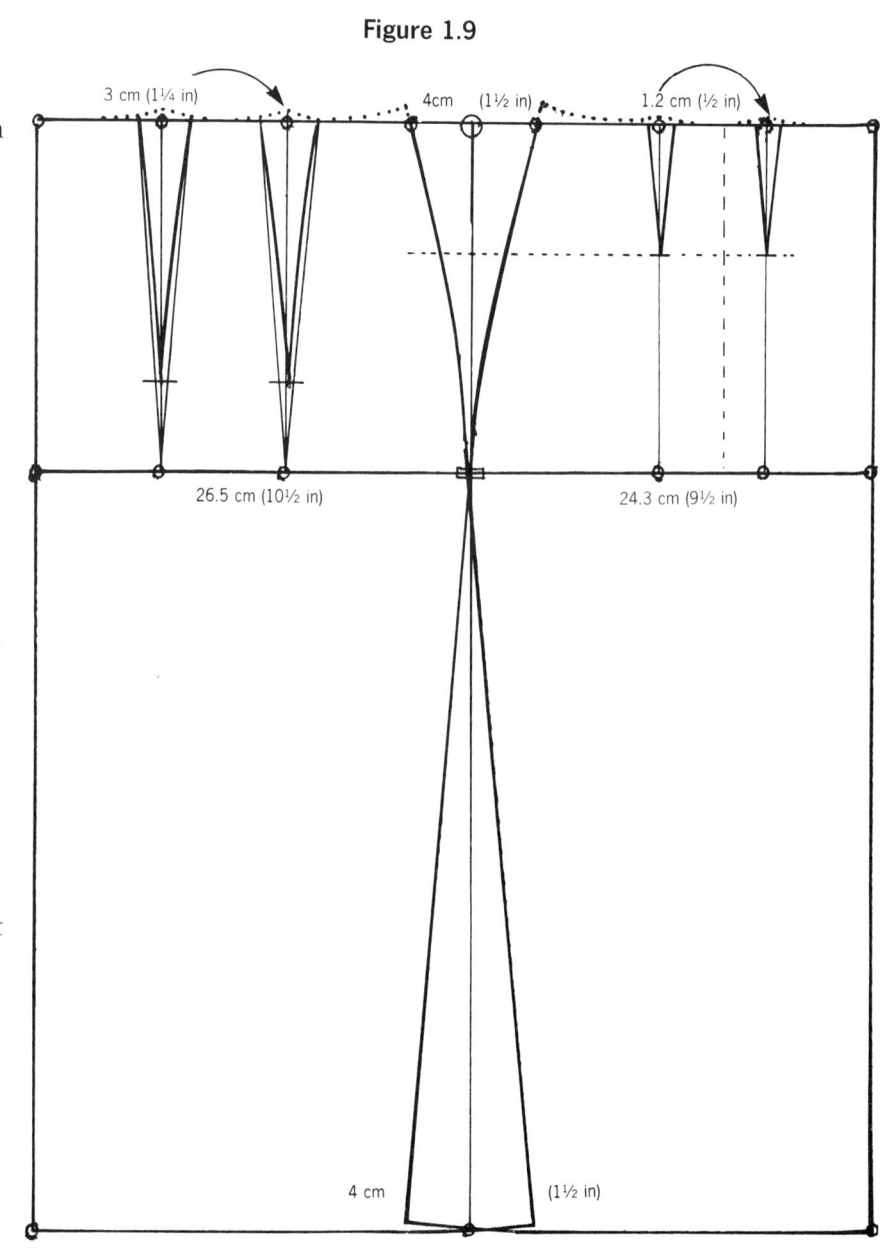

14

Size 12 – Finished measurements include all tolerances

	cm	in
Sleeve length from shoulder to wrist over slightly bent elbow	57.2	22½
Upper arm girth, taken high at armhole point	34.2	13½
Armhole	42.0	16½
Wrist (for this draft)	25.3	10
Elbow	30.5	12

The central tree

1	Figure 1.10	
	0–1 Equals sleeve length measurement Draw centre sleeve line Square at 0 to left and right; name **shoulder level line** Square out at 1 to left and right; name **wrist line**	57.0 cm (22½ in)
	0–2 Equals ⅓ of armhole circumference Square left and right; name **crown level line**	14.0 cm (5½ in)
	2–3 Equals half 2–1 minus 2.5 cm (1 in); name **elbow line**	19.0 cm (7½ in)
2	Figure 1.11	
	1–1¹ & 1–1² Equals half wrist measurement	12.7 cm (5 in)
	2–2¹ & 2–2² Equals half upper arm girth	17.1 cm (6¾ in)
	1¹–2¹ –4 & 1²–2² –4¹ Connect	
	Draw vertical guide lines halfway between 0–4 and 0–4¹ and 1–1¹ and 1²–1	
3	Figure 1.12	
	0–5 & 0–5¹ Equals one quarter of 0–4 and 0–4¹	approx. 4.4 cm (1¾ in)
	2¹–6 Equals one sixth of 2¹–2	2.7 cm (1⅛ in)
	2²–6¹ Equals one quarter of 2²–2	4.1 cm (1⅝ in)
	Connect 6–5 and 6¹–5¹ with straight guide lines	
	From 6, 5 & 5¹ draw diagonal guide lines	1.2 cm (½ in)
	From 6¹ draw guide line	1.0 cm (⅜ in)
	Curve the sleeve head as shown	

The basic sleeve block

Cut pattern paper 63.5 cm (25 in) long by 48 cm (17 in) wide, crease widthwise. This represents the centre line 0–1.

Figure 1.10

Figure 1.11

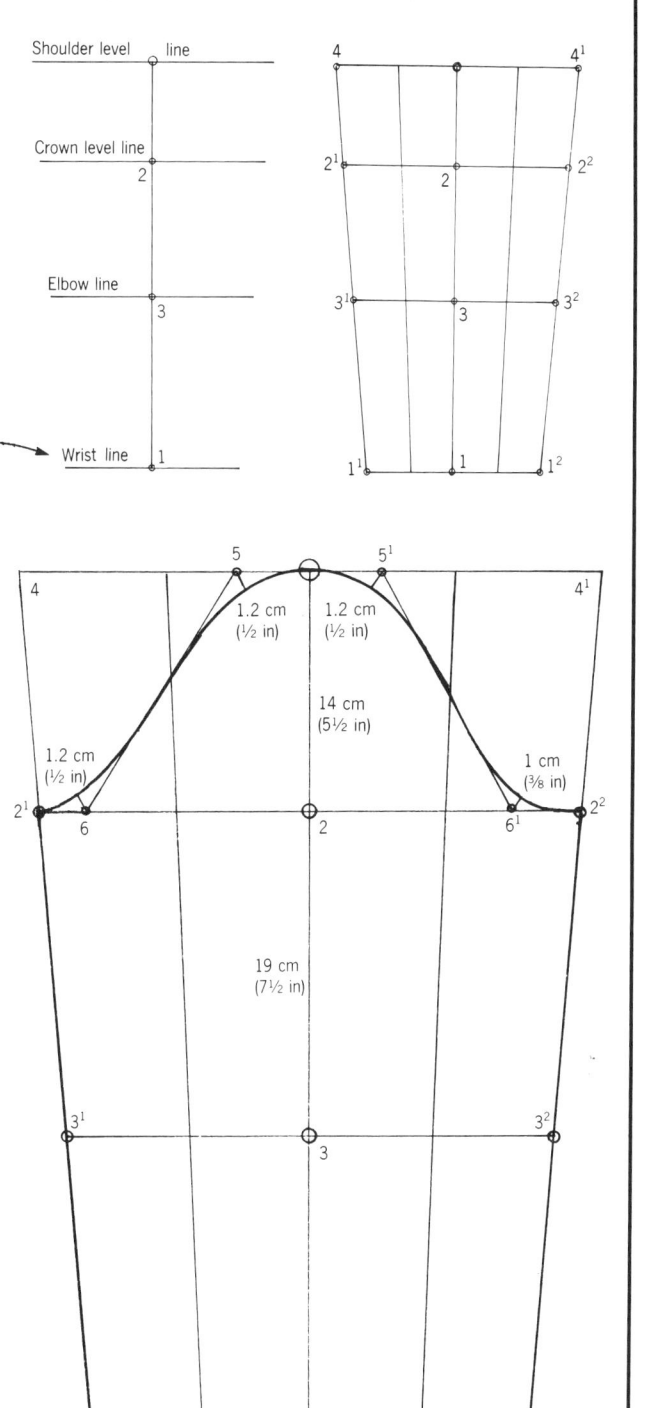

Figure 1.12 Completed sleeve block

Drafting the basic blocks

1

15

The trouser block draft

This trouser draft is a useful basis for developing other trouser silhouettes and styles. It is included for readers who prefer to draft the block rather than develop it from the skirt block. After the initial stages however, block adaptations and style developments are identical.

The back crutch seam must be longer than the front crutch seam to fit comfortably when the wearer is in a sitting position. Fashion plays a part in this and sometimes the back is deliberately not extended.

Figure 1.13a Slash from 10–2, open 3 cm (1–1¼ in).

Figure 1.13b Shows final outline.

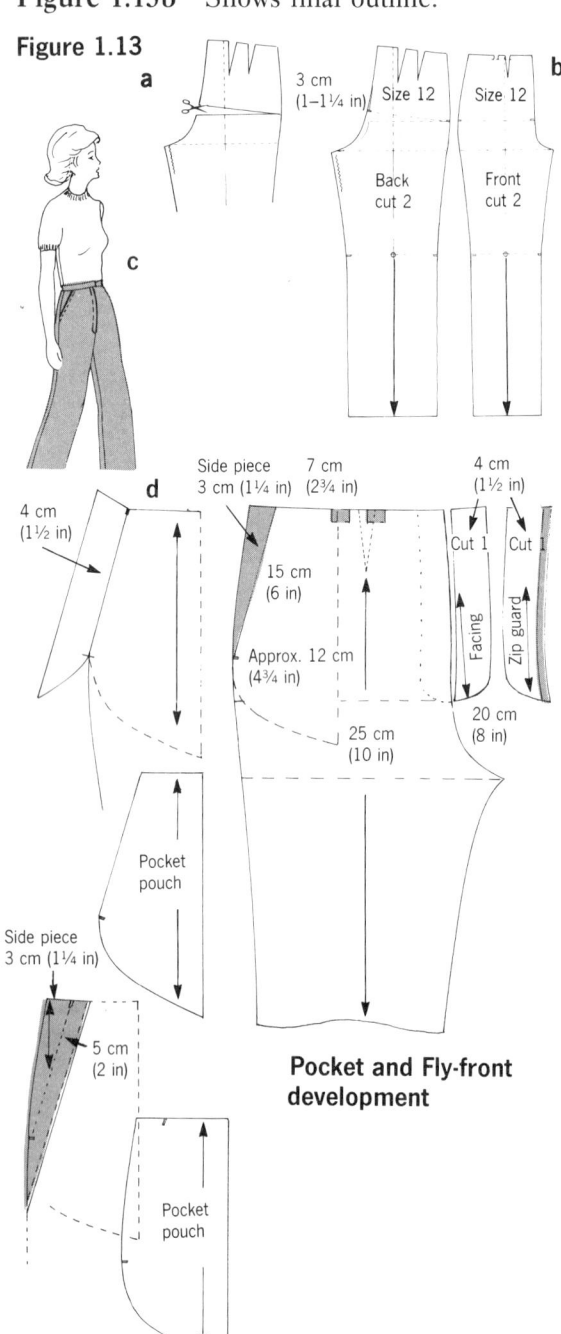

Figure 1.15

		cm	in
0–1	Side seam (outside leg) measurement; square across 0 and 1	104	41
0–2	Hip level; square across	20	8
0–3	Body rise; square across	28	11
0–4	Knee level; square across	59	23¼
Front			
2–5	Quarter hip measurement minus 7mm (¼ in); square down to 5^1 and up to 5^2	24	9½
5^1–6	5 cm (2 in); square down to 6^1 and 6^2	5	2
6–5^2	Curve up as shown		
6^1–7 6^2–7^1 4–4^1	Connect 6–7–7^1 for inside leg and 1–1^1	4	1½
0–8	Connect 8–2 and 3–4^1–1^1	3.5	1⅜
9–9^1 9^2–9^3	Halve trouser bottom; square up to waist line. This is the straight grain and also the crease line		
Back			
2–10	Quarter hip measurement plus 8 mm (¼ in); square down to 10^1 and up to 10^2	25.5	10
10^1–11	Square down to 11^1 (1 cm (⅜ in) –11^2–11^3	12	4¾
10^1	Draw 4 cm (1½ in) diagonal line		
10^2–10 –11^1	Connect for crutch seam		
11^2–12 11^3–12^2		4	1½
11^1–12 –12^1	Connect for inside leg seam		
0–14		3.5	1⅜
4–4^2		4	1½
1–1^2	Connect 14–2 and 3, 4^2–1^2	4	1½
13–13^1 –13^2– 13^3	Halve back trouser bottom; square up to waist line; this is the straight grain and also the crease line. Waist darts vary according to waist measurement. In this case all darts (or tucks) are 2 cm (¾ in) deep. In addition 5 mm (¼ in) suppression was taken out at CF waist line (5^3) and waist line lowered by 5 mm (¼ in)		
10^2–13^4		6	2½
14–14^1		7	2¾
5^3–9^4		7	2¾
8–8^1		7.5	3

Pocket and Fly-front development

Figure 1.15

a — Outside leg

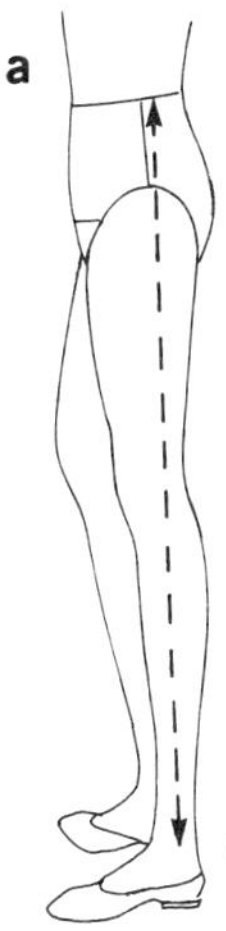

b — Body rise

c — High thigh circumference

d — Crutch seam

Figure 1.17 Finished measurements (ease included) in order of drafting.

Size	10		12		14		16	
	cm	in	cm	in	cm	in	cm	in
a Side seam (outside leg)	103	40½	104	41	104	41	104.5	41⅛
Hips 20 cm (8 in) from waist	94	37	99	39	104	41	109.2	43
b Body rise	27.5	10¾	28	11	28.5	11¼	29	11½
Knee circumference: 58/60 cm (22½/24 in) from waist	47.6	18¾	48.1	19	48.6	19¼	49.5	19½
Trouser bottom circumference	47.5	18¾	48	19	48.5	19¼	49.4	19½
c High thigh circumference	61	24	64	25¼	67	26½	71	28
d Crutch seam	64	25¼	67	26½	70	27¾	74	29¼
Waist	66	26	71	28	76	30	81	32

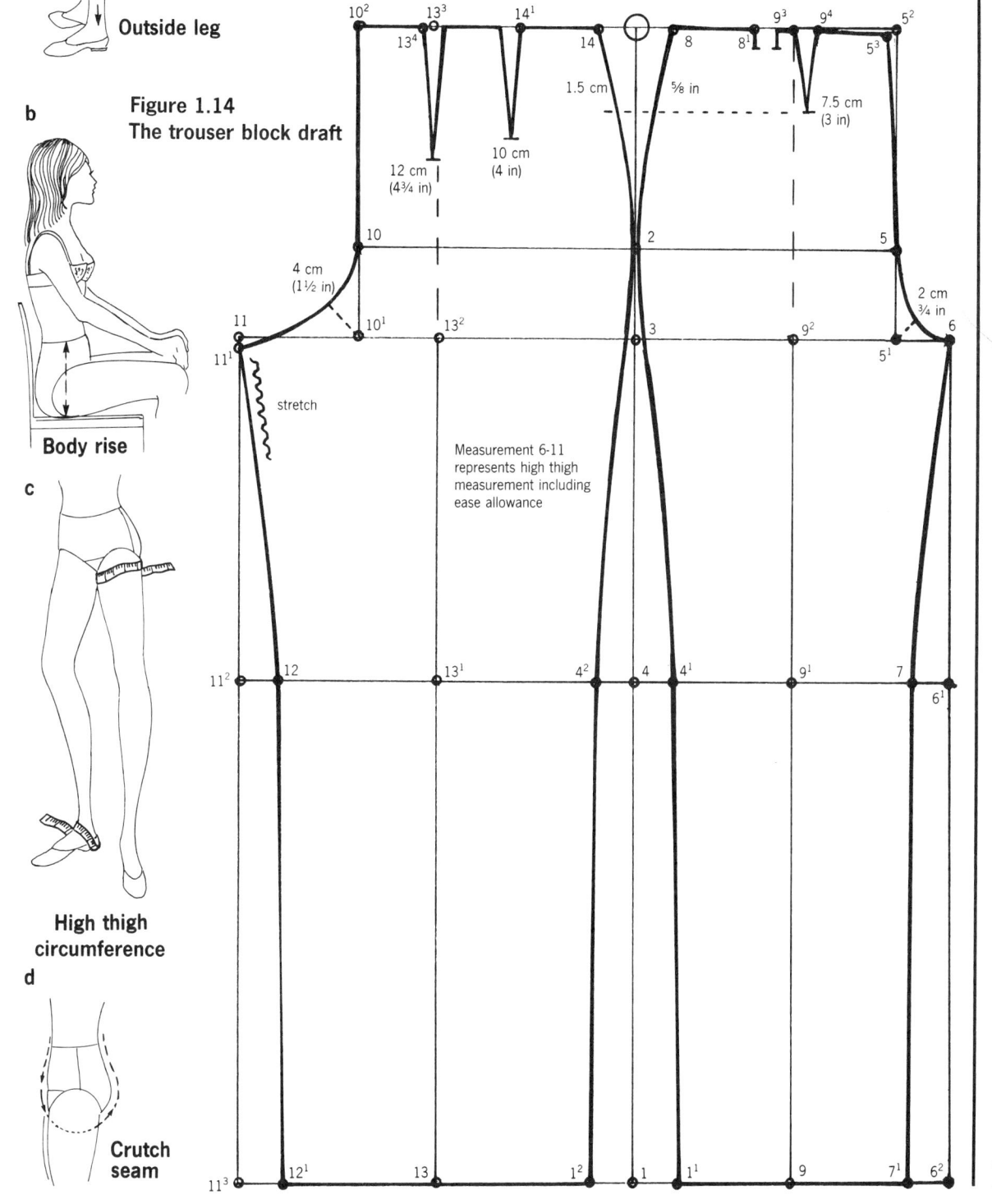

Figure 1.14 The trouser block draft

Measurement 6–11 represents high thigh measurement including ease allowance

1

Drafting the basic blocks

17

2 | Waist bodice and darts
Preparing the dress form for modelling

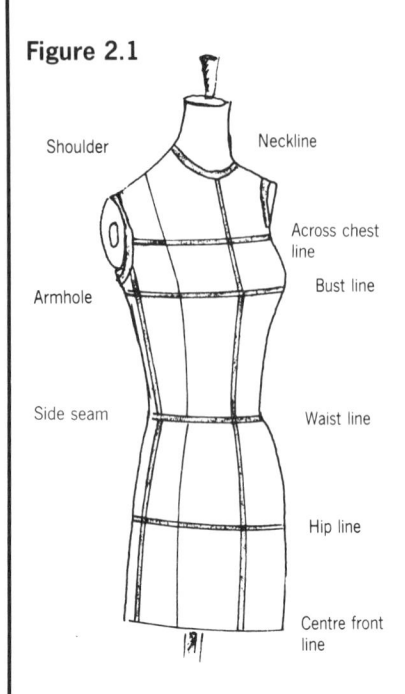

Figure 2.1

Figure 2.2

Sew narrow black tape over seams and important pattern construction lines. The taped lines can be seen through the modelling material and serve as a guide while modelling.

Note measurements as you go along; compare them with those taken on a person of apparently the same size and with those given in the size chart.

Neck line
Figure 2.5 Pin black tape around base of neckline and sew to dress form with diagonal stitches.

Bust line
Figures 2.1 and 2.2 Sew tape over highest part of bust beginning approximately 2.5 cm (1 in) below taped base of armhole, raising the tape slightly at the back.

Figure 2.3

Waist line
Figures 2.1 and 2.2 Around smallest part of waist.

Hip line
Sew tape 20 cm (8 in) below waist line. This is an average measurement and varies between 18–23 cm (7–9 in) depending on height of person.

Centre front line
From pit of neck crossing bust line, waist line and hip line to end of dress form.

Across chest line
From bust line up 4 cm (1½ in), sew at right angles to centre front.

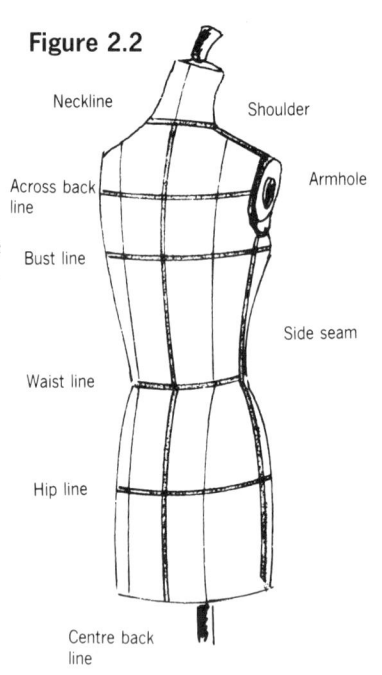

Figure 2.4

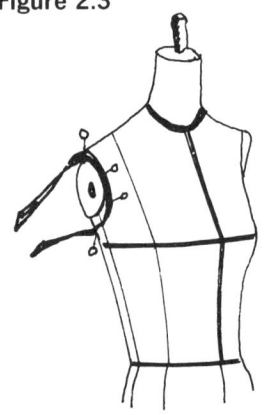

Shoulder line
On seam line from neck to armhole or according to fashion.

Across back line
From nape of neck.

Centre back line
Figure 2.2 As for centre front but starting from nape of neck.

Figure 2.5

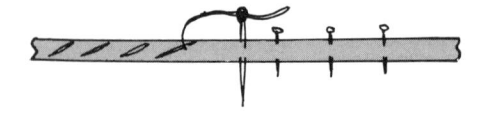

Armhole
Figures 2.1, 2.2 and 2.3 The average size 12 **armhole** measures 41–42 cm (16–16½ in). Lower tape in curved line if armhole of form measures less than this.

Figure 2.4 As a guide, measure 14–15.5 cm (5½–6 in) from shoulder point across armhole to underarm side seam position and mark this point with a pin to indicate position of tape for measuring armhole.

Side seam
Figures 2.1 and 2.2 The tape should be in line with the shoulder seam, usually covering the existing dress form seam.

Modelling the front waist block

Figure 2.6

All sorts of materials can be used for modelling. Some designers work with tissue paper or 'spot' paper when working on simple 'tailored' styles; others use the more pliable unbleached cottons, calicoes and muslins. Gingham, because of its woven check pattern and its easily discernible warp and weft threads, often helps the beginner to recognise 'grain' and is used as a modelling fabric. Experience will tell which materials to use. If paper is used, it must be remembered that it has no natural grain lines, e.g. warp and weft; these will have to be drawn on paper. Tissue paper is excellent for the beginner, being pliable and cheap. It can be purchased in large quantities of small sized sheets.

Cutting the modelling fabric

Figure 2.7 Measure from shoulder neck point over bust to waist line, approximately 26.5 cm (16½ in) and add 10 cm (4 in) for manipulation and seams.

Take half front bust line measurement from centre front to underarm point, approximately 25.5 cm (10 in) and add 5 cm (2 in) for manipulation and side seam. Record half bust width measurement from centre front point **B** to bust point **A** as you measure.

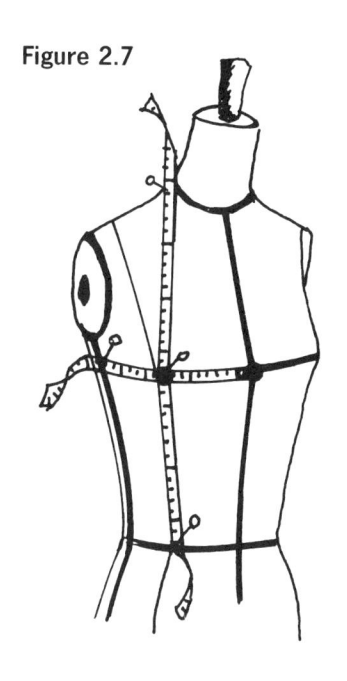

Figure 2.7

Figure 2.8

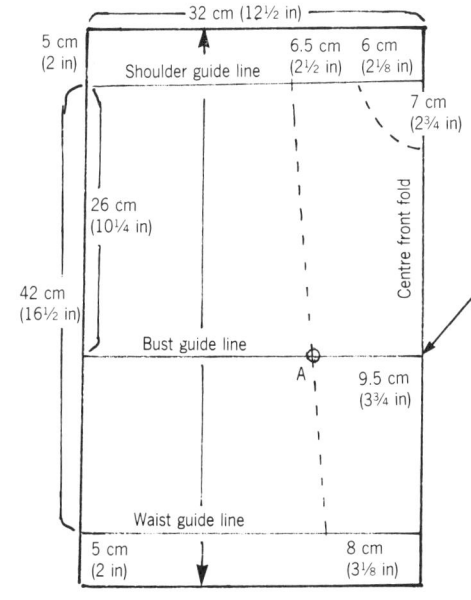

Figure 2.8 Cut a rectangle of modelling material 52 cm (20½ in) long and 32 cm (12½ in) wide. If paper is used, work with the rough side uppermost. Draw the following guide lines on it:

The long right-hand edge of the paper represents the **centre front**. The **shoulder guide line** is 5 cm (2 in) below the upper edge of the paper and parallel to it. **Waist guide line** is 5 cm (2 in) above lower edge of paper and parallel to it. The **bust guide line** is at right angles to the centre front and approximately 25.5 cm (10 in) down from shoulder guide line.

Mark half **bust width** measurement on bust line (approximately 9.5 cm or 3¾ in. Locate bust point **A**. Indicate **neckline curve** as shown in diagram. A **dart guide line** may be drawn from shoulder guide line through bust point to waist guide line as shown. Measurements are given in the diagram. Draw the **grain line** parallel to centre front.

With practice and experience the guide lines can be entirely disregarded. They are included solely for the benefit of the beginner and should always be regarded as a guide only. Dress form measurements and dart placements can vary considerably with dress forms of different manufacture.

2 Waist bodice and darts

Figure 2.9

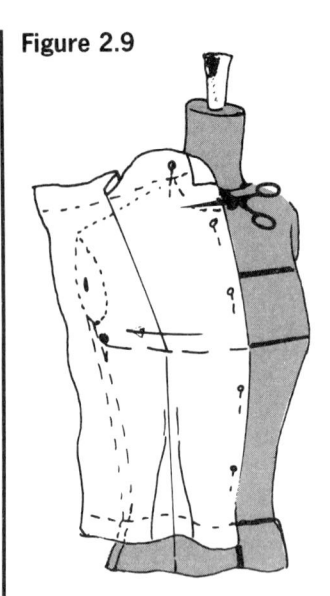

Figure 2.9 Pin rectangle of modelling material with drawn guide lines to right side of dress form with centre front of material covering centre front line on dress form and bust guide line on modelling material matching bust line on dress form.

Pin as shown, one pin near shoulder-neck point position, four pins down centre front and one pin on bust line at underarm position.

Roughly cut away the top right hand corner of the material to within 2.5 cm (1 in) of the neck guide line and snip the curved edge. Smooth the material and pin the neckline slightly below the position of the taped seam on the dress form.

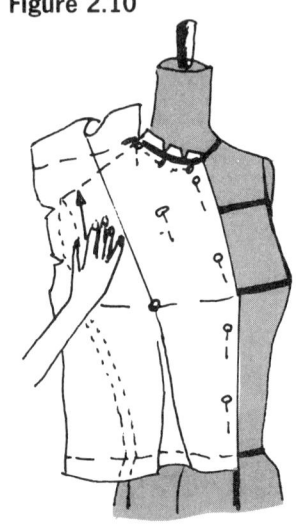

Figure 2.10

Figure 2.10 Mark **neckline** with soft pencil and cut to within 1 cm (⅜ in). Roughly cut away some excess material at armhole position and slash edge. Smooth paper upwards from underarm point towards shoulder point and pin armhole line.

Figure 2.11 Fold **shoulder dart** 5–8 cm (2–3 in) deep by creasing the material on or near the previously drawn guide line to bust point. The depth of the dart can vary; the fuller the bust, the deeper the dart. The shoulder dart should rest in the centre of the shoulder seam and should be folded as a lapped seam. Mark the lapped shoulder dart edge and the edge meeting the lapped edge with soft pencil. Mark the previously pinned **armhole line** and cut paper to within 1.3 cm (½ in). Snip edges.

Figure 2.11

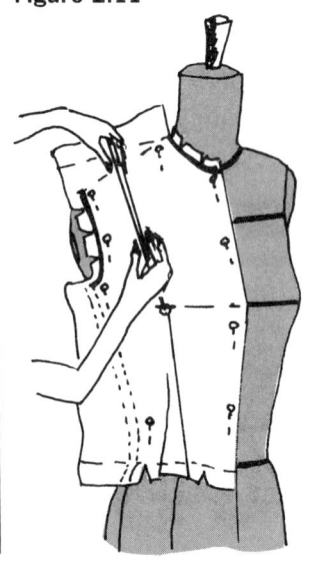

Figure 2.12 With shoulder dart closed, place two pins slightly below shoulder guide line, fold material back upon itself along the shoulder seam line on the dress form, and crease **shoulder line.** Mark creased shoulder line with soft pencil.

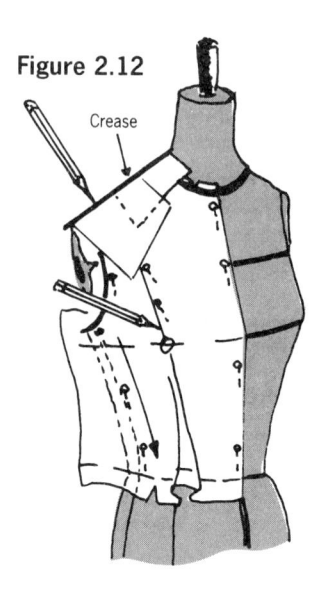

Figure 2.12

Crease

Figure 2.13

Figure 2.13a Cut modelling fabric to within 2 cm (¾ in) of pencilled shoulder line. Smooth fabric at side seam towards waist line and snip at waist line.

Fold fabric back upon itself and proceed as for shoulder line.

b Mark **side seam**.

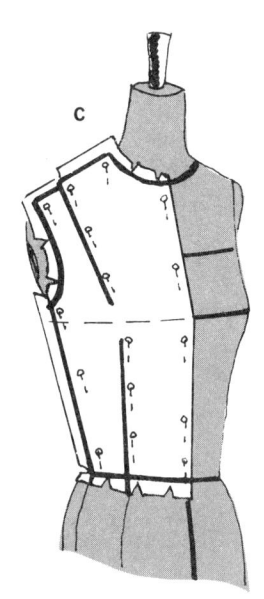

c Roughly cut away modelling fabric below waist line and snip. Fold surplus fullness at waist into **waist dart,** matching dart seam line on dress form. Mark two meeting lines with soft pencil. Pin waist line and cut away any more surplus paper and snip edge. Mark **waist line** and cut fabric to within 2 cm (¾ in).

Figure 2.14 Remove modelled shape from dress form, unpin darts, true all pencilled lines, ensure that all intersections are at right angles to each other and recut all jagged edges. Draw arrowed grain line parallel to centre front.

Most designers in industry use block patterns with seam allowances, and for this reason recommended seam allowances are included in the size charts, pages 6 and 7. These allowances vary with individual manufacturers and because of this, and to facilitate the construction of more intricate patterns, block patterns without seam turnings are often preferred. Seam allowances are then added to the final pattern.

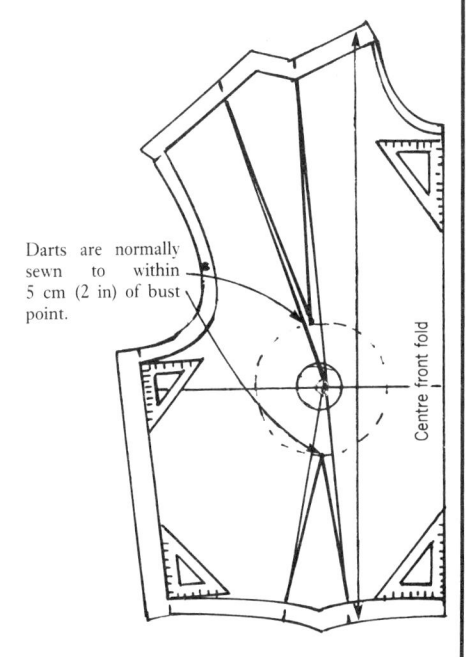

Darts are normally sewn to within 5 cm (2 in) of bust point.

Figure 2.14 Completed pattern

Waist bodice and darts

2 Waist bodice and darts

Modelling the back waist block

Figure 2.15

Figure 2.15a Pin front waist block with darts closed back onto dress form.

Take measurements as for front waist block (Figure 2.8) and cut rectangle of tissue paper or other modelling fabric. Mark left long side **centre back**. Draw **bust guide line** as for front block at right angles to centre back.

Shoulder guide line is 5 cm (2 in) below upper edge of paper, and **waist guide line** 5 cm (2 in) above lower edge. The **back neck guide line** is shallower than the front neck guide line.

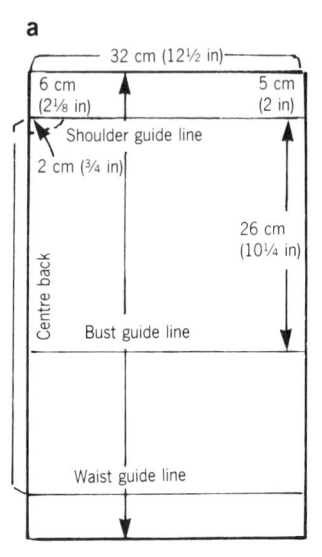

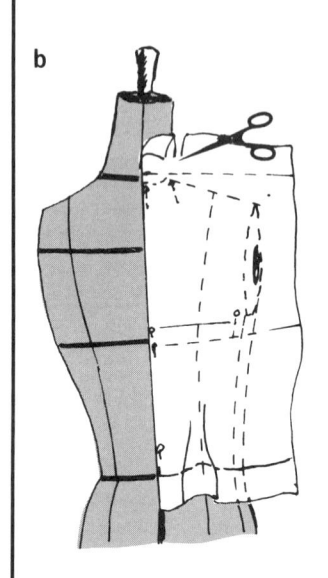

a
- 32 cm (12½ in)
- 6 cm (2⅛ in)
- 5 cm (2 in)
- Shoulder guide line
- 2 cm (¾ in)
- 26 cm (10¼ in)
- Centre back
- Bust guide line
- Waist guide line

b Pin modelling fabric to right side of back of dress form covering centre back seam of dress form with centre back line of modelling fabric. Match bust guide line with taped bust line on dress form. Pin as shown.

c Pin and mark **neckline.** Snip edge and cut to within 1 cm (⅜ in). Roughly cut away some surplus paper at armhole position and slash. Smooth paper towards shoulder and pin. This provides a small amount of ease for the back shoulder dart.

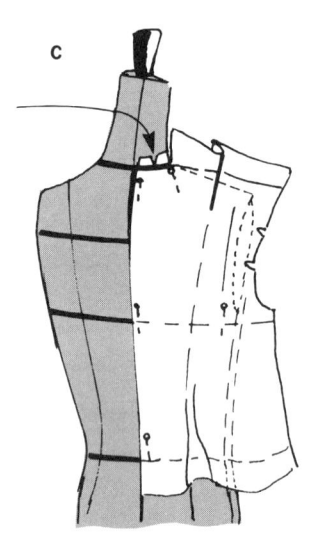

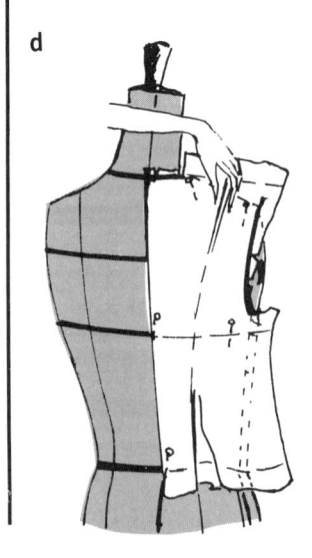

d Fold small **shoulder dart** as lapped seam 5–13 mm (¼–½ in) deep and 7.5 cm (3 in) long to correspond with front dart position at shoulder. The rounder the back, the deeper this dart will be; it can be from 5–20 cm (¼–¾ in). It should run parallel to the armhole seam line. Mark dart with soft pencil. Smooth armhole, pin and mark **armhole line** and cut paper to within 1.3 cm (½ in) of it.

e Proceed as for front block (Figure 2.12)

Crease modelling fabric back upon itself and mark **shoulder seam line** where it matches the shoulder seam on the dress form.

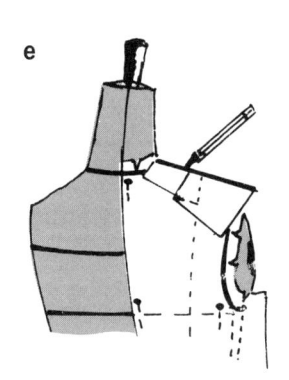

Figure 2.15 cont.

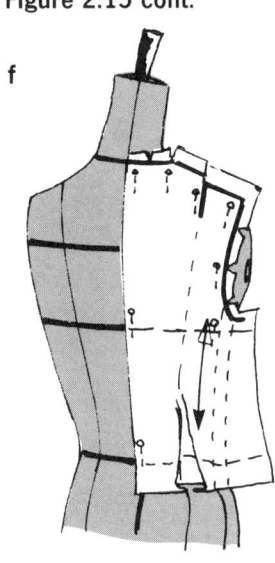

f Smooth fabric down **towards** waist line.

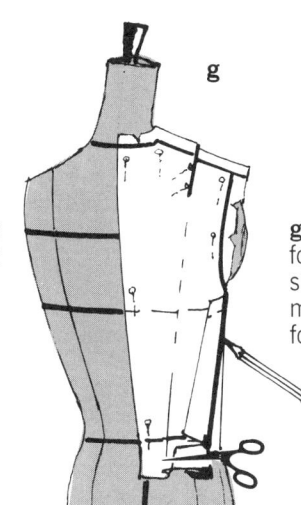

g Crease modelling fabric, fold back upon itself and mark side seam line where it matches side seam on dress form.

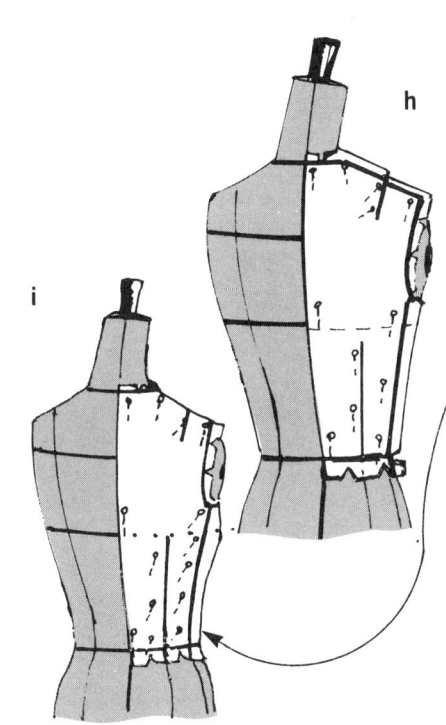

h Fold **waist dart** making it approximately 4 cm (1½ in) deep and 19 cm (7½ in) long and matching seam on dress form. Fold with lapped seam and mark dart lines.

Pin and mark waist line and trim excess modelling fabric to within 2 cm (¾ in) of it.

i With lapped seam pin back shoulder seam over front shoulder seam and back side seam over front side seam and make sure bodice fits well. Refit if required and mark alterations with coloured pencil.

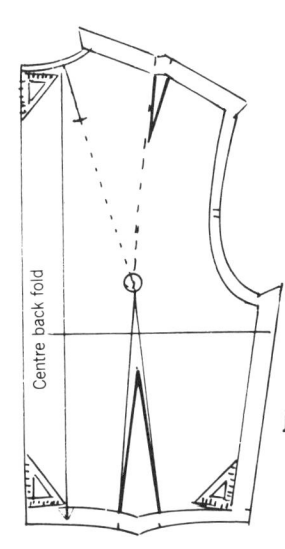

j Remove modelled back bodice from form, unpin darts and true all marked lines. Check back and front side seams and shoulder seams for equal length, excluding darts in your measurements.

k Pin **neck dart** instead of shoulder dart if preferred. This dart is more becoming for some figures and can be used for raglan and kimono patterns.

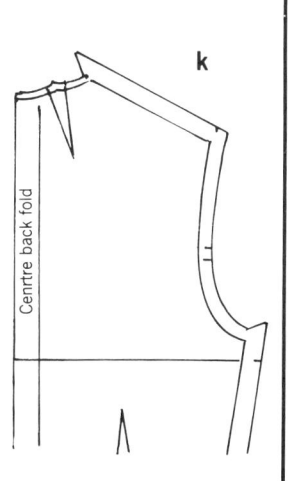

j Completed back waist block

Modelling the bodice darts

Figure 2.16

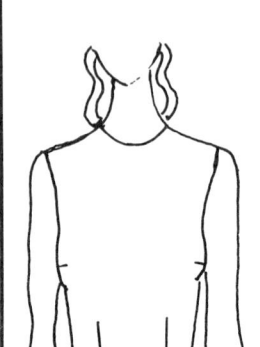

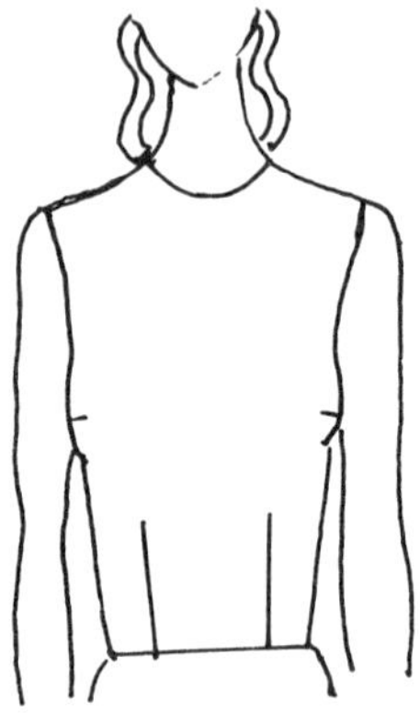

Underarm dart

Figure 2.16a Cut the modelling fabric as for Figure 2.8. Pin to centre front of dress form and match bust lines of dress form and modelling fabric from centre front to bust point only.

Place one pin at shoulder/neck position and cut away excess fabric at neckline to within 2.5 cm (1 in) of neckline. Snip neckline edge.

Smooth modelling material at shoulder position and pin as shown. Note that whereas the two bust lines were matched throughout from centre front to side seam and the material was smoothed upwards, in this case the reverse is happening: fabric is smoothed down from the shoulder area, displacing the grain line at underarm area. Roughly cut away some excess fabric at armhole and slash.

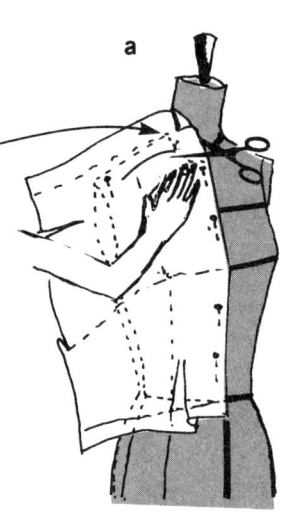

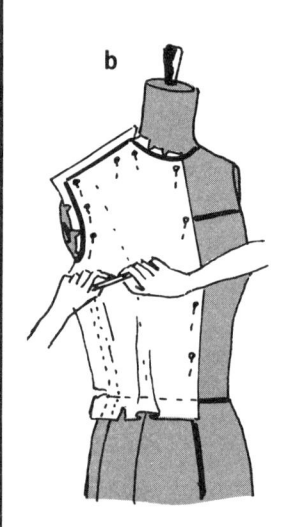

b Crease and mark shoulder line. Smooth material downwards towards underarm point and pin armhole. Mark armhole and cut to within 2 cm (¾ in). Place one pin at underarm point, then fold underarm dart and pin.

The modelling material should hang straight at side seam. If it does not, the dart is either too deep or too shallow. Experiment until a good fit is achieved. The dart should be approximately 4.5 cm (1¾ in) deep and should, at this stage, be tapered to the bust point.

c Place one pin at side seam/waist line position. Crease and mark side seam. Fold and mark waist dart and mark the waist line.

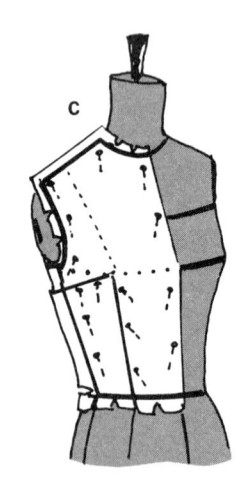

Foreshorten darts to within 5 cm (2 in) of bust point

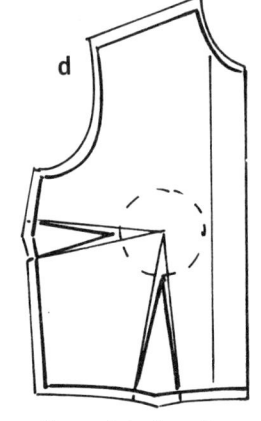

Completed pattern

Neck dart

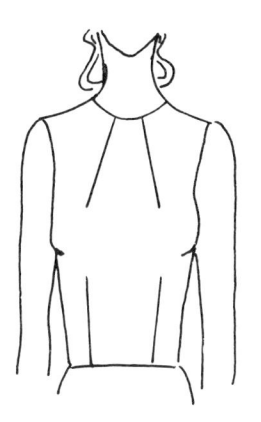

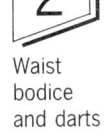

Figure 2.17

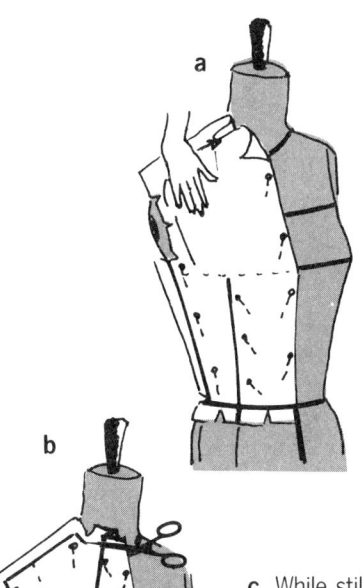

Figure 2.17a Pin rectangle of modelling fabric to dress form at centre front and at underarm/bust line point (as if modelling the front waist block, Figure 2.9). Model lower part of bodice first; fold waist dart, pin side seam. Snip waist line and intersection with side seam and mark dart, side seam and waist line.

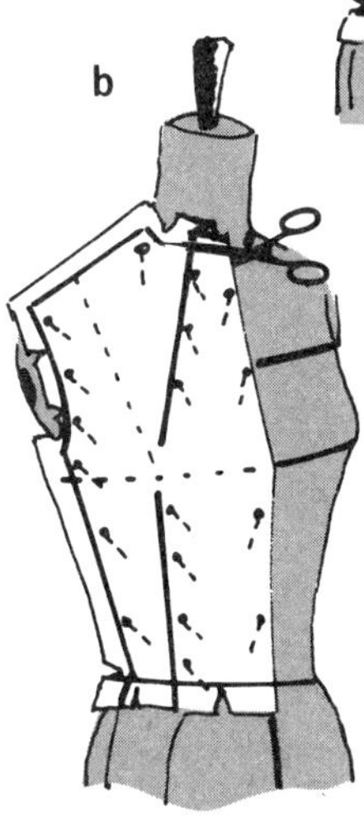

b Smooth material up over armhole towards shoulder and slash at armhole position. Pin. Smooth shoulder area. Pin at shoulder/neck point. Form **neck dart**. Mark dart, neckline, shoulder and armhole.

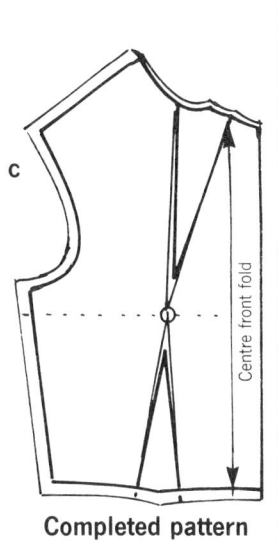

c While still pinned, trim seam allowances at neck to within 13 mm (½ in) and at waist to within 2 cm (¾ in) of marked seam lines. Remove from form, reduce and true seam allowances as required (see size charts).

Completed pattern

2 Waist bodice and darts

Large waist dart

Figure 2.18

This is a very flattering dart which is used mainly in fitted waist-length designs. The block itself (**b**) is an important block which is often used for the development of other designs.

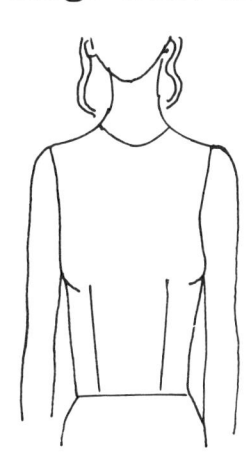

Figure 2.18a Proceed as for modelling underarm dart (Figure 2.16). Having modelled neck, shoulder and armhole areas, pin at underarm point. Smooth down side seam, making allowances for one large waist dart. Mark all lines with a soft pencil and remove from dress form. True all lines.

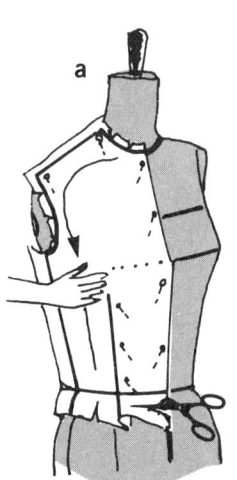

b Mark grain line, centre front and add seam allowances if required.

Note grain line at side seam.

Curve dart for closer fit.
With thick material cut away and sew as seam

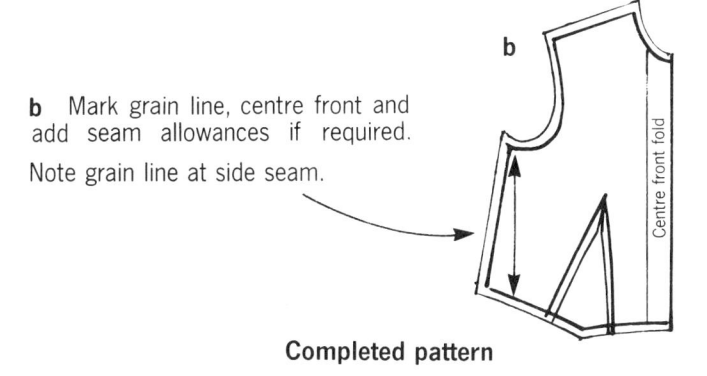

Completed pattern

25

Modelling the hip blocks or dress foundation

Hip block patterns are essential for designing garments that extend below the waist line.

Figure 2.19a Model as for the waist blocks, but cut the modelling material 21 cm (8 in) longer.

Note that the waist darts are shallower and the side seams less fitted than those of the waist blocks. This is due mainly to the absence of a waist seam which also functions as a fitting line.

b For the same reason the waist line position on the hip block is approximately 1.3 cm (½ in) above the waist line of the waist block. Unless this is observed, the pattern will not fit well, and the finished dress will tend to 'ride up' and throw wrinkles in the region of the waist line.

c Mark all dart and seam lines. Place balance marks at waist line level. Improve any uneven lines.

The waist dart below the waist line is 15 cm (6 in) long but can be extended to the hip line if wished.

Figure 2.19

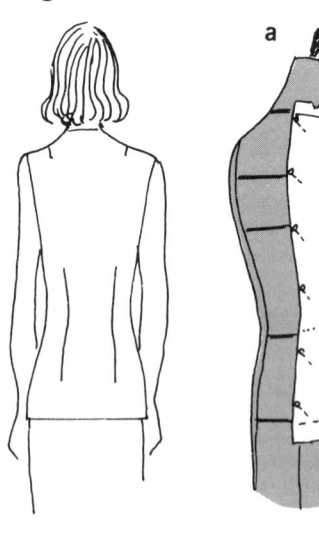

Figure 2.20

Figure 2.20a Proceed as for back waist block (Figure 2.15) and as above.

b Waist darts extend 15 cm (6 in) below waist line, but can be lengthened to hip line. Hip blocks can be extended to dress length.

Square down from hip line and add 5 cm (2 in) for stride room as shown.

This block can be used to construct light suits and coats, provided adjustments are made (See page 177–80).

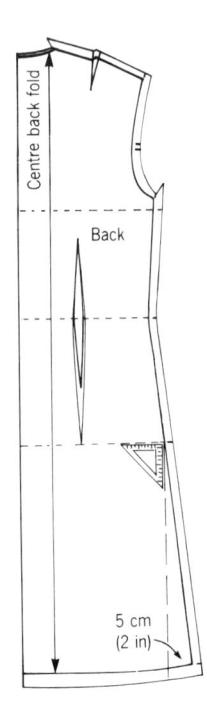

b Completed pattern

Moving darts by the slashing method

From underarm to shoulder dart

Figure 2.21

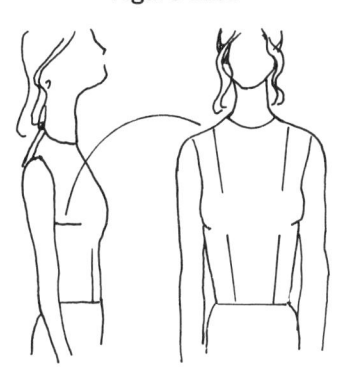

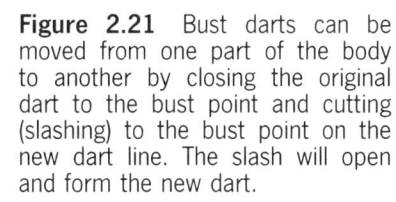

Figure 2.21 Bust darts can be moved from one part of the body to another by closing the original dart to the bust point and cutting (slashing) to the bust point on the new dart line. The slash will open and form the new dart.

a Outline block (Figure 2.16d). Cut out; close waist and underarm dart by either pinning or sticking with tape and pin to dress form or thinly clad figure.

b Pin black tape from bust point to centre of shoulder and mark with soft pencil. Remove from form.

c Unpin waist dart but keep original undearm dart closed. Cut on new marked shoulder line to bust point. Trace on to new sheet of paper and complete shoulder dart block as shown in **d**.

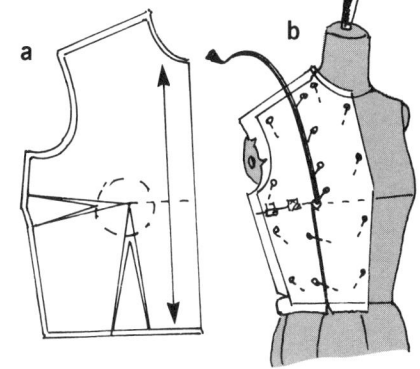

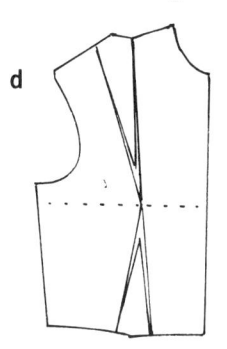

Completed pattern

Block development – from waist block to dress foundation

Figure 2.22

Completed patterns

Figure 2.23

Completed patterns

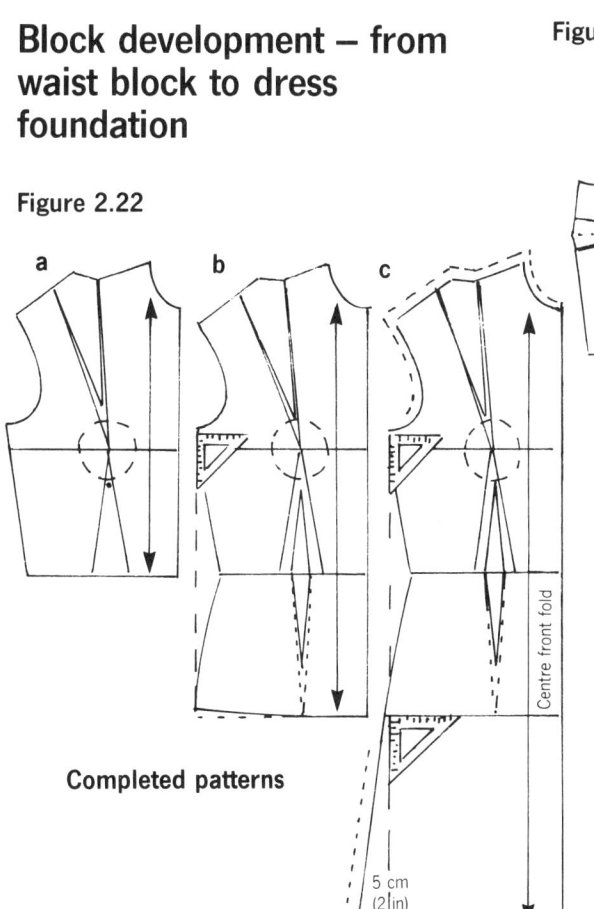

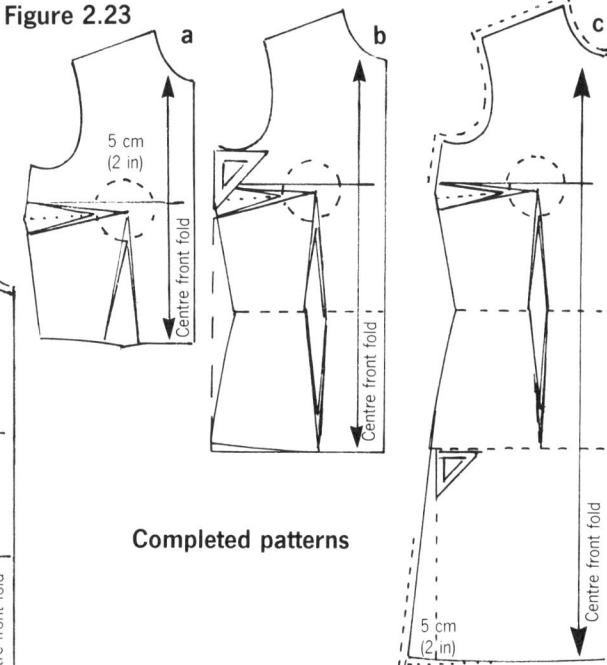

1 For hip block, square down from widest part above bust line to hip line 21 cm (8 in) below waistline.

2 For dress foundation, square down further to desired length.

3 Reduce depth of waist darts and foreshorten where required to within 5 cm (2 in) from bust point.

Centre front dart

Figure 2.24

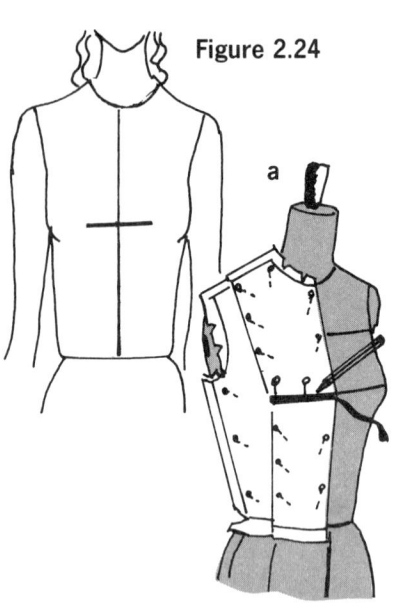

Figure 2.24a Close shoulder dart and waist dart and pin waist block to dress form. Mark position of centre front dart and remove front pattern from dress form.

b Cut through new dart line to bust point and open out.

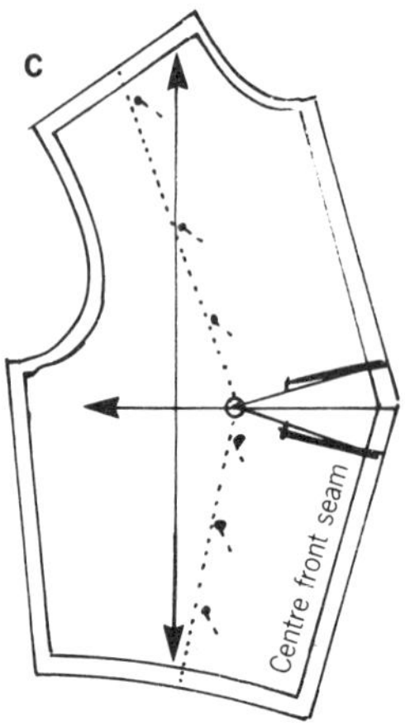

c Curve dart for a closer fit or shorten dart for an open tuck appearance.

d The dart or tuck can be replaced by gathers.

Various designs can be created by placing the pattern on different grains of the fabric.

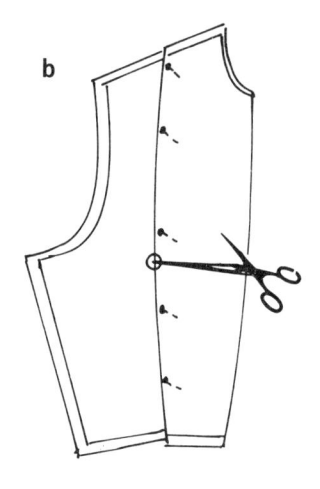

Figure 2.25

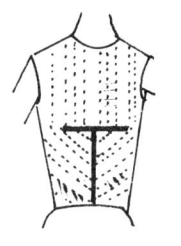

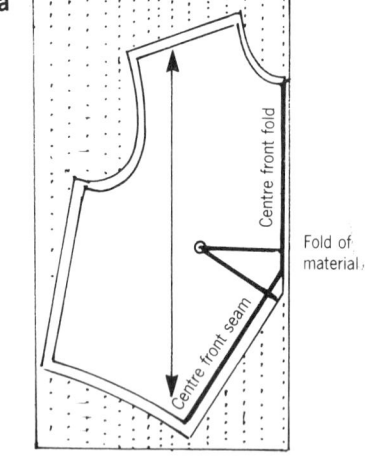

Figure 2.26

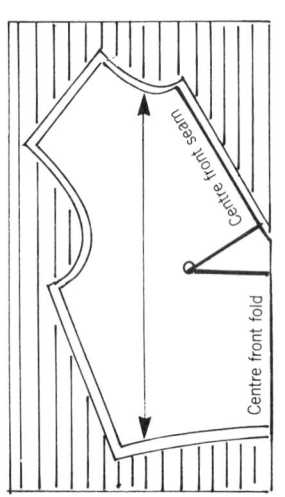

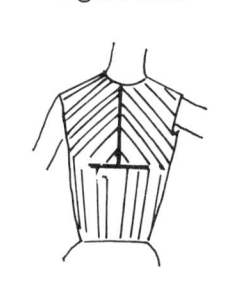

Figure 2.27

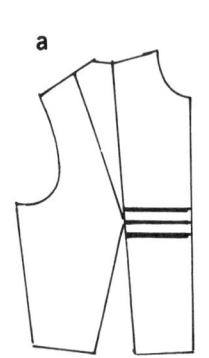

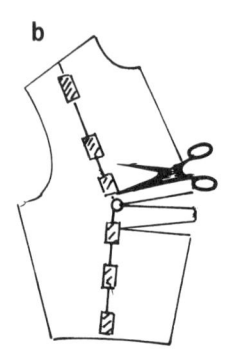

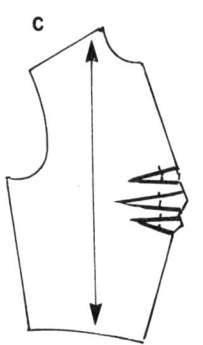

Figure 2.28 Armhole dart and neck darts

This armhole dart was developed from the basic underarm dart block pattern, but any other dart block would have been suitable.

Figure 2.28a Cut on new dart line to bust point and open out.

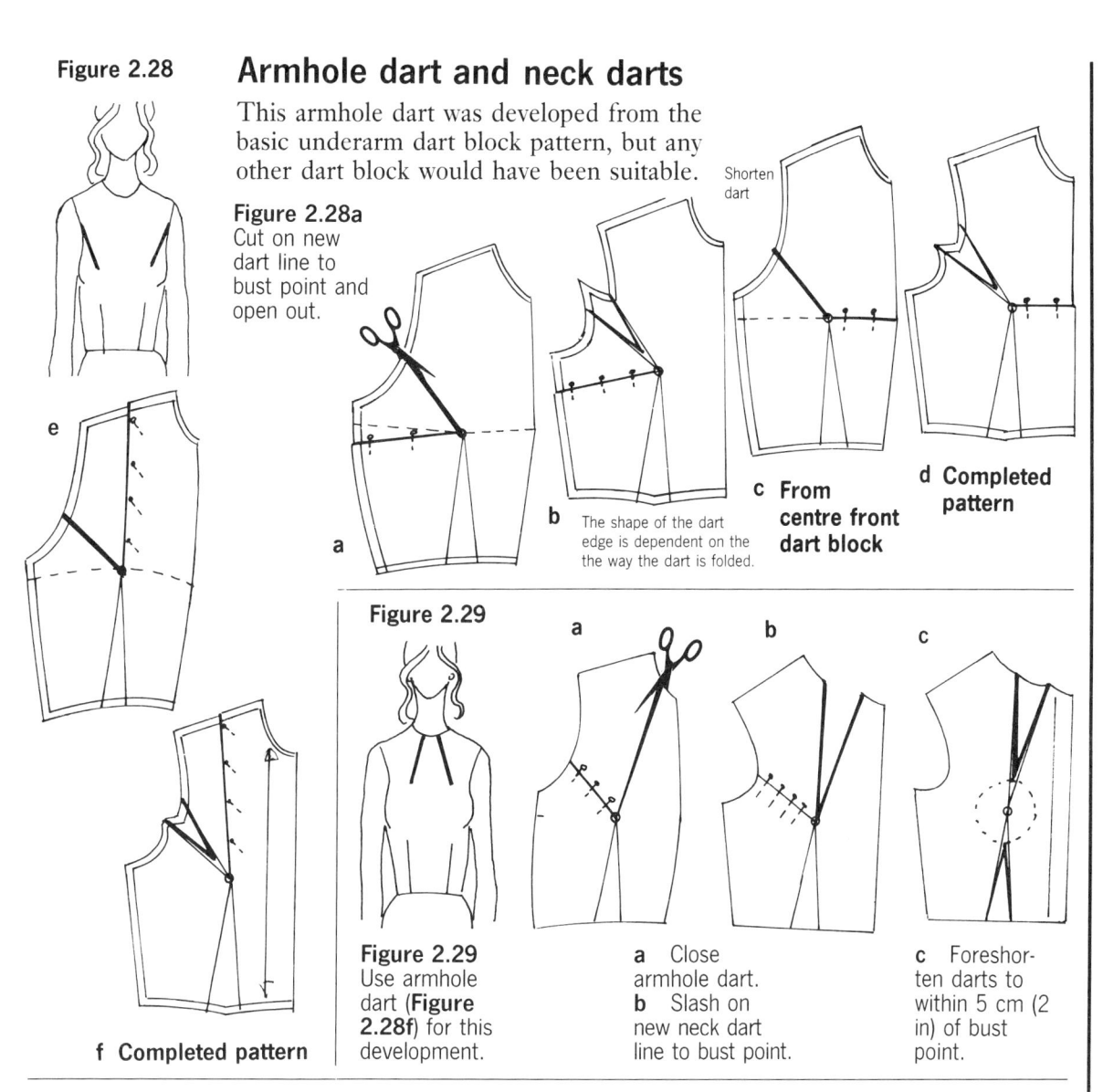

Shorten dart

a

b The shape of the dart edge is dependent on the the way the dart is folded.

c From centre front dart block

d Completed pattern

e

f Completed pattern

Figure 2.29

Figure 2.29 Use armhole dart (**Figure 2.28f**) for this development.

a Close armhole dart.
b Slash on new neck dart line to bust point.
c Foreshorten darts to within 5 cm (2 in) of bust point.

Figure 2.30

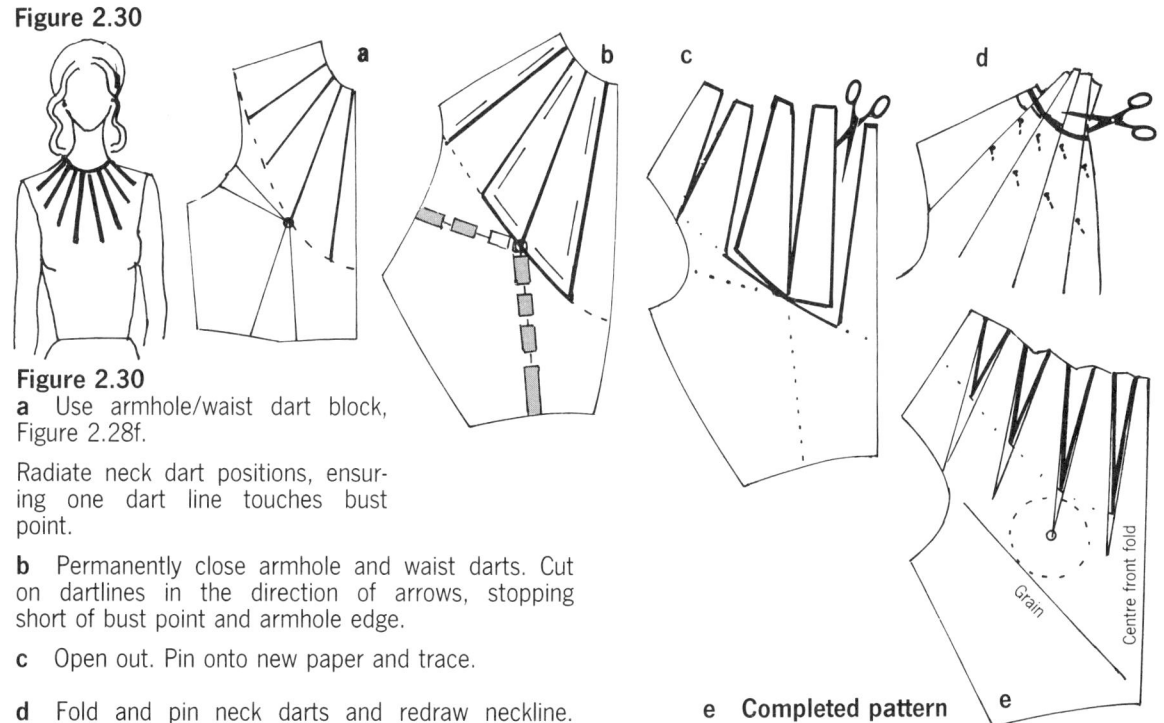

Figure 2.30
a Use armhole/waist dart block, Figure 2.28f.

Radiate neck dart positions, ensuring one dart line touches bust point.

b Permanently close armhole and waist darts. Cut on dartlines in the direction of arrows, stopping short of bust point and armhole edge.

c Open out. Pin onto new paper and trace.

d Fold and pin neck darts and redraw neckline. Use block neckline as template. Cut through folds.

e Completed pattern

2 Waist bodice and darts

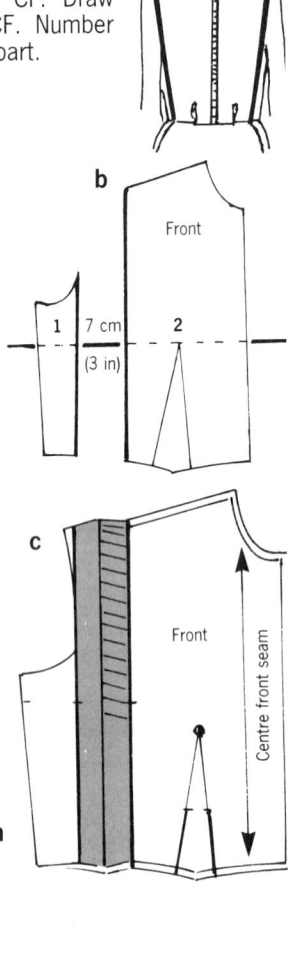

Shoulder flanges

Figure 2.31a Pin waist block with shoulder and waist dart closed to dress form. Pin narrow tape from end-of-shoulder point to bust point. When satisfied with the new dart line, mark with soft pencil.

b Remove pattern from dress form with original shoulder dart closed. Open waist dart.

c Cut on new pencilled dart line and open out.

Sew as dart or as top-stitched pleat

Completed pattern

Figure 2.32

Figure 2.32 For a softer effect cut the bodice on the bias and omit the waist dart.

Proceed as for Figure 2.31b but keep both shoulder **and** waist dart closed. Cut on new dart line as before.

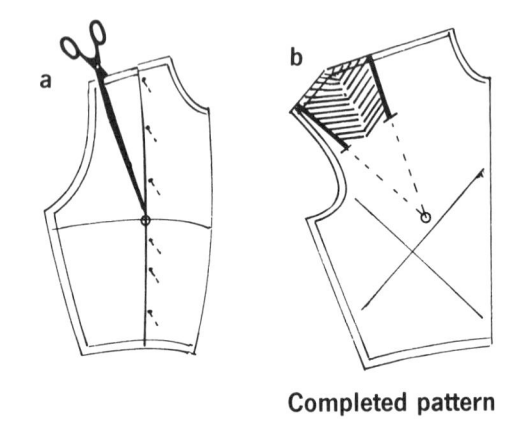

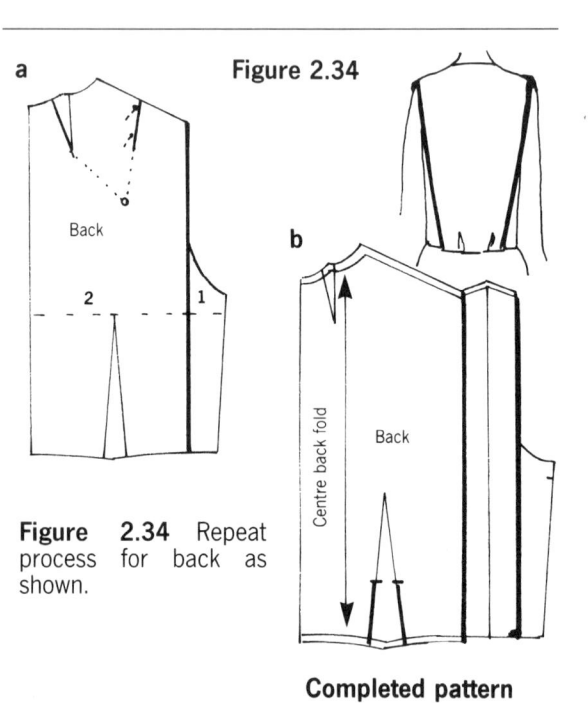

Completed pattern

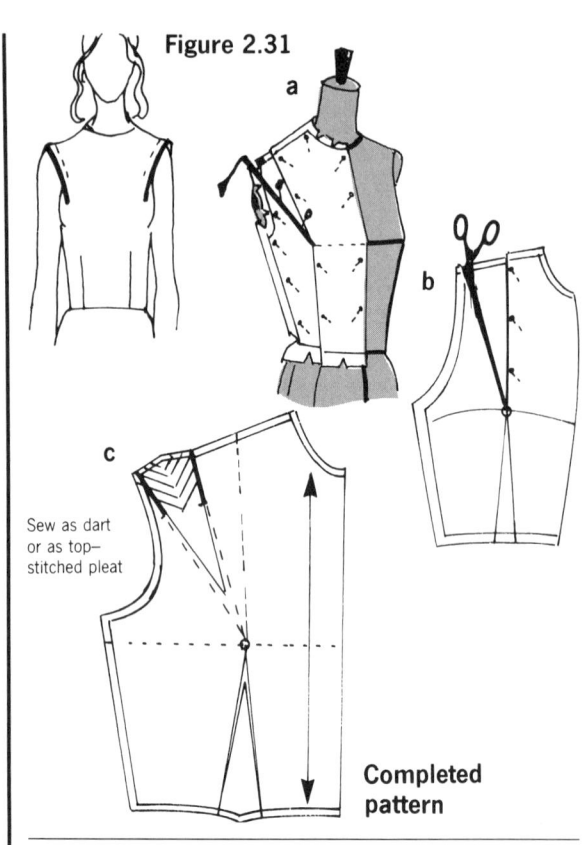

Figure 2.33

Figure 2.33a Outline front block with one large waist dart. Reduce dart and side seam at waist level by 4 cm (¾ in). Draw dotted bust line at right angles to CF. Draw flange line parallel to CF. Number parts **1** and **2** and cut apart.

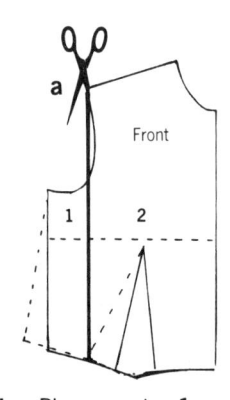

b Place parts **1** and **2** (in this case) 7 cm (3 in) apart with dotted bust line aligning previously drawn horizontal line. Fold and crease flange and cut out through folded shoulder and waist.

c Unfold and add seam allowances.

Completed pattern

Figure 2.34

Figure 2.34 Repeat process for back as shown.

Completed pattern

French darts

Figure 2.35 The French dart can be obtained by modelling as in previous examples or by the flat pattern cutting – dart manipulation – method:

a Outline large waist dart block (**Figure 2.18b**). Cut out.

b Draw position of French dart to bust point.

Close waist dart with pins and cut on French dart line as shown.

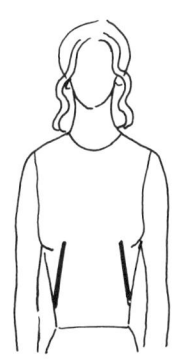

Figure 2.35

Curve dart for closer fit

Cut away excess material

Completed pattern

Waist bodice and darts

Figure 2.36

Figure 2.36a Cut on both new dart lines to bust point and open out.

Completed pattern

Waist darts

Figure 2.37

Figure 2.37a Cut on both new dart lines to bust point and open out.

Two waist darts

Completed pattern

Figure 2.38

Low centre front darts

Figure 2.38a Cut on new centre front line to bust point and open out.

b Sew as dart or open end tuck. Curve dart for closer fit.

Centre front seam

Completed pattern

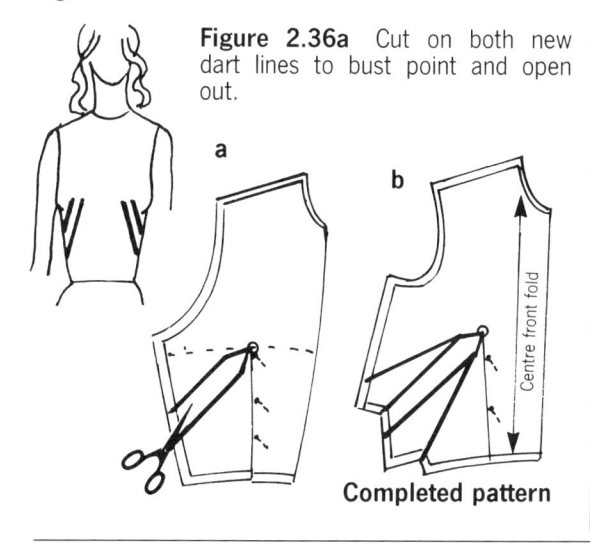

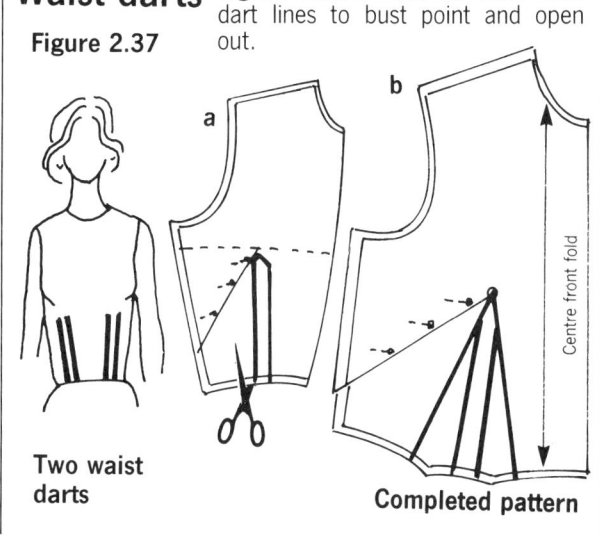

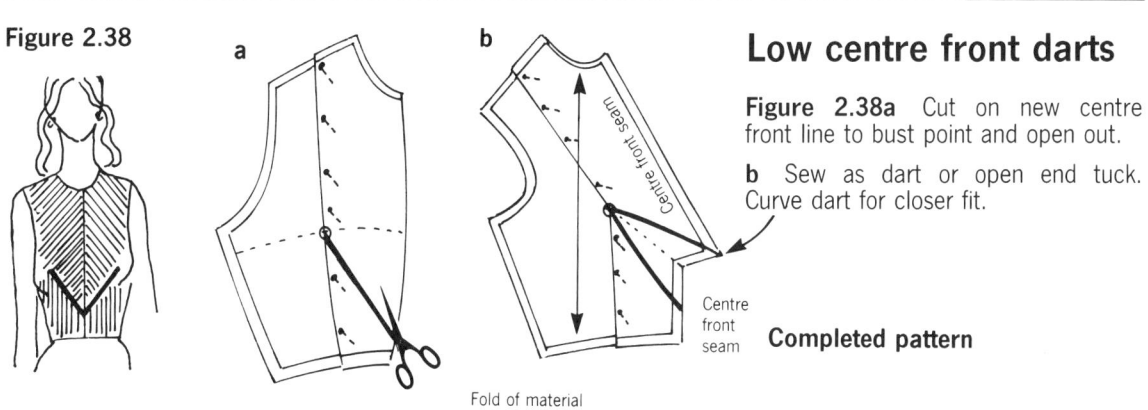

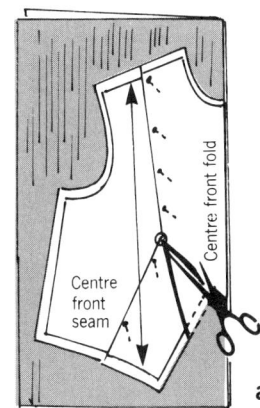

Fold of material

Figure 2.39

Figure 2.39a Allow 6 mm (¼ in) seam turning on pointed flap and cut on this line. Apply facing and make buttonhole.

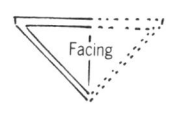

Facing

Note: The same pattern as Figure 2.38b but placed on different grain line, creating different effects.

Centre front seam

a **Completed pattern**

31

Application of centre front dart – cross over style

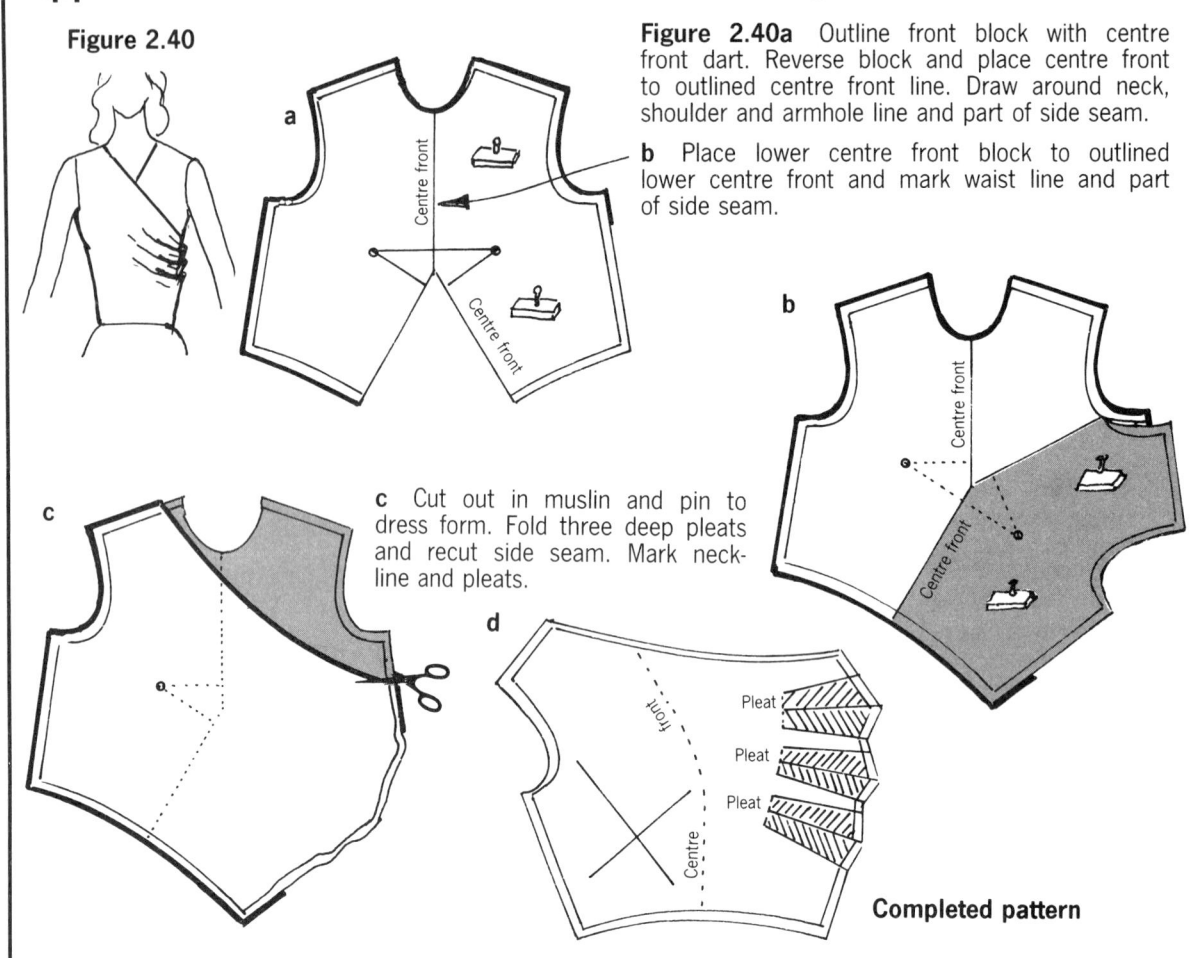

Figure 2.40

Figure 2.40a Outline front block with centre front dart. Reverse block and place centre front to outlined centre front line. Draw around neck, shoulder and armhole line and part of side seam.

b Place lower centre front block to outlined lower centre front and mark waist line and part of side seam.

c Cut out in muslin and pin to dress form. Fold three deep pleats and recut side seam. Mark neckline and pleats.

Completed pattern

Application of large waist dart – 'no dart' dress

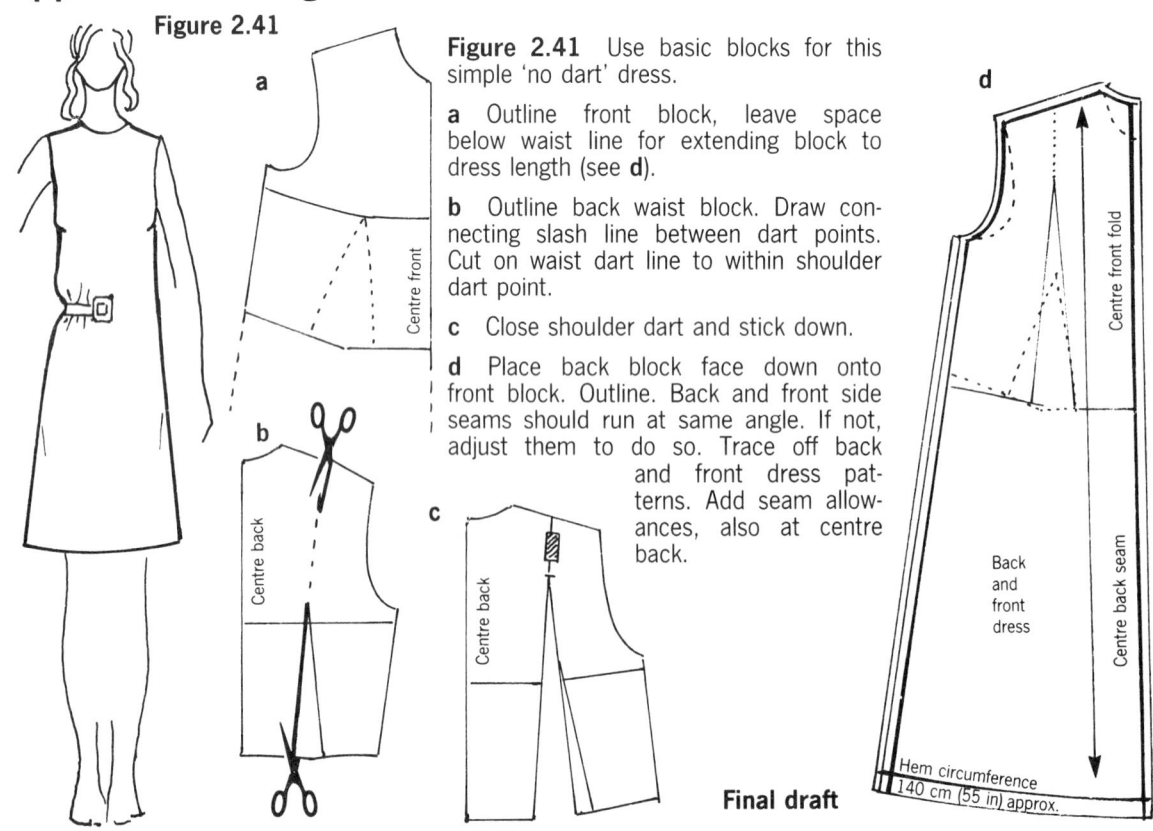

Figure 2.41

Figure 2.41 Use basic blocks for this simple 'no dart' dress.

a Outline front block, leave space below waist line for extending block to dress length (see **d**).

b Outline back waist block. Draw connecting slash line between dart points. Cut on waist dart line to within shoulder dart point.

c Close shoulder dart and stick down.

d Place back block face down onto front block. Outline. Back and front side seams should run at same angle. If not, adjust them to do so. Trace off back and front dress patterns. Add seam allowances, also at centre back.

Hem circumference 140 cm (55 in) approx.

Final draft

Principles of pivoting

An existing bust or waist dart can be pivoted on its pivoting point to other positions on the pattern, providing the amount of control remains constant and it originates from an outside seam. Although the fit of the bodice remains the same a new design is created, as the following examples show.

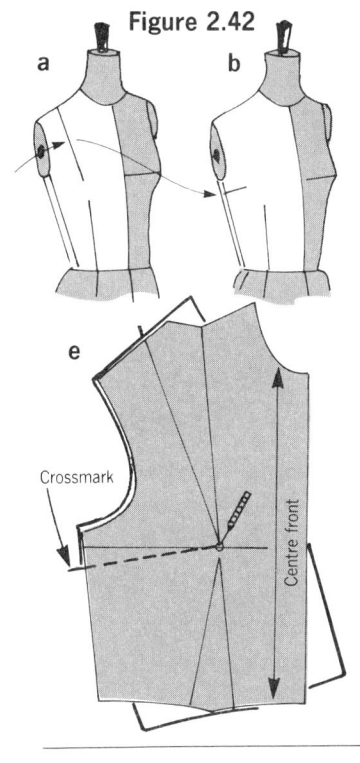

Figure 2.42

Shoulder to underarm dart

Figure 2.42a shows the shoulder dart before it is pivoted to underarm seam **(b)**.

c Draw new dart position clearly on a card waist block

d Place waist block on to pattern paper and outline **constant part** of waist block and **crossmark** clearly.

e On pivoting point, pivot shoulder dart out. Outline remaining block section and crossmark new dart position.

f Remove waist block and complete new waist block with underarm dart.

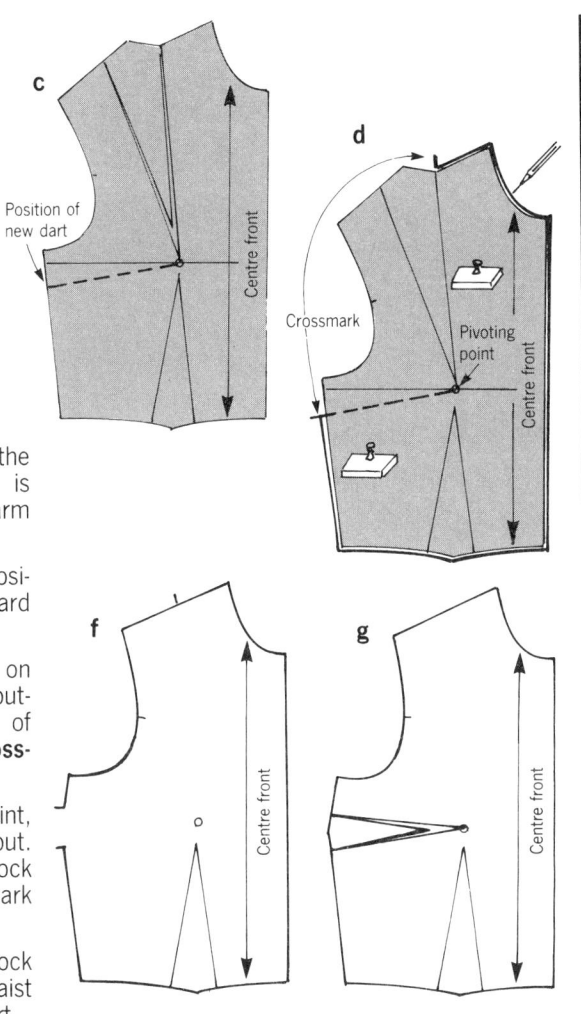

Completed block

Figure 2.43

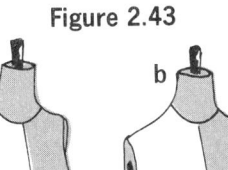

From shoulder to larger waist dart

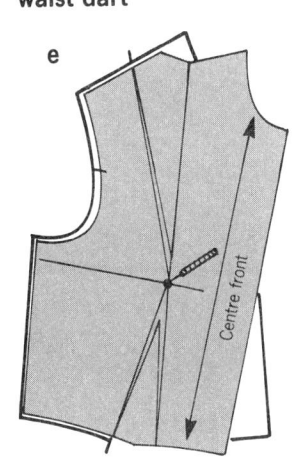

Shoulder to larger waist dart

Figure 2.43c Draw new dart position clearly on card waist block.

d Place waist block on to pattern paper and outline constant part of waist block and crossmark clearly.

e On pivoting point, pivot shoulder dart out. Outline remaining block section and crossmark new dart position.

f Remove waist block and complete new waist block with one large waist dart.

g This block can be used to cut bias styles with or without a centre front seam.

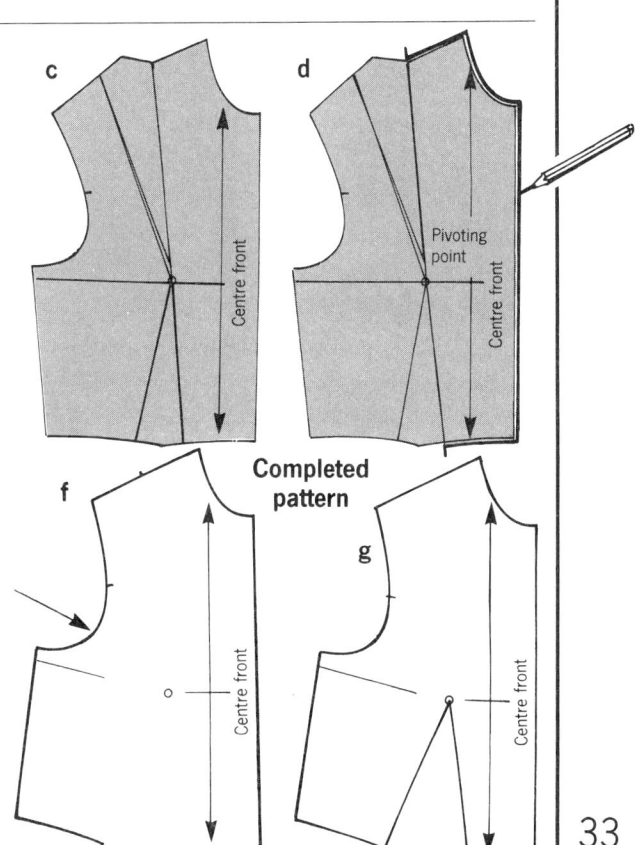

Completed pattern

2 Waist bodice and darts

33

From shoulder to neck dart

Figure 2.44

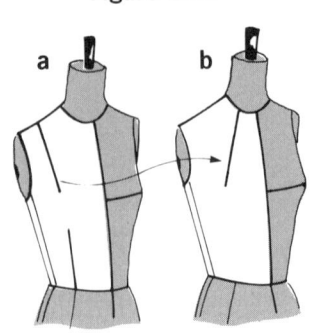

Figure 2.44c Draw new dart position clearly on card waist block.

d Place waist block on to pattern paper. Outline constant part of waist block and crossmark clearly.

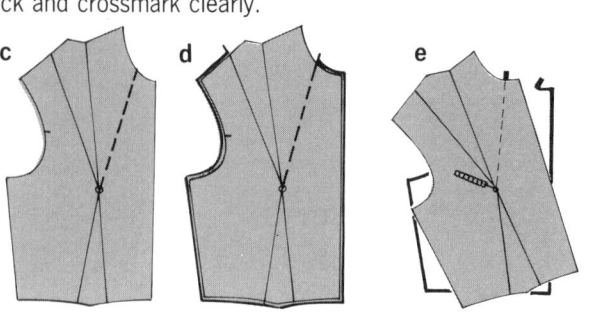

e On pivoting point, pivot shoulder dart out. Outline remaining block section and crossmark new dart position. Outline CF and short distance of neck and waist lines. Crossmark inner dart line positions.

f Remove waist block, complete drafting and cut out.

g Pivot waist dart out, outline remaining block section and crossmark new dart position. Remove waist block.

h Shows the completed block with one neck dart.

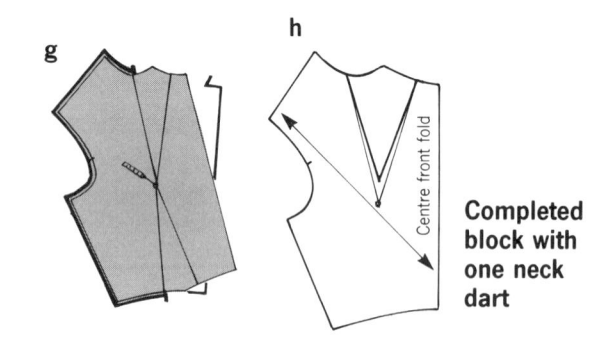

Completed block with one neck dart

From waist to centre front dart

Figure 2.45

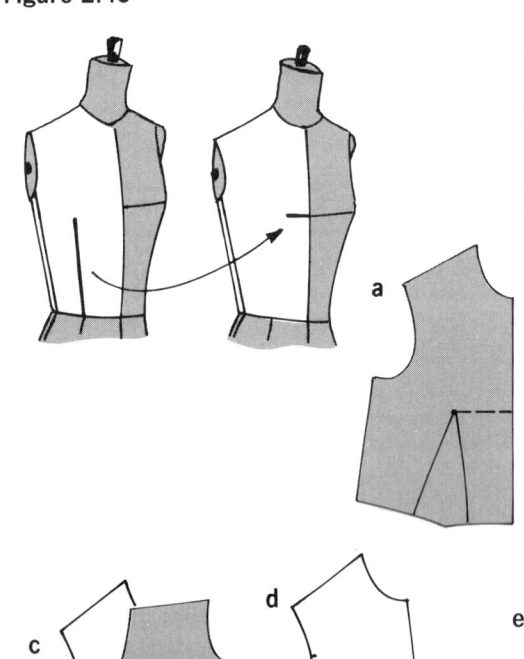

Figure 2.45a Draw clearly new dart position on card waist block.

b Place waist block on to pattern paper. Outline constant part of waist block and crossmark clearly.

c On pivoting point, pivot waist dart out. Outline remaining block section and crossmark new dart position.

d Remove waist block from pattern paper and complete drafting new waist block with centre front dart.

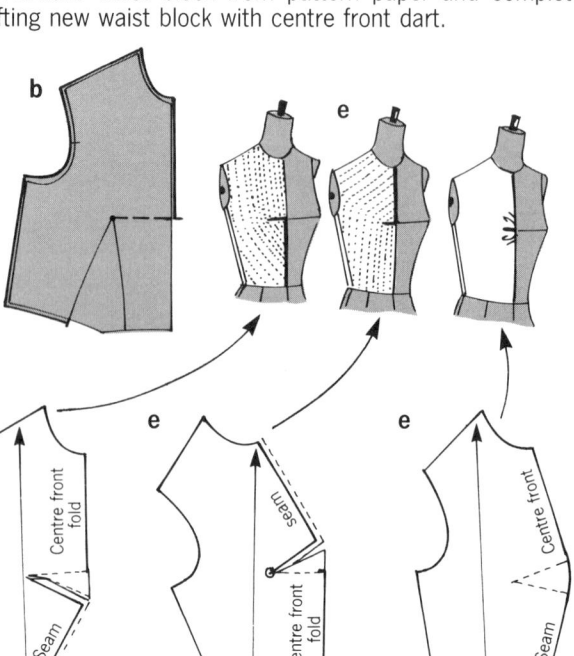

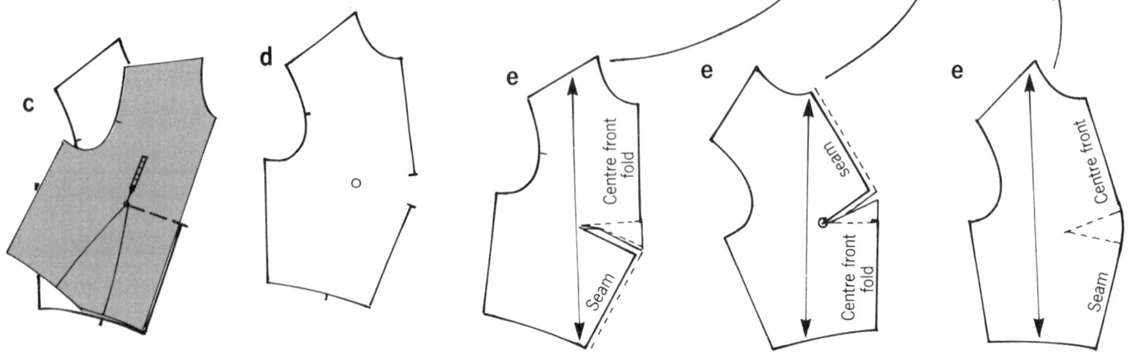

Completed blocks

From back shoulder to back neck dart

Figure 2.46

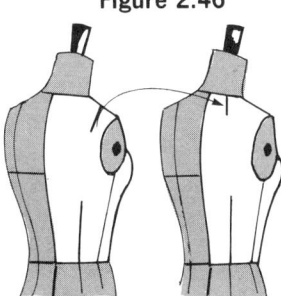

For fitting or stylistic reasons the back shoulder dart or its ease allowance is sometimes moved to other positions. The process of pivoting this dart is the same as for front bodice darts.

Figure 2.46a Draw clearly new dart position on card back waist block and place on pattern paper.

b Outline constant part of back waist block and crossmark clearly.

c On pivoting point, pivot shoulder dart out. Outline remaining block section and crossmark new dart position.

d Remove back waist block from pattern paper and complete drafting new back waist block with back neck dart.

e Shows the complete new block.

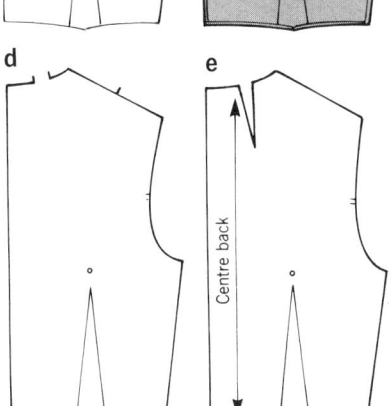

Completed new block

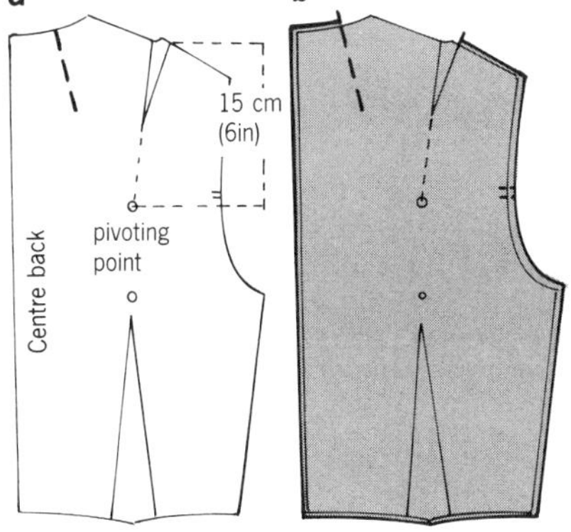

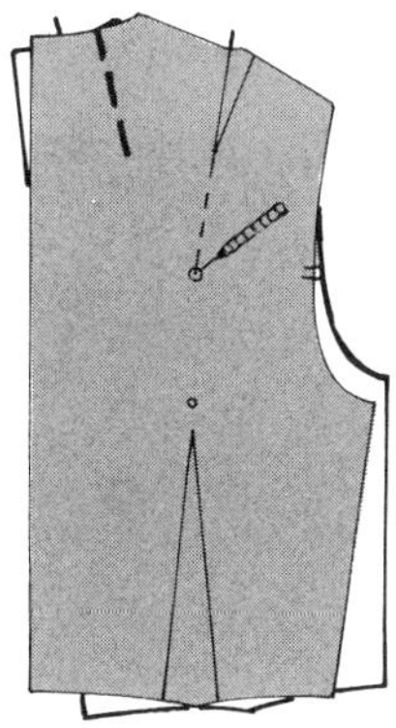

Slashing method

Figure 2.47

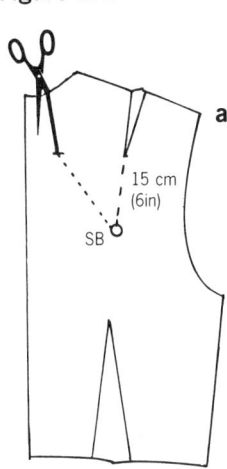

From back shoulder to back neck and to armhole dart by the slashing method.

Figure 2.47a Outline back waist block and mark position of new neckline dart, 6 cm (2½ in) long. Connect to highest point of shoulder blade (SB) approx. 15 cm (6 in) down from centre of shoulder.

b Cut to SB and overlap shoulder dart.

c Draw in new neck dart as shown. Cut neckline through folded neck dart.

Figure 2.48 This suppression is seldom used as a dart in its own right but rather in conjunction with the princess line seam development. Proceed as for back neck dart.

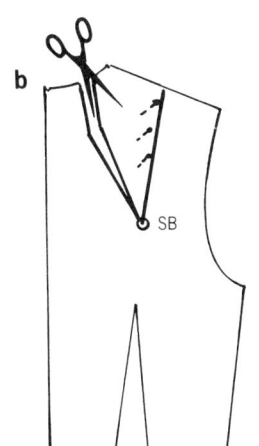

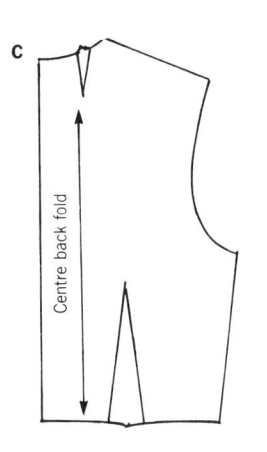

Figure 2.48

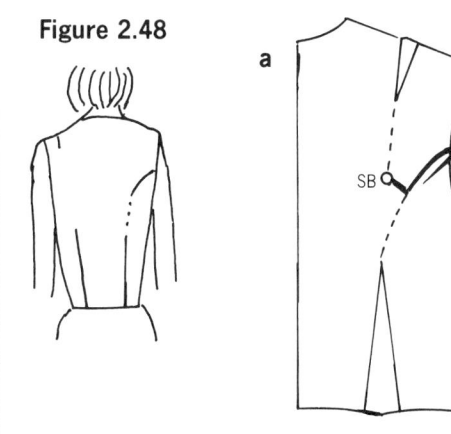

Completed pattern

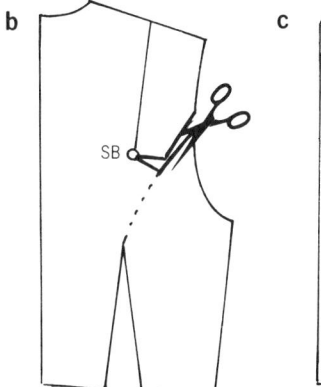

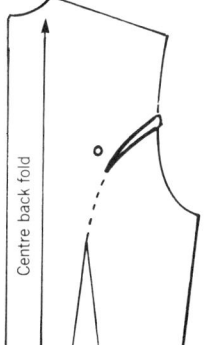

Completed pattern

Waist bodice and darts

Making the card block or foundation pattern

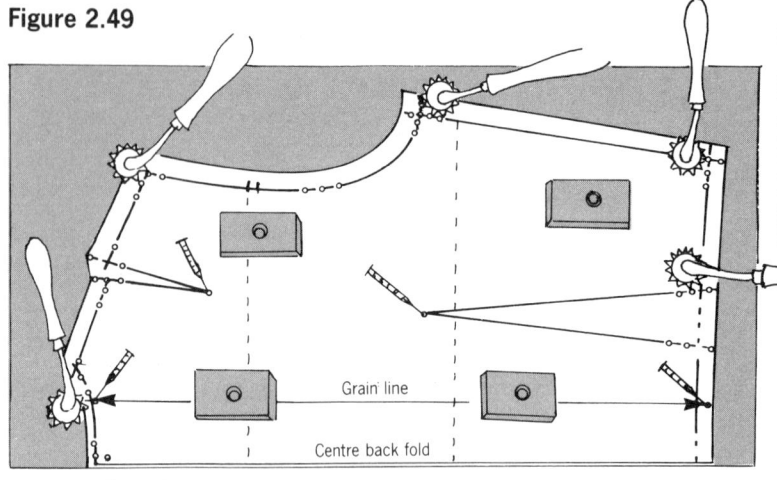

Waist bodice and darts

Figure 2.49

Completed muslin or paper patterns

Figure 2.49 Place pattern onto heavy pattern card or plastic pattern board with centre back of pattern to straight edge of cardboard. Hold down with weights.

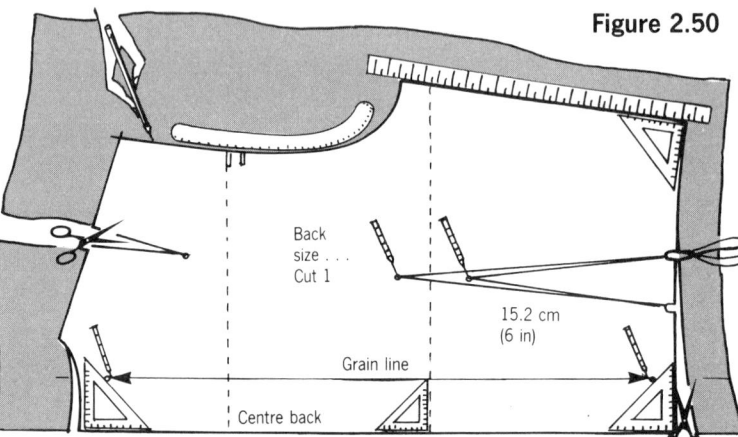

Figure 2.50

Figure 2.50 Connect tracing wheel marks with aid of a ruler, a tailor's curve and set square.

Draft alternative shorter waist dart, 15.2 cm (6 in) and cut out small shoulder dart.

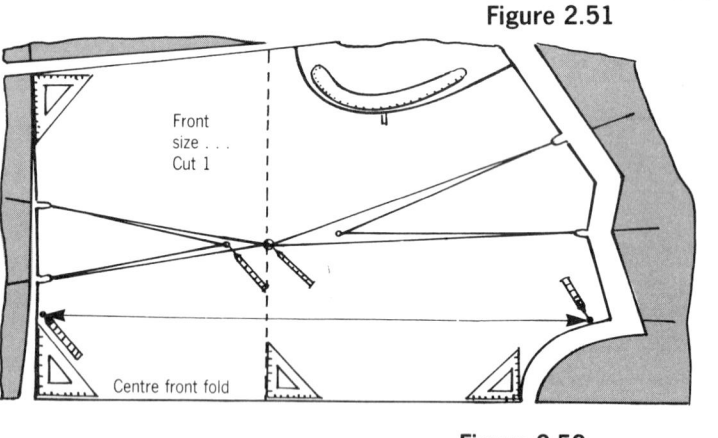

Figure 2.51

Figure 2.51 Pierce dart points and grain line points with scriber or small-hole perforator. Extend drafted grain lines to edges of cardboard.

Figure 2.52 Cut with long even strokes on drafted seam lines. (Blocks do not generally carry seam allowances.) Notch darts.

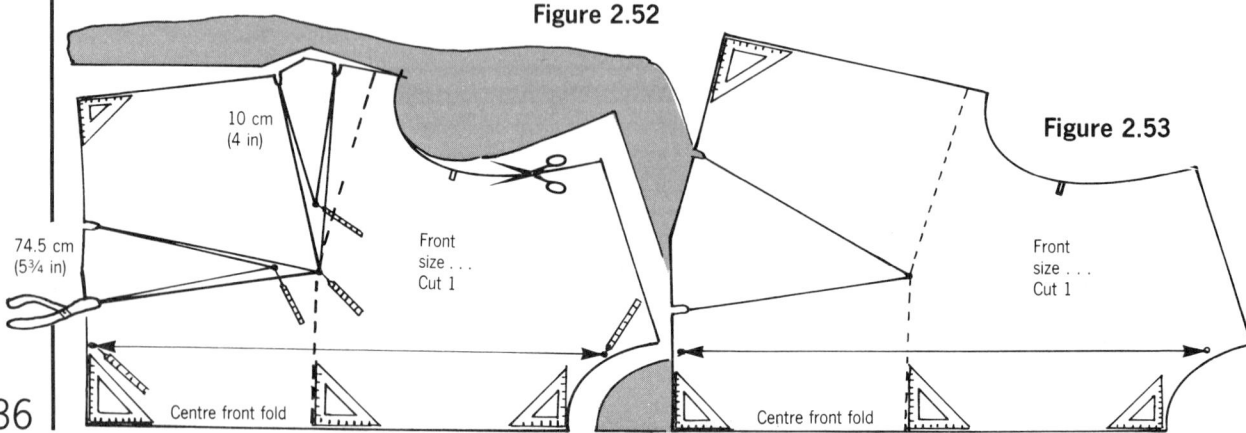

Figure 2.52

Figure 2.53

Figure 2.54

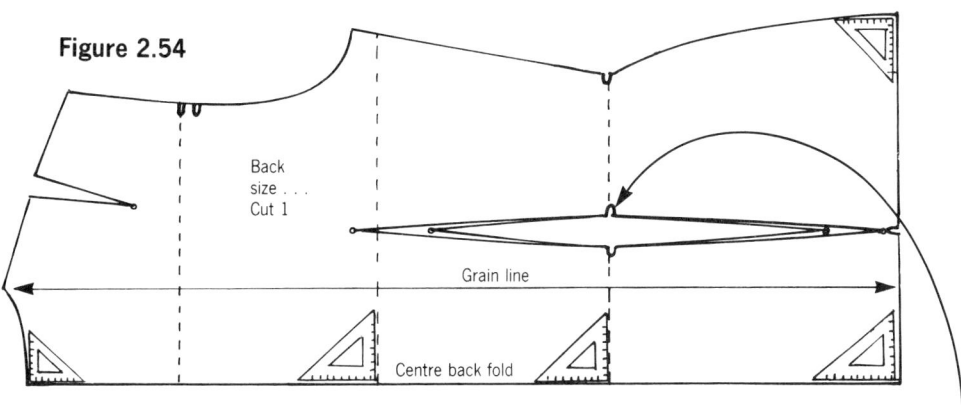

Back size... Cut 1

Grain line

Centre back fold

Figure 2.54 Either cut out darts and notch waist line or perforate dart points and waist position (Figure 2.55).

Figure 2.55

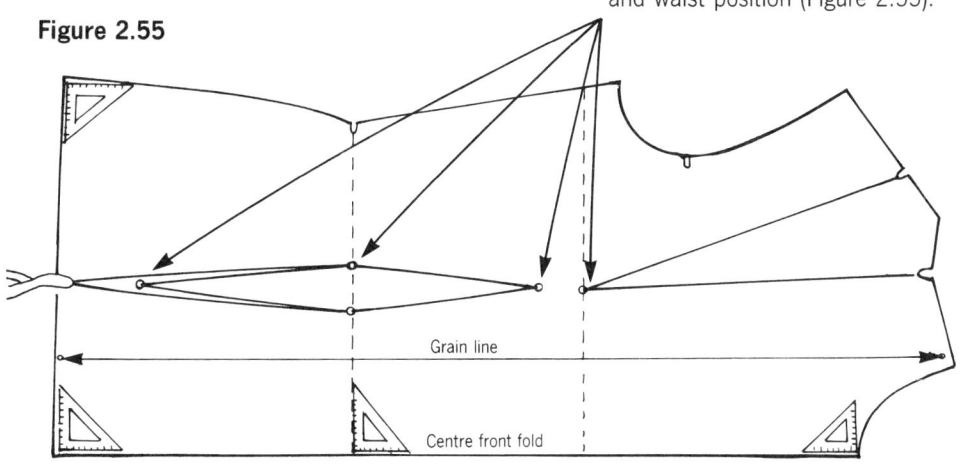

Grain line

Centre front fold

Figure 2.56 Important block pattern

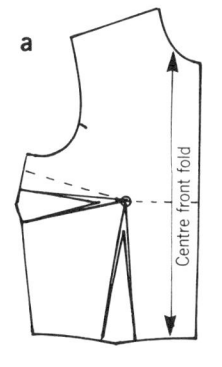

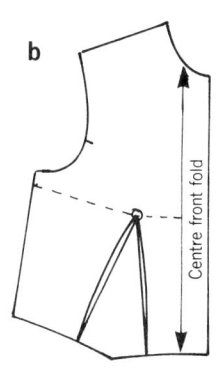

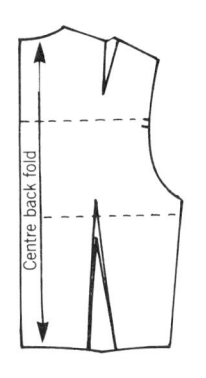

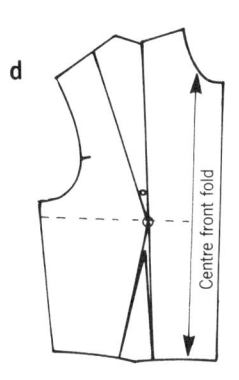

a b c d e f

Figure 2.56 From the preceding examples of pattern development it can be seen that some block patterns are frequently used to develop new and more intricate patterns.

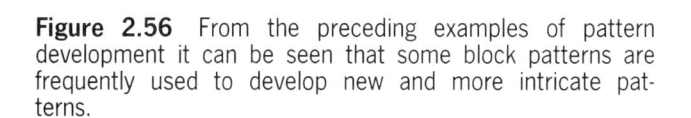

Cut these block patterns in **a–f** in heavy card and hang up ready for use.

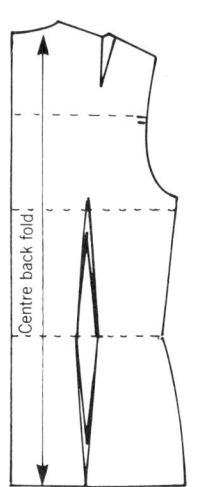

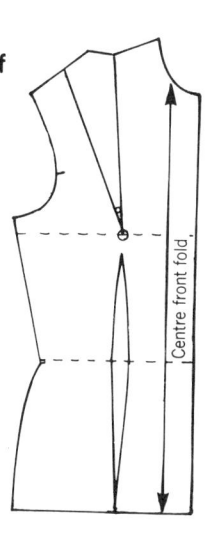

2

Waist bodice and darts

3 Bodice styling
Gathers, yokes and pleats

Bust formation influences pattern development of horizontal seams and yokes.

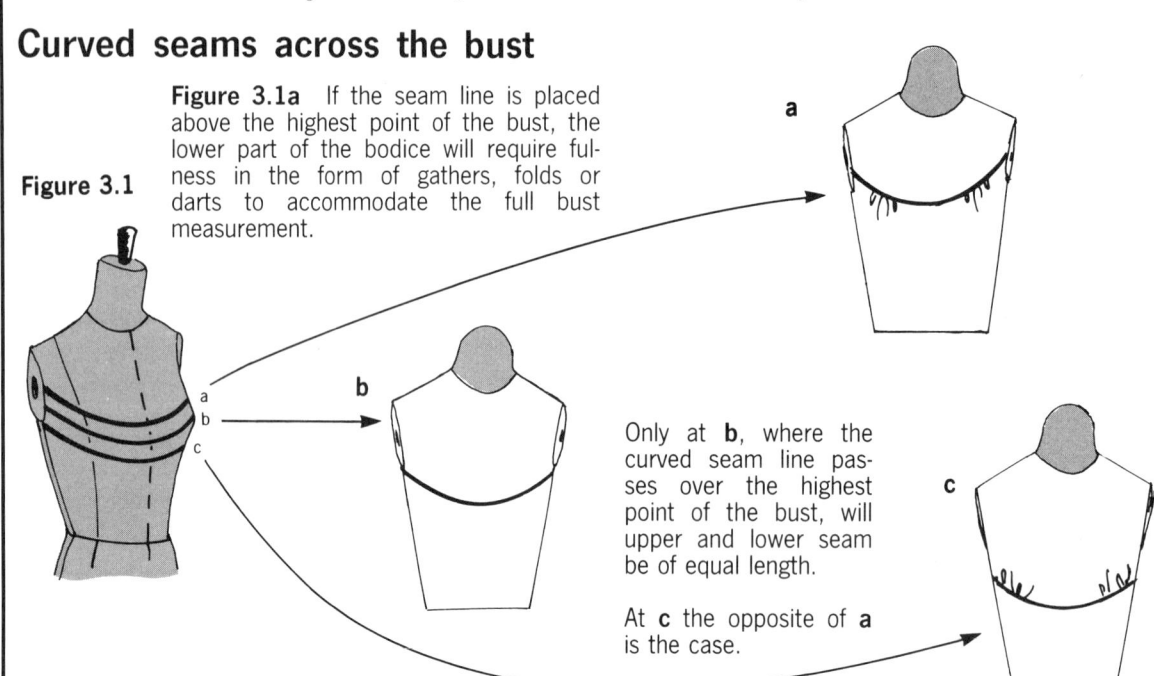

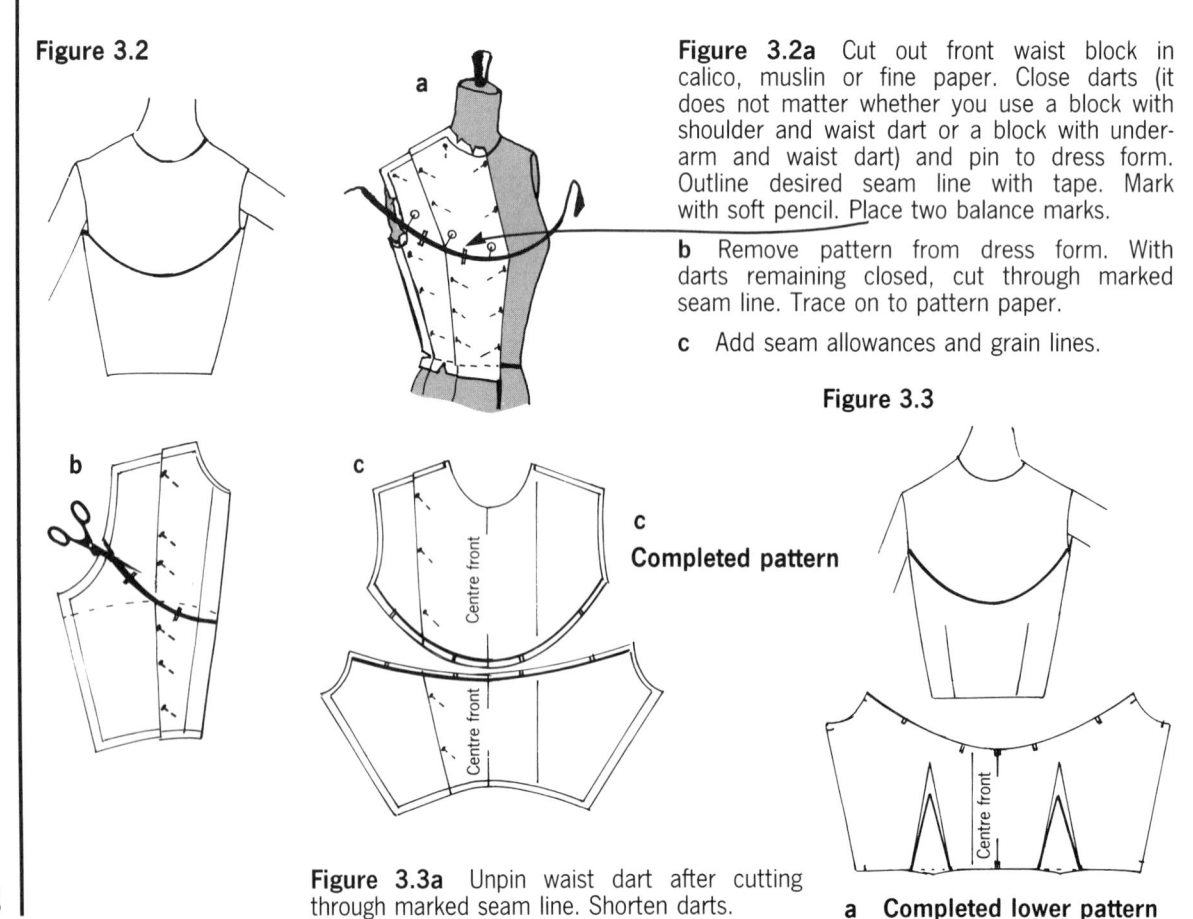

Curved seams across the bust

Figure 3.1

Figure 3.1a If the seam line is placed above the highest point of the bust, the lower part of the bodice will require fulness in the form of gathers, folds or darts to accommodate the full bust measurement.

Only at **b**, where the curved seam line passes over the highest point of the bust, will upper and lower seam be of equal length.

At **c** the opposite of **a** is the case.

Figure 3.2

Figure 3.2a Cut out front waist block in calico, muslin or fine paper. Close darts (it does not matter whether you use a block with shoulder and waist dart or a block with underarm and waist dart) and pin to dress form. Outline desired seam line with tape. Mark with soft pencil. Place two balance marks.

b Remove pattern from dress form. With darts remaining closed, cut through marked seam line. Trace on to pattern paper.

c Add seam allowances and grain lines.

Figure 3.3

c **Completed pattern**

Figure 3.3a Unpin waist dart after cutting through marked seam line. Shorten darts.

a **Completed lower pattern**

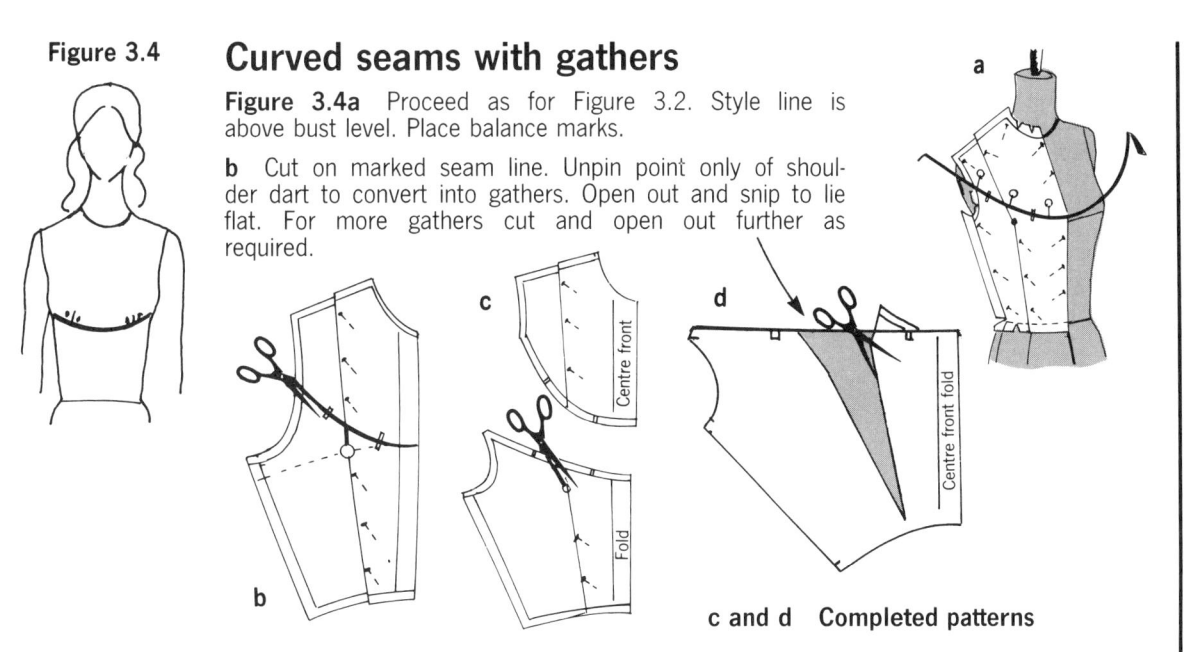

Curved seams with gathers

Figure 3.4

Figure 3.4a Proceed as for Figure 3.2. Style line is above bust level. Place balance marks.

b Cut on marked seam line. Unpin point only of shoulder dart to convert into gathers. Open out and snip to lie flat. For more gathers cut and open out further as required.

c and d Completed patterns

Figure 3.5

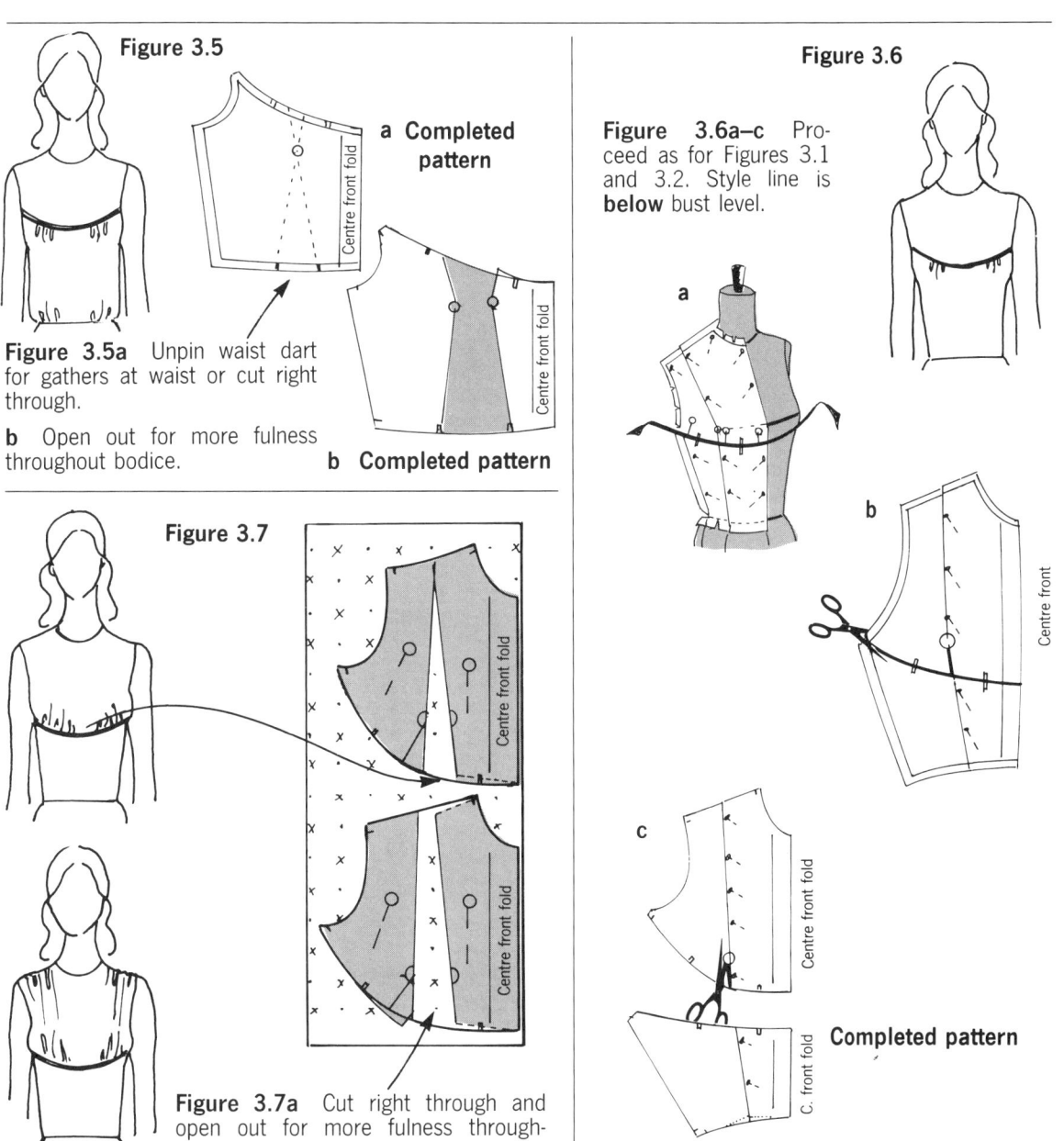

Figure 3.5a Unpin waist dart for gathers at waist or cut right through.

b Open out for more fulness throughout bodice.

a Completed pattern

b Completed pattern

Figure 3.6

Figure 3.6a–c Proceed as for Figures 3.1 and 3.2. Style line is **below** bust level.

Completed pattern

Figure 3.7

Figure 3.7a Cut right through and open out for more fulness throughout.

3 Bodice styling

39

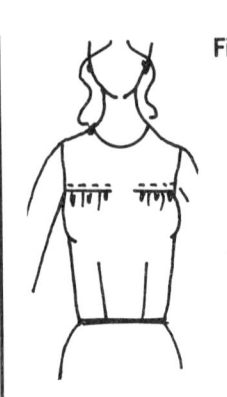

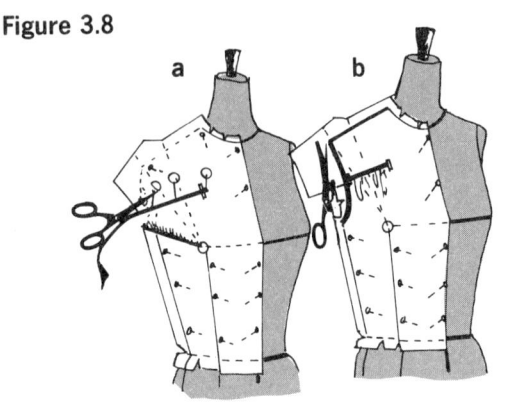

Partial yoke with gathers

Figure 3.8

Figure 3.8a Cut shoulder and waist dart block in muslin. Close waist dart and pin to dress form. Smooth shoulder seam and pin, ignoring original shoulder area. Pin tape for style line and gathers. Mark with soft pencil. Cut on line.

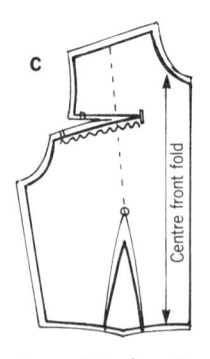

b Arrange gathers over bust position. Unpin shoulder section and fold cut edge over gathered section allowing 1.3 cm (½ in) seam turning tapering to nothing at inner end. Pin and mark new lines. Place balance marks. Redraw shoulder and part of armhole line and cut away surplus muslin.

d and **e** The same style, but cut flat.

Completed pattern

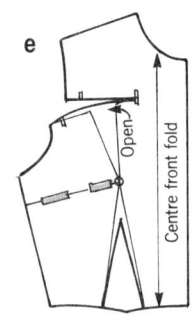

Draft   Completed pattern

Partial yoke with centre front neck seam and gathers

Figure 3.9

Figure 3.9a Roughly cut out in muslin front waist block with one large shoulder dart (waist dart having previously been moved into the shoulder dart). Pin to dress form but leave shoulder and neck area unpinned.

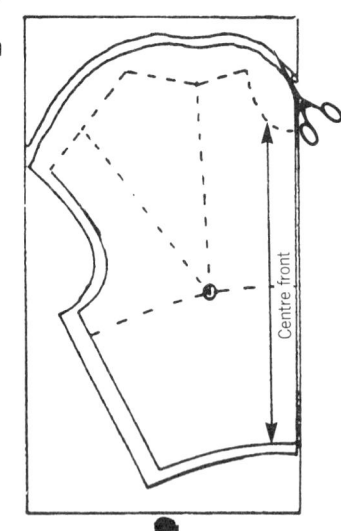

b Mark position of style line approximately 7.5 cm (3 in) below pit of neck and cut.

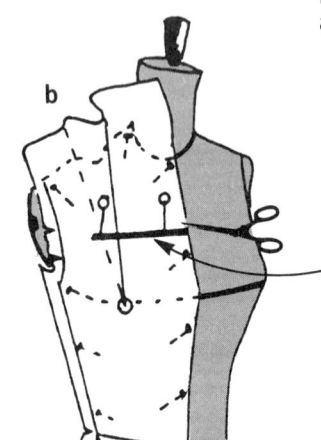

c Fold back upper section. Arrange excess fulness into gathers and pin.

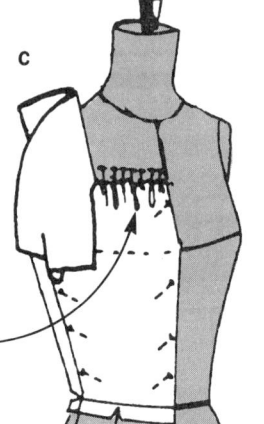

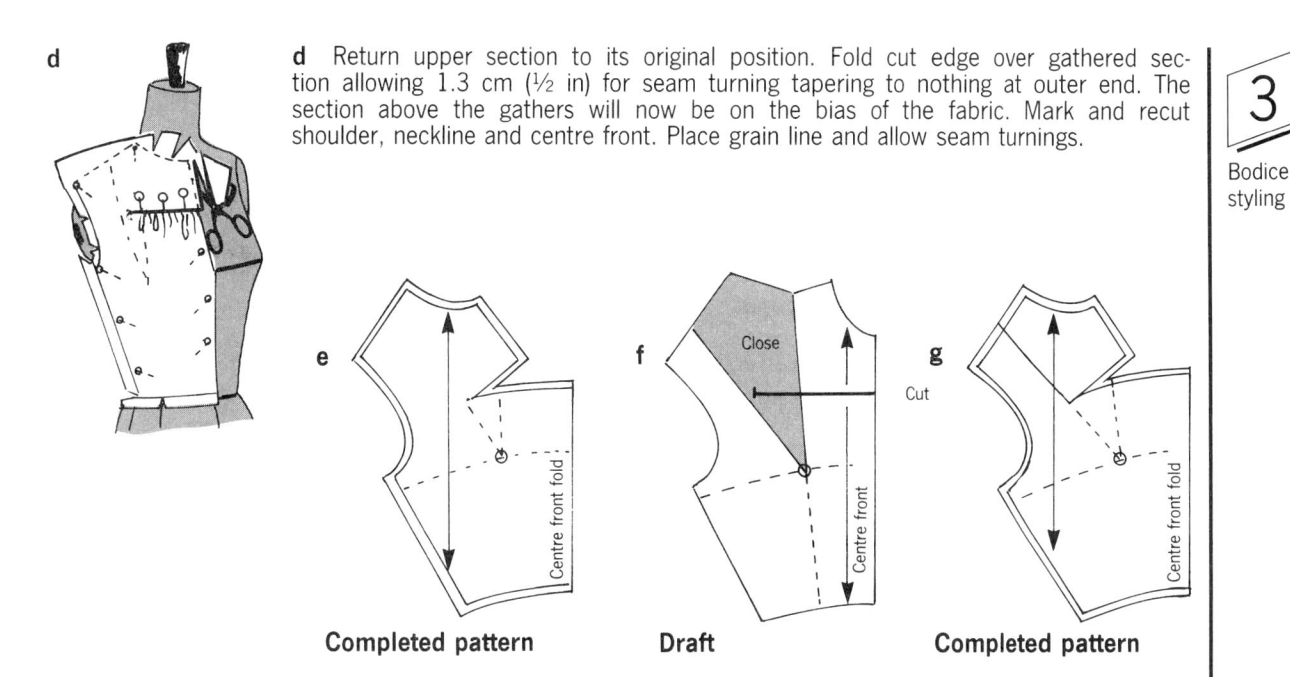

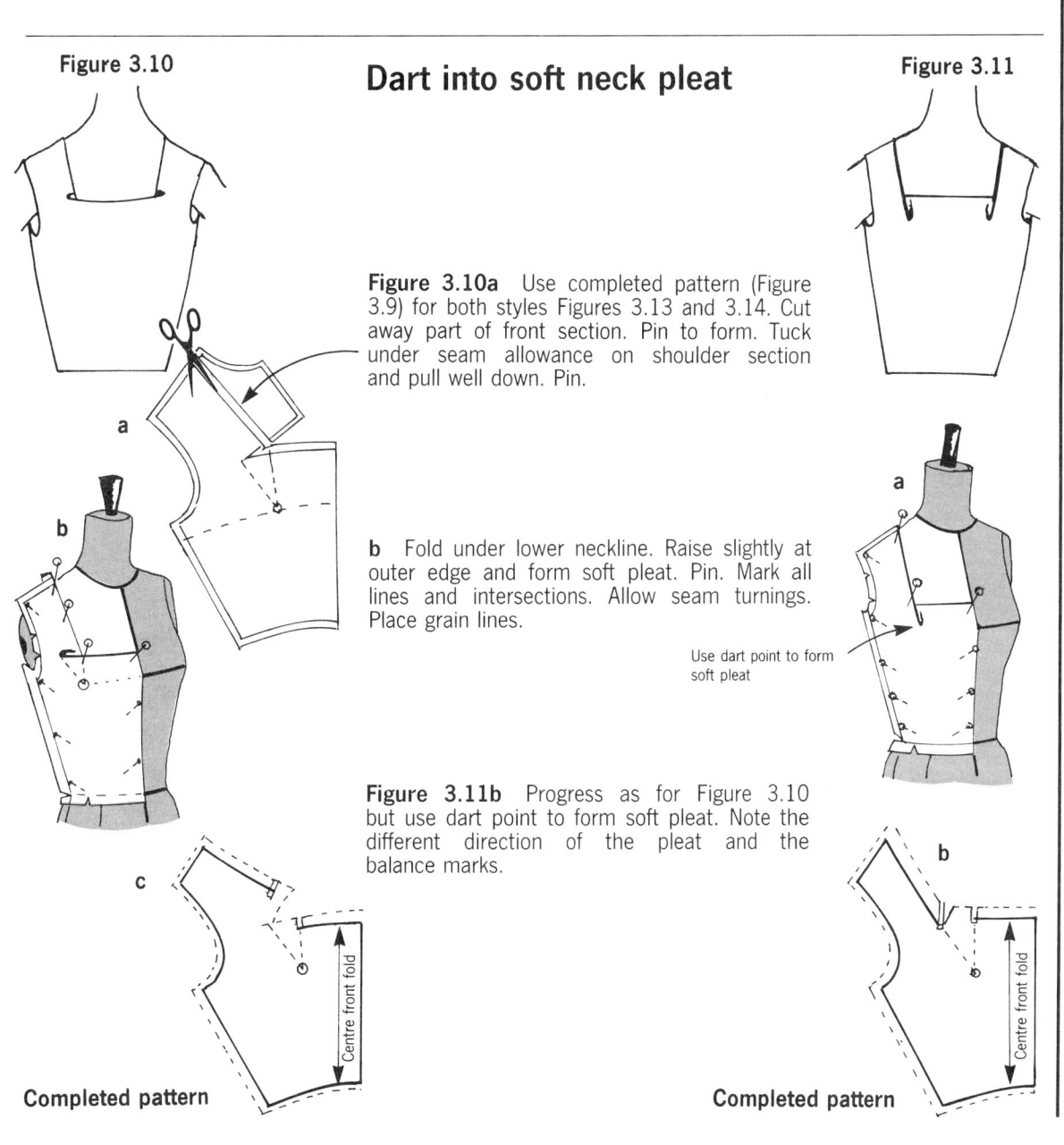

d Return upper section to its original position. Fold cut edge over gathered section allowing 1.3 cm (½ in) for seam turning tapering to nothing at outer end. The section above the gathers will now be on the bias of the fabric. Mark and recut shoulder, neckline and centre front. Place grain line and allow seam turnings.

3

Bodice styling

e Completed pattern

f Draft — Close / Cut

g Completed pattern

Dart into soft neck pleat

Figure 3.10

Figure 3.11

Figure 3.10a Use completed pattern (Figure 3.9) for both styles Figures 3.13 and 3.14. Cut away part of front section. Pin to form. Tuck under seam allowance on shoulder section and pull well down. Pin.

b Fold under lower neckline. Raise slightly at outer edge and form soft pleat. Pin. Mark all lines and intersections. Allow seam turnings. Place grain lines.

Use dart point to form soft pleat

Figure 3.11b Progress as for Figure 3.10 but use dart point to form soft pleat. Note the different direction of the pleat and the balance marks.

Completed pattern

Completed pattern

41

Shoulder-neck yoke with gathers

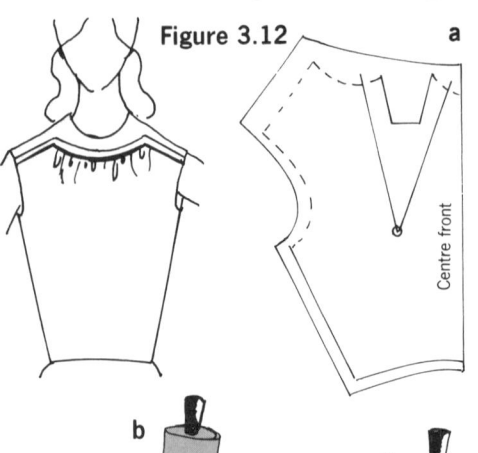

Figure 3.12a Cut out front waist block with one large neck dart (see Figure 3.9a). Use muslin or fine calico. Allow larger turnings at shoulder and neckline. Close neck dart.

b Pin to dress form. Outline yoke with tape. Mark with soft pencil. Place balance mark. Cut 6 mm (¼ in) above pencilled line.

c Temporarily fold back yoke. Unpin dart point. Arrange as gathers between balance mark and centre front.

d Unpin yoke, turn under lower edge and pin over gathered section. Correct part of armhole, shoulder line and neckline. Mark yoke style line and adjoining gathered section. Transfer to pattern paper.

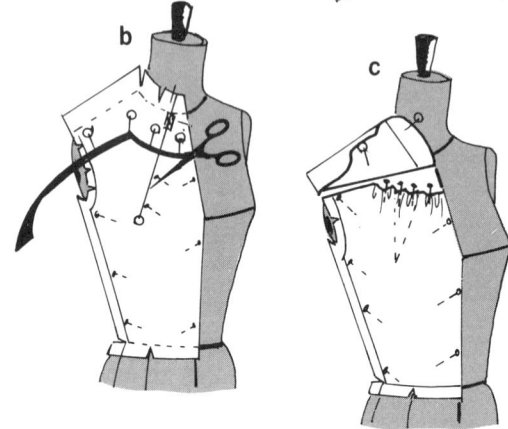

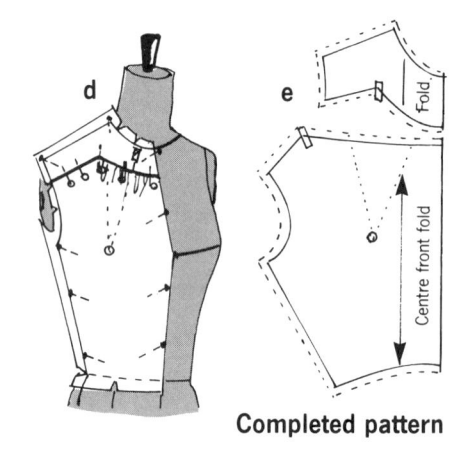

Completed pattern

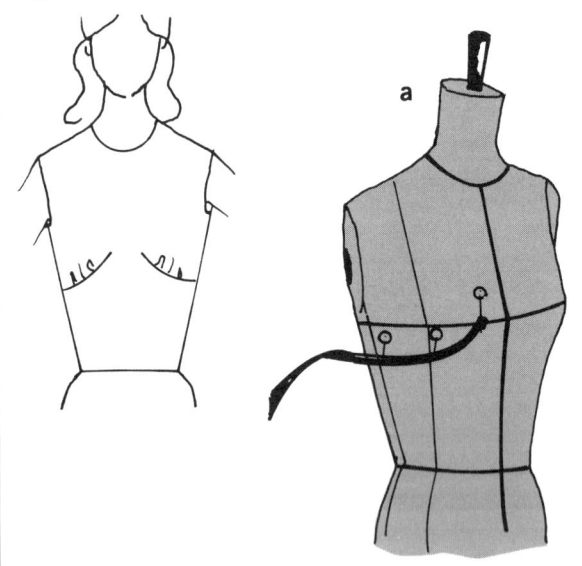

Partial under bust seam and gathers

Figure 3.13a Experiment with different style lines on dress form. When a pleasing line has been established, transfer final information to flat pattern.

b Use block with one large shoulder dart. Draw style line and place balance marks confining position of gathers immediately under bust. Cut on arrowed line. Cut to bust point. Close shoulder dart and add seam allowances all around. For more fulness, cut to shoulder line and open (see Figure 3.7a).

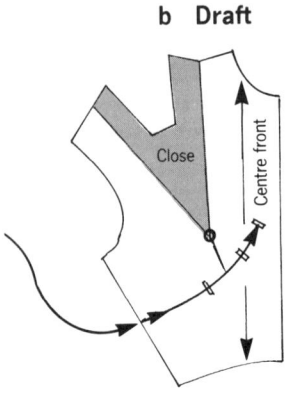

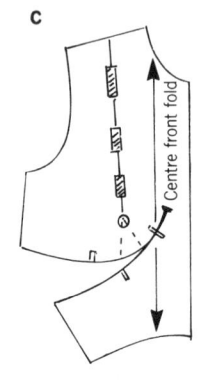

Completed pattern

Button closings and facings

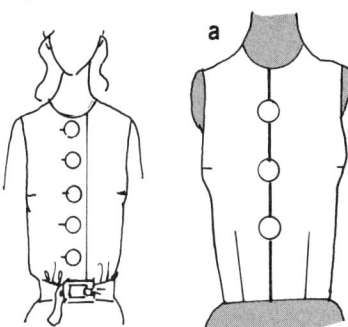

Figure 3.14

Figure 3.14a Buttons rest in the centre of all single-breasted garments. When fastened, the button will extend half to the right and half to the left of the centre. Because of this, and to allow for buttonholes, a button stand, extension or wrap must be provided.

b The width of the button stand depends mainly on the size of the button, but also on fashion trends and the thickness of the fabric. The minimum width is equal to the diameter of the button. Add 1.3 cm (½ in) or more for thick fabrics.

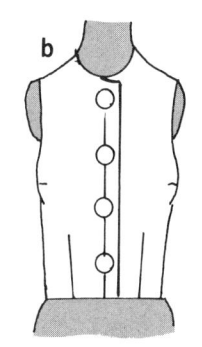

c Buttonholes are on average 3 mm (⅛ in) longer than the diameter of the button. When the button is flat and smooth, less than this amount is required to pass the button easily through the buttonhole.

Slightly more than 3 mm (⅛ in) will be needed for a chunky ball button. Try out before deciding on the exact size.

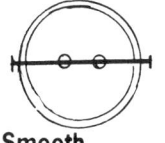

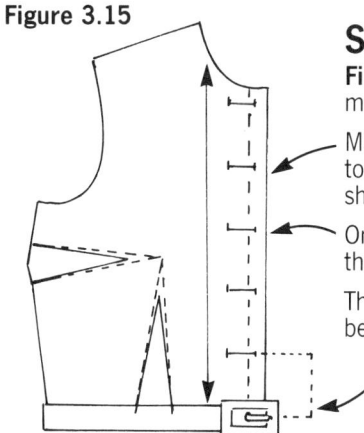

Smooth flat button

Chunky ball button

Figure 3.15

Single-breasted fastenings and facings

Figure 3.15 The distance from neckline to first buttonhole is normally the same as the width of the button stand.

Mark the average addition of 3 mm (⅛ in) to the length of the buttonhole to the right of the centre front. This will provide for the shank of the button.

One button should be placed at or near the point of greatest strain, the bust line.

The space between waist line and button should be the same as between the other buttons.

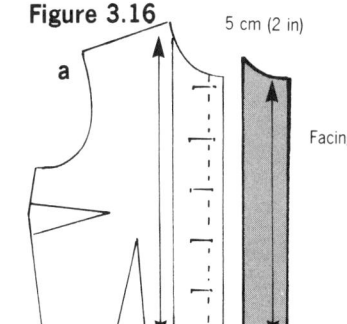

Figure 3.16

Facings

Facings can be cut in three ways: in **Figure 3.16a** the garment is always worn closed at the neckline; in **b** it is worn open or closed at the neck and in **c**, having the same dual purpose as **b**, the facing is cut in one with the front bodice. This method, while preferable in some ways, is less economical as regards fabric.

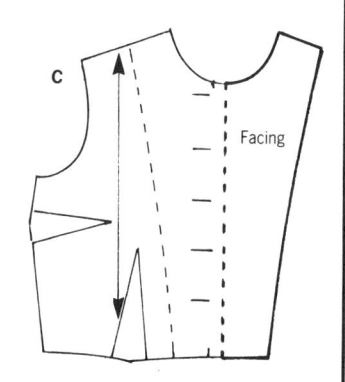

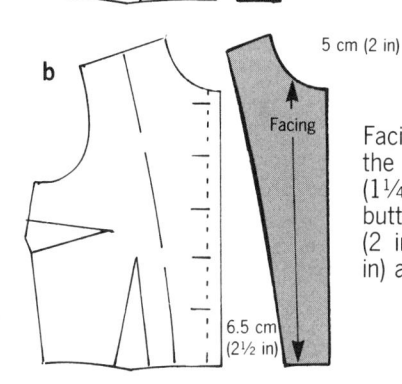

Facings must be wide enough to cover the buttonholes and should extend 3 cm (1¼ in) or more beyond the end of the buttonhole. As a guide, measure 5 cm (2 in) at shoulder and 5–6.5 cm (2–2½ in) at waistline and connect.

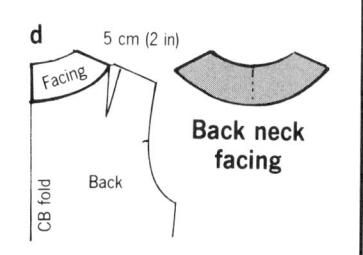

Back neck facing

Double-breasted fastening and facing

Figure 3.17

Figure 3.17a Outline hip block (Figure 12.1, page 176). Determine width of extension or wrap beyond centre front – approximately 6 cm (2⅜ in). Shape neckline. Shape edge of extension – slightly wider at neckline narrowing towards waistline.

Buttonholes are marked from the edge of the wrap, generally 1.5 cm (⅝ in) away from it. Measure from centre front to outer edge of buttonhole. Apply this measurement to the placing of the 'double-breasted' row of buttons.

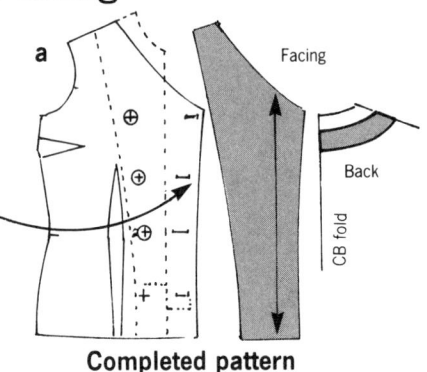

Completed pattern

Shirt band opening

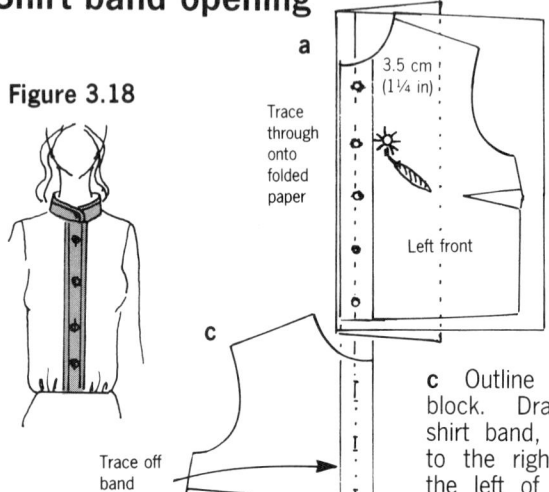

Figure 3.18

Figure 3.18a The left front pattern has a grown-on facing. Draw width of band (3.5 cm) (1¼ in) half to left and half to right of CF. Trace through onto folded paper.

b Open out. This determines width of grown-on facing. Add seam allowances.

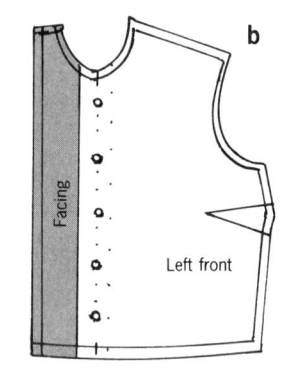

c Outline right front block. Draw width of shirt band, extending half to the right and half to the left of CF as above. Trace off band, but leave front block intact – (**d** and **e**). Band can be cut on bias (**f**) or on reverse grain if in striped fabric. Apply by placing right side of band to wrong side of bodice. After stitching, band is turned to right side of bodice. Turn under band seam allowance. Stitch down.

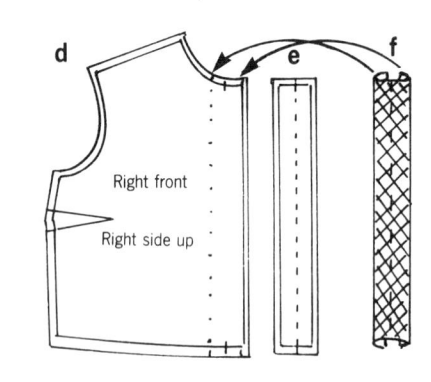

Fly front opening

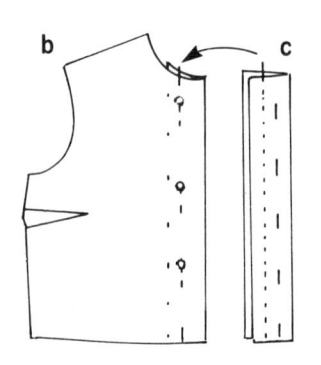

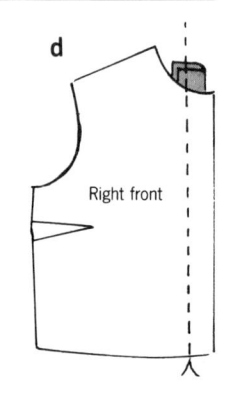

Figure 3.19

Figure 3.19a Proceed as for Figure 3.18a and **c** above. **b** and **c** Cut double band 6 mm (¼ in) narrower than drawn lines.

Neck finishes and buttonholes are completed before band is attached. The double band should not be visible from the right side, having been set back 6 mm (¼ in) from the edge.

Blouse and shirt developments

Bodice with detachable yoke

Figure 3.20

This yoke is detachable. Experiment on dress form to obtain the most pleasing yoke line.

Figure 3.20a Transfer final information to draft. Trace each pattern part onto new sheet of paper. Add seam allowances.

Develop facings as in **Figure 5.7b** and **5.16**.

The detachable yoke is lined throughout.

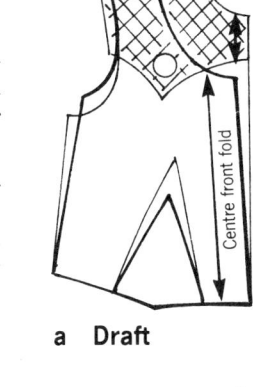

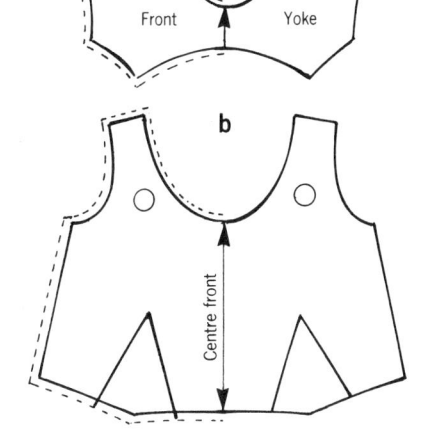

Figure 3.21

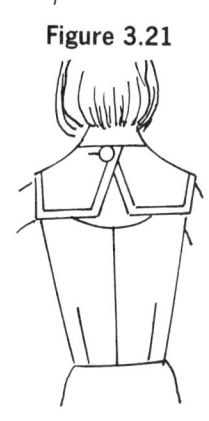

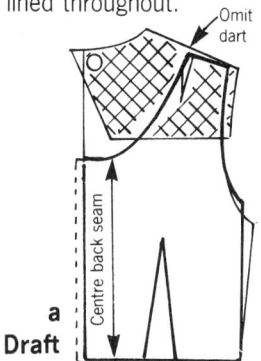

a **Draft**

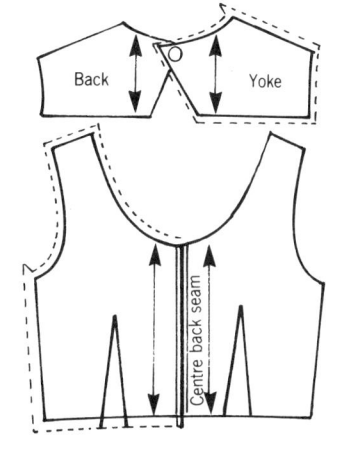

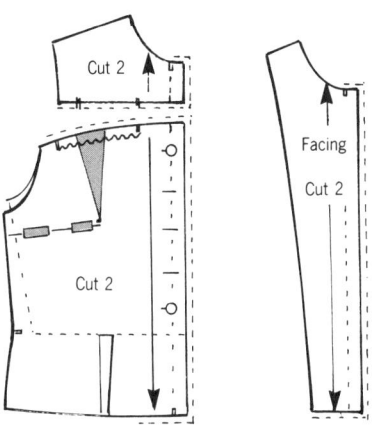

b **Completed pattern**

Figure 3.21 Back: proceed as for front. Add seam allowance at centre back.

Figure 3.22

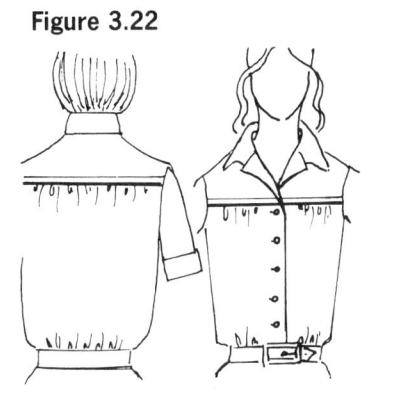

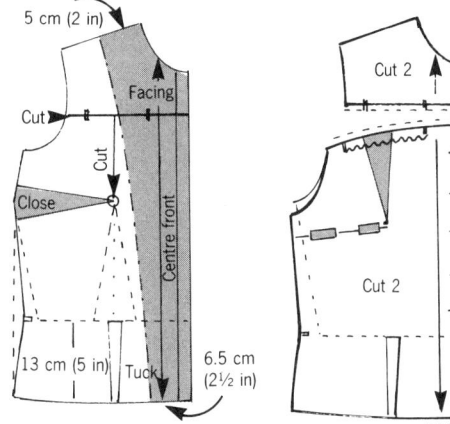

a **Front draft**

b **Completed pattern**

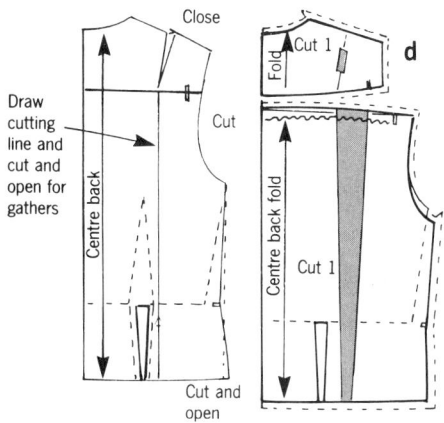

c **Back draft**   **Completed pattern**

Figure 3.22a Front draft: Outline front waist block with underarm dart. Draw yoke line. Lengthen waist block by at least 13 cm (5 in). Add button stand. From yoke line draw slashing line to bust point. Draw 2.5 cm (1 in) tuck instead of waist dart from hip to waist line. Redraw side seam.

a Draw facing and balance marks. Trace pattern parts onto new sheet of paper.

b Add seam allowances, grain lines, button and buttonhole spacing and cutting instructions. See page 43 for facings, etc.

c Proceed for back as shown.

Important! See also pages 47–9.

Bodice styling

45

Shirt with yoke and pleats

Figure 3.23

a **Draft**

b **Completed pattern**

Shirt with yoke and pleats

Figure 3.23a Use shirt pattern drafts, Figure 3.22a and c. Draw line through bust point and waist tuck, parallel to CF. Cut on line. Open 15 cm (6 in) for inverted pleat. Pin onto new sheet of paper. Distribute ease evenly each side of pleat. Draw line for centre of pleat. Indicate manner of folding by balance marks.

b Place balance marks throughout. Trace pattern sections onto new sheet of paper. Add seams. Facing is as in Figure 3.22b. (See also page 43 on buttons and buttonholes.)

d For back proceed as illustrated.

d **Completed pattern**

Shirt with shoulder yoke

Figure 3.24

Figures 3.24a On narrow shoulder yokes the shoulder seam is omitted. Use shirt pattern drafts Figure 3.22a and c. Place onto sheet of paper with shoulder seams touching. Outline yoke. Reduce back of yoke at armhole level by width of dart. Dart point is used as either small pleat or ease allowance in the final pattern. Place balance marks. Trace sections through. Add seam allowances. See also pages 47–9.

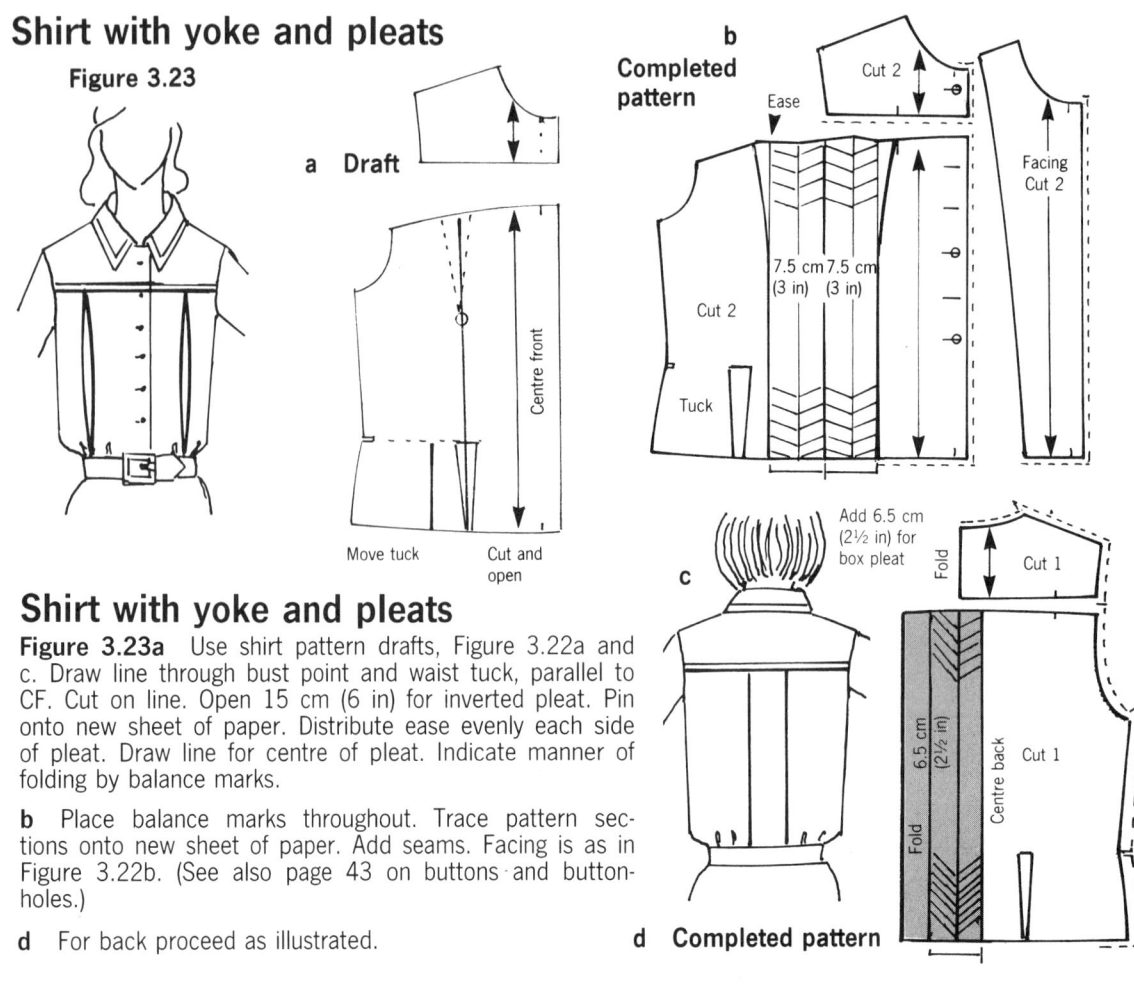

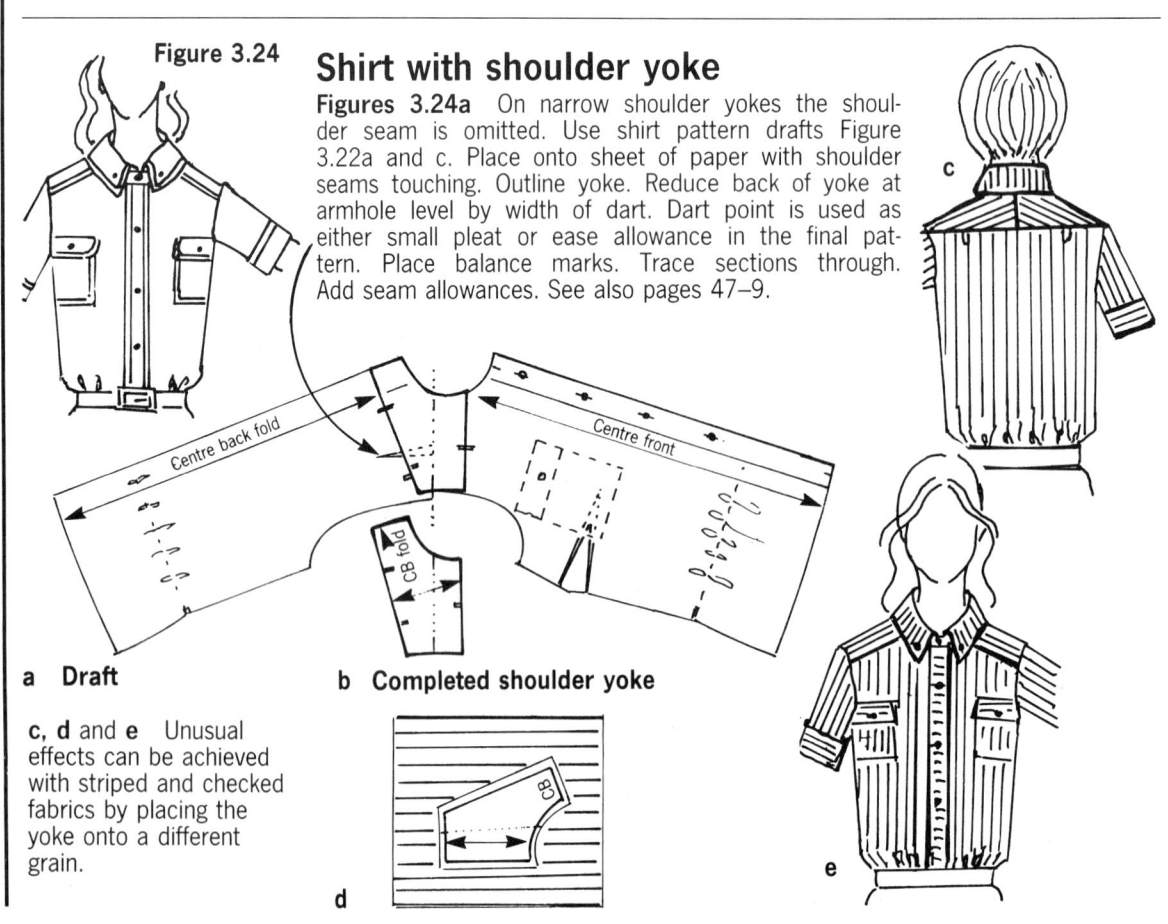

a **Draft**

b **Completed shoulder yoke**

c, d and **e** Unusual effects can be achieved with striped and checked fabrics by placing the yoke onto a different grain.

Figure 3.25

The shirt or blouse block with low armhole and slim shirt sleeve

The average dress block does not incorporate the ease allowances required for a loose-fitting shirt or blouse

Measure your blocks carefully; compare measurements with those given in the size chart.

Figure 3.25a Illustrates the adjustments that may have to be made to obtain a basic shirt or blouse block from which designs, such as are shown in previous pages, can be developed.

The basic blocks and size charts in this book include ample tolerance allowances; thus the hip block will be found to require only minor width adjustments.

b Outline **hip block** (Figure 12.11 page 176). Lower armhole by amount shown. Extend side seams according to size chart.

c Widen sleeve seams, conforming with hip block side seam extension.

d Develop sleeve; raise its underarm seam by amount armhole was lowered. Use pivoting method (Figure 7.30, page 98). With this basic block develop any shirt or blouse style you wish.

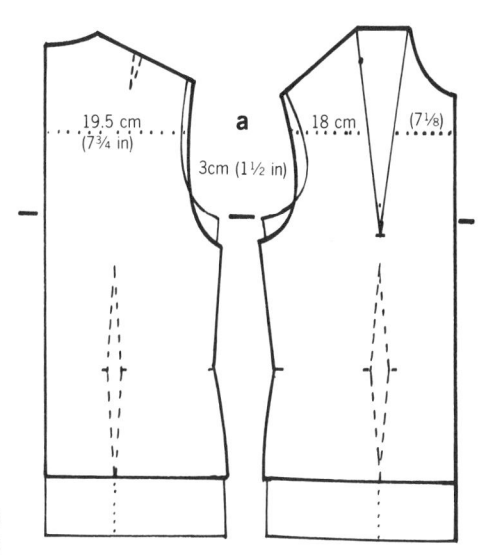

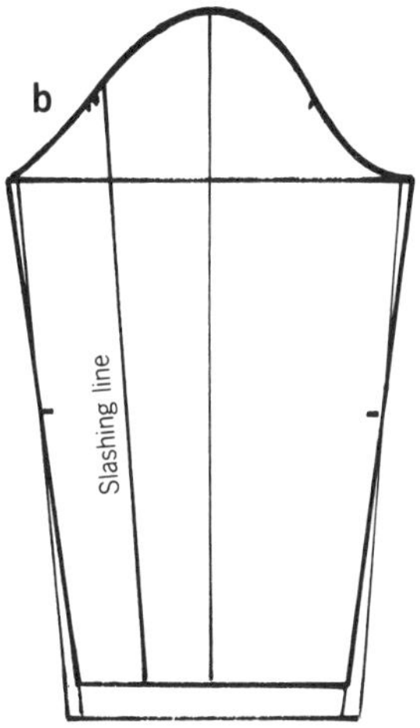

d Slim shirt sleeve

Size chart Shirt or blouse block – Size 12: Recommended minimum/finished measurements

	cm	inches
Bust	99	39
Waist	86	34
Hem circumference	100.5	39½
Length from nape	56	22
Neck	37.6	14¾
Across chest 5 cm (2 in) from neck base	36	14¼
Across back 11 cm (4¼ in) from nape	39	15⅜
Shoulder seam	13.5	5¼
Armhole (measured inside)	44.5	17½
Underarm sleeve seam	42	16½
Cuff	20	8

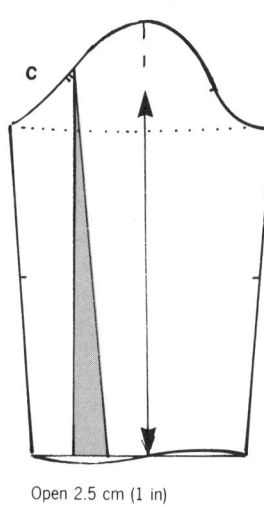

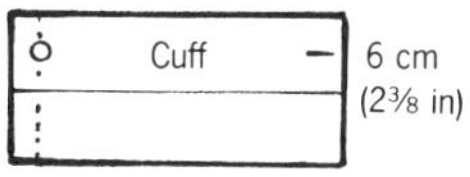

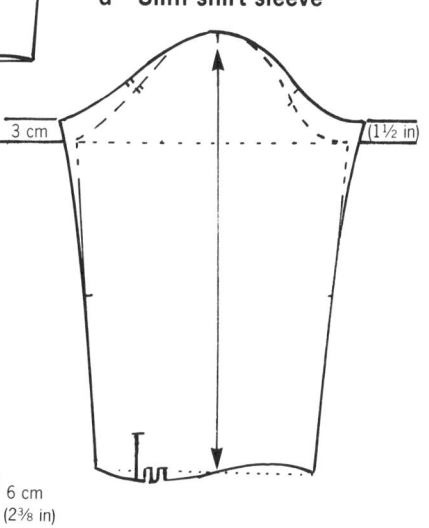

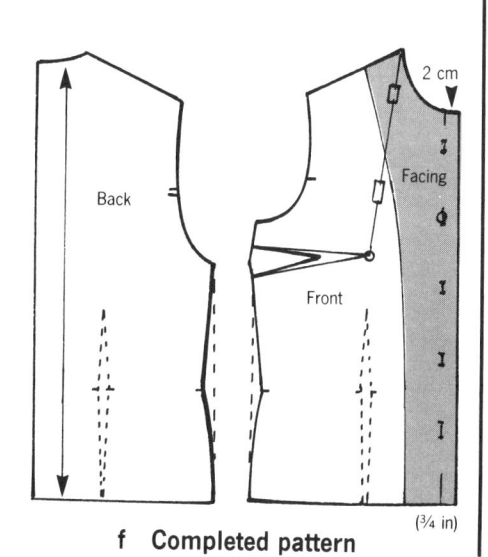

f Completed pattern

3 Bodice styling

Dartless drop-shoulder shirt

Size 12 – Finished measurements

	cm	inches
Bust	122	48
Hip	123	48⅓
Drop-shoulder length	18	7
Armhole circumference	56	22
Neck (at base of neck)	39.5	15½
Across back, 11 cm (4¼ in) from nape	47	18½
Across chest, 5 cm (2 in) from base of neck	45	17¾
Full length	72.5	28½
Underarm sleeve length	42	16½
Top-arm sleeve length, from drop-shoulder – minus half cuff width	48.5	19
Cuff length	20	8
Cuff width	5	2

Figure 3.26

Use hip block Figure 12.11 page 176.

Figure 3.26a Move half shoulder dart into armhole by slashing or pivoting. Draw new shoulder and armhole lines.

b Centralise side seams (and shoulder seams if needed). See page 94 for details.

c Draw two parallel vertical lines, 15 cm (6 in) apart, 76 cm (30 in) long. Draw bust guide line at right angle 27.5 cm (10¾ in) down; extend to right and left.

d Place centralised front block to the right of right vertical line with underarm point and hip line touching vertical line.

Place centralised back block to the left of left vertical line, aligning bust, hip and waist lines as far as possible.

Extend shoulders by 3 cm (1¼ in) to 18 cm (7 in).

Extend side seams by 5 cm (2 in). Square down. Extend CF and CB lines 6 mm (¼ in). Draw button stand 1.5 cm (⅝ in); draft facing 3.5 cm (1¾ in) beyond button stand.

Raise shoulder/armhole points 2 cm (¾ in); connect to neckline shoulder points.

Draft new armhole, having checked across back and across chest measurements.

Determine full length measurement (72.5 cm (28½ in) in this case). Shape side seams and tail hem as shown.

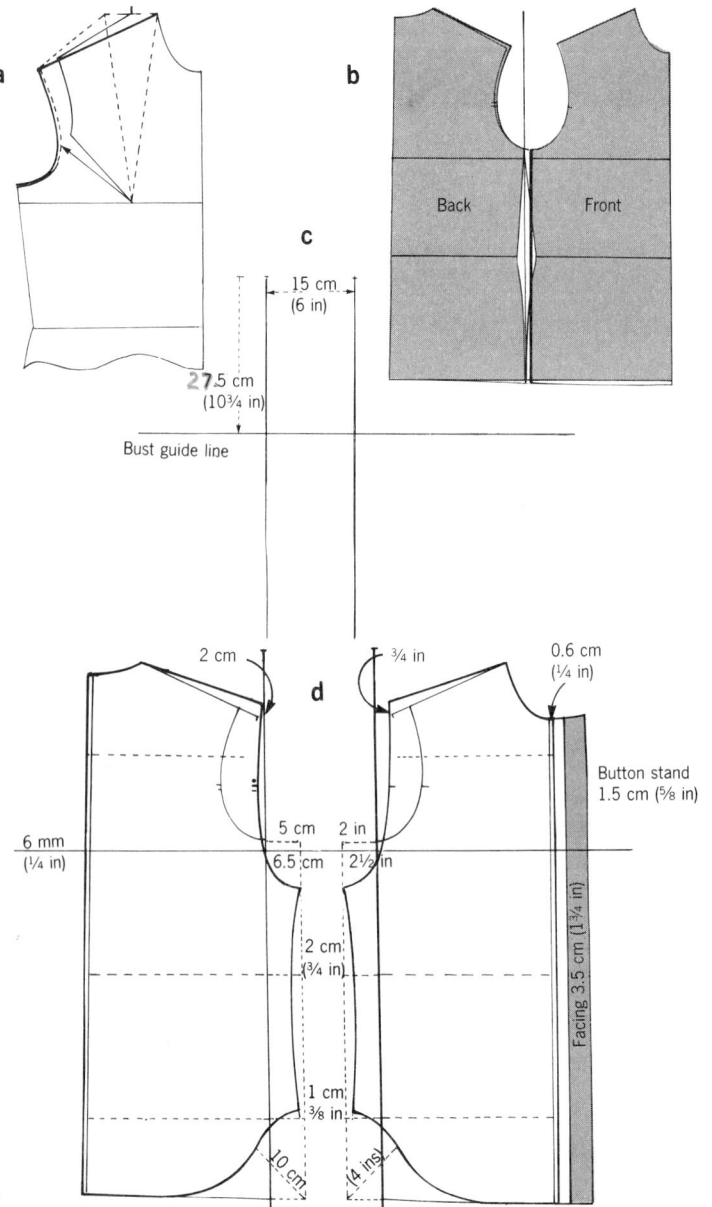

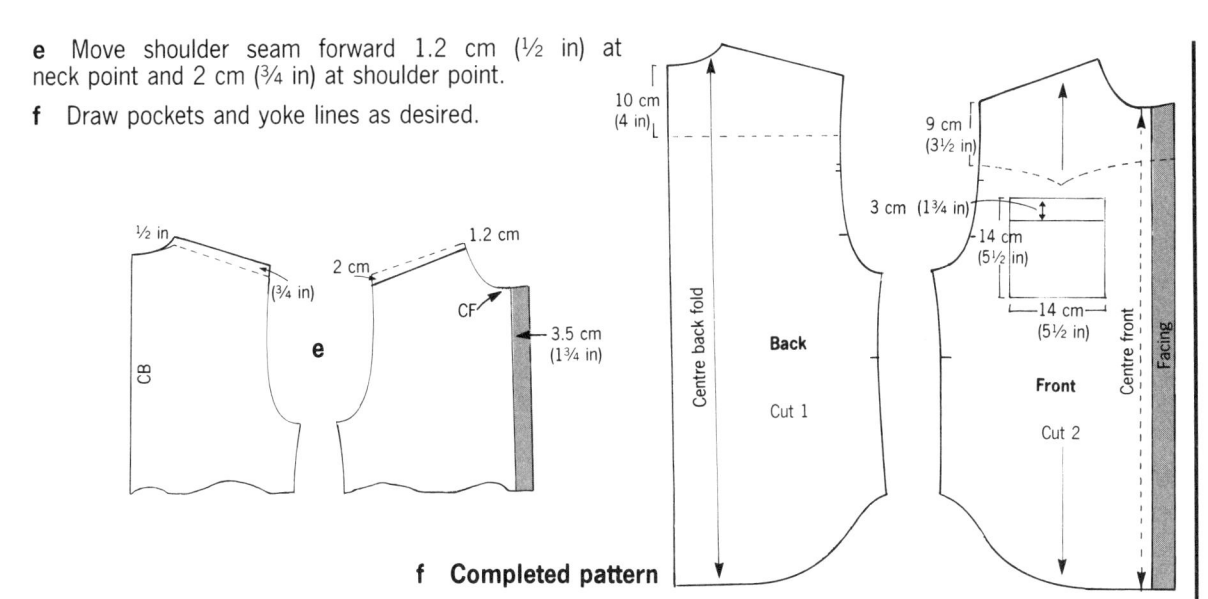

e Move shoulder seam forward 1.2 cm (½ in) at neck point and 2 cm (¾ in) at shoulder point.

f Draw pockets and yoke lines as desired.

f Completed pattern

The two-piece collar

Figure 3.27

d Collar stand

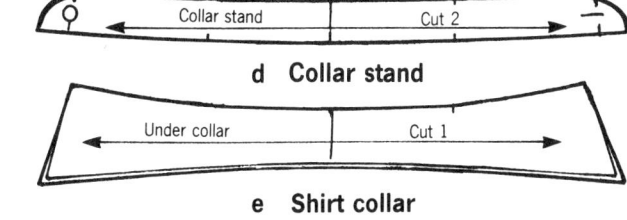

e Shirt collar

Figure 3.27a Construct a rectangle, half neck measurement by width of collar stand (3.5 cm (1⅜ in) in this case). Name left edge CB and right edge CF. Measure half back neck measurement from CB; crossmark shoulder position.

Raise neckline 1.2 cm (½ in) at CF; draw new neckline from shoulder position, having the same measurement as the original line. Square up 3.5 cm (1⅜ in) for new CF. Connect to shoulder position on upper line.

b Add extension to CF for button stand (this must be the same measurement as the button stand on the shirt front (1.5 cm (⅝ in) in this case). Shape upper edge as shown.

c Draft the collar from upper construction line according to desired shape. Add 1 cm (⅜ in) to collar width at CB; blend into collar point shape. This is the under collar. Construct the top collar as shown (see also page 71).

The sleeve and cuff

Figure 3.28 Shorten sleeve block (Figure 1.12, page 15) at wrist line to 'top-arm measurement, (see size chart above).

Draw long vertical line. Place shortened sleeve block on to it, centre sleeve line aligning with vertical line. Outline with dotted line. Draw crown level line at right angle to vertical line, aligning with crown level line of outlined sleeve block.

Increase wrist measurement to 28 cm (11 in).

Draw parallel horizontal line 6.5 cm (2½ in) above crown level line. This is the amount by which the armhole was lowered.

From ◯ draw guide lines measuring half armhole circumference plus 6mm (⅛ in) to left and right, touching upper horizontal line at **A**. Connect underarm points **A** to wrist line.

Shape sleeve head as shown. This seam should be 1.5–2.5 cm (¾–1 in) longer than the armhole circumference for ease.

This wrist opening is 7 cm (2¾ in) long and halfway between back seam and centre sleeve.

Draw two 4 cm (1½ in) pleats at 1.2 cm (½ in) at intervals towards front of sleeve to fit a 20 cm (8 in) cuff.

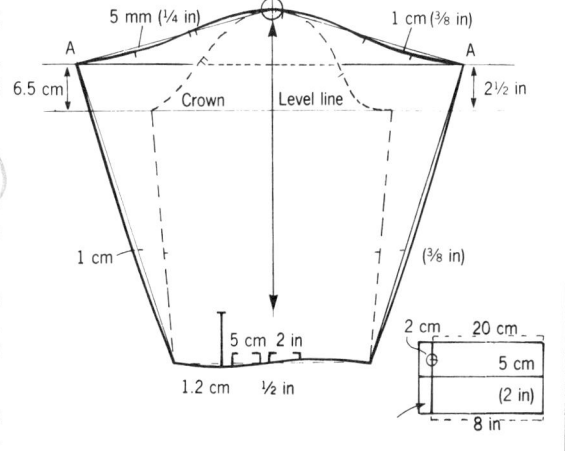

Figure 3.28 Shirt sleeve and cuff

4 | Strapless bodices and vertical seams

Figure 4.1

a Snake Goddess, Palace of Knossus, Crete c. 1600 BC

b Mosaic, Sicily, AD 200

c A corslet, 1870

d A suntop, 1948

e An evening dress, 1953

Figure 4.2

A problem was created when fashion made it desirable for women to wear bodices which revealed a bare or partially covered bosom, or displayed the shoulders. The problem was, and still is, how to support the fabric on and around the body without using the shoulder area from which to suspend the bodice.

Bodices can be either fashionable silhouette-foundations on to which the garment style is constructed (draping, shirring, pleating), or they can be styled garments in themselves (corslet, bra, suntop).

In the past, support was achieved by wiring the shaped seaming, applying wood, steel, cane stays and tight lacing. More recently, whale, feather and nylon boning, and elasticated fabrics have been used.

Figure 4.2a and **b** A basic boned strapless bodice with centre front seam.

This can be worn as foundation or as a garment style in its own right.

c Boned strapless bodice but with a horizontal centre front dart.

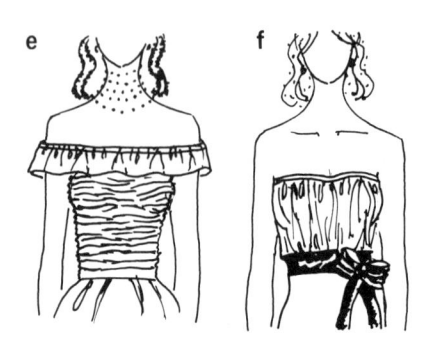

d Draped folds applied over the foundation bodice.

e Irregular small folds (or ruches) are shown draped horizontally over the foundation bodice and in **f** they are shown draped vertically.

Comparison of measurements

Figure 4.3

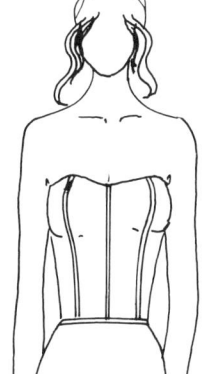

Figure 4.4

Compare the measurement taken around a size 12 figure, in the position shown in **Figure 4.4a**, with the measurement taken in the corresponding position around a size 12 dress form (**b**).

Note that the measurement taken on the human body is smaller than that taken on the dress form. This discrepancy is due to a deliberate addition of tolerance by the designers of dress forms and is a significant part of the construction of dress forms in order to obtain a solid base suitable for the fitting and modelling of garments with shoulders, armholes and sleeves.

The human body, or a specially constructed form for swimwear, which closely follows the anatomy of the body, are ideally the best bases for modelling strapless bodices.

For practical reasons, the dress form is being used more often, and good results are achieved when small fitting adjustments are made immediately above and below the bust area.

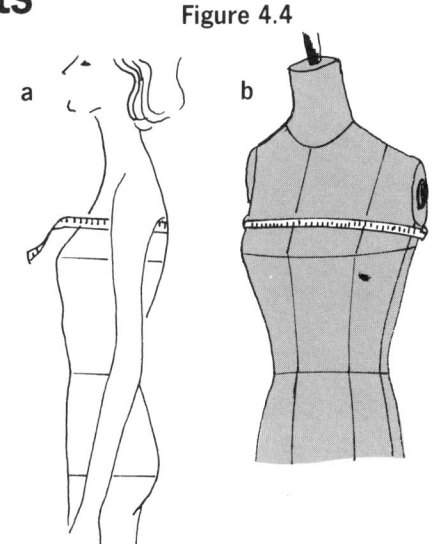

Figure 4.5

Constructing the strapless bodice

Figure 4.5a On dress form outline with tape front and back upper edge of strapless bodice.

b Model centre front section first and follow grain and seaming of canvas covering of form. Pin straight warp grain of rectangular piece of modelling fabric of sufficient length and width along centre front of dress form, extending approximately 2 cm (¾ in) beyond centre front seam and vertical shoulder-bust seam, thus planning for required seam allowances.

Fold slightly wider piece of fabric for side section and crease on straight warp grain. Pin this fabric to front side of dress form, aligning with straight grain of dress form canvas.

Pin lapped seam over modelled front section following seam line and contours of dress form. Pin modelled front to tape and cut fabric. Cut around armhole area and trim.

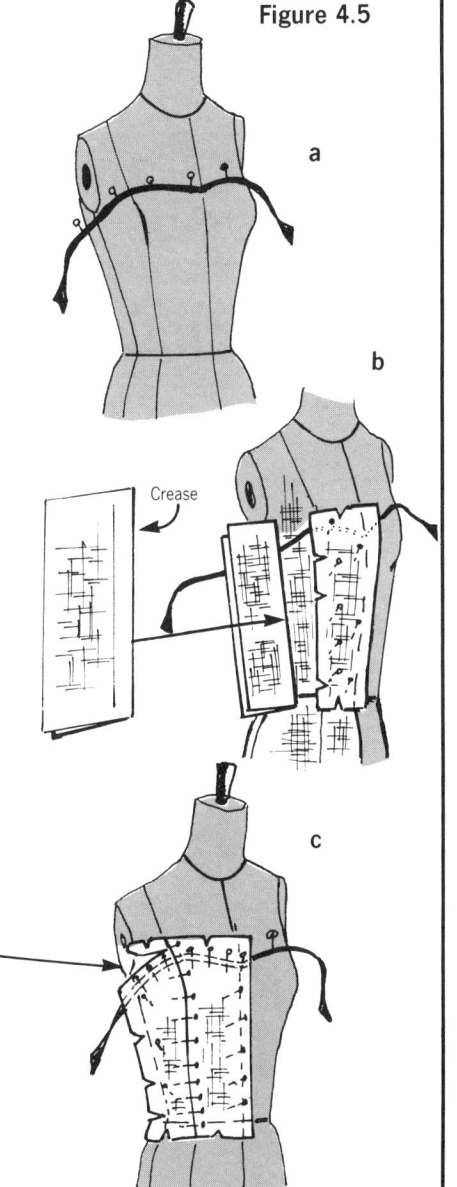

4 — Strapless bodices and vertical seams

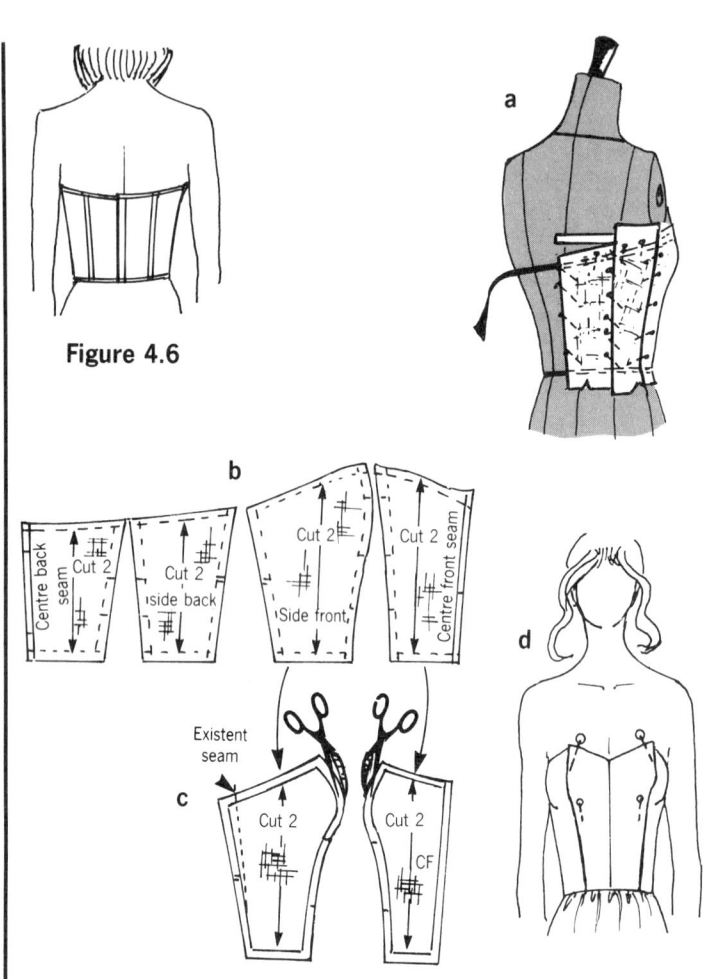

Figure 4.6 Model back of bodice in same manner as front, beginning with centre back.

a Mark all pinned seam and style lines and balance marks.

b Remove from dress form; true all marked lines. Trim.

c Cut corresponding left sections. Tack or machine bodice. Fit on live model with same bust size as dress form.

d If required, take in bust seam at upper edge of bodice, and below bust, at diaphragm level. Further slight adjustments may be required, mainly at upper edge of bodice, but also at side and back seams. Graduate these adjustments to existent seam (see **c**).

Mark and recut front bodice sections. Sew sections together again, attach light boning. Refit. Make any final adjustments. Trace onto pattern card. Include all cutting information.

Figure 4.6

Bust formation influence on seam placement

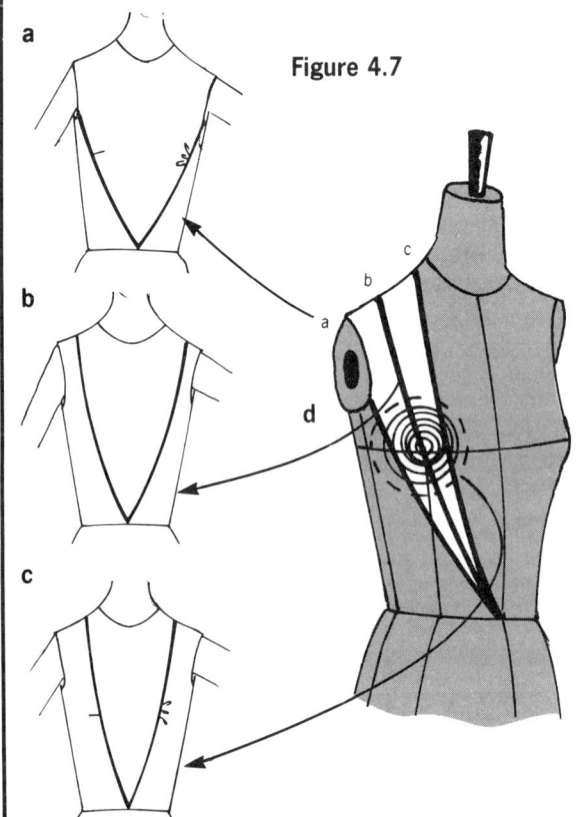

Figure 4.7

Figure 4.7a If the seam is placed outside the highest part of the bust, the centre section of the bodice requires darts, pleats or gathers to accommodate the full bust measurement.

b Where the seam passes over the highest point of the bust, the seam lines of both, the centre and the side panels of the bodice, are of equal length.

c If the seam is placed inside the highest part of the bust, the side panels of the bodice require darts, pleats or gathers to accommodate the highest part of the bust.

Princess lines

V-shape princess lines from shoulder

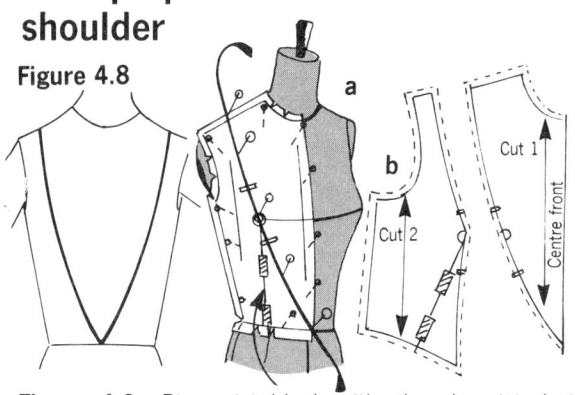

Figure 4.8

Figure 4.8 Pin waist block with closed waist dart to dress form. Outline seam line from mid-shoulder over bust point to shown waist point. Mark. Place balance marks and grain lines. Remove from dress form. Cut on marked line.

Figure 4.10

Princess lines from armhole

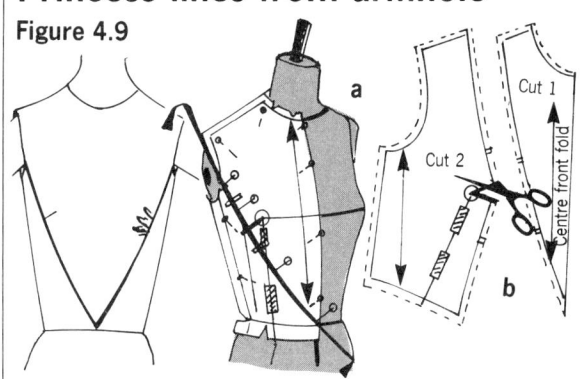

Figure 4.9

Figure 4.9 Proceed as for Figure 4.8 but outline and mark panel seam as shown, slightly to the left, outside bust point. Place three balance marks (one on bust point). Cut on marked seam line. Snip to bust point for dart or gathers.

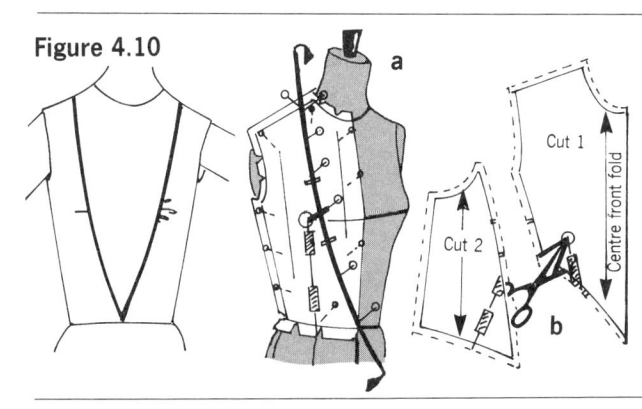

Figure 4.10 Proceed as for Figure 4.9 but outline and mark panel seam line as shown, to the right, inside bust point. Cut through marked seam line, snip to bust point for dart, pleat or gathers.

For all styles, always true and check all seams before adding seam allowances.

Figure 4.11

Figure 4.11a Pin waist block with closed underarm dart and waist dart to dress form. Outline a pleasing curved seam line from armhole over bust point and over original waist dart. Mark. Place balance marks. Remove from dress form.

With both darts remaining closed, cut on new style line. Place grain lines. Add seam allowances.

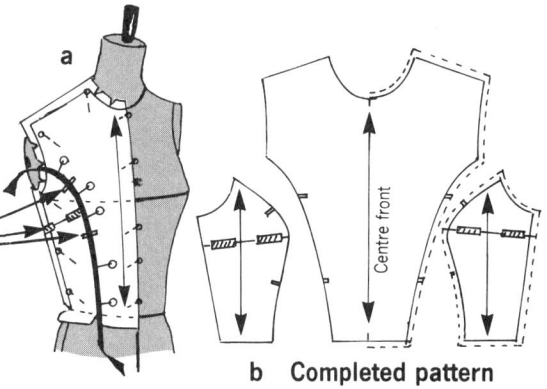

b Completed pattern

Figure 4.12

Figure 4.12a Proceed as above but outline and mark panel seam line slightly away from bust point and original waist dart as shown. Place balance marks. Cut on new line. Unpin dart point only of underarm dart. Additionally, snip to bust point. Mark grain lines.

b This style can be cut by the flat cutting method. Outline block with waist and underarm dart. Draw new style line including moved dart. Cut and close dart as shown.

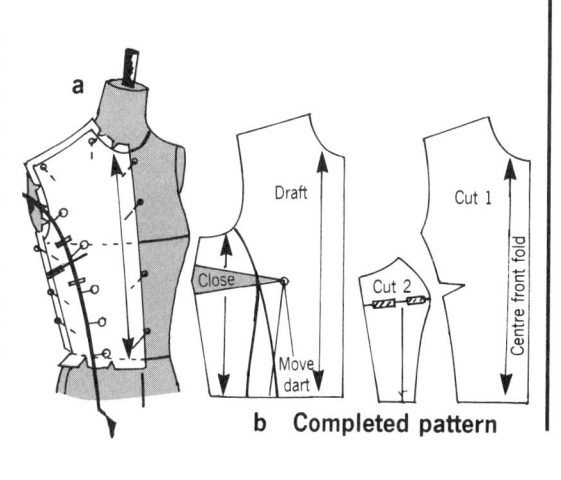

b Completed pattern

4

Strapless bodices and vertical seams

53

4 Strapless bodices and vertical seams

Dress with Princess line from shoulder

Figure 4.13

Figure 4.13a and **b** Tear on grain two rectangles of calico, both 110 cm (43¼ in) long.

Side panel is 30 cm (11¾ in) wide.

Centre front panel 24 cm (9½ in).

Press rectangles. Ensure they are on perfect grain.

Draw shoulder guide lines 5 cm (2 in) away from torn horizontal **a** and **b** edges.

Draw panel guide lines 6 cm (2½ in) away from torn vertical edges, except centre front line, as shown.

c Draw horizontal guide lines as in **a** and **b**.

Pin **b** to dress form. Align centre fronts up to hip level. Cut away surplus fabric. Snip curved areas. Added fabric below hip level is used to create 'flare' and increase hem width.

Fold side panel **a** in half and press crease for straight grain indication. Pin crease line to centre of side section of dress form.

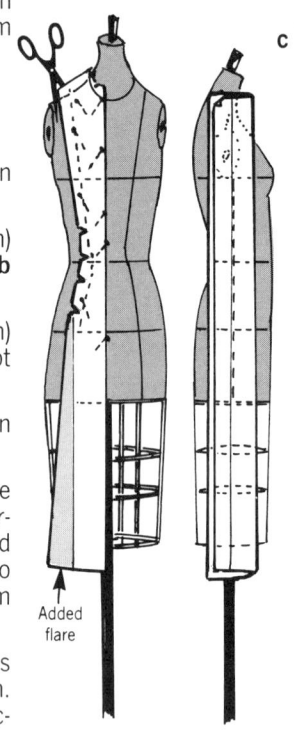

d Open folded fabric. Smooth to dress form. Cut away surplus fabric. Pin, overlapping front panel seam to hip level.

e Continue to hemline, gradually releasing added flare allowance on both front and side panel seams.

Mark all seams; place balance marks.

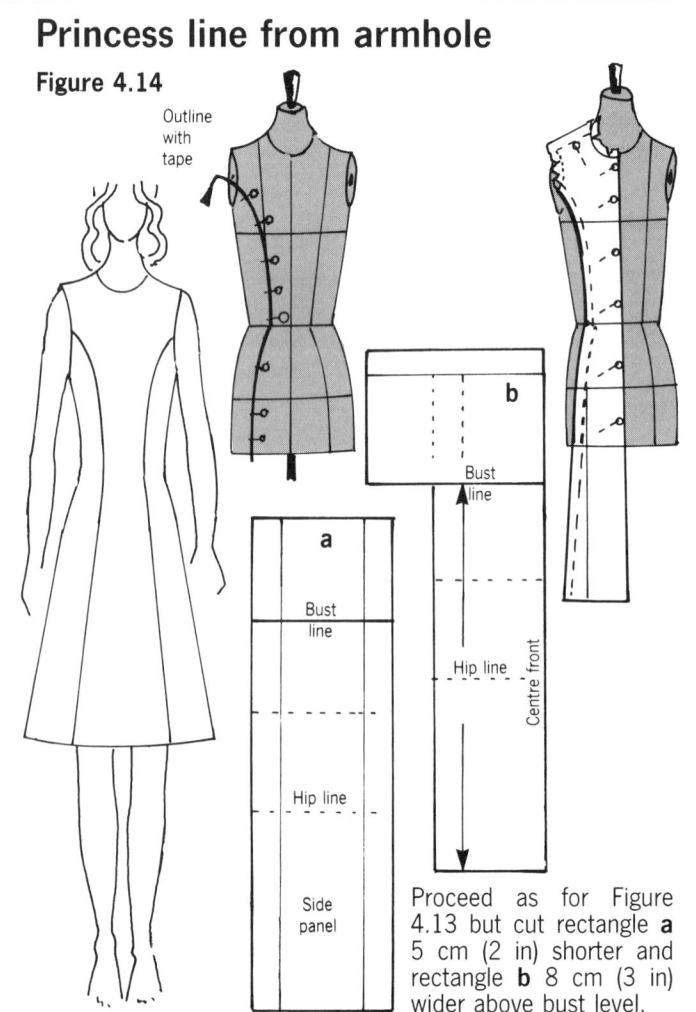

Princess line from armhole

Figure 4.14

Proceed as for Figure 4.13 but cut rectangle **a** 5 cm (2 in) shorter and rectangle **b** 8 cm (3 in) wider above bust level.

Princess lines – cut flat

Figure 4.15

Figure 4.15 Outline dress blocks (Figures 2.20b and 2.20c, pages 26 and 27) without seam allowances. Extend shoulder and upper section of waist darts to bust level and lower section to hip level. Dart points on hip level must be the same distance away from CF and CB as centre of darts at waist.

Drop a line, parallel to CF and CB, through centre of waist darts, dart points to hemline in preparation for introducing flare into the hemline.

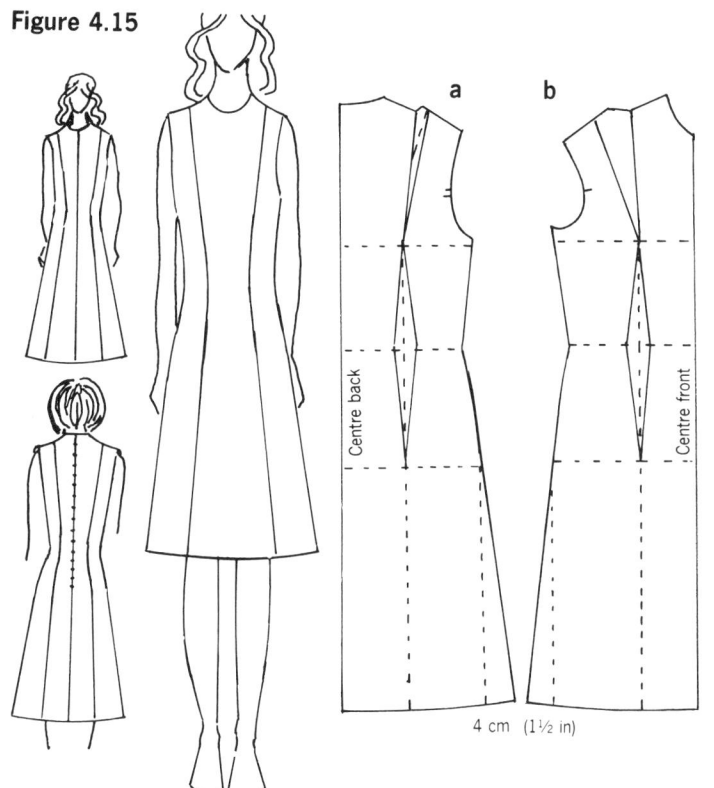

Figure 4.16

Figure 4.16 The draft Mark 2.5 cm (1 in) at hemline each side of dropped line (this amount can be larger depending on the amount of flare desired). Connect lines as shown and, aiming at a less pointed effect, round off the panel line with a line between original shoulder dart and new (lengthened) dart line. Centre back seam can be shaped as shown. Place balance marks and grain lines and trace pattern parts onto new paper (Figure 4.17).

Add seam allowances all around, including at centre front if wished.

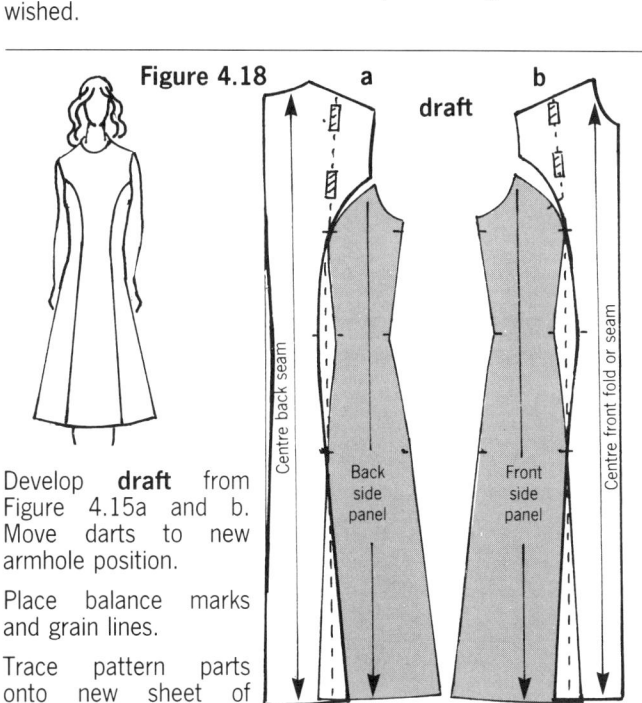

Figure 4.18

Develop **draft** from Figure 4.15a and b. Move darts to new armhole position.

Place balance marks and grain lines.

Trace pattern parts onto new sheet of paper. Add seam allowances as for Figure 4.17.

Figure 4.17

Completed pattern

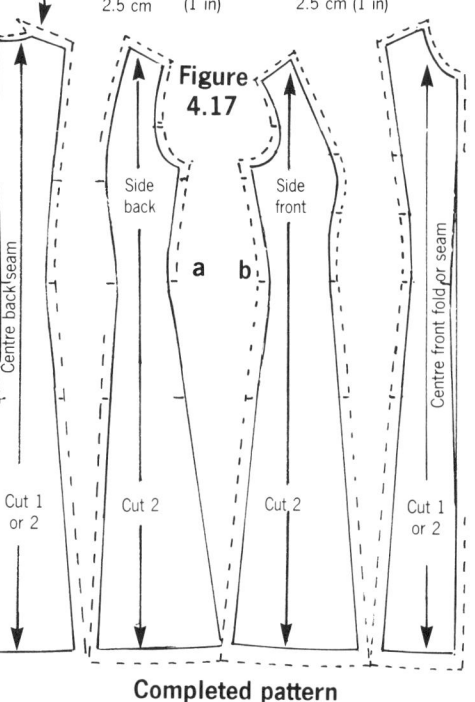

4 — Strapless bodices and vertical seams

'A'-line dress block without darts

This block will be useful when designing tent-shaped garments and certain types of Princess line designs. In the first instance the original darts are ignored altogether and in the second the large gap between the dart lines can be employed to introduce design features, e.g. straight and scalloped seams, cut-on pocket stands, etc. (see Figure 4.20 c, d and e).

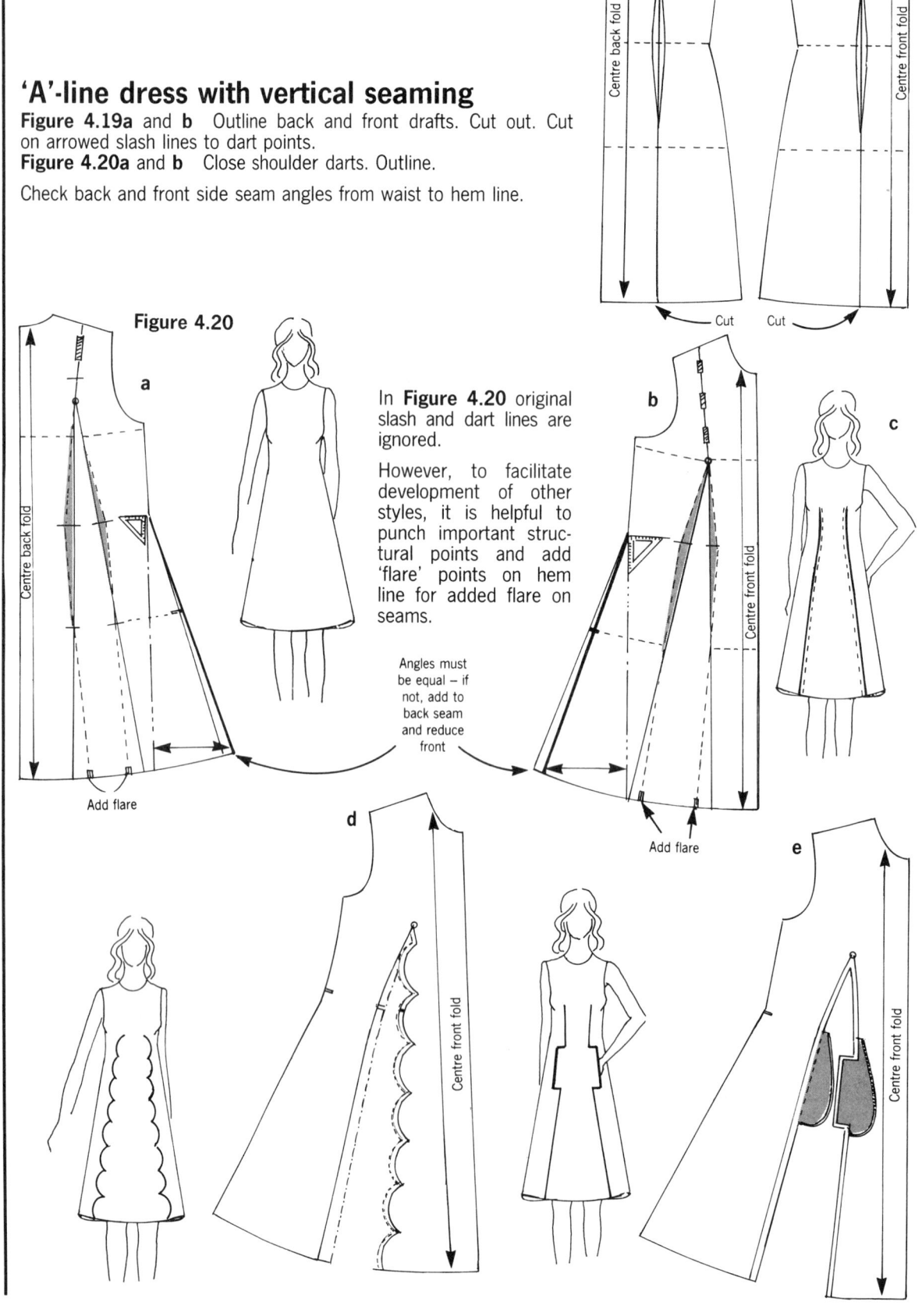

'A'-line dress with vertical seaming

Figure 4.19a and **b** Outline back and front drafts. Cut out. Cut on arrowed slash lines to dart points.

Figure 4.20a and **b** Close shoulder darts. Outline.

Check back and front side seam angles from waist to hem line.

In **Figure 4.20** original slash and dart lines are ignored.

However, to facilitate development of other styles, it is helpful to punch important structural points and add 'flare' points on hem line for added flare on seams.

Angles must be equal – if not, add to back seam and reduce front

Dress with Princess line and empire waist

Figure 4.21

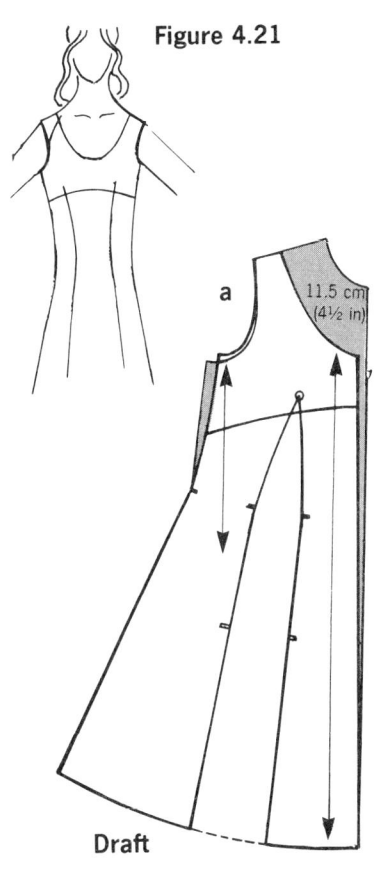

Figure 4.21a Outline dress block Figure 4.20b. The original waist dart line becomes the Princess line. Draw neckline and under bust style line.

Reduce neckline by 5 mm (³⁄₈ in), raise and take in armhole (see Figure 5.3b page 60 and Figure 5.17a, page 64).

b Pin pattern to dress form. Confirm position of under bust line. Outline with tape if uncertain; also neckline.

Cut through under bust style line. Trace all seam lines onto pattern paper. True lines. Add seam allowances. Develop back pattern.

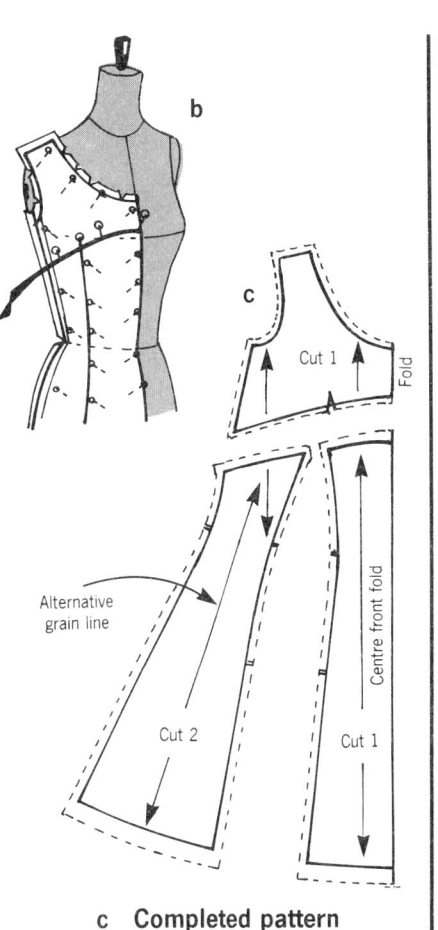

11.5 cm (4½ in)

a Draft

c Completed pattern

Dress with curved Princess line styling

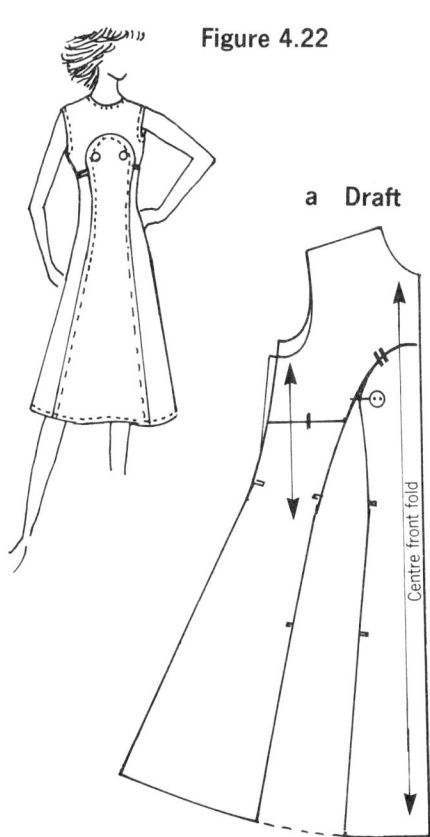

Figure 4.22

Figure 4.22 As above, this design is based on dress block Figure 4.20 and is developed in the same way as Figure 4.21 above.

a Draw style lines on the draft by first measuring distances on the dress form.

Pin, cut out. Pin to dress form to confirm correct interpretation.

Develop back pattern from Figure 4.20a.

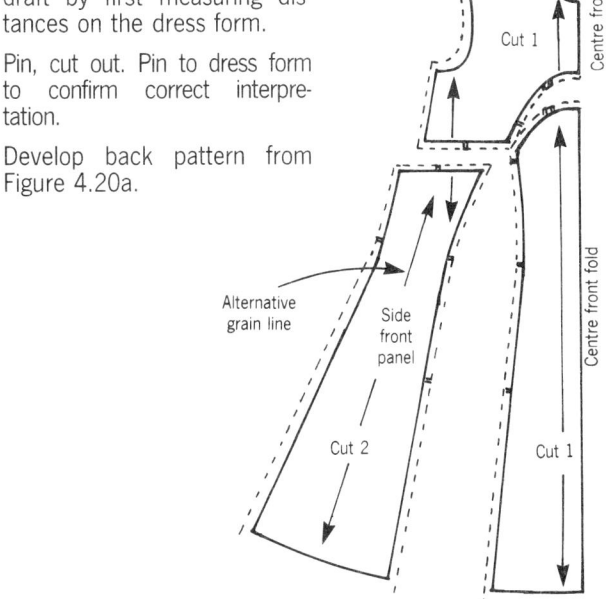

a Draft

b Completed pattern

Strapless bodices and vertical seams

4

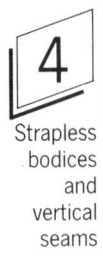

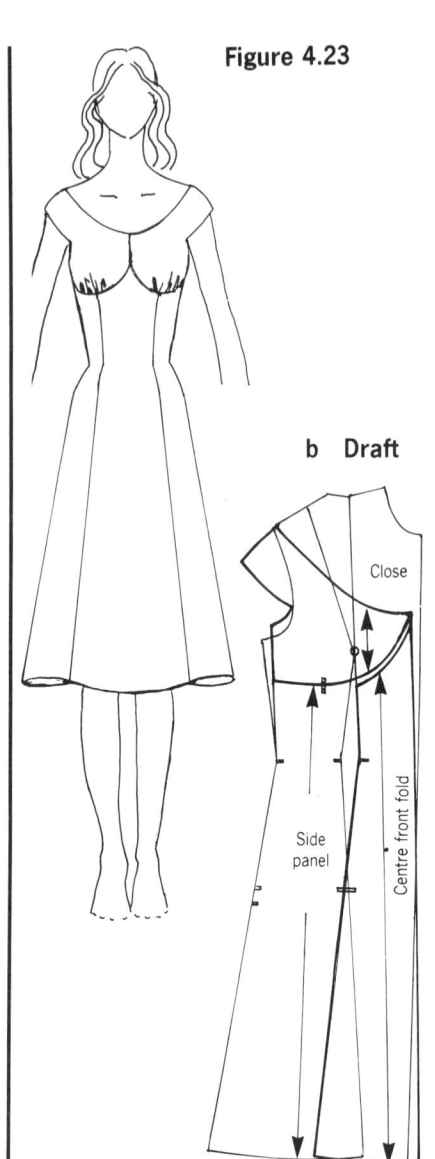

Princess line dress with bra-style seaming and gathers under bust

Figure 4.23

Figure 4.23a Try out a variety of style lines on dress form. Transfer final information to flat pattern on dress block draft (Figure 4.19b, page 56).

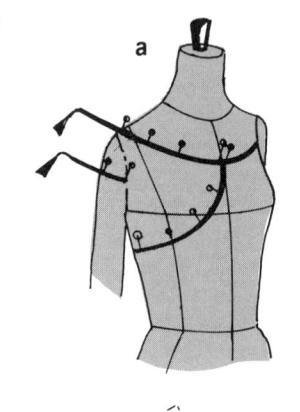

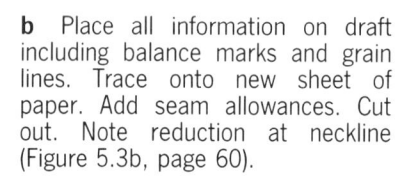

b Draft

b Place all information on draft including balance marks and grain lines. Trace onto new sheet of paper. Add seam allowances. Cut out. Note reduction at neckline (Figure 5.3b, page 60).

c For additional fulness under bust draw slash line, cut and open 5 cm (2 in) or more **d**, depending on thickness of fabric to be used.

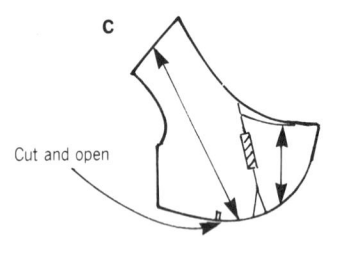

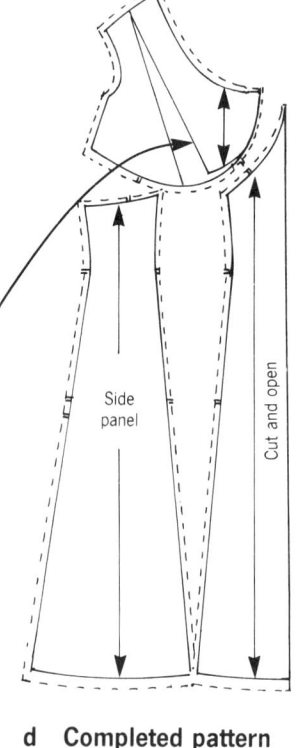

d Completed pattern

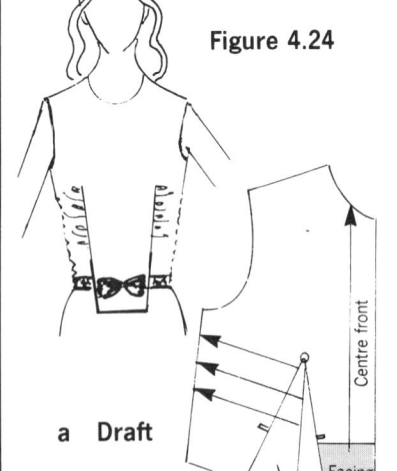

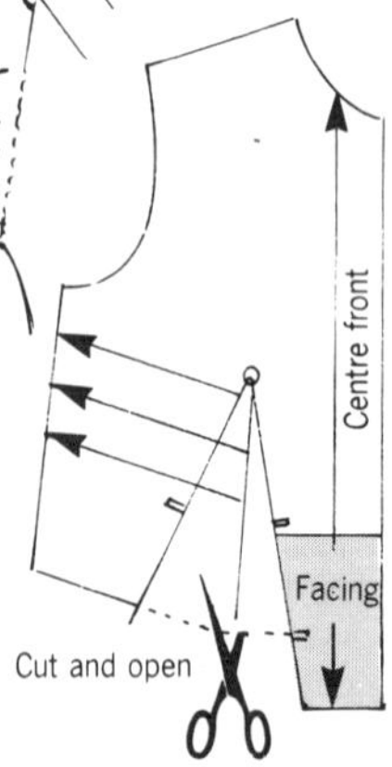

Bodice with vertical seams and gathers

Figure 4.24 Outline front waist block with one large waist dart. Place balance marks on both dart lines 7.5 cm (3 in) above waist line to confine gathers position. Draw three slash lines above balance mark. Lengthen CF section 6 cm (2¼ in) below waist line. Place balance mark at waist line.

Cut on dart lines and on slash lines to just short of side seam. Open slashes. Here 10.5 cm (4⅛ in) overall is allowed for gathers, but amounts vary with fabric.

a Lower part of CF section is unattached to allow a belt to pass underneath. This section, therefore, requires a facing. Cut facing 3 cm (1¼ in) above waist line.

b An extension is added to the side section to provide a backing for the unattached centre section.

a Draft

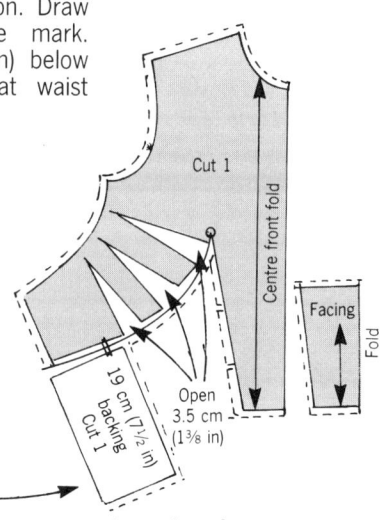

b Completed pattern

Jacket

Figure 4.25

Jacket with curved seam and centre fastening

Figure 4.25a Outline hip block with underarm dart. Add button extension. Close underarm dart. Pin to dress form.

Move waist dart 2.5 cm (1 in) towards side seam. Pin and mark. Pin tape, following style line of sketch. Mark with soft pencil. Place balance marks. Determine button position.

b Remove from dress form. Unpin waist dart. Draft facing and trace onto new sheet of paper. Cut on style line. Snip into underarm dart point.

c Place flat on pattern paper. Outline and trace all new lines, balance marks and seam allowances.

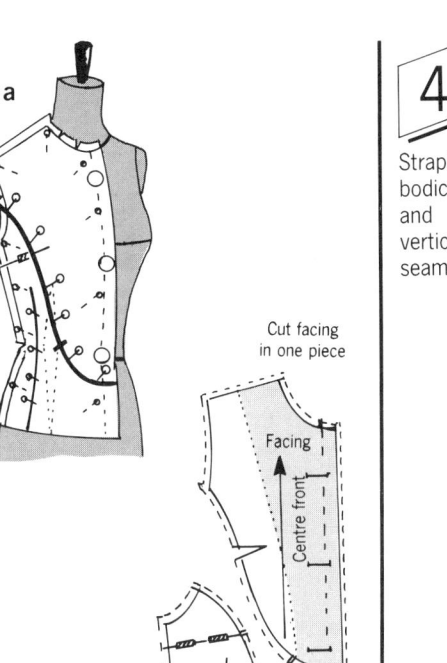

c Completed pattern

Vertical seam and pocket combined

Figure 4.26

Figure 4.26a Cut out dress block (Figure 2.23c, page 27) in fine paper and, with underarm dart closed, pin to dress form. Pin tape, beginning 2.5 cm (1 in) away from underarm dart point, curving very slightly to meet dart at waist level. Continue pinning tape to approx. 7.5 cm (3 in) below waist level.

b Mark style line with soft pencil. Mark position of pocket stand. Place balance marks. Cut on style line. Snip into under arm dart point.

c Release remainder of lower waist dart point. This will cause the pocket mouth to stand away slightly.

c Completed pattern

5 Necklines and collars

Bateau and round necklines

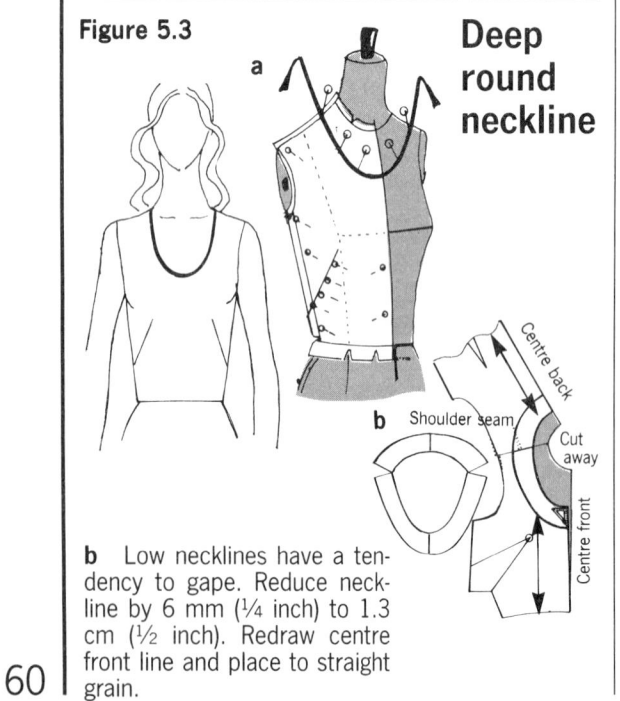

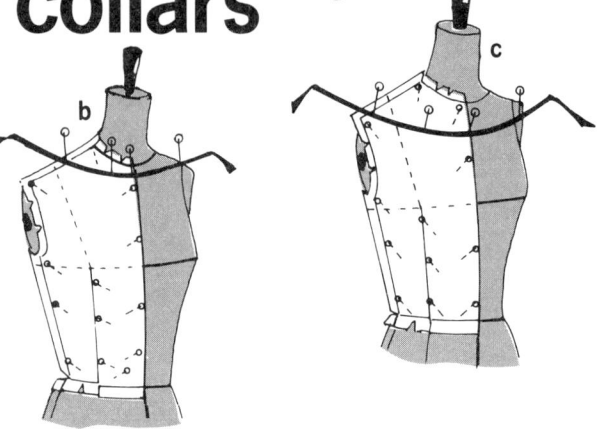

Figure 5.1

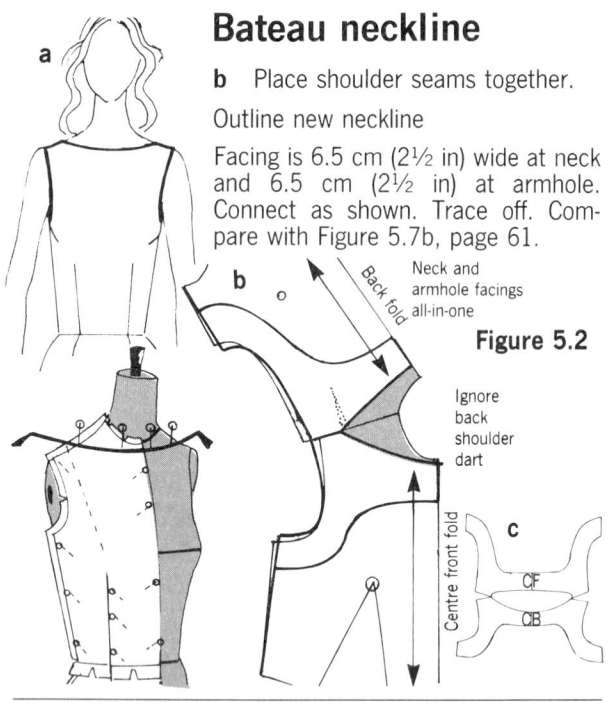

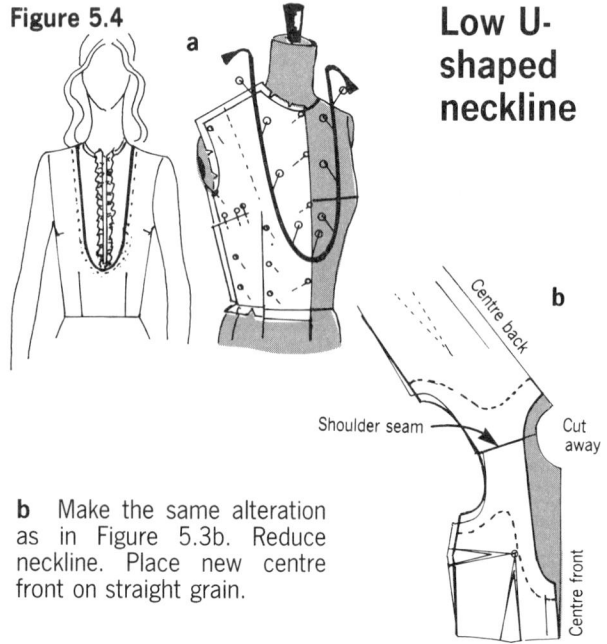

Figure 5.1a, b and **c** show how tape can be changed around until you are satisfied that the most pleasing effect has been achieved.

d Ensure that the back neckline follows the front neckline at shoulder/neck position.

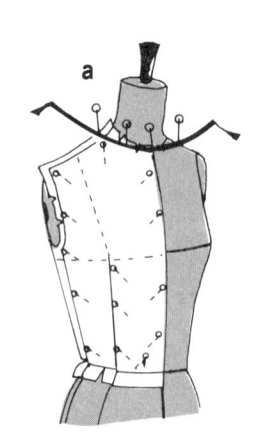

Lightly mark new neckline. Remove back and front patterns from dress form. True lightly drawn necklines and add seam allowances in preparation for drafting neck facings.

See Figure 5.17a for rules on tightening armholes on sleeveless bodices.

Bateau neckline

b Place shoulder seams together.

Outline new neckline

Facing is 6.5 cm (2½ in) wide at neck and 6.5 cm (2½ in) at armhole. Connect as shown. Trace off. Compare with Figure 5.7b, page 61.

Figure 5.2

Neck and armhole facings all-in-one

Ignore back shoulder dart

Figure 5.3 — Deep round neckline

b Low necklines have a tendency to gape. Reduce neckline by 6 mm (¼ inch) to 1.3 cm (½ inch). Redraw centre front line and place to straight grain.

Figure 5.4 — Low U-shaped neckline

b Make the same alteration as in Figure 5.3b. Reduce neckline. Place new centre front on straight grain.

Square and V-necklines

Figure 5.5

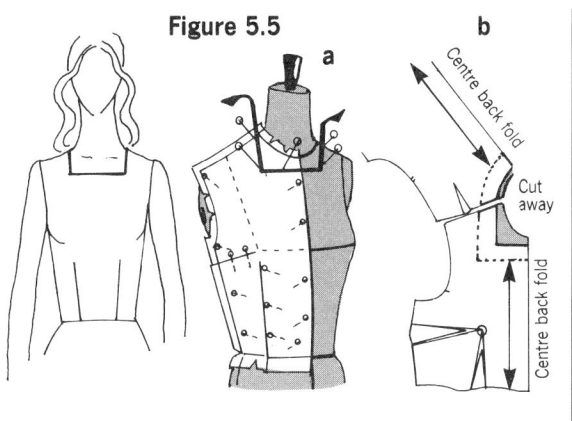

Figure 5.6

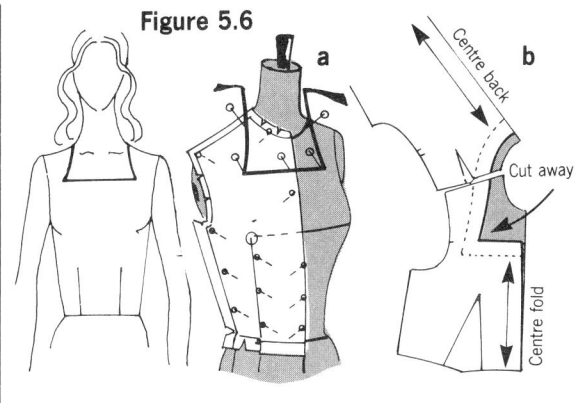

Figure 5.7

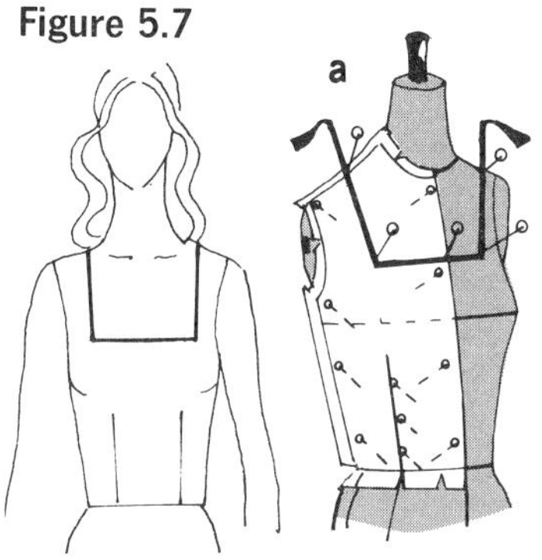

Figure 5.7a Low necklines tend to gape. Reduce neckline by 6 mm (¼ in) to 1.2 cm (½ in). Redraw centre front line and place to straight grain.

b Neckline and armhole facings are cut-in-one for sleeveless garments, see Figure 5.2b, page 60.

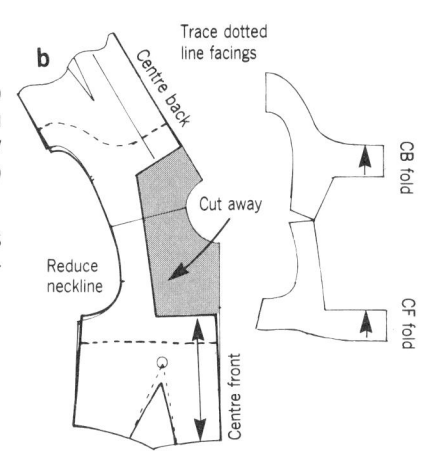

V-neckline variations

Figure 5.8

Figure 5.8a Apply this neck band like a facing, but turn to the right side of the neckline.

Assess desired neckline and width of band.

b Trace neck band. Omit shoulder seam.

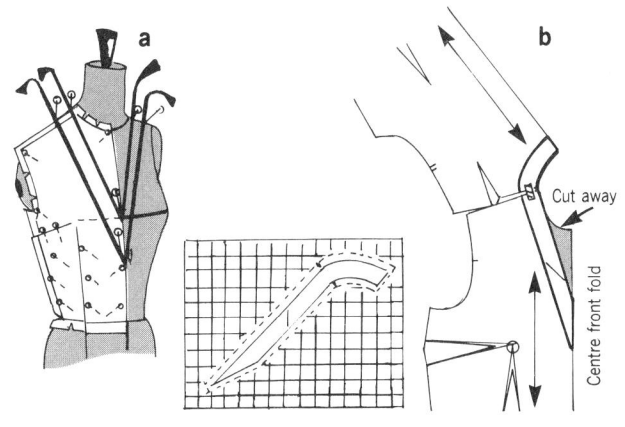

Figure 5.9

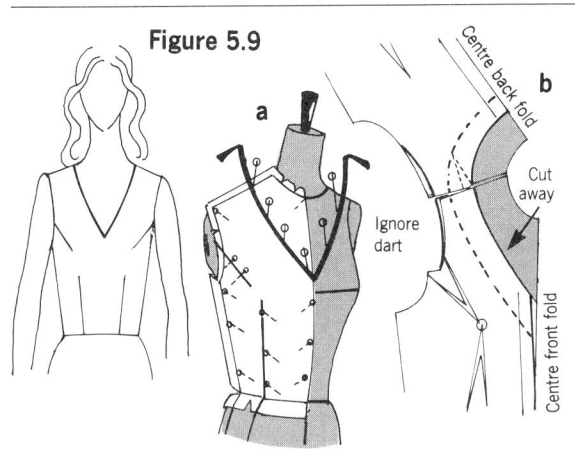

Figure 5.10

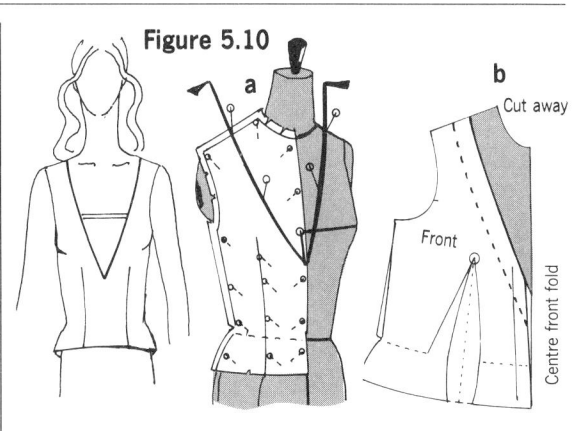

5
Necklines and collars

Raised necklines

Raised neckline with centre front opening

Figure 5.11

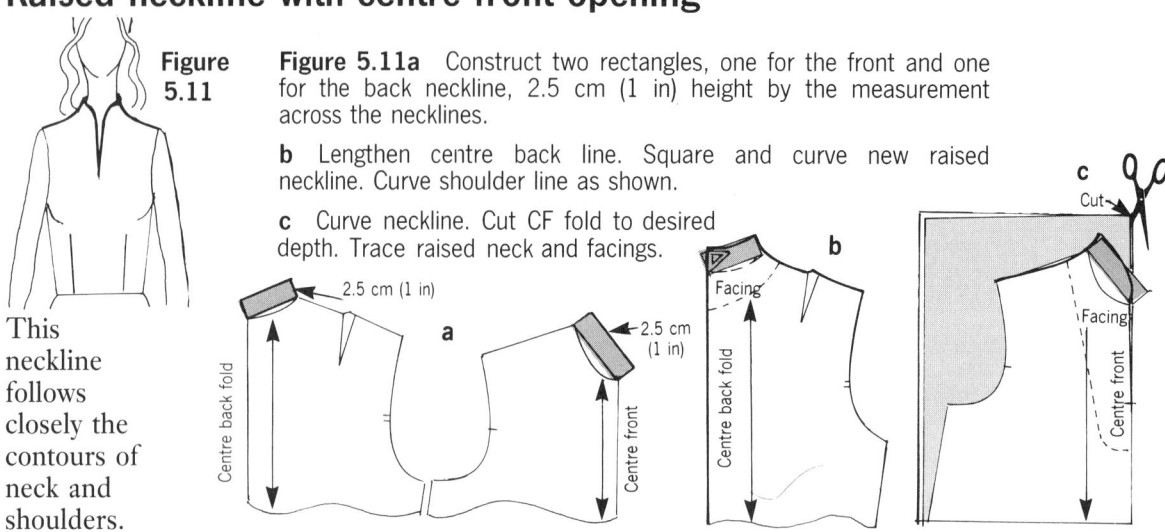

This neckline follows closely the contours of neck and shoulders.

Figure 5.11a Construct two rectangles, one for the front and one for the back neckline, 2.5 cm (1 in) height by the measurement across the necklines.

b Lengthen centre back line. Square and curve new raised neckline. Curve shoulder line as shown.

c Curve neckline. Cut CF fold to desired depth. Trace raised neck and facings.

Raised neckline standing away from the neck

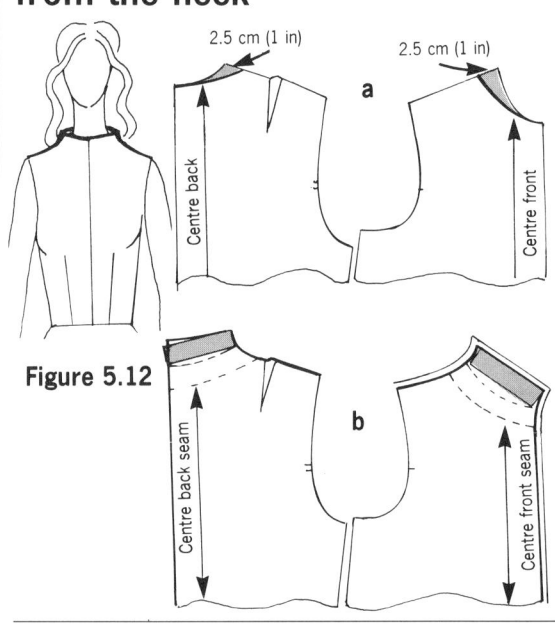

Figure 5.12

Figure 5.12a Lower neckline at shoulder by 2.5 cm (1 in).

b Construct rectangles on this larger neckline as above.

Lengthen centre back neckline. Add seam allowance for back opening.

Lengthen centre front line and curve away slightly. Add seam allowance.

V-neck, fold-down lapels

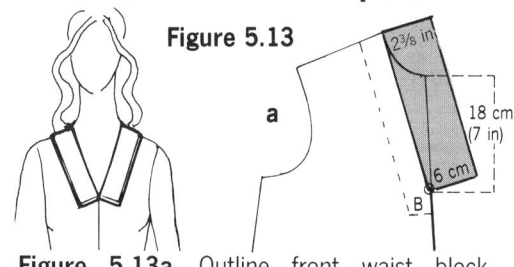

Figure 5.13

Figure 5.13a Outline front waist block. On centre front line mark point B down 18 cm (7 in). Connect with shoulder/neck point. Construct collar rectangle on this line. Trace facing.

The basic hood

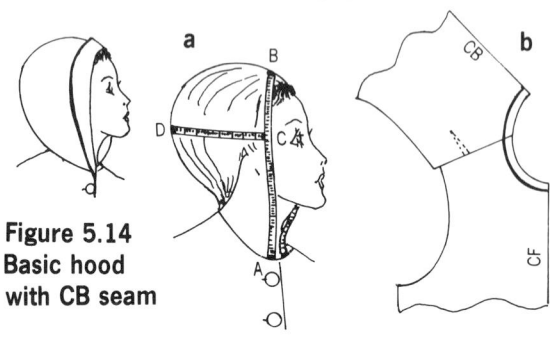

Figure 5.14 Basic hood with CB seam

a Measurements
A–B 38 cm (15 in)
B–C eye level 15 cm (6 in)
C–D 26 cm (10¼ in)

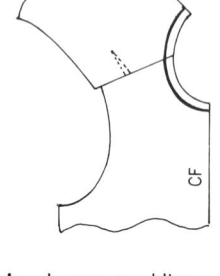

b Lower neckline by at least 1.2 cm (½ in); finally blend to shape of hood neckline.

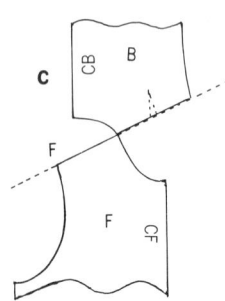

c Draw dotted guide line (continuation of **F** shoulder line). Place **B** block face downwards, shoulder points meeting.

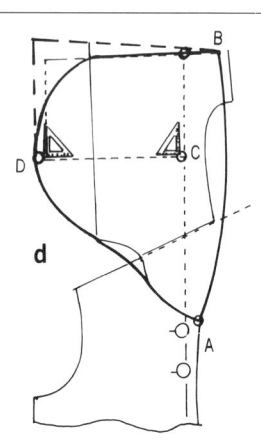

d Draw desired hood shape and 'cuff' extension. Trace off.

Figure 5.15

Detachable hood

This hood has a gusset section running down centre.

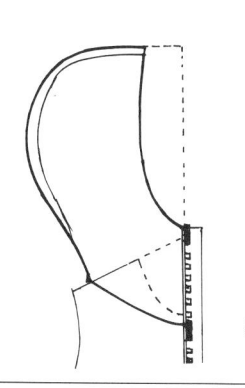

a

Necklines of sleeveless bodices

Semi-fitted sleeveless bodice and facing

Figure 5.16

Figure 5.16a Outline back and front hip blocks. Determine back and front necklines and armhole line. As this garment is semi-fitted, add 6 mm (¼ in) to side seams and make darts shallower and shorter. Neck and armhole facings are 6 cm (2½ in) wide.

b Edge seams of facings should not be visible on the right side of garments. They should be well set back from edges. Understitching and good pressing helps towards this end, but to ensure a permanent good appearance and fit, facings must be cut 3 mm (⅛ in) away from the edge to force the outer edge to the under side.

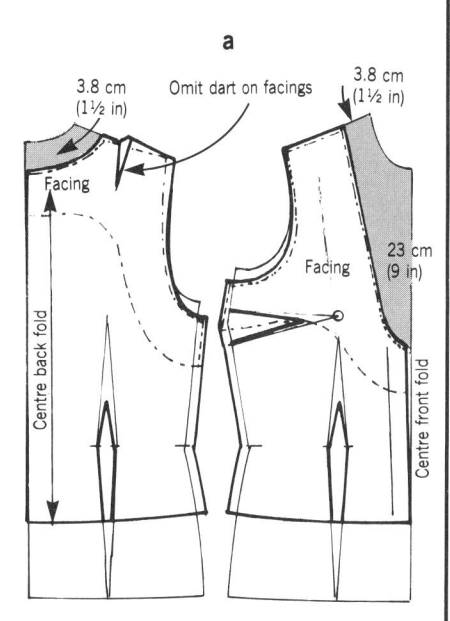

Pattern
With tracing wheel trace each pattern piece onto new paper in turn, including facings.

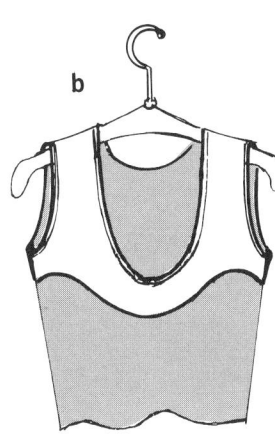

c Completed pattern

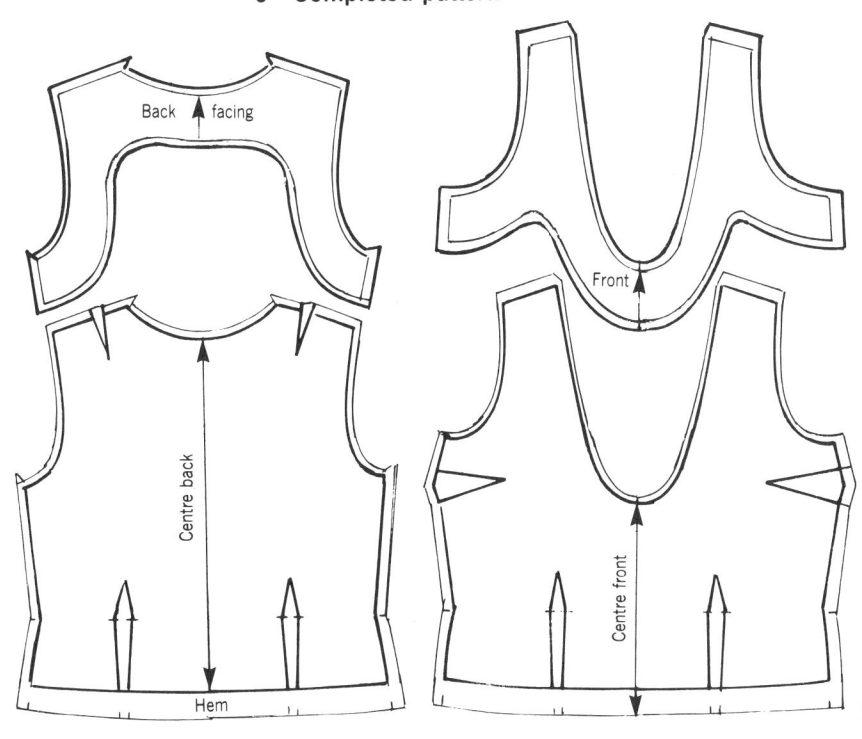

c Add 6 mm (¼ in) seam allowances to neck and armhole lines and the same amount to neck and armhole facings. 6 mm (¼ in) allowance is also added to the outer edge of facing for overlocking or any other form of neatening.

Allow 1.3 – 2 cm (½–¾ in) seam turnings for side seams and shoulder seams.

Add a hem allowance of 2.5–5 cm (1–2 in).

5 Necklines and collars

Round neck

Figure 5.17

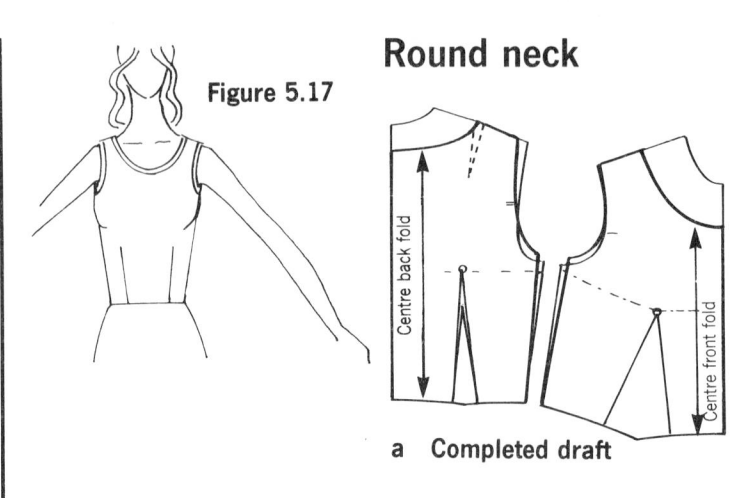

a Completed draft

Sleeveless garments require a closer fit around the armhole than garments with sleeves.

Adjustments to front and back waist blocks must be made to tighten and raise the armhole.

Figure 5.17 At underarm points, take in back and front side seams by 1.3 cm (½ in). Draw new side seam lines from original waist line to 1.3 cm (½ in) above original armhole line as shown. Trace new construction and style lines on to new paper.

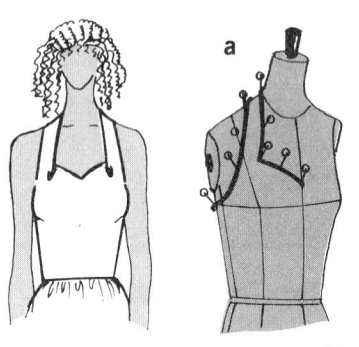

Halter neckline and facing

Figure 5.18

Figure 5.18a Outline with tape on dress form desired style lines for halter neckline.

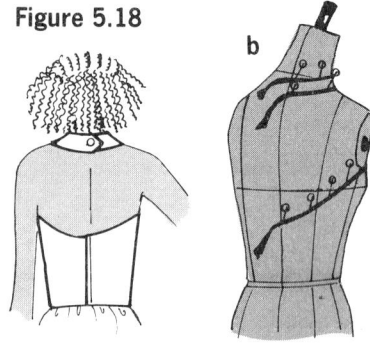

b Use basic back block and front block with one large waist dart. Outline on paper. Reduce side seams at underarm points as for Figure 5.17a. Also reduce centre front at neck (see wide, low-cut necklines Figure 5.3b and 5.7b) to avoid gaping.

c Draw halter neck style lines as established on dress form onto outlined blocks producing the basic draft.

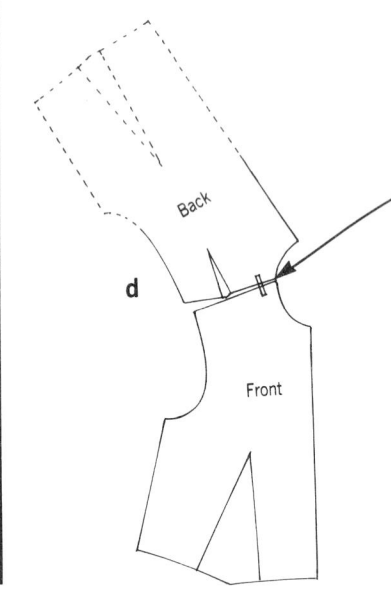

d Cut away back neck halter section and join to front shoulder, having previously placed balance marks, to obtain the characteristic 'halter' as shown.

e Close front waist dart and slash from corner of neckline to bust point, thus transferring bust dart to neck position. This dart will be sewn as unpressed pleat and can be tightened to improve the fit of neckline. The pleat is, however, omitted when constructing the facing. This garment fits even better when cut on the bias.

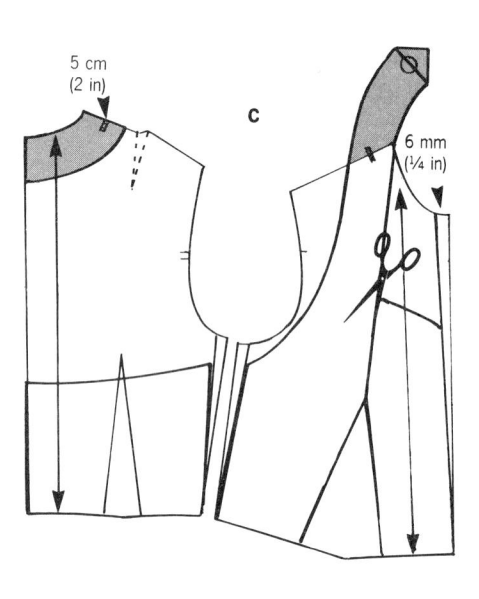

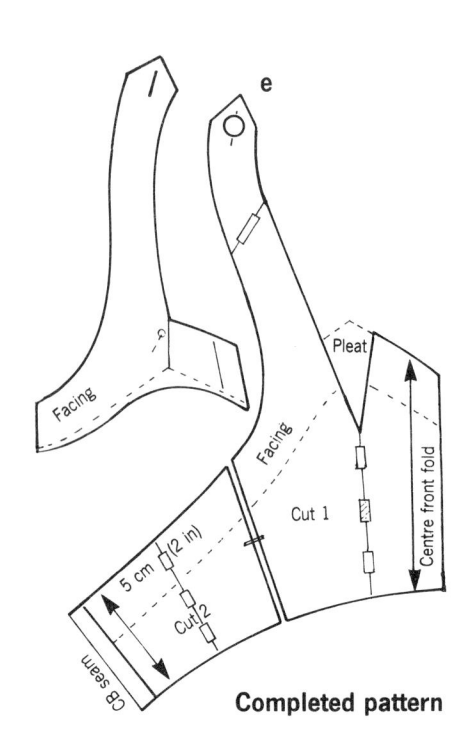

Completed pattern

64

Flat collars

Principles of cutting

Figure 5.19a Draw rectangle of calico with circle for neckline.

b Fold and crease.

c If used to model a flat collar as illustrated, a wedge of surplus fabric would form at shoulder position. This is due to the natural slope of the shoulders.

Without using darts or seams, the collar can be made to lie flat over the shoulders by carefully smoothing the fabric around from CB to CF thus changing the grain and shape of the neckline.

d Note on the back of the dress form the position of the cut out semi-circle. This is much too low, compared with the anatomical position of the prominent vertebra – the nape of the neck.

Figure 5.19

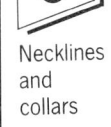

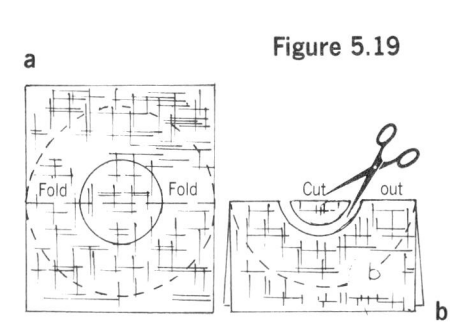

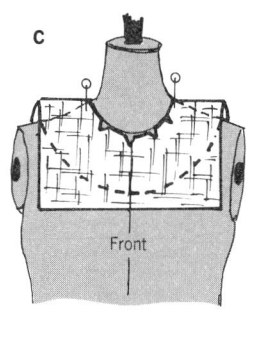

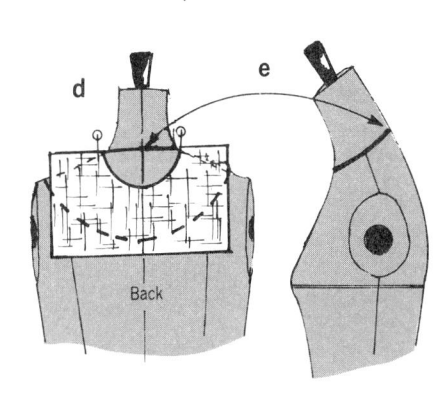

Figure 5.20

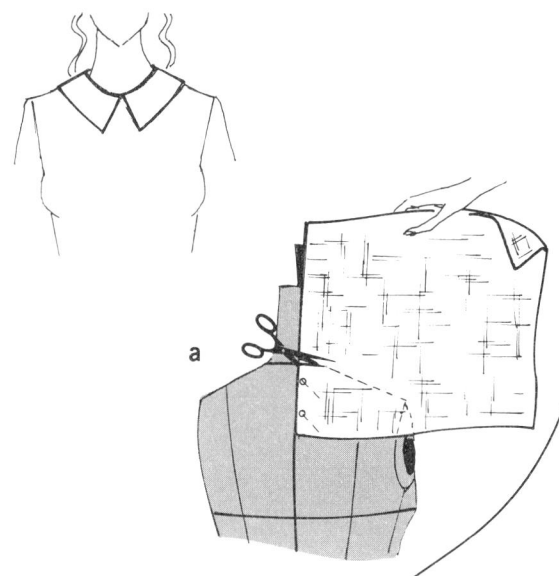

Peter Pan collar – modelled

Figure 5.20a Cut a rectangle of muslin 30.5 × 35.5 cm (12 × 14 in).

Pin warp edge of muslin to centre back of dress form. Raise or lower muslin according to desired finished depth of collar at centre back.

Pin and mark back neckline to shoulder line. Place shoulder balance mark. Cut to within 13 mm (½ in) of neckline and snip edge.

b Cut muslin to shoulder/neck point, smooth over shoulder towards centre front and pin. Slash outer edge of muslin. Turn dress form to front and pin, mark and snip front neck line.

c and **d** Outline desired shape of collar with tape. Mark with soft pencil and remove from dress form.

e Lower front neckline by 6–13 mm (¼–½ in) and add 6 mm (¼ in) seam turnings.

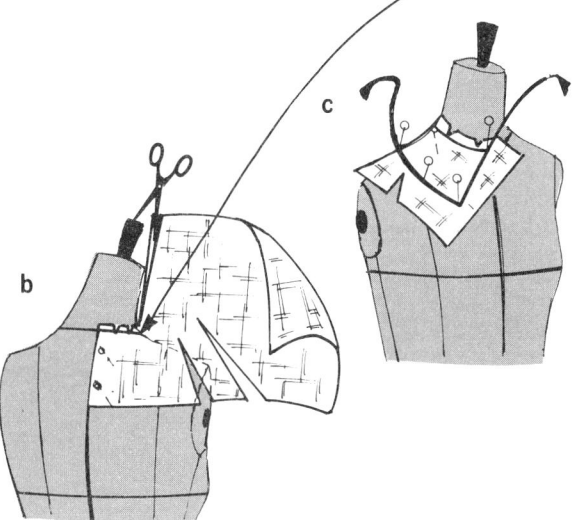

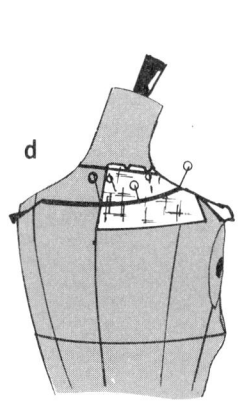

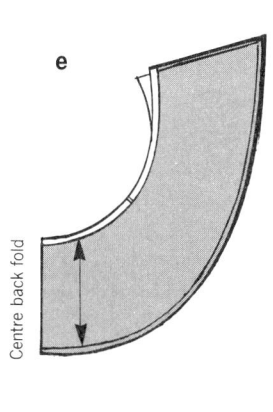

Completed pattern

Flat jabot collar

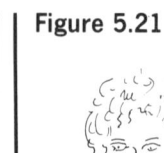

Figure 5.21 Begin modelling as for Peter Pan collar, Figure 5.20, continuing from **(a)**; pin modelling fabric firmly at shoulder seam area; smooth remaining fabric around to front of dress form.

b The grain of the fabric must be dropped to create the flare shown in the illustration. The upper warp-grain edge will become the centre front of the collar. Drop point A to CF neckpoint on dress form. Immediately form half of inverted pleat shown. Pin firmly. A deep flare will have formed in the shoulder area.

c Distribute deep flare by slashing and pinning neckline until a pleasing all-over flare is achieved.

d and **e** Trim and mark lower edge; also back collar line.

f Transfer to paper for final pattern.

Try cutting this collar by the **flat pattern cutting method.**

Outline upper parts of back and front blocks, overlapping shoulder points as in Figure 5.36b.

g Draw outline of collar and slash lines. Trace on to new paper.

h Cut on slash lines to neckline but not through it. Open as shown. Outline and complete pattern.

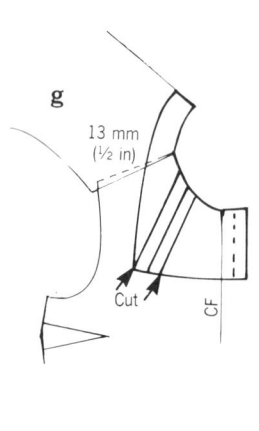

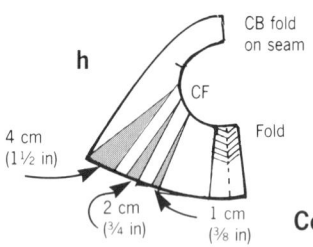

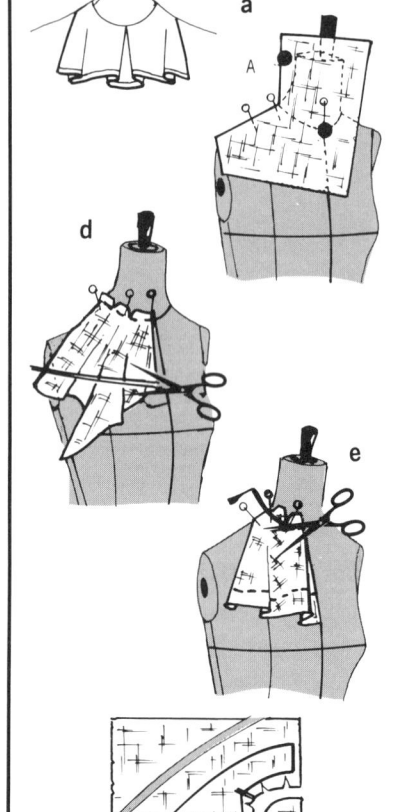

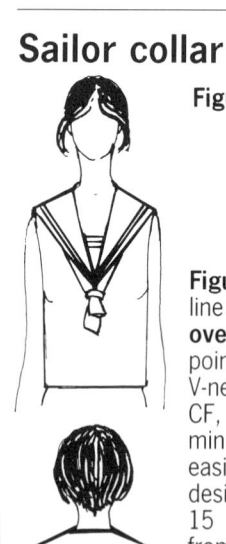

Sailor collar

Figure 5.22

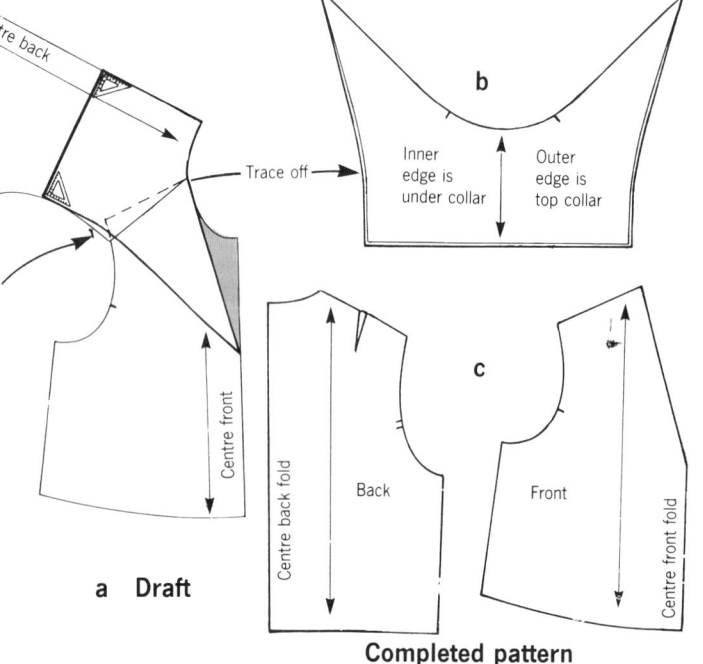

Figure 5.22a and **b** Outline back and front blocks; **overlap** shoulder armhole points 2 cm (¾ in). Draw V-neck 15 cm (6 in) down CF, 13 cm (5 in) is the minimum depth to pull easily over the head. Draw desired collar shape, here 15 cm (6 in), down CB from nape of neck. Place balance marks at shoulder position. Trace through. Draft top collar from under collar, (see Figure 5.37d and e). Add seams and grain lines.

Bertha collar

Figure 5.23 Proceed as for flat collar but cut a larger rectangle of muslin or calico 46 × 32 cm (18 × 13 in).

Capes

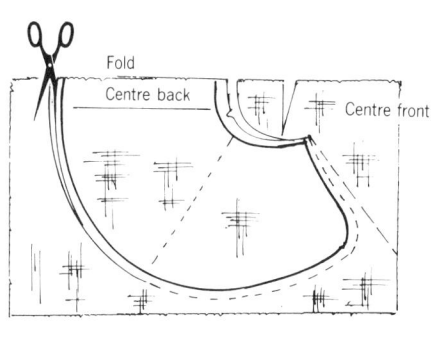

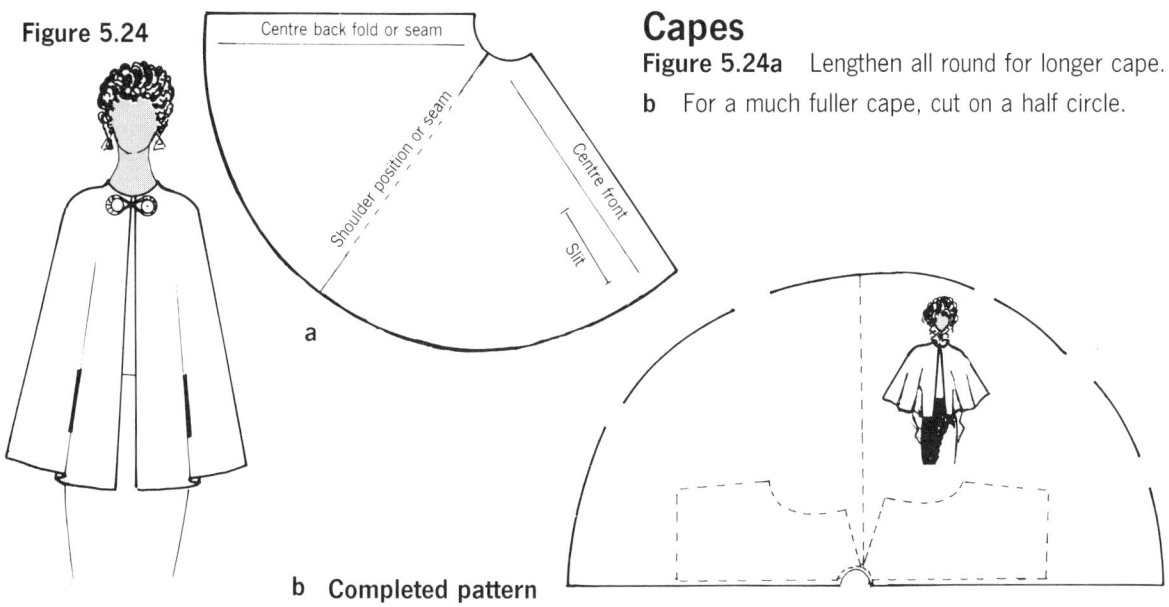

Figure 5.24a Lengthen all round for longer cape.

b For a much fuller cape, cut on a half circle.

Figure 5.24

b Completed pattern

Flared capelet

Figure 5.25a Cut piece of muslin 64 × 36 (25 × 14). Pin to centre back of dress form. Snip as shown.

b Continue pinning and cutting around neckline and allow muslin to drop at intervals. This throws fullness towards the back, thus forming a soft flare.

c Continue pinning over shoulder to front neckline.

Outline shape of cape with tape, mark and remove from form.

d Recut muslin, trace onto paper with tracing wheel and make pattern.

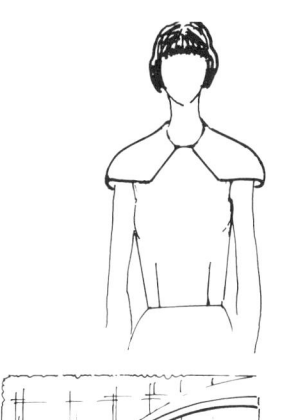

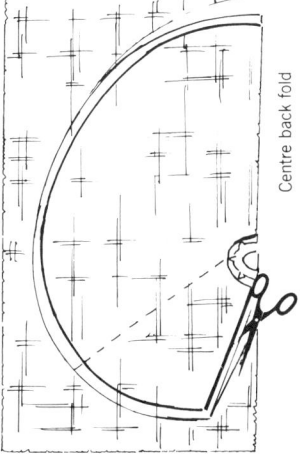

d Completed pattern

5 Necklines and collars

Roll collars

Figure 5.26

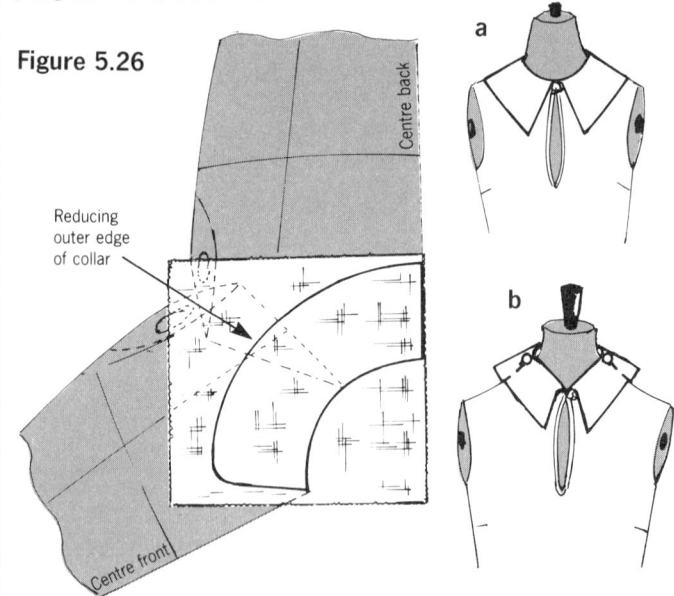

Principles of cutting

By reducing the outer edge of a flat collar, a roll collar can be obtained. The collar edge is forced up to rest more comfortably higher up on a level where the body–shoulder circumference is equal to the reduced collar circumference, at the same time producing the desired 'fold' or 'roll' near to the neck.

At no time, however, is the collar neckline reduced. Its measurement must always remain the same as that of the garment neckline.

Figure 5.27

Eton-type collar

Figure 5.27a Cut rectangle of muslin, width of finished collar plus 5 cm (2 in) by half neckline measurement plus 6 cm (2½ in).

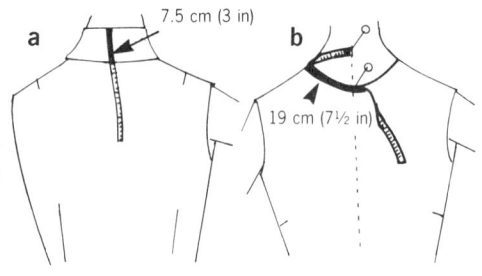

b Name short left hand side '**Centre back**' (**CB**). Cut away narrow section of muslin 1.3 cm (½ in) at CB tapering to nothing, as shown. This represents the slightly curved neckline.

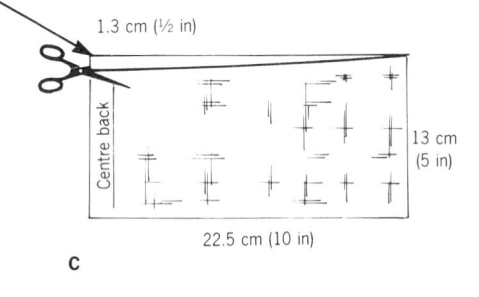

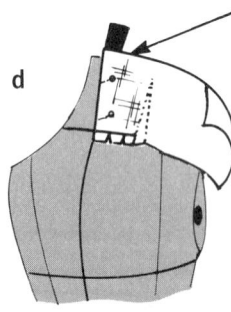

d – g Pin CB edge of muslin to centre back of form arranging bulk of muslin above neckline. Allow 1.3 cm (½ in) below this line. Pin to shoulder position and place balance mark. Pin around to front easing muslin a little over shoulder area. Outline desired shape with tape. Mark. Trace onto pattern paper and true all lines.

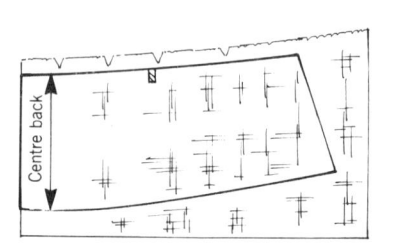

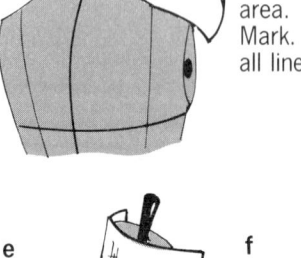

a 7.5 cm (3 in)
b 19 cm (7½ in)

Take measurements

1.3 cm (½ in)
13 cm (5 in)
22.5 cm (10 in)

c

h Completed pattern

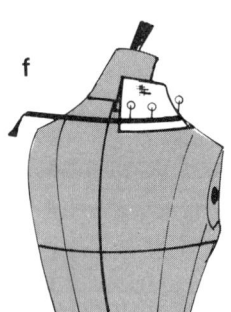

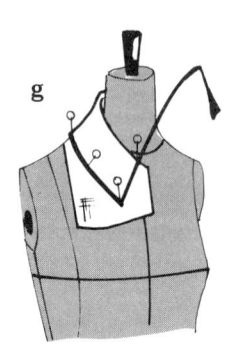

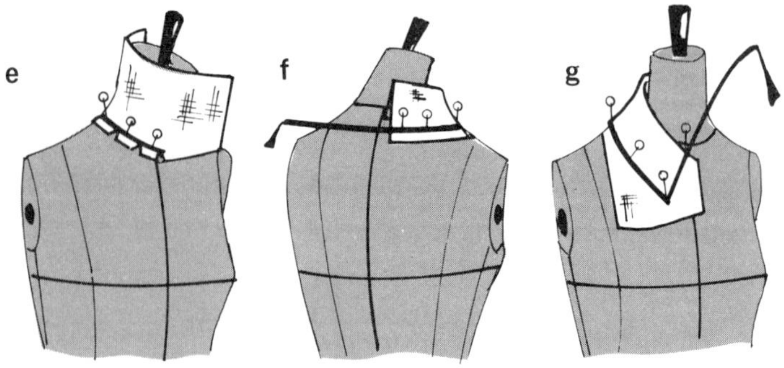

Revers collars

Modelling the revers collar

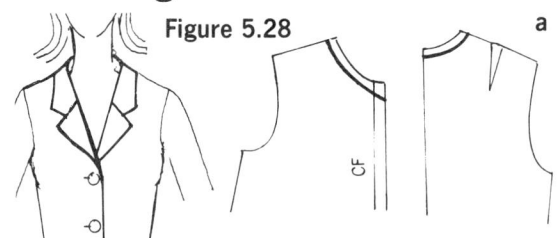

Figure 5.28

Figure 5.28a Outline back and front blocks. Add 2.5 cm (1 in) to right of centre front line for button stand. Lower back and front necklines by 1.3 cm (½ in). Straighten front neckline.

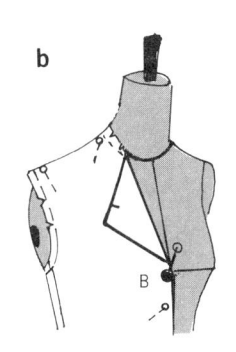

b Pin back and front patterns to dress form, fold over lapel. Mark breakline and break point **B**.

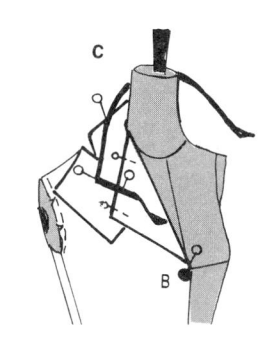

c Cut rectangle of fabric 12.5 × 25.5 cm (5 × 10 in). Model back and shoulder area of collar as Figure 5.27. Place modelling fabric under lapel. Pin. Outline shape of collar. Balance mark collar position on lapel and mark width of collar.

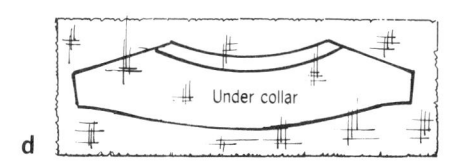

d Remove collar shape from form and true all lines. This collar is the **under collar**. It is sometimes cut on the bias with a centre seam.

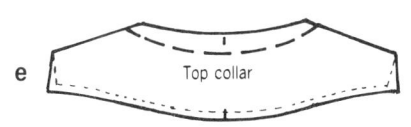

e The **top collar** is cut larger from nothing at this point to 3 mm (⅛ in) all around the outer edge of the collar. (See also pages 76–9.)

The grown-on collar (high shawl variation)

Figure 5.29

Figure 5.29a Cut rectangle of modelling fabric in size of front block plus 20 cm (8 in) above shoulder and 20 cm (8 in) to right of CF. Front block may be outlined on fabric as shown.

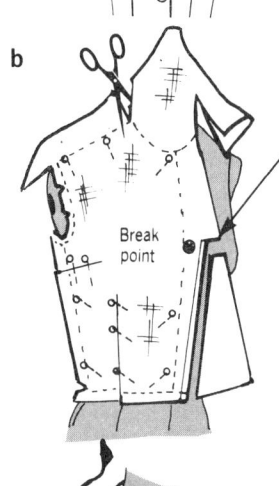

b Pin to dress form. Locate break point. Mark button stand. Cut away excess fabric. Cut to shoulder/neck point at neckline and pin.

c Fold back fabric at break point and pivot remaining fabric to CB. Collar can be made to rest close to neck or lie somewhat flatter, slightly away from it. In the first case, CB seam of collar is on the bias, whereas in the second, seam is on straight grain of the fabric.

When satisfied with appearance of collar, remove from form, true all marked lines and recut.

Experiment with other shapes, e.g. shawl collar.

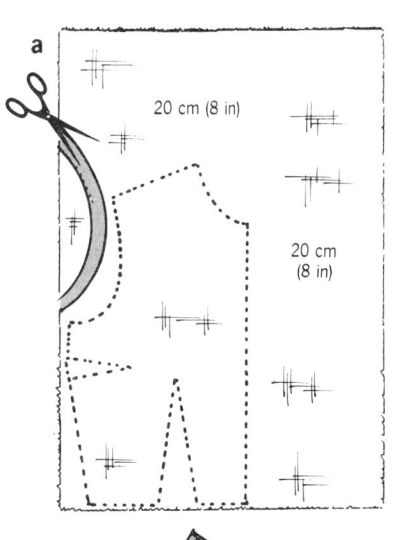

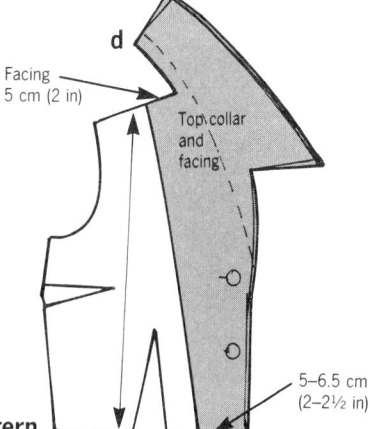

Completed pattern

5 Necklines and collars

Stand collars

Figure 5.30

The stand collar is the easiest collar to model, yet it is the most flattering and versatile of all collar styles with many adaptations throughout the ages (Figure 5.30).

The straight stand collar stands upright enveloping the neck and, in its basic form, is set on to the natural neckline.

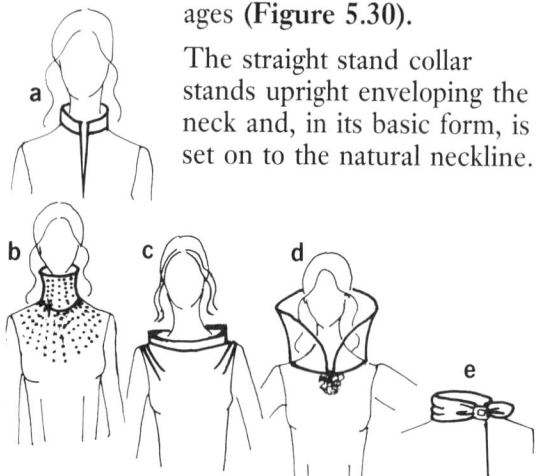

Figure 5.31

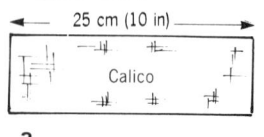

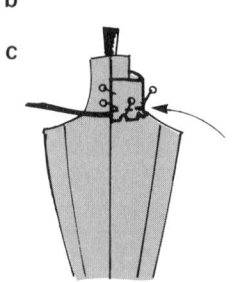

Figure 5.31a Tear or cut on straight grain a piece of modelling fabric half neck circumference plus 2.5 × 7.5 cm (1 × 3 in).

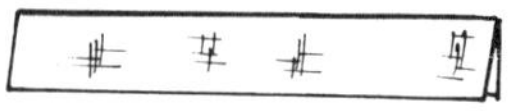

b Fold in half lengthwise. Establish desired neck circumference measurement on the dress form and outline with tape.

c Pin double collar band from CB around neckline to CF, following taped outline. Take care not to stretch collar band.

Balance mark shoulder position. Shape and mark CF collar edge as desired.

Mandarin collar

The mandarin collar is slightly more shaped and fits closer to the neck.

Figure 5.32 Tear or cut on straight grain a piece of modelling fabric half neck measurement plus 5 × 7 cm (2 × 2¾ in).

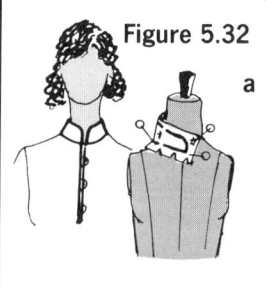

Figure 5.32 Establish neck circumference measurement (as above).

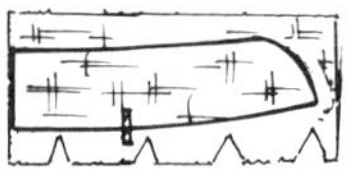

a Pin single layer fabric collar band to CB and pin around neckline to shoulder position; balance mark. Continue pinning, slightly dropping grain of modelling fabric and in doing so, causing fabric collar edge to rest closer to the neck.

b Shape CF collar points. Mark neckline and upper edge of collar. Remove. True all marked lines. Transfer to pattern paper. This is the under collar.

c Develop top collar by adding 3 mm (⅛ in) to outer edge.

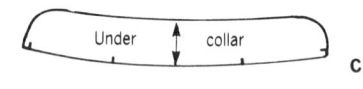

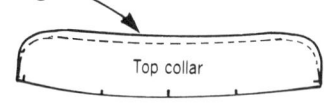

Standing wing collar

Based on the mandarin collar. Develop top collar from under collar.

Figure 5.33

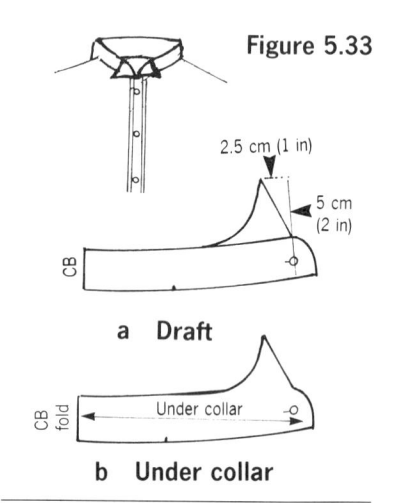

a Draft

b Under collar

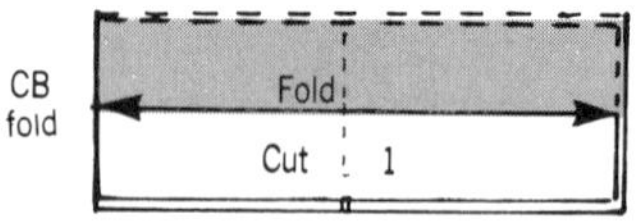

Straight stand collar cut flat

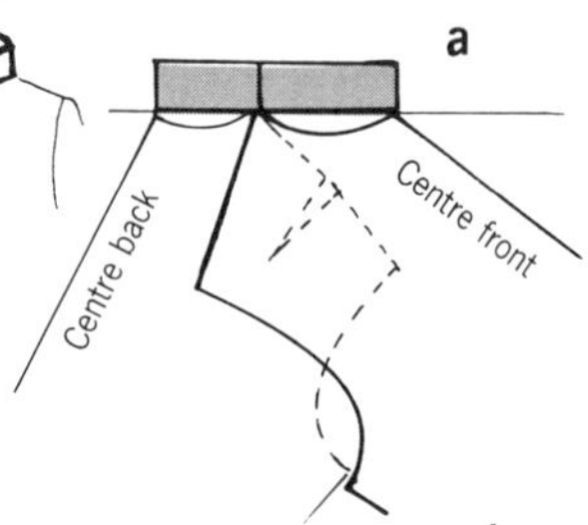

Figure 5.34a Draw horizontal line. Place back and front necklines to it. Draw rectangles 2.5 cm (1 in) high. Trace off as one collar band. Check measurements.

b Upper edge of collar is on fold. Draft double width collar. Place shoulder balance mark. Add seam allowances on CF and lower neck edge.

Mandarin collar cut flat

Figure 5.35

Figure 5.35a Outline basic collar rectangle. Divide front section into three parts.

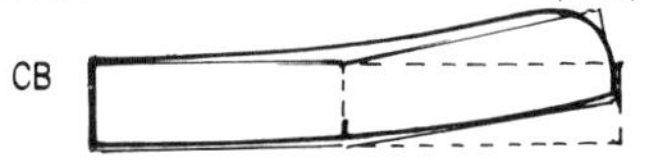

b Overlap each division by 2 mm (1/16 approx.) on top collar edge only. Lower edge must remain same measurement as neck. Cut top collar as Figure 5.32.

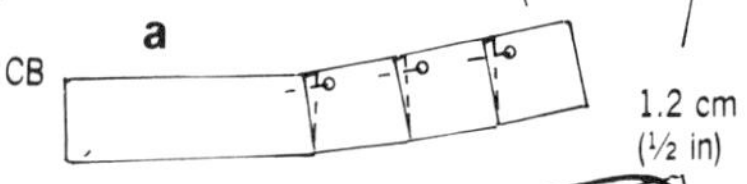

Flat cutting of collars

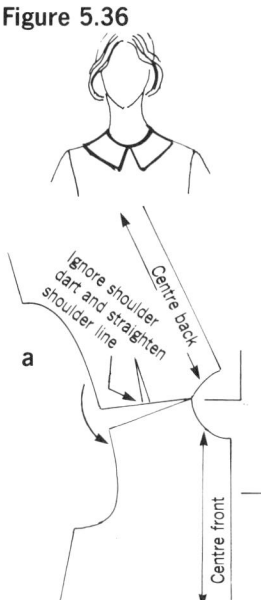

Figure 5.36

Refer to Figures 5.19, 5.26 and 5.38 where the basic principles of constructing collars are discussed.

Figure 5.36a Outline upper section of front block as shown. Place back waist block with shoulder neck point touching front shoulder neck point.

b Overlap shoulder points by 1.3–2.5 cm (½–1 in). This reduces outer collar edge, slightly straightens the collar neckline curve and effects a slight roll at the neckline. The roll conceals the neckline seam which would otherwise show.

Outline neckline, part of CB and CF lines. Place shoulder/neck balance mark and draw part of armhole for orientation.

Remove blocks. Draw in desired shape of collar lowering the curve by approximately 6 mm (¼ in) at CB.

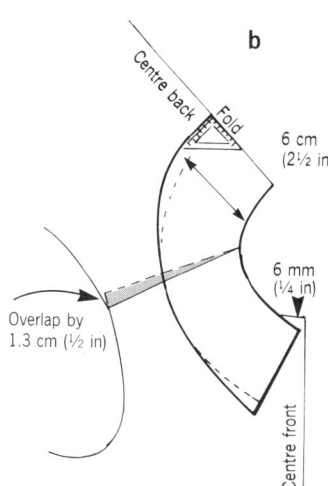

Lower CF of collar neckline by 6 mm (¼ in). This will cause the collar to roll slightly at this point and will conceal the neckline seam. Trace collar onto new paper. Add **6 mm (¼ in)** seam allowance all round except to CB line which is placed on straight grain fold of fabric.

Peter Pan collar

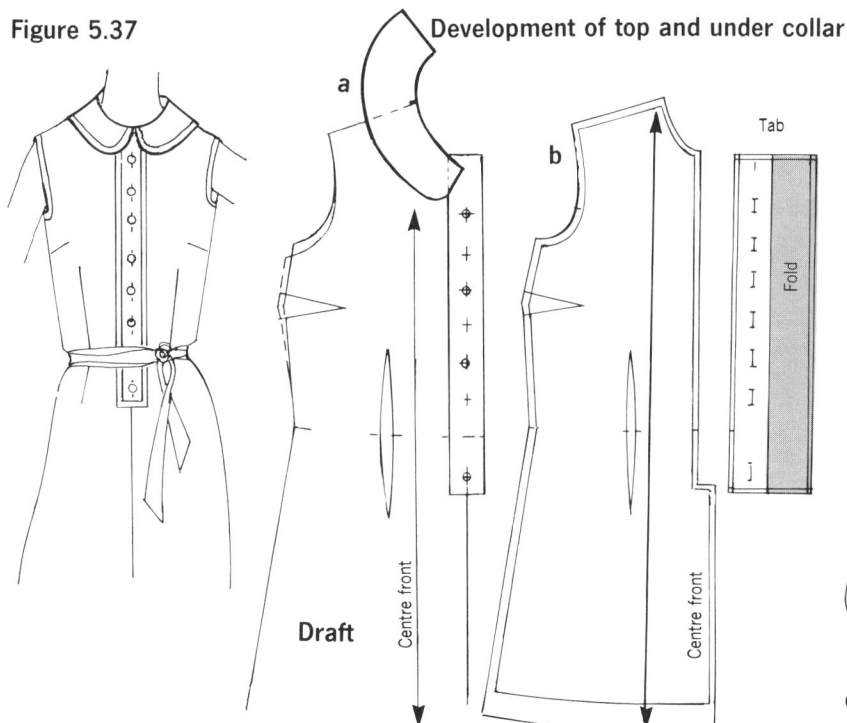

Figure 5.37

Development of top and under collar

Draft

d Increase top collar from nothing at CF neck to 3 mm (⅛ in) on back outer edge.

Inner necklines of both top and under collars must remain the same. Add 5 mm (¼ in) seam allowances.

Completed dress and collar patterns

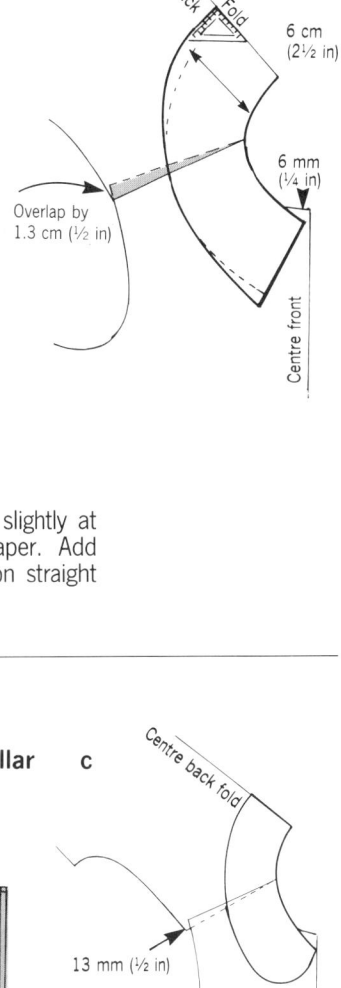

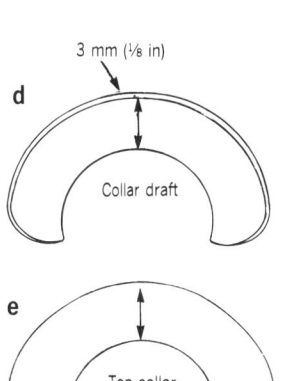

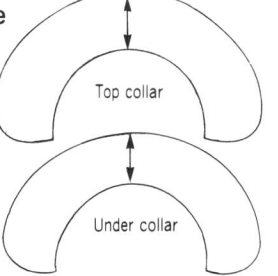

Necklines and collars

Roll collars – cut flat

Figure 5.38

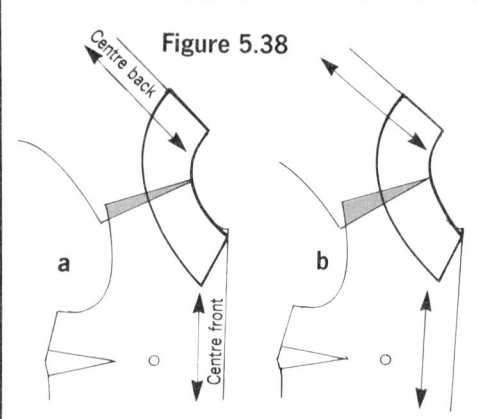

The more the outer edge of the collar is reduced, the more the collar rolls at the neckline. The best way to achieve this is to overlap the shoulder points of the back and front waist blocks each time more than before. Note that both the neckline and the outer edge of the collar become less curved the more the shoulder points overlap, until finally (e) the straight collar as we know it on shirt necklines is arrived at.

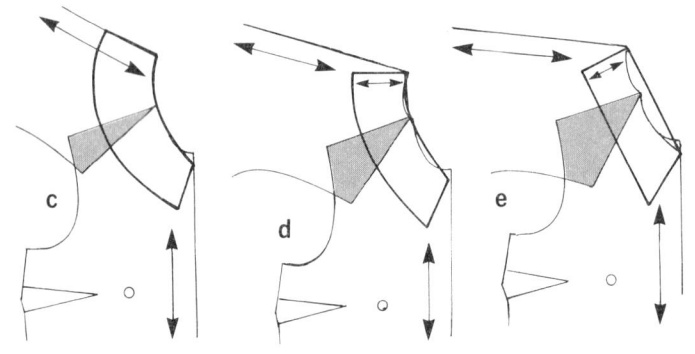

Collars are easily identifiable: the more curved the inner neckline, the flatter is the fit of the collar; the straighter the inner neckline, the higher it fits and rolls at the back of the neckline.

Three shirt collars

Convertible shirt collar A

Figure 5.39

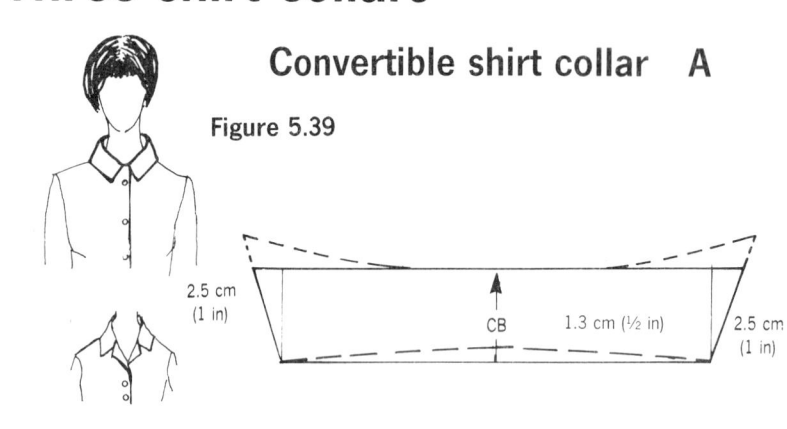

Figure 5.39 Draw rectangle, length of neckline circumference by width of desired collar including 'neck roll'. The neckline is straight, but can be slightly curved.

Shape collar points as desired.

This is the under collar. Develop top collar as Figure 5.37d and e.

Convertible shirt collar B

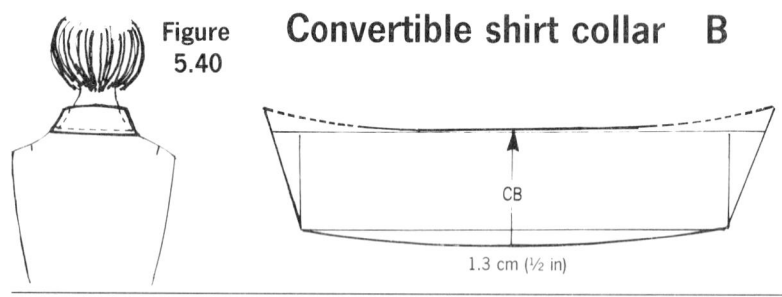

Figure 5.40

This collar has an added stand and fits higher at the back of the neck.

Develop top collar as Figure 5.37d and e.

Shirt collar with stand C
(Cut in one and two-piece variety)

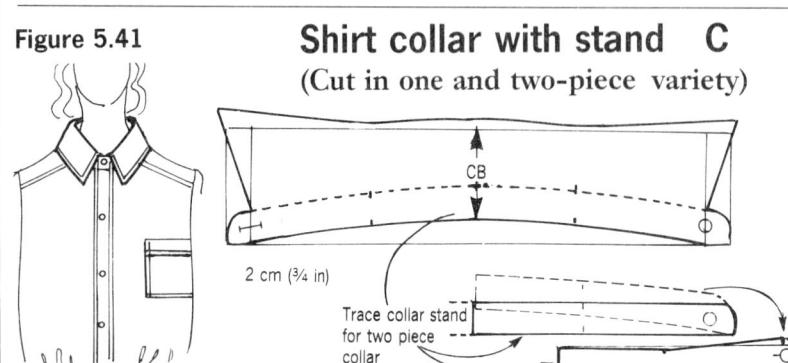

Figure 5.41

This collar is an adaptation of the curved neck shirt collar **A** above, and the mandarin stand collar.

Figure 5.35b combined. It can be cut in two pieces (indicated by the dotted line) or in one as shown here.

Develop shirt tab opening as Figures 5.37 and 3.18, pages 71 and 44.

Trace collar stand for two piece collar

Adding collar stands

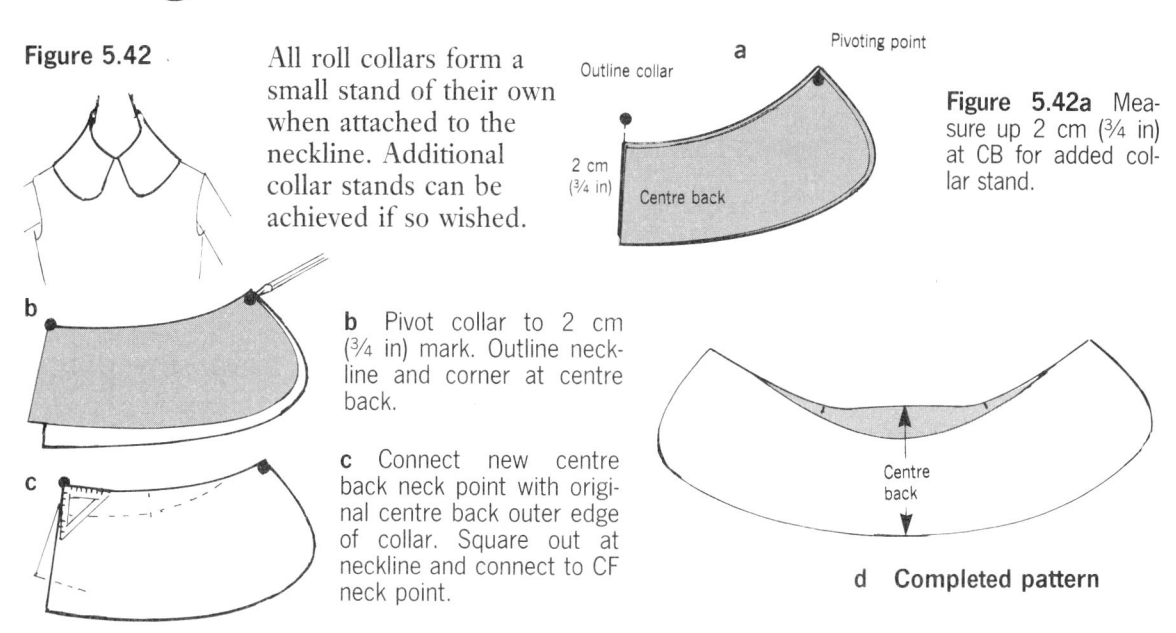

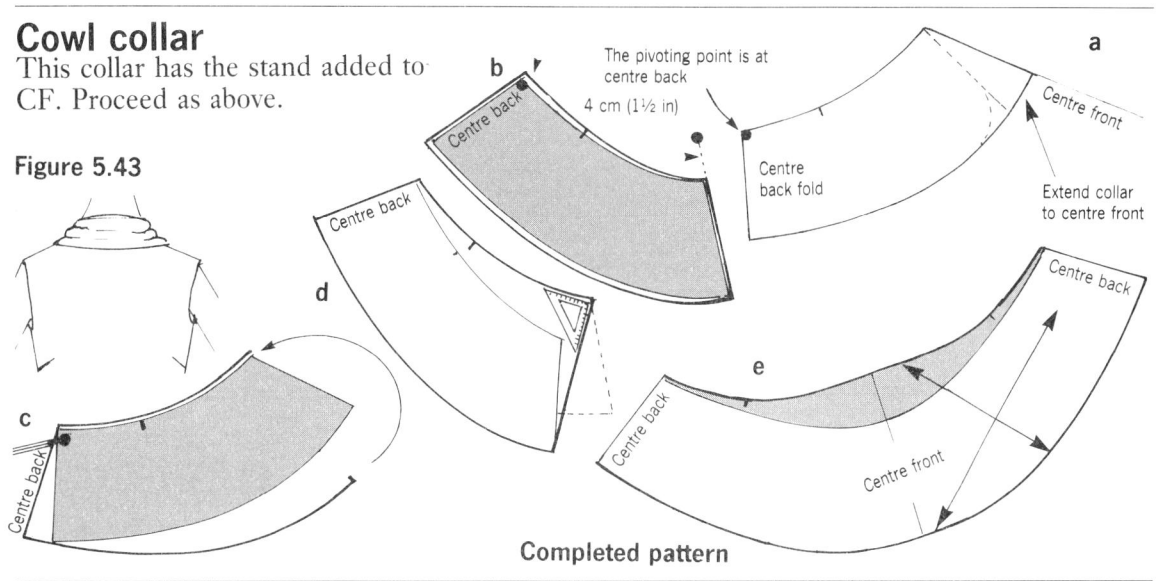

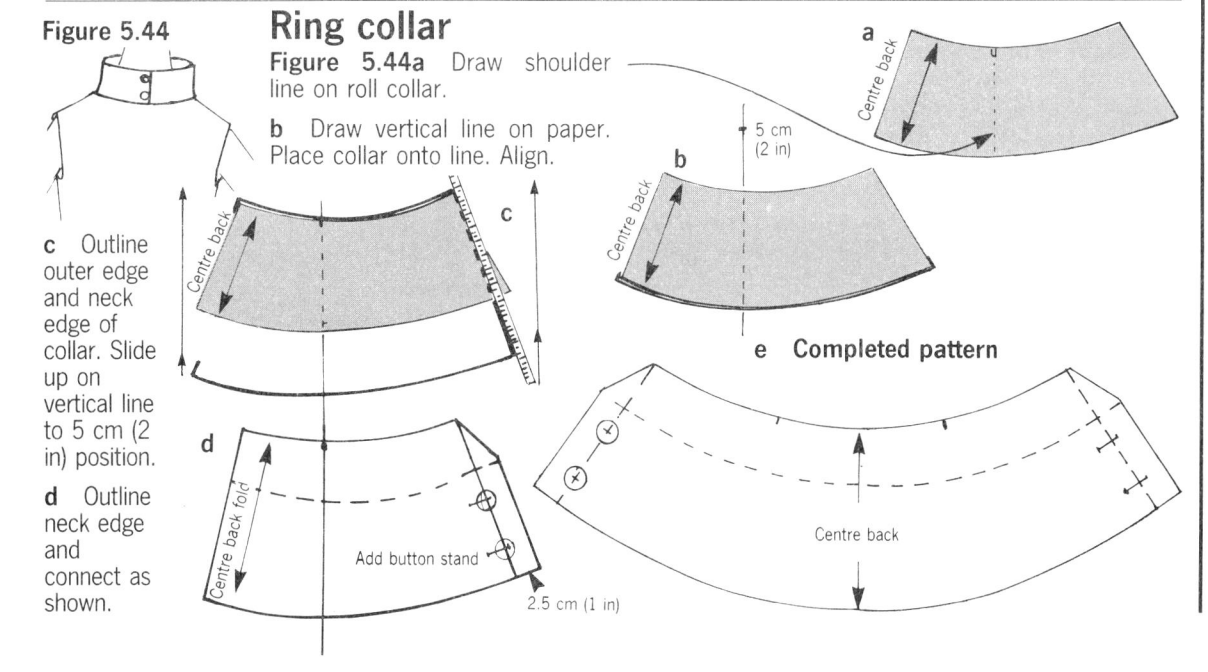

Figure 5.42

All roll collars form a small stand of their own when attached to the neckline. Additional collar stands can be achieved if so wished.

Figure 5.42a Measure up 2 cm (¾ in) at CB for added collar stand.

b Pivot collar to 2 cm (¾ in) mark. Outline neckline and corner at centre back.

c Connect new centre back neck point with original centre back outer edge of collar. Square out at neckline and connect to CF neck point.

d Completed pattern

Cowl collar

This collar has the stand added to CF. Proceed as above.

Figure 5.43

Completed pattern

Ring collar

Figure 5.44

Figure 5.44a Draw shoulder line on roll collar.

b Draw vertical line on paper. Place collar onto line. Align.

c Outline outer edge and neck edge of collar. Slide up on vertical line to 5 cm (2 in) position.

d Outline neck edge and connect as shown.

e Completed pattern

Basic collars on different necklines

High roll-collar

Collars can be attached to almost any type of neckline. In doing so an entirely new design can be created. The high roll collar is a stand collar to which a 'fall' has been added which must be 6 mm (¼ in) to 13 mm (½ in) deeper than the stand to cover neck seam line.

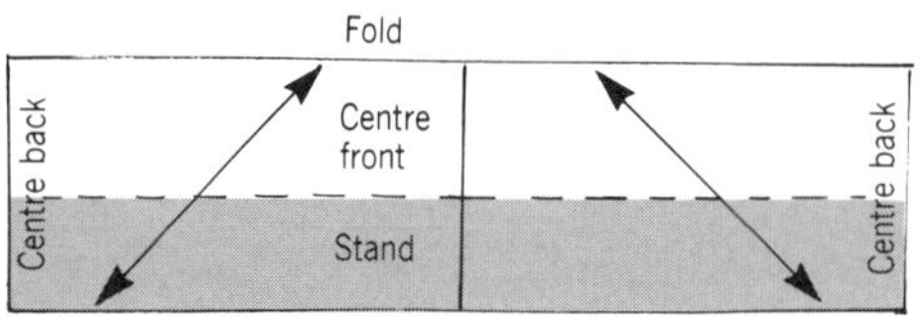

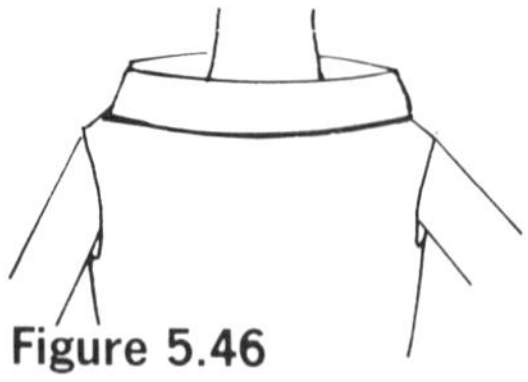

Figure 5.46

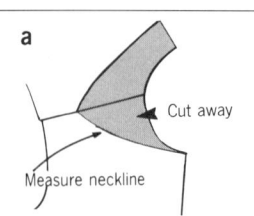

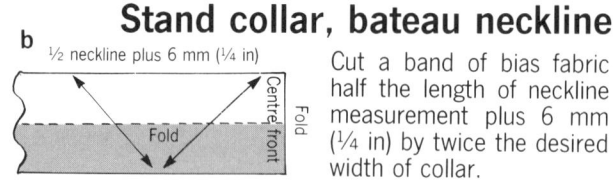

Stand collar, bateau neckline

Cut a band of bias fabric half the length of neckline measurement plus 6 mm (¼ in) by twice the desired width of collar.

Figure 5.47

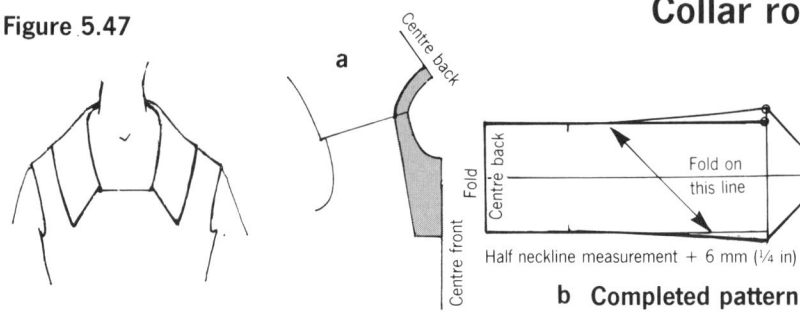

Collar rolling at back of neck

Construct a rectangle, half the length of neckline measurement plus 6 mm (¼ in), by twice the desired width of collar.

Raise line 6 mm (¼ in). Extend folding line by 5 cm (2 in) beyond CF. Draw new, slightly curved neckline and collar point.

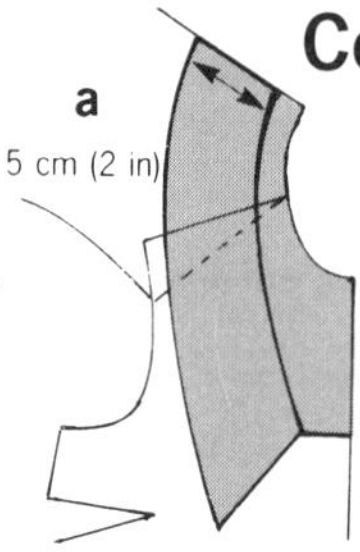

b Completed pattern

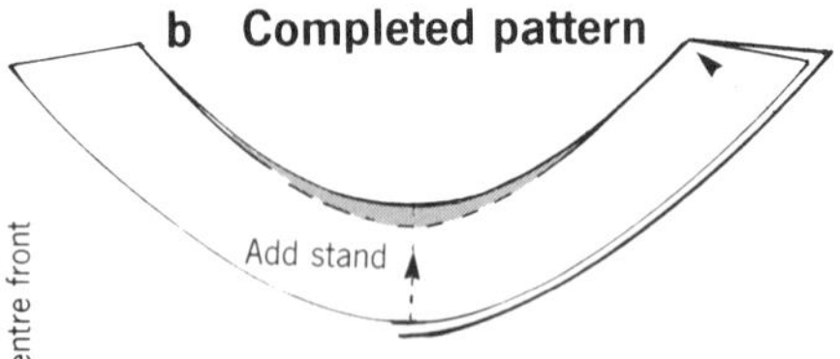

Collar rolling at back of neck, square neckline

Compare cut and fit of this collar with previous one.

For top collar add 3 mm (⅛ in) to outer edge of collar from nothing at neck point.

Trace collar from draft.

Figure 5.48

b Completed pattern

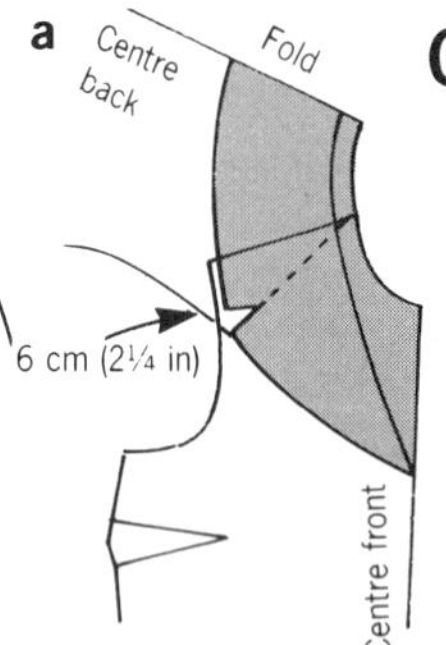

Collar rolling at back of neck, V-neckline

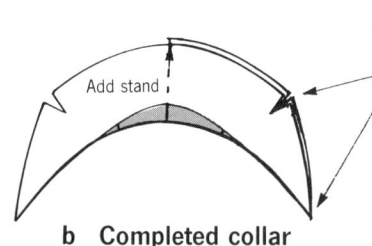

For top collar add 3 mm (⅛ in) to outer edge of collar from nothing at neck point and collar step.

Trace collar from draft.

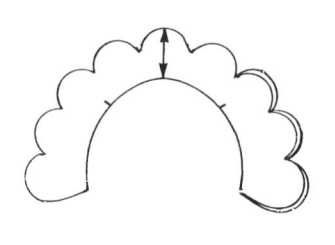

Figure 5.49

b Completed collar

Flat collar

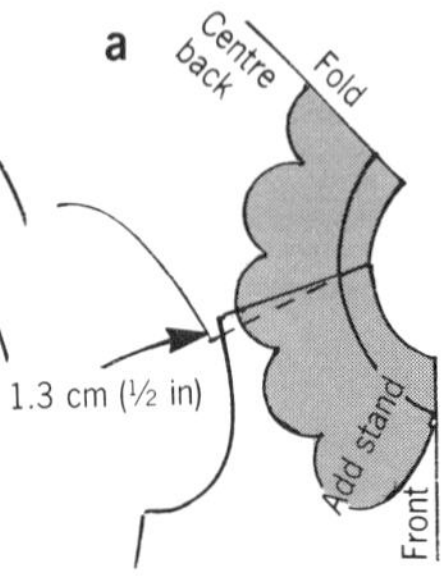

For top collar add 3 mm (⅛ in) to outer edge of collar from nothing at neck point and each scallop.

Trace collar from draft.

Figure 5.50

b Completed pattern

Grown-on wing collar cut flat

Figure 5.51

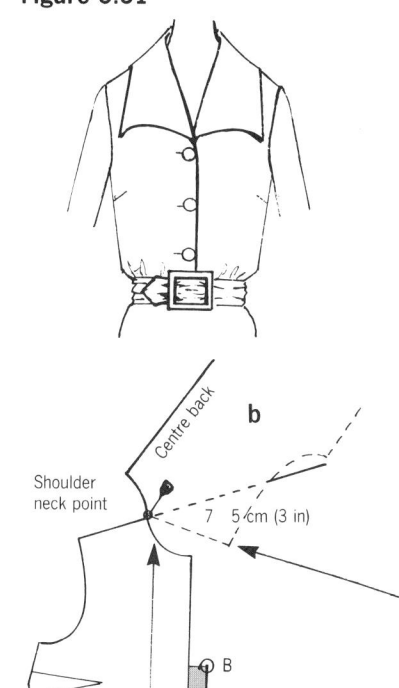

Compare the method of cutting this collar with the method of modelling the grown-on collar **Figure 5.29**. the underlying principle is the same and the final appearance of the pattern, apart from the difference in design, is similar.

Figure 5.51a Outline front waist block. Add 2.5 cm (1 in) button stand. Locate break point B 16.5 cm (6½ in) down from CF neck point. Extend shoulder line by approximately 16.5 cm (6½ in).

b Place back waist block face downwards with shoulder-neck points meeting, shoulder line resting on extended shoulder line.

Drop back shoulder point 7.5 cm (3 in) below extended shoulder line. Outline back neckline and part of CB line.

c Draw prospective collar stand and break line 2 cm (¾ in) away from back neckline and connect to break point B.

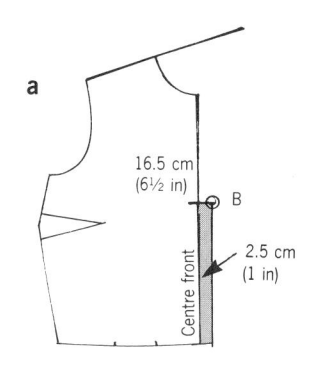

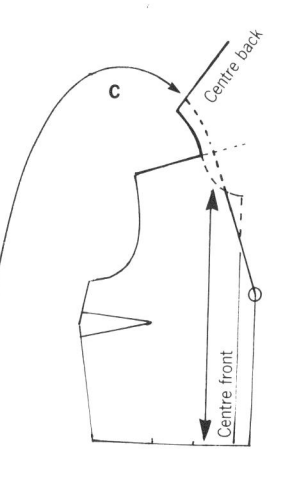

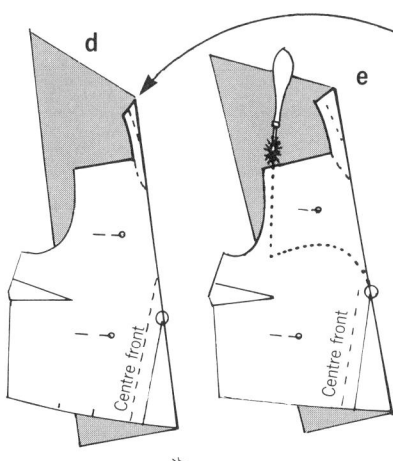

d Fold paper under on break line and crease.

e Draw desired shape of collar. Trace through with tracing wheel.

f Unfold paper. Draw collar outline to CB.

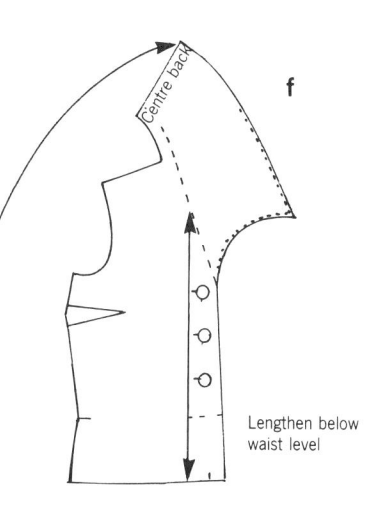

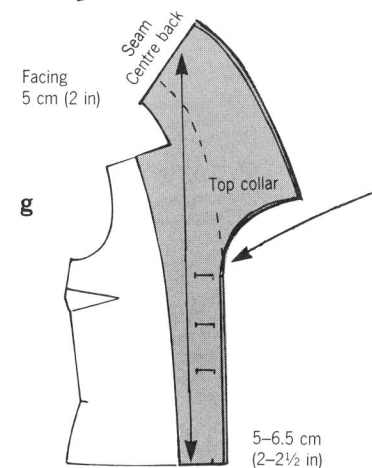

g Facing is cut in one with top collar. There is a seam at CB. Add 3 mm (⅛ in), depending on thickness of fabric, around outer edge of top collar from nothing at break point.

h The seam at CB of top collar can be avoided by cutting the collar on the straight grain. The facing is then joined below the first buttonhole.

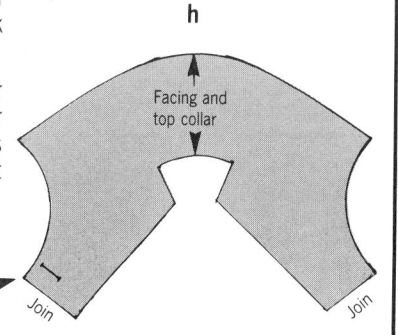

5 Necklines and collars

Tuxedo collar

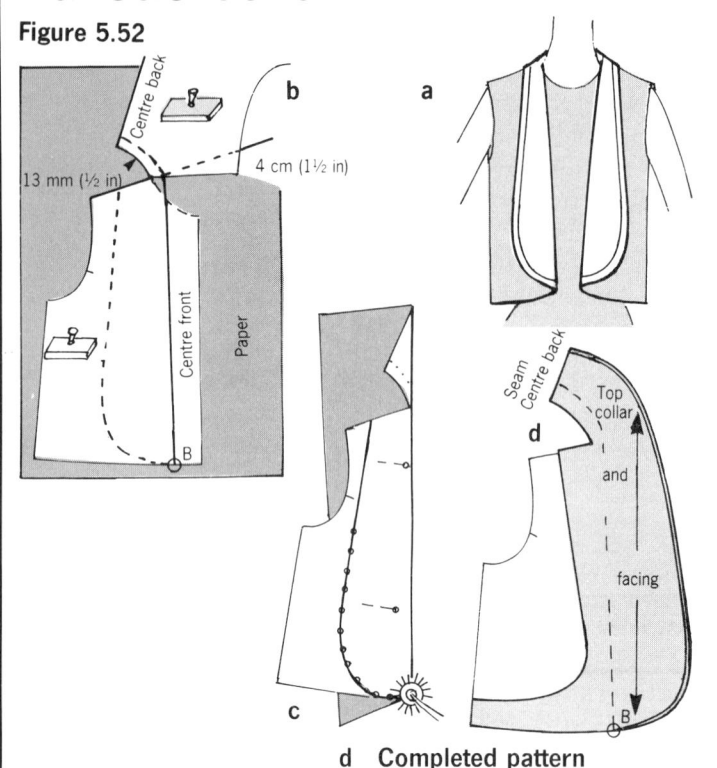

Figure 5.52

Figure 5.52a Outline front block. Extend paper 5 cm (2 in) to the right of CF line. Indicate shape of collar as sketch.

b Extend shoulder line as in Figure 5.51a. Place back block face down onto it with shoulder-neck point meeting. As this collar lies fairly flat around the neckline, a larger circumference for the collar edge is required. Therefore drop back shoulder point only 4 cm (1½ in) below extended shoulder line. Draw back neckline and part of CB line. Draw shallow collar stand 13 mm (½ in) deep. Connect with break line and break point B at waist level.

c Fold paper under at break line. Redraw shape of collar if required. Trace through collar outline.

d Unfold paper. Complete back of collar as in Figure 5.51g. Develop facing and top collar as in Figure 5.51h. Add 3 mm (⅛ in) around outer edge to nothing at **B**.

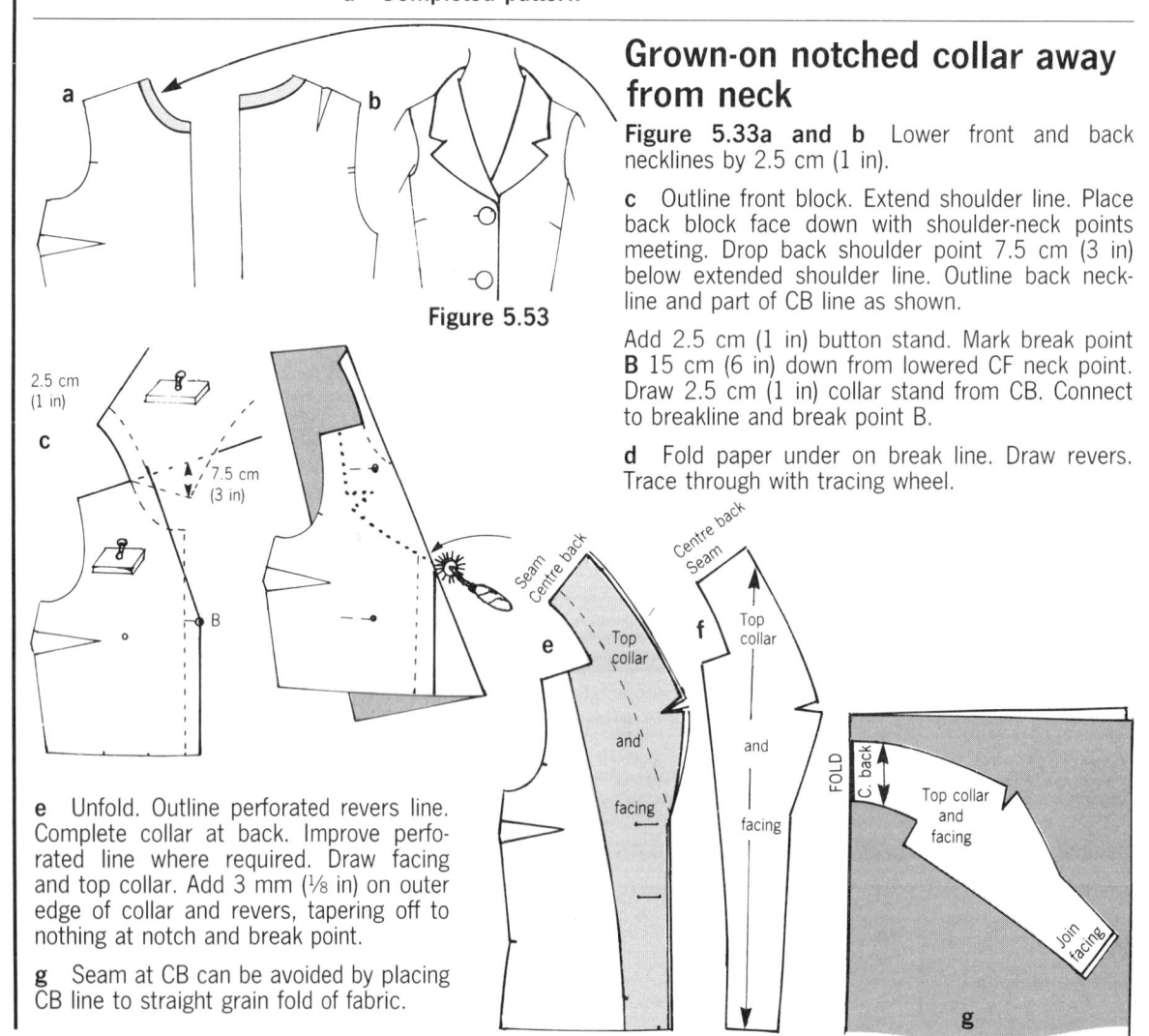

d Completed pattern

Grown-on notched collar away from neck

Figure 5.33a and b Lower front and back necklines by 2.5 cm (1 in).

c Outline front block. Extend shoulder line. Place back block face down with shoulder-neck points meeting. Drop back shoulder point 7.5 cm (3 in) below extended shoulder line. Outline back neckline and part of CB line as shown.

Add 2.5 cm (1 in) button stand. Mark break point **B** 15 cm (6 in) down from lowered CF neck point. Draw 2.5 cm (1 in) collar stand from CB. Connect to breakline and break point B.

d Fold paper under on break line. Draw revers. Trace through with tracing wheel.

Figure 5.53

e Unfold. Outline perforated revers line. Complete collar at back. Improve perforated line where required. Draw facing and top collar. Add 3 mm (⅛ in) on outer edge of collar and revers, tapering off to nothing at notch and break point.

g Seam at CB can be avoided by placing CB line to straight grain fold of fabric.

Figure 5.54

For a softer roll and a more curved neckline away from the neck, introduce a 'fish dart'.

Figure 5.54 Draw line from shoulder-neck point to break point **B**. Take out 13 mm (½ in) deep dart from just below shoulder-neck point to within 7–10 cm (3–4 in) of break point.

When a still more curved neckline is desired, the depth of this dart is increased up to 2.5 cm (1 in).

The 'fish dart' is hidden from view on the right side by the revers collar and on the wrong side by the facing and top collar.

In thick materials the fish dart is cut and pressed open.

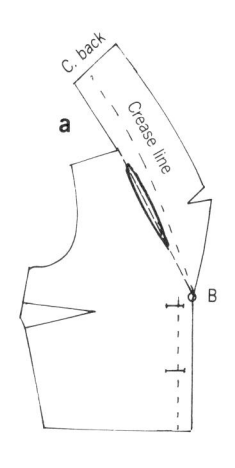

Completed pattern

Two-piece notched or revers collar

The collar and revers can be developed from the closer fitting patterns (Figure 5.51), from the lowered neck pattern (Figure 5.53) or from the above curved neckline pattern (Figure 5.54).

Figure 55a and b Lengthen lower notch line to touch fish dart.

c Outline and trace through collar.

d Develop facing and top collar: see Figure 5.53e.

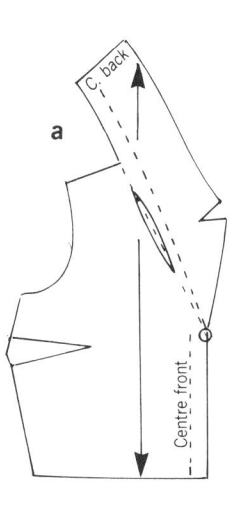

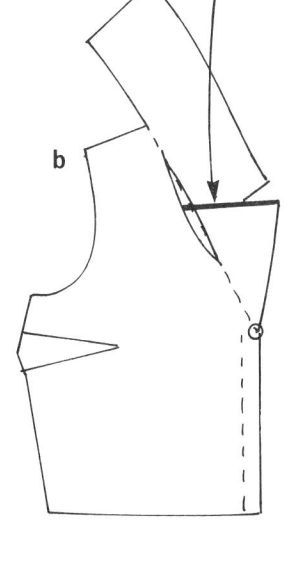

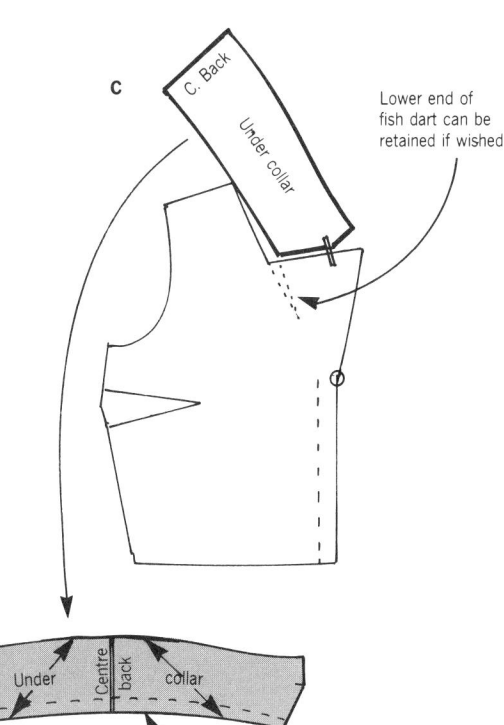

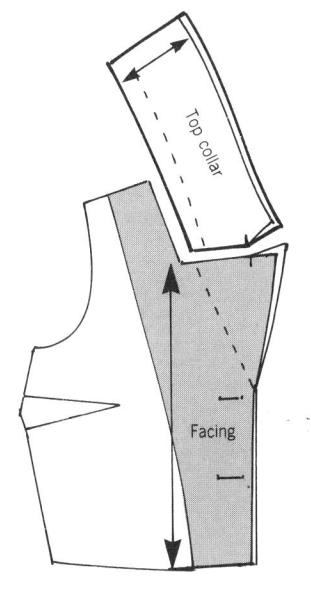

Figure 5.55

Lower end of fish dart can be retained if wished

d **Completed pattern**

5 Necklines and collars

Jabot and other neck finishes

Cravat
Figure 5.56

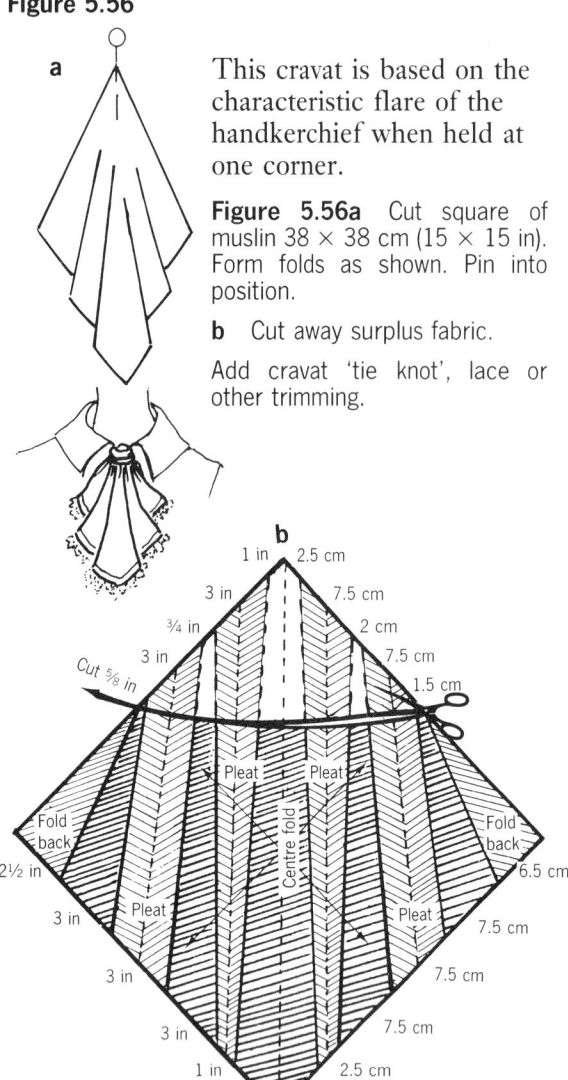

This cravat is based on the characteristic flare of the handkerchief when held at one corner.

Figure 5.56a Cut square of muslin 38 × 38 cm (15 × 15 in). Form folds as shown. Pin into position.

b Cut away surplus fabric.

Add cravat 'tie knot', lace or other trimming.

Jabot

This **jabot** is detachable or inserted in the CF seam.

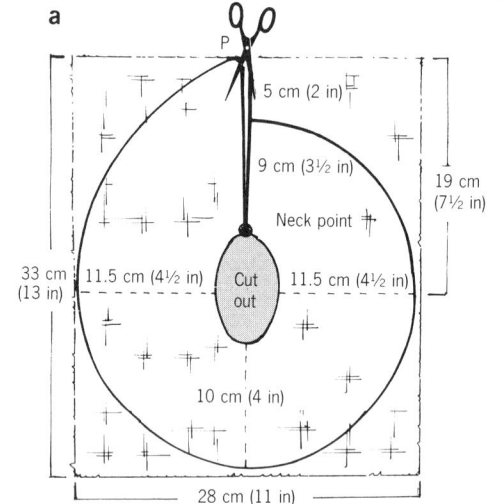

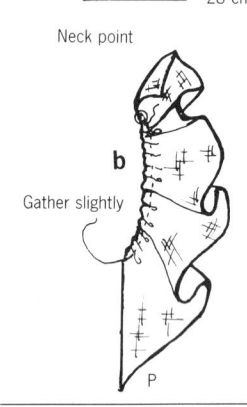

Figure 5.57

Figure 5.57a Cut rectangle of muslin 33 × 28 cm (13 × 11 in). Draw line through lengthwise centre. Draw line at right across, 19 cm (7½ in) down from top of rectangle.

Follow diagram: cut to neck point. Cut out oval centre piece. Point **P** is lower point of jabot.

Circular frill

Join as many circular pieces as are required and gather slightly.

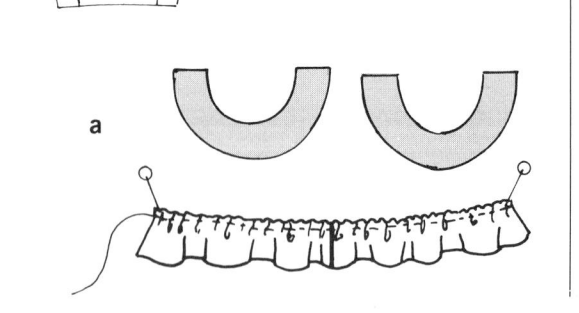

Figure 5.58

Circle collar

Figure 5.59

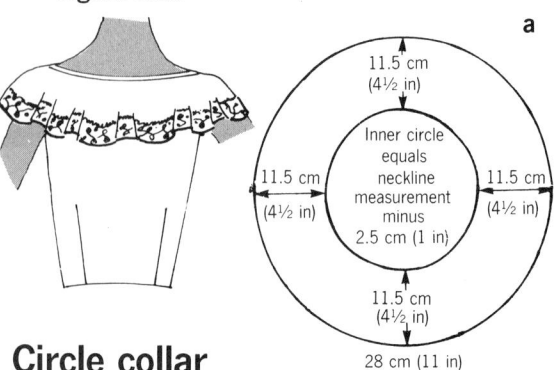

Circle collar

Draw inner circle equal to neckline measurement minus 2.5 cm (1 in) equals approx. measure 80.5 cm (32 in). Determine width of collar. Draw outer circle accordingly. Add beading, embroidery or other trimmings.

Modelling in the garment fabric

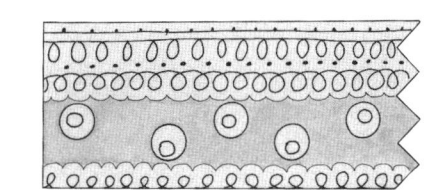

Many designers prefer to create their designs by draping the actual garment fabric on to a dress form or a figure rather than develop design ideas by sketching on paper. By handling the fabric and feeling its weight and texture, as well as seeing the visual effect of the fabric, the weave and the colour when pinned first one way and then another, designers are also able to consider a number of other potential styles before modelling the garment of their final choice.

The characteristics of the fabric in question – for example, the crispness of sheer organzas and organdies or the heavier taffetas and brocades, the drapability of soft and sheer chiffons and crepes, the bulkiness of tweed, the special qualities of satins and velvets and the stretch properties of knitted fabrics – will be reflected in the silhouette of the garment. The designer may wish to employ gathering rather than pleating and pleating rather than draping or tucking, or may wish to use seams rather than darts in order to create shape, fulness or design interest.

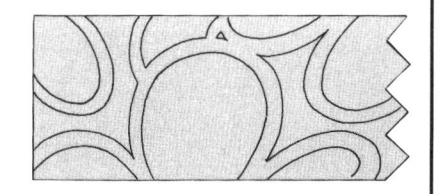

While modelling, the designer may wish to experiment with trimmings and note what effect one or the other has on the design of the garment. Designers must select trimmings compatible with the natural or synthetic fibre composition of the fabric(s) in question. The selection of piping, braiding, frilling and buttons will depend very much on whether the garment is washable or requires dry cleaning.

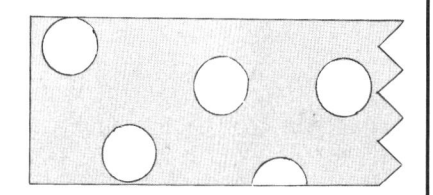

Finally, the designers' ideas will be greatly influenced by the woven or printed pattern of the fabric, for example, geometric checks and stripes, florals and paisleys or dot and spot patterns. Thought will have to be given to possible 'up and down', 'one way' and 'multiple-direction' prints. The frequency with which a pattern is repeated and the width of the fabric are other important considerations.

The reader will appreciate the advantages of modelling in the actual garment fabric compared with working in muslin or calico which necessitates visualising the factors already mentioned.

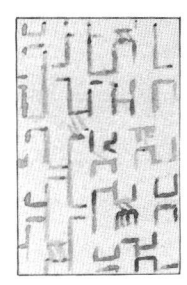

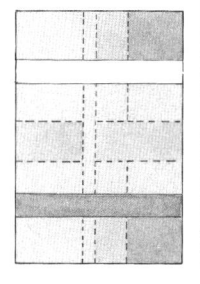

6 Modelling in the garment fabric

Developing the design

Figure 6.1

Border print fabric is used here as an example, but the approach to modelling in the garment fabric remains the same for whatever fabric is selected.

Heavy border cut and placed at centre front, with a horizontal stripe on the midriff

Heavy border at neckline

Heavy border at hem line

Method of working

Figure 6.1a and b The designer must first consider the design potential of the fabric chosen.

c The heavy border cut design is now developed.

d After experimenting with possible styles in the given fabric, outline style lines with narrow black tape on dress form

Estimate required length and width of fabric pieces for both right and left side of garment. Tear fabric sections whenever possible in order to establish straight grain. Some fabrics do not respond to tearing and must be cut following the pattern of the fabric.

e Before pinning centre front fabric section to dress form, place large CF tacking stitch a seam width away from one long edge of fabric. Pin to dress form. Trim neckline.

f Pin side front section over CF section turning raw edge under as raised seam. Feel and follow black style tape line underneath. Mark meeting edges and any small pleats with pins. Pin shoulder, armhole and side seam areas inside, away from, actual seams.

g Fold fabric piece intended for midriff, carefully matching any printed or woven pattern. Tack CF line.

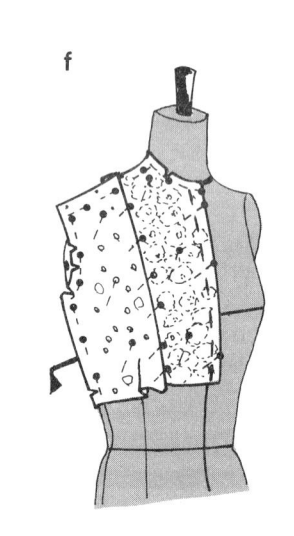

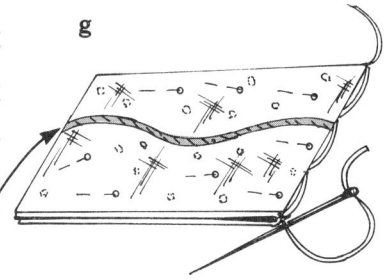

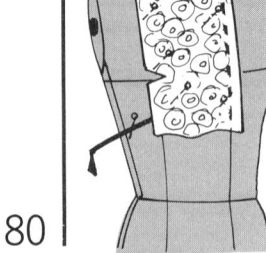

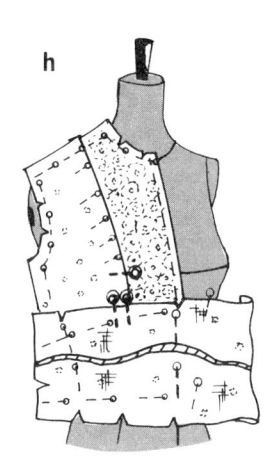

h Smooth and mould right side of midriff to shape of dress form. Leave left side temporarily pinned as shown. Place pins for trace-tacking balance marks to indicate positions of panel seam and small pleats.

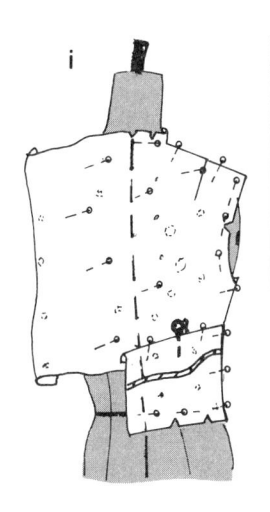

i Proceed for back as shown, having previously sewn a centre back tack mark. The midriff has a short centre back seam opening. In its place a longer opening can be placed in the side seam of the centre back seam.

6

Modelling in the garment fabric

j Remove modelled shape from dress form. Trace-tack garment sections along marked pin lines.

k and **l** Take garment sections apart. Place on to cut out counterpart fabric pieces. Pin on trace-tacked fitting lines through both layers of fabric. Trace-tack pin lines showing on counterpart garment section, taking care to catch one layer of fabric only. Cut out, using modelled garment sections as pattern guide.

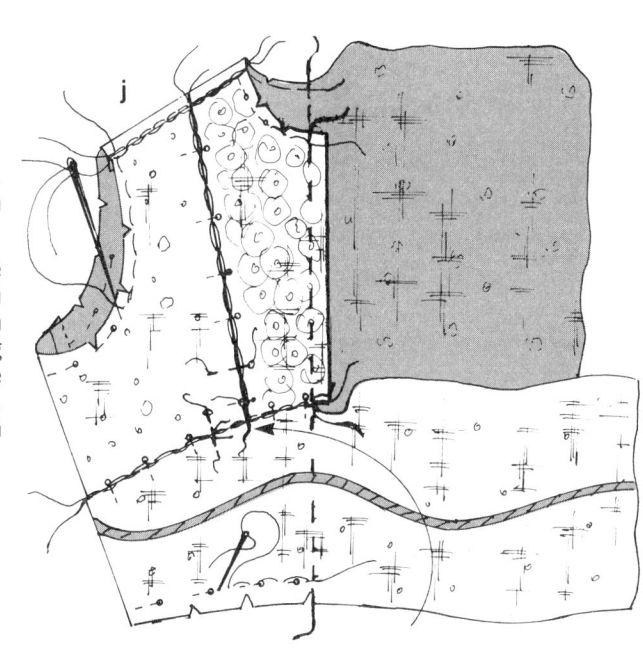

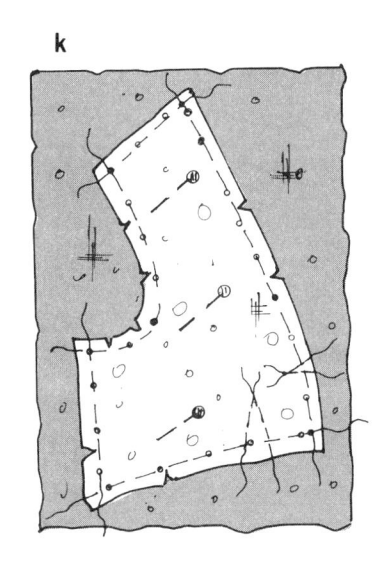

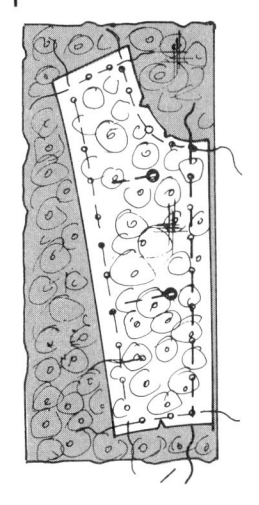

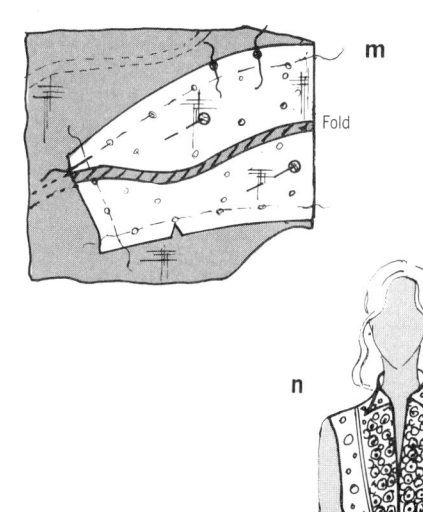

m Fold midriff on tacked centre front line. Pin both layers together. Proceed as for **k** and **l**.

n Tack garment together. Ask model to try it on. Make any necessary alterations. Model collar suitable for style of garment. Model or trace off centre front facing. Before making up the garment, develop a sample pattern with correct seam allowances and cutting directions.

Completed garment

6 Modelling in the garment fabric

Cutting on the bias of the fabric

Figure 6.2

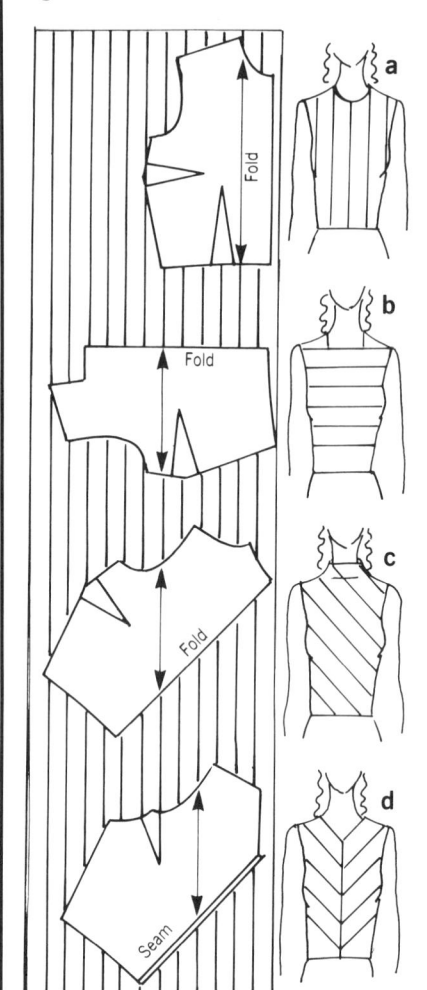

Figure 6.2a Garments can be cut on the lengthwise (warp) grain, the crosswise (weft) grain (**b**), or on the bias of the fabric (**c** and **d**).

The lengthwise grain, parallel to the selvage, has little or no elasticity and is stronger than the crosswise grain which, because of its construction, is more elastic and has a somewhat weaker thread (**e**). The bias of the fabric (**f**), because of its much geater elasticity and flexibility, combines the properties of stretch with those of clinging to the figure and also with good draping qualities.

As a general rule, in order to ensure good fit and hang, as well as long wear, garments are cut with the warp grain running down the centre of the pattern pieces.

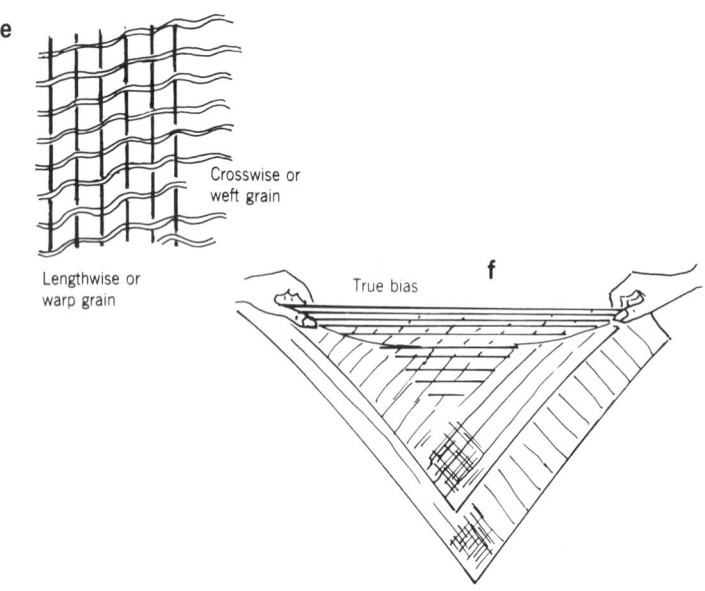

Figure 6.3

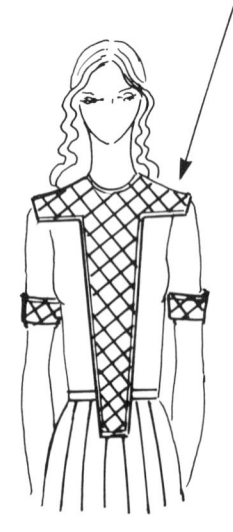

Figure 6.3a There are, however, exceptions to the rule. In the case of striped or checked fabrics, interesting designs can be created by placing pattern pieces on varying grains of the material.

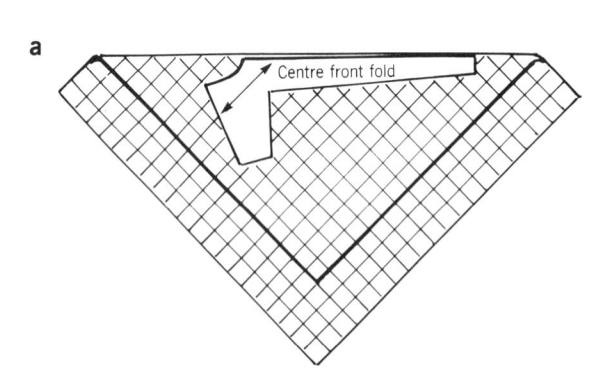

b Sometimes fashion decrees that entire garments be cut on the bias in order to produce the characteristic 'cling' and 'fluted' hem line which the fashion silhouette demands.

Suitability for the figure type in question must also be considered by the designer. Only the slim and perfect figure is flattered by bias-cut garments.

b An evening dress cut on the bias, 1932

82

Figure 6.4

Experimentation with bias fabric

Figure 6.4a and **b** Before cutting a garment on the bias, experiment with the garment fabric or with a trial fabric of similar stretch properties. It has been found that when a piece of bias fabric is stretched in a given area, it will contract immediately above and below that area. Not only will the fabric become narrower, but it will also become shorter. Some knitted fabrics behave in a similar way.

c and **d** Further, it will be noted that often the weft grain stretches and drops more than the warp grain due to the greater elasticity of weft threads. This will cause the garment to swing slightly to one side and can also affect the balance of the hem line.

Allowing the garment to hang for a day or two before levelling the hem helps only temporarily and is impractical for wholesale production.

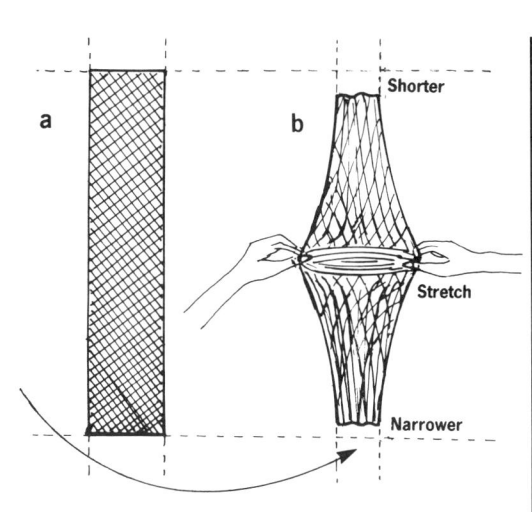

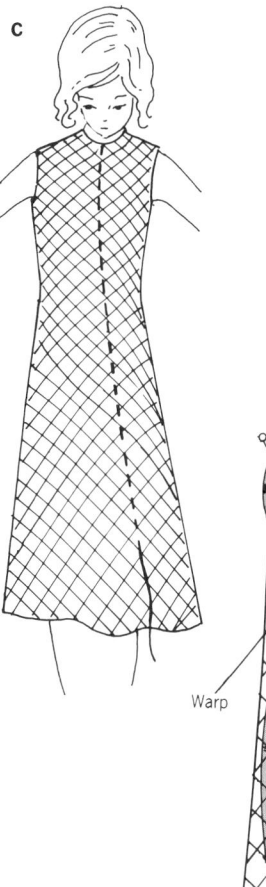

Behaviour of bias fabric seen on the human figure

6

Modelling in the garment fabric

e A centre front and centre back seam should be considered if the weft grain stretches badly. In this way, both left and right sides are cut on the same grain and an even balance is ascertained. **Bias garments should always be cut longer than garments cut on the straight grain** (see **a** and **b**).

Normal ease allowances are usually reduced but are sometimes actually increased depending on the type of fabric and style of the garment. The dress would have had extra width allowed throughout, particularly if the fabric were a heavy slippery satin, to cause the fabric to drop, touching the hips, skimming the waist and causing the characteristic ripple at the hem. Width can be reduced at the fitting stage if needed.

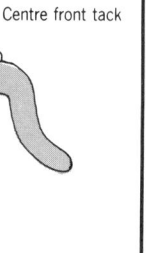

7 | Sleeves

Sleeves fall into two main categories; **a** the set-in sleeve and **b** the sleeve cut in one with the bodice (Figure 7.1).

Each category has a variety of styles, but it is sometimes possible to use the same style in both categories as in **a** and **b**. While category **a** embraces variations of raglan styles and drop shoulder styles, variations of style in category **b** are limited to the kimono (or magyar) and to styles with gussets. Dolman sleeves belong to this category and often have the characteristic simulated armhole seam introduced to create interest (**e**).

The methods used to develop basic sleeves by modelling and flat pattern cutting will enable the reader to evolve more intricate sleeve patterns.

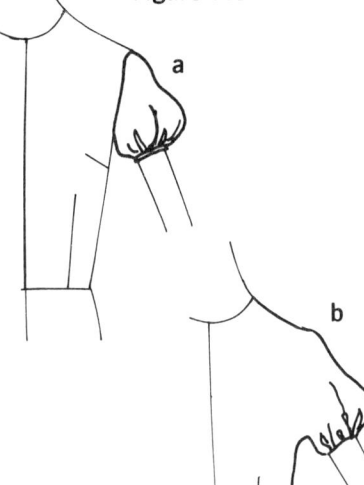

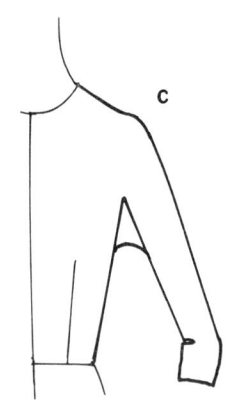

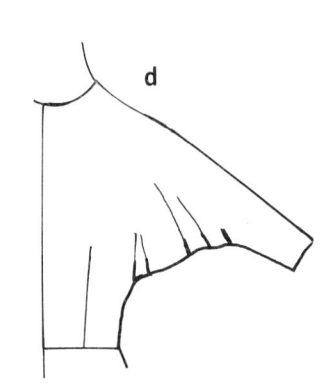

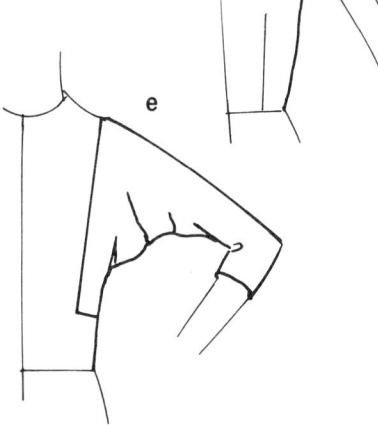

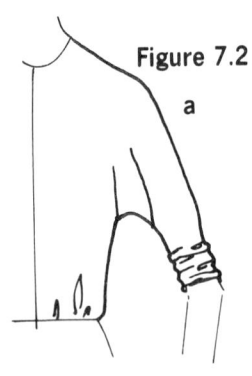

Figure 7.1

Figure 7.2

Figure 7.2a The selection of sleeve styles is governed by the prevailing fashion silhouette and the function the garment is expected to fulfil. For example, the kimono sleeve will be a good choice at a time when a sloping, shoulder-hugging silhouette, with a soft undefined underarm line is in fashion. Because of this quality it will also lend itself well for over-garments and wraps.

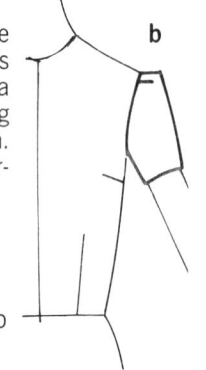

b The set-in sleeve with darted sleeve crown will give a crisp and square silhouette.

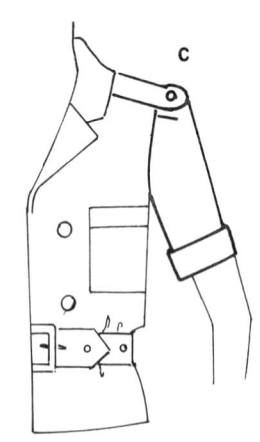

c A more severe variation of this sihouette is the 'military' look, often with padded shoulders.

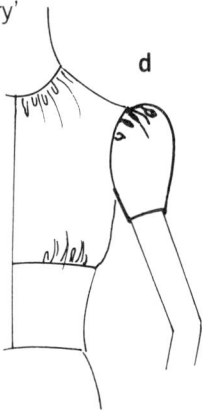

d A softer interpretation is this puffed sleeve.

Set-in sleeves cut flat

Semi-fitted sleeve with elbow dart

Figure 7.3

Figure 7.3a Reduce Figure 1.12 sleeve block measurements to:

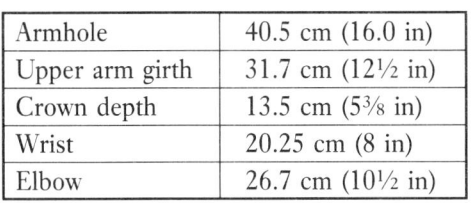

Armhole	40.5 cm (16.0 in)
Upper arm girth	31.7 cm (12½ in)
Crown depth	13.5 cm (5⅜ in)
Wrist	20.25 cm (8 in)
Elbow	26.7 cm (10½ in)

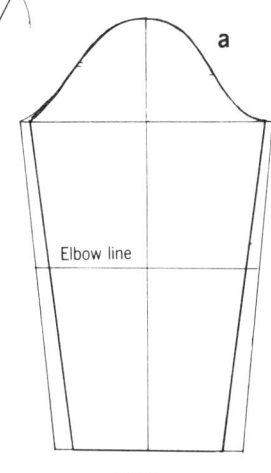

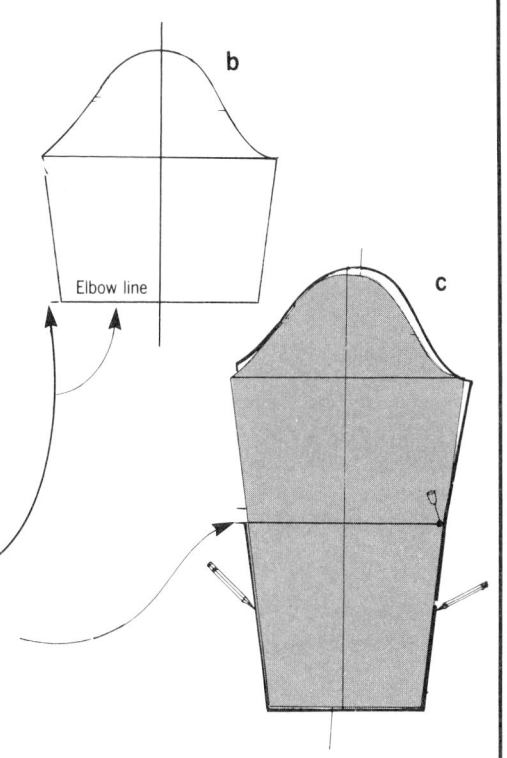

b Place new, reduced sleeve block on to drawn vertical line, aligning with centre sleeve grain line. Outline upper section to elbow line; crossmark.

Place a crossmark 2 cm (¾ in) below back elbow level mark.

c Pivot back elbow line point down to 2 cm (¾ in) mark. Outline.

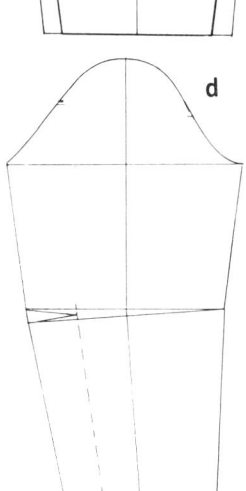

d Remove sleeve block. Divide back sections of wrist and elbow lines in half. Draw elbow dart to this point.

e Fold sleeve block edges (particularly from wrist to elbow level) to meet centre sleeve line. Straighten wrist line, draw new line and cut through folded wristline.

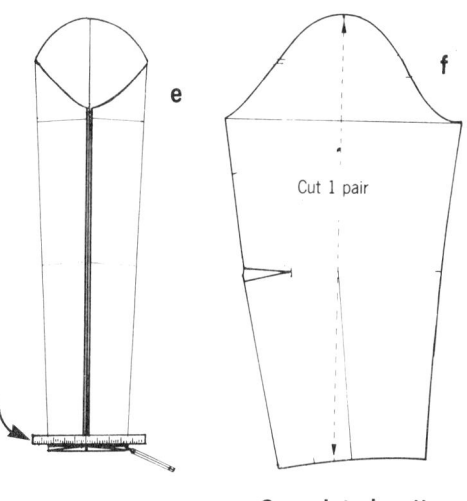

Completed pattern

Figure 7.4

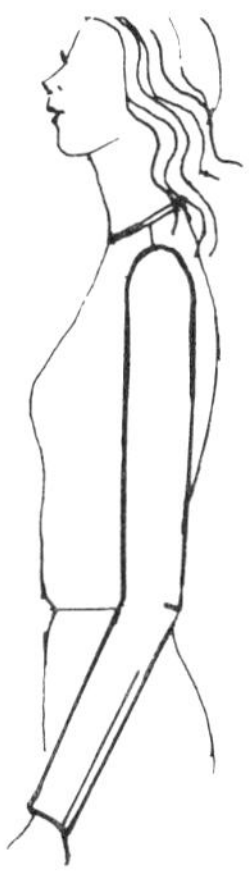

Semi-fitted sleeve with wrist dart or wrist opening

Figure 7.4a Outline sleeve block with elbow dart Figure 7.3d. Close elbow dart. Cut from wrist to elbow dart point; open up.

b Outline. Place balance marks, grain line, cutting instructions and seam allowances.

See also Figure 10.22, page 147 for bias-cut fitted sleeve.

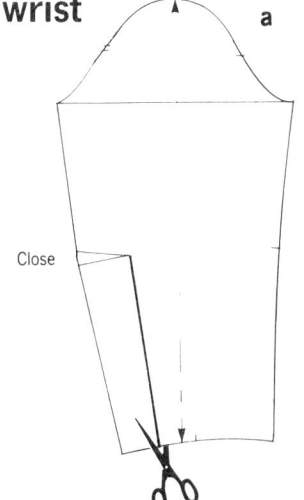

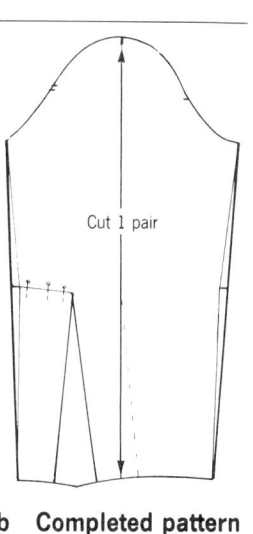

b Completed pattern

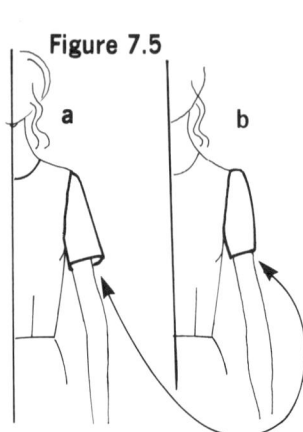

Fitted short sleeve

Figure 7.5a and **b** If a more fitted short sleeve is required adjustments have to be made.

c Outline semi-fitted block. Mark desired length. Cut out. Fold dart at hem.

d Snip centre line at crown. Continue as shown.

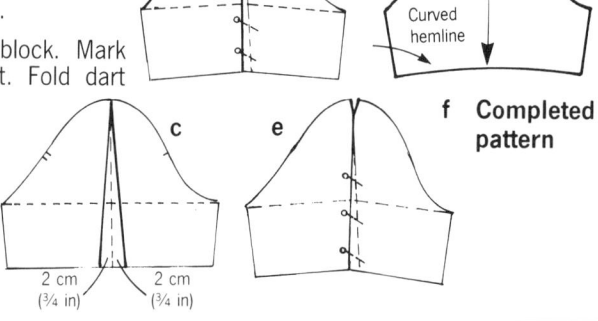

f Completed pattern

2 cm (¾ in)   2 cm (¾ in)

Curved hemline

Wrist flounce

Figure 7.6

Figure 7.6a Outline area of flounce on semi-fitted block. Trace.

Divide as shown. Slash and open

c Completed pattern

Flared cuff

Figure 7.7

Figure 7.7a and **b** Proceed as for Figure 7.6. Balance marks and slashing are different.

c Completed pattern

Simulated cuffs

Use block **Figure 7.3a** above.

Figure 7.8a and **b** Shaped facings turned to right side of garment and top stitched.

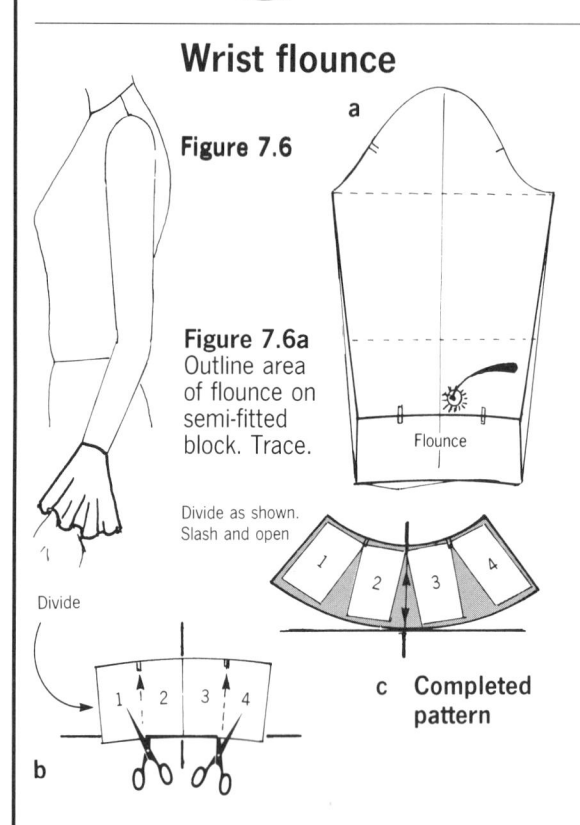

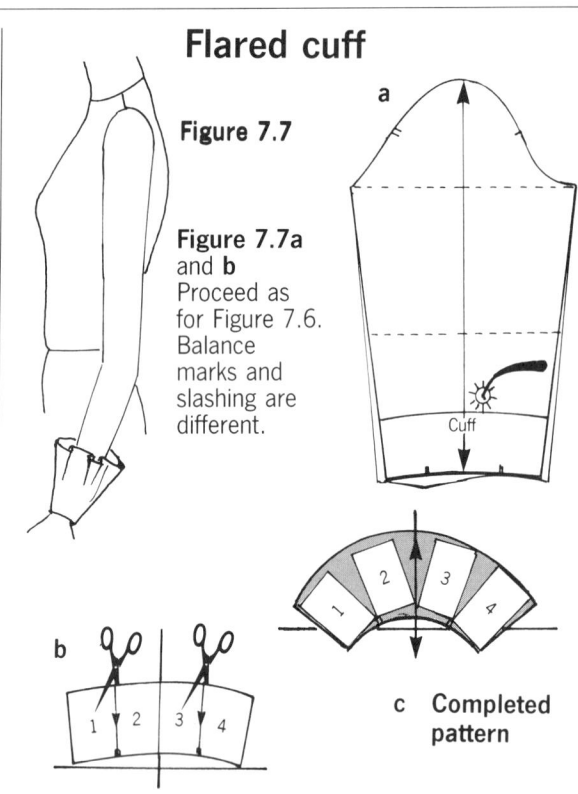

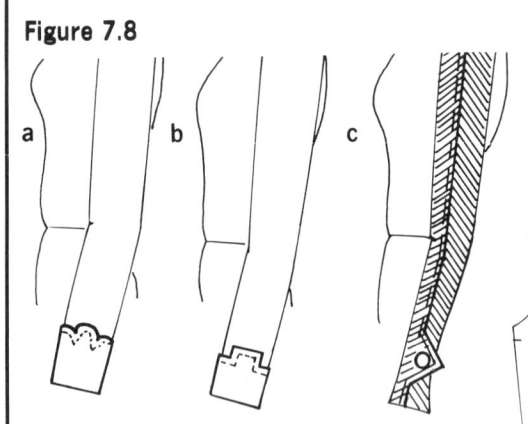

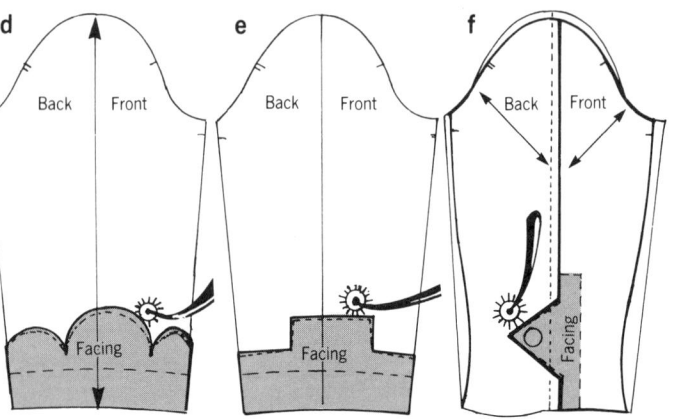

Figure 7.8

c Bias cut sleeve. Note the slimmer fit, also in the pattern (**f**). Design interests, and centre seam, are moved forward 1.3 cm (½ in) towards front of sleeves.

The shirt sleeve

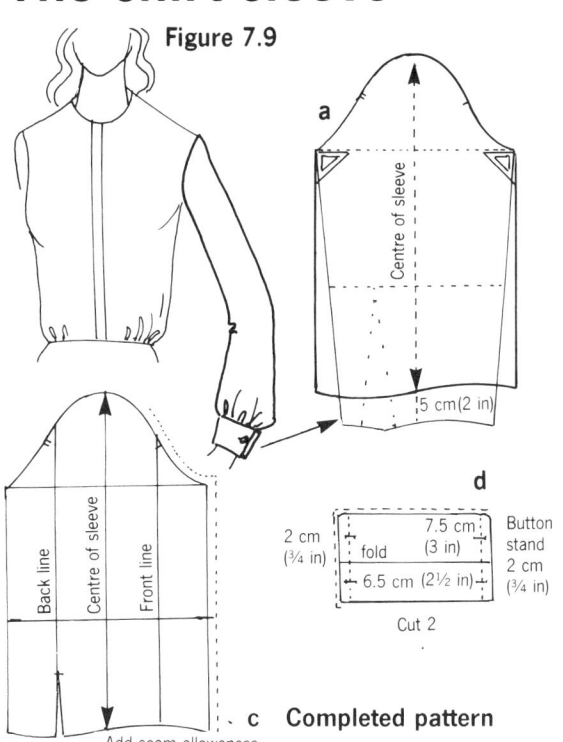

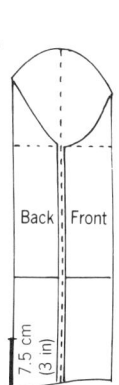

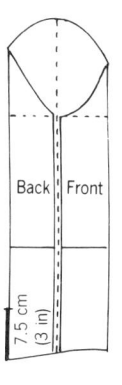

Figure 7.9

Figure 7.9a Outline semi-fitted sleeve Figure 7.4b. Square down from crown level line for new side seams. Shorten sleeve by 5 cm (2 in) for cuff 7.5 cm (3 in) wide. 2.5 cm (1 in) is allowed for 'pouching'. Cut out.

b and **c** Fold side seams to centre line. Crease back and front lines. On creased back line measure 6.5–7.5 cm (2½–3 in) up for sleeve opening.

d For double cuff draw rectangle 19 cm (7½ in) multiplied by twice desired width of cuff, 14 cm (5½ in) in this instance. Add 2 cm (¾ in) button stand each end. Add seam allowances.

See also sleeve, page 47.

The bishop sleeve

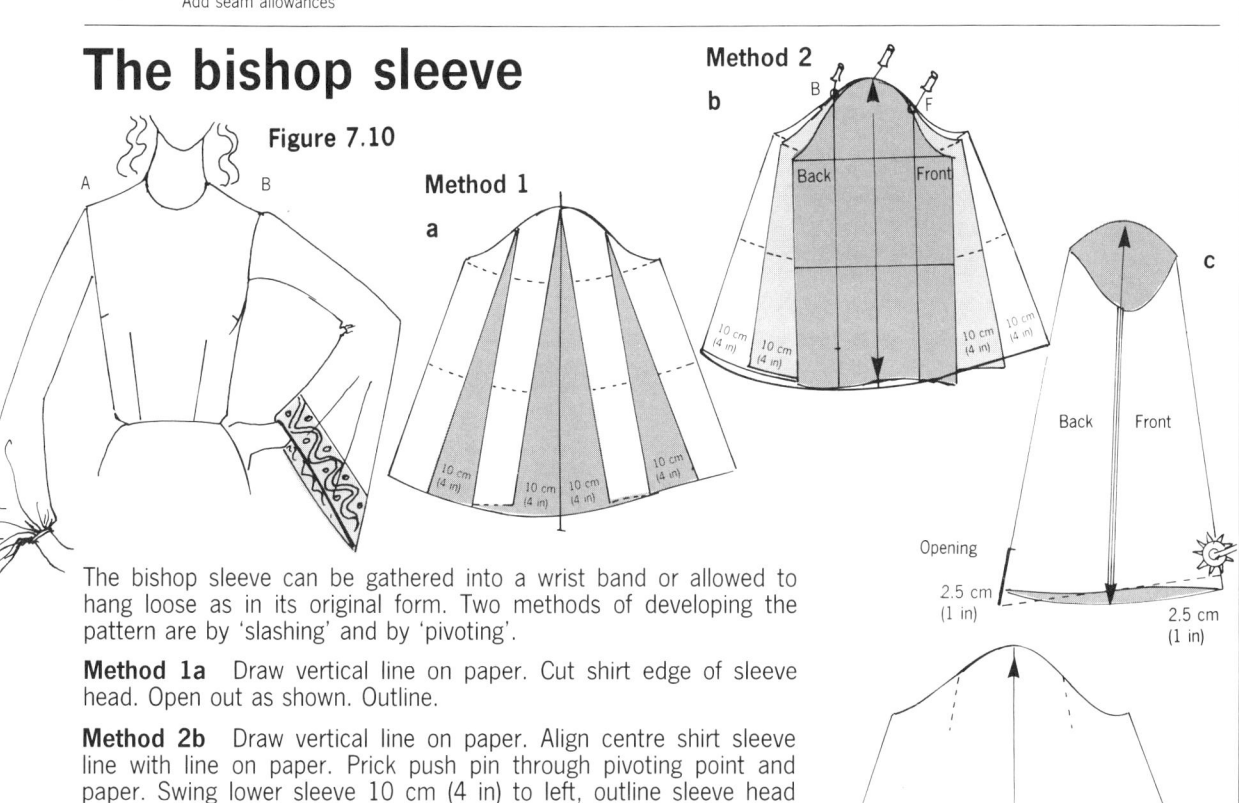

Figure 7.10

The bishop sleeve can be gathered into a wrist band or allowed to hang loose as in its original form. Two methods of developing the pattern are by 'slashing' and by 'pivoting'.

Method 1a Draw vertical line on paper. Cut shirt edge of sleeve head. Open out as shown. Outline.

Method 2b Draw vertical line on paper. Align centre shirt sleeve line with line on paper. Prick push pin through pivoting point and paper. Swing lower sleeve 10 cm (4 in) to left, outline sleeve head and lower sleeve to this new point. Swing lower sleeve to the right and repeat in same way. Now prick push pin through **B** (back line) pivoting point. Swing lower sleeve 10 cm (4 in) to left. Outline. Repeat to right from **F** (front line) and outline.

c Both methods. Fold sleeve seams to meet centre line. Crease back and front lines. Shorten front line and lengthen back line 2.5 cm (1 in). Draw line. Trace through with tracing wheel.

Sleeve opening is as in Figure 7.9b above. If sleeve has no wrist band, as in Figure 7.10b, a facing must be made following the sleeve shape.

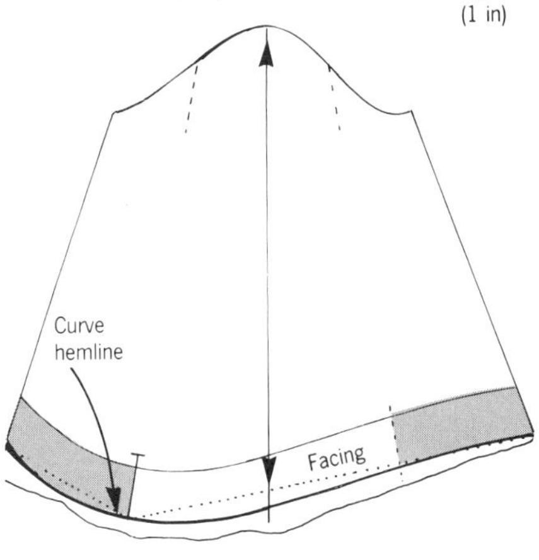

7 Sleeves

87

Sleeves gathered at crown

Figure 7.11

Figure 7.11a This sleeve pattern can be developed by two methods, by 'slashing' or by 'pivoting'. Use the fitted short sleeve, Figure 7.5f for both methods.

Slashing

b Slash centre, front and back line to within hem line. Open out as shown. Outline new crown line (sleeve head). Curve hem line.

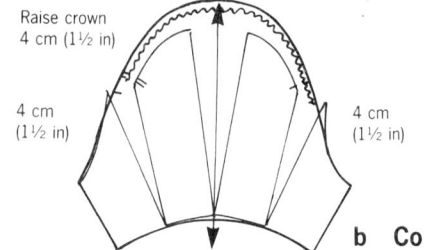

b Completed pattern

Figure 7.12

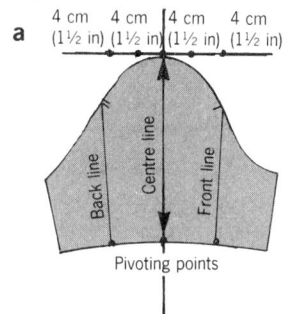

Pivoting

Figure 7.12a Draw vertical line. Cross at right angle by horizontal line. Place sleeve onto it with centre sleeve line covering vertical line. Mark three pivoting points as shown. Mark distances on horizontal line.

b Place scriber or pencil point on centre pivoting point. Pivot sleeve 4 cm (1½ in) to left. Outline hemline from centre line to back line.

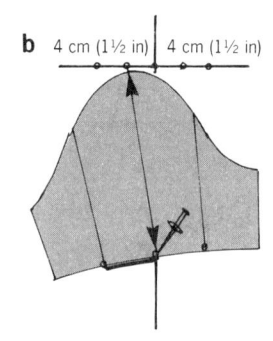

c From back pivoting point, pivot sleeve a further 4 cm (1½ in) to left. Outline back sleeve head and remaining hemline and underarm seam line.

d Return sleeve to centre position. From centre pivoting point, pivot sleeve 4 cm (1½ in) to right. Outline hemline from centre line to front line.

e From front pivoting point, pivot sleeve a further 4 cm (1½ in) to right. Outline front sleeve head, underarm seam line and hemline.

f Remove sleeve from paper. Raise sleeve crown by 4 cm (1½ in) above centre sleeve line. Connect to previously outlined back and front crown line.

g Place balance marks to define area that is to be gathered.

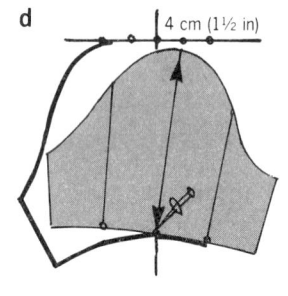

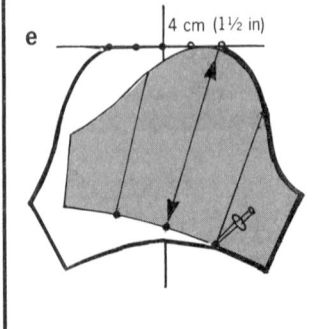

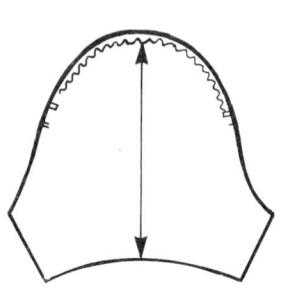

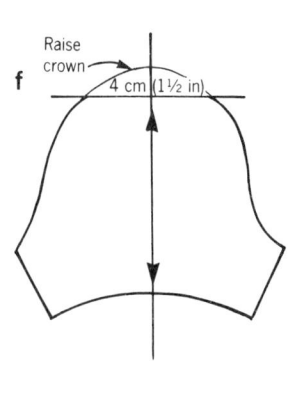

g Completed pattern

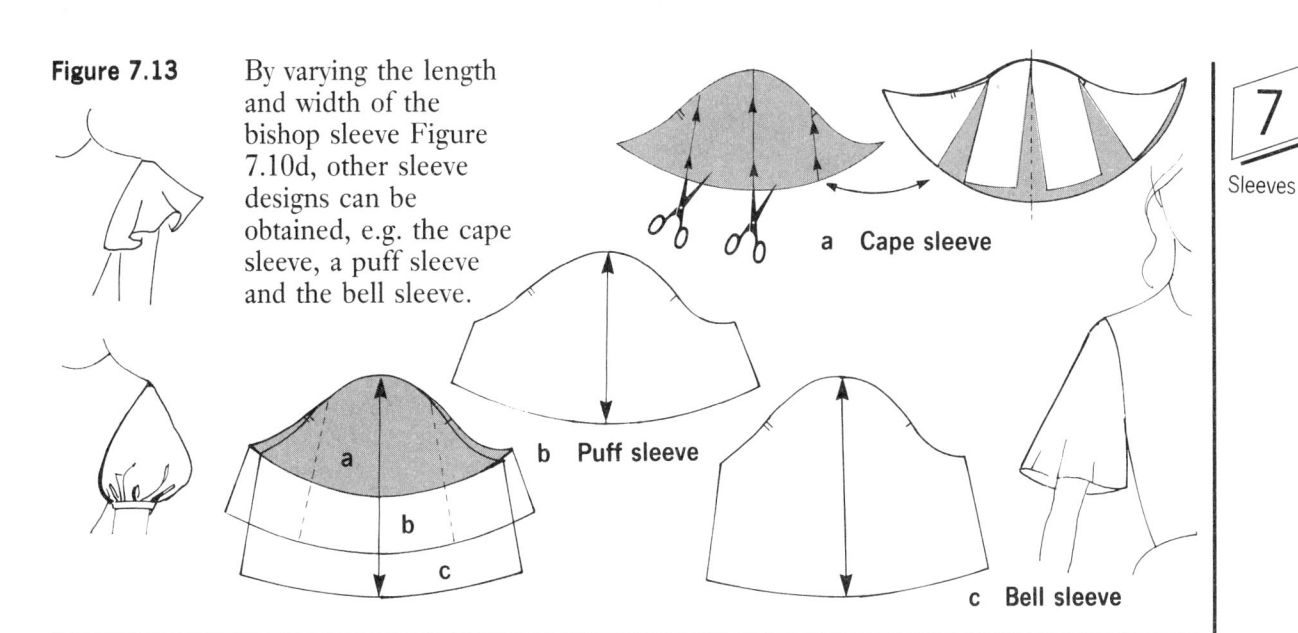

Figure 7.13 By varying the length and width of the bishop sleeve Figure 7.10d, other sleeve designs can be obtained, e.g. the cape sleeve, a puff sleeve and the bell sleeve.

a Cape sleeve

b Puff sleeve

c Bell sleeve

Full puff sleeve

Figure 7.14

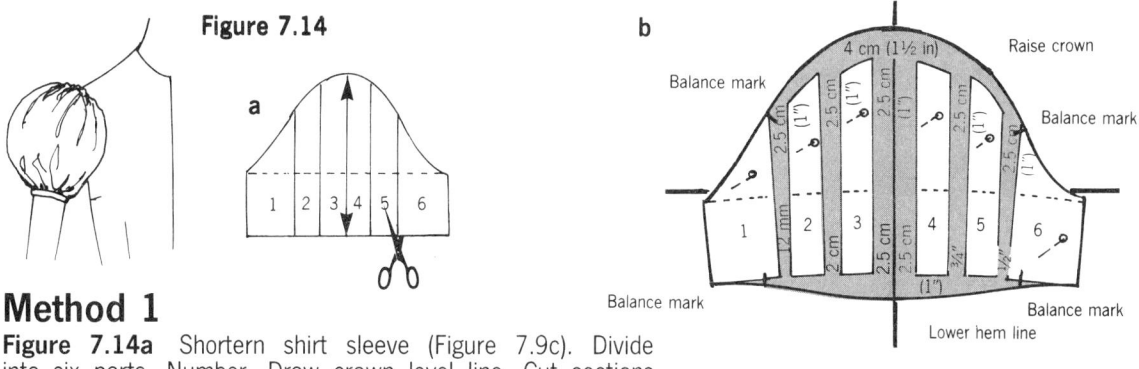

Method 1

Figure 7.14a Shortern shirt sleeve (Figure 7.9c). Divide into six parts. Number. Draw crown level line. Cut sections apart.

b Assemble on crossed lines.

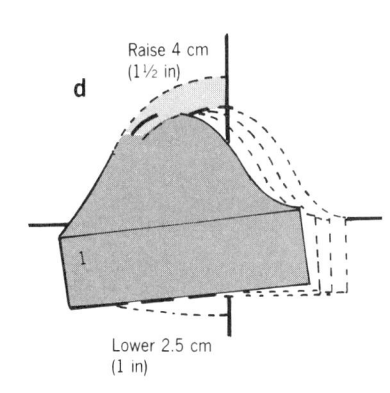

Method 2

Divide sleeve block into six parts, draw crown level line as above but do not cut sections.

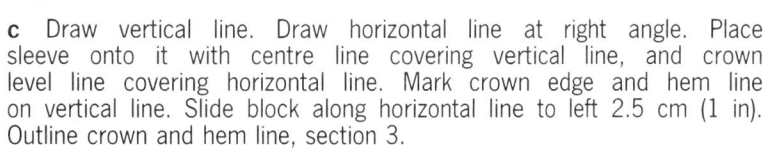

c Draw vertical line. Draw horizontal line at right angle. Place sleeve onto it with centre line covering vertical line, and crown level line covering horizontal line. Mark crown edge and hem line on vertical line. Slide block along horizontal line to left 2.5 cm (1 in). Outline crown and hem line, section 3.

d Slide block further along horizontal line, 2.5 cm (1 in) at crown edge, but 2 cm (¾ in) at hem. Outline crown and hemline of section 2.

Slide block further to left, tilting it somewhat. Gap at crown is now 2.5 cm (1 in); at hem it is 1.3 cm (½ in). This causes crown level line to curve slightly at underarm point below horizontal line. Outline crown edge and hemline of section 1.

e Repeat process to right of centre line or fold paper on centre line. Trace completed back through to front. Curve front underarm section. Raise sleeve crown 4 cm (1½ in) above centre line. Connect to sections 1 and 6. Lower hem line 2.5 cm (1 in) below centre line. Connect as shown.

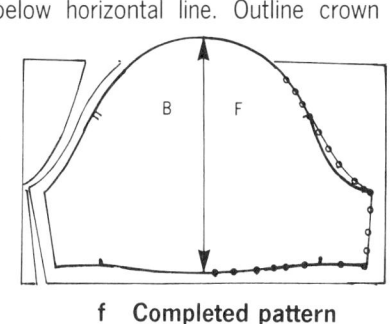

f Completed pattern

Sleeve with two parallel darts or pleats

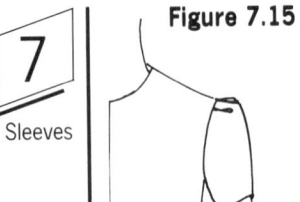

Figure 7.15 Outline short fitted sleeve (Figure 7.5f). Draw two parallel lines to crown level line, each 3 cm (¼ in) away from centre line.

b Cut on arrowed lines to within 3 mm (⅛ in) of underarm points.

c Raise back and front sections by 2.5 cm (1 in) or more, depending on the desired depth of darts or pleats.

d Pin sleeve to new sheet of paper. Raise centre sleeve section by 5 cm (2 in), draw darts and outline sleeve. Cut out except for crown section.

e Fold darts and redraw crown line. Cut out.

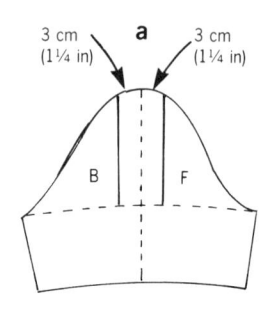

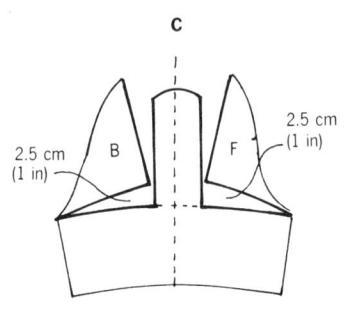

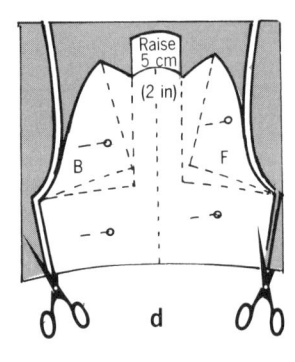

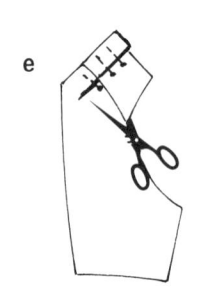

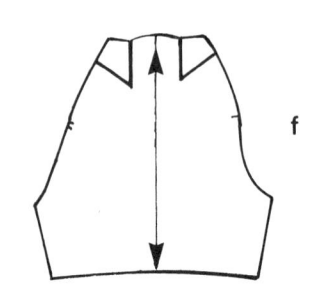

f Completed pattern

Epaulet sleeve

Figure 7.16a Draw vertical line on sheet of paper. Place back and front shoulder seams to it. Ignore back shoulder dart.

Place centre line of two-darted sleeve, Figure 7.15 onto vertical line with back dart slightly overlapping back armhole.

b Trace epaulet, darts and sleeve with balance marks.

Add seam allowances to complete pattern.

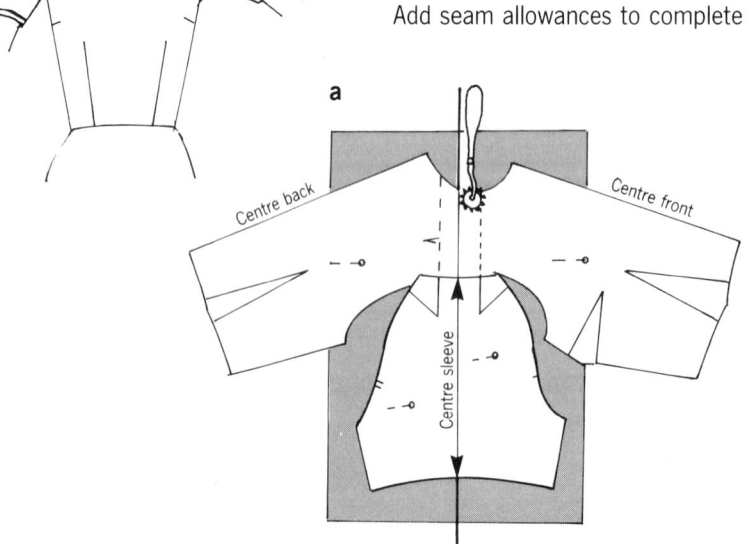

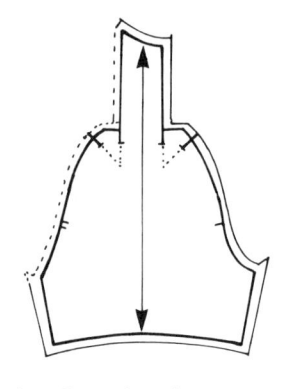

b Completed pattern

Raglan sleeves

Figure 7.17

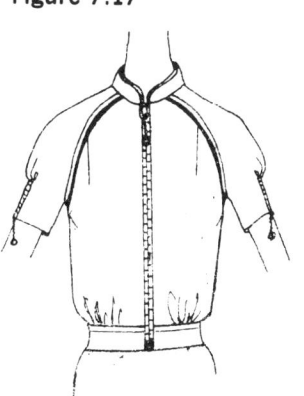

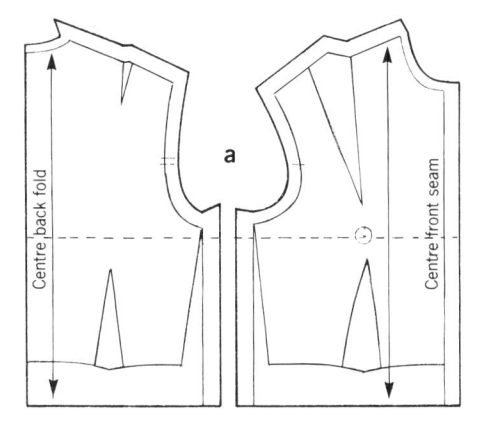

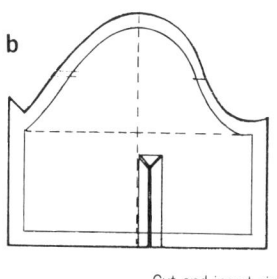

Figure 7.17a Outline back and front waist blocks on calico. Mark waist darts, straighten side seams and lengthen 4 cm (1½ in) for pouched effect. Allow larger seam turnings all around. Cut out, pin darts and seams. Pin to dress form.

b Cut and insert zip.

c Pin already constructed calico sleeve to armhole or stick with masking tape. Outline desired raglan line with tape.

d Arrange gathers mainly in areas where darts were. Define waist line with tape and pin waist band over this. Mark all new seam lines, dart and balance marks. Remove from dress form. Cut on raglan lines.

e Open shoulder seam. Snip 2.5 cm (1 in) into crown of sleeve.

f This causes the sleeve to lie flat when unpinned and removed from the lower part of the armhole. It may be necessary to snip the sleeve edges at shown points.

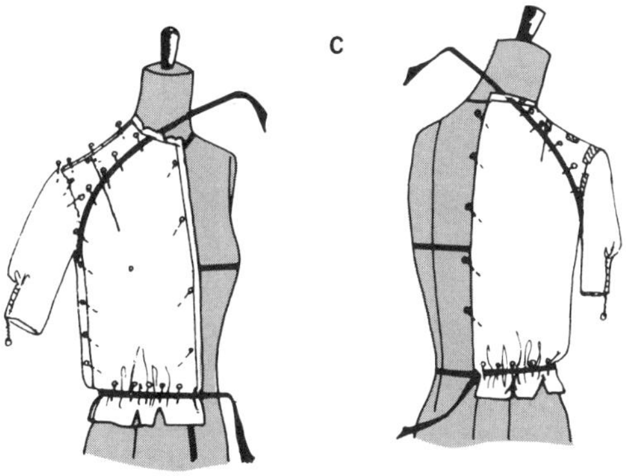

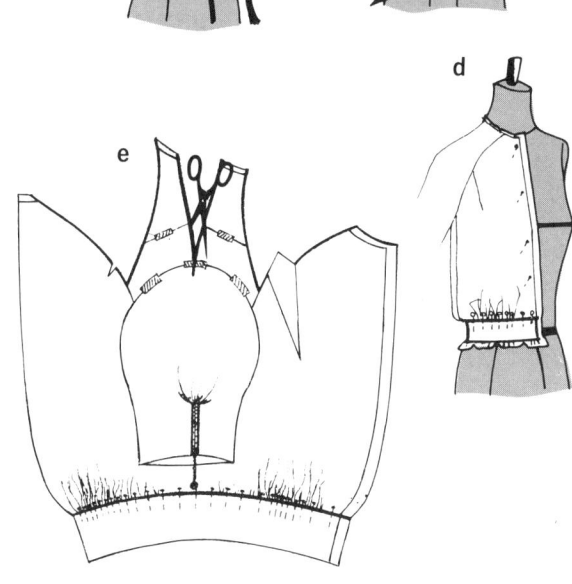

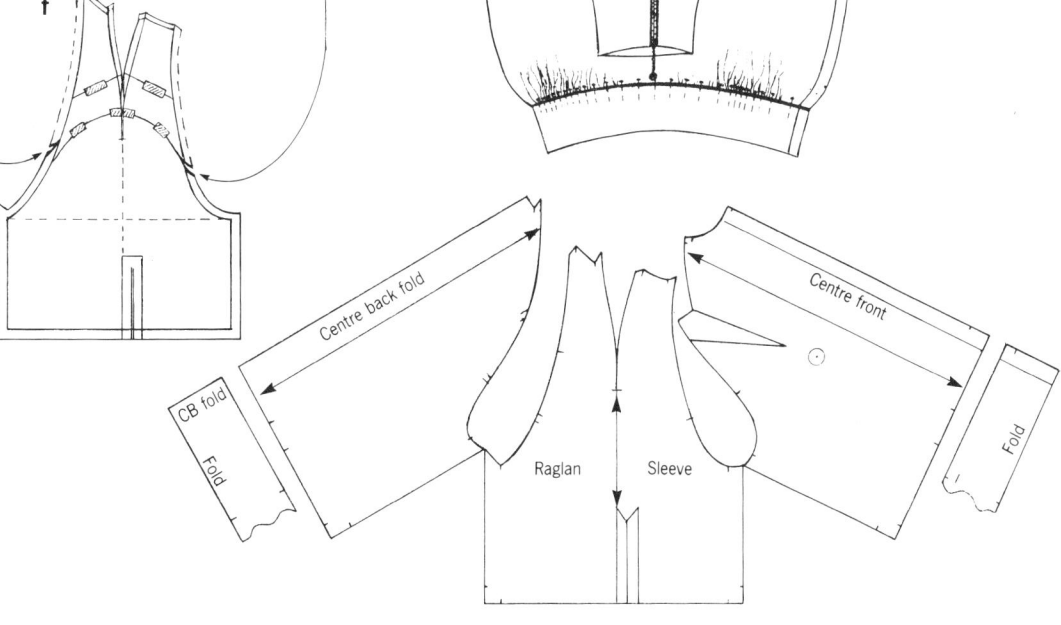

g Completed pattern

Raglan-type sleeve

Figure 7.18a Develop two French darts on hip block according to Figure 2.36, page 31.

Pin back and front shoulder and side seams together. Pin to dress form.

Attach sleeve to armhole with masking tape. Outline new sleeve lines with tape. Mark, including balance marks.

b Cut on new sleeve line, unpin and snip edge of crown, so that sleeve lies flat. When sewn, this sleeve seam will be 'eased' into the corresponding 'armhole'. Place shoulder balance mark on sleeve.

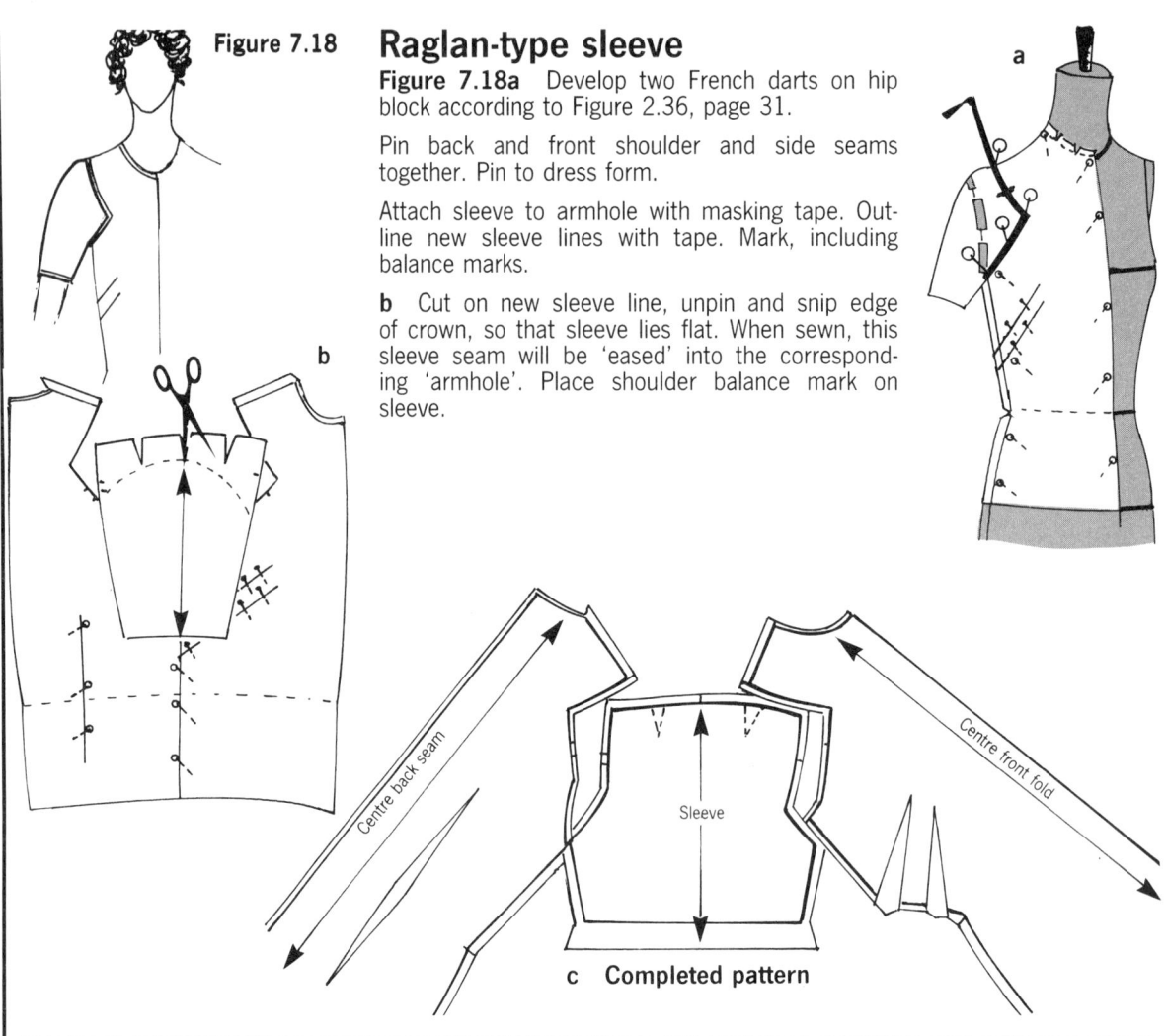

c Completed pattern

Drop shoulder sleeve

Figure 7.19a Cut in modelling fabric: back and front bodice with dart at side seam, short straight sleeve and allow seam turnings all around. Pin bodice seams together. Pin to dress form. Pin sleeve, with seams closed, to armhole and stick down upper section.

Outline dropped shoulder line with tape. Lengthen and tape shoulder seam to this point. Mark all new lines, also sleeve length.

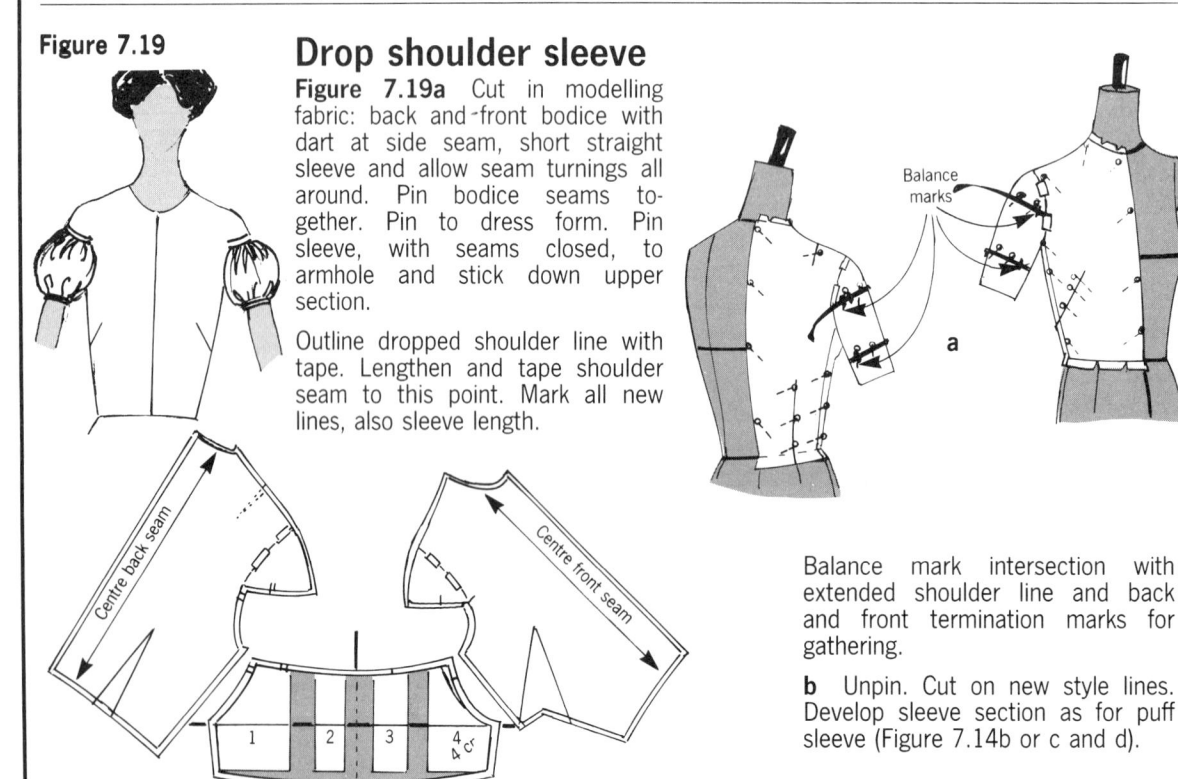

Balance mark intersection with extended shoulder line and back and front termination marks for gathering.

b Unpin. Cut on new style lines. Develop sleeve section as for puff sleeve (Figure 7.14b or c and d).

b Completed pattern

Position of the shoulder seam

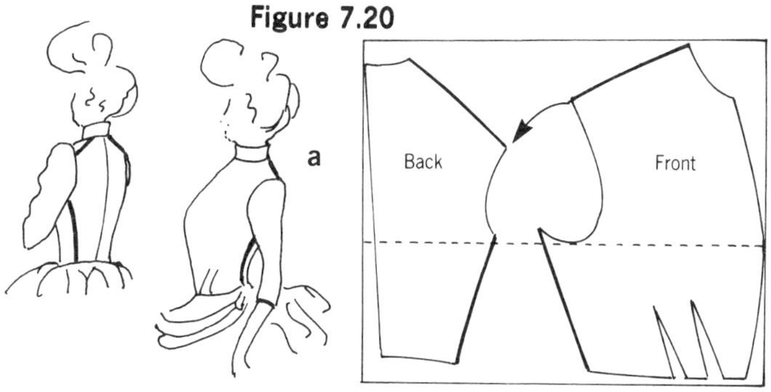

Current fashion has always influenced the position of the shoulder seam. A study of twentieth-century historic costume reveals that the shoulder seam was often set so far back to the back of the bodice that to the modern eye it resembled a yoke line. This was in harmony with the then fashionable sihouette, which aimed at creating an illusion of straightness combined with the characteristic narrow back and well developed front (Figure 7.20).

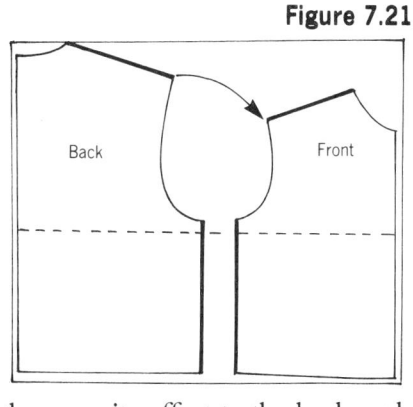

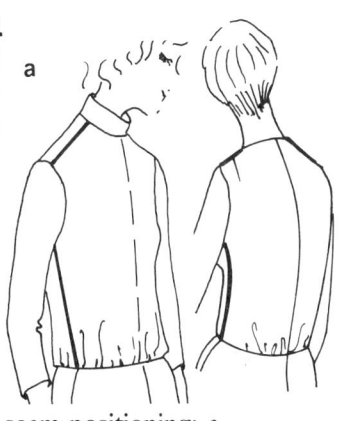

Gradually, over the years, the shoulder seam moved forward to a more central position and in more recent years designers, encouraged by the prevailing fashion silhouette, sometimes placed shoulder and side seams towards the front of the bodice. This positioning aimed at creating the opposite effect to the backward seam positioning: a shallow front and a more rounded back (Figure 7.21).

Skilfully used, a slightly forward-placed shoulder seam can ensure that a design feature is not lost but can be seen when viewed from the front (Figure 7.22a–e except d).

Indeed, this is the main reason why, in the development of raglan and kimono styles, it is customary to move the shoulder seam forward. Another important factor contributes to the practice of 'centralising' shoulder and side seams. It was found that, if the shoulder seam was placed exactly in the centre of the shoulder (and it must be remembered that back and front shoulder lines of most currently-used block patterns are still constructed so as to produce shoulder seams that run slightly towards the back of the bodice) and carried on through the centre of the sleeve, this seam, when worn, would be seen to run off centre towards the back (Figure 7.22d). To avoid this happening, it is essential that both the shoulder seam and the sleeve centre seam be moved forward slightly. Correspondingly, the side seam of the bodice should also be moved towards the front of the bodice.

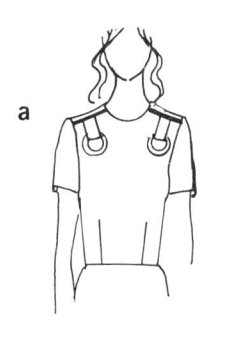

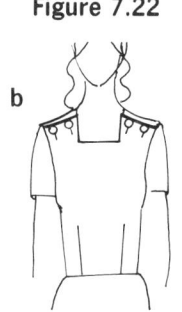

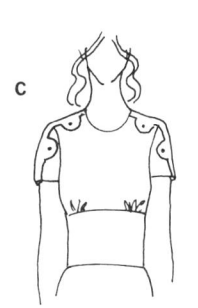

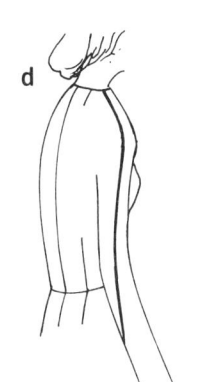

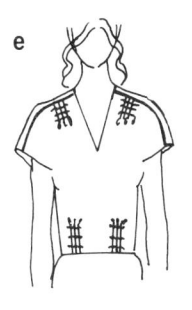

Centralising the bodice blocks in preparation for the kimono block

Figure 7.23

Centralising side seams

Figure 7.23a Place back and front side seams together. Measure across. Half-way is position of new side seam. Cut out for further development.

b Pivot (or use slashing method) back shoulder dart into waist dart. Cut out.

c Shows first development.

d Cut on determined armhole slash line to bust point and close shoulder/neck dart.

e Outline new front block with now larger armhole on new sheet of paper. Place back waist block face down onto outlined front block and outline, using back armhole curve as template for outlining front armhole. Front and back armholes and side seams should now be alike.

Centralising shoulder seam

Redraw front shoulder angle to conform to that of back block.

f But for the necklines, front and back blocks should now be exactly alike.

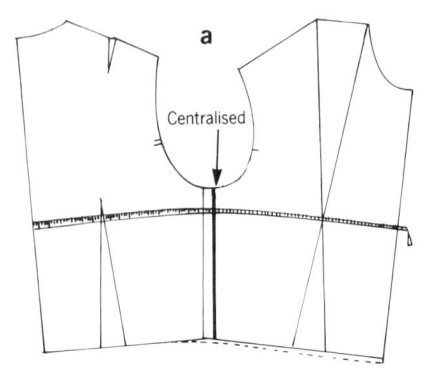

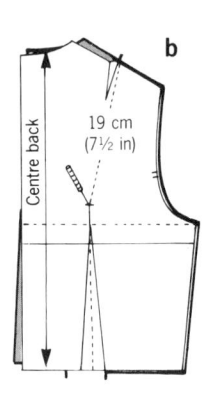

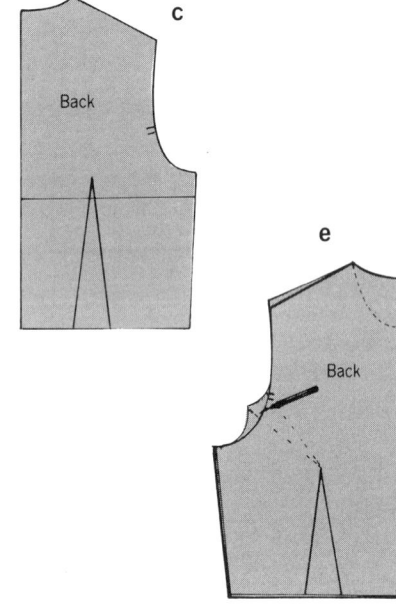

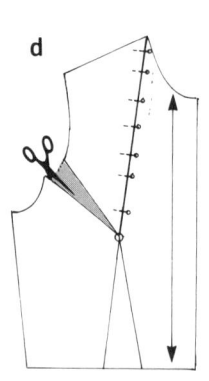

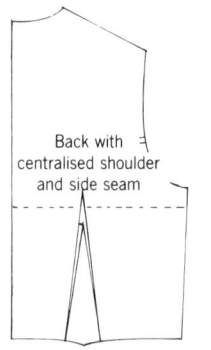

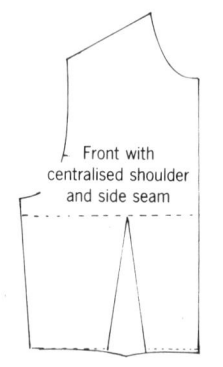

Figure 7.24

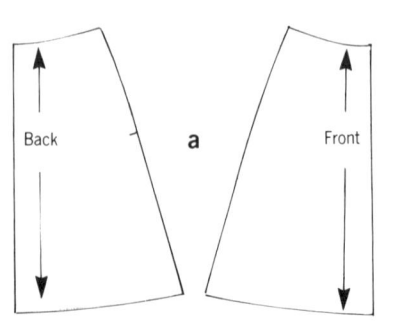

Centralising skirt blocks

Figure 7.24 Place together back and front side seams. Measure across pattern. Half way is position of new seam.

a shows completed back and front flared skirt with centralised side seams.

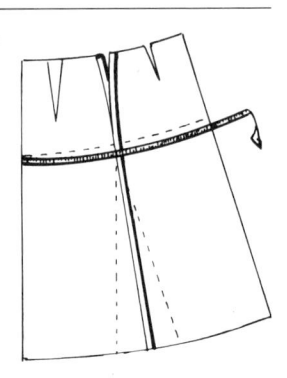

Kimono block development

Figure 7.25

Style 1

Two variations are shown here: Figure 7.25 has more room for movement at underarm while Figure 7.26 is more restricting in arm movement.

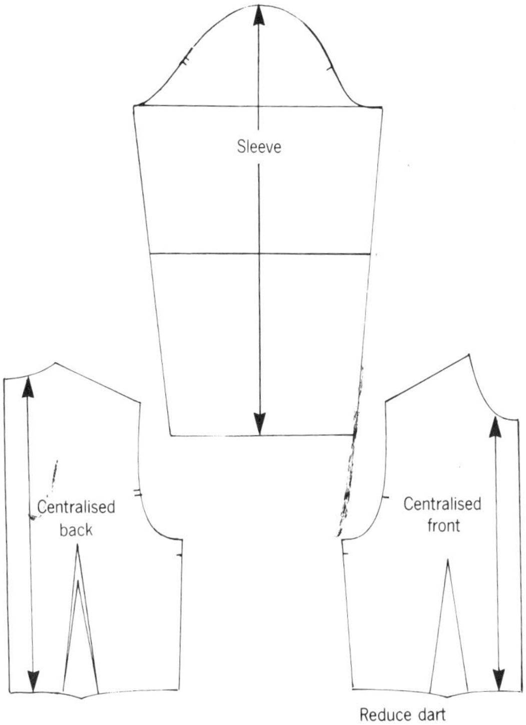

b Completed draft

Figure 7.25a Check back, front and sleeve blocks. Draw horizontal and vertical lines at right angles to each other (note measurements).

b Place pattern pieces to these lines. Complete draft using a template to draw identical underarm lines. (See **b**).

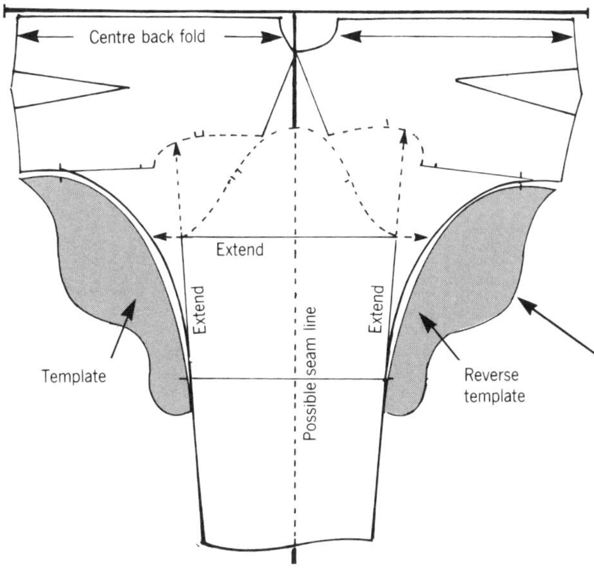

Figure 7.26

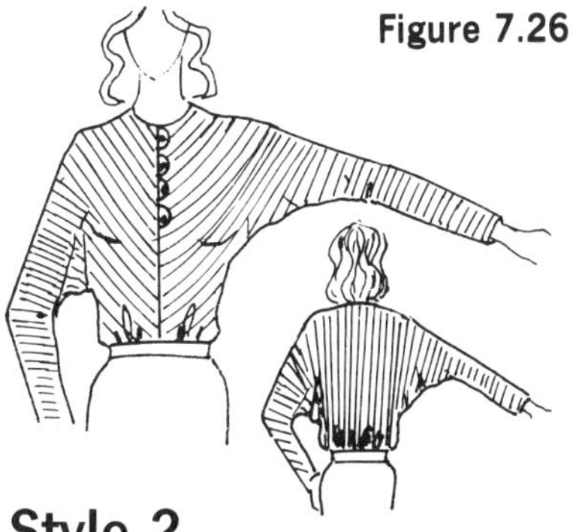

Style 2

Figure 7.26 Proceed as for Figure 7.25, but move back and front shoulder points nearer together (approx. 2 cm (¾ in) each side of centre line). This reduces underarm fullness and achieves a closer fit to the body.

Two possible underarm seam curves are shown which should be drawn with the aid of a template to obtain identical back and front curves.

Interesting effects with striped and checked fabrics can be obtained by placing the pattern on different grain lines, or cutting it in two pieces with a shoulder-top sleeve seam as indicated in Figure 7.25**b** and Figure 7.26**a**.

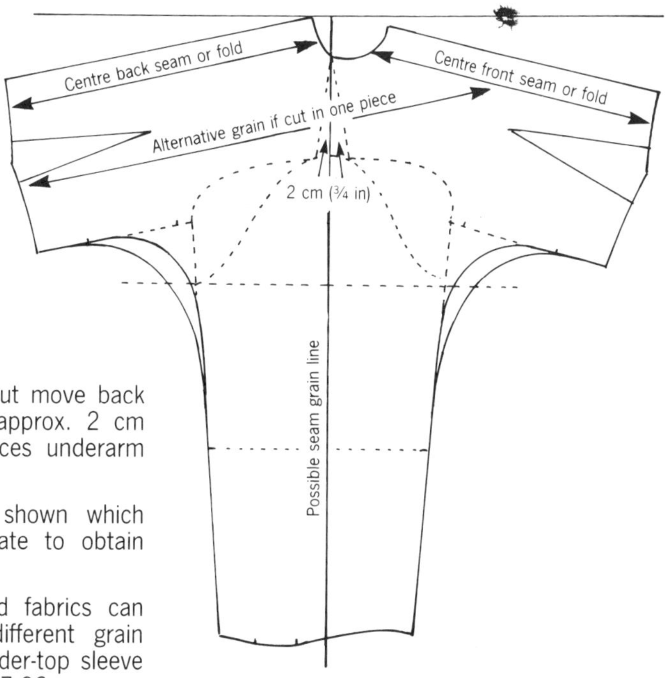

a Completed draft

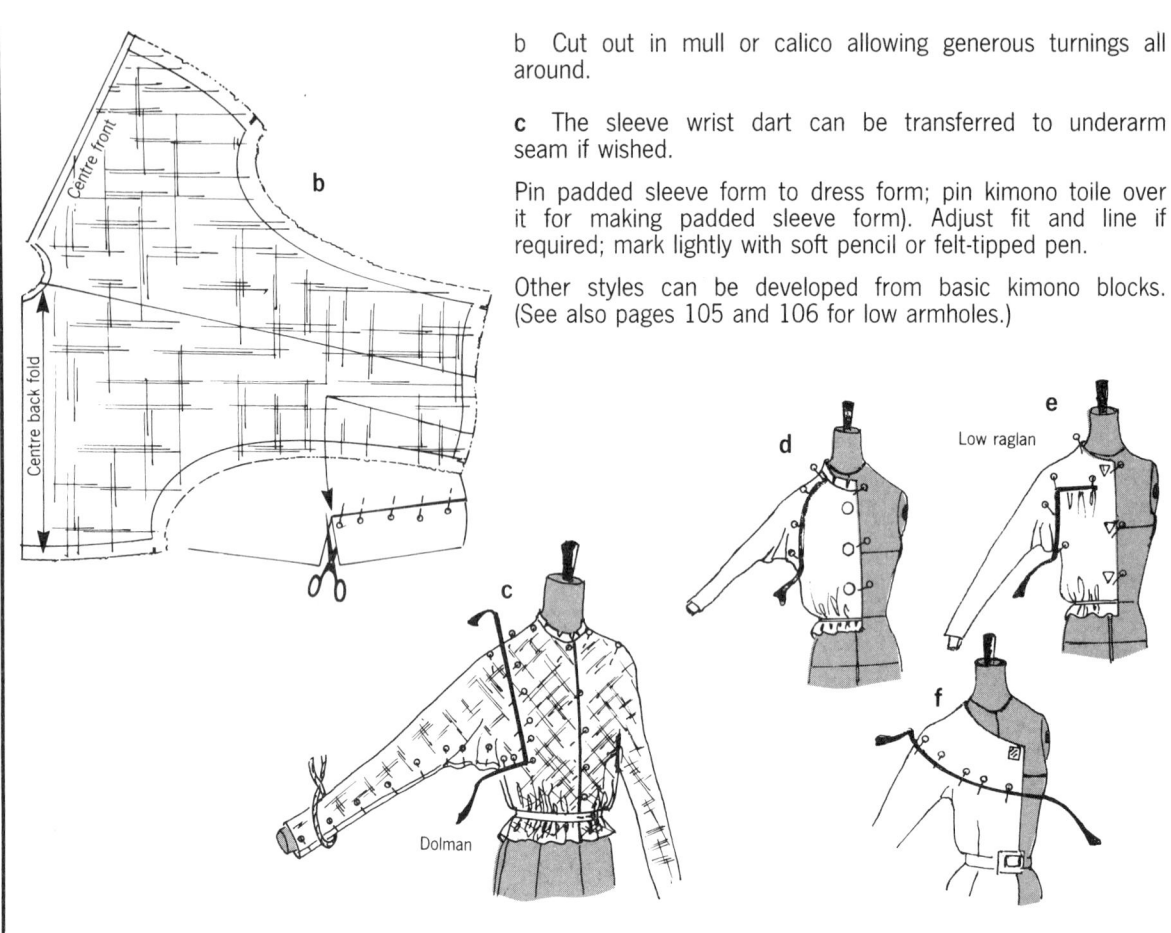

b Cut out in mull or calico allowing generous turnings all around.

c The sleeve wrist dart can be transferred to underarm seam if wished.

Pin padded sleeve form to dress form; pin kimono toile over it for making padded sleeve form). Adjust fit and line if required; mark lightly with soft pencil or felt-tipped pen.

Other styles can be developed from basic kimono blocks. (See also pages 105 and 106 for low armholes.)

Style 3 Fitted kimono block

Figure 7.27

Figure 7.27 Proceed as for Styles 1 and 2 but place shoulder-neck points touching horizontal line 2.5 cm (1 in) away from vertical shoulder line.

This further reduces the underarm fulness and provides an opportunity to fit the shoulder contours.

a Insert gusset as shown to provide for arm movement.

This style can be cut with a shoulder dart or with a continuous overarm seam. Chevron effects can be obtained by placing the centre front and centre back on either the warp or the weft grain.

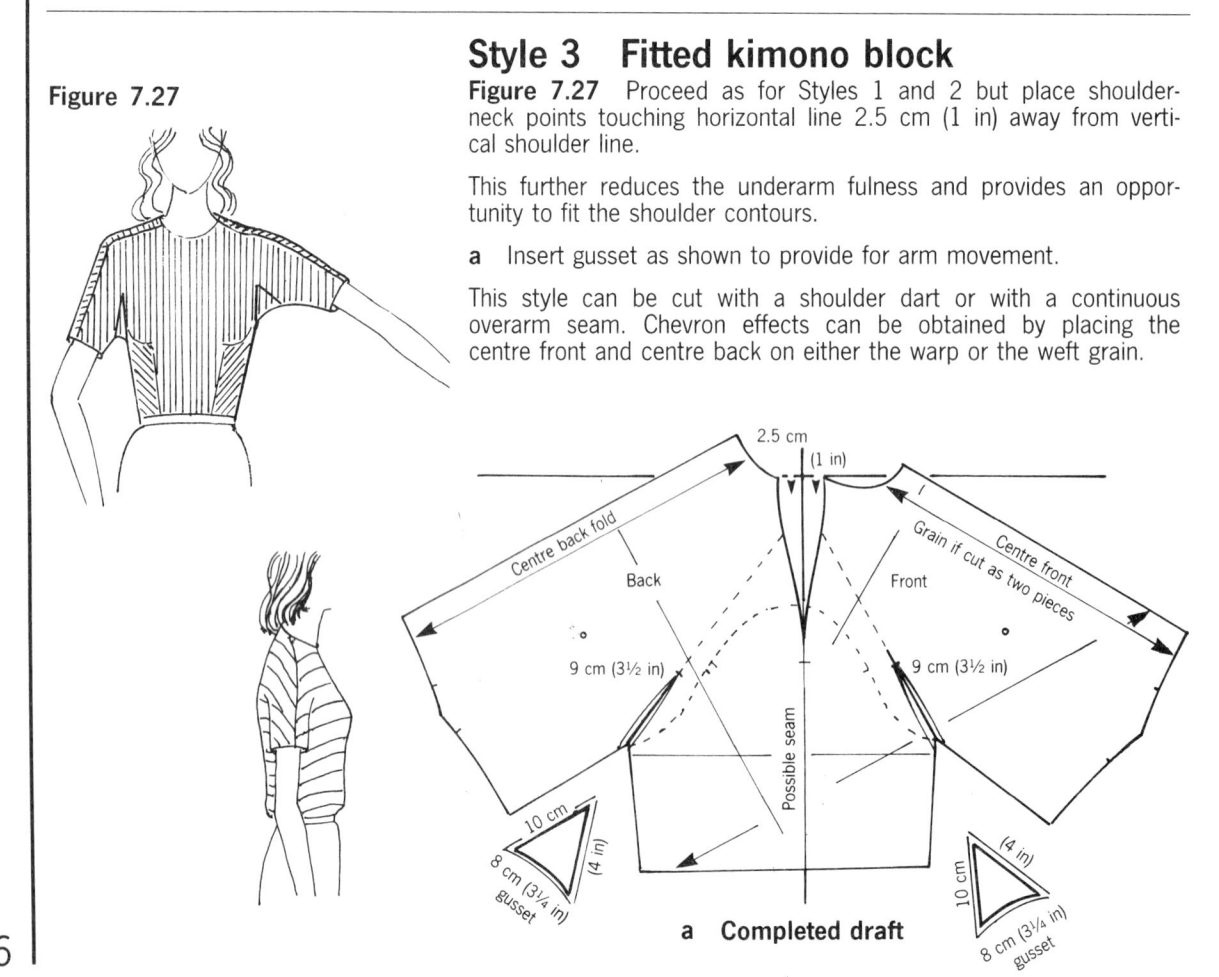

a Completed draft

Dolman sleeve lowered armhole development

Figure 7.28

Once the reason for this development is understood, it is possible to apply its basic principles to other low armhole designs (see Figure 7.26 **c**, **d** and **e** on page 96).

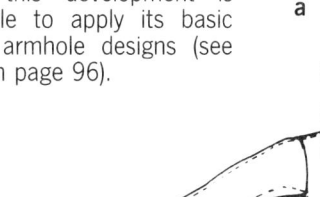

Figure 7.28a The construction of the basic waist blocks and set-in sleeve is based on the anatomy of the human figure, allowing for comfort and ease of movement.

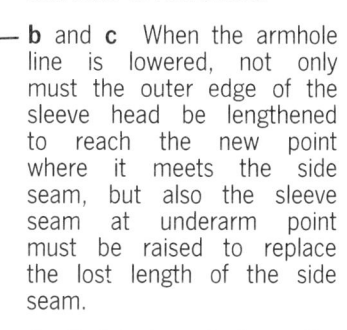

b and **c** When the armhole line is lowered, not only must the outer edge of the sleeve head be lengthened to reach the new point where it meets the side seam, but also the sleeve seam at underarm point must be raised to replace the lost length of the side seam.

d If this is not done, the side seam will 'pull', resulting in an uncomfortable and ill-fitting garment.

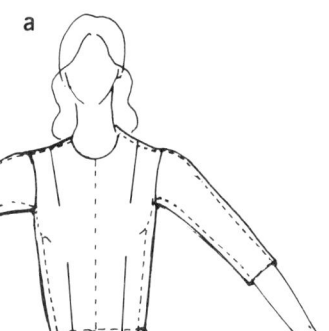

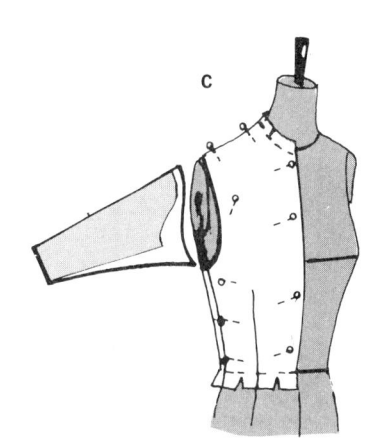

Slashing method

Figure 7.29 Outline back and front waist blocks. Join half sleeve block to back and front; outline. Lower armhole by required amount, 4 cm (1½ in) in this case, and draw new armhole line. Ensure that distance from waist to lowered armhole point on side seam is equal on back and front. Cut out on new lowered armhole line.

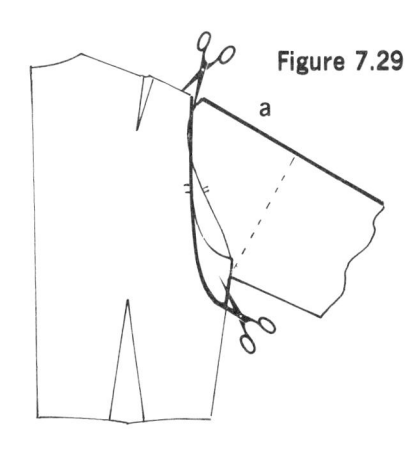

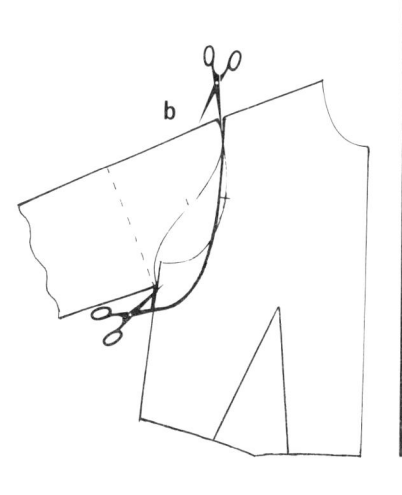

Figure 7.29

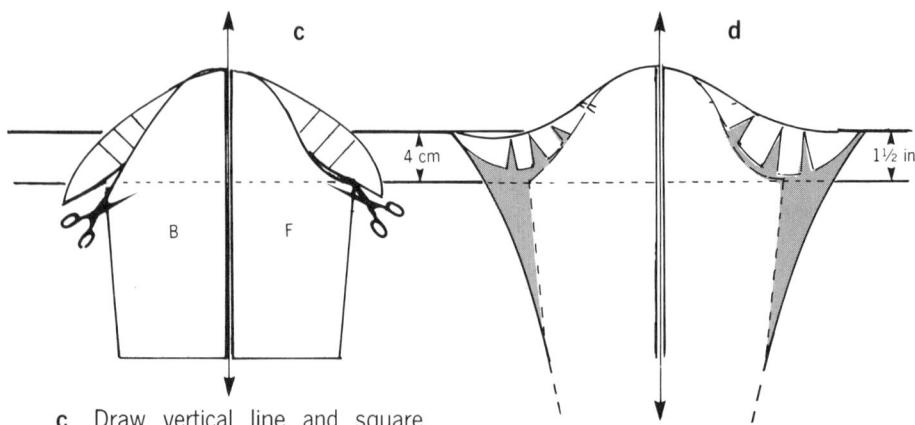

c Draw vertical line and square two parallel lines 4 cm (1½ in) apart. Place **B** and **F** sleeve sections to vertical line aligning crown level line with lower horizontal line. Draw three slash lines each side at approximate right angle to existing lines. Cut upwards to sleeve head line, but not through it.

d Cut up each slash line and open up, touching upper horizontal line; outline.

Pivoting method

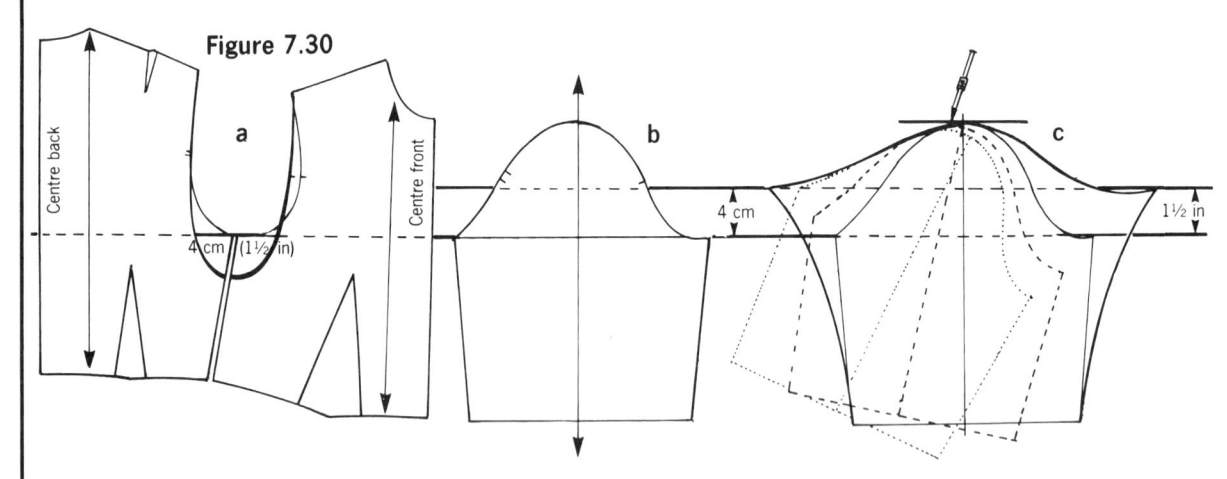

Figure 7.30

Figure 7.30a and b Outline back and front waist blocks. Draw vertical line and square two parallel lines 4 cm (1½ in) apart to it. Place sleeve on to vertical line aligning crown level line with lower horizontal line. Draw short horizontal T-line at top of sleeve head.

c Pivot sleeve from centre of sleeve head and at intervals (see dots) first to left and then to right side until sleeve underarm point touches upper horizontal line. Measure back and front armhole line and lengthen sleeve head seam if required. Alternatively, outline sleeve head to 1.3 cm (½ in) below back and front armhole balance marks and pivot from there.

Figure 7.31 Final patterns of both slashing and pivoting methods should be identical.

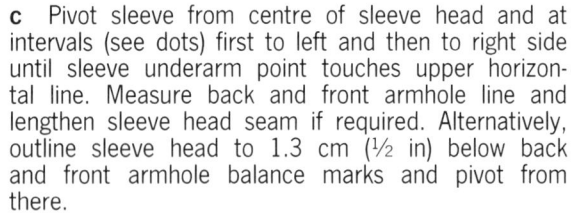

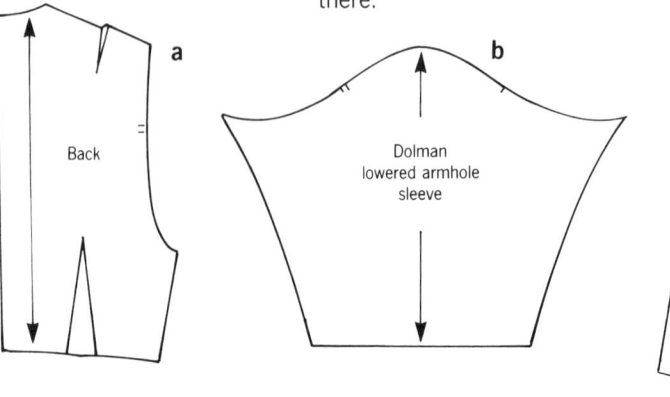

Figure 7.31 Completed patterns

Modelling of basic sleeves

Figure 7.32
Each square represents
2.5 cm (1 in)

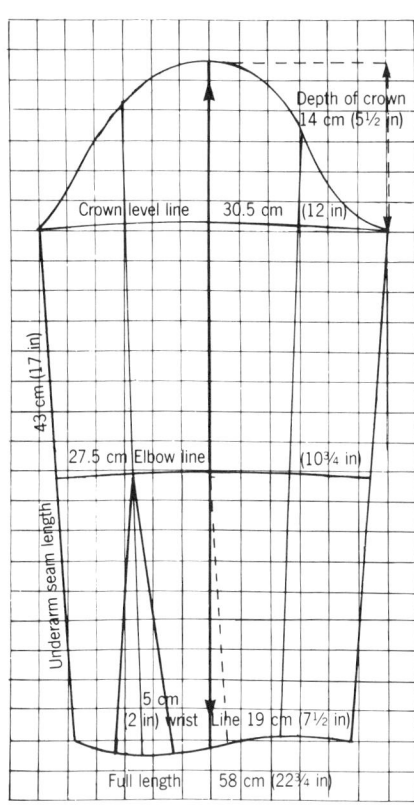

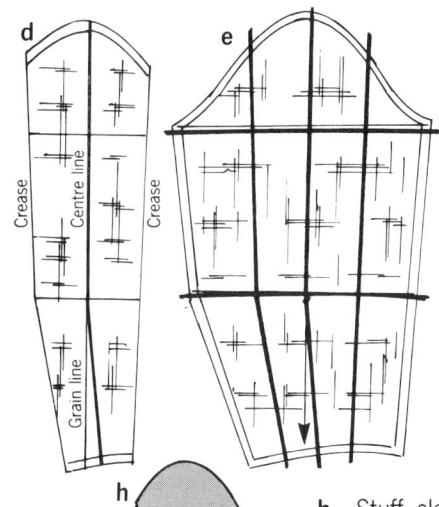

Making padded sleeve form for modelling

Measurements represent: Size 12 (38) equals body measurements plus ease allowances.

Upper arm girth	33 cm (13 in)
Wrist	20.5 cm (8 in)
Sleeve length	68.5 cm (23¼ in)

Add 13 mm (½ in) seam allowances all around sleeve pattern. Cut out in tailor's canvas or strong calico.

Right arm
Figure 7.32a Cut out sleeve. Machine wrist dart. Press towards centre of sleeve.

b and **c** Fold sleeve seams to meet centre line. Crease. Draw straight line across crown level line and elbow line.

d Halve folded wrist line. Draw new centre sleeve line to elbow line.

e Unfold. Machine black narrow tape along creased and newly established lines, including wrist dart.

f Machine underarm seam. Press. Turn to right side.

g Cut crescent-shaped piece of canvas on fold and two oval-shaped pieces. Add 1 cm (⅜ in) seam allowance.

h Stuff sleeve tightly with cotton or wool flock or similar material. Sew larger oval piece of canvas over armhole. Sew smaller piece over wrist opening.

i Turn raw edges of crescent-shaped piece towards each other. Machine. Machine folded straight edge to sleeve crown. It forms the means of pinning the arm securely to the shoulder of the dress form. Press arm firmly. It should not be too round and should rest naturally against the side of the dress form when pinned to the shoulder.

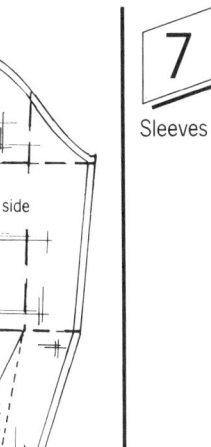

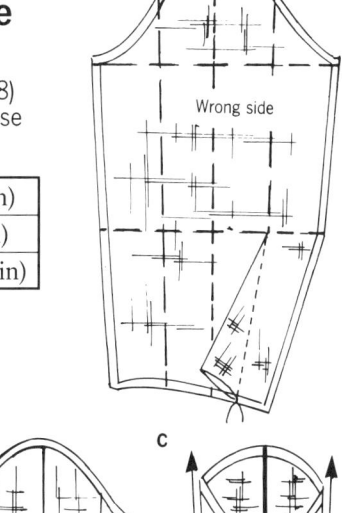

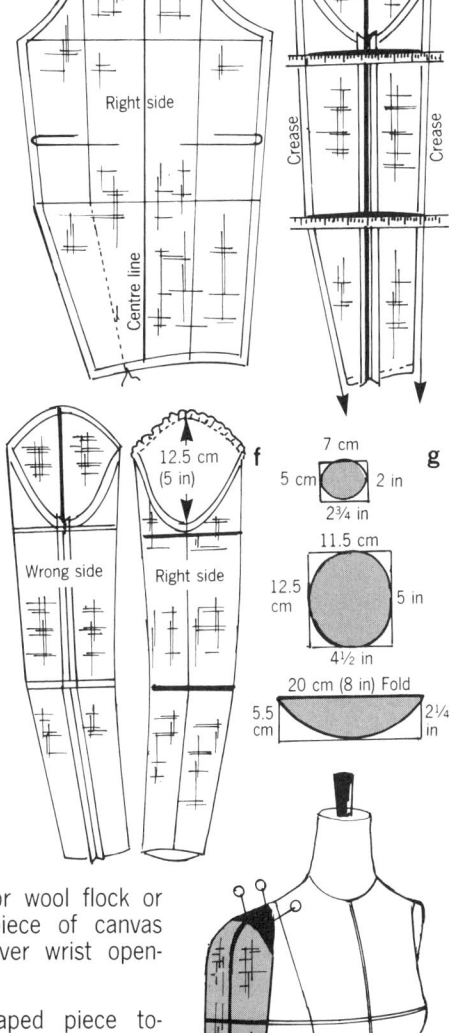

i Completed sleeve form

Modelling the shirt sleeve

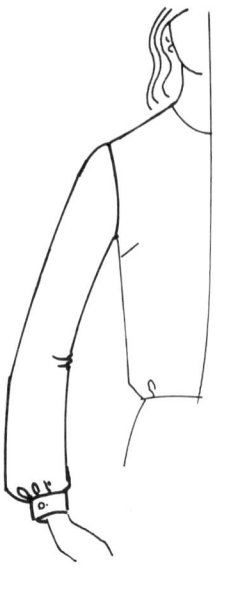

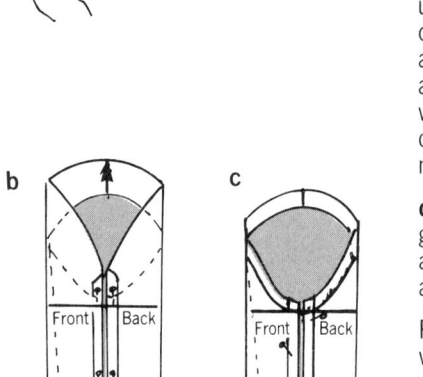

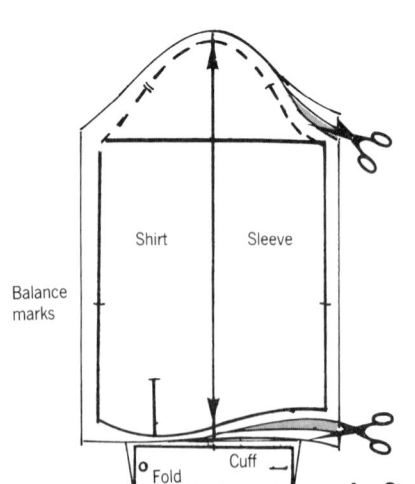

Figure 7.33

Figure 7.33a Cut rectangle of fine paper or calico: length of arm plus 5 cm (2 in) by width of upper arm plus 5 cm (2 in).

Fold paper in half lengthwise; crease and mark centre line. Draw horizontal line at right angle to centre line 17 cm (6¾ in) down from top edge. This represents crown level line. Curve paper at top as shown. Pin to arm, matching taped centre and crown level line.

b and **c** Turn arm over with underarm uppermost. Smooth paper or calico around to underarm seam, matching crown level line with that on arm. Crease seam allowances and pin. Continue in this way to wrist. Mark armhole line and cut away excess modelling material.

d Turn arm over. Arrange gathers at wrist. Pull paper up a little to cause sleeve to pouch at this point.

Pin black tape around wrist where cuff will be attached and mark.

Pin sleeve crown to top of arm allowing a small amount of ease (2.5–3.5 cm (1–1½ in)) at shoulder position. Mark sleeve head curve, balance marks. Cut away excess paper.

e The wrist opening is 6.5 cm (2½ in) long and is placed in line with the taped back line on the arm. Cut wrist opening through wrist tape. Pin strip of calico into position, representing the finished cuff.

f Remove from arm and unpin. Make good any uneven lines and markings and trim to desired seam allowances.

See also slim shirt sleeves, page 47.

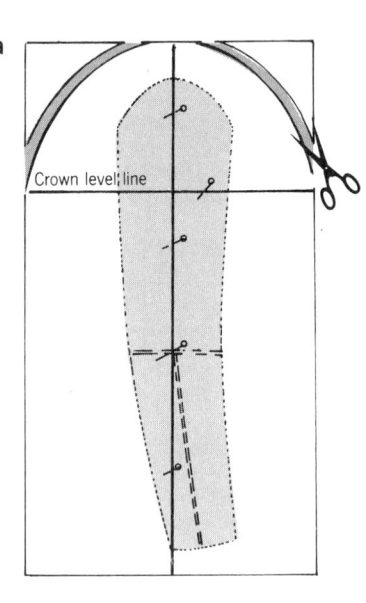

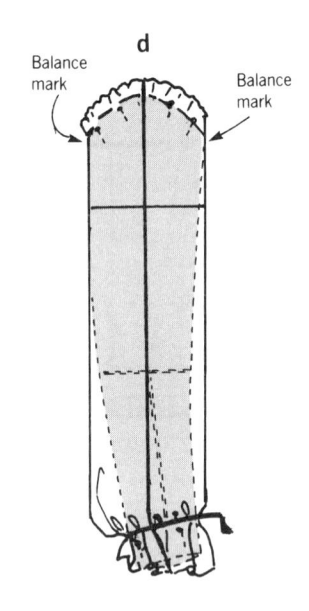

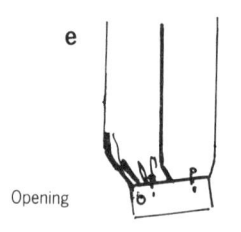

f **Completed pattern**

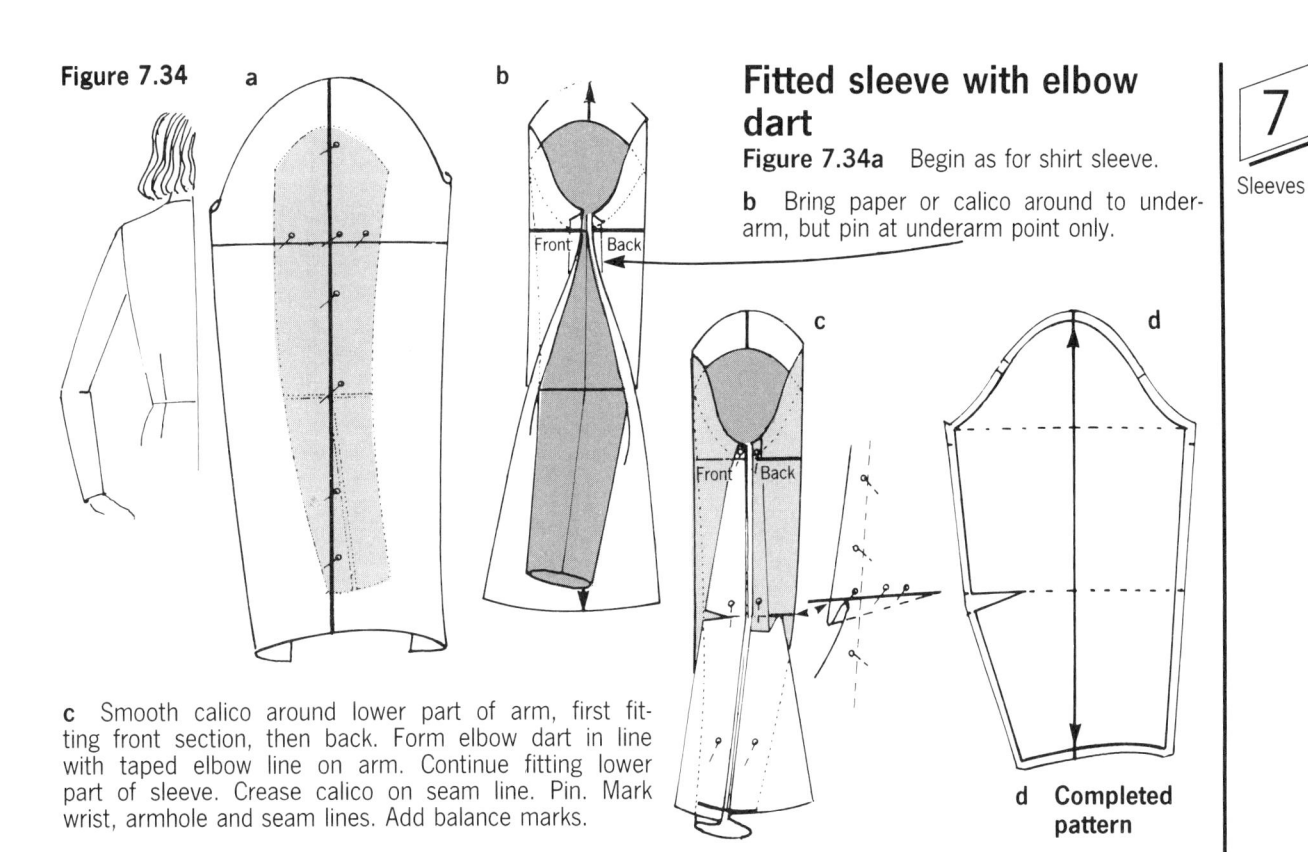

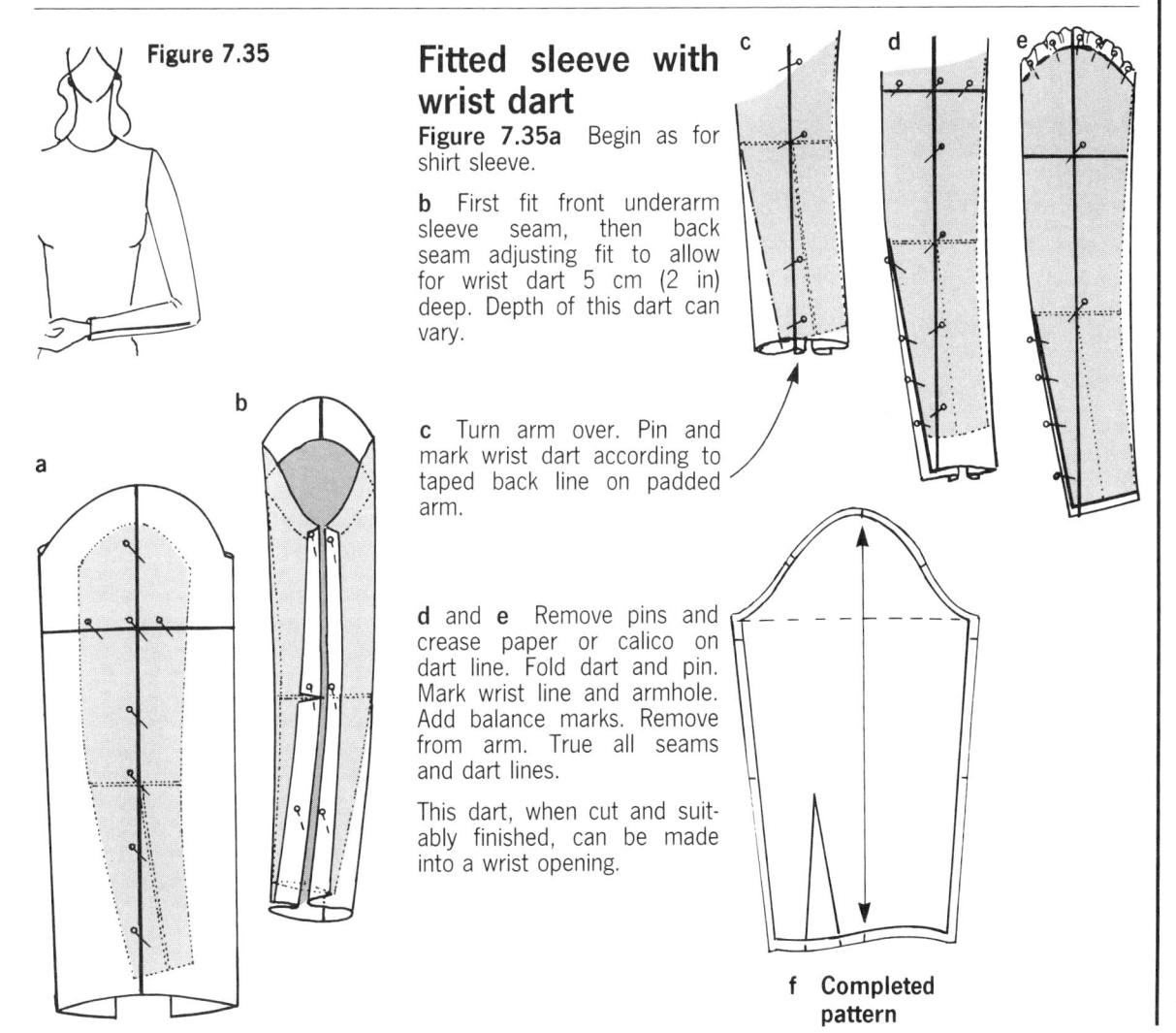

Figure 7.34

Fitted sleeve with elbow dart

Figure 7.34a Begin as for shirt sleeve.

b Bring paper or calico around to underarm, but pin at underarm point only.

c Smooth calico around lower part of arm, first fitting front section, then back. Form elbow dart in line with taped elbow line on arm. Continue fitting lower part of sleeve. Crease calico on seam line. Pin. Mark wrist, armhole and seam lines. Add balance marks.

d Completed pattern

Figure 7.35

Fitted sleeve with wrist dart

Figure 7.35a Begin as for shirt sleeve.

b First fit front underarm sleeve seam, then back seam adjusting fit to allow for wrist dart 5 cm (2 in) deep. Depth of this dart can vary.

c Turn arm over. Pin and mark wrist dart according to taped back line on padded arm.

d and **e** Remove pins and crease paper or calico on dart line. Fold dart and pin. Mark wrist line and armhole. Add balance marks. Remove from arm. True all seams and dart lines.

This dart, when cut and suitably finished, can be made into a wrist opening.

f Completed pattern

Three quarter sleeve with elbow fulness

This sleeve is best modelled in calico or muslin.

Figure 7.36 Cut rectangle of modelling fabric as for shirt sleeve, but allow 9 cm (3½ in) extra width across back section of sleeve. Pin to top of arm.

b Turn arm over and model front underarm sections as for fitted sleeve, Figure 7.34c.

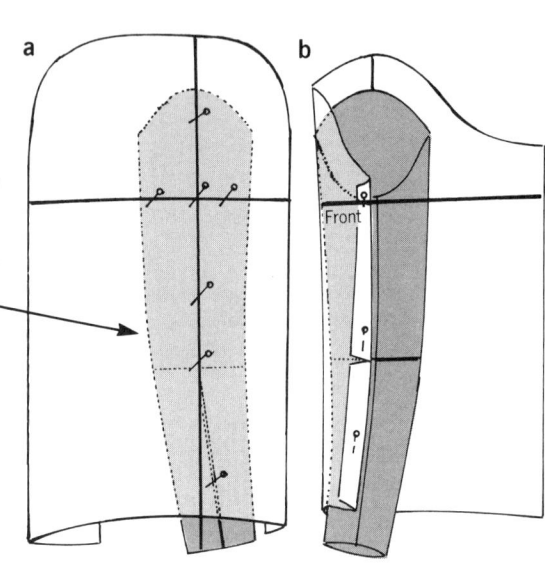

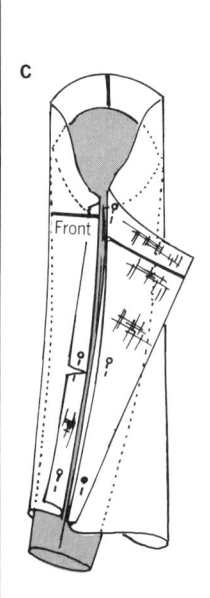

c Bring over back sleeve section. Pin at underarm point with back crown level line at a lower level than front. In this way more fulness is moved to lower arm level where it is needed.

d Turn arm over. Pin tape from centre of sleeve to underarm seam as shown. Mark position of style line and gathers.

Determine length of sleeve in relation to style line. Mark tentatively at this stage.

e Unpin gathers and cut on fold where marked. Smooth cuff section around to underarm seam.

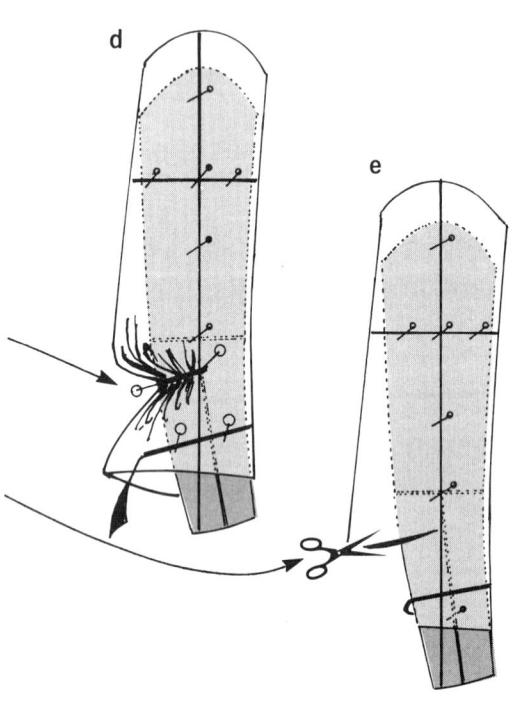

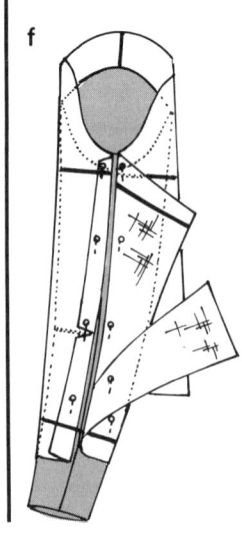

f Crease and pin underarm seam at 'cuff' position and cut away excess fabric.

Mark all new seams. Improve lines and shape where required. Place balance marks and grain line.

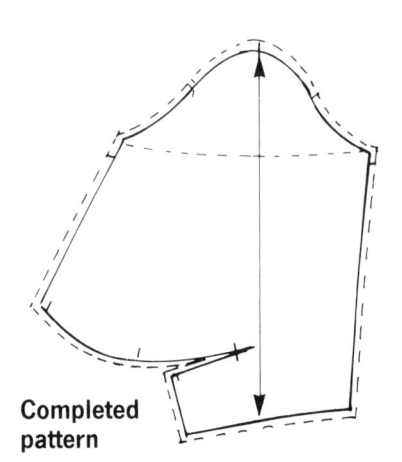

g Completed pattern

Leg-of mutton sleeve

Figure 7.37a Draw fitted sleeve block (Figure 7.35f) on modelling fabric. Draw centre line and crown level line. Extend width and length beyond sleeve outline as shown.

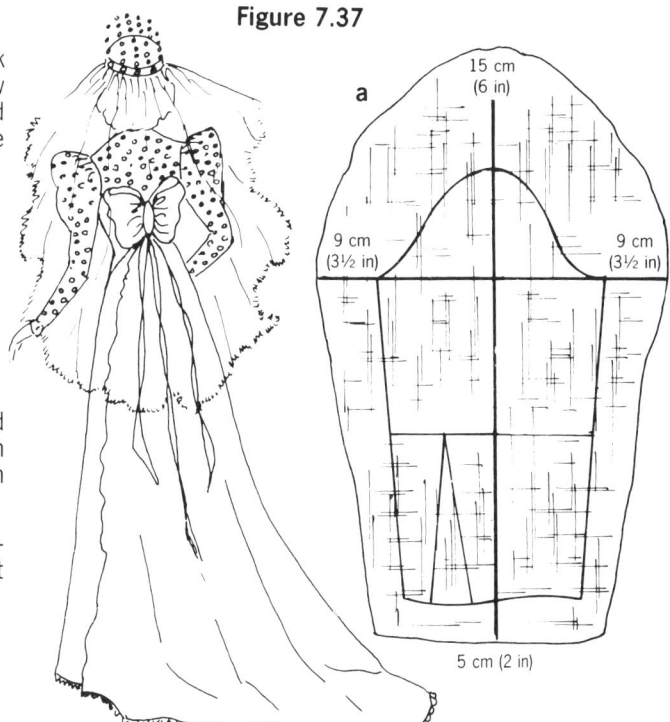

b Close wrist dart; pin to padded sleeve, aligning centre sleeve and crown level lines with taped centre and crown level lines on sleeve form.

c Turn sleeve form over and pin modelling fabric to it experimentally; first one side and then the other.

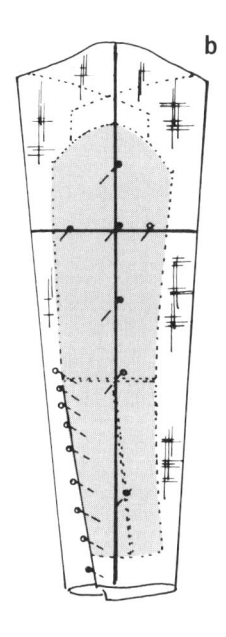

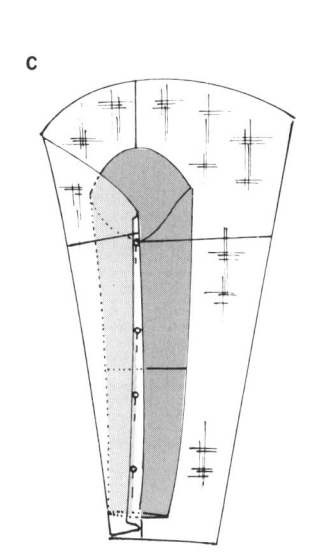

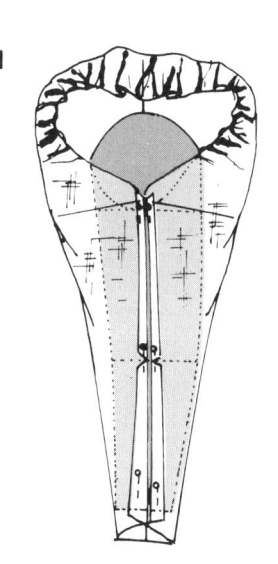

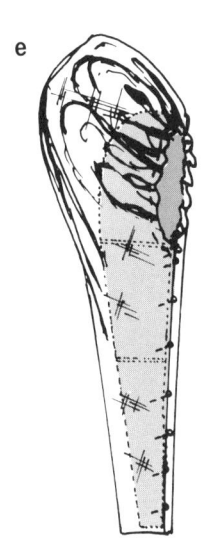

d Turn sleeve form back. Place hand between head of sleeve form and crown section of modelling fabric, and 'puff' material 'out', bringing down excess fabric from above normal sleeve head, which was planned for this purpose.

e Pin temporarily, as if you were gathering this area, and look at the sleeve sideways to take note of the effect. Reduce or increase amount of 'puff' until the desired silhouette is achieved.

The underarm sleeve seam may now require adjustment.

Figure 7.37

A more extreme example of a leg-of-mutton sleeve.

7 Sleeves

g

h

i

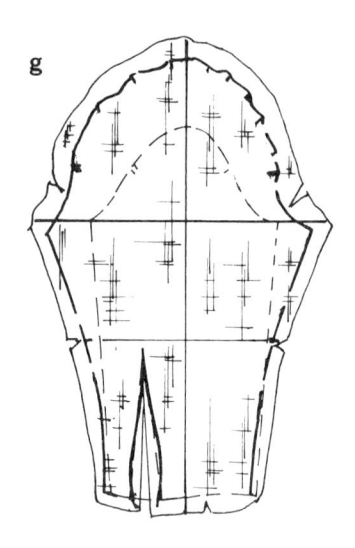

g Mark all seam lines, dart and balance marks and remove from sleeve form.

True uneven lines and transfer all relevant information to pattern paper or card.

h Pin sleeve to garment on figure and make final adjustments.

i A stiff net frill helps to support the gathered sleeve.

Gather

Sleeve

Cut 2

Transfer to pattern paper and add seam allowances

j Completed pattern

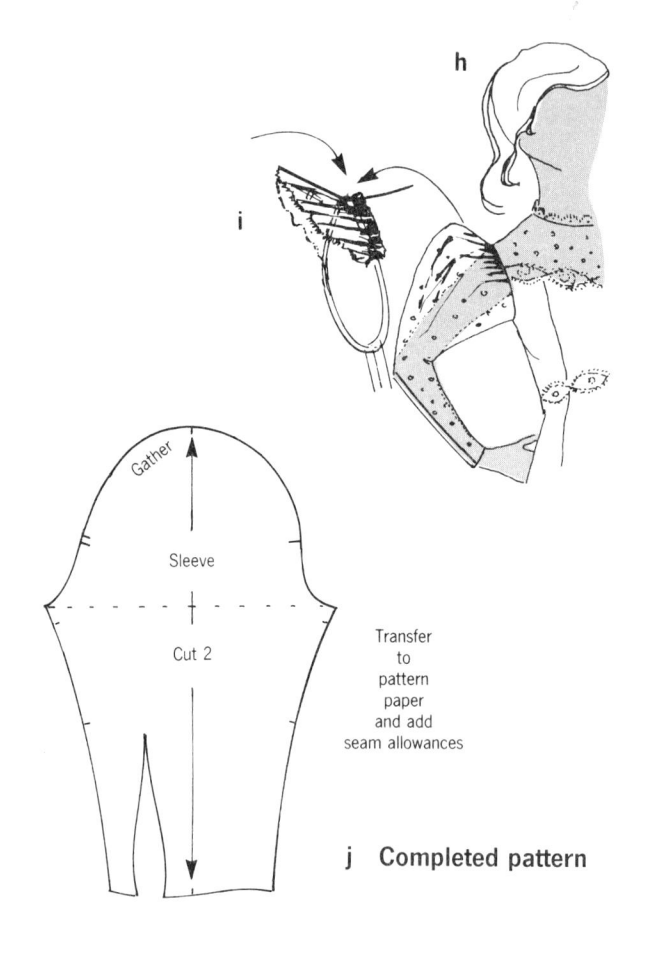

Figure 7.38

Leg-of-mutton sleeve cut flat

Figure 7.38a Outline block (Figure 7.34f). Draw cutting lines as shown or where fulness is required.

b Cut and open out as shown. Cut out in muslin or calico; compare fit of this sleeve with that of the modelled one.

Make adjustments; complete pattern adding seam allowances, balance marks, grain line and cutting directions.

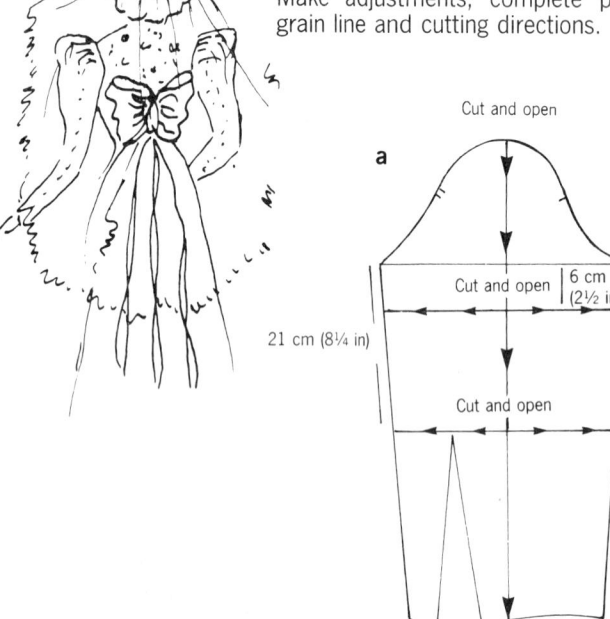

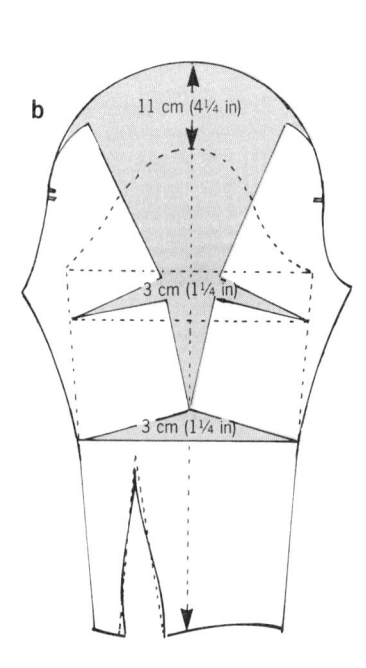

a

Cut and open

Cut and open | 6 cm (2½ in)

21 cm (8¼ in)

Cut and open

b

11 cm (4¼ in)

3 cm (1¼ in)

3 cm (1¼ in)

Completed pattern

The kimono sleeve

Classic kimono sleeves allow ample ease under the arm when raised but tend to pull over the shoulder when the arm is lowered. By changing the sleeve angle and inserting an underarm gusset, a contoured shoulder-overarm silhouette can be achieved and ease for movement at underarm can be provided.

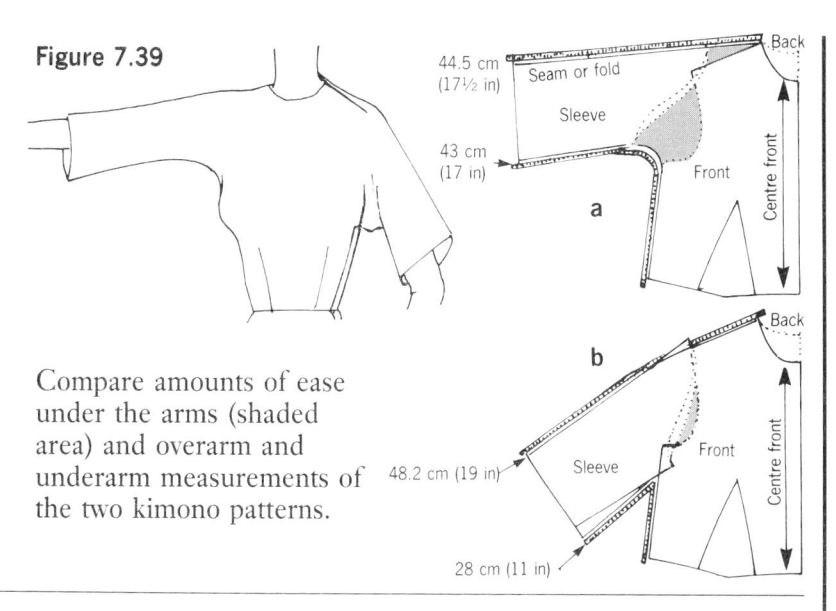

Figure 7.39

Compare amounts of ease under the arms (shaded area) and overarm and underarm measurements of the two kimono patterns.

Kimono sleeve with gusset

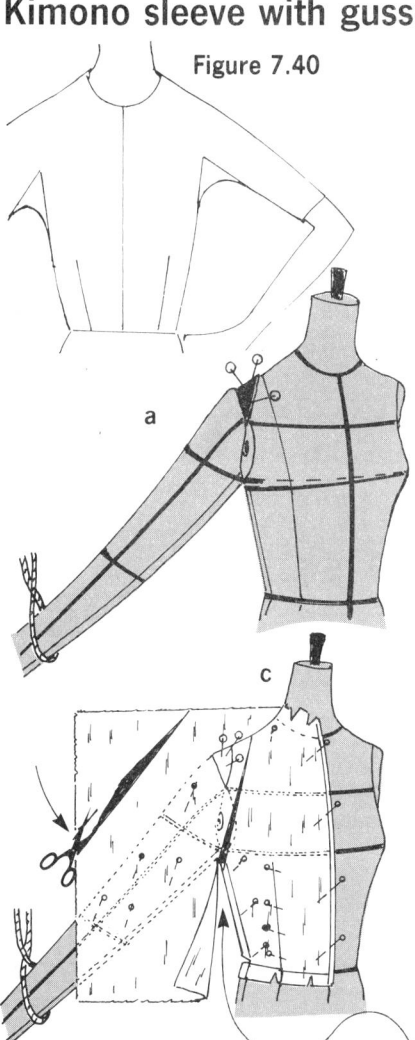

Figure 7.40

Figure 7.37a Pin arm securely to dress form. Suspend at 45° to side seam.

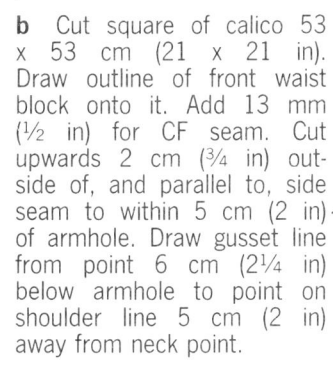

b Cut square of calico 53 x 53 cm (21 x 21 in). Draw outline of front waist block onto it. Add 13 mm (½ in) for CF seam. Cut upwards 2 cm (¾ in) outside of, and parallel to, side seam to within 5 cm (2 in) of armhole. Draw gusset line from point 6 cm (2¼ in) below armhole to point on shoulder line 5 cm (2 in) away from neck point.

c Close waist dart. Pin square of calico to dress form. Cut away left hand corner at neck. Snip neck and waist edges.

Cut 9 cm (3½ in) on gusset line from side seam towards shoulder line.

d Fold calico on underarm seam. Crease and pin.

For back pattern follow same instructions. Extend shoulder-overarm seam by 13 mm (½ in) to meet front shoulder. Mark sleeve length.

e Cut two-piece gusset 10 x 10 cm (4 x 4 in).

f Add seam turnings. Insert as shown.

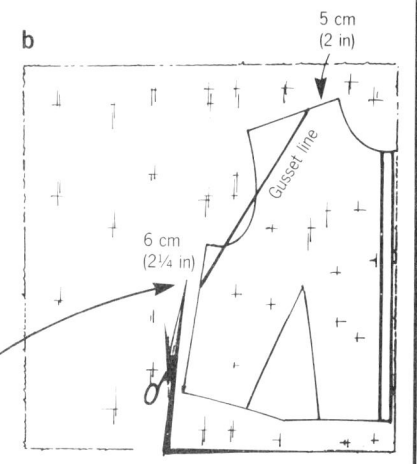

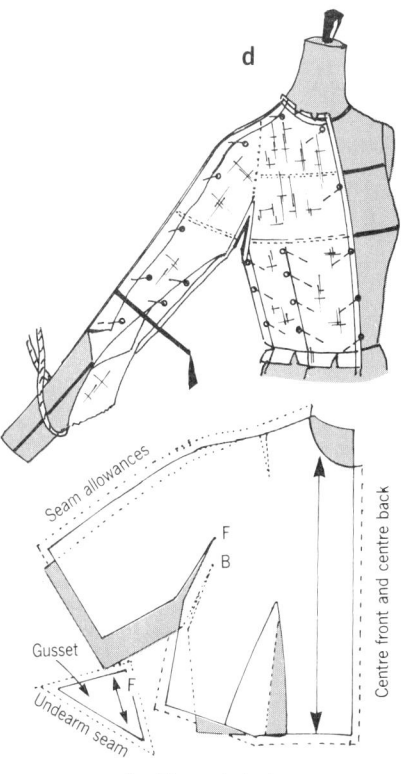

f Completed pattern

8 Skirts

Figure 8.1

Figure 8.2

Preparing the form

For the modelling of short skirts no additional preparations to the dress form are required. Ideally however, the form used for modelling skirts, should have a firm base representing the leg area of the body. The special skirt forms which extend only to slightly above the waist provide this. Some dress forms have a wire frame attached for the purpose and this forms a very satisfactory support.

Otherwise, a large sheet of strong paper, wrapped around, pinned and tacked just below the hip line level is very effective, especially for modelling long skirts. The base thus obtained is slightly cone shaped and helps to avoid modelling the skirt too tightly at knee level. The base can, however, be shaped to follow a body-fitting silhouette suitable for modelling slim skirts when wished.

Draw continuation of side seam lines, centre front and centre back lines on the paper base.

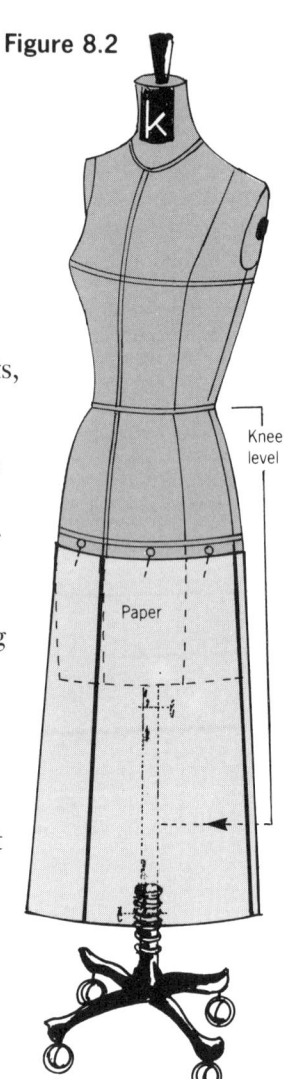

Modelling the straight two-piece skirt

Figure 8.3

Skirt front
Figure 8.3a Cut rectangle of fine pattern paper or calico the desired length of skirt plus 8 cm (3 in) by one quarter of hip measurement plus 5 cm (2 in). Right hand long edge of paper or calico represents centre front fold line. Draw dotted waist line 2.5 cm (1 in) below top short edge of material, and dotted hip line 20 cm (8 in) below waist line. Both these lines are approximate and serve only as guides. Their shape may have to be slightly altered in the course of modelling.

b Pin centre front of paper to centre front of dress form matching waist and hip lines with those on the form. Smooth fabric on hip line towards side seam. Drop dotted hip line 6 mm (¼ in) below taped hip line on form. Pin. Smooth fabric up towards waist line. Pin at side seam point. Fold surplus fabric at waist into short shallow dart 9 × 2 cm (3½ × 2¾ in), using seam line on form as guide. Smooth fabric towards hem line. Pin on lowest point.

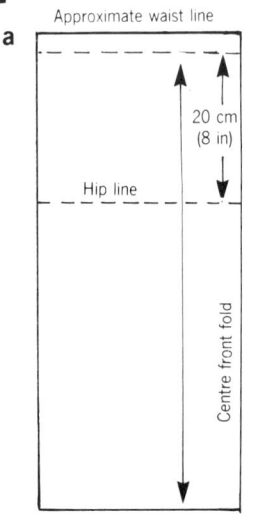

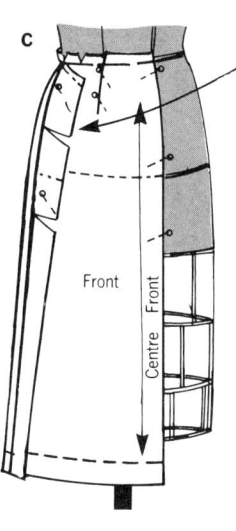

c Fold fabric back upon itself. Crease side seam as in **c** and **d**. Mark waist line, hip line and desired hem line, dart and side seam.

Skirt back

d Proceed as for front. Back dart is longer and deeper due to the lower and more curved body formation, approx. 14 cm (5½ in) long and 3.5 cm (1½ in) deep. Two shallower darts can be substituted for one deeper dart, if so wished.

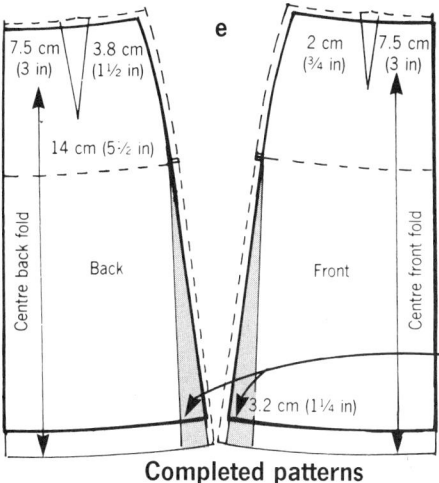

e Remove modelled patterns from form. Unpin darts. Improve seam and dart lines. Check hem line. Finished hem width of this basic skirt should be 8–13 cm (3–5 in) greater than hip circumference. If this is not the case, add the appropriate amounts to side seams. Make up as toile to ascertain fit. Transfer final checked pattern to heavy card as basic skirt block.

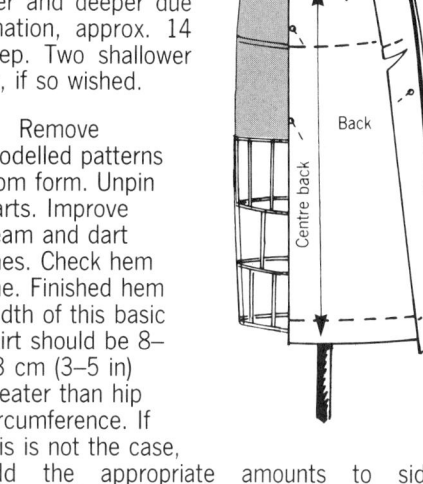

Completed patterns

Gathered waist skirts

This skirt is lightly gathered at the waist. Use hem width throughout. The waist opening is at centre back.

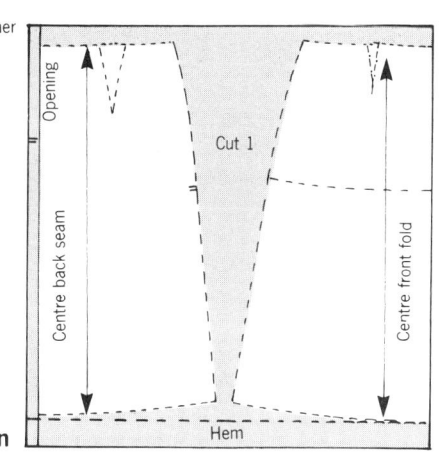

a Completed pattern

Figure 8.4

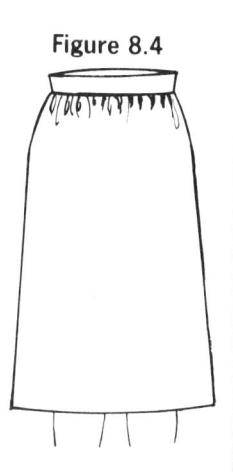

Figure 8.5

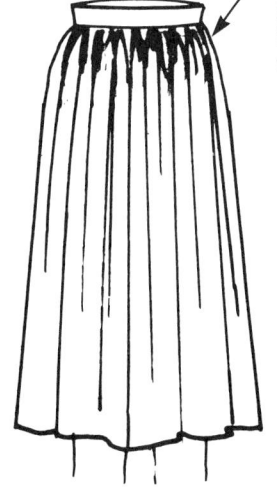

Twice the hem width is used here to achieve a fuller gathering at waist and wider hem line. Side seams can be slanted as shown to reduce waist fulness yet retain full hem circumference. When still more width is needed, as with very fine fabrics of limited width, more seams can be introduced. These seams will not be noticeable in a very full skirt.

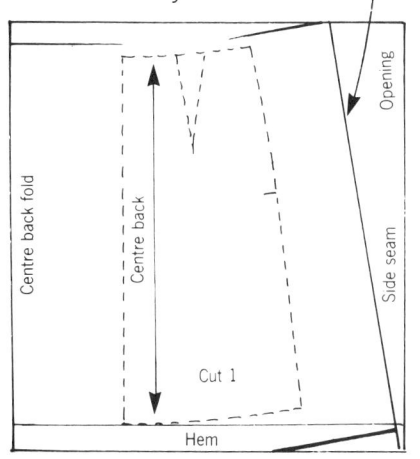

a Completed pattern 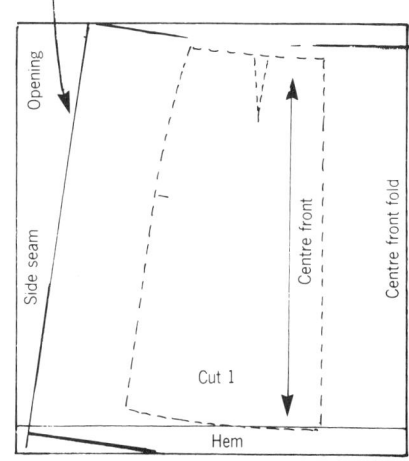   **b Completed pattern**

8 Skirts

107

Gathered tiered skirt

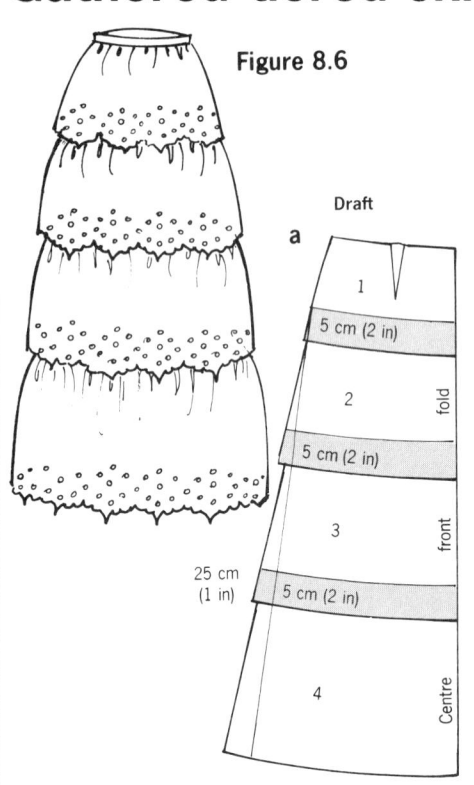

Figure 8.6

Figure 8.6a Draft: outline straight skirt front block. Add 2.5 cm (1 in) to side seam at hem line. Lengthen skirt to 81 cm (32 in).

Experiment on the form with tiers of differing depths. Transfer the most pleasing design to the draft. Here, tiers are graduated, tier 4 being the deepest. Add 5 cm (2 in) for underlap above tiers 2, 3 and 4. Place balance marks and grain lines.

b Trace through to new sheet of paper. Increase width of tiers by half its present width for gathers. Add seam turnings where required. The tiers are stitched onto an underskirt.

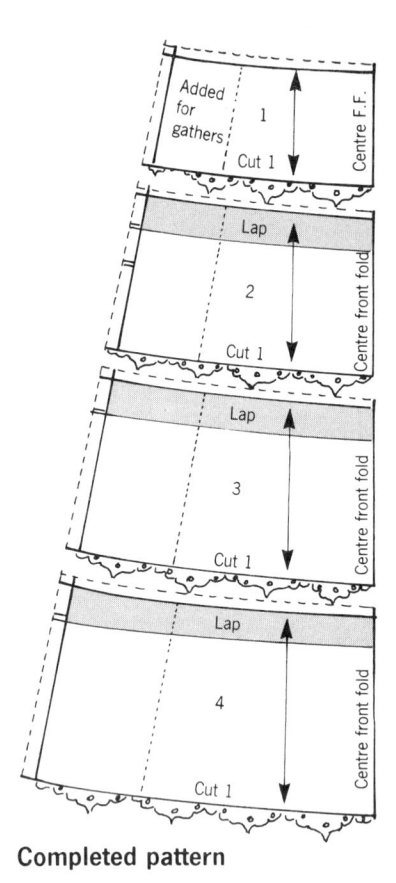

b Completed pattern

Long skirt with godets

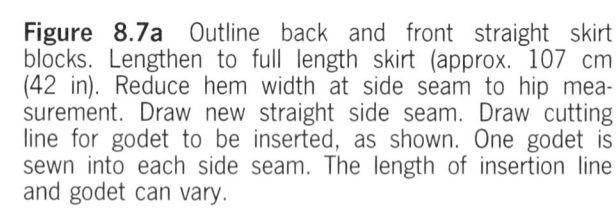

Figure 8.7a Outline back and front straight skirt blocks. Lengthen to full length skirt (approx. 107 cm (42 in). Reduce hem width at side seam to hip measurement. Draw new straight side seam. Draw cutting line for godet to be inserted, as shown. One godet is sewn into each side seam. The length of insertion line and godet can vary.

Godets can become a focal point when cut in a contrasting colour or texture, or when pleated in accordion 'sunray' pleating.

d Godets stand out more when cut as quarter or half circles.

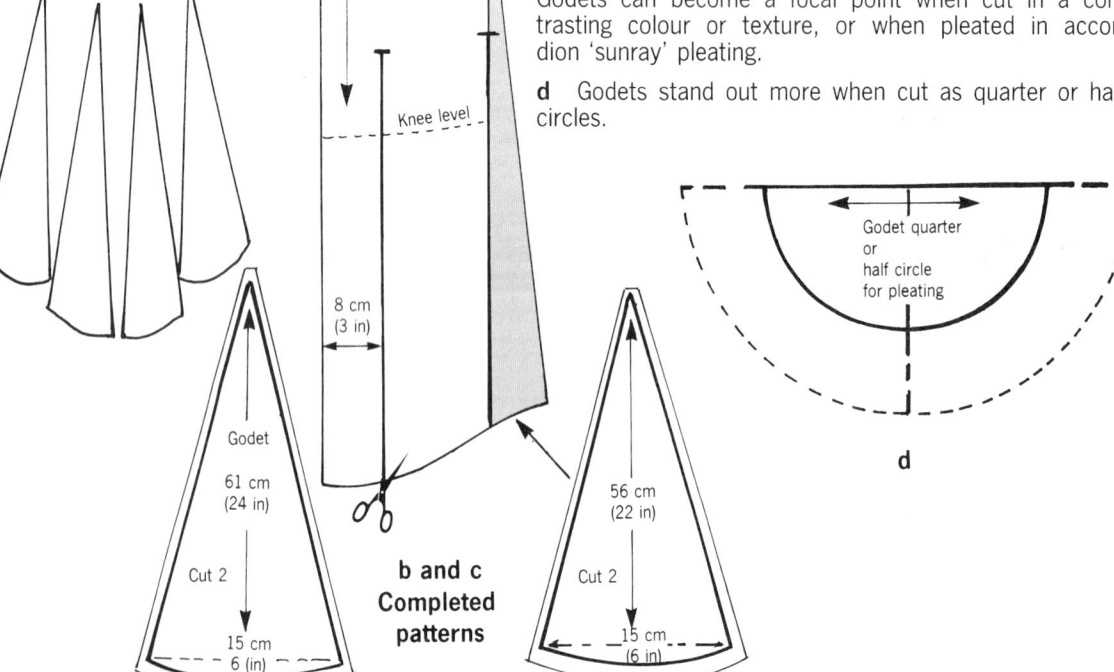

b and c Completed patterns

Modelling the flared skirt

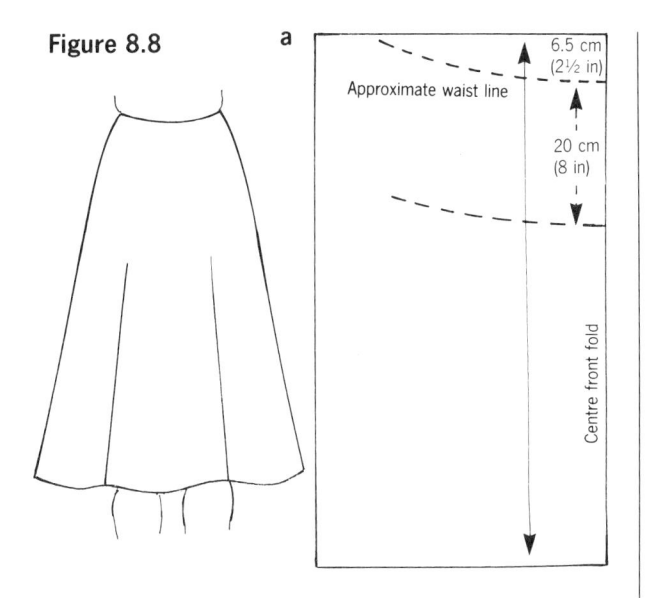

Figure 8.8

Figure 8.8a Cut rectangle of fine calico, the desired length of skirt plus 12 cm (5 in) by quarter hip measurement plus 15 cm (6 in). Draw approximate waist and hip lines as shown.

b Pin to dress form. Snip excess fabric above waist. Smooth material at waist line towards side seam. Pin. By raising or lowering waist side seam point** more or less flare can be produced. When a satisfactory appearance has been obtained, fold side seam back upon itself and crease. Mark side seam, waist and hem line. Place balance mark at hip line level. Finished hem width is approx. 30 cm (12 in) larger than that of **Figure 8.3e**.

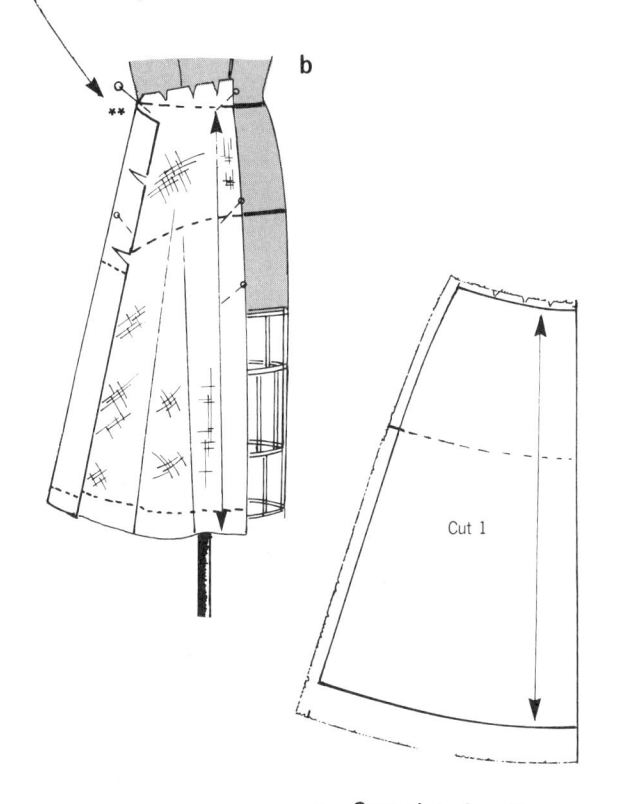

c Completed pattern

Flared skirt – cut flat

Figure 8.9a Outline front straight skirt block. Lower dart point to make dart 15 cm (6 in) long.

b Connect dart lines to new dart point. Draw cutting line parallel to centre front line. Cut on line to dart point. Cut on one dart line to dart point but not through it. Close dart. Repeat for back skirt.

c and **d** Compare front skirt hem width and angle of side seam with that of back skirt. Add to front side seam or reduce back side seam to make both patterns equal.

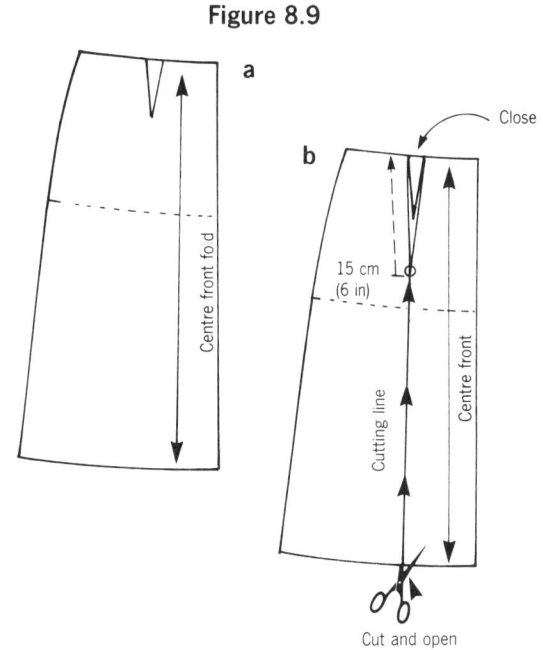

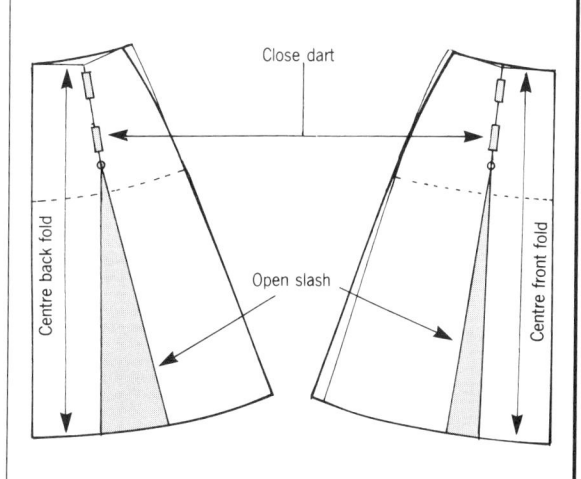

Figure 8.9

c and d Completed patterns

Flared skirt – pivoted

Figure 8.10a Lower dart point on straight skirt block. Perforate. Place on new sheet of paper.

b Outline centre section to first dart line. Cross mark.

c Pivot pattern. 'Close' dart. Outline side section.

Figure 8.10

Figure 8.11

d Completed pattern

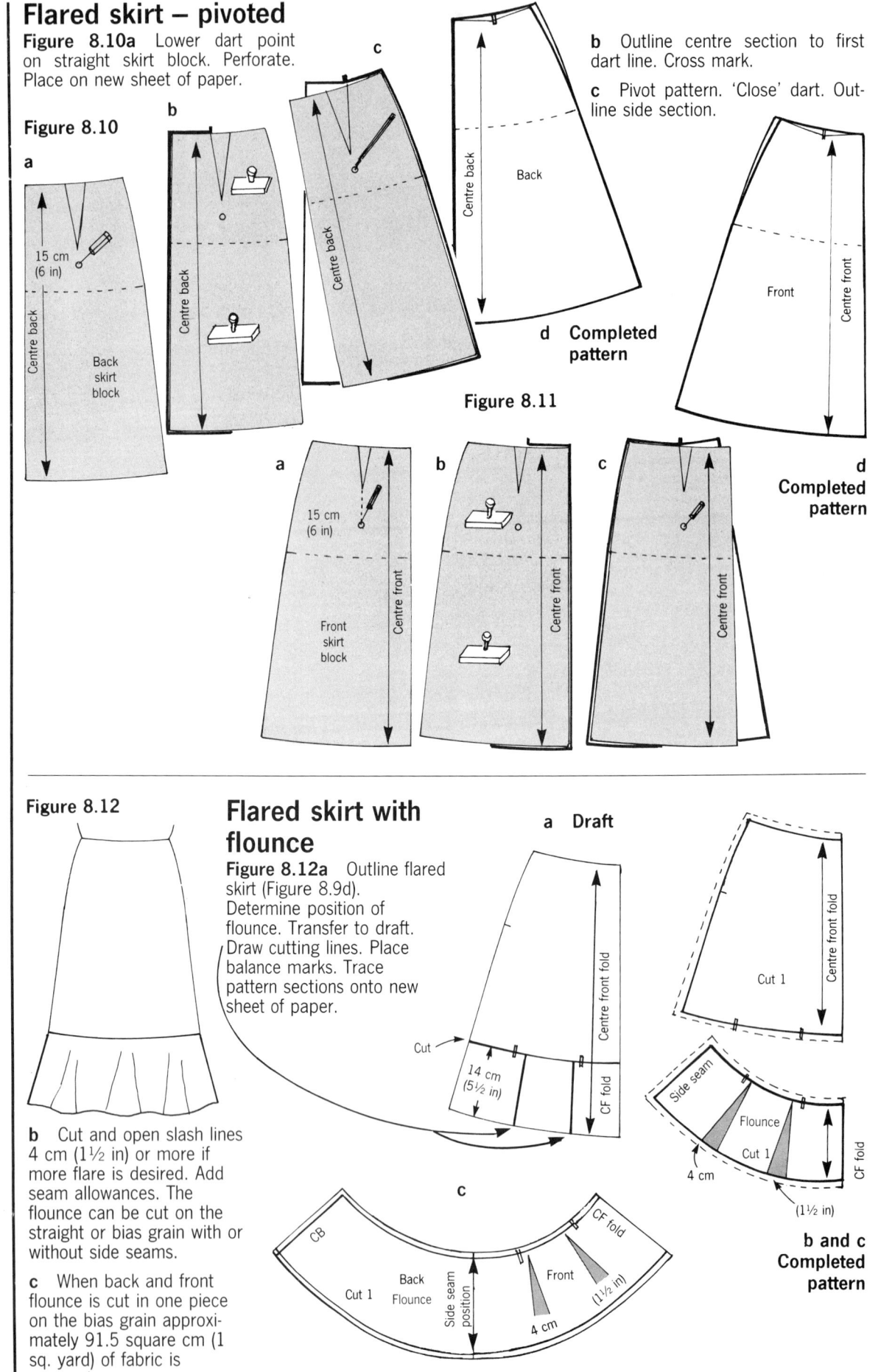

Flared skirt with flounce

Figure 8.12a Outline flared skirt (Figure 8.9d). Determine position of flounce. Transfer to draft. Draw cutting lines. Place balance marks. Trace pattern sections onto new sheet of paper.

Figure 8.12

a Draft

b Cut and open slash lines 4 cm (1½ in) or more if more flare is desired. Add seam allowances. The flounce can be cut on the straight or bias grain with or without side seams.

c When back and front flounce is cut in one piece on the bias grain approximately 91.5 square cm (1 sq. yard) of fabric is required.

b and c Completed pattern

Gored skirts

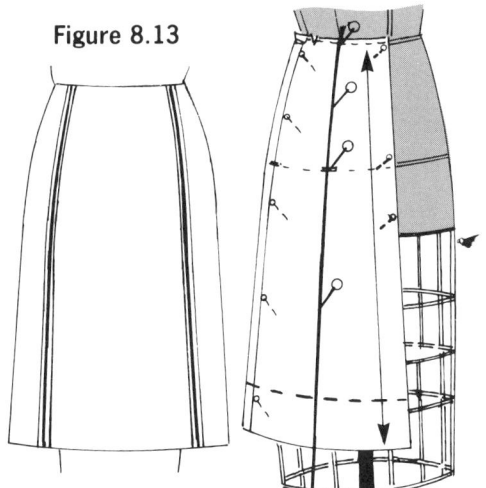

Figure 8.13

Straight six-gored skirt

Figure 8.13a Close front waist dart of straight skirt block, Figure 8.3e. Keep dart permanently closed by sticking down with masking tape. Pin black tape over closed dart and continue to hem in a continuing pleasing line. Pin. Mark with soft pencil. Place balance marks. Remove from form.

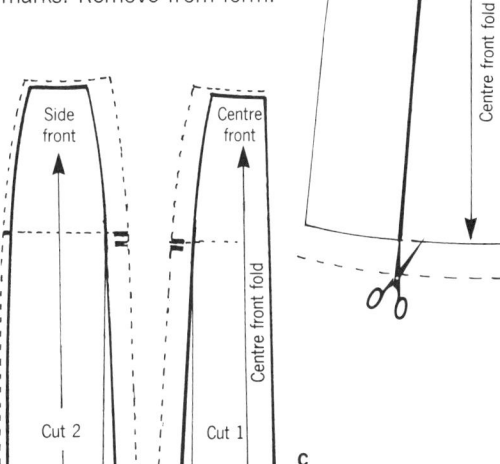

b Straighten marked line. Cut. Place newly cut side gore seam on front gore seam. Ensure that both seams run at the same angle from hip line down. If not add more 'flare' to one or the other gore seam. Add 2.5 cm (1 in) seam turnings on gore (panel) seam for a wider than usual top stitching.

Repeat for back skirt.

c Completed pattern

Figure 8.14

Flared six-gored skirt – cut flat

Figure 8.14a Outline flared skirt (Figure 8.9c and d). Draft gore (or panel) line according to design. Place balance marks and grain lines.

b Trace pattern sections onto new sheet of paper. Add seam allowances.

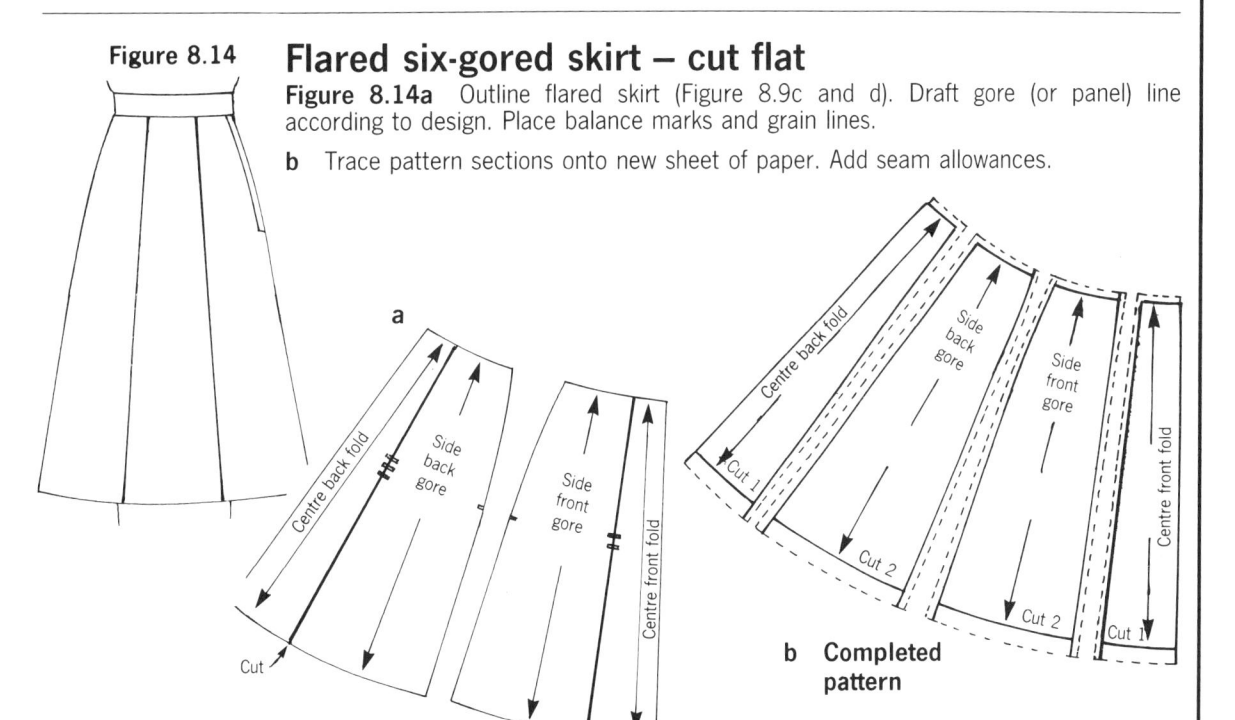

b Completed pattern

Figure 8.15

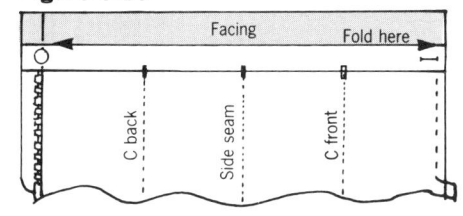

Waistband with side opening

Measure waist, eliminating darts and seams. Determine band width – here 3 cm (1¼ in). Add facing of equal width – cut on fold. Add extension 2.5 cm (1 in) for button/metal bar. Add seam turnings, balance marks, grain line.

This basic waistband can be used also for back and front openings by turning band around.

8 Skirts

Six-gored long skirt with deep frill

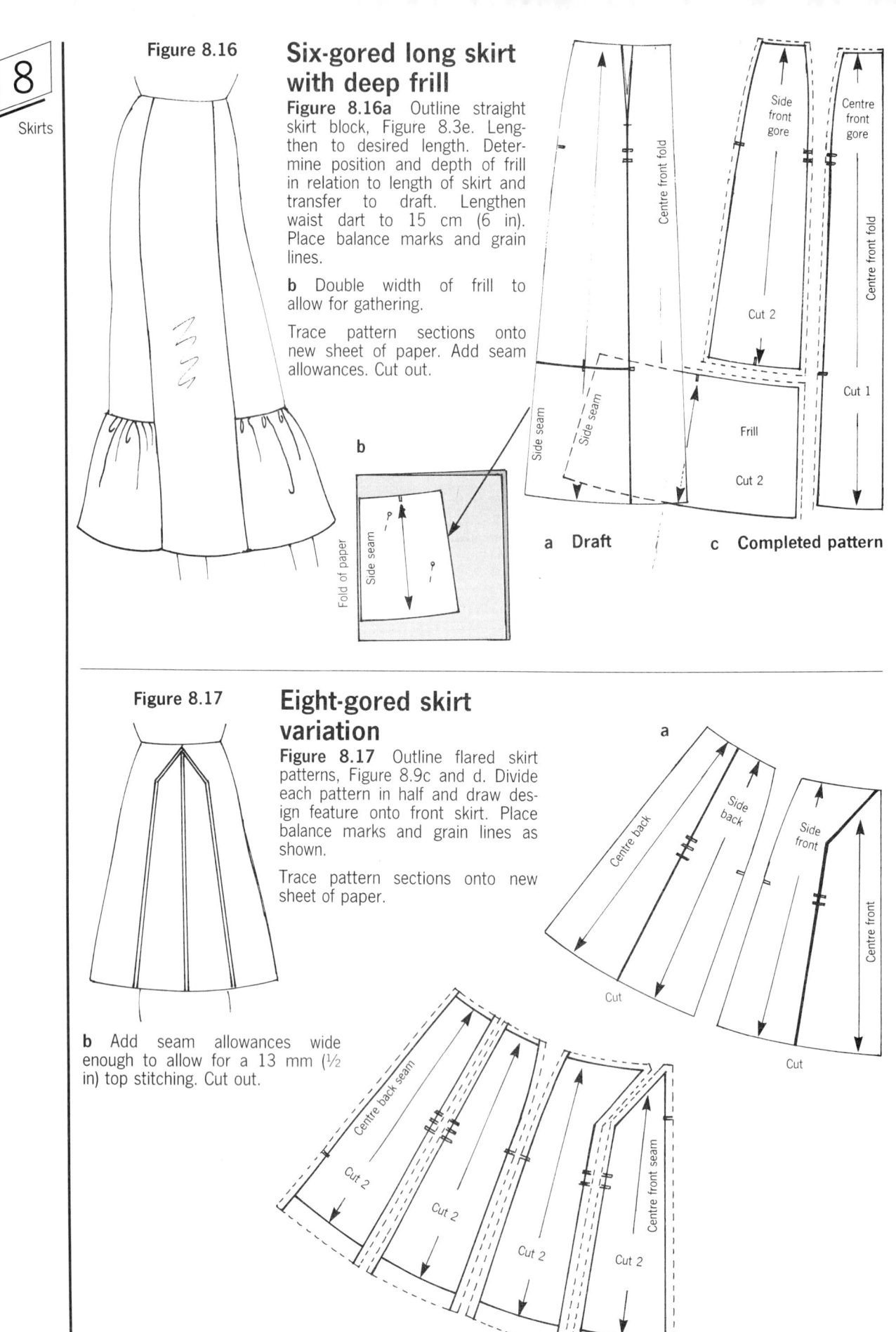

Figure 8.16a Outline straight skirt block, Figure 8.3e. Lengthen to desired length. Determine position and depth of frill in relation to length of skirt and transfer to draft. Lengthen waist dart to 15 cm (6 in). Place balance marks and grain lines.

b Double width of frill to allow for gathering.

Trace pattern sections onto new sheet of paper. Add seam allowances. Cut out.

Figure 8.16

a Draft

b

c Completed pattern

Eight-gored skirt variation

Figure 8.17 Outline flared skirt patterns, Figure 8.9c and d. Divide each pattern in half and draw design feature onto front skirt. Place balance marks and grain lines as shown.

Trace pattern sections onto new sheet of paper.

b Add seam allowances wide enough to allow for a 13 mm (½ in) top stitching. Cut out.

Figure 8.17

a

b Completed pattern

Figure 8.18

Twelve-gored skirt

Figure 8.18a Outline flared skirt patterns, Figure 8.9c and d. Divide each pattern into three equal sections. Grain line runs down centre of each gore. Place balance marks. Trace pattern sections onto new paper.

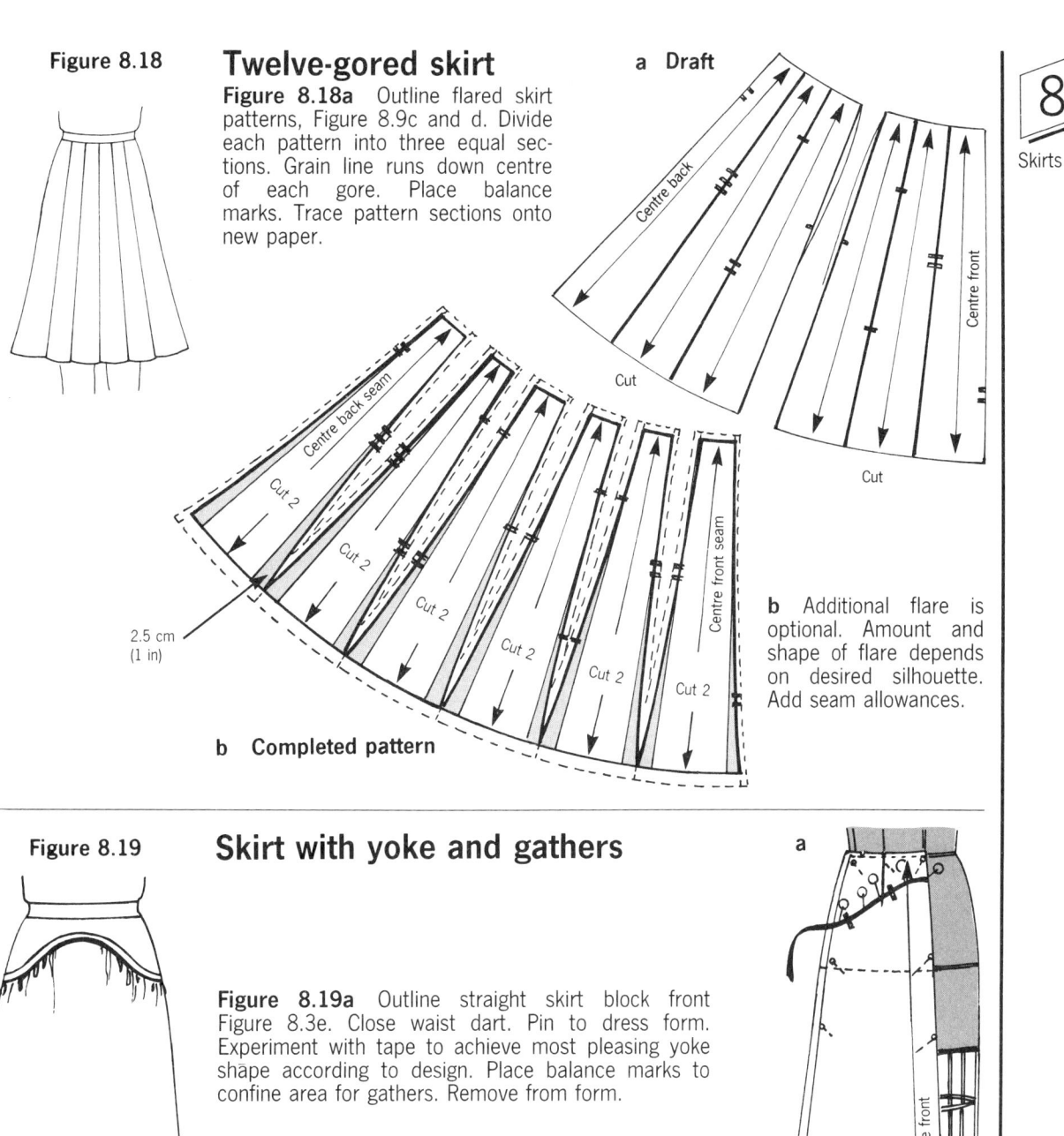

a Draft

b Additional flare is optional. Amount and shape of flare depends on desired silhouette. Add seam allowances.

b Completed pattern

2.5 cm (1 in)

Figure 8.19

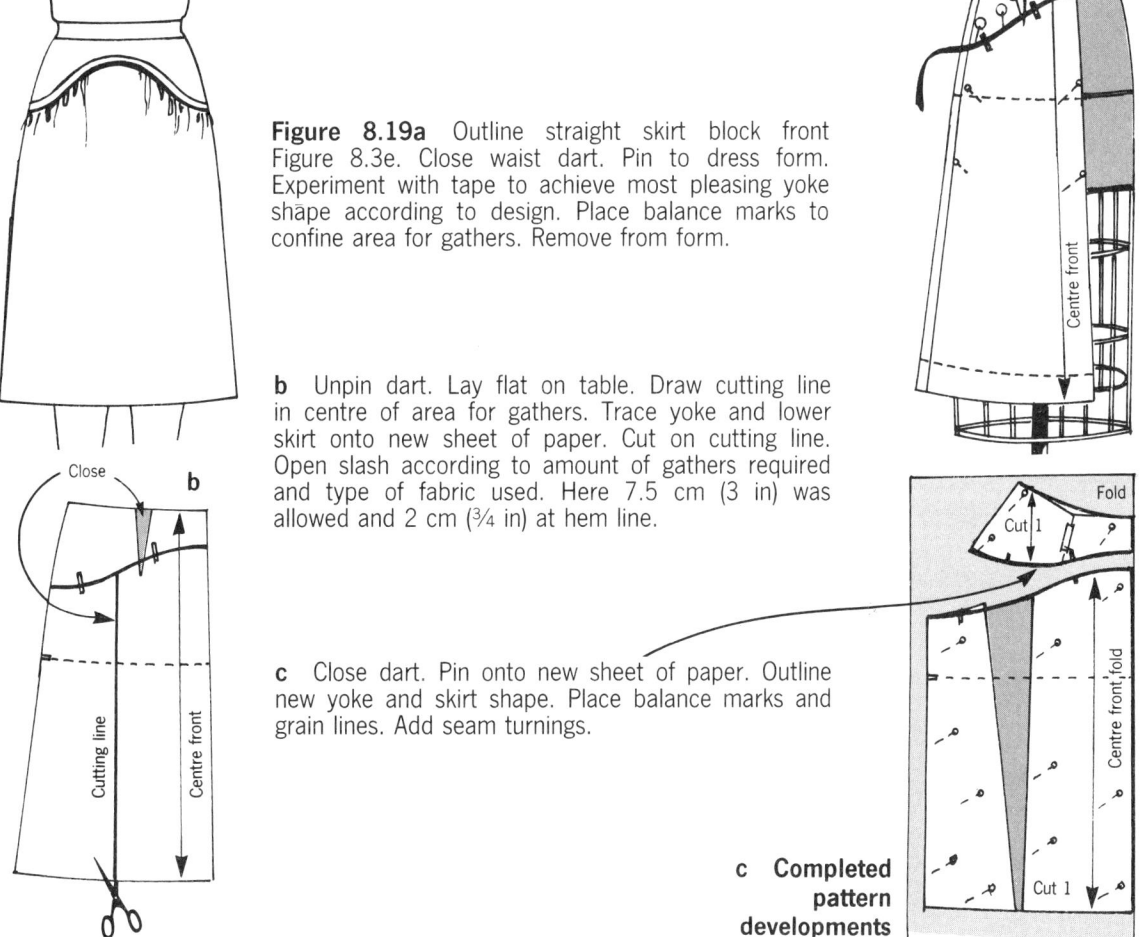

Skirt with yoke and gathers

Figure 8.19a Outline straight skirt block front Figure 8.3e. Close waist dart. Pin to dress form. Experiment with tape to achieve most pleasing yoke shape according to design. Place balance marks to confine area for gathers. Remove from form.

b Unpin dart. Lay flat on table. Draw cutting line in centre of area for gathers. Trace yoke and lower skirt onto new sheet of paper. Cut on cutting line. Open slash according to amount of gathers required and type of fabric used. Here 7.5 cm (3 in) was allowed and 2 cm (¾ in) at hem line.

c Close dart. Pin onto new sheet of paper. Outline new yoke and skirt shape. Place balance marks and grain lines. Add seam turnings.

c Completed pattern developments

Six-gored flared skirt with knife pleats

Figure 8.20a Outline straight skirt block, Figure 8.3e. Lengthen waist dart to 15 cm (6 in). Draw dotted line from dart point parallel to centre front line.

b Add 2.5 cm (1 in) flare to side seam. Measure 5 cm (2 in) each side of dotted line at hem line. Connect to dart (flare) point. Place balance marks and grain lines. Trace sections to new paper.

c Add 5 cm (2 in) for pleat each side of dotted line. Add seam allowances.

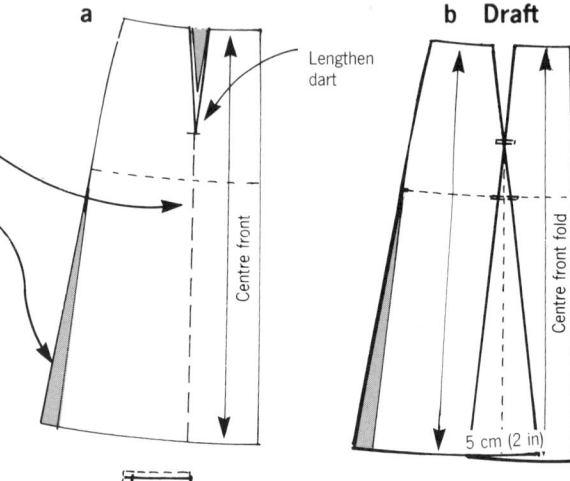

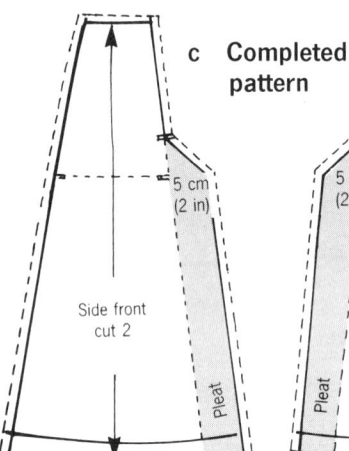

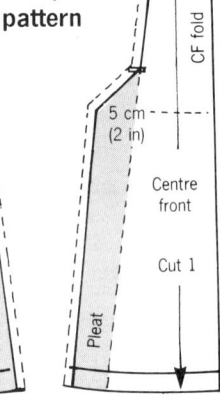

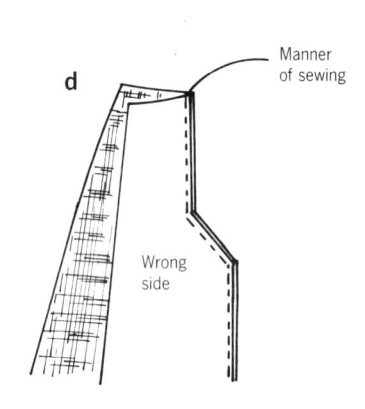

Six-gored skirt with inverted pleats, pockets and flaps

Figure 8.21a Draw a 76 cm (30 in) long vertical line on paper. Using completed pattern Figure 8.20c fold under front and side gore pleats. Crease. Place to vertical line. Outline. Remove pattern.

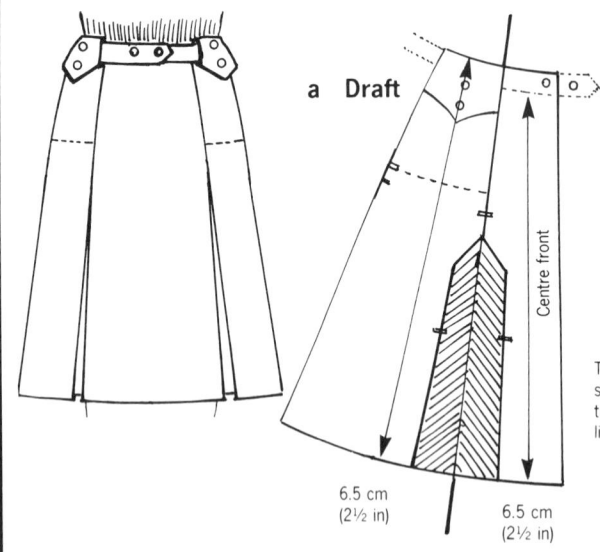

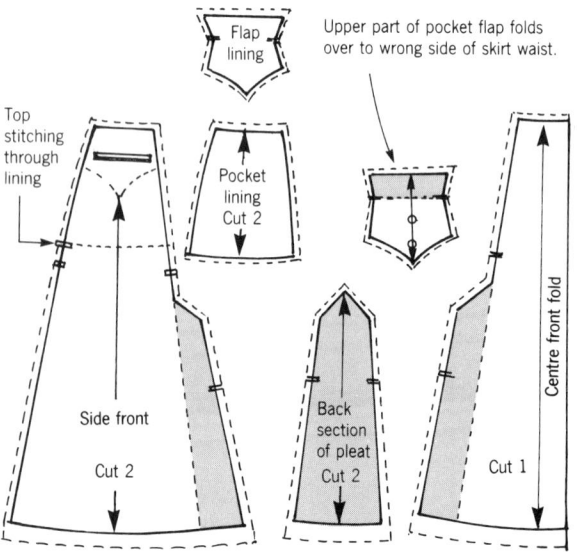

b Complete draft recording all relevant information including position of pocket and flap. Trace all pattern sections onto new sheet of paper. Cut pocket flap lining 3 mm (1/8 in) smaller on outer edge.

Skirt with front seaming and gathers – modelled

Figure 8.22

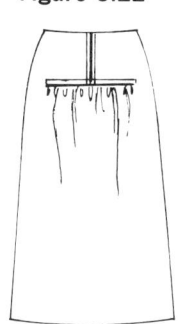

b Draw hip line at right angle to CF to align with hip line on dress form. Outline side seam of straight skirt Figure 8.3e allowing 2.5 cm (1 in) seam turning. Drop straight grain line at right angle from hip to hemline. Pin to dress form aligning side seams from waist to hip line.

Smooth waistline to dress form. Slash at intervals. Pin.

c Cut from CF edge in line with marked style tape to within end of taped style line for gathering.

Complete pinning waistline until CF style tape is reached. The marked waistline should be slightly curved upwards. Trim excess fabric beyond CF seam.

Gather lower section according to desired fulness.

d Pin upper 'yoke' section over lower gathered section turning under a narrow seam allowance. Mark all new seam and style lines. Place balance marks.

Remove from form. True all newly created lines. Trace onto paper. Add seam allowances, grain line and cutting instructions. The finished pattern should look very similar to Figure 8.23b (cut flat).

Figure 8.22a Outline position of design feature with style tape.

Tear on grain calico or muslin: Length of skirt plus hem allowance plus 7.5 cm (3 in) above waist multiplied by width: ¼ hip measurement plus at least half this amount for gathers. Add 1.2 cm (½ in) ease plus 2.5 cm (1 in) side seam allowance equals approx. 71 × 43 cm (28 × 17 in).

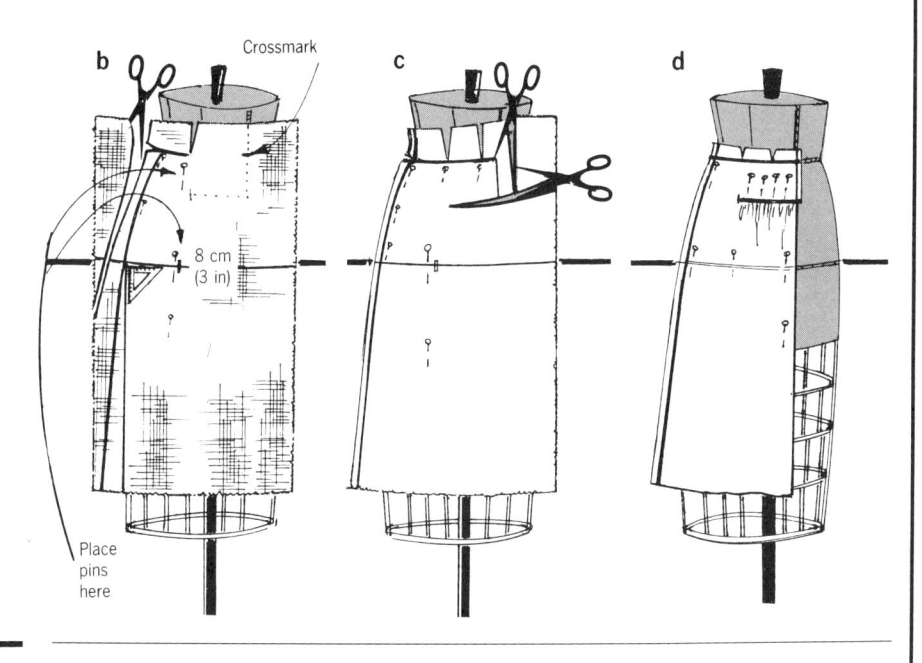

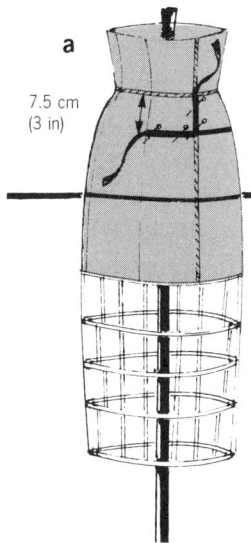

Skirt with front seaming and gathers – cut flat

Figure 8.23a Draft: outline straight skirt **Figure 8.3e**.

Draw style line 7.5 cm (3 in) below waistline and at right angle to CF.

Add a minimum of 4–5 cm (1½–2 in) for gathers beyond centre front.

b Cut on style line. Close waist dart. Add seam allowances, balance marks and cutting instructions.

Figure 8.23

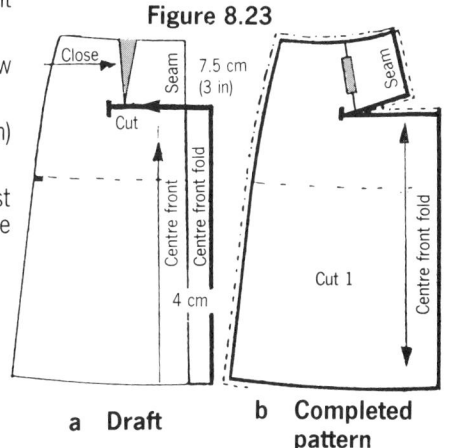

a Draft   b Completed pattern

Skirt with yoke feature and gathers – modelled

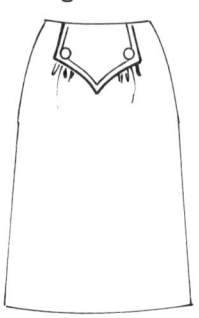

Figure 8.24

Figure 8.24a Outline design feature with style tape.

Tear on grain calico or muslin: length of skirt plus hem allowance plus 7.5 cm (3 in) above waist x width: ¼ hip measurement plus at least half this amount for gathers.

Add 1.2 cm (½ in) ease plus 2.5 cm (1 in) side seam allowance equals approximately 71 × 43 cm (28 × 17 in).

b Draw hip line to CF to align with hip line on dress form. Pin CF of muslin to CF of dress form. Mark waistline to 5 cm (2 in) from CF.

Pin. Slash as shown. Place two more pins, one at hip level the other 13 cm (5 in) further down; both are 5 cm (2 in) from CF. Taped outline on dress form indicates gathering should begin from this point.

Lift and smooth fabric largely from side waist and upper hip area and to a lesser extent from below hip line towards the gathering area.

c Pin into tiny pleats between pin and point of taped style feature on dress form.

Fold short waist dart in line with taped style line (this should coincide with the normal position of this dart). Mark dart lines. Complete waistline and mark side seam. Cut away small section at CF.

d Tear muslin to cover taped design feature on dress form, (approximately 15 cm (6 in) x 13 cm (5 in). Mark style line. Remove from form. Recut with even seam allowance.

e Turn under seams. Return to form. Pin into place.

Mark edges and fitting lines. Place balance marks for confining position of gathers. Remove from form. True all new lines. Trace onto pattern paper. Add seam allowances, grain lines and cutting instructions.

The finished pattern should look very similar to Figure 8.25a (cut flat).

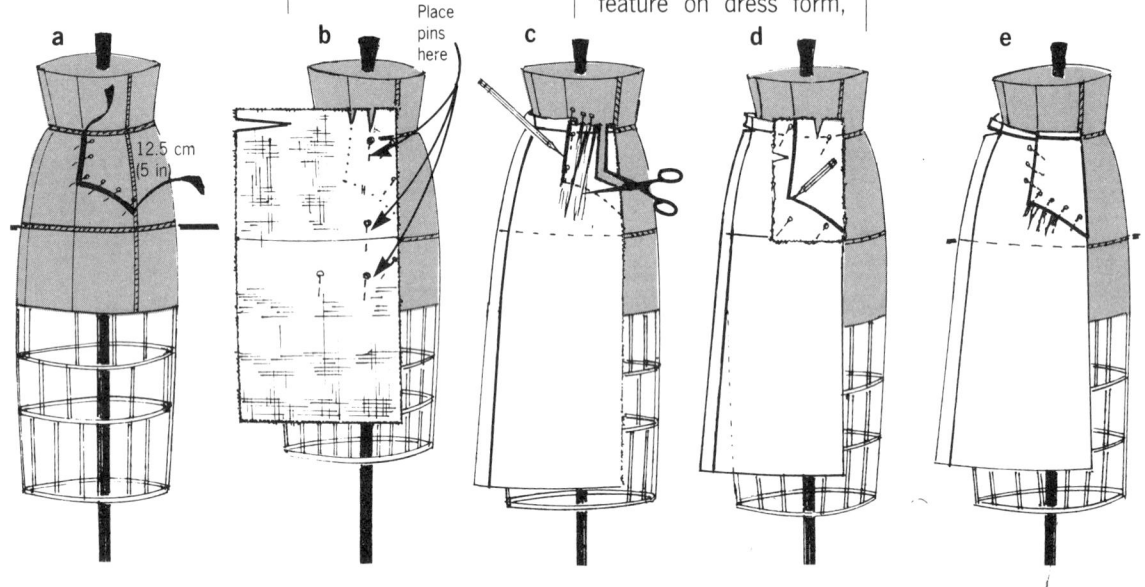

Skirt with yoke feature and gathers – cut flat

Figure 8.25a Outline straight skirt, Figure 8.3e. Draw hip line.

Draw style line using inner waist dart line, as shown in diagram.

Draw slash line, balance mark, grain line.

b Trace sections onto pattern paper. Cut and open slash line by amount shown. True all lines. Add seam allowances and cutting instructions.

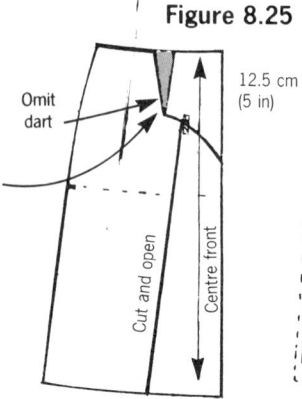

Figure 8.25

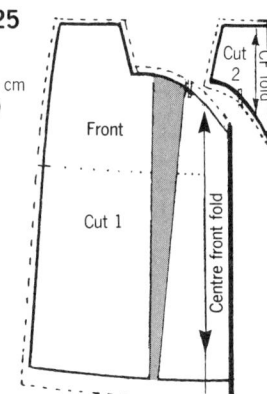

a Draft   b Completed pattern

Figure 8.26

Skirt with gathered centre front panel

Experiment on dress form with possible style lines before transferring lines to draft. For this design outline flared skirt, Figure 8.9d (page 107).

Add 4 cm (1½ inches)

4 cm (1½ in)

a Draft

b Completed pattern

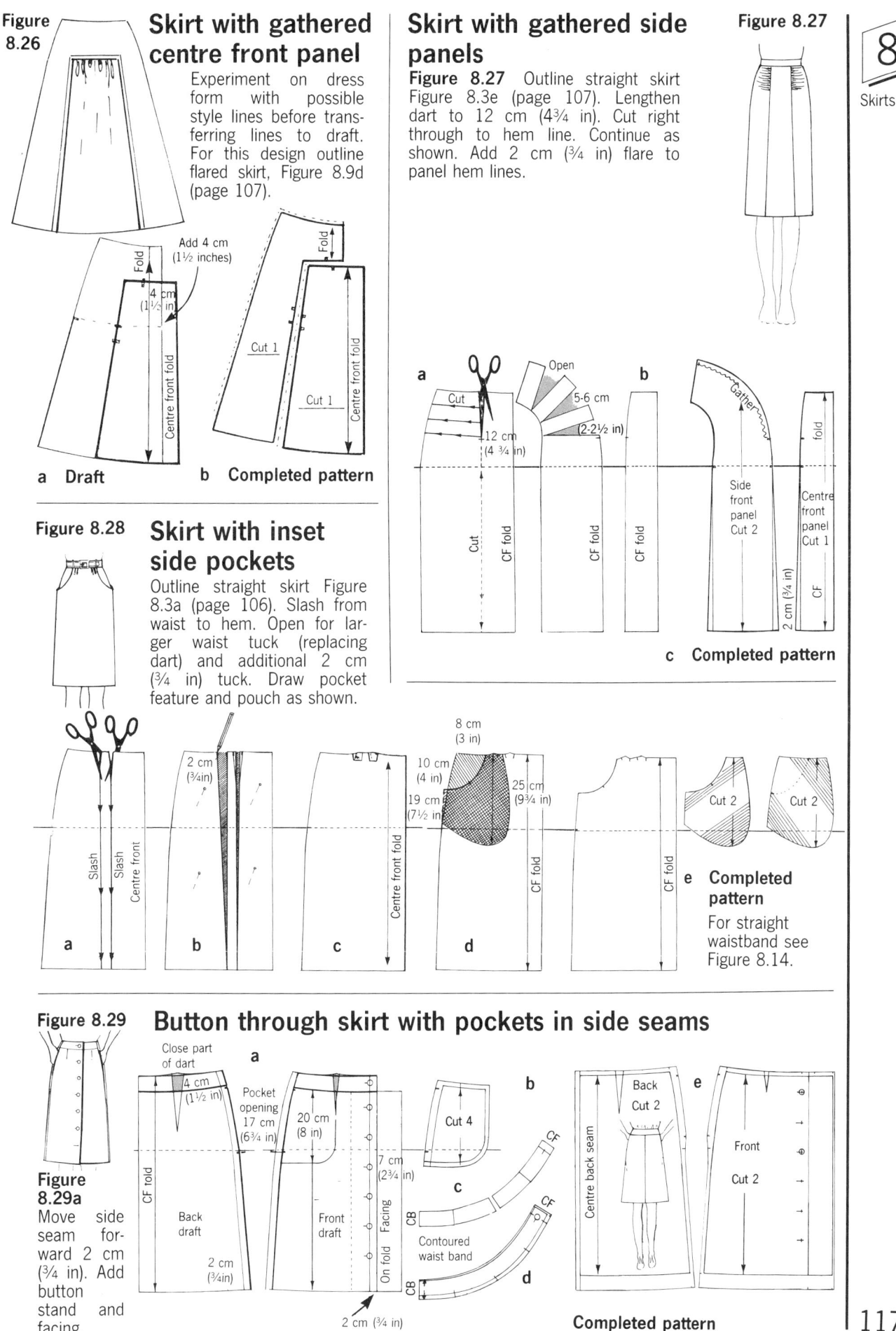

Skirt with gathered side panels

Figure 8.27 Outline straight skirt Figure 8.3e (page 107). Lengthen dart to 12 cm (4¾ in). Cut right through to hem line. Continue as shown. Add 2 cm (¾ in) flare to panel hem lines.

Figure 8.27

8 Skirts

a Cut — 12 cm (4¾ in) Open 5–6 cm (2–2½ in)

b Gather Side front panel Cut 2 Centre front panel Cut 1 2 cm (¾ in)

c Completed pattern

Figure 8.28

Skirt with inset side pockets

Outline straight skirt Figure 8.3a (page 106). Slash from waist to hem. Open for larger waist tuck (replacing dart) and additional 2 cm (¾ in) tuck. Draw pocket feature and pouch as shown.

a Slash Slash Centre front

b 2 cm (¾ in)

c Centre front fold

d 8 cm (3 in) 10 cm (4 in) 19 cm (7½ in) 25 cm (9¾ in) CF fold

Cut 2 Cut 2

e Completed pattern

For straight waistband see Figure 8.14.

Figure 8.29

Button through skirt with pockets in side seams

Figure 8.29a Move side seam forward 2 cm (¾ in). Add button stand and facing.

a Close part of dart 4 cm (1½ in) Pocket opening 17 cm (6¾ in) 20 cm (8 in) 7 cm (2¾ in) CF fold Back draft Front draft Facing On fold 2 cm (¾ in) 2 cm (¾ in)

b Cut 4

c CF CB Contoured waist band

d CB CF

e Back Cut 2 Centre back seam Front Cut 2

Completed pattern

117

Wrap-over skirt with side pleats

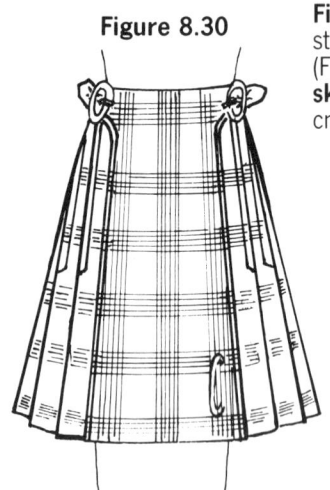

Figure 8.30

Figure 8.30a Cut two whole straight skirt fronts in calico (Figure 8.3e). Mark one **under skirt**, the other **front wrap**. Add 5 cm (2 in) above waistline.

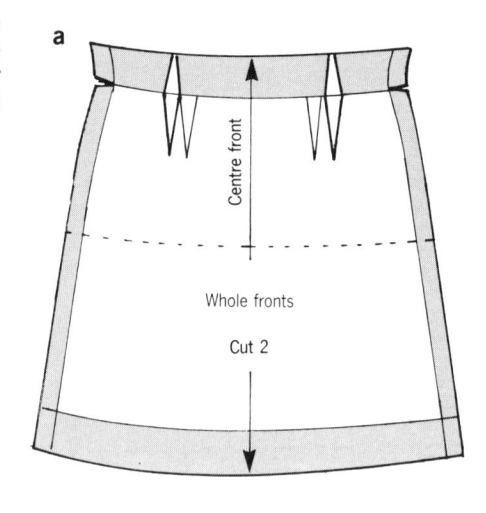

Centre front — Whole fronts — Cut 2

b Cut one whole skirt back in calico. Raise waist line by 5 cm (2 in) as above.

Move waist darts 2.5 cm (1 in) towards side seams.

c Pin together left front under skirt side seam and left back side seam. Pin to dress form. Roughly pin together right side seam to keep in position.

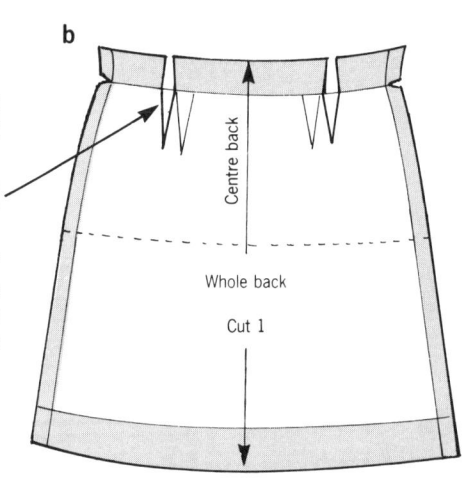

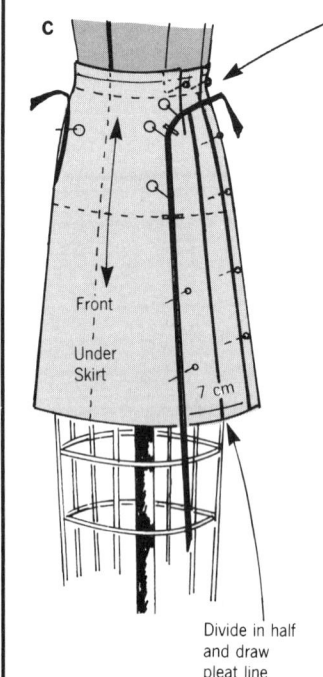

Centre back — Whole back — Cut 1

Front Under Skirt — 7 cm — Divide in half and draw pleat line

d With tape outline style lines on right and left side, back and front, and outline both sides as much as possible.

The distance from side seam to style line at hem level is approximately 7 cm (2¾ in). Divide this area evenly for pleats (ignore darts). The side seam will become one pleat. There are three pleats altogether.

Mark all new lines with soft pencil, true them as you go along. Place balance marks and grain lines.

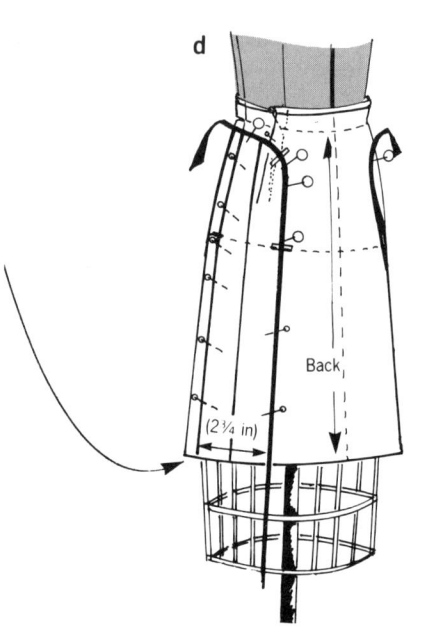

Back (2¾ in)

e Unpin right side seam to waist. Cut away right side front section of under skirt. Leave right back section undisturbed. The cut-away section can be discarded.

f Pin front wrap to right side seam. Wrap over to left side seam. Pin.

g Mark style line in accordance with previously drawn line on under skirt. Cut away excess fabric adding 13 mm (½ in) to cover style line on under skirt. This reveals marked pleats section of under skirt. Mark slightly raised waist line.

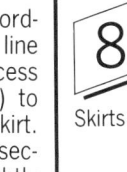

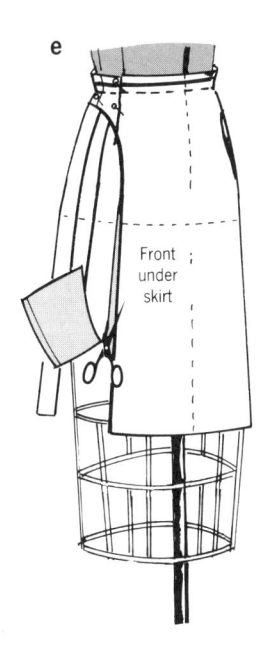

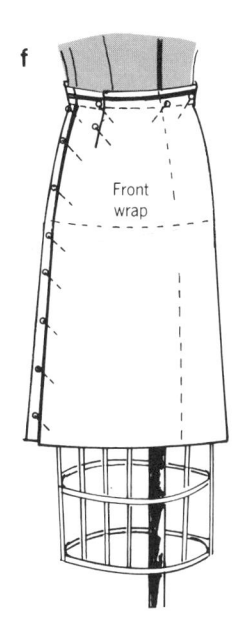

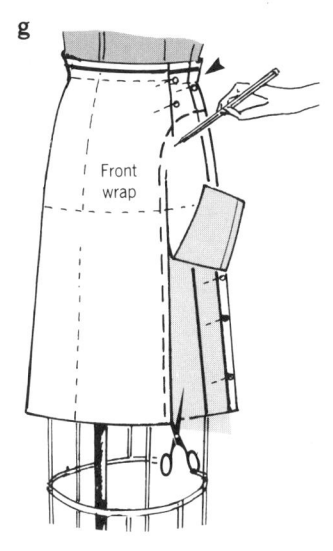

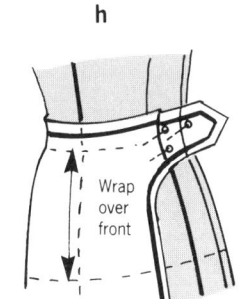

h Pin small piece of calico belt to side seam.

Right side view

i Mark anew all style lines. Place balance marks. Remove from form. Cut on style line. Close darts permanently.

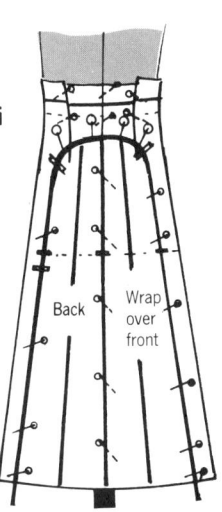

j Draw long, horizontal hip level line on paper.

Number and cut pleat sections. Pin to sheet of paper aligning hip lines. Draft pleats between each section as shown.

Lay flat on table. True new lines. Trace onto new pattern paper. Add seam allowances.

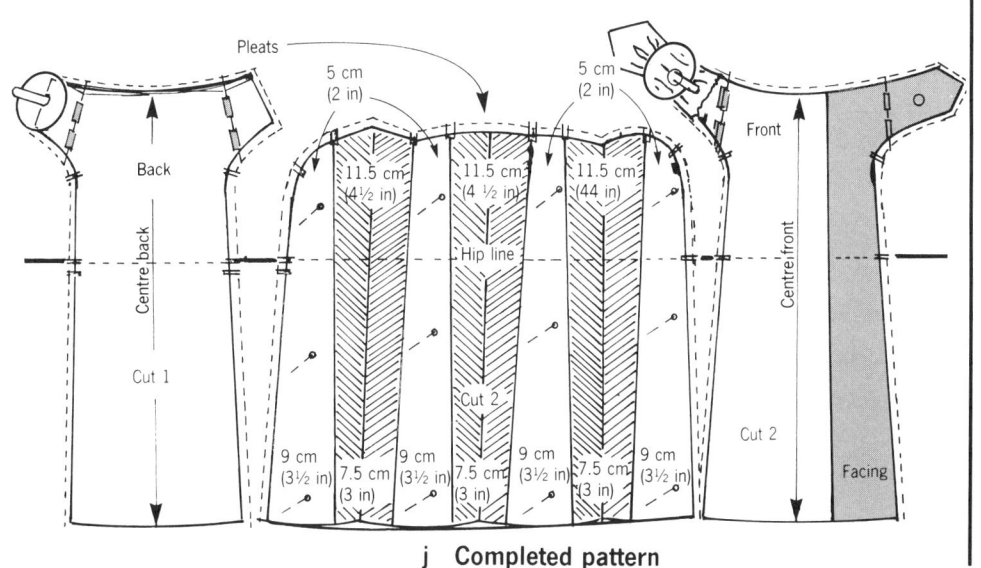

j Completed pattern

Half circle skirt – modelled

Figure 8.31

Waist measurement: 64 cm (25 in)

Figure 8.31a Tear square calico or muslin 76 × 76 cm (30 × 30 in) Mark right straight grain edge centre front, and straight edge at right angles to it, centre back. Mark short guide lines 20.5 cm (8 in) from point ○.

b Pin to dress form with CF short guide line matching waistline on form. Slash as shown.

c, d and **e** Allow grain to drop and pin. Continue in this way pinning and dropping grain line periodically at waistline until arrived at CB guide line. Observe hip line. Mark waist and hem lines.

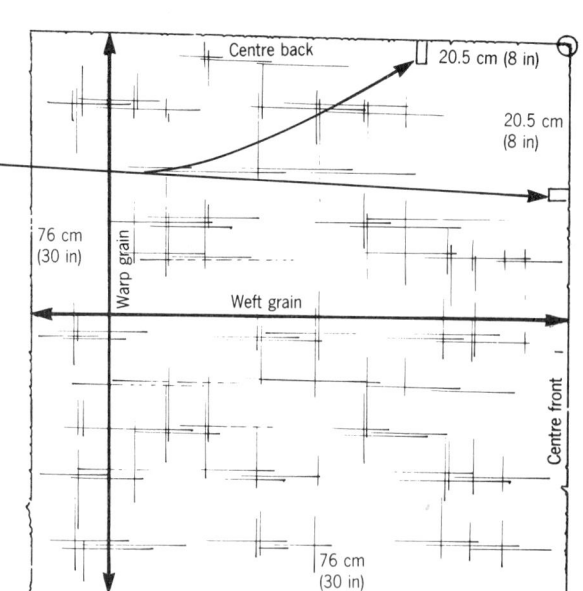

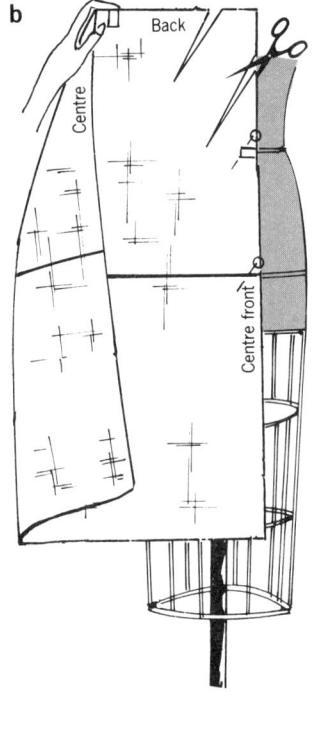

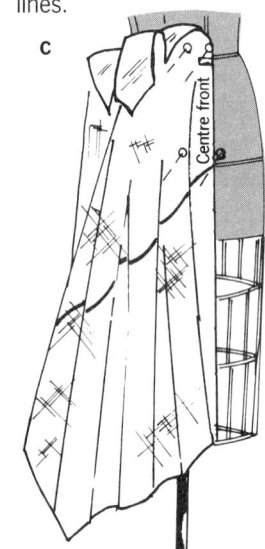

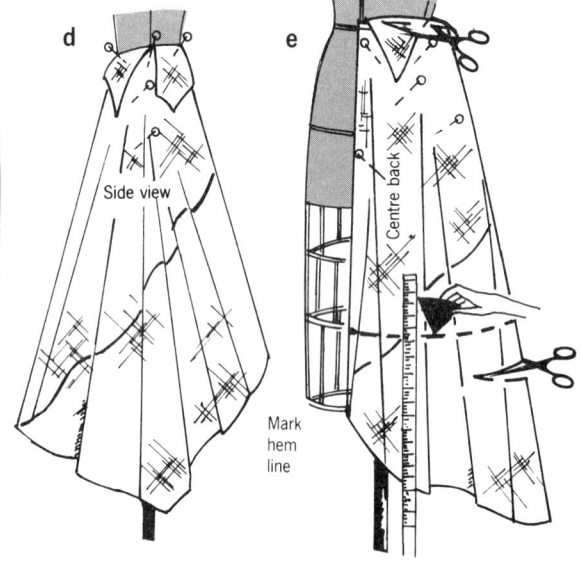

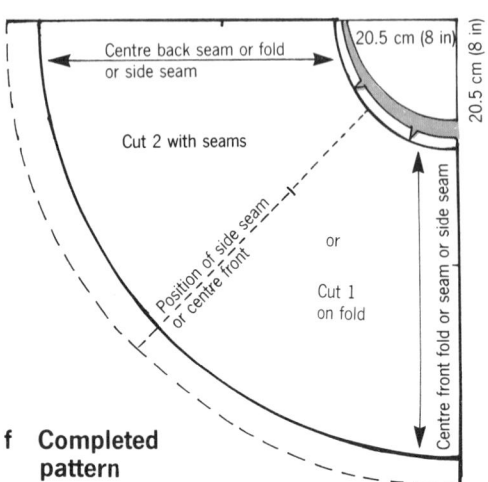

Remove toile from form, lay flat and true waist and hem lines. Transfer to pattern paper. Add seam allowances, grain lines and cutting instructions.

This pattern can be used in different ways according to design and width of material.

f Completed pattern

Figure 8.32

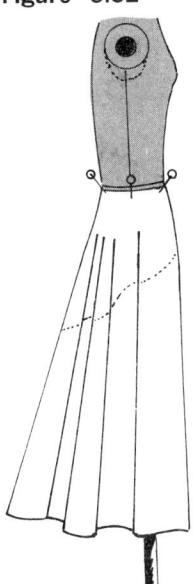

Half circle skirt with flare at back – modelled

Figure 8.32a When modelling the half circle skirt Figure 8.31, it was observed that it was possible to influence the hang and flare of the skirt by lowering or raising the grain of the modelling fabric at specific points, pinning as one went along to obtain a smooth waistline.

Whereas the flare in the half circle skirt, Figure 8.31, is evenly distributed around the dress form, in this skirt the flare has a higher concentration at the back. The length of the modelling fabric is the same as in Figure 8.31 but the modelling technique is somewhat different and would be further affected if a fabric of another weight or texture was used.

All guide lines and approximate measurements are suggestions for the beginner and should be disregarded once a greater facility in modelling has been achieved.

Waist measurement: 64 cm (25 in)

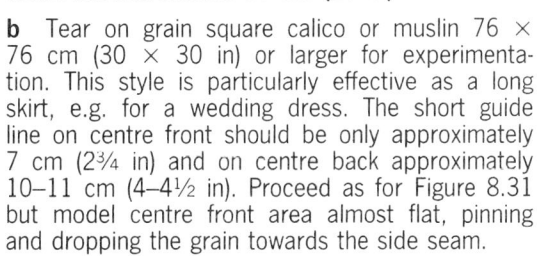

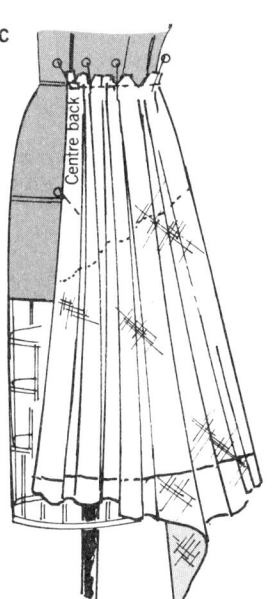

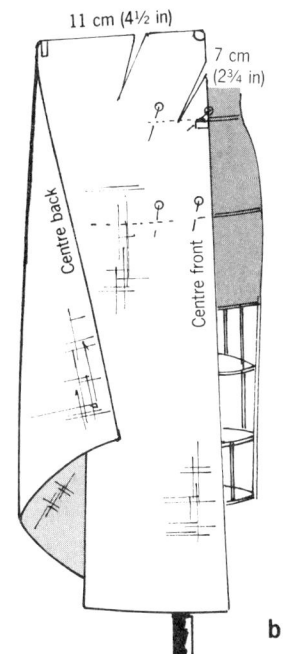

b Tear on grain square calico or muslin 76 × 76 cm (30 × 30 in) or larger for experimentation. This style is particularly effective as a long skirt, e.g. for a wedding dress. The short guide line on centre front should be only approximately 7 cm (2¾ in) and on centre back approximately 10–11 cm (4–4½ in). Proceed as for Figure 8.31 but model centre front area almost flat, pinning and dropping the grain towards the side seam.

c Gradually raise grain as you approach centre back waist area. This will create a greater concentration of flare beginning above hip level.

Mark waist and hem lines. Remove from form. True these lines. Trim excess fabric. Return to form for final check for fit. Transfer to pattern paper. Add seam allowances, grain lines and cutting instructions.

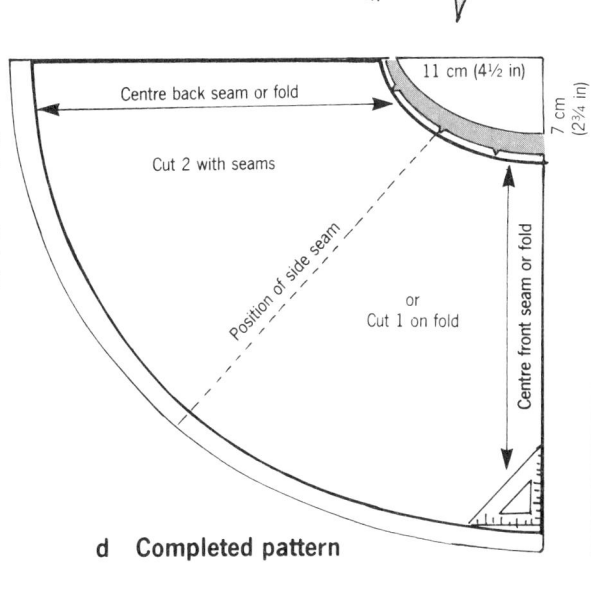

d Completed pattern

Figure 8.33

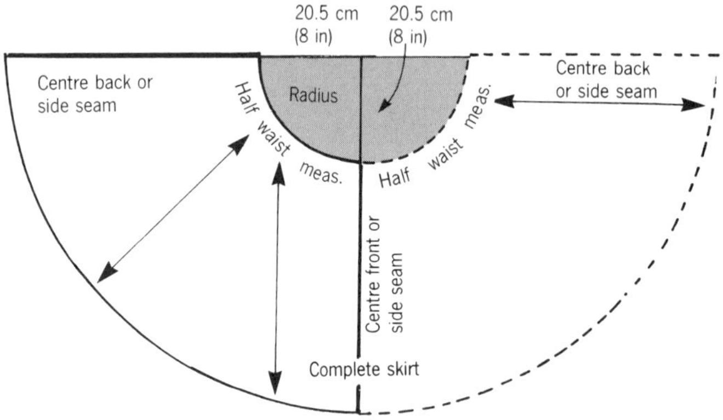

Waist measurement: 64 cm (25 in)
Bias waist lines of circular skirts have a tendency to stretch. This makes it necessary to deduct 2.5 cm (1 in) from the waist measurement before constructing the pattern.

This skirt has one seam, either at centre back or at centre front. Side seams and/or an additional centre seam can be introduced. The choice is often governed by the width of the fabric to be used. Long skirts require a greater width of fabric than very short ones.

Method of construction:
The radius is one third of the waist measurement, i.e. 64 − 2.5 = 61.5 cm ÷ 3 = 20.5 cm (25 − 1 = 24 in ÷ 3 = 8 in).

Full circle skirt – cut flat

Waist measurement: 64 cm (25 in)

Radius equals half of 20.5 cm (8 in) (see Figure 8.33).

Figure 8.34

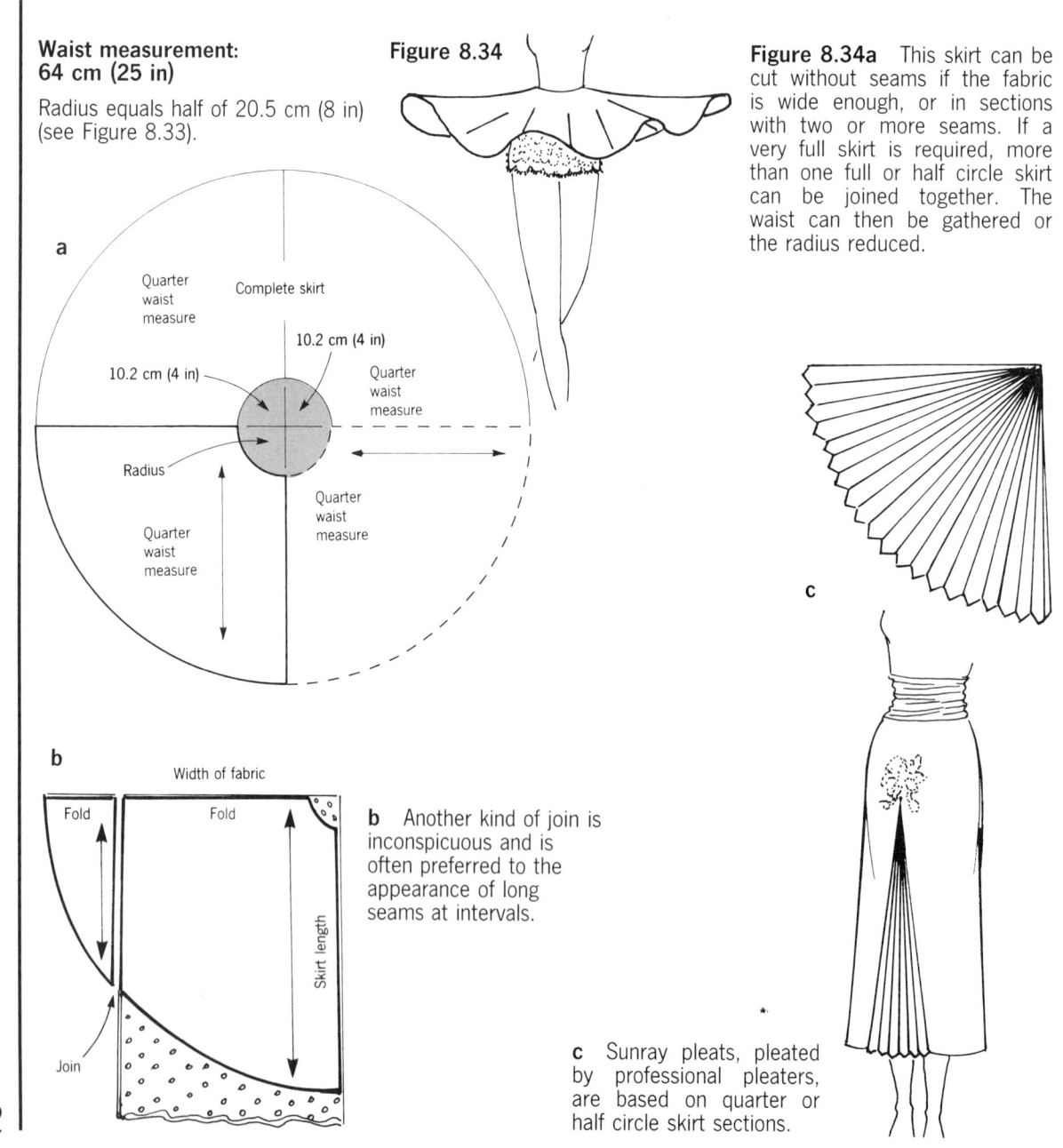

Figure 8.34a This skirt can be cut without seams if the fabric is wide enough, or in sections with two or more seams. If a very full skirt is required, more than one full or half circle skirt can be joined together. The waist can then be gathered or the radius reduced.

b Another kind of join is inconspicuous and is often preferred to the appearance of long seams at intervals.

c Sunray pleats, pleated by professional pleaters, are based on quarter or half circle skirt sections.

Quarter circle skirt – cut flat

Figure 8.35

Figure 8.35a Dotted line indicates a possible seam line. Chevron effects can be achieved by varying the grain line.

Basic circular skirt block
Test and perfect full, half and quarter circle skirts. Incorporate them in one basic circular skirt block. Cut in card. Notch and punch the three waist lines for easy marking. Use as shown lengthening the skirt as required.

Waist measurement: 64 cm (25 in)

Radius is twice that shown in Figure 8.33 i.e. 41 cm (16 in)

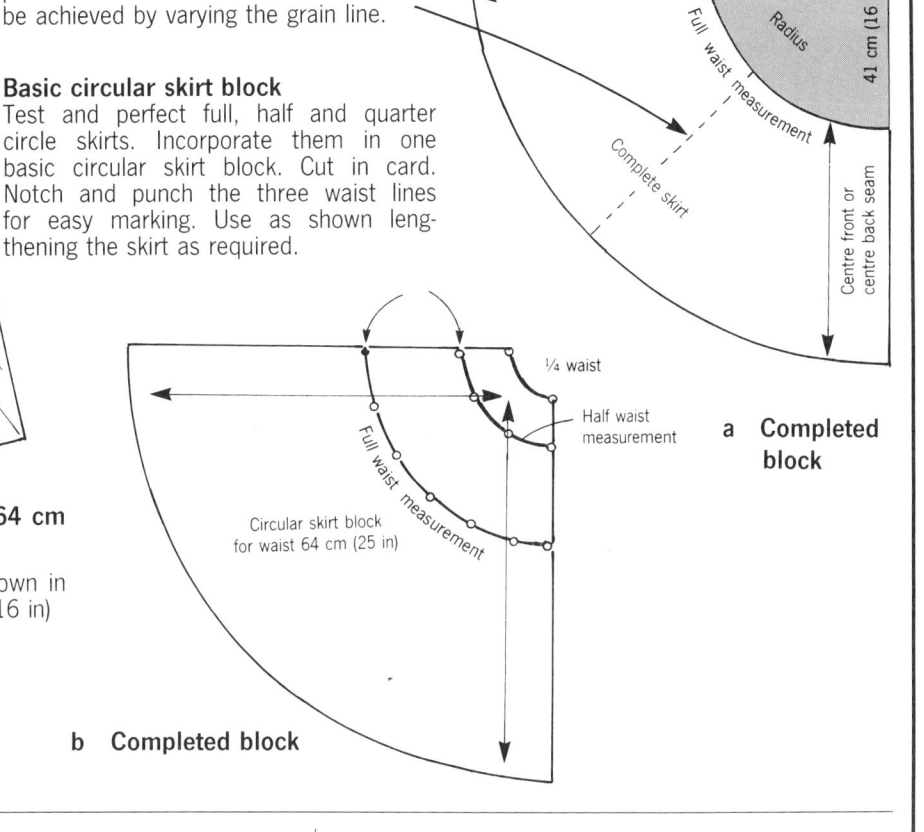

a Completed block

b Completed block

Straight skirts

Figure 8.36

Straight slim-fitting skirt

Figure 8.36 The characteristic of this skirt is its narrow hem line. The width is equal to the hip measurement which tends to restrict movement. For this reason a slit is often introduced.

a Outline straight skirt, Figure 8.3e. Drop a line at right angle from hip line to hem. This line becomes the new side seam.

Straighten waist and hem line.

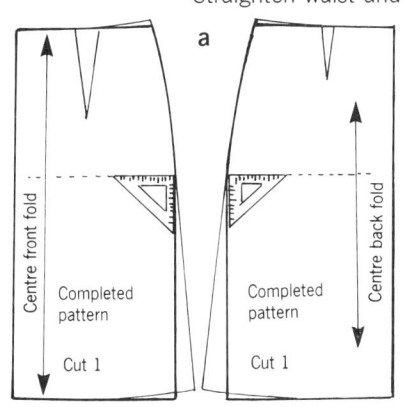

Peg-top skirt

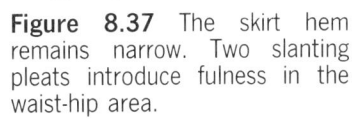

Figure 8.37 The skirt hem remains narrow. Two slanting pleats introduce fulness in the waist-hip area.

a Draw two slash lines. Open out approximately 5 cm (2 in) or according to desired effect.

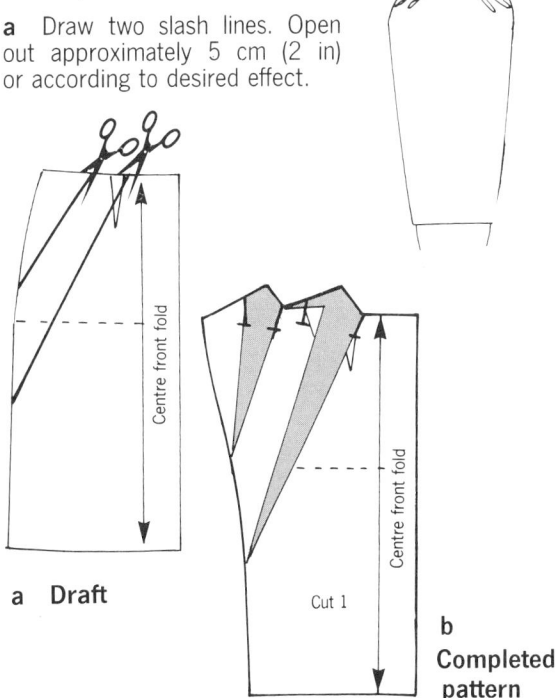

Figure 8.37

a Draft

b Completed pattern

9 Cowl drapery

Figure 9.1 Monk's hood or cowl

Figure 9.2 Doric chiton, 550 BC

The cowl, as we know it today, is named after the hood or cowl worn by monks during the twelfth to fifteenth centuries (Figure 9.1). However, the principle of draping fabric in this way dates back to the Greeks, who draped and pinned their garments to differing effects as long ago as 500 BC (Figure 9.2). The idea was passed on through the ages, influenced by the fashion of the day (Figure 9.3) to the present time (Figure 9.4).

Cowls express a feeling of softness and fluidity; their pleasing folds and play of light and shade enhance the beauty of a fabric and flatter the figure. Cowls are seen on back and front bodices, sleeves, and skirts, in a variety of designs. The kind of fabric used, whether it be rich velvet, slinky silk jersey or shiny slipper satin, greatly influences the appearance. It also has a bearing on the quantity of fabric needed to form pleasing cowl folds.

Initially, cowl features can be cut by the flat pattern cutting method, but it will be found that the desired effect is best achieved by experimenting – by moulding and adjusting folds and drapery, the designer modelling on the figure or on the dress form, preferably in the actual fabric.

The modelling material should resemble as near as possible the weight and handling qualities of the garment fabric. Select from soft muslins and calicoes, cheap jersey fabrics, silky lining material and fabric remnants.

The modelled toile should be carefully marked, with seam allowances, position of darts, folds and gathers indicated clearly. To ensure a good 'hang' of the final garment also place balance marks and grain lines. These data are transferred to the paper pattern for further development and the final making of the planned garment.

Figure 9.3 A day dress incorporating a cowl, 1946

Figure 9.4 A more modern cowl dress

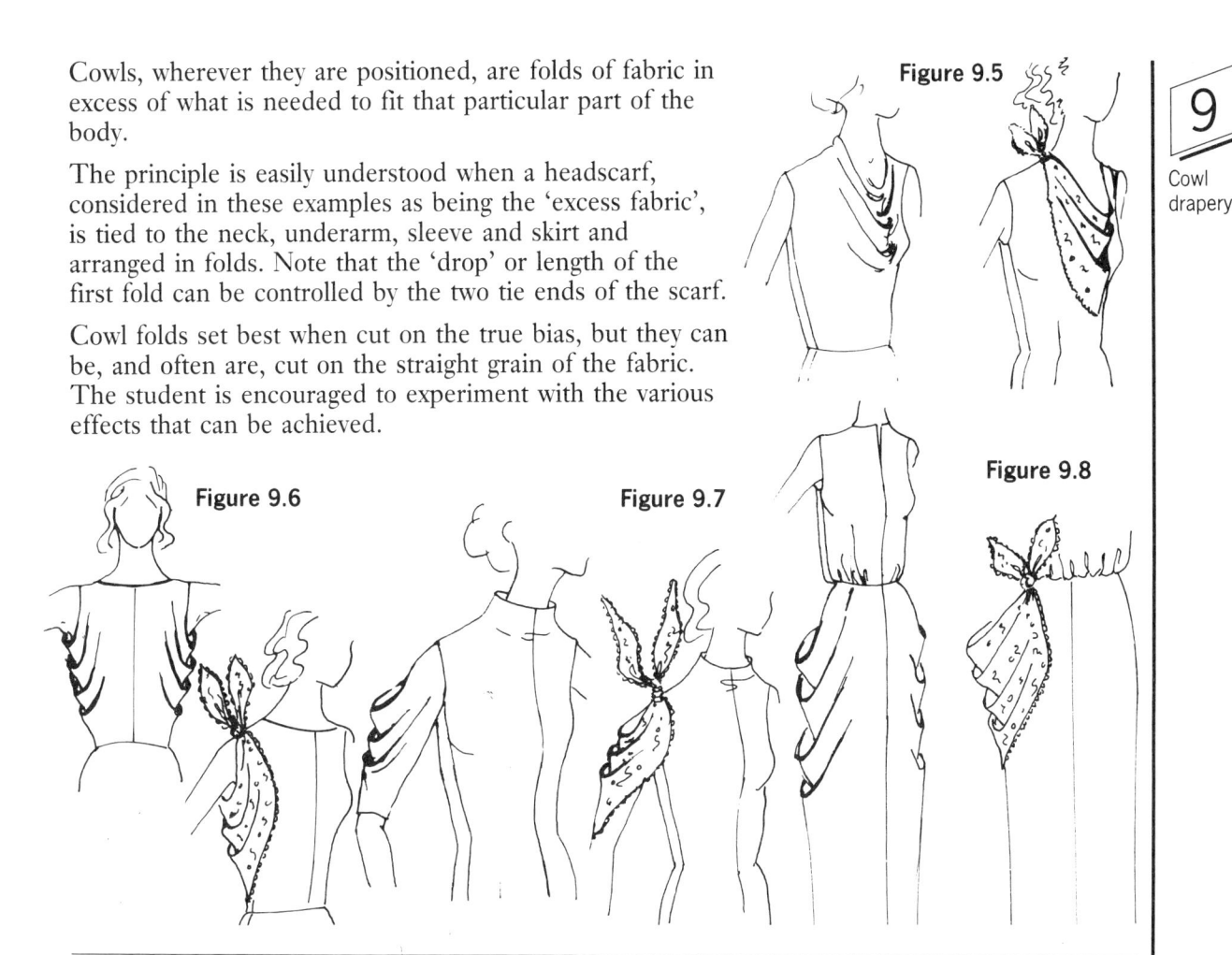

Cowls, wherever they are positioned, are folds of fabric in excess of what is needed to fit that particular part of the body.

The principle is easily understood when a headscarf, considered in these examples as being the 'excess fabric', is tied to the neck, underarm, sleeve and skirt and arranged in folds. Note that the 'drop' or length of the first fold can be controlled by the two tie ends of the scarf.

Cowl folds set best when cut on the true bias, but they can be, and often are, cut on the straight grain of the fabric. The student is encouraged to experiment with the various effects that can be achieved.

9 Cowl drapery

Figure 9.5

Figure 9.6

Figure 9.7

Figure 9.8

Cowl necklines

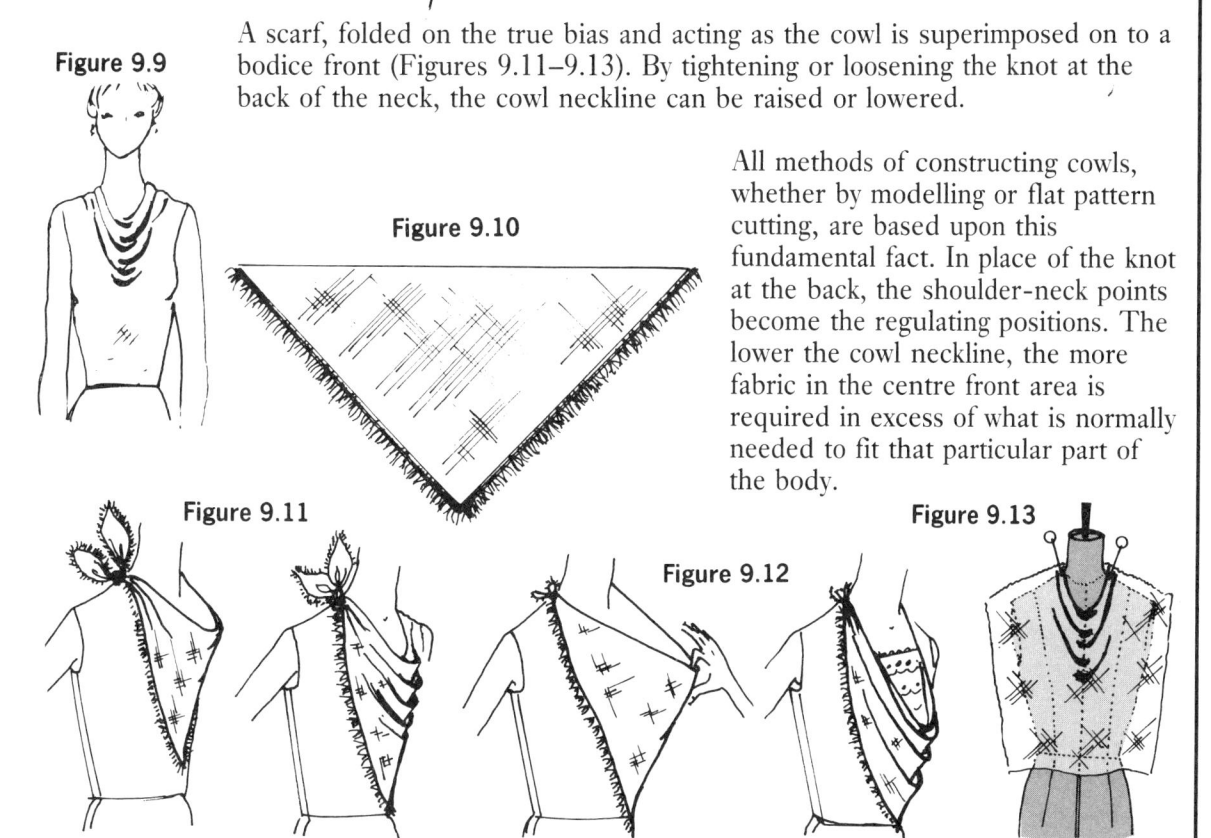

Figure 9.9

A scarf, folded on the true bias and acting as the cowl is superimposed on to a bodice front (Figures 9.11–9.13). By tightening or loosening the knot at the back of the neck, the cowl neckline can be raised or lowered.

Figure 9.10

All methods of constructing cowls, whether by modelling or flat pattern cutting, are based upon this fundamental fact. In place of the knot at the back, the shoulder-neck points become the regulating positions. The lower the cowl neckline, the more fabric in the centre front area is required in excess of what is normally needed to fit that particular part of the body.

Figure 9.11

Figure 9.12

Figure 9.13

125

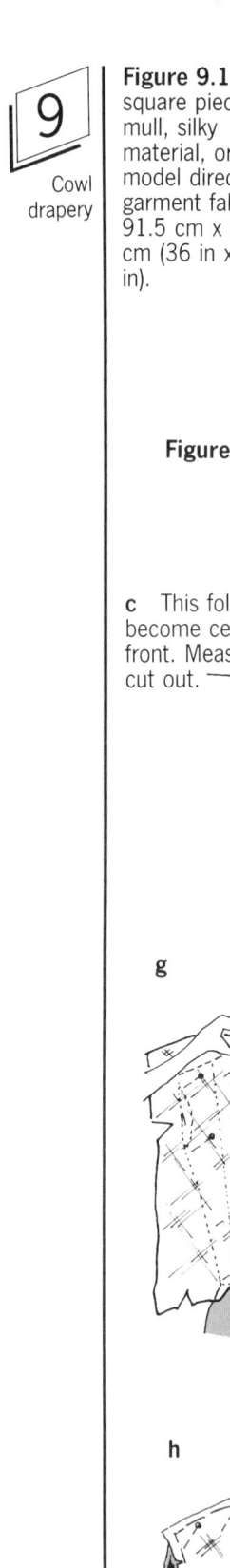

Figure 9.14a Cut square piece of mull, silky material, or model directly in garment fabric, 91.5 cm x 91.5 cm (36 in x 36 in).

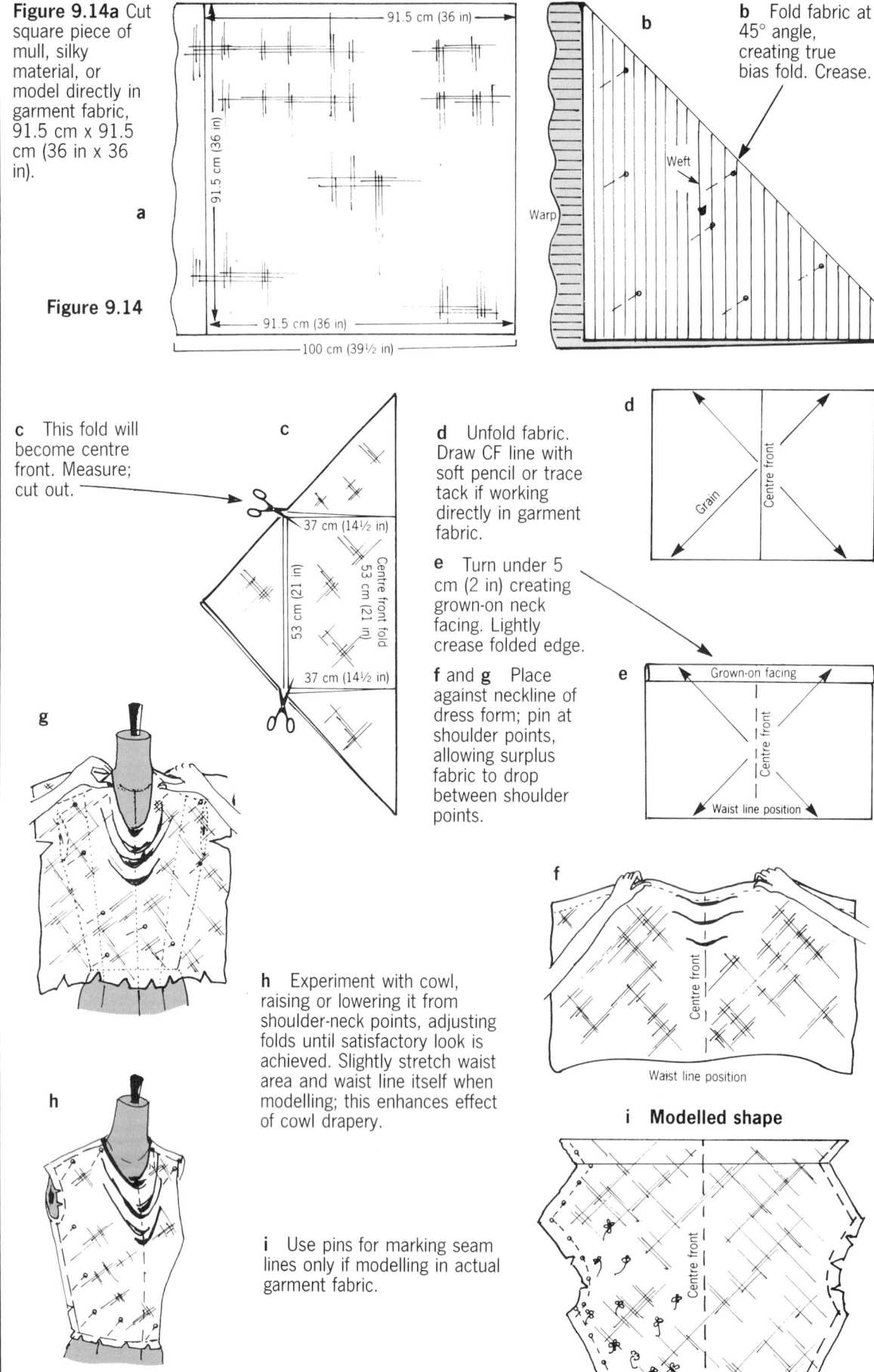

Figure 9.14

b Fold fabric at 45° angle, creating true bias fold. Crease.

c This fold will become centre front. Measure; cut out.

d Unfold fabric. Draw CF line with soft pencil or trace tack if working directly in garment fabric.

e Turn under 5 cm (2 in) creating grown-on neck facing. Lightly crease folded edge.

f and **g** Place against neckline of dress form; pin at shoulder points, allowing surplus fabric to drop between shoulder points.

h Experiment with cowl, raising or lowering it from shoulder-neck points, adjusting folds until satisfactory look is achieved. Slightly stretch waist area and waist line itself when modelling; this enhances effect of cowl drapery.

i Use pins for marking seam lines only if modelling in actual garment fabric.

i Modelled shape

Figure 9.15

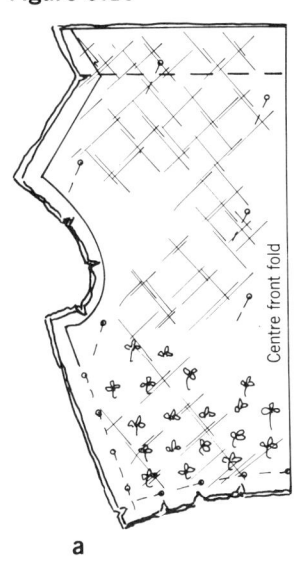

Transfer of markings

Figure 9.15a Whenever an entire garment part, as opposed to only half, is modelled, the marked seam lines of right and left sides will vary, if only slightly. It is essential that both sides are alike. This is achieved by tracing through the markings of the 'better' side to the other side using either a tracing wheel and carbon paper or, when working with garment material, by trace-tacking and pinning through to the other side.

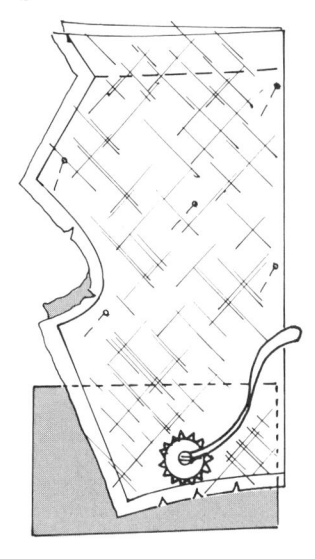

b Working flat on a table, fold model shape on CF (or CB) line without pulling or distorting grain; pin left and right sides together. Markings are transferred from right to left side or vice versa, depending on which side is considered the 'better side'.

Slip carbon paper between two layers at relevant points. With plastic tracing wheel, trace all final markings from one side to the other.

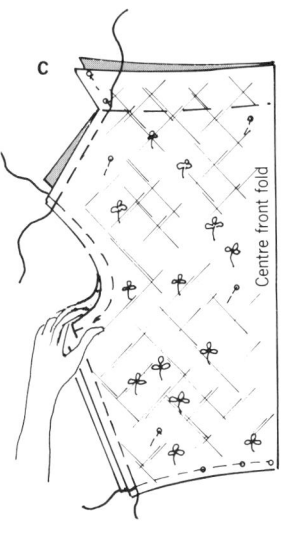

c If final garment fabric was used for modelling, realign and pin on 'better side', true all marked lines and curves, pinning through both layers of fabric. Recut double layer edges of fabric. Trace-tack first one side, pin through to the other, then trace-tack the other side, taking care not to catch the underneath layer when tacking. Remove all pins.

d Transfer modelled shape to pattern paper. Add seam allowances, balance marks and grain lines.

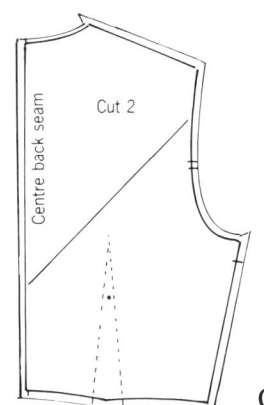

d and e Completed pattern

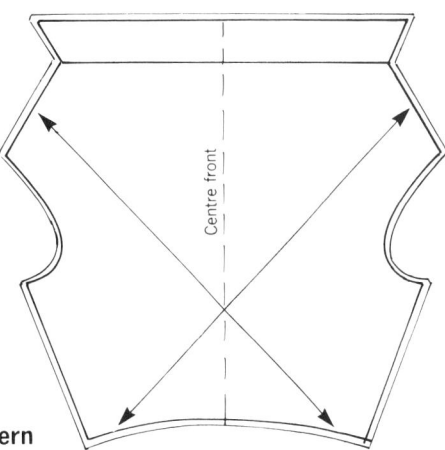

9 Cowl drapery

Cowl neckline cut on the straight grain

Figure 9.16

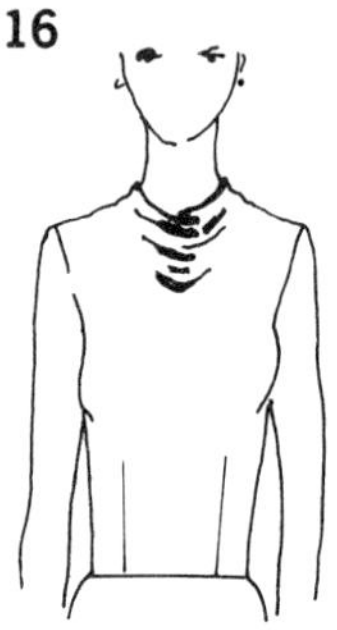

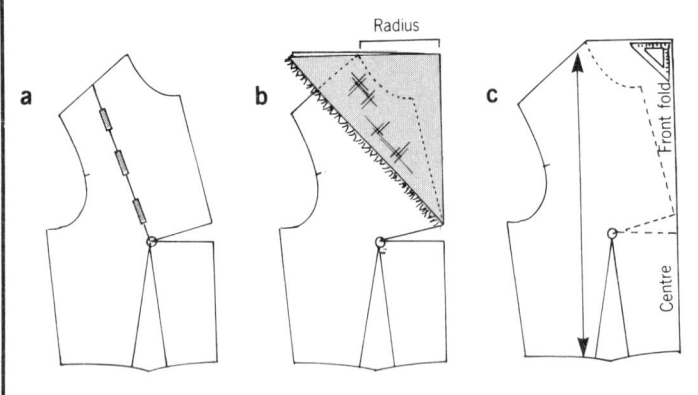

This pattern is cut on the straight grain. The waist dart is retained and produces a high and relatively shallow cowl effect.

Figure 9.16a Outline front bodice. Move shoulder dart to CF.

b Radius is 13 cm (5⅛ in).

d The excess fabric created is indicated by the shaded area.

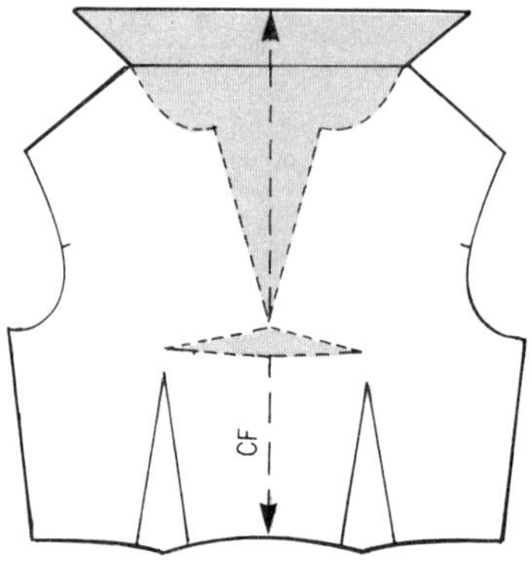

d Completed cowl neck pattern

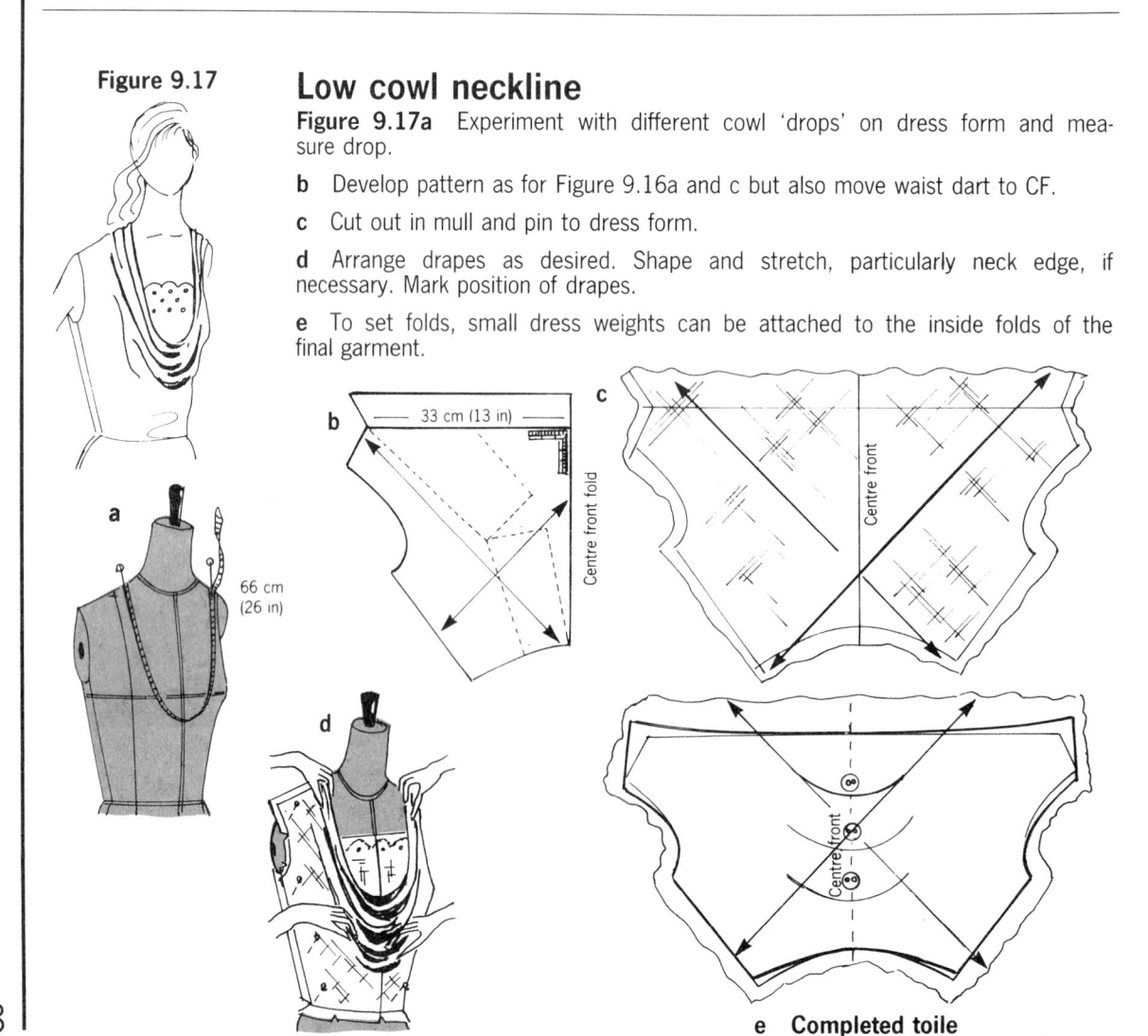

Low cowl neckline

Figure 9.17a Experiment with different cowl 'drops' on dress form and measure drop.

b Develop pattern as for Figure 9.16a and c but also move waist dart to CF.

c Cut out in mull and pin to dress form.

d Arrange drapes as desired. Shape and stretch, particularly neck edge, if necessary. Mark position of drapes.

e To set folds, small dress weights can be attached to the inside folds of the final garment.

e Completed toile

Cowl necklines cut on the straight grain or on the bias

Figure 9.18 shows that the cowl drop, or radius, can be measured from the shoulder neck point to the desired depth of the cowl neckline. From this determined point, square new centre front fold line to centre front waist point. The pattern, complete with turnings and grown-on facing, is placed on either the bias or the straight grain fold of the fabric.

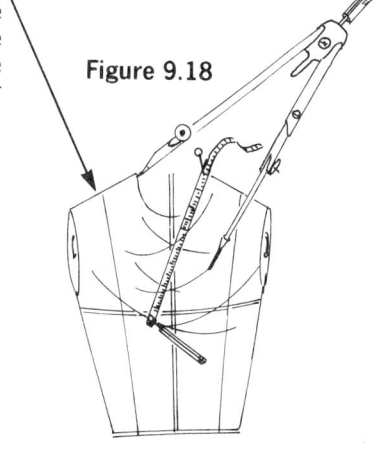

Figure 9.18

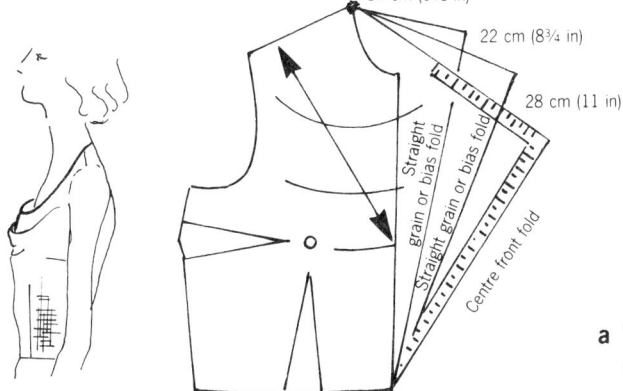

a This style has a waist and an underarm dart

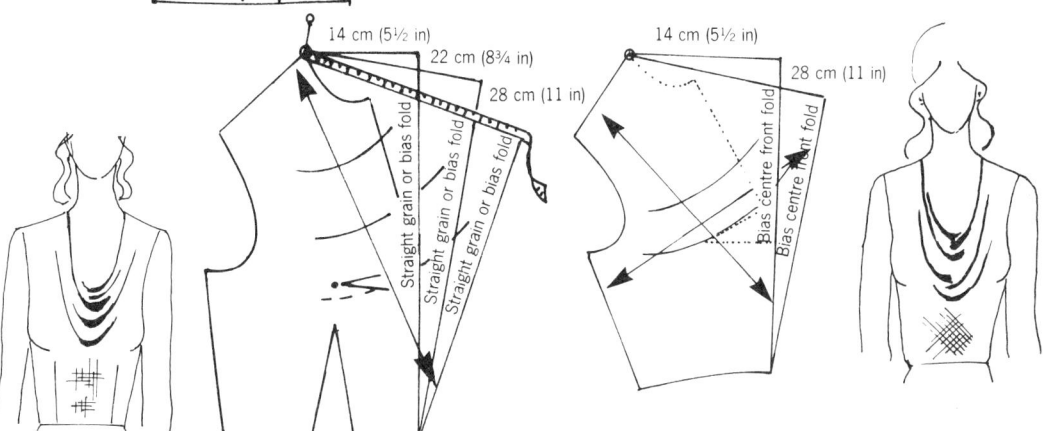

b This style has waist darts only

c This style has no darts and must be cut on the bias

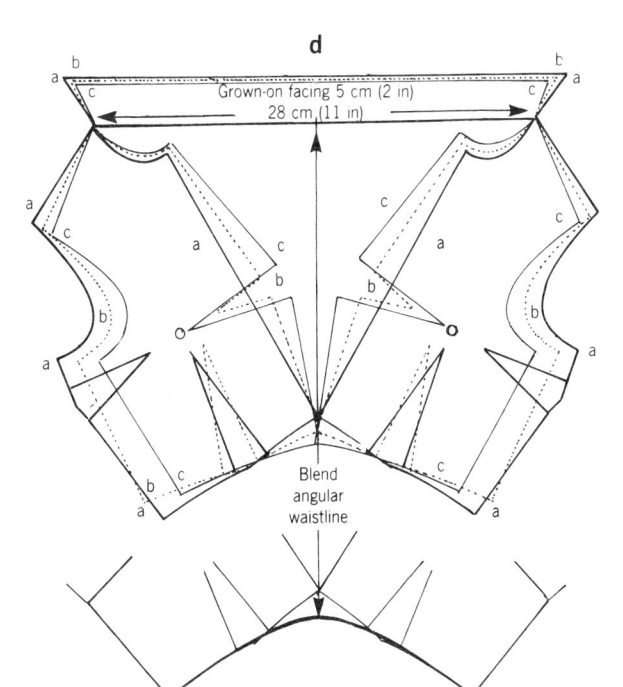

d Although drafts **a**, **b** and **c** have the same radius applied, the completed front patterns differ in each case in the amount of fabric distributed over the whole front area in general, and the centre front cowl area in particular.

When these drafts are superimposed upon each other pattern **a**, irrespective of whether it is cut on the bias or the straight grain, covers a larger area than pattern **c**. Experiment to find out in what way the final appearance of the cowl differs, and which pattern you would use to interpret your design.

Cowl drapery

Figure 9.19

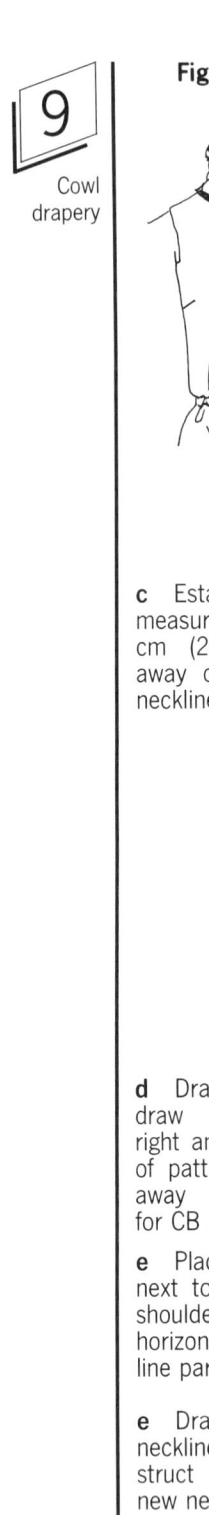

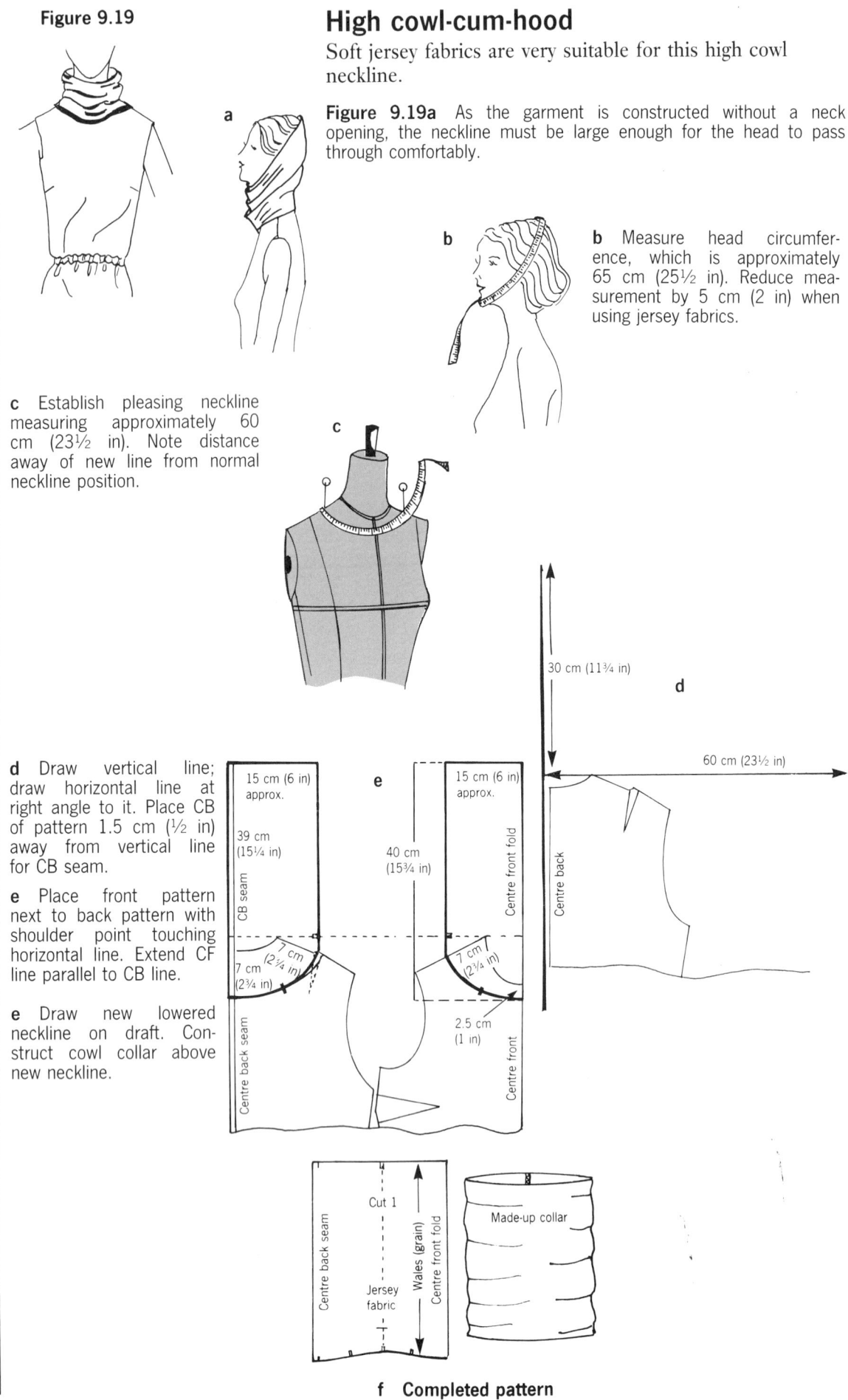

High cowl-cum-hood

Soft jersey fabrics are very suitable for this high cowl neckline.

Figure 9.19a As the garment is constructed without a neck opening, the neckline must be large enough for the head to pass through comfortably.

b Measure head circumference, which is approximately 65 cm (25½ in). Reduce measurement by 5 cm (2 in) when using jersey fabrics.

c Establish pleasing neckline measuring approximately 60 cm (23½ in). Note distance away of new line from normal neckline position.

d Draw vertical line; draw horizontal line at right angle to it. Place CB of pattern 1.5 cm (½ in) away from vertical line for CB seam.

e Place front pattern next to back pattern with shoulder point touching horizontal line. Extend CF line parallel to CB line.

e Draw new lowered neckline on draft. Construct cowl collar above new neckline.

f Completed pattern

Cowl neckline styles

Figure 9.20

Cowl neckline with shoulder pleats

Figure 9.20a Cut muslin wider and longer than required for modelling on dress form.

b Form folds. The completed pattern is similar to that in **c**.

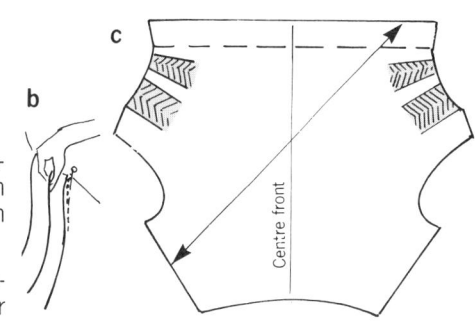

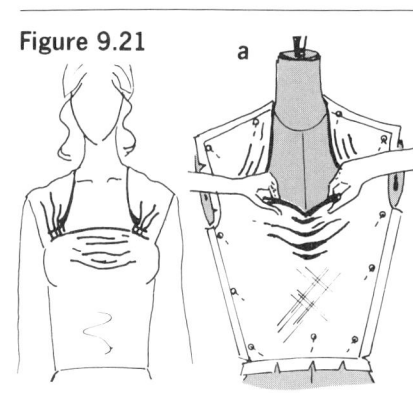

Figure 9.21

Cowl neck variations

Cowl neckline patterns **Figure 9.21a** and **Figure 9.22a** would be suitable to shape these necklines.

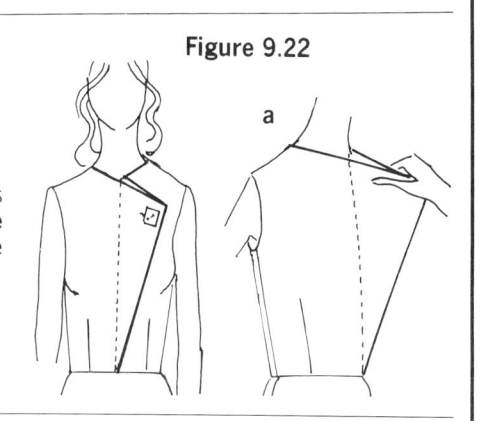

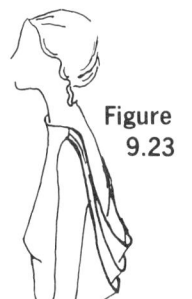

Figure 9.22

Back cowls

Figure 9.23 The back cowl is obtained in the same way as the front cowl, Figure 9.17b. Set neckline 4 cm (1½ in) away from normal shoulder-neck point on dress form. Pin folds as shown in Figure 9.20b and set permanently with small dress weights (see Figure 9.17e).

Figure 9.24

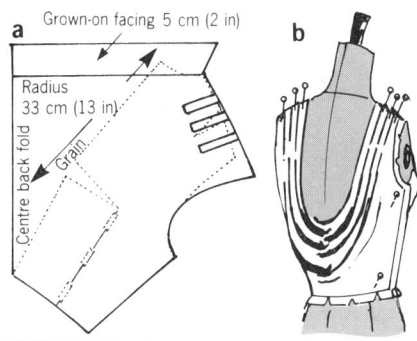

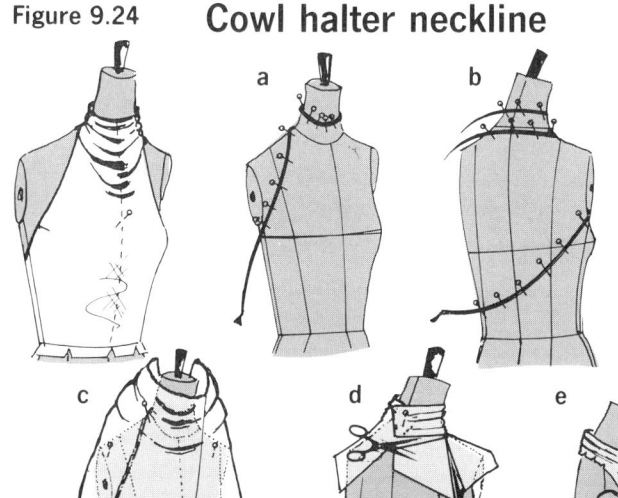

Cowl halter neckline

Figure 9.24a and **b** Outline style lines with black tape.

c, d and **e** Pin CF of modelling fabric to CF of dress form. Drape fabric towards back, following black style tape, moulding and slashing fabric to obtain the required shape. Set folds as desired with the help of small dress weights.

The pattern can be cut with or without side seams. Small darts improve the fit at armhole.

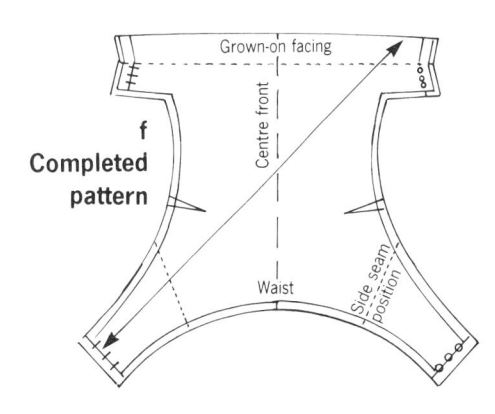

f Completed pattern

9 Cowl drapery

Underarm cowl

Figure 9.25

Use centralised blocks, Figure 7.23g, for this development; see page 94 for centralising instructions.

Figure 9.25a and **b** Move back and front waist darts to underarm seams where fulness is required. Draw neck style lines.

c Square out two lines. Name left line CB, and right line CF. Draw centre line; place blocks to back and front lines with side waist points touching centre line.

Outline new pattern; add grown-on facing, good seam allowances, including CB and CF.

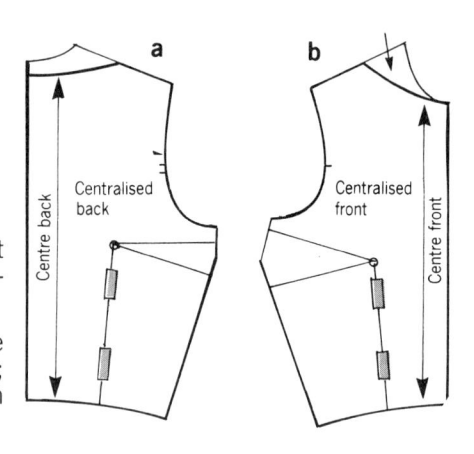

d Cut out pattern in a trial fabric similar to final garment material, e.g. soft muslin for fine woven fabric; inexpensive nylon jersey for good quality silk jersey.

Generally, 'wales' in knit fabric, or warp in woven fabric would be expected to run down CF or CB seam; in this instance it is cut on the 'courses' (knitted fabric) and weft (woven fabric).

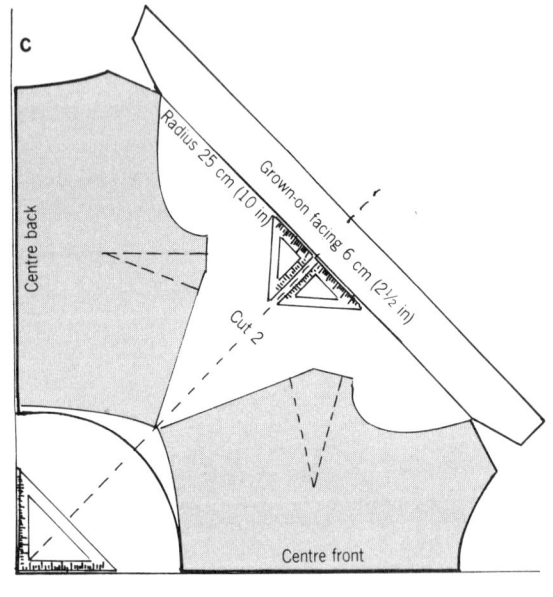

e, f and **g** These folds, like any other cowl folds, can be 'set' by means of covered lead weights sewn to the wrong side of the inside folds.

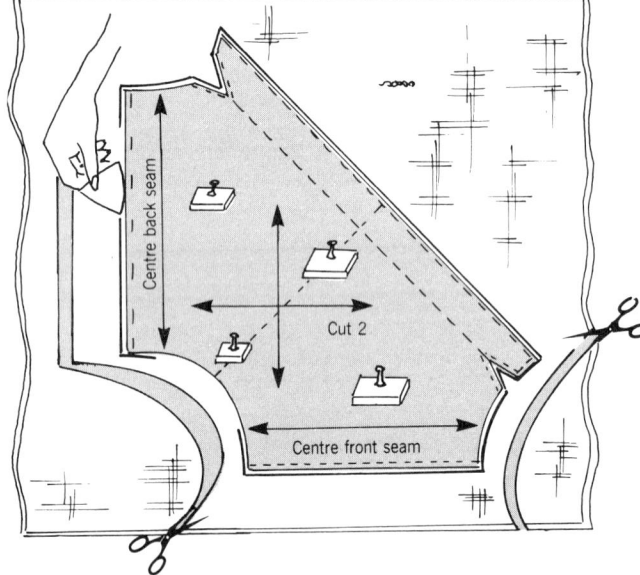

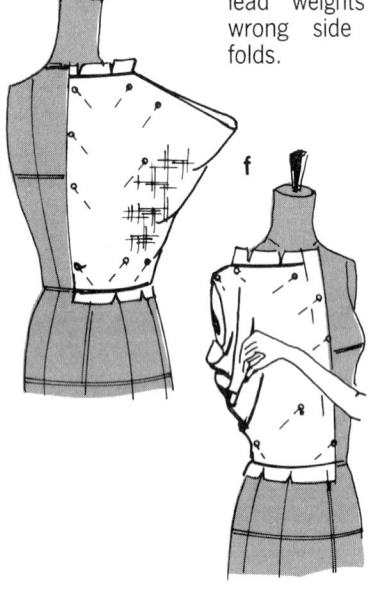

The cowl will at first appear as in **e** and must be arranged into pleasing folds. Make use of the large seam turnings which have been allowed. Transfer all newly found lines to the pattern; compare with the original pattern.

Cowl drapery in sleeves

Figure 9.26

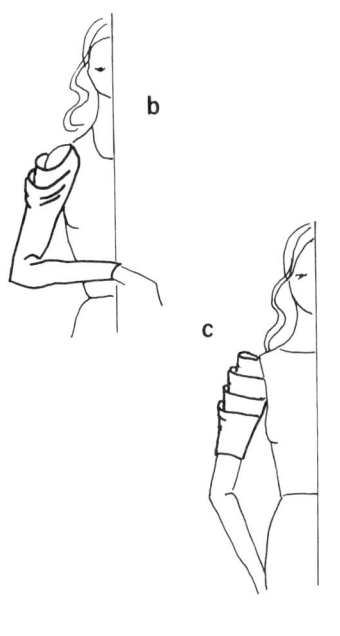

It is possible here to establish only the *basic principles* of constructing cowl drapery in sleeves. The reader is encouraged to experiment with a number of other styles as and when they are in fashion, or when developing a particular design.

The construction and design of the basic cowl sleeve allows a little of the upper arm and shoulder to be visible Figure 9.26a.

At a time when a lady's exposed shoulder was considered most alluring, all kinds of designs were created to emphasise and enhance the beauty of that part of the body (**b**).
The squarer design shown in **c** would allow for a tantalising peep.

As the methods of constructing cowl effects vary, the knowledge of a variety of methods will enable the student to choose the one most relevant to the design under consideration and to develop an individual approach and understanding. Three basic methods are now considered.

Figure 9.27

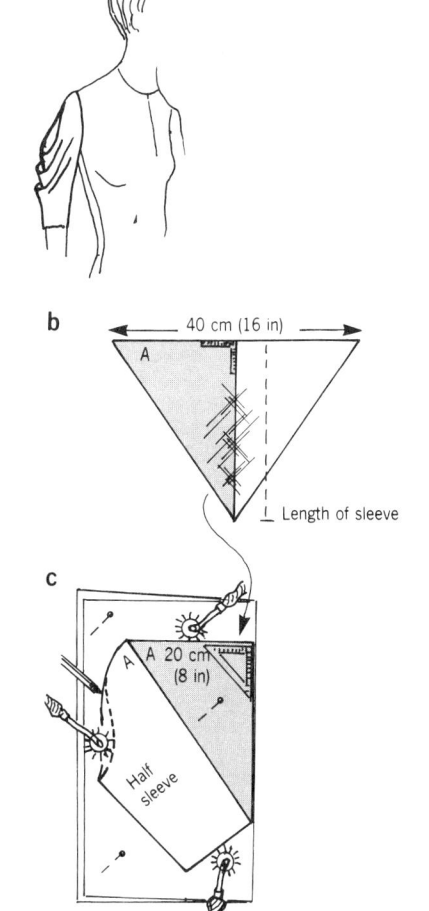

Cowl sleeve method 1

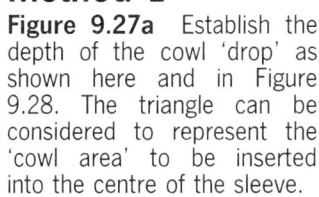

Figure 9.27a Establish the depth of the cowl 'drop' as shown here and in Figure 9.28. The triangle can be considered to represent the 'cowl area' to be inserted into the centre of the sleeve.

b and **c** Draw half of triangle **b** on folded sheet of paper **c**.

Join back half of sleeve to triangle and outline in pencil. Place front half of sleeve face down over outlined back and trace through front sleeve curve through paper with tracing wheel.

d Unfold paper and outline pattern in preparation for completion as in Figure 9.29d.

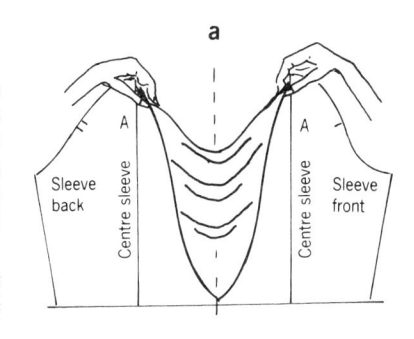

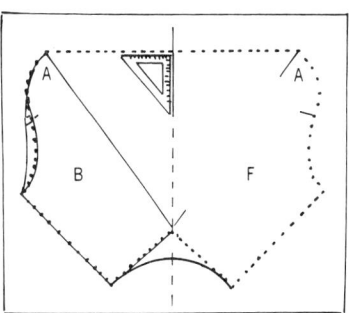

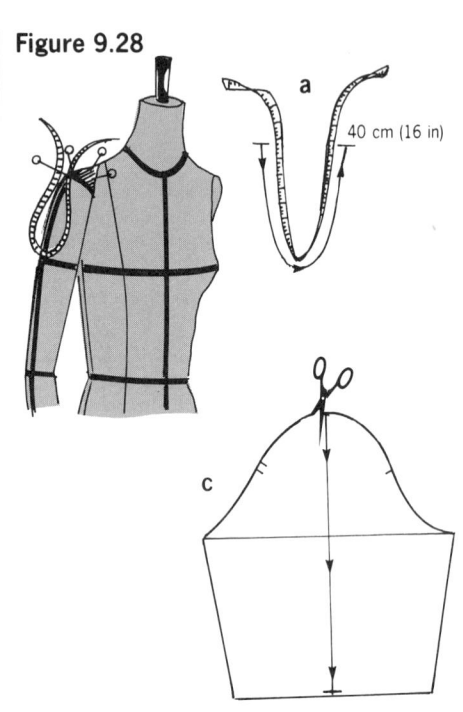

Cowl sleeve method 2
Slashing method

Figure 9.28a and **b** Measure depth of cowl 'drop' on person's arm, padded sleeve form, or on sleeve pattern.

c Cut sleeve on centre line; open out.

d Draw vertical (centre) line and position sleeve sections as shown. Outline and complete pattern as below in **Figure 9.29d**.

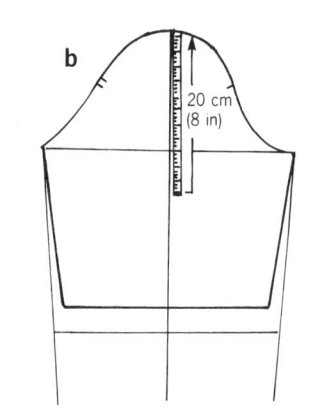

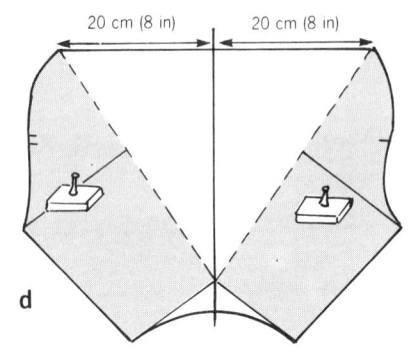

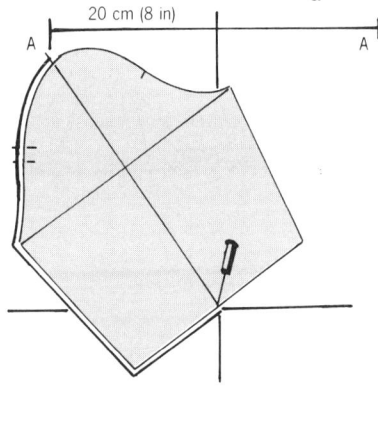

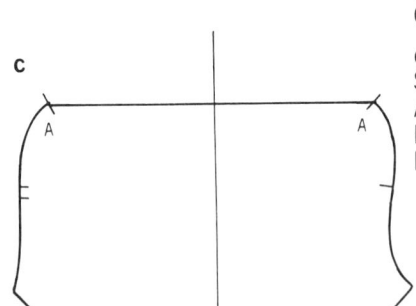

Cowl sleeve method 3
Pivoting method

Figure 9.29a Draw vertical line; square out using cowl drop (radius) measurement.

Position sleeve with centre on vertical line. Pivot to predetermined point and outline left half of sleeve.

b and **c** Pivot to right of vertical line by same measurement and outline right half of sleeve. Connect points A and A.

d Add grown-on facing; Shape hem line as shown. Add seam allowances, balance marks and grain lines to complete pattern.

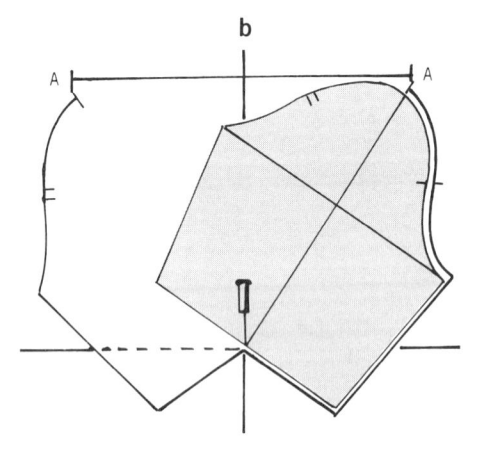

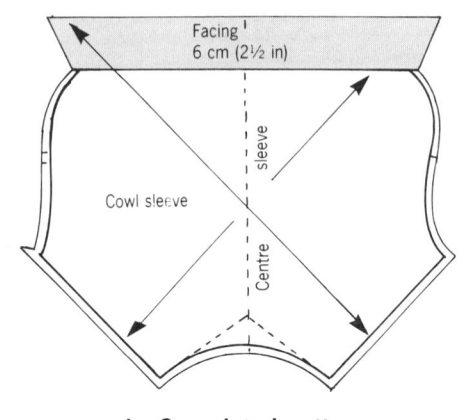

d Completed pattern

Cowl skirts

Figure 9.30

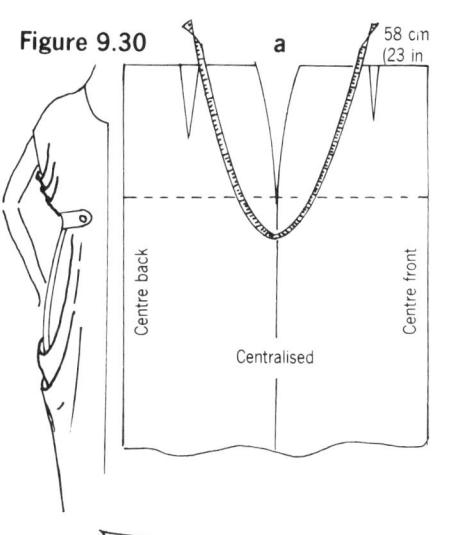

Low hip level

Figure 9.30a Centralise skirt blocks (see page 94). Use back block for this development. Establish desired cowl 'drop' (see preceding pages).

b Place back block on folded paper. Trace through; open up. Cut out in drapeable trial fabric; pin to dress form. Shape cowl folds using dart as means to setting cowl drapery. Mark all new lines carefully, including inside folds.

*A fuller effect, with more folds at waist, can be created by using a peg-top skirt (page 123) for the development.

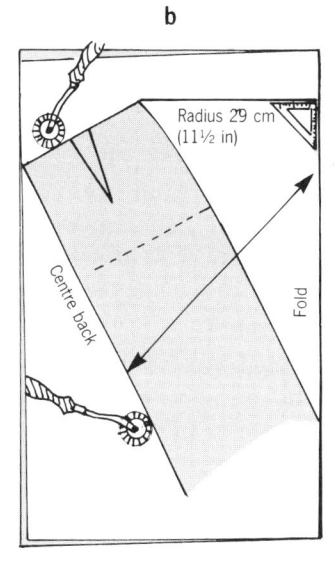

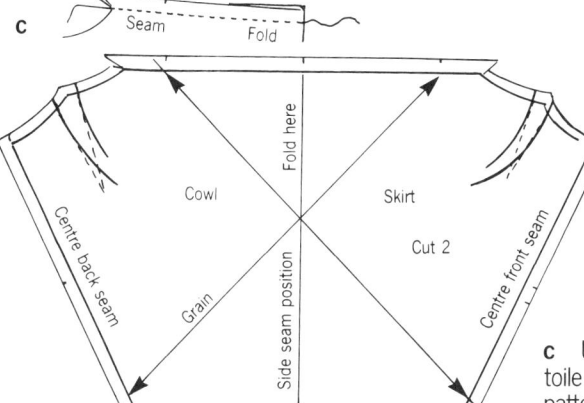

c Use marked toile to complete pattern.

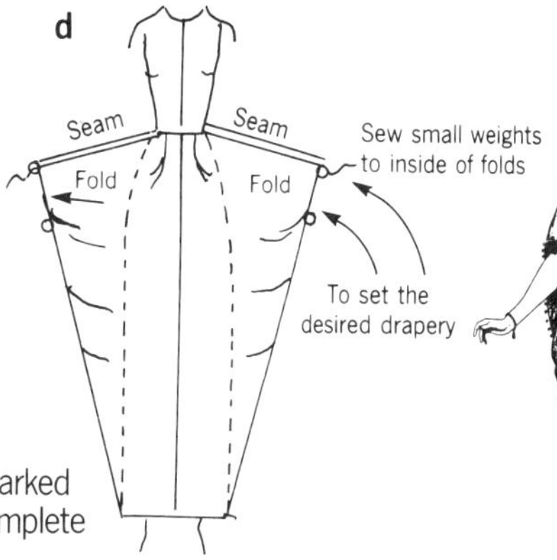

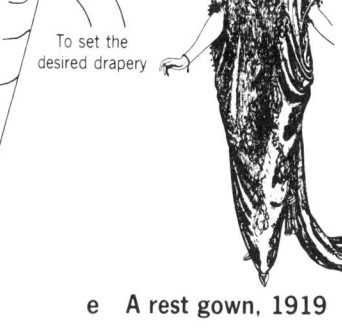

e A rest gown, 1919

Figure 9.31

Long, low-level cowl skirt

In this long, slim skirt the cowl drapery is placed lower down the side seam. Stride room can be increased, if wished, by eliminating the waist dart and flaring the hem at CB seam. The principle of cutting this skirt is the same as for other cowl features.

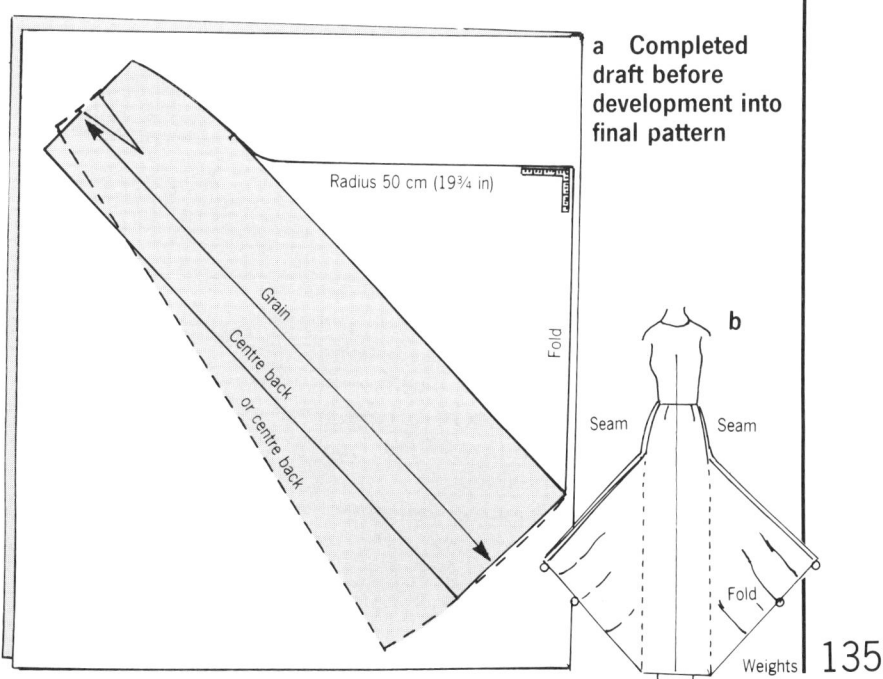

a Completed draft before development into final pattern

10 Wedding dresses

The history of the wedding dress is a fascinating subject, and is worthy of exploration in greater detail than is possible here. A broad knowledge of the history will help students to understand the symbolic reasons for certain features that are associated with wedding dresses and will inspire them with new ideas for designs that can be adapted to today's fashions.

Certain features, such as the train, can be traced back to the fourteenth century when the garments of women displayed added length to the backs of their already long garments. Thus, it was discovered centuries ago how flattering to the figure this feature is, whether the wearer is in a standing position or moving about. Royal ladies of the past recognised that wearing long and beautifully embroidered trains with their garments imparted a sense of importance to a special occasion, and they exploited this style to the full whenever it was demanded that an 'entrance' be made. These two factors strongly contributed to the popularity of the train as a feature in modern wedding dresses.

Early fifteenth-century Italian paintings of wedding scenes depict wedding dresses in strong plain colours, sometimes with an overall pattern in a different colour, and a short veil, long enough to cover the face of the bride. A Rubens painting of 1600 shows a richly-embroidered ivory satin gown with an almost full-length veil of fine gauze material, and a train held by a young boy attendant.

A 1770 ivory satin wedding dress, embroidered in silver with a train attached high to the back and shoulders, can be seen in the Barcelona Arts Museum.

Literature of the past is also an important source for research into the fashions and customs of the period it seeks to describe. For example, the wedding dress of Jane Austen's Emma, in 1880: '... where the parties had no taste for finery or parade, had very little white satin, very few lace veils; a most pityful business...' It was the empire line which influenced Jane Austen's period of dress (Figure 10.3). From 1832 to 1837, ivory faille, Indian muslin, white satin and lace are mentioned.

Figure 10.1

Figure 10.2

A wedding dress, 1485

Figure 10.3

A wedding dress, c. 1800

Figure 10.4

A 1920s wedding dress

Figure 10.5

Wedding dress, 1931

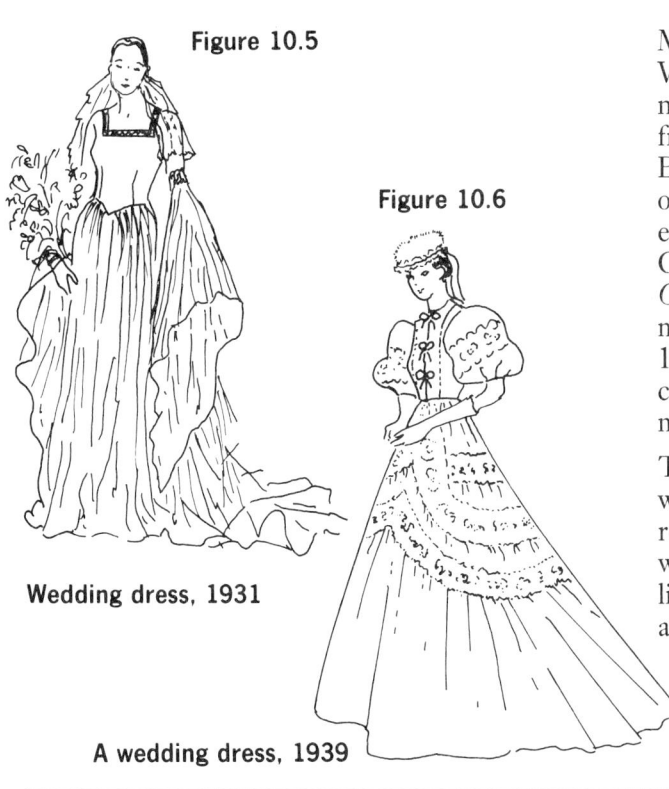

Figure 10.6

A wedding dress, 1939

Much more information is available on the Victorian and Edwardian eras, and numerous examples of wedding dresses from 1920 can be seen in museums in Bath, Manchester and London. A number of smaller 'folk museums' hold excellent exhibitions of local history. C. Willet Cunnington, in his book *English Women's Clothing in the Present Century*, describes many wedding dresses in detail (Figures 10.4, 10.5 and 10.6) and more knowledge can be gained from costume societies and modern literature.

Thus wedding dresses have a history which we seek to perpetuate with one romantic aim in mind: to create a garment which makes a woman, for one day in her life, appear more graceful, more beautiful and more lovely than seems possible.

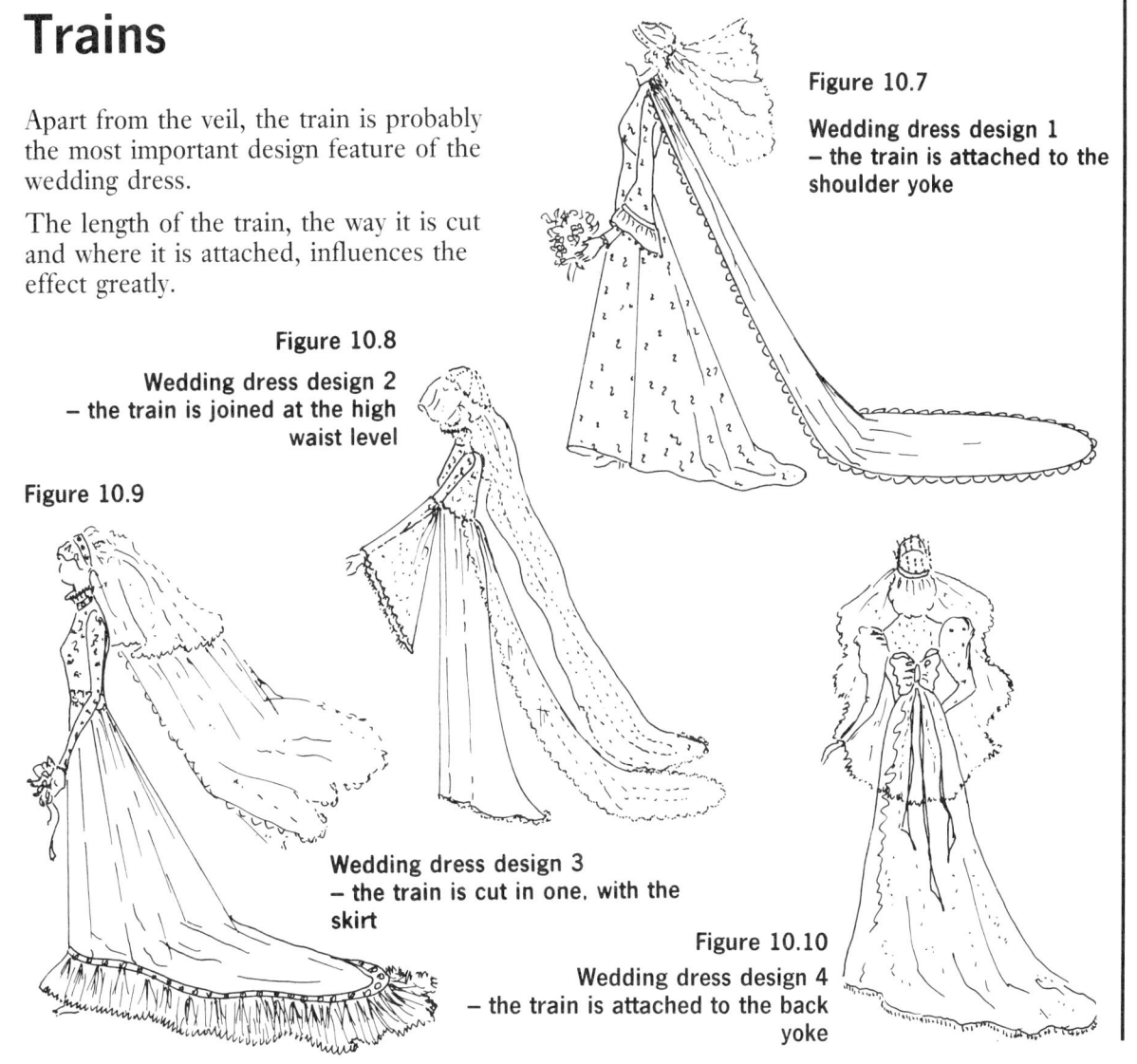

10 Wedding dresses

Trains

Apart from the veil, the train is probably the most important design feature of the wedding dress.

The length of the train, the way it is cut and where it is attached, influences the effect greatly.

Figure 10.7

Wedding dress design 1 – the train is attached to the shoulder yoke

Figure 10.8

Wedding dress design 2 – the train is joined at the high waist level

Figure 10.9

Wedding dress design 3 – the train is cut in one, with the skirt

Figure 10.10

Wedding dress design 4 – the train is attached to the back yoke

137

Wedding dress 1

Figure 10.11

Construct an underskirt that follows the desired silhouette of the garment skirt (see Figure 10.25). This forms a firm base on to which the wedding dress is modelled (not shown in the illustration).

Model this garment on a figure or on the dress form. The approximate fabric measurements here are for size 12.

Figure 10.11a Outline desired midriff position with narrow black tape.

b Pin modelling fabric of suitable weight to dress form (approx. 46 × 33 cm (14 × 13 in). Smooth fabric from neckline over shoulder and armhole towards side seam, as if modelling a bodice front with one deep waist dart, thus creating fulness under bust.

c Arrange this fulness into pleasing gathers. Mark underbust style line; trim surplus fabric in preparation for attaching the skirt. Remove from form.

d True all marked lines.

6 cm (2½ in) fabric above neck base

d The shape of the modelled pattern when finally removed from the dress form

Figure 10.12 For front and back skirts fold fabric 132 cm (52 in) or more in width on the true bias. With wider fabric allow CB seam. More width can then be added to hem line, see example Figure 10.14. Alternatively, use two lengths of fabric to cut back skirt.

b When shaping the waist and midriff, any excess fabric at side seam, due to greater width of garment fabric, can be utilised to form a soft fold, thus creating additional width and 'sweep' to the hem.*

c Pin folded bias fabric to dress form with point turned under or cut away in order to achieve the rounded line required for this style.

Experiment by slightly lifting or dropping modelling fabric at centre front or side seam points until desired silhouette is achieved. (See skirt Figure 8.32a page 121).

The aim is to throw fulness towards the back. Smooth and mould fabric as much as possible to dress form or figure at midriff and waist level. Cut and shape side seam. A close fit at waist level **cannot** be achieved with this bias-cut skirt; the bias fabric 'skims' the waist.

10

Wedding dresses

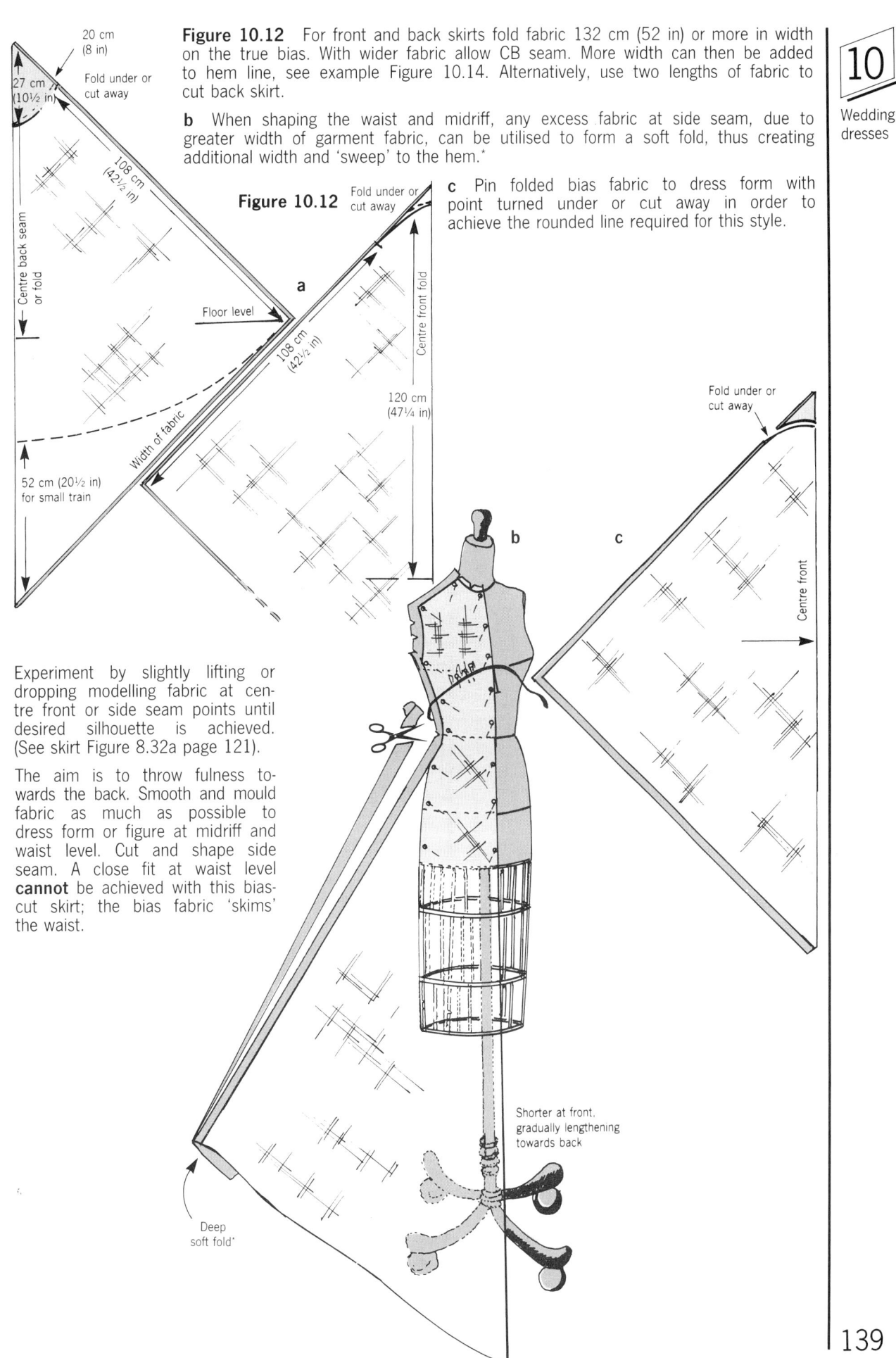

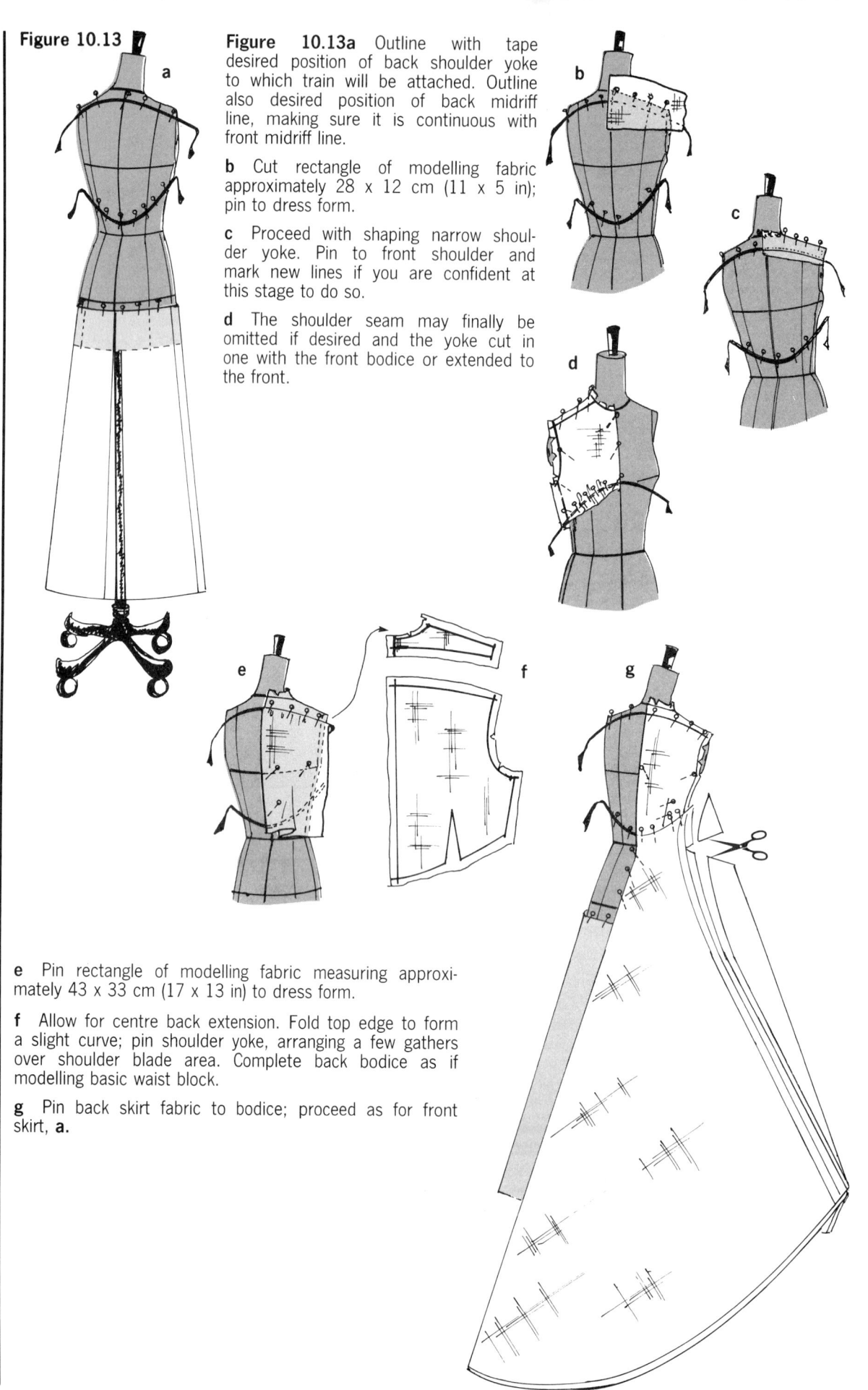

Figure 10.13

Figure 10.13a Outline with tape desired position of back shoulder yoke to which train will be attached. Outline also desired position of back midriff line, making sure it is continuous with front midriff line.

b Cut rectangle of modelling fabric approximately 28 x 12 cm (11 x 5 in); pin to dress form.

c Proceed with shaping narrow shoulder yoke. Pin to front shoulder and mark new lines if you are confident at this stage to do so.

d The shoulder seam may finally be omitted if desired and the yoke cut in one with the front bodice or extended to the front.

e Pin rectangle of modelling fabric measuring approximately 43 x 33 cm (17 x 13 in) to dress form.

f Allow for centre back extension. Fold top edge to form a slight curve; pin shoulder yoke, arranging a few gathers over shoulder blade area. Complete back bodice as if modelling basic waist block.

g Pin back skirt fabric to bodice; proceed as for front skirt, **a**.

Figure 10.14

Centre front fold ↑

Deep fold (see text Figure 10.12b*)

Cut 1

Centre back fold

Cut 1

Fold back side seam over front seam

Grain

Underlay

Fold over

Grain

Centre back seam

Cut 2

Small train

Figure 10.14 Completed skirt pattern for wedding dress 1

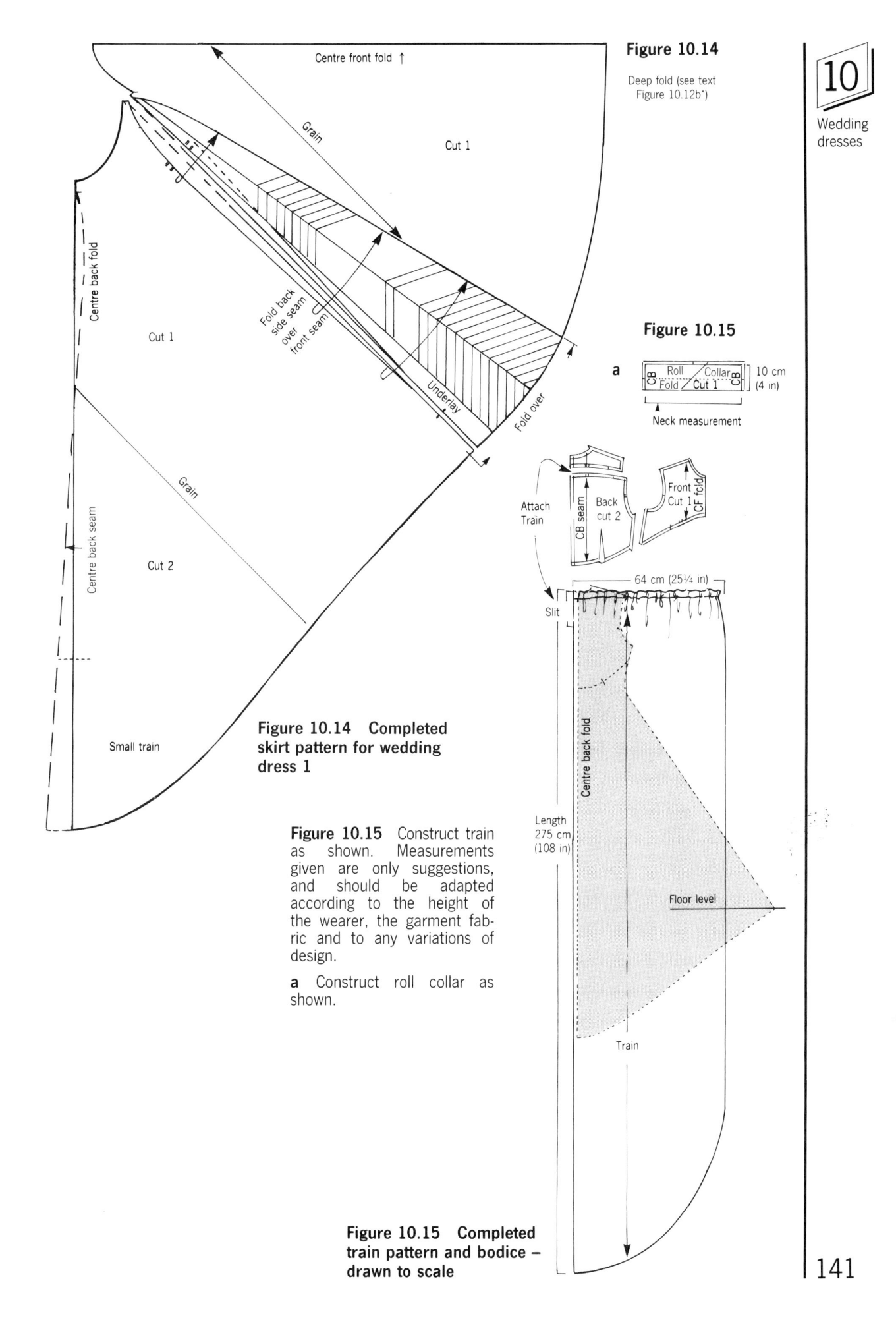

Figure 10.15

a

CB	Roll Collar	
	Fold / Cut 1	CB	10 cm (4 in)

Neck measurement

Attach Train

CB seam — Back cut 2

Front Cut 1 — CF fold

Slit

64 cm (25¼ in)

Centre back fold

Length 275 cm (108 in)

Floor level

Train

Figure 10.15 Construct train as shown. Measurements given are only suggestions, and should be adapted according to the height of the wearer, the garment fabric and to any variations of design.

a Construct roll collar as shown.

Figure 10.15 Completed train pattern and bodice – drawn to scale

10 Wedding dresses

141

Finished measurements of the sleeve

Sleeve length	59 cm (23 in)
Upper arm circumference	33 cm (13 in)
Elbow circumference	30 cm (11¾ in)
Wrist circumference	17 cm (6¾ in)
Bell sleeve hem circumference	41 cm (16 in)

Figure 10.16

Figure 10.16a Outline shirt sleeve (see page 87 or 100); cut out. Fold shaded sections to meet centre line.

a Crease and stick down. Use size 12 measurements given above or others desired for this Victorian-influenced sleeve.

b Turn sleeve over; complete two-piece-based fitted sleeve draft. Cut on inner sleeve line, from wrist to elbow point, through both thicknesses of paper.

c Draw your own cuff and frill style lines or as shown here.

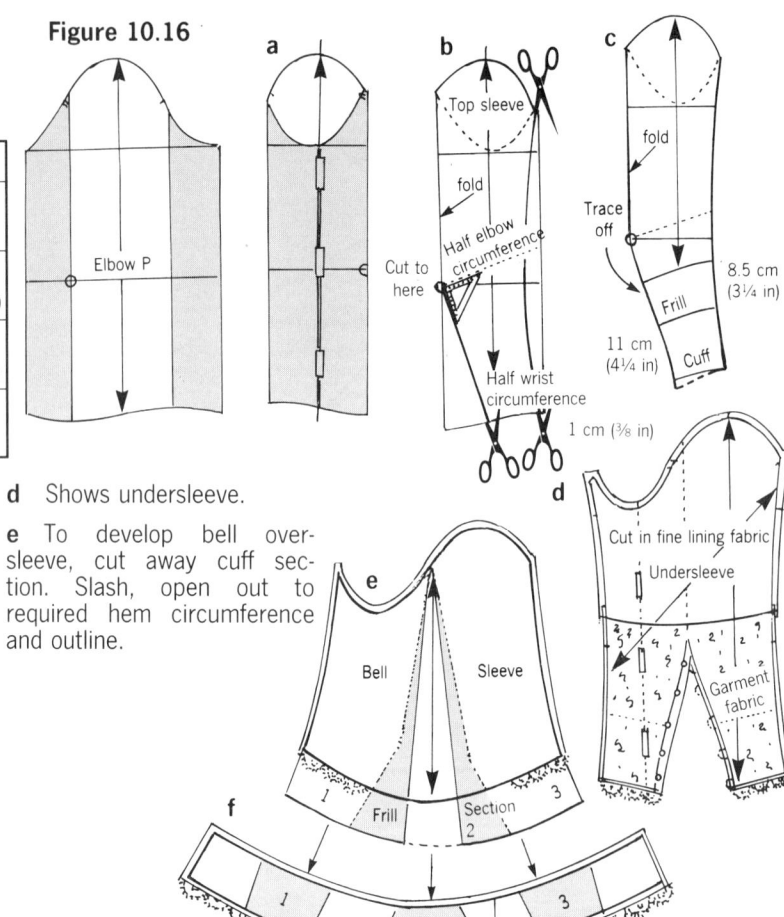

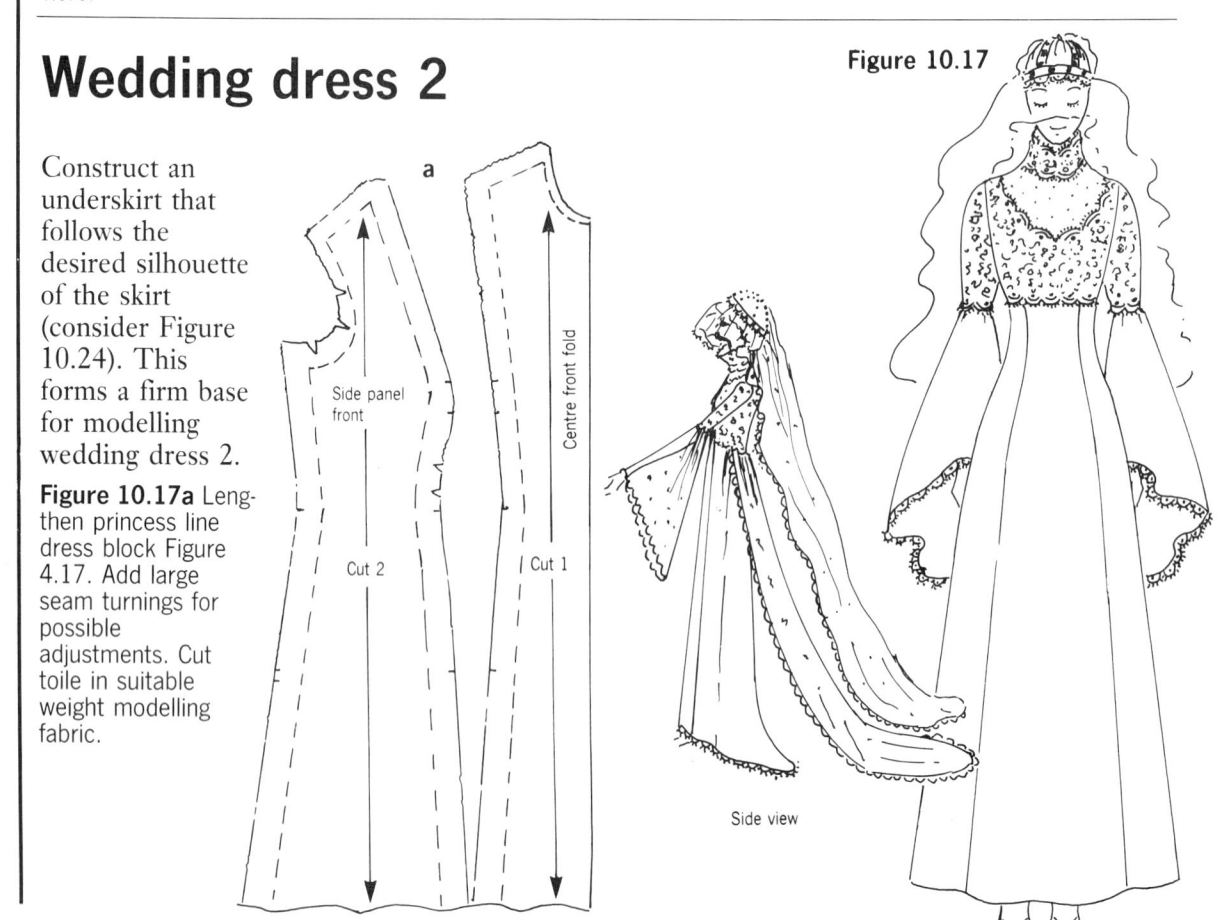

d Shows undersleeve.

e To develop bell oversleeve, cut away cuff section. Slash, open out to required hem circumference and outline.

Wedding dress 2

Construct an underskirt that follows the desired silhouette of the skirt (consider Figure 10.24). This forms a firm base for modelling wedding dress 2.

Figure 10.17a Lengthen princess line dress block Figure 4.17. Add large seam turnings for possible adjustments. Cut toile in suitable weight modelling fabric.

Figure 10.17

Side view

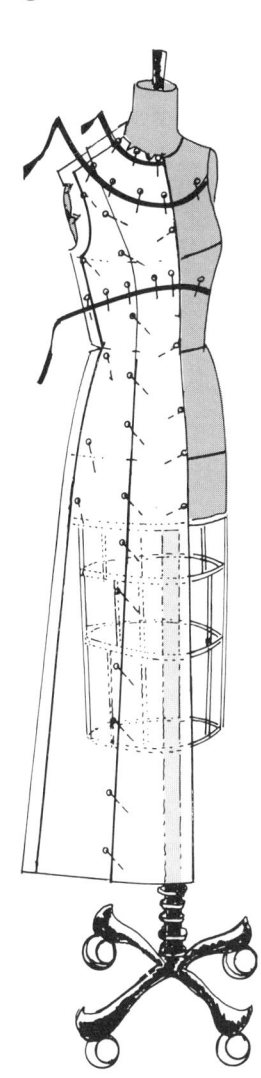

Figure 10.18

Figure 10.18 and a Pin front and side princess line sections together; pin to dress form. Outline desired style lines with tape; mark with soft pencil. Remove and trace off bodice section. Retain two front skirt panels for later development (one for the development of the back skirt).

The bodice loses its princess line seams, but the closer-fit seams can be retained for the lace bodice which can be cut in three sections, provided that motifs on the lace pattern can be overlaid and joined inconspicuously without a seam showing (Figure 10.21a and b). Otherwise, eliminate princess line seam.

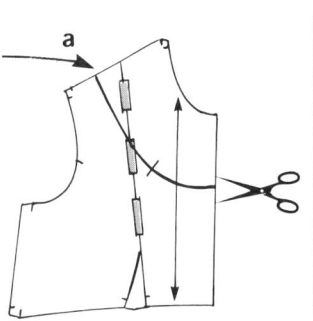

b Develop back bodice from basic waist block; add large CB seam for either button stand or loops and button placement. Establish style lines and proceed as for front bodice.

c Develop back skirt from the two front princess line panels.

Place CF skirt panel face down; outline. Join side front panel to CF panel; outline.

d Add 10 cm (4 in) flare to CB hemline. Lower back waist line approximately 7.5 cm (3 in) and curve. Cut away what was originally the raised waist front.

Use this basic skirt for still further development.

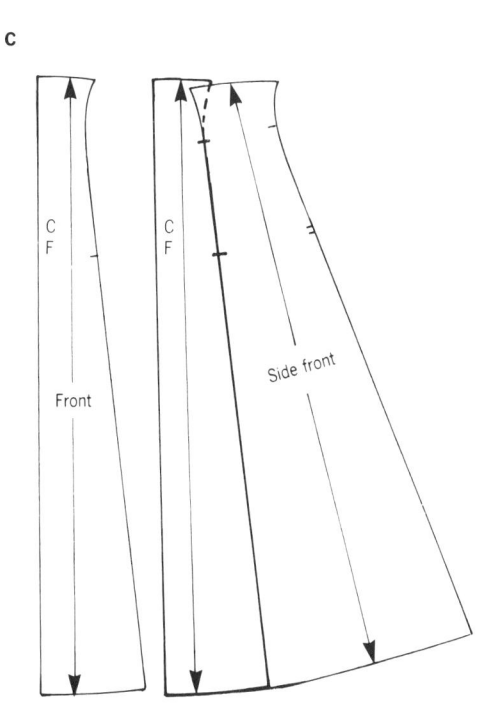

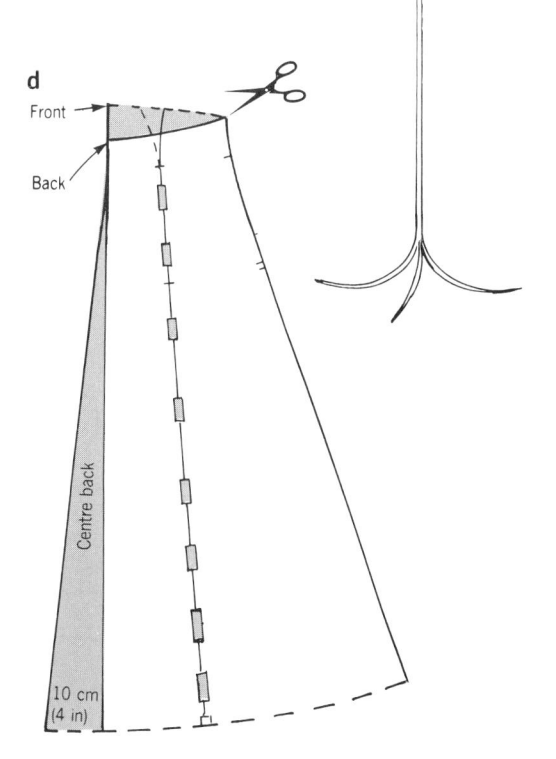

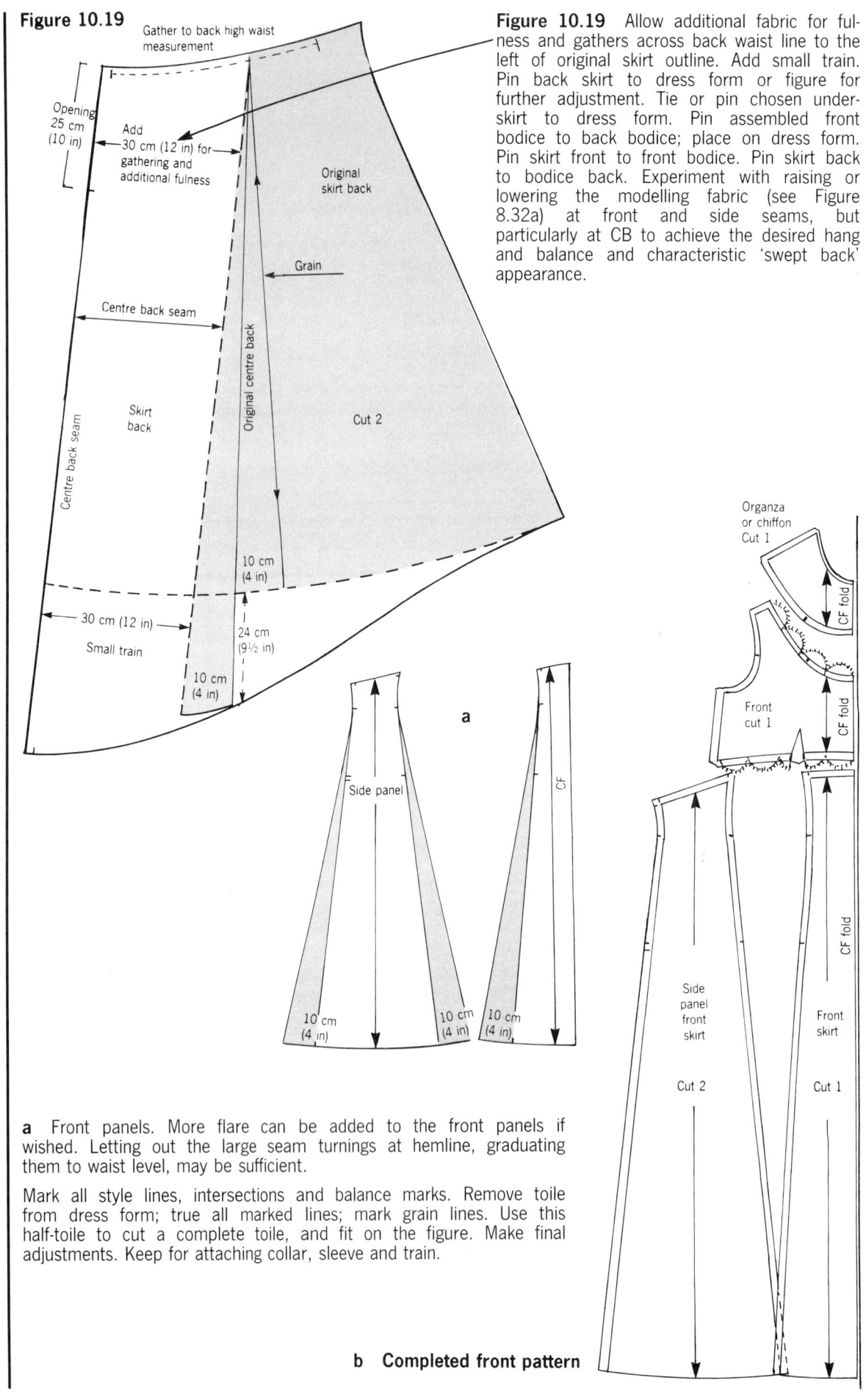

Wedding dresses

Figure 10.19

Figure 10.19 Allow additional fabric for fulness and gathers across back waist line to the left of original skirt outline. Add small train. Pin back skirt to dress form or figure for further adjustment. Tie or pin chosen underskirt to dress form. Pin assembled front bodice to back bodice; place on dress form. Pin skirt front to front bodice. Pin skirt back to bodice back. Experiment with raising or lowering the modelling fabric (see Figure 8.32a) at front and side seams, but particularly at CB to achieve the desired hang and balance and characteristic 'swept back' appearance.

Labels on back skirt diagram: Gather to back high waist measurement; Opening 25 cm (10 in); Add 30 cm (12 in) for gathering and additional fulness; Original skirt back; Grain; Centre back seam; Skirt back; Original centre back; Cut 2; 30 cm (12 in); Small train; 10 cm (4 in); 24 cm (9½ in); 10 cm (4 in)

a Front panels. More flare can be added to the front panels if wished. Letting out the large seam turnings at hemline, graduating them to waist level, may be sufficient.

Labels on panel a: Side panel; CF; 10 cm (4 in); 10 cm (4 in); 10 cm (4 in)

Mark all style lines, intersections and balance marks. Remove toile from dress form; true all marked lines; mark grain lines. Use this half-toile to cut a complete toile, and fit on the figure. Make final adjustments. Keep for attaching collar, sleeve and train.

Labels on completed front pattern: Organza or chiffon Cut 1; CF fold; Front cut 1; CF fold; Side panel front skirt Cut 2; CF fold; Front skirt Cut 1

b Completed front pattern

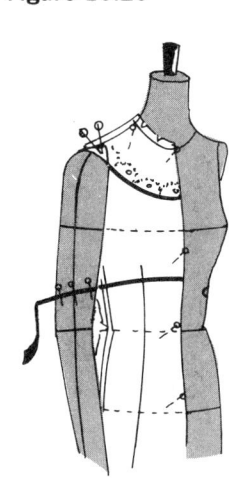

Figure 10.20

Figure 10.20 Measure on padded sleeve or arm of model from shoulder point to desired level in line with seam on bodice.

a Transfer this measurement to fitted sleeve block draft. Divide lower sleeve section into four equal parts, ignoring wrist dart; number parts 1–4. Cut off lower sleeve section. Cut upwards on each division line to within cut edge.

b Spread sections as shown; pin to paper. Measurements are approximate. Add extra length from above elbow to little finger/wrist position. Introduce small pleats on back (above elbow) section.

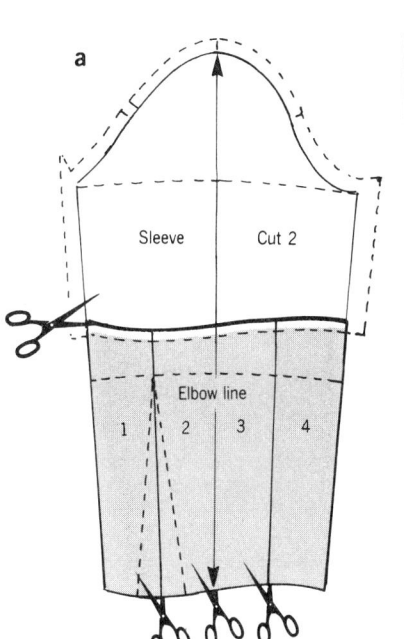

c This flounce can be cut without an underarm sleeve seam in fabric 92–102 cm (36–40 in) wide.

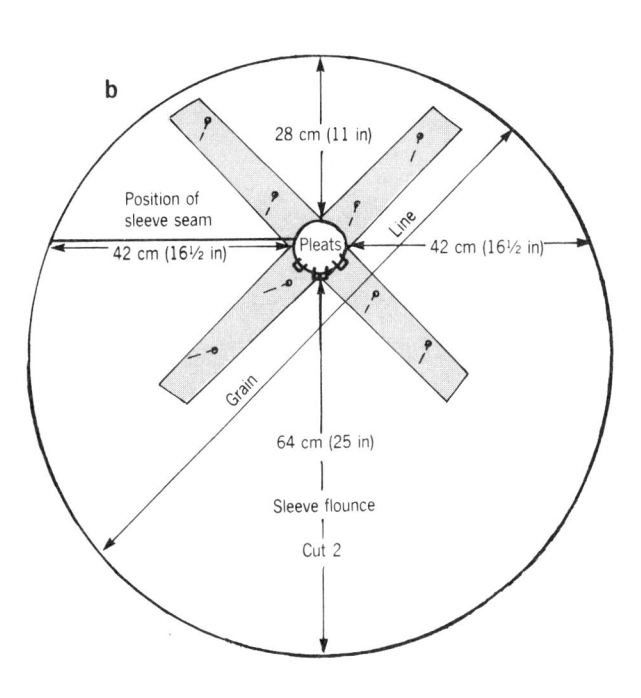

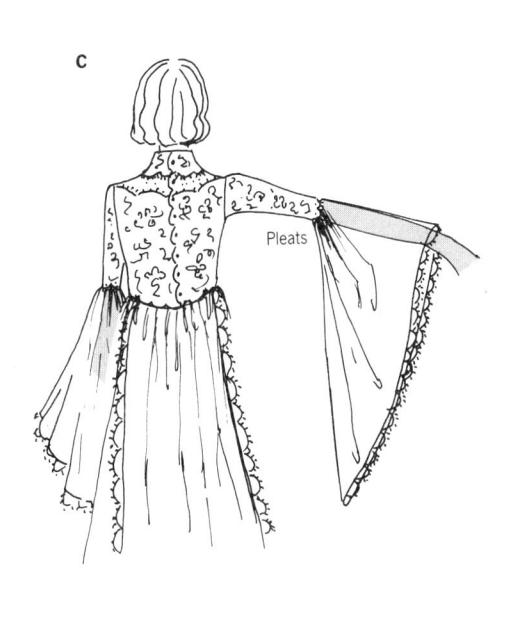

d This flattering bias-cut stand collar stands slightly away from the neck and is set on to a lowered neckline. The collar is made up in the usual way and lace, if used, is shaped over the collar after it has been joined to the bodice neckline.

Draw rectangle representing neckline measurement by desired width of collar. Shape as shown. Add button stand if required. Develop top and undercollar; add seam allowances.

d Bias stand collar set on lowered neckline

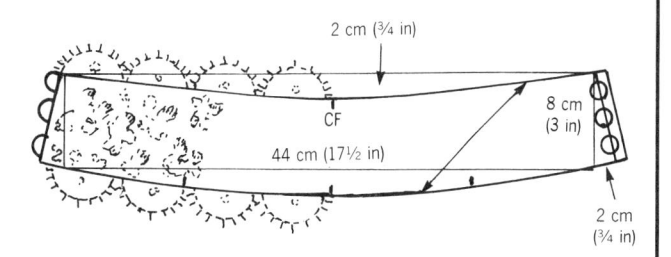

10 Wedding dresses

Wedding dress 3

Figure 10.21

Because the bodice of this garment is close-fitting, it is developed from the princess line block (see Figure 4.17, page 55). If it is to be cut in lace, it is worthwhile selecting the fabric carefully with the design, pattern and making taken into consideration. Flouncing, which has one or both edges scalloped, can be the means of emphasising a design feature, and lace, with very definite raised embroidered motifs, can be shaped to the body by overlaying garment sections or cut darts, and closely zigzag stitching the motif outline of one section on to the adjoining and underlying one.

Excess lace beneath the lapped edge is cut away close to the stitching. In this way a moulded fit is achieved without the appearance of darts or seam lines.

Joining lace

Figure 10.21a Cut around raised outlines of motifs and lay over adjoining seam.

b Use motif outline as guide for zigzag stitching one section on to the other. Cut away excess lace from beneath lapped edge.

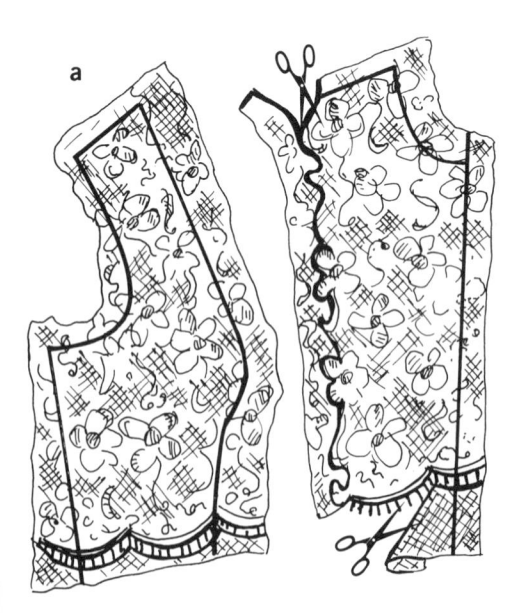

Tight-fitting sleeve

This sleeve style is usually cut on the bias of the fabric. The stretch property of bias-cut sleeves insures ease of movement for the wearer and also a tight-fitting appearance. Add approximately 4 cm (1½ in) more sleeve length (see page 83).

Tight-fitting sleeves and garments are fitted more successfully on an individual person. For wholesale manufacturing purposes however, when saleability is a major consideration, a size 12 garment must fit a variety of size 12 women and, therefore, more tolerance and ease must be added when constructing the wholesale pattern.

Figure 10.22

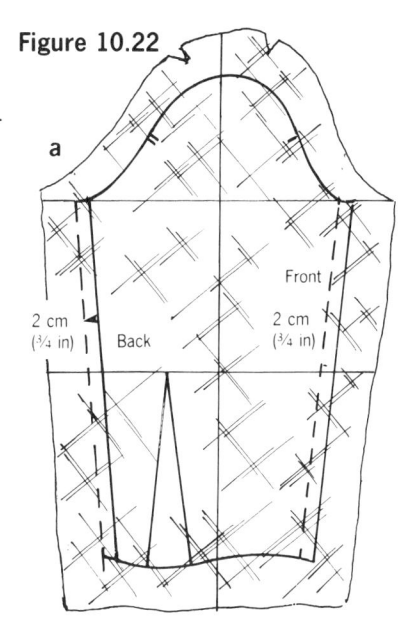

Figure 10.22a Outline fitted sleeve block on soft bias, modelling fabric. Move sleeve seam forward by taking away 2 cm (¾ in) from front sleeve seam and adding this amount to back seam (dotted lines).

This seam position makes it possible to follow the contours of a slightly bent arm when fitting the sleeve.

Cut out sleeve, having allowed seam turnings.

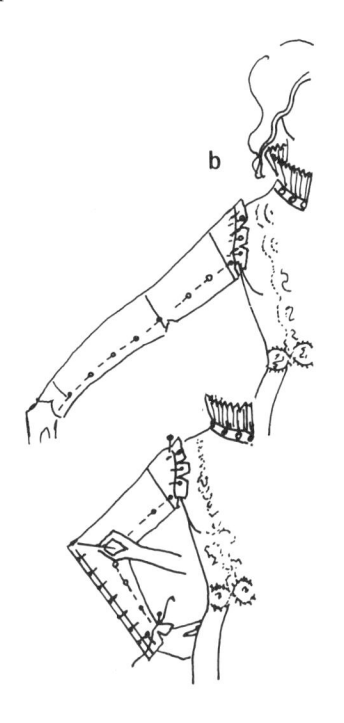

b Fold and pin wrist dart. Pin sleeve seam and pin to armhole of bodice on figure or dress form with padded sleeve. This seam will not align with bodice side seam. Experiment with fitting more tightly if necessary; also try to introduce more ease on back seam over elbow area in order to give more 'shape' to the sleeve: unpin lower section of sleeve seam to just above elbow and 'ease' back seam into front seam over elbow area. Repin sleeve seam. Back seam will now be slightly shorter than front by approximately 1–2.5 cm (½–1 in). Try pinning a small fish dart, where shown, to improve fit even further.

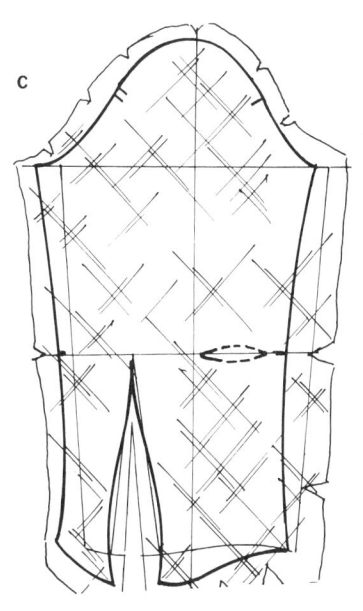

c Mark all new lines and balance marks; remove from arm and transfer to pattern paper, having previously improved all uneven lines.

d Draw grain line and add seam allowances and small button extension if required.

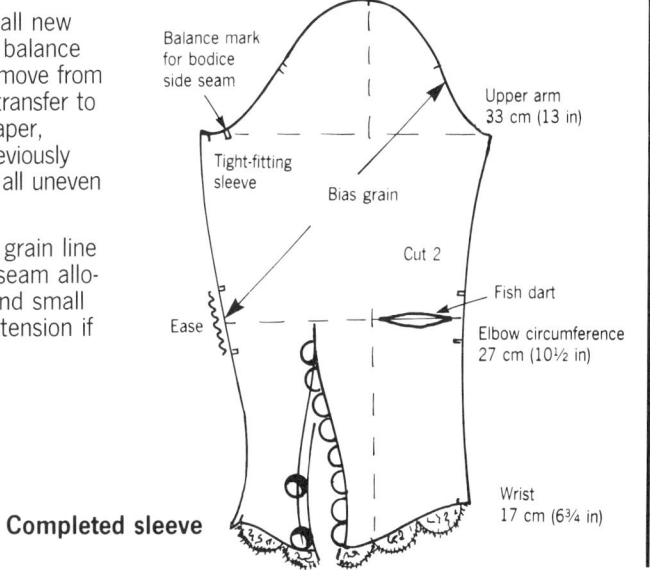

d Completed sleeve

Balance mark for bodice side seam
Tight-fitting sleeve
Upper arm 33 cm (13 in)
Bias grain
Cut 2
Ease
Fish dart
Elbow circumference 27 cm (10½ in)
Wrist 17 cm (6¾ in)

Wedding dresses

Figure 10.23 Completed skirt pattern for wedding dress 3

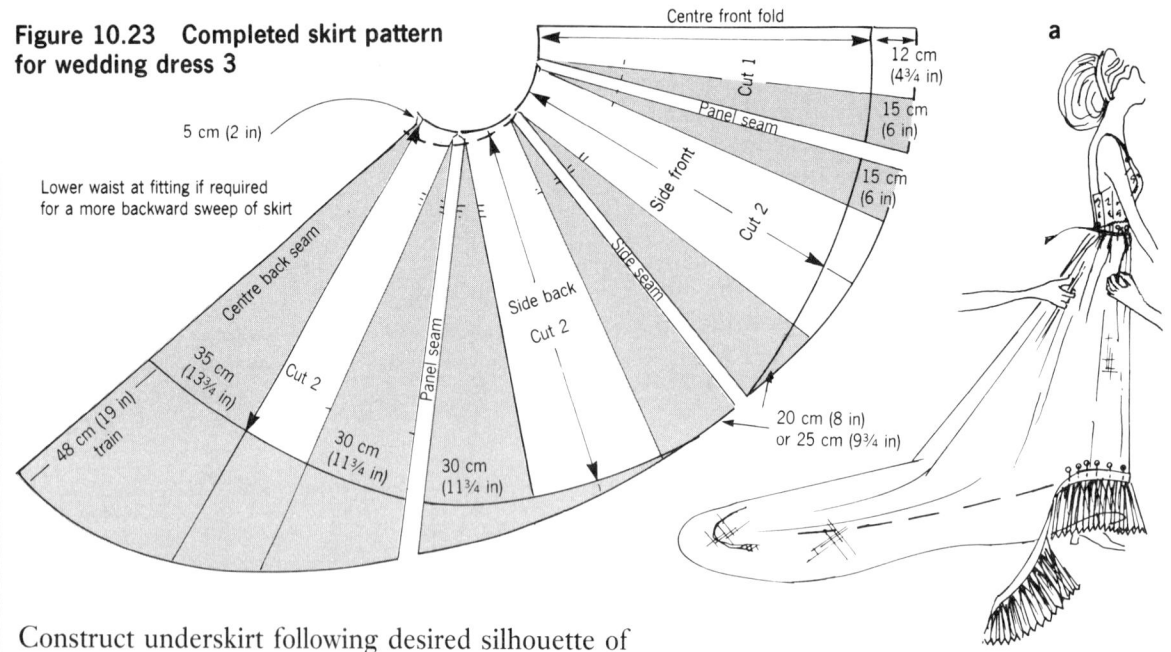

Construct underskirt following desired silhouette of garment skirt (see pages 148–50). This forms a firm base on to which the wedding dress is modelled (not shown in the illustration).

The train for this dress is cut in one with the skirt. It is developed from the wedding dress 2 princess line skirt (Figure 10.18 and 10.19). Much more fulness is required for this train at hem line, particularly at centre back.

Figure 10.23 shows the development which increases the hem measurement to more than 6 metres (6½ yards).

Underskirts

Underskirt 1

Figure 10.24

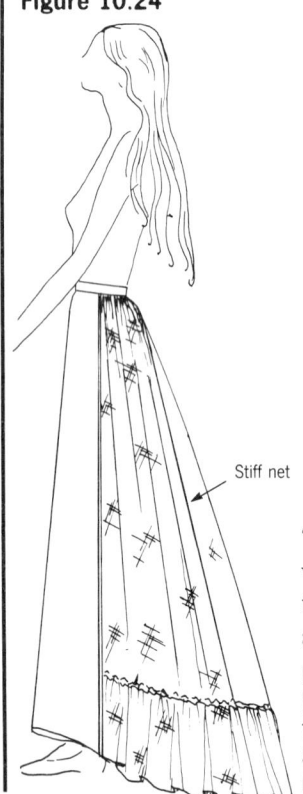

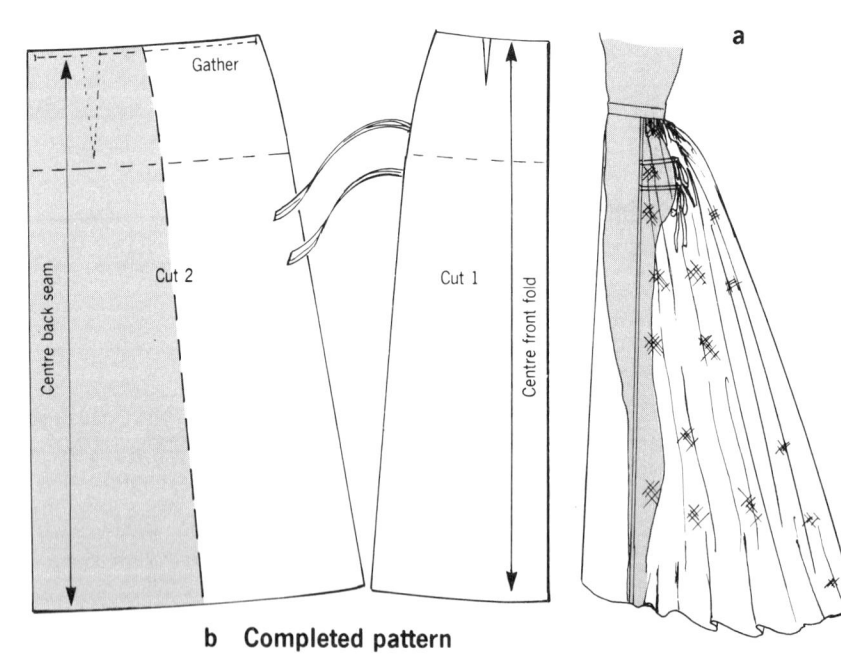

This underskirt is a suitable foil for a skirt of almost straight silhouette with some fulness at the back, such as dress Figure 10.17. In this case, twice the back skirt width is allowed, but more or less fulness can be added as wished.

Figure 10.24a In order that the front skirt remains straight and flat against the body, tapes are attached to the inside of the side seams at hip position. When tied at the back against the body, the fulness remains confined to the back area and side seams are not pushed forward. See also Figure 10.25c for another method.

Underskirt 2

This underskirt is suitable for the Figure 10.21 wedding dress skirt.

Figure 10.25a Cut basic, slightly flared skirt. Superimpose skirt **b** onto this skirt. Machine stitch through both layers of skirt where side seam and side seam position of top skirt overlap. This ensures that the long, sweeping train section remains confined to the intended area (see also Figure 10.24 where tapes are used for the same purpose).

c Rows of frills can be sewn on top or on the inside of the back section to give more support. In this 1870 skirt the frilly back section was buttoned on to the side seams.

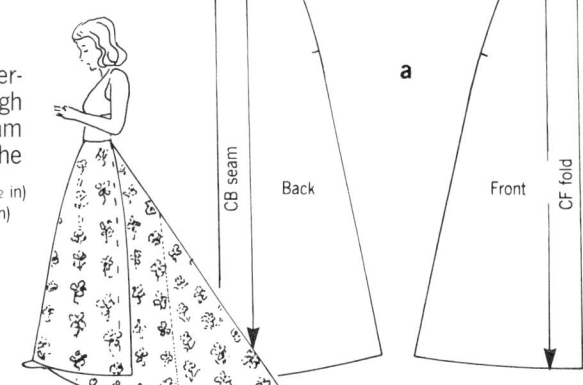

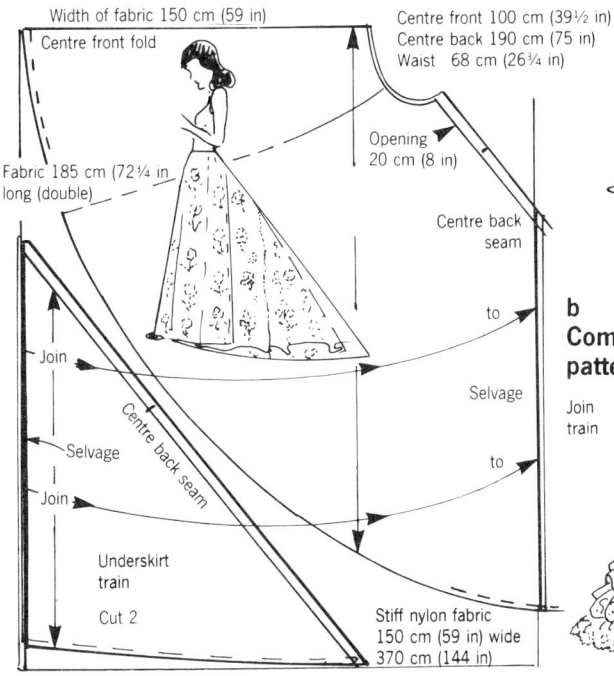

b Completed pattern

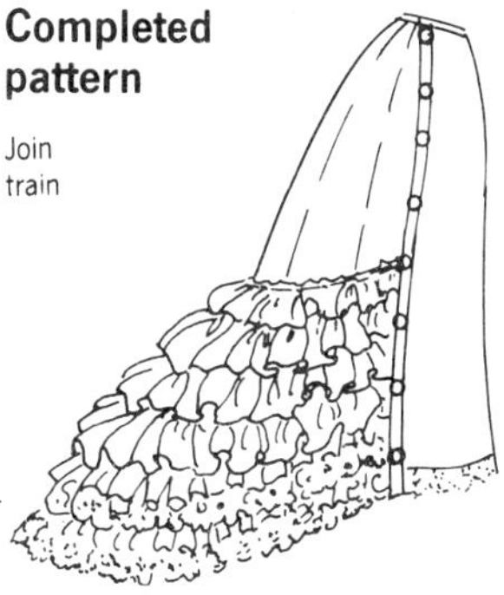

Tiered underskirt 3

Figure 10.26

Figure 10.26a Outline long skirt block. Divide into four sections (see suggested measurements).

b Gather each section into previous one. Waist dart can be pivoted out or used for elasticated waist.

Repeat for back. Trace off. Add seam allowances, etc.

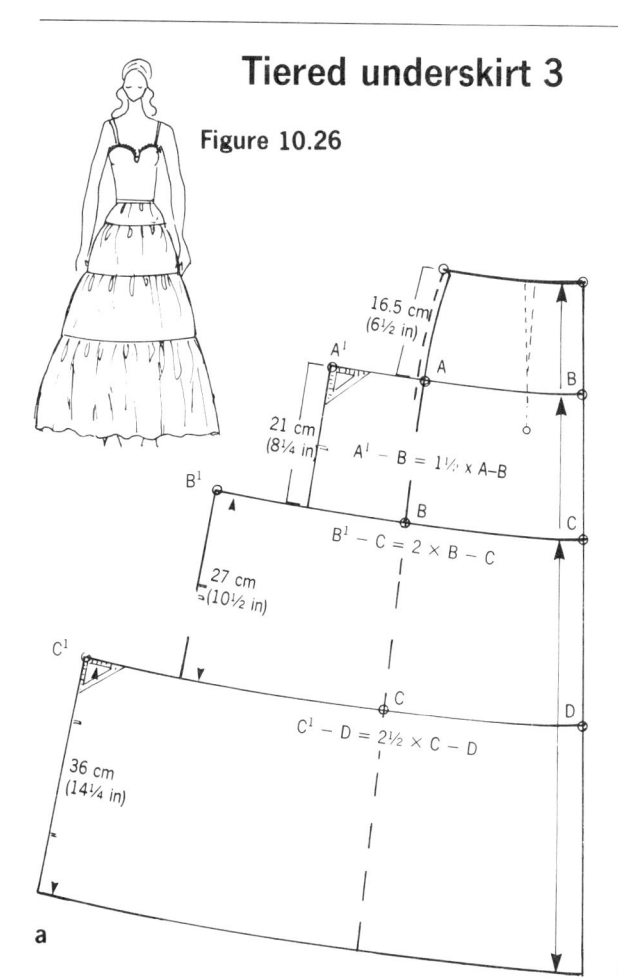

$A^1 - B = 1\frac{1}{2} \times A-B$

$B^1 - C = 2 \times B - C$

$C^1 - D = 2\frac{1}{2} \times C - D$

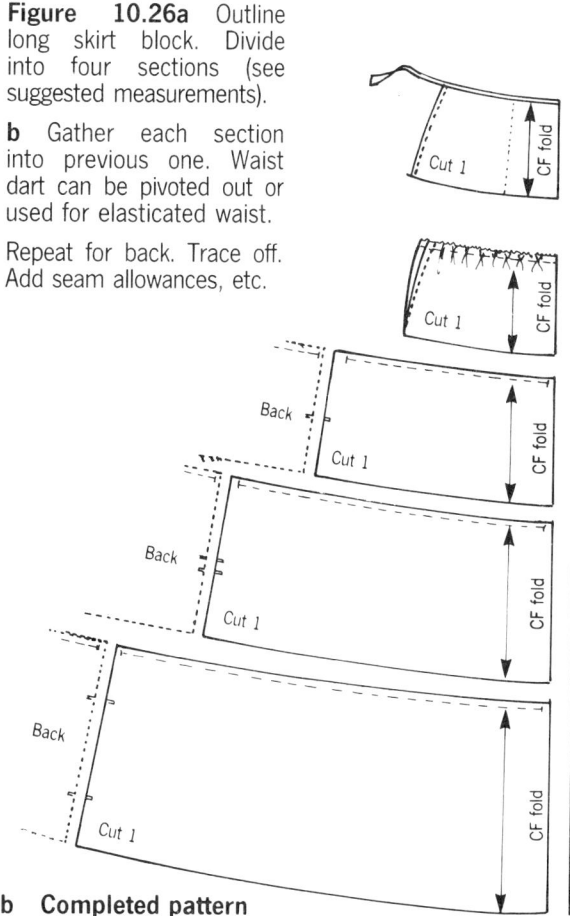

b Completed pattern

Underskirt 4 with rigilene bands

Probably the most popular underskirt for wedding dresses that demand a crinoline silhouette.

Finished measurements	Size 12
1 Full length	104 cm (41 in)
2 Waist circumference	66 cm (26 in)
3 Below hip circumference	115 cm (45¼ in)
4 Above knee circumference	136 cm (53½ in)
5 Hem circumference	173 cm (68¼ in)

Figure 10.27

Figure 10.27a Draft back and front long skirt based on straight skirt block. Rigilene bands are stitched at given intervals (without horizontal seams).

b Net is attached at band 2. Length 73 cm (29 in), circumference 258 cm (102 in).

The CB seam is left unstitched to form a waist opening

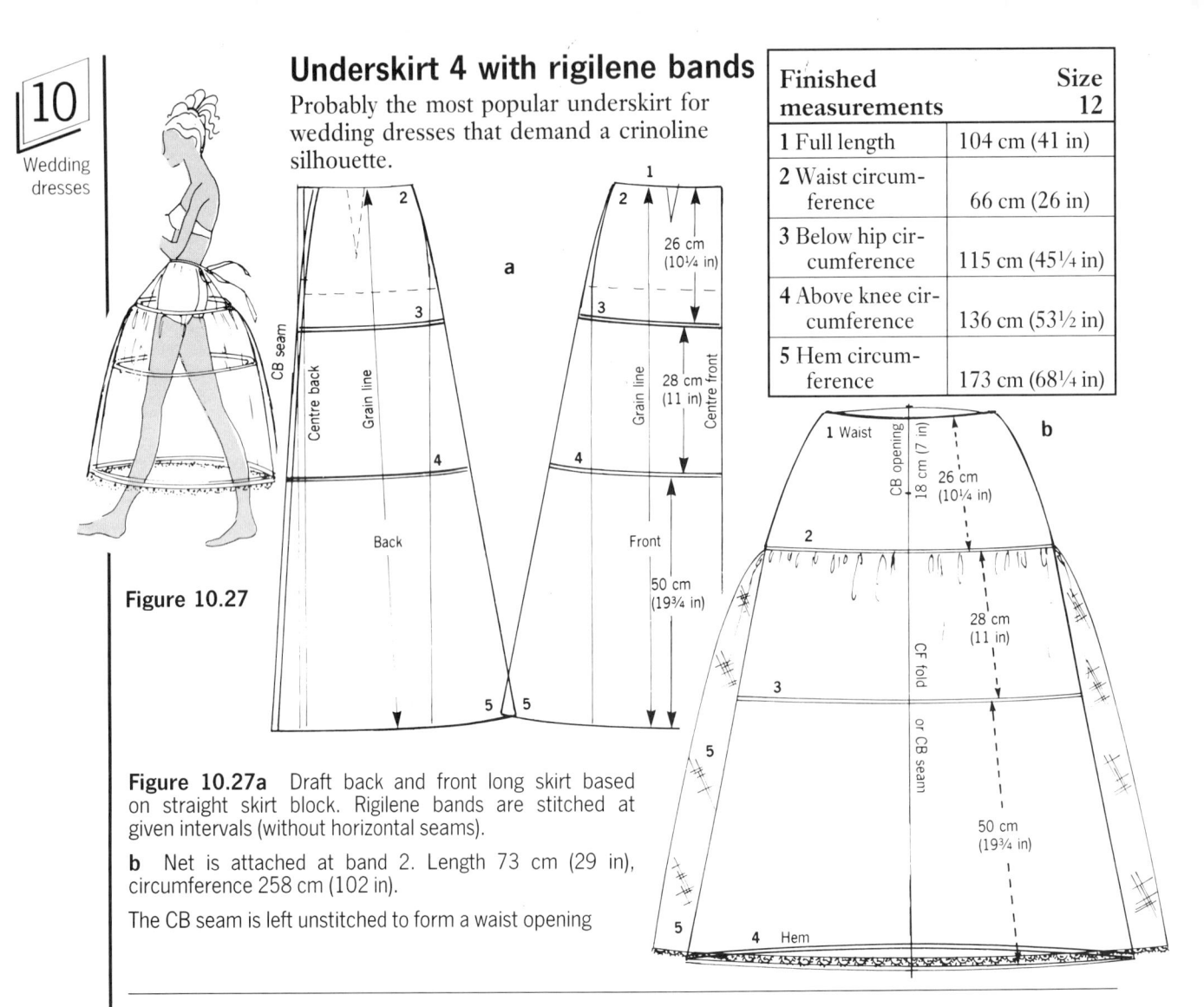

Full length veil

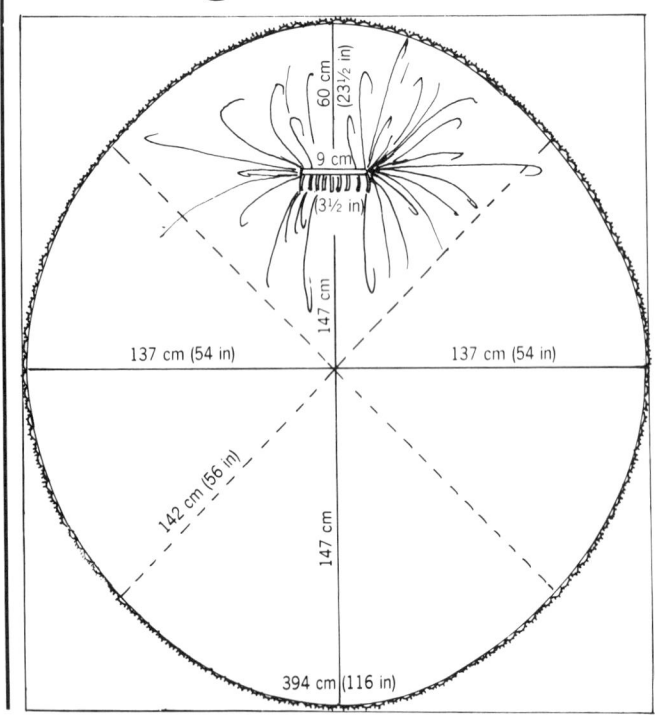

Figure 10.28 Draw vertical line – length 294 cm (116 in). Divide in half; square horizontal line 137 cm (54 in) each side of vertical line. Draw diagonal guide lines 142 cm (56 in). Connect in slightly oval shape. Measure 60 cm (23½ in) down from top; square out 15 cm (6 in) each side of vertical line. Machine two rows of gathering stitches; gather to length of 9 cm (3½ in). Machine short inside seam to create a ridge to which a 8.5 cm (3½ in) padded combe is sewn by hand.

Figure 10.28 Completed full length veil pattern

Trousers

Trousers are not only a useful and practical item of clothing but have now become an important garment of fashion. The one sociological factor most probably responsible for the great popularity of trousers in Western society is women's acknowledged status of equality with men regarding work and way of life in general. Trousers provide both cover up and freedom of movement, and further lend themselves well to periodic fashion changes and style permutations as other articles of clothing.

As with other garments, it is possible to model trousers entirely on a trouser form (Figures 11.1 and 11.2), or directly on the human figure, but a quicker and more assuredly successful method is to begin with a well-constructed basic block. Major silhouette changes (Figure 11.7a and d) are made on the flat and the pattern is then cut out in a trial fabric, for example, muslin or unbleached calico, and made up as an experimental garment, a trouser 'toile'. It is subsequently seen on a figure with the same measurements as those used in the construction of the original trouser block or on a trouser form representing these measurements.

At this point three-dimensional designing begins. The fit, shape and length is checked; the placing of seams, yokes and style lines explored and marked; and the positioning of pockets, buttons and belts, use of trimmings, contrast fabric and top stitching considered in relation with the other garments that will be worn with the trousers.

The study of national characteristics and traditions, and the history and development of trousers is a most fascinating and rewarding subject for the designer, and his or her imagination will be stimulated by it (Figures 11.3 – 11.6). But most importantly, when creating new and pleasing designs, the shape of the female figure must always remain the governing factor in the designer's mind.

Figure 11.1

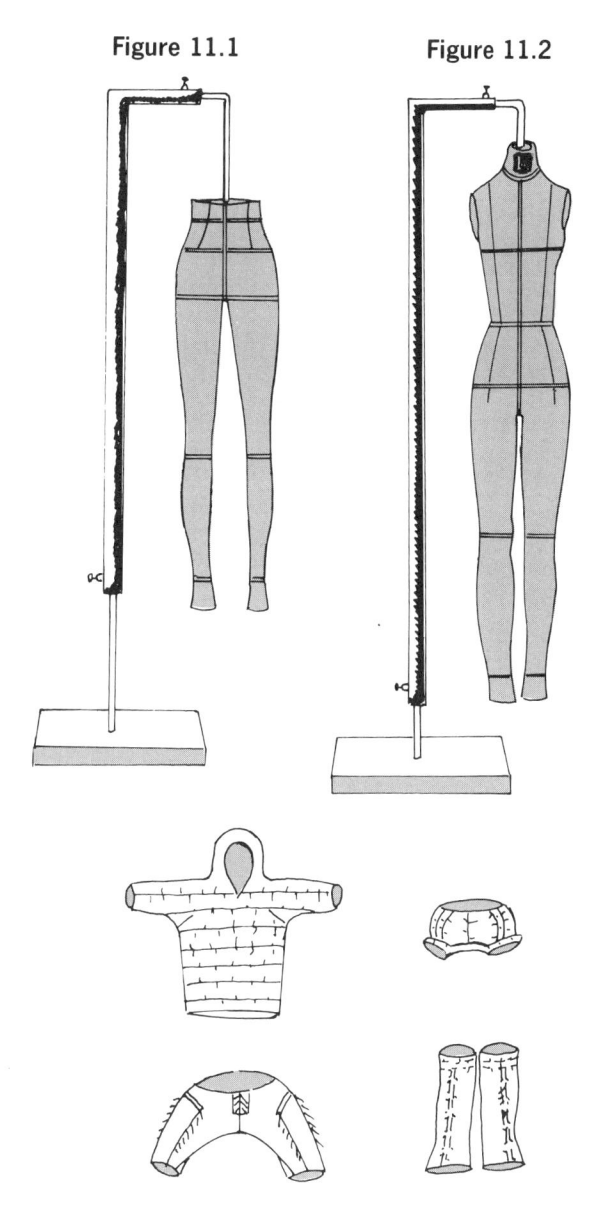

Figure 11.2

Figure 11.3 Eskimos' clothing

Figure 11.4 Mandarin

Figure 11.5 Gentleman's outfit, 1818

Figure 11.6 Working woman's outfit, 1917

11

151

Trouser silhouettes

Figure 11.7

The shape of trousers is influenced mainly by the prevailing fashion silhouette, particularly that of the skirt, but also by the function for which they are intended, and the fabric to be used.

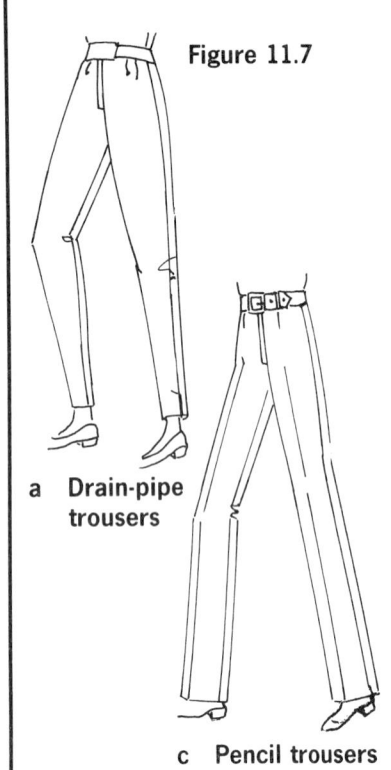

Figure 11.7a Ankle-hugging 'drainpipes' develop into 'flared bottoms' (b), often with the introduction of seams.

c 'Pencil' trousers are straight throughout, yet slimfitting at the waist and hips.

d 'Oxford bags' hang straight and loose, with characteristic pleats at the waistline.

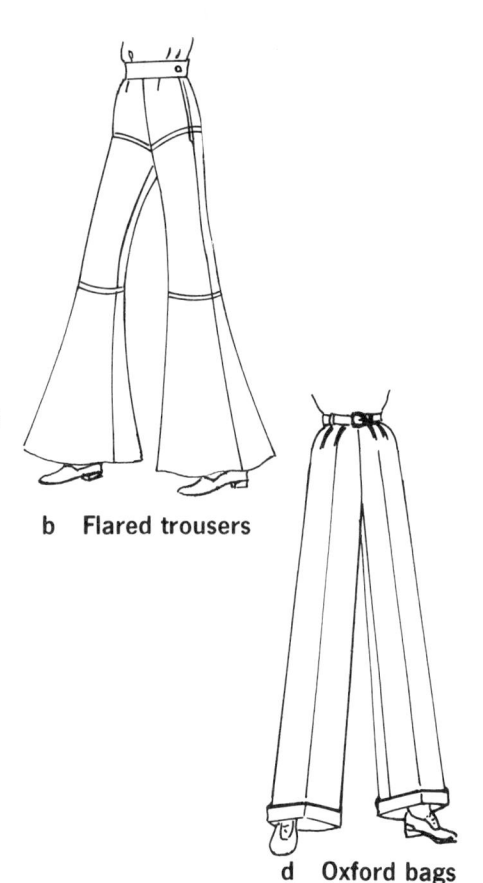

a Drain-pipe trousers
b Flared trousers
c Pencil trousers
d Oxford bags

Trouser development

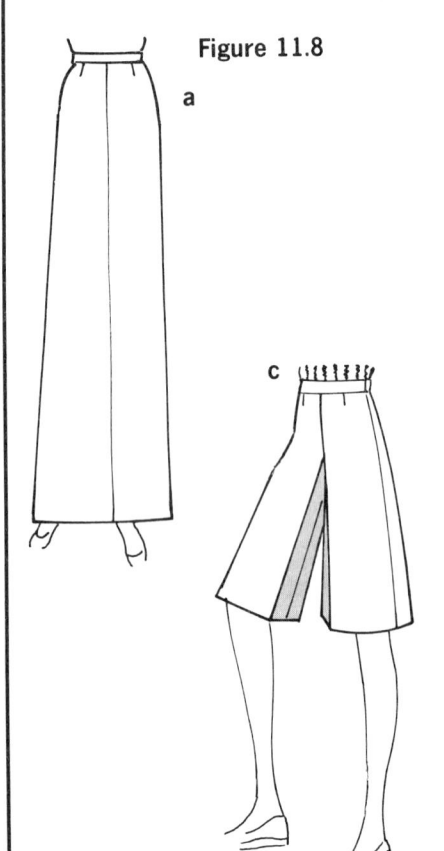

Figure 11.8

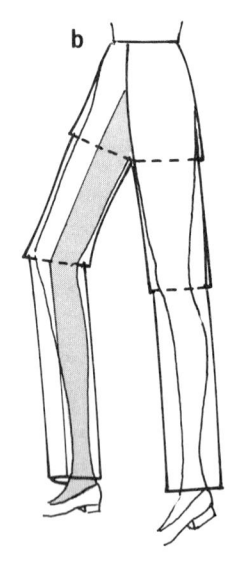

Figure 11.8a and b Except for the inner thigh, trousers cover the same surface area on the body as a skirt.

c and d It will be found, therefore, that a trouser pattern can be developed from a skirt pattern by adding to it a section of paper representing the size and shape of the inner thigh surface.

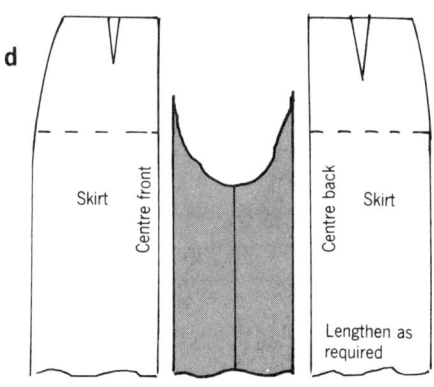

Constructing the trouser block

This trouser block is developed from the straight skirt block shown in Figure 11.9b. See also the scale blocks on page 2 and the trouser block construction, pages 16–17.

Figure 11.9 Basic trousers

Knee level 58 cm (22¾ in)
To fit waist 66 cm (26 in) hip 94 cm (37 in)

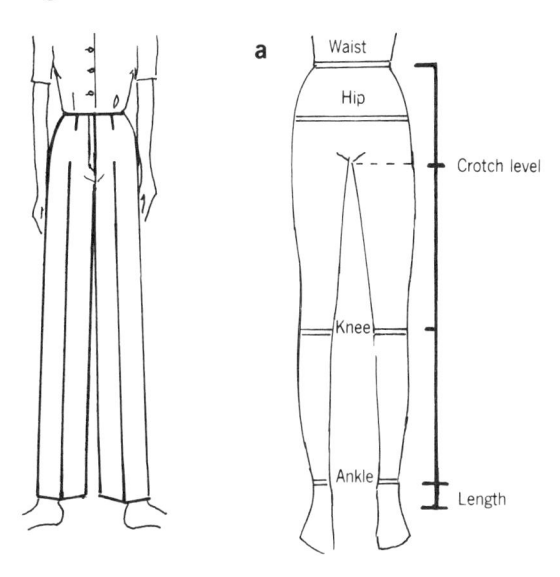

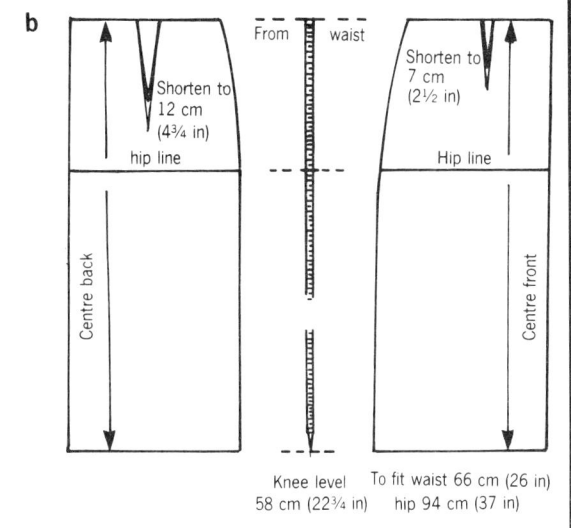

Figure 11.9a and **b** As the skirt blocks already contain the basic shape and measurements, only three more measurements are required to construct the basic trouser block. These are:

1. Outside leg
2. Body rise or crotch level
3. Width of trouser bottom

For comparison of other measurements see the size charts on pages 6 and 7.

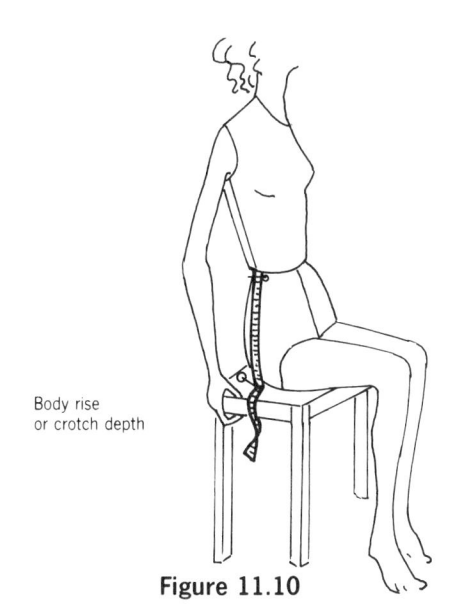

Figure 11.10 The position of the crotch level is determined primarily by the body rise measurement. Added to this measurement is a variable amount of tolerance for ease of movement and comfort in wear. See Table 11.1.

The actual amount allowed over and above the body measurements is influenced by a number of factors. For example, the function – jodhpur and ski trousers, lingerie panties, cami-knickers, pyjama trousers, low-cut 'baggy' trousers or figure-hugging leotard type trousers. The fabric that is to be used is another factor for example, soft stretch fabric instead of a bulky fabric. Probably the most decisive factor regarding everyday-wear garments is the prevailing fashion mood which will 'date' more than anything a trouser crotch line that is considered too high or too low.

Figure 11.10

Table 11.1 Average ease allowances on body rise measurements

Size	10 cm	10 in	12 cm	12 in	14 cm	14 in	16 cm	16 in	18 cm	18 in
Body rise	26.5	10¼	27	10½	27.5	10¾	28	11	29	11½
With ease	27.5	10¾	28	11	28.5	11¼	29	11½	30	12

11 Trousers

Measurement for constructing the size 12 trouser blocks are:

Waist	66 cm (26 in)
Hip	96 cm (37¾ in)
Knee length	58 cm (22¾ in)
Outside leg	102 cm (40 in)
Crotch level from waist	28 cm (11 in)
Bottom of trousers width	60 cm (23½ in)
Knee circumference	60 cm (23½ in)

Figure 11.11 Draw vertical line 102 cm (40 in) long and 15 cm (6 in) away from edge of paper and parallel to it.

Place back skirt block on paper with centre back touching vertical line. Outline to knee level.

Extend waist, hip and knee level lines across paper.

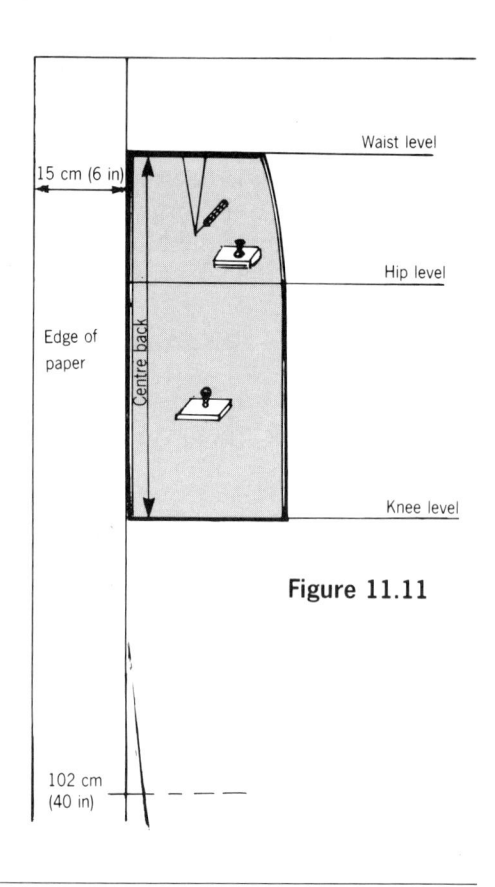

Figure 11.11

Figure 11.12 Place front skirt block to back side seam line with all level lines aligning. Outline. Lengthen and complete centre front, side seam and bottom of trouser lines.

Draw crotch line 28 cm (11 in) down from waist line and parallel to it. Extend this line 12 cm (4¾ in) beyond centre back* and 7 cm (2¾ in) beyond centre front**. Square down to bottom of trousers.

Amounts allowed for extensions are based on the average high thigh measurement and are further influenced by the depth of the crotch level (the higher the level the longer the extension) – 2 or 3 cm (1 in) more or less, do not influence the fit greatly.

An approximate yet reliable calculation is: Back extension* equals half back crotch line plus 3 mm (⅛ in), for example A–B = 23.5 cm (9¼ in). Half A–B is 11.7 + 0.3 = 12 cm (4⅝ + ⅛ = 4¾ in).

Front extension** equals one quarter of front crotch line minus 1 cm (⅜ in), for example, B–C = 24.5 cm (9⅝ in). Quarter B–C is 6.1 – 1 = 5 cm (2⅜ – ⅜ = 2 in).

Figure 11.12

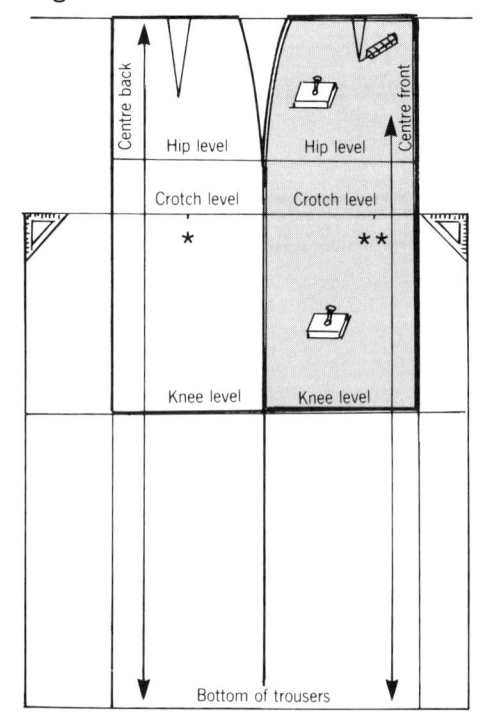

Table 11.2 Examples of crotch line extensions

Size	10	12	14
Back	11.7 cm (4⅝ in)	12 cm (4¾ in)	12.4 cm (4⅞ in)
Front	4.5 cm (1¾ in)	5 cm (2 in)	5.5 cm (2¼ in)

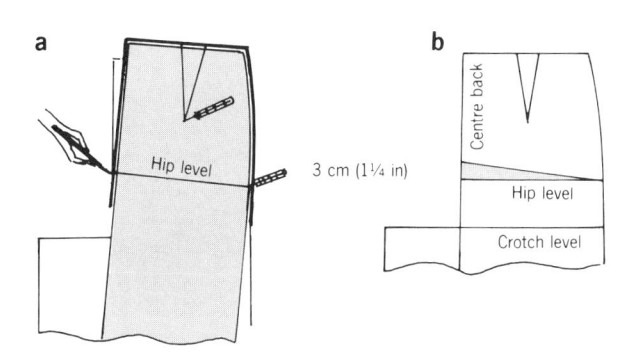

Figure 11.12a On centre back line, where hip line intersects, measure 3 cm (1¼ in) upwards. Connect this point to side seam-hip line intersection.

b Cover back trouser draft with back shirt block and pivot hip line up by 3 cm (1¼ in), as shown. Outline new slanting centre back, waist line, dart and side seam.

c Draft back crotch seam line 1 cm (⅜ in) below crotch level at A. Draft front crotch curve. Replace front waist dart with two small tucks and make waist wider by width of one tuck.

Bottom width can be adjusted (see Figures 11.13b, 11.14b and 11.15a). This basic draft is suitable for Oxford bags-type trousers. Add crease line, seam allowances, balance marks and turn-ups if required.

Side seam can be moved forward by 1 cm (⅜ in) if wished.

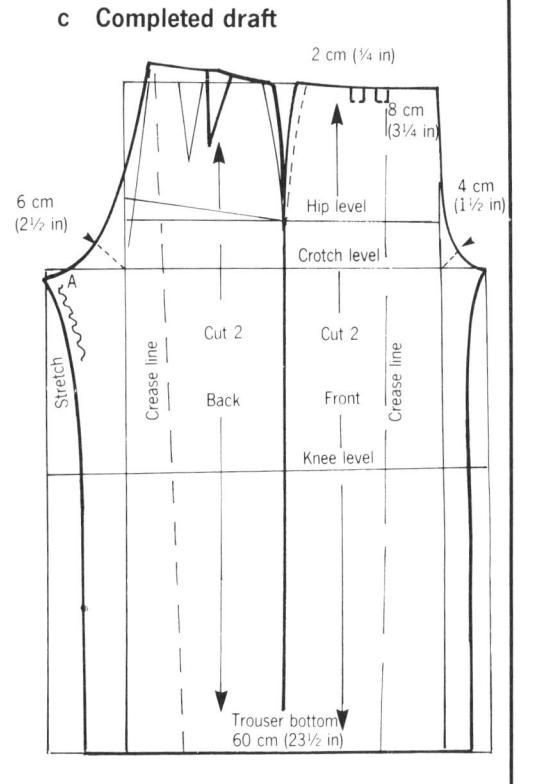

Trouser block adaptations

Figure 11.13

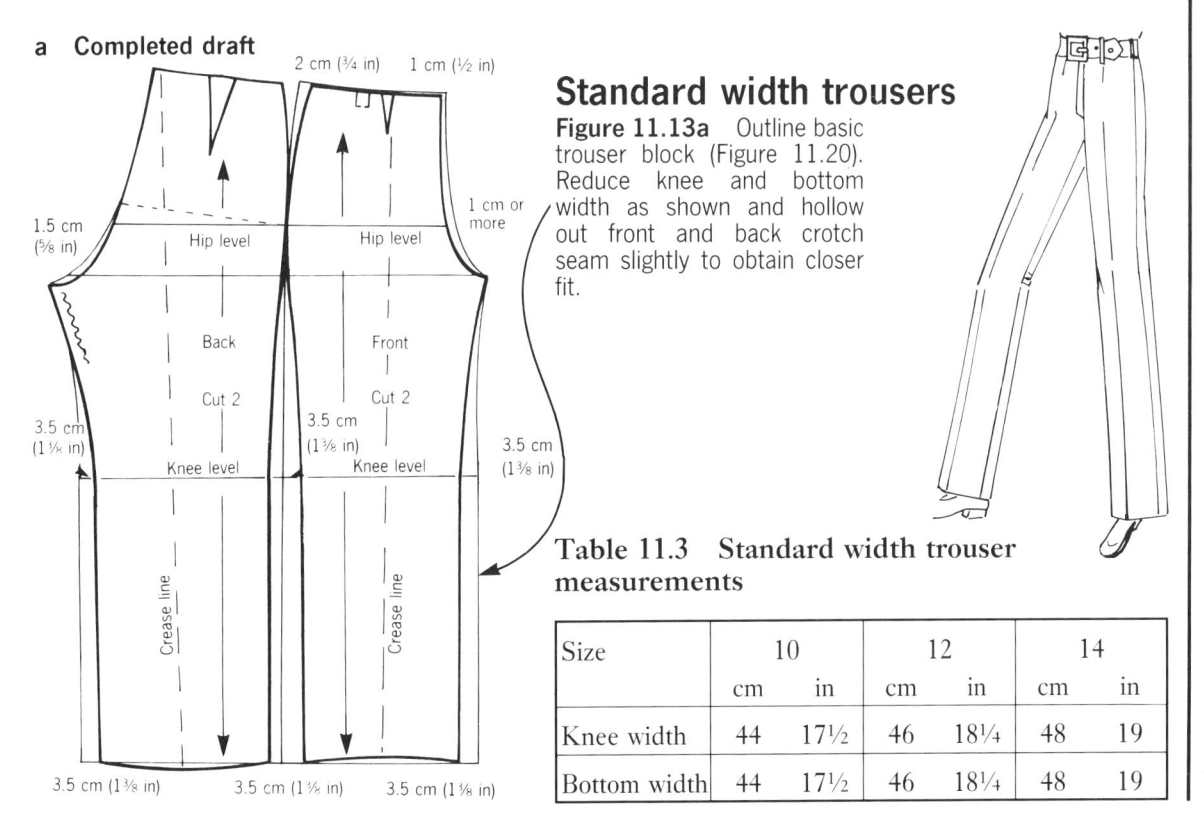

Standard width trousers

Figure 11.13a Outline basic trouser block (Figure 11.20). Reduce knee and bottom width as shown and hollow out front and back crotch seam slightly to obtain closer fit.

Table 11.3 Standard width trouser measurements

Size	10 cm	10 in	12 cm	12 in	14 cm	14 in
Knee width	44	17½	46	18¼	48	19
Bottom width	44	17½	46	18¼	48	19

Figure 11.14

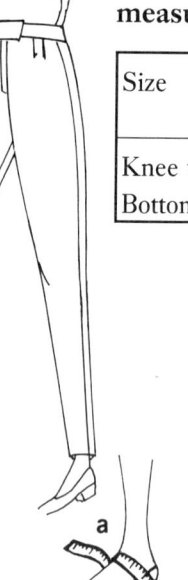

Table 11.4 Tapered width trouser measurements

Size	10 cm	10 in	12 cm	12 in	14 cm	14 in
Knee width	43	16¼	44	17¼	45	17¾
Bottom width	31	12	32	12½	33	13

Tapered trousers

Outline basic trouser block (Figure 11.12c). Reduce knee and bottom width as shown in Figure 11.13b. Bottom width is 2–3 cm (1 in) wider than ankle measurement.

Measurements above are suitable for ankle-fitting trousers that slip easily over a foot's heel. For a tighter, 'drainpipes' fit, a short vent must be introduced.

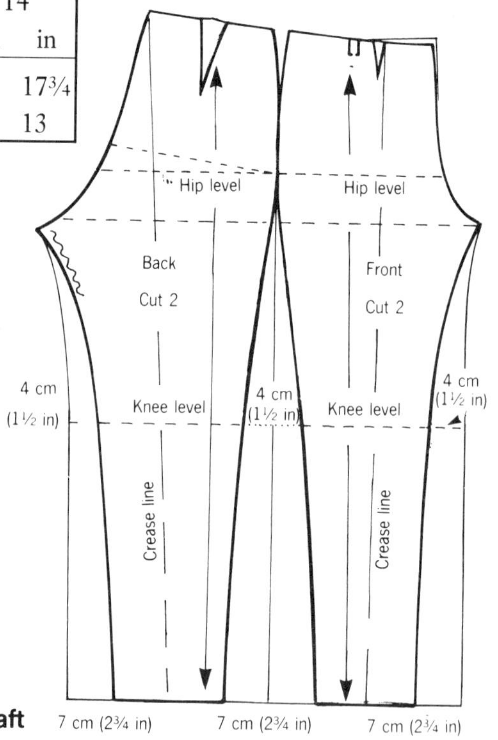

b Completed draft

Figure 11.15

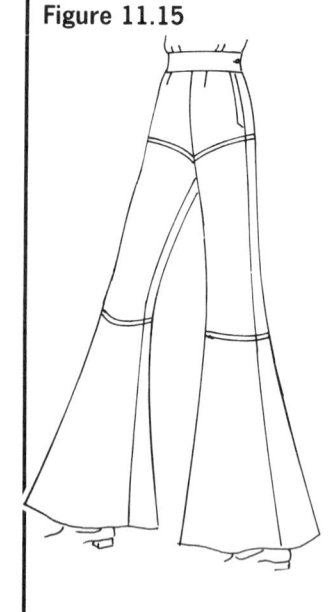

Flared trousers

Outline tapered trouser block (Figure 11.14b). 'Flare' bottom of trousers according to chosen design by adding equal amounts as shown in Figure 11.15a. Make up trousers in a trial fabric and try on. Evaluate fit and shape, and complete final pattern accordingly (see fitting problems, page 157–8).

Look at the silhouette and make any necessary alterations, for example, raising or lowering, decreasing or increasing the flare until the desired effect is achieved. Mark these alterations carefully and recut the pattern.

The bottom width is 70 cm (27½ in), 10 cm (4 in) wider than the basic block shown in Figure 11.12c.

a Completed draft

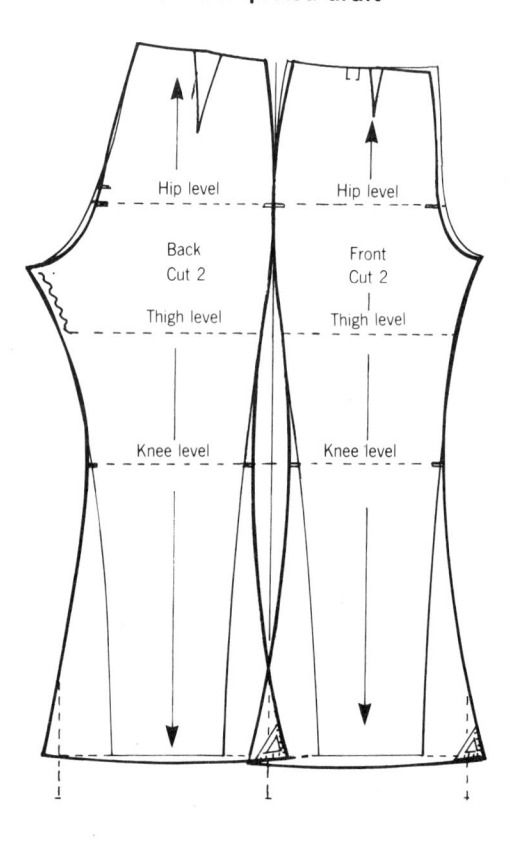

Fitting the trouser block   Figure 11.16   Figure 11.17

The basic trouser blocks shown in Figure 11.12–Figure 11.15 are drafted to the average stock size measurements, and the resulting patterns fit the majority of women with such measurements. Due to differences of body structure in women who otherwise have identical waist and hip measurements, variations in fit may occur, and, therefore, alterations are required. Other reasons for a designer wishing to adapt the fit of trouser blocks are the changes of styles and fashion silhouettes.

Examples of the most frequently encountered alterations

Figure 11.16 Very tight-fitting trousers have fitting problems entirely divorced from the usual adjustments. Unless a stretch material is used, or a seam or horizontal dart introduced, it is impossible to fit trousers immediately below the seat without wrinkles appearing.

This fitting problem is again encountered when trousers are expected to flare out suddenly from a previously leg-hugging fit without causing the side seam to pull; a seam placed in this position is a great fitting aid.

Figure 11.17a Oxford bags are much easier to fit provided sufficient fulness for pleats at waist level is allowed.

b If wrinkles appear across the seat, and side seams swing slightly forward, this denotes either a 'flat seat' or prominent abdomen.

c To correct this, raise the back waist line by pinning a horizontal dart and, if required, let out some of the front waist seam allowance until a satisfactory fit and hang is achieved.

d Mark any alterations with a soft pencil and alter the pattern accordingly.

e If the trousers are too short at the back this denotes a large seat and the crotch length is too short for the wearer. Let out the waist seam allowance at centre back and graduate towards the front, and lengthen the back crotch seam on the pattern as shown in **f**. Sometimes two waist darts achieve a better fit.

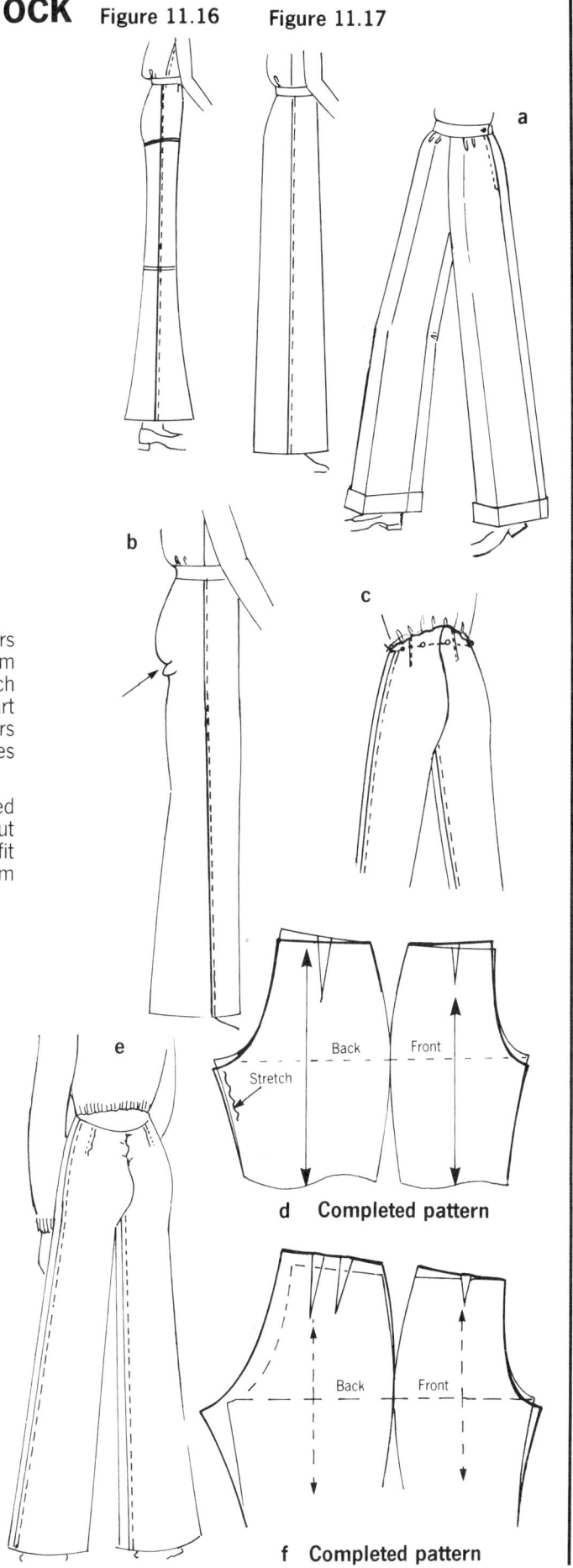

d Completed pattern

f Completed pattern

Figure 11.18

Figure 11.18 Where wrinkles occur in the front, and sometimes in a similar manner at the back, it means that the crotch length is too short and not shaped enough.

a Pin the crotch seam and mark the alterations carefully with a soft pencil.

b Transfer these markings to the pattern and lengthen the crotch seam.

c Assemble one trouser leg at a time and stitch the crotch seam last of all. Press in leg creases before trying on.

a

b Completed alteration

c

Jeans

Figure 11.19 Outline standard width trouser block (Figure 11.13a, page 155).

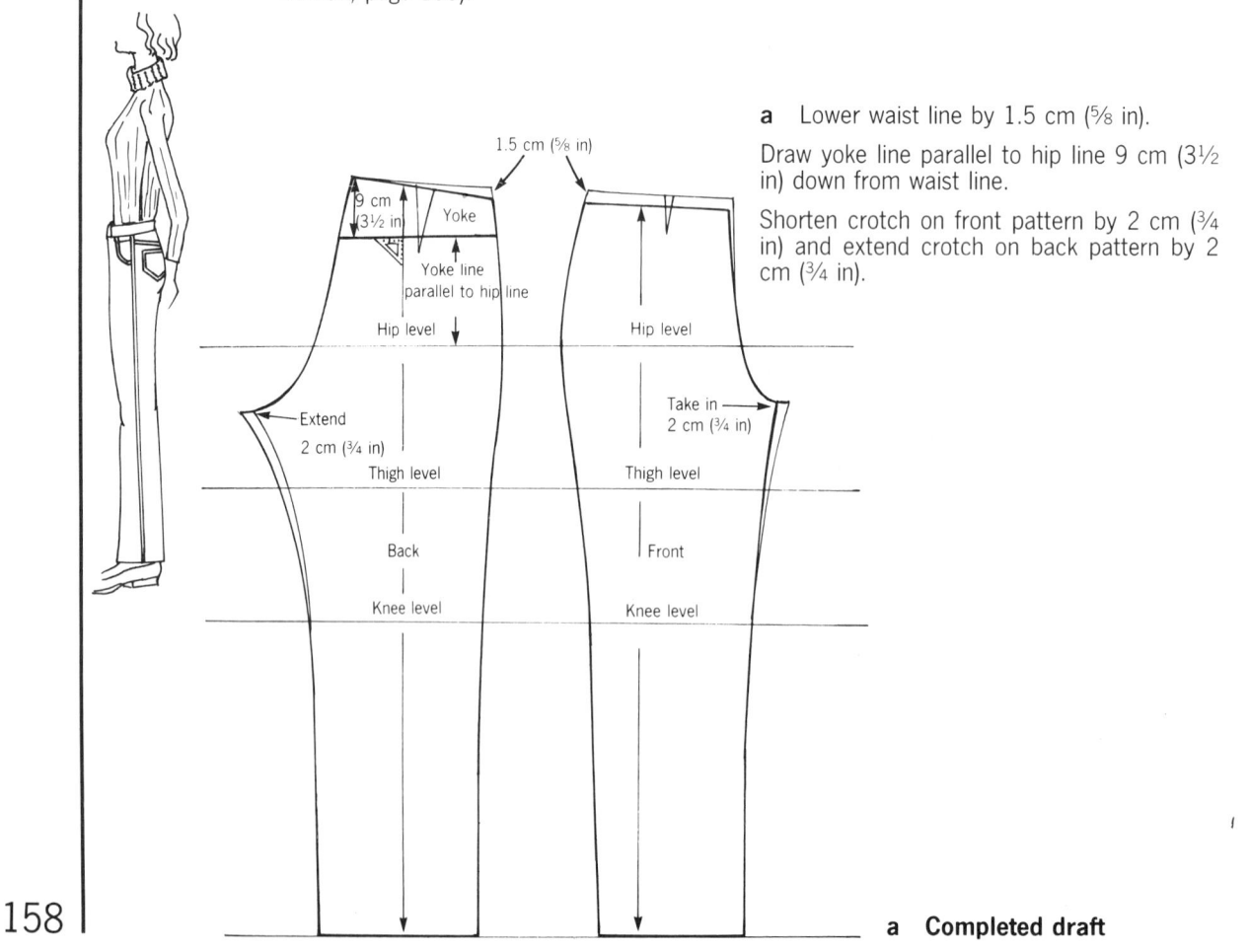

a Lower waist line by 1.5 cm (⅝ in).

Draw yoke line parallel to hip line 9 cm (3½ in) down from waist line.

Shorten crotch on front pattern by 2 cm (¾ in) and extend crotch on back pattern by 2 cm (¾ in).

a Completed draft

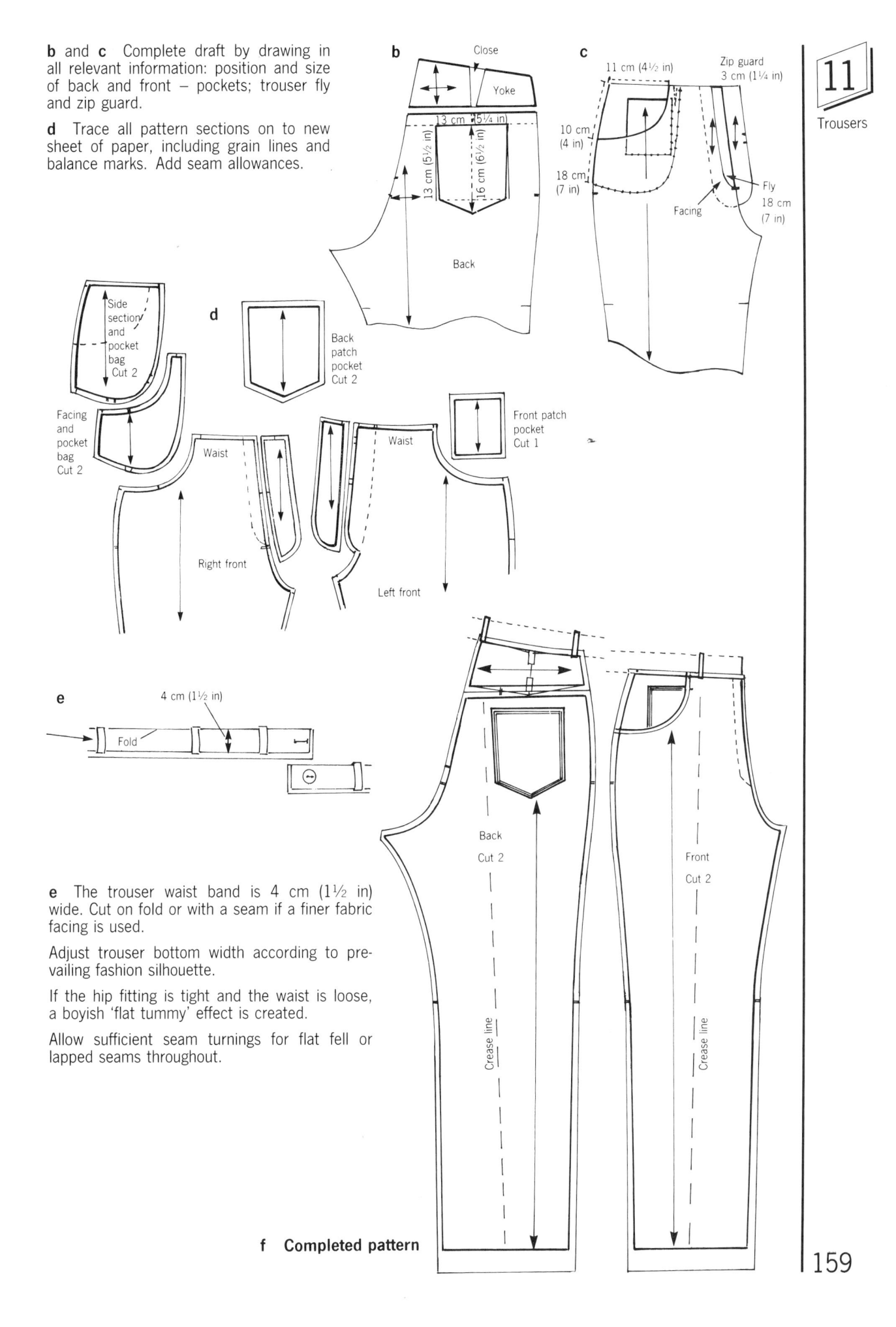

b and **c** Complete draft by drawing in all relevant information: position and size of back and front – pockets; trouser fly and zip guard.

d Trace all pattern sections on to new sheet of paper, including grain lines and balance marks. Add seam allowances.

b Close Yoke
13 cm (5¼ in)
13 cm (5½ in) 16 cm (6½ in)
Back

c 11 cm (4½ in) Zip guard 3 cm (1¼ in)
10 cm (4 in)
18 cm (7 in)
Facing Fly 18 cm (7 in)

d
Side section and pocket bag Cut 2
Facing and pocket bag Cut 2
Back patch pocket Cut 2
Waist — Right front
Waist — Left front
Front patch pocket Cut 1

e 4 cm (1½ in) Fold

e The trouser waist band is 4 cm (1½ in) wide. Cut on fold or with a seam if a finer fabric facing is used.

Adjust trouser bottom width according to prevailing fashion silhouette.

If the hip fitting is tight and the waist is loose, a boyish 'flat tummy' effect is created.

Allow sufficient seam turnings for flat fell or lapped seams throughout.

Back Cut 2 — Crease line
Front Cut 2 — Crease line

f Completed pattern

11 Trousers

Bloomers

An American lady, Amelia Jenks Bloomer, was responsible for the creation of the bloomer suit, and for the success it enjoyed with female cyclists in the second half of the nineteenth century.

Figure 11.20a The fashionable twill bathing-suit of 1890 was adapted from the long, tailored jacket and knee-length baggy pants of the bloomer suit.

b The cami-bockers appeared in 1929.

c The gradual merging of the style of bloomers with the then new divided skirt, and later the trousers, led to a more fitted garment which retained the characteristic fulness at the bottom of the trouser leg.

By using a basic block, new designs can be created, based on the demands of fashion trends and functional needs.

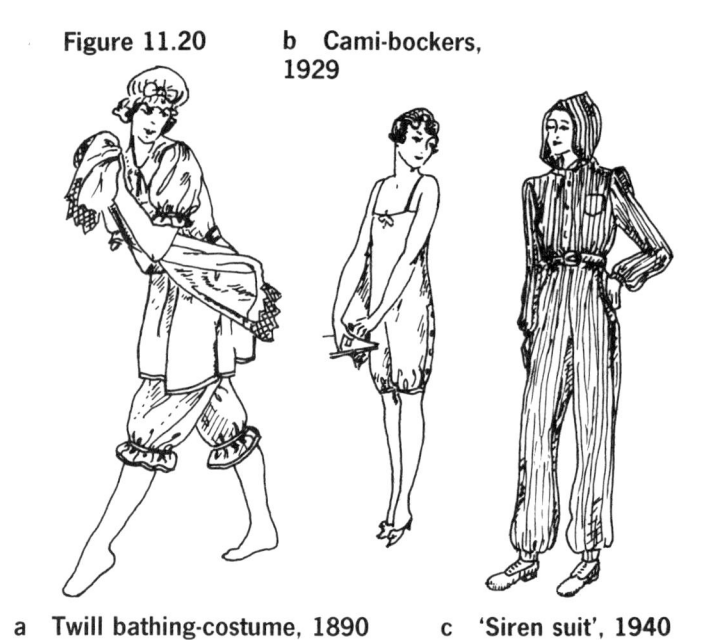

Figure 11.20

a Twill bathing-costume, 1890
b Cami-bockers, 1929
c 'Siren suit', 1940

Tracksuit trousers

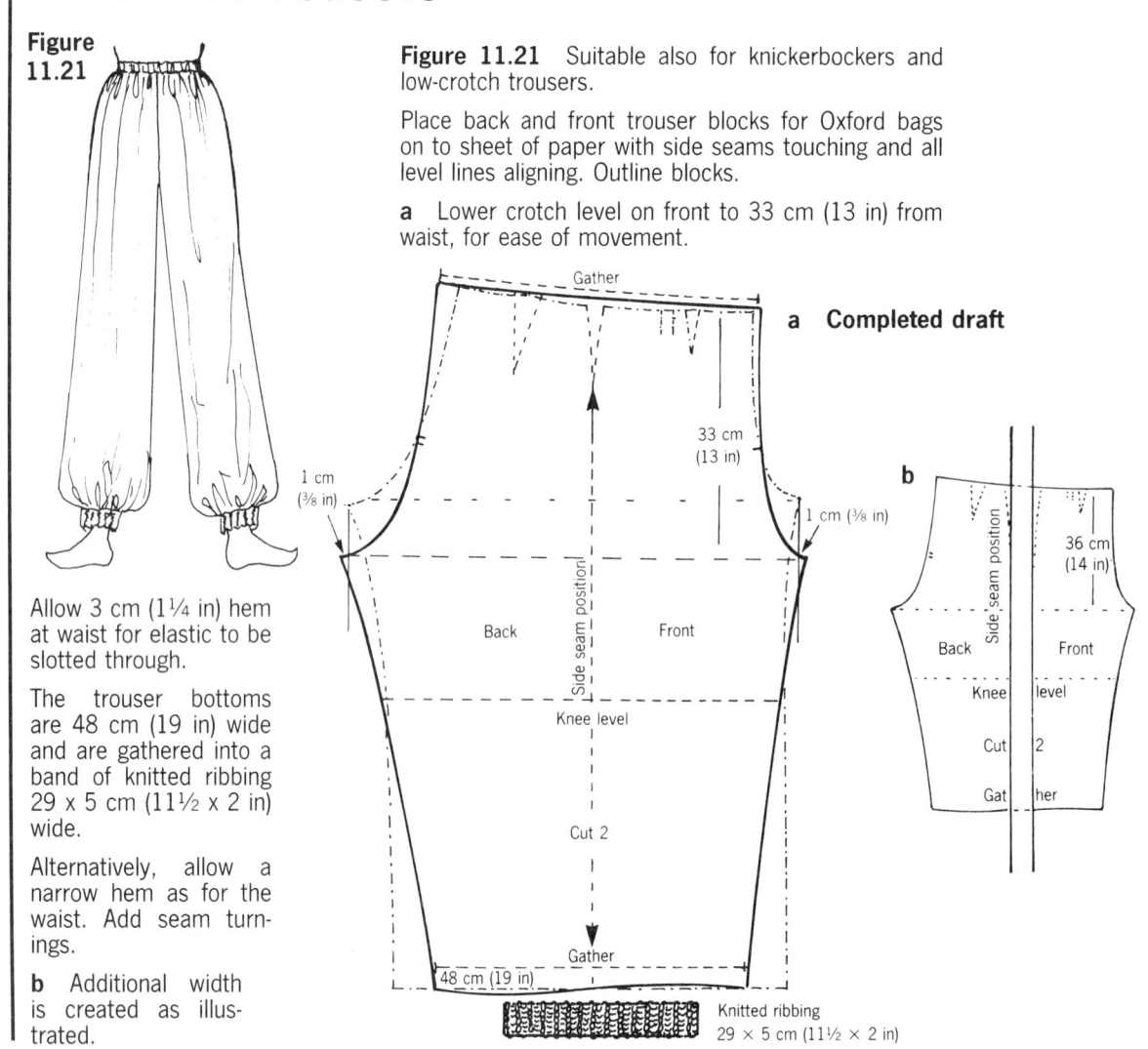

Figure 11.21

Figure 11.21 Suitable also for knickerbockers and low-crotch trousers.

Place back and front trouser blocks for Oxford bags on to sheet of paper with side seams touching and all level lines aligning. Outline blocks.

a Lower crotch level on front to 33 cm (13 in) from waist, for ease of movement.

a Completed draft

b

Allow 3 cm (1¼ in) hem at waist for elastic to be slotted through.

The trouser bottoms are 48 cm (19 in) wide and are gathered into a band of knitted ribbing 29 × 5 cm (11½ × 2 in) wide.

Alternatively, allow a narrow hem as for the waist. Add seam turnings.

b Additional width is created as illustrated.

Jodhpur trousers

Figure 11.22

Figure 11.22a Draw horizontal line on pattern paper representing trouser crotch level. Place back and front tapered leg trouser blocks (Figure 11.14b) on to paper aligning crotch level lines. Outline as shown.

Lower crotch level lines and crotch points by 4 cm (1½ in) and extend widths by amounts given.

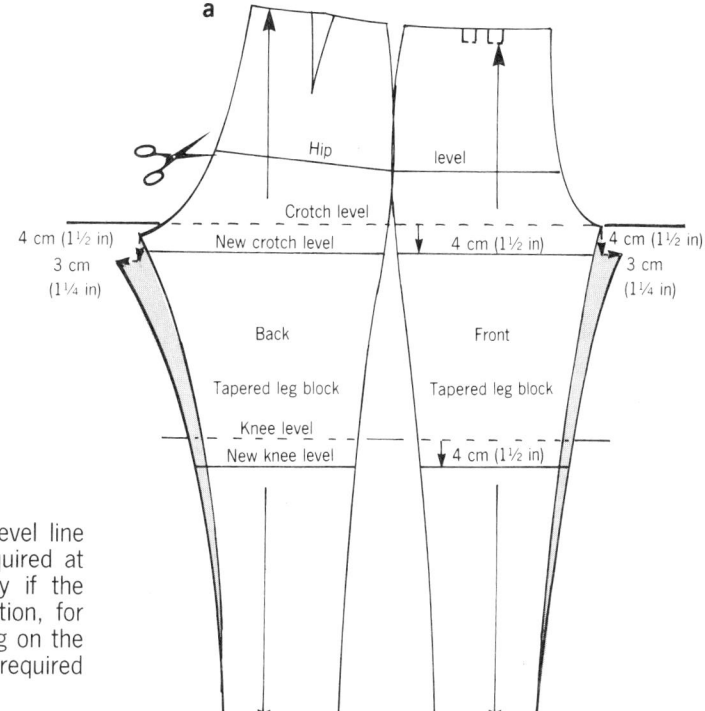

Draw new inner leg seams. Lower knee level line by 4 cm (1½ in). Additional length is required at the centre back crotch seam, particularly if the trousers are to be worn in a sitting position, for example, riding. This is achieved by cutting on the back hip line and opening the slash by the required amount.

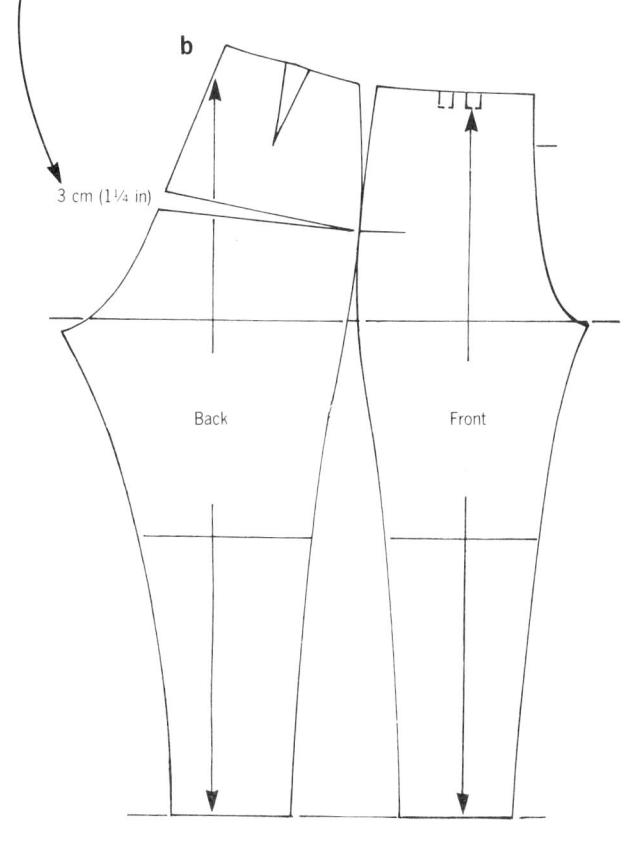

b Cut on back hip level line from centre back to side seam. Open slash 3 cm (1¼ in) and outline new centre back crotch seam line and back waist line including waist dart.

The trouser block is now ready for development into jodhpur-style trousers.

Jodhpur trousers and breeches are sometimes in fashion, but primarily they are worn for riding and other sports activities. The wearer must feel comfortable in movement and in a sitting position.

c Shape side seams. Add seam allowances, balance marks, grain lines and cutting instructions.

Cut out in calico allowing large seam turnings for possible adjustment. Fit on a figure to see trousers in movement.

Fulness around hip area can be reduced or increased as desired until satisfactory effect is achieved. Add pockets, waistband and, if required, fly-front opening); see pages 17 and 159.

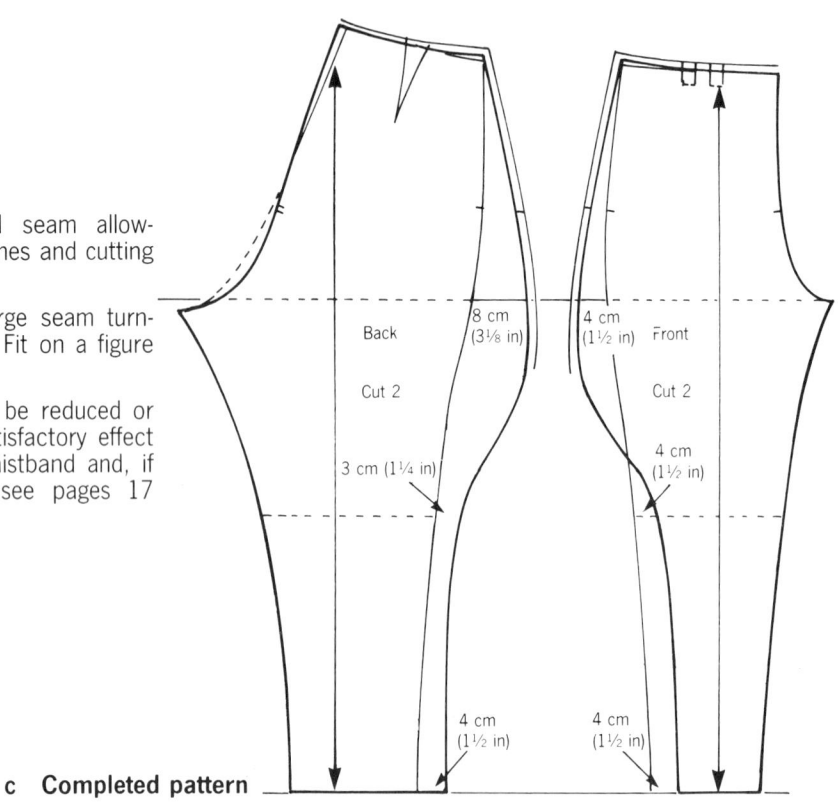

c Completed pattern

Jodhpur breeches

Figure 11.23

Figure 11.23 Outline jodhpur trouser pattern (Figure 11.21c). Shorten trouser legs 8 cm (3⅛ in). Make front leg pattern narrower and back wider by amounts shown. The underknee horizontal seam or dart achieves a closer fit in this area. The dart at hem level creates shape for the calf of the leg and reduces surplus fabric.

Cut facings and pocket pouches. Add all required data and cutting instructions. Cut out in calico. Fit the toile on a moving figure.

a Completed pattern

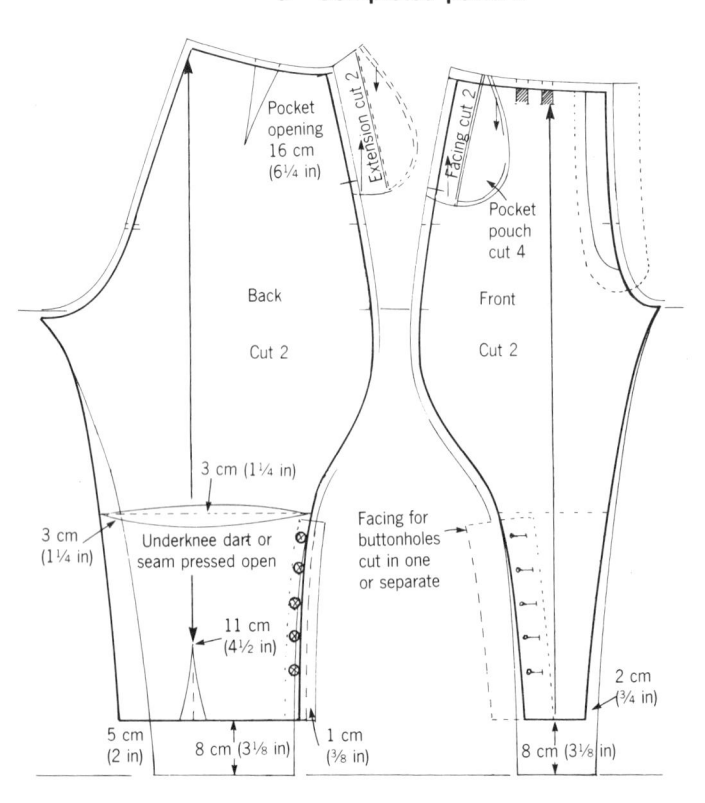

Jumpsuit

Figure 11.24

Figure 11.22 Use hip blocks (Figure 2.19d and 2.20b, page 26) and trouser block (Figure 1.15, page 16 or Figure 11.12c, page 155). Draft on to sheet of paper measuring 150 x 90 cm (59 x 35½ in).

a Draw centre back line 15 cm (6 in) away from left-hand side of paper and parallel to it. Square out a line.

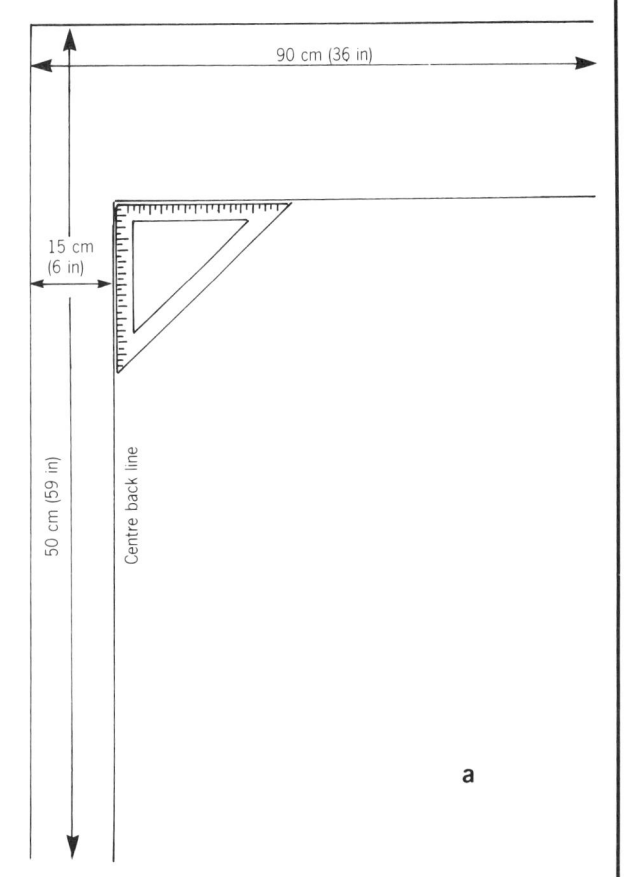

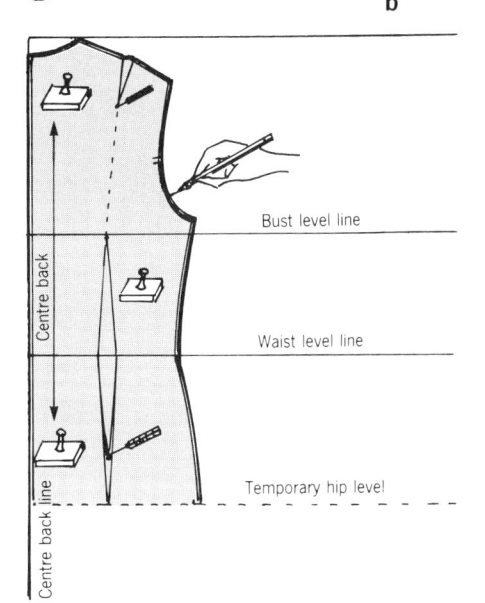

b Place back hip block to centre back line and outline.

Draw bust and waist lines, and dotted temporary hip line.

c Place front hip block 15 cm (6 in) away from outlined back block. Align bust, waist and hip lines and outline.

Draw new permanent hip line 5 cm (2 in) below dotted line to allow for extra ease in movement.

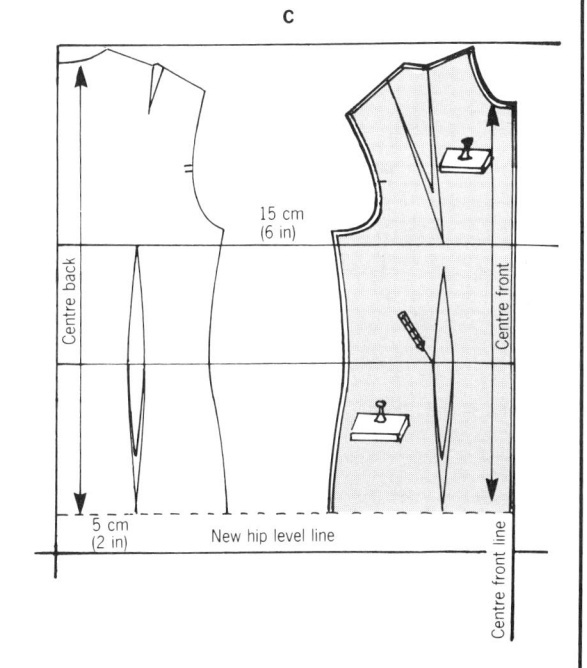

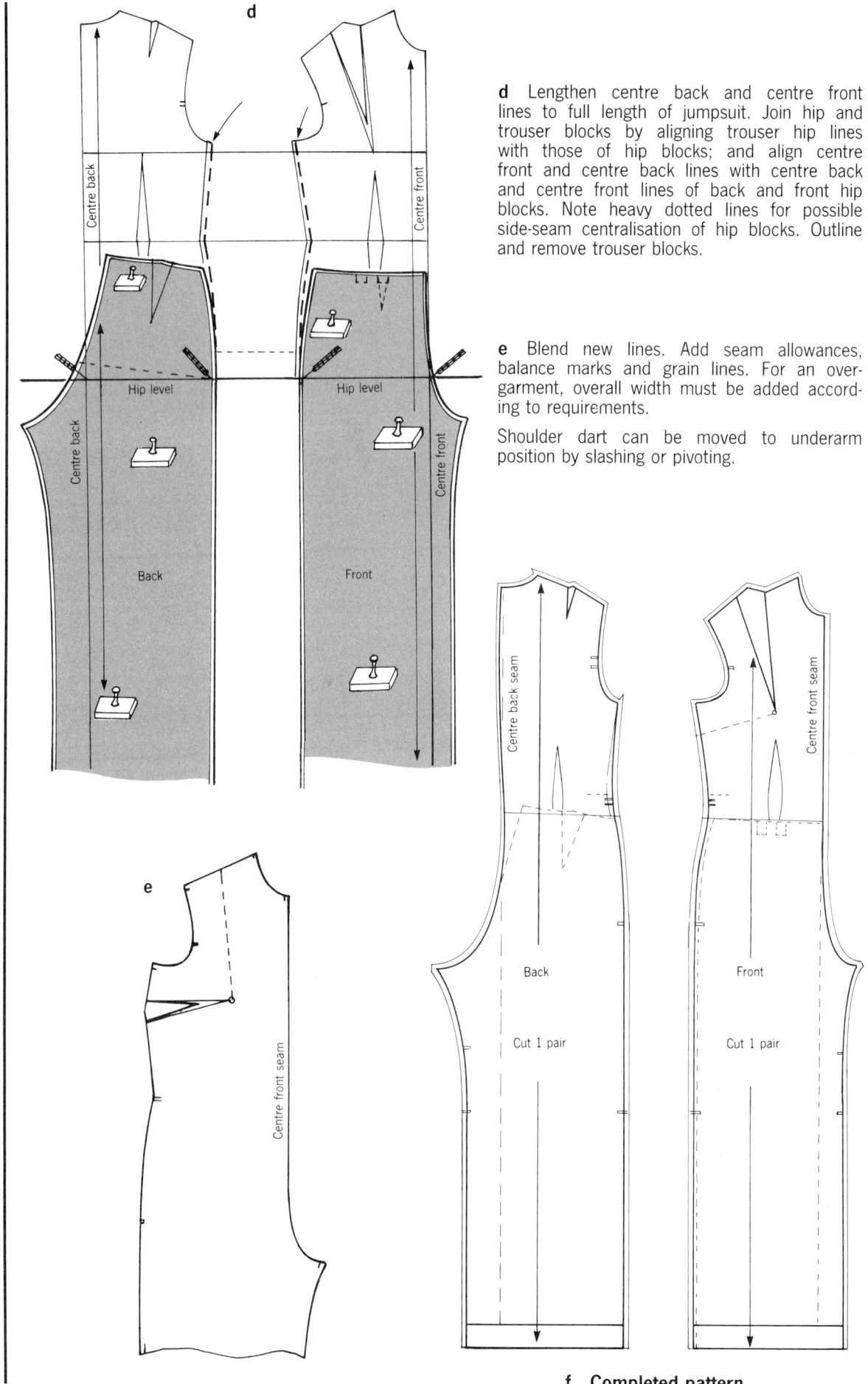

d Lengthen centre back and centre front lines to full length of jumpsuit. Join hip and trouser blocks by aligning trouser hip lines with those of hip blocks; and align centre front and centre back lines with centre back and centre front lines of back and front hip blocks. Note heavy dotted lines for possible side-seam centralisation of hip blocks. Outline and remove trouser blocks.

e Blend new lines. Add seam allowances, balance marks and grain lines. For an over-garment, overall width must be added according to requirements.

Shoulder dart can be moved to underarm position by slashing or pivoting.

f Completed pattern

Dungarees

Made in strong denim, khaki and drilling, overalls and dungarees were (and still are) worn as protective overgarments by men at work. During the Second World War, factory girls tackled the jobs of men, and began to wear slacks and dungarees. Today, dungarees have become a fashion garment for women, with a unisex look, and their function is now perhaps associated more with leisure than work. By their nature, dungarees still remain loose and unrestricting, but the fabrics in which they are now being made are often lighter in weight and more varied in colour and design.

The dungarees shown in Figure 11.25 are cut flat, but pattern parts can be tried out on the figure or on the dress form, in paper or in modelling material, until the desired effect is achieved (a and b).

Figure 11.25

Dungarees, 1939

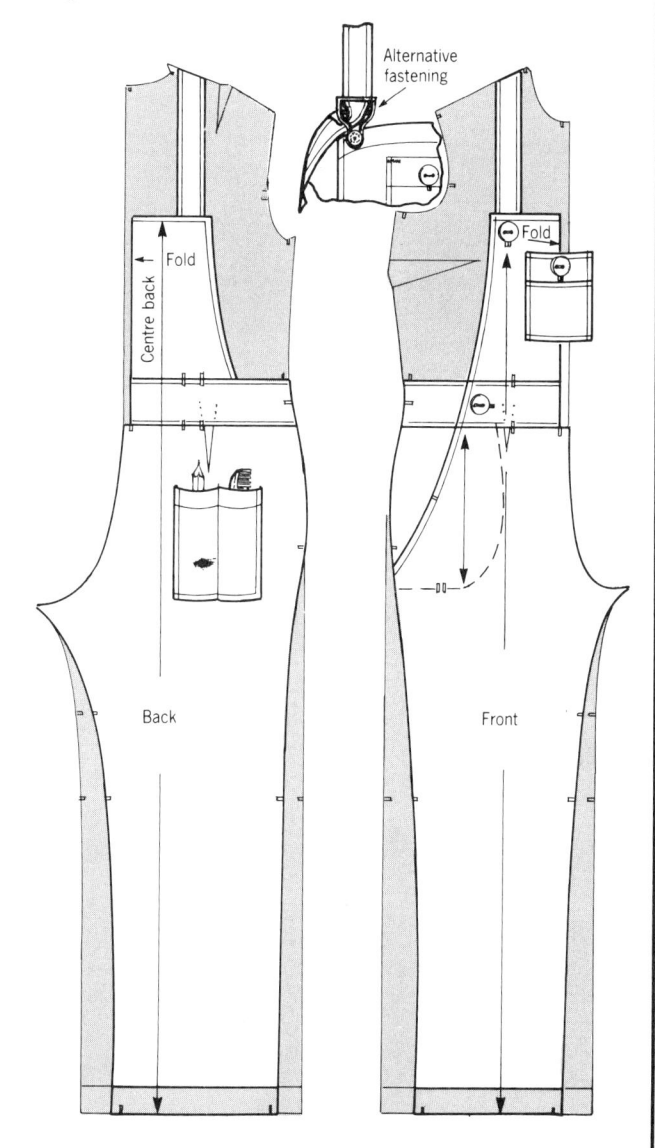

Figure 11.26

Figure 11.25a Outline basic jumpsuit block (Figure 11.24e). Reduce trouser bottom width as desired.

Draft style lines, pockets, mark button positions and holes, balance marks and other relevant information.

a **Completed draft**

11
Trousers

b Trace pattern sections on to new paper and add seam allowances only where required, according to seam type.

b Completed pattern

Ski-suit

Figure 11.27

The function of the ski-suit must be carefully considered before the pattern is made. It is an outer garment worn over layers of other clothing and could also be interlined with thick wadding. It must, therefore, be loosely fitting and allow for much ease in movement.

This ski-suit is based on the basic jumpsuit construction (Figure 11.24e, page 164), which has already extra length allowed from nape to waist, and from waist to crotch level. But in addition it is recommended that the still lower-level crotch lines of the track-suit trousers (Figure 11.21, page 160) or the pyjama trousers (Figure 13.26i, page 203) be given consideration with added width as required. (See also relatively small adjustments for jacket development, page 177.) Also consult British Standard Institution's guidelines for the sizing of sports- and outerwear.

Figure 11.27 has elasticated straps at the wrists and ankles, and has an elasticated waist belt. A long zip at back waist line and part of side seams can be included in the design for practical considerations (a).

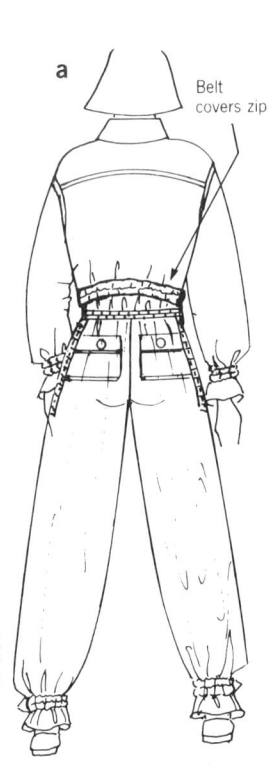

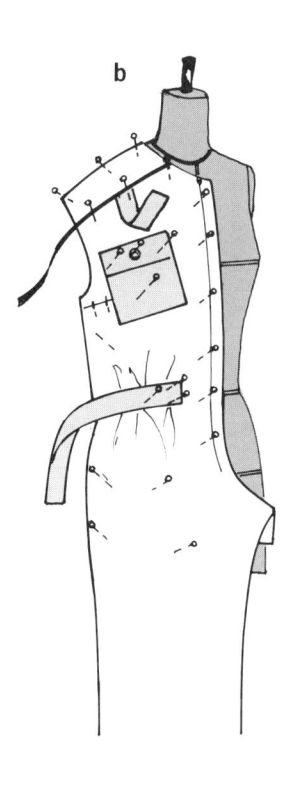

b Outline **jumpsuit** (Figure 11.24e, page 164), having made above suggested adjustments to it. Reduce width of trouser bottoms to 50 x 55 cm (19¾ x 21½ in). Lower neckline by 2 cm (¾ in) all around. Move underarm dart to armhole (see page 48, Figure 3.26a). Tentatively draw yoke lines, position of waist line and pockets. Cut out and pin back and front shoulders and side seams together with a lapped seam. Pin this paper shell to the dress form.

c With tape, outline the most pleasing effect for front and back yoke lines. Cut out paper shapes for pockets, buttons, straps and belt, and experiment with them in different positions. Tuck crotch under for a more realistic trouser effect. Model collar in calico (Figure 11.28) or cut flat by either of two methods shown in Figures 11.29 and 11.30.

Assess appearance of garment. A long zip down centre front could be improvised to make the pattern look more realistic. Mark all lines, positions of pockets, etc. and balance marks lightly. Remove pattern from dress form, unpin and hold ready for later development.

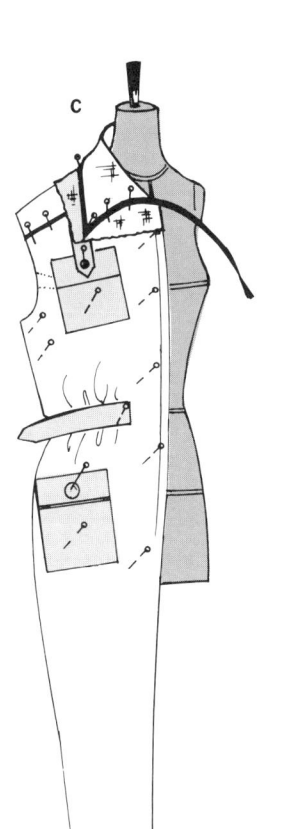

Modelling the collar for the ski-suit

Figure 11.28

Figure 11.28 Cut piece of muslin approximately 25 x 30 cm (9¾ x 12 in) Mark left edge centreback. Cut away a triangle section 4 x 30 cm (1½ x 12 in).

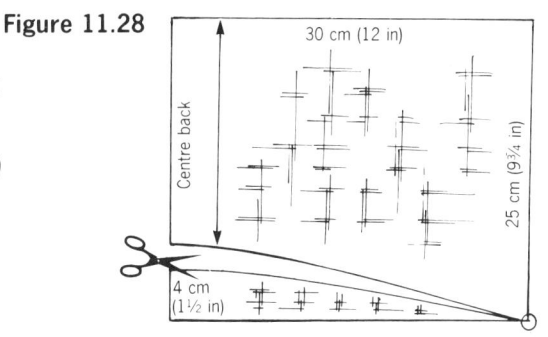

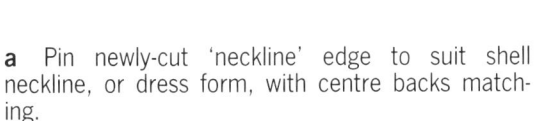

a Pin newly-cut 'neckline' edge to suit shell neckline, or dress form, with centre backs matching.

b Keeping bulk of muslin above neckline, pin and ease muslin around neck to centre front.

c Turn down collar and assess result. If in doubt continue raising or lowering parts of the collar neckline, thereby causing it to be more or less curved, until desired degree of roll is achieved.

d Outline with tape possible collar shapes until desired shape is established. Mark; outline lightly with dots using a soft pencil or felt-tipped pen. Mark also centre back, neckline and centre front point.

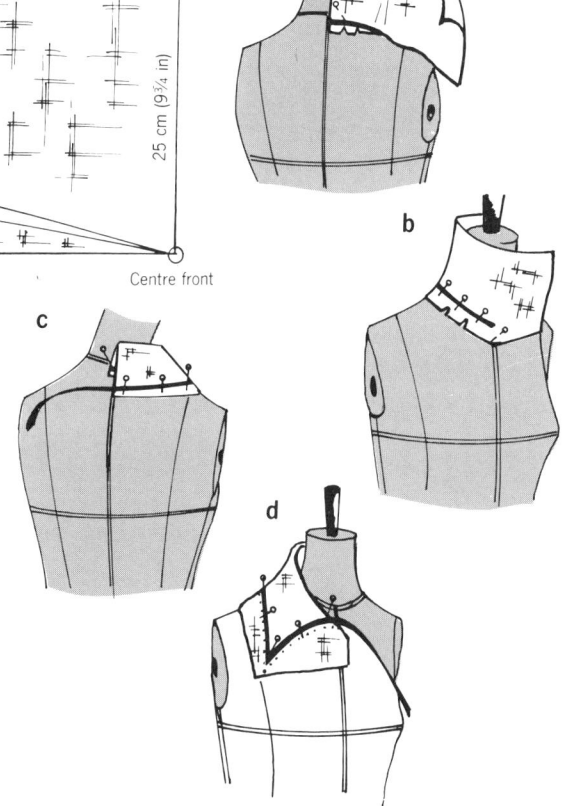

e and **f** Remove pattern from dress form; lay flat. True all dotted lines.

g Trace through onto folded pattern paper. Unfold and redraw marks. This pattern represents the undercollar. Add 5 mm (¼ in) around outer edge of collar from nothing at CF points. Trace through; draft top collar with relevant information (**h**).

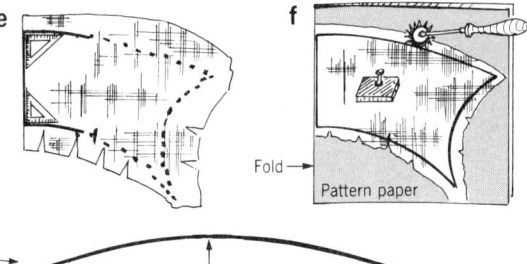

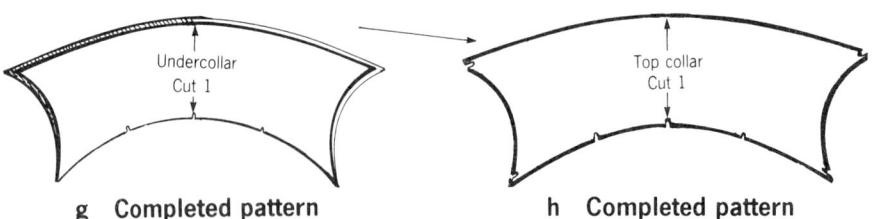

g Completed pattern

h Completed pattern

Ski-suit collar cut flat – method 1

Figure 11.29a Outline upper part of front pattern. Mark pivoting point where shown.

Figure 11.29

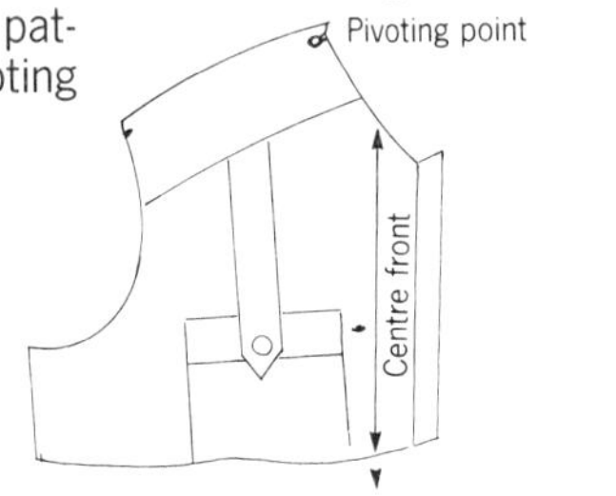

b Place back pattern on to outlined front with pivoting points meeting. Pivot back shoulder point down, 13 cm (5 in) away from front shoulder point. Outline CB line and neckline.

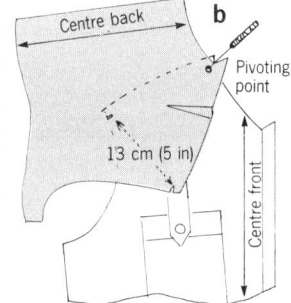

c Draw collar shape; trace off.

d Add seams to outer edge of collar. Develop top collar as Figure 11.28 g and h.

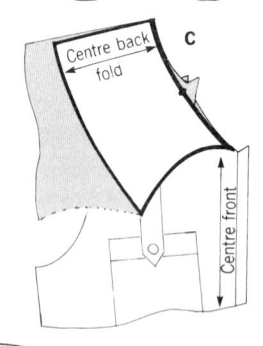

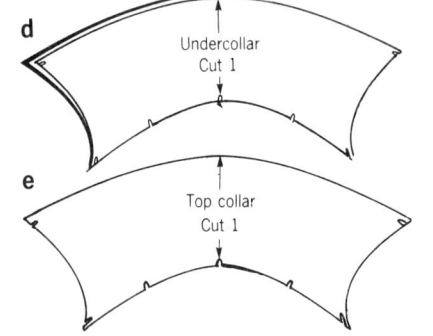

Ski-suit collar cut flat – method 2

Figure 11.30 Outline upper part of front pattern. Draw shape of collar as seen from front.

b Extend shoulder by approximately 25 cm (10 in).

Figure 11.30

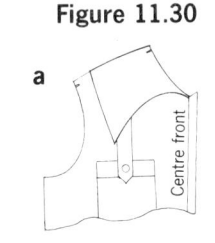

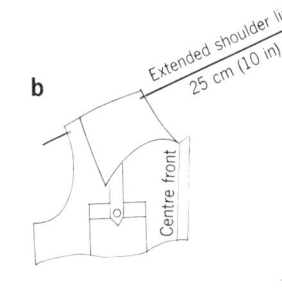

c Place back pattern face down with shoulder/neck points meeting. Drop back shoulder point 8 cm (3¼ in) below extended shoulder line. Outline back neck and CB line. Fold paper under and crease. Trace through collar outline.

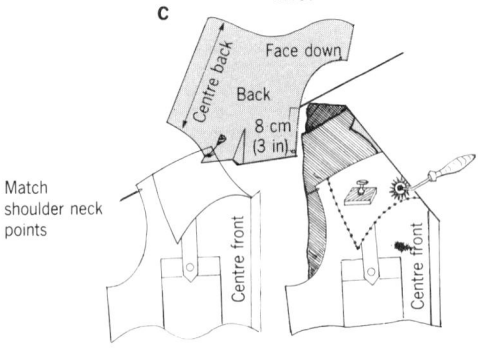

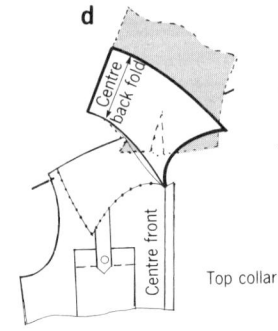

d Unfold paper; draw collar outline on tracing wheel marks; extend to CB. Complete under and top collars as for Figure 11.26g and h.

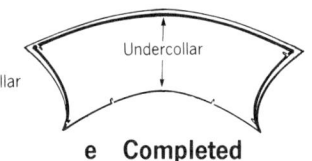

e Completed collar draft

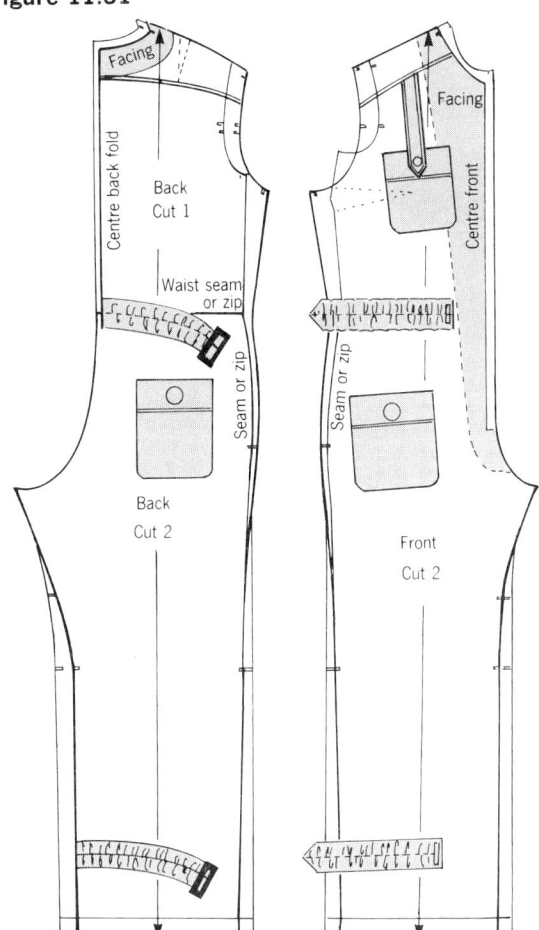

Figure 11.31

Figure 11.31 Lay draft flat on the table. Perfect and redraw all lines tentatively pencilled while on the dress form. Place balance marks and draft facings. Mark positions of belt, straps and pockets.

If preferred, this suit can be cut without waist seam/zip and side seam zips.

Overall width, nape to waist and body rise measurements were all increased when ski-suit was developed from the jumpsuit (see Introduction, page 166 and Figure 11.27), to allow for greater ease of movement.

Keep this draft for reference. It contains all the relevant information and will be useful throughout the making of the pattern.

11 Trousers

Figure 11.32 Trace off all pattern pieces. As the original jumpsuit pattern had seam allowances, only new style lines in this pattern will require seam turnings.

Cut the pattern out in calico and make a toile for final proving and adjustments. Record any changes on the draft.

Trouser bottoms can be more tapered to fit into ski-boots. Storm linings should be sewn inside trouser and sleeve hems.

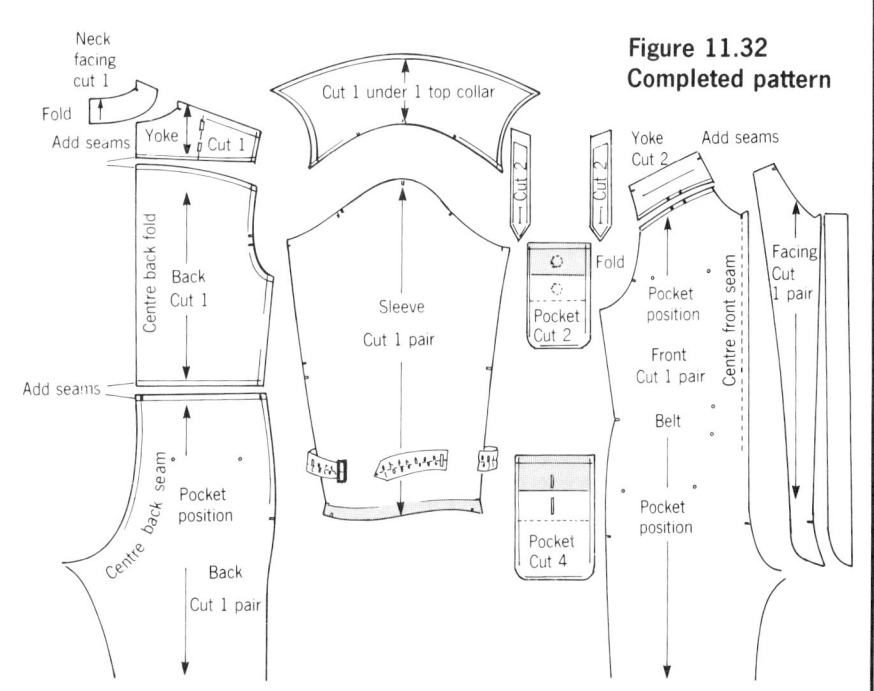

Figure 11.32 Completed pattern

Culottes

This sports garment first became fashionable at the beginning of the twentieth century as the 'divided cycling skirt' (Figure 11.33). The garment hangs loosely and is intended to look like a skirt. Only in movement does the division become apparent (Figure 11.34). Most skirt shapes, except peg-top skirts, can be used to construct divided skirts, whether they are straight, circular or pleated, provided that they have a centre front and centre back seam.

Measurements for size 12 culottes are:

Hip level	20 cm (8 in)
Finished hip measurement	99 cm (39 in)
Crotch level = body rise + ease. Body rise 25.5 cm (10 in) + ease 5 cm (2 in)	30.5 cm (12 in)

Figure 11.34a Draw two parallel lines one quarter of hip measurement 25 cm (9¾ in) away from each other. Mark left line centre front and right line centre back. Mark also hip level position.

Figure 11.33 The 'divided cycling skirt'.

b Place front and back skirt blocks to their respective lines, and outline. Draw crotch level line 30.5 cm (12 in) down from waist line; remove blocks.

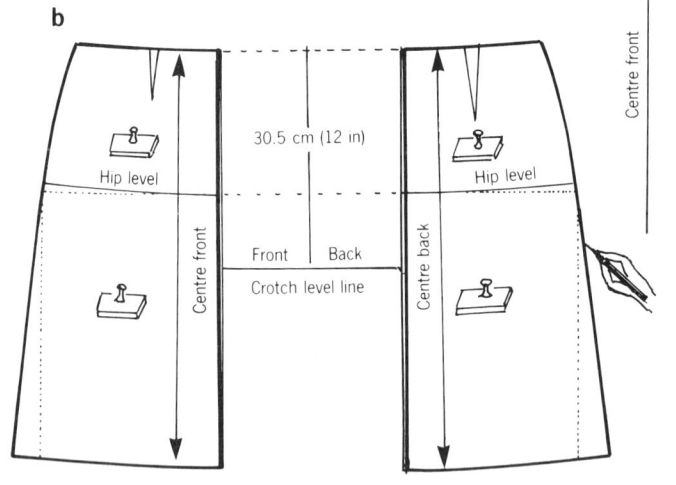

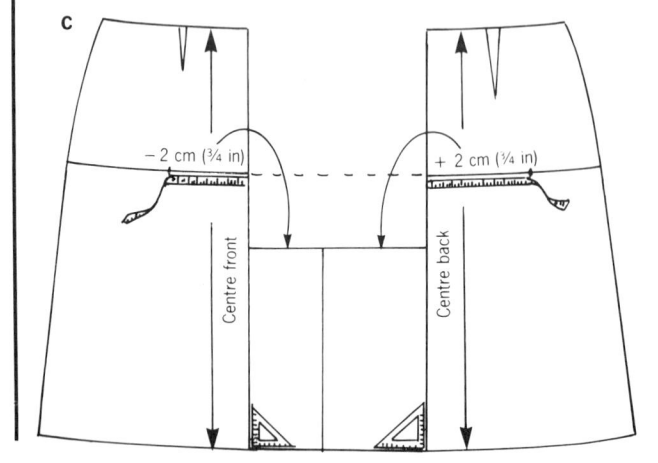

c On front section of crotch line mark half front hip measurement minus 2 cm (¾ in); on back section of crotch line mark half back hip measurement plus 2 cm (¾ in). Square line down and complete hem line.

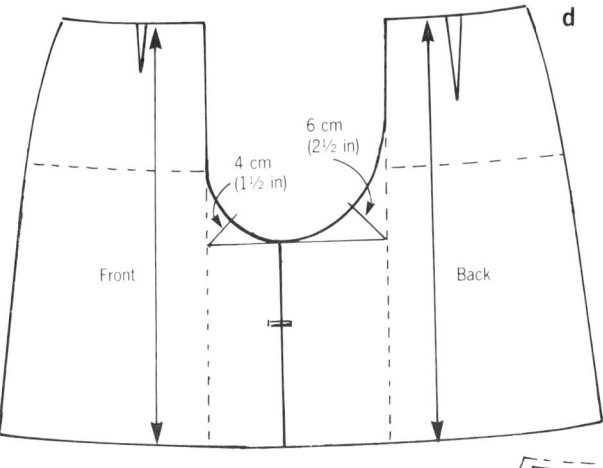

d Complete crotch seam curve as shown. Place balance marks to indicate joining of seams. Add seam allowances, grain line and other relevant information.

When making culottes, assemble one leg at a time. Machine outside leg seam first, then inside leg seam. Repeat procedure for other leg. Finish by stitching crotch seam (see Figure 11.18c, page 158). Leave opening for zip where required.

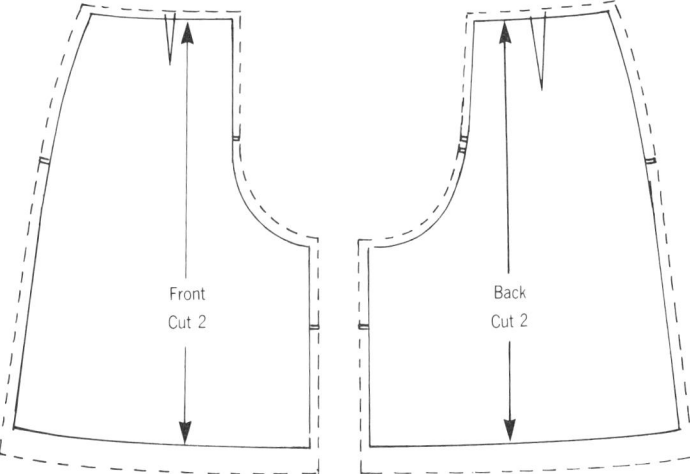

e Completed pattern

Flared culottes

Figure 11.35 'Flare' is achieved by increasing hem circumference and eliminating darts as a means of fitting the waist. This can be achieved by the slashing method (see skirts, page 109) or by pivoting (compare skirts, page 110). Here, pivoting point of culotte front is immediately below dart point whereas pivoting point of culotte back is on hip level line. This makes it possible to obtain the same degree of flare in both back and front completed patterns.

Figure 11.35a Establish pivoting point. Place pattern on sheet of paper; outline centre front section as shown.

b Crossmark position of inner dart line and balance marks.

c With scriber on pivoting point, pivot pattern to right until outer dart line meets previously drawn crossmark.

d Draw remaining outline of culotte. Remove pattern and complete.

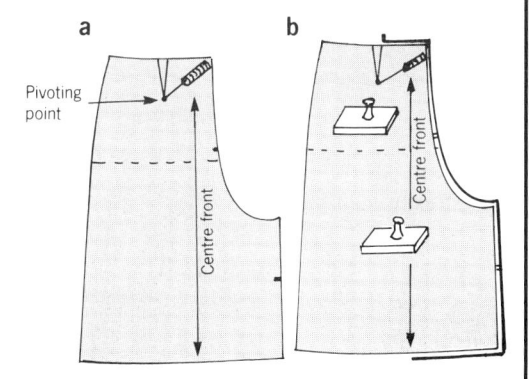

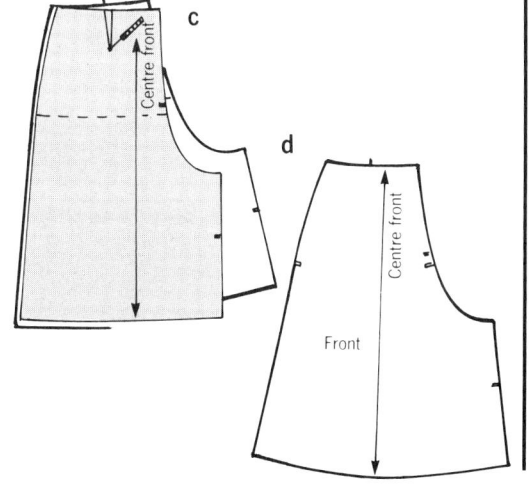

11 Trousers

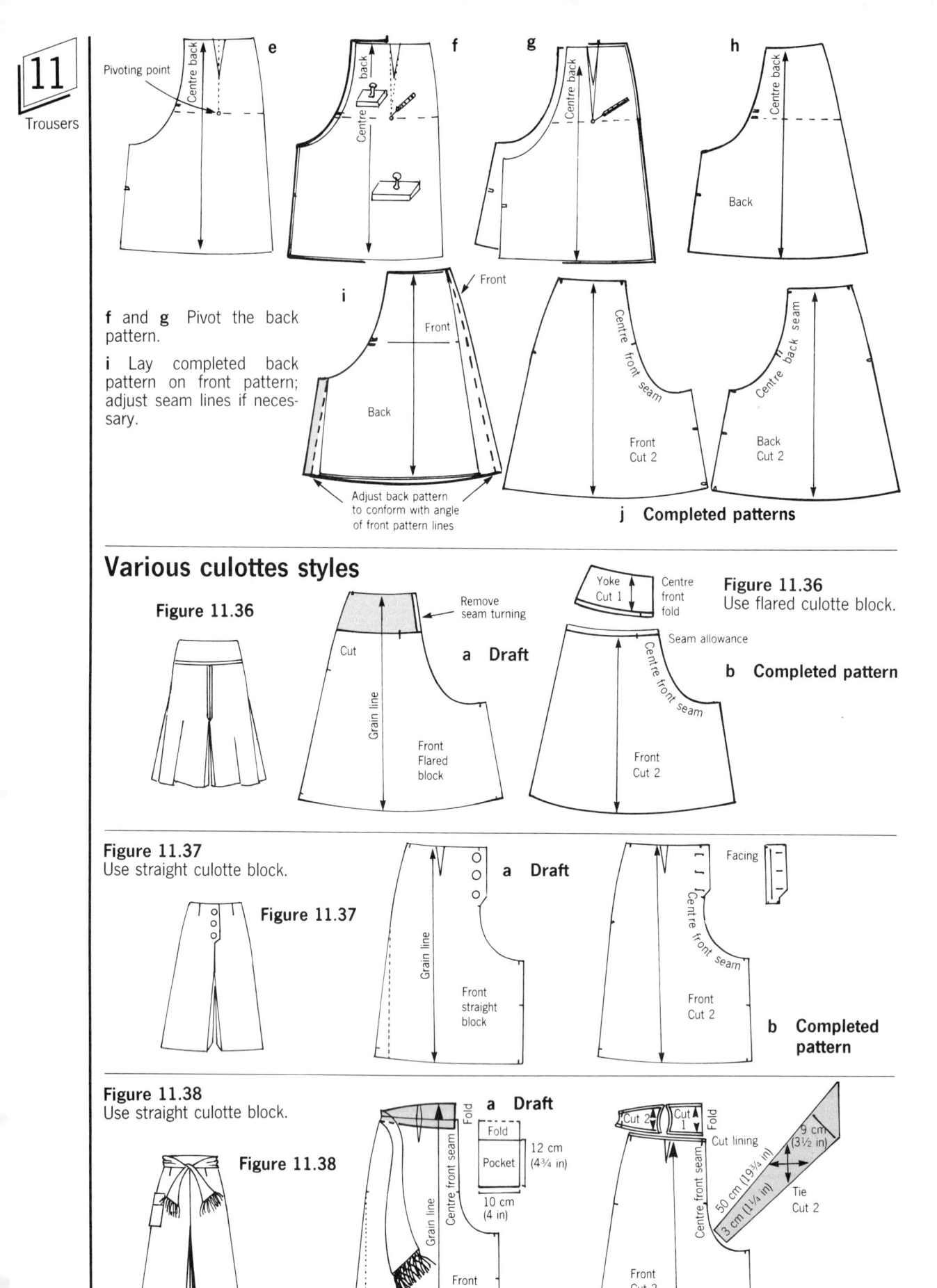

f and **g** Pivot the back pattern.

i Lay completed back pattern on front pattern; adjust seam lines if necessary.

j Completed patterns

Various culottes styles

Figure 11.36
Use flared culotte block.

a Draft
b Completed pattern

Figure 11.37
Use straight culotte block.

a Draft
b Completed pattern

Figure 11.38
Use straight culotte block.

Pocket 12 cm (4¾ in) × 10 cm (4 in)

Tie Cut 2: 50 cm (19¾ in) × 3 cm (1¼ in), 9 cm (3½ in)

a Draft
b Completed pattern

172

Figure 11.39

Culottes with inverted pleat

Figure 11.39a Outline straight skirt block 26 cm (10¼ in) away from edge of paper. Draw line for inverted pleat at distance of 10 cm (4 in) from CF and parallel to it.

b Fold and crease inverted pleat.

c Join inside leg section to CF.

d Shows completed pattern with inverted pleat extended to waist line.

e Fold inside pleat allowance towards CF and cut surplus paper away; an open seam will result. This, when pressed open, is less bulky at waist. Fold inside pleat back to its original inverted pleat position. When culotte is made up, stitch pleat in position.

Repeat process for development of culotte back.

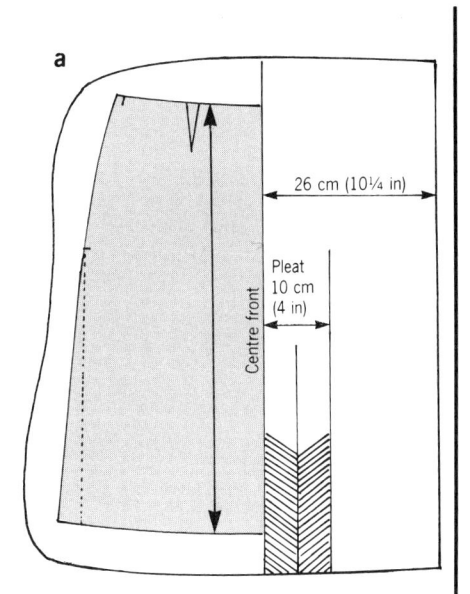

d Completed pattern

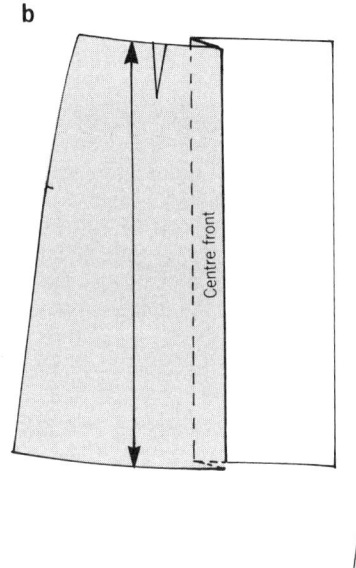

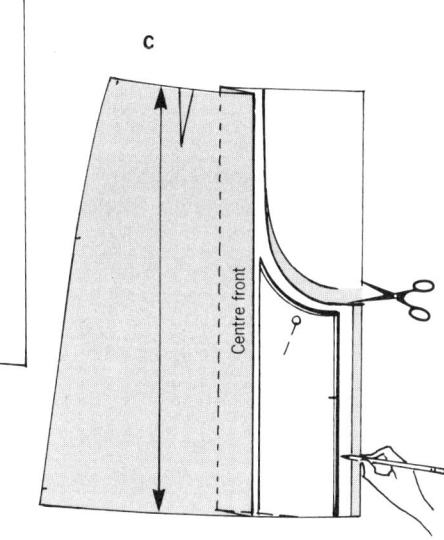

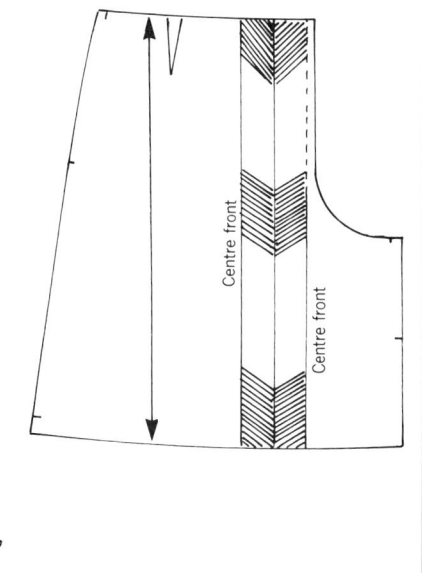

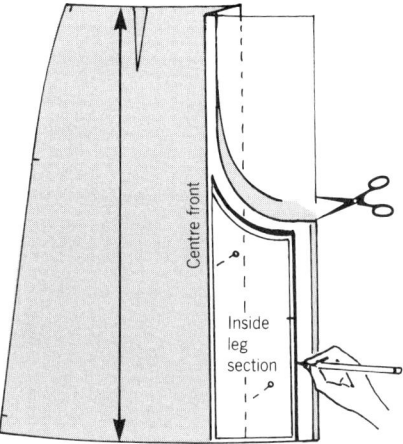

f Completed pattern

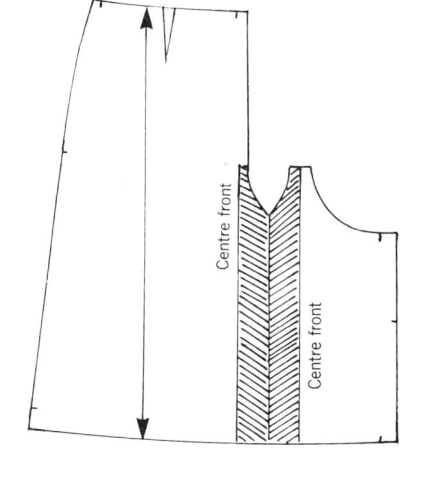

11 Trousers

173

Long half-circle culottes cut flat

Measurements for size 12

Waist	64 cm (25 in)
Length	100 cm (39½ in)

Method of construction

Subtract 2.5 cm (1 in) from the waist measurement (64 − 2.5 = 61.5 cm). One third of this measurement is the radius for drafting the waist line, that is: 61.5 cm (24 in) ÷ 3 = 20.5 cm (8 in).

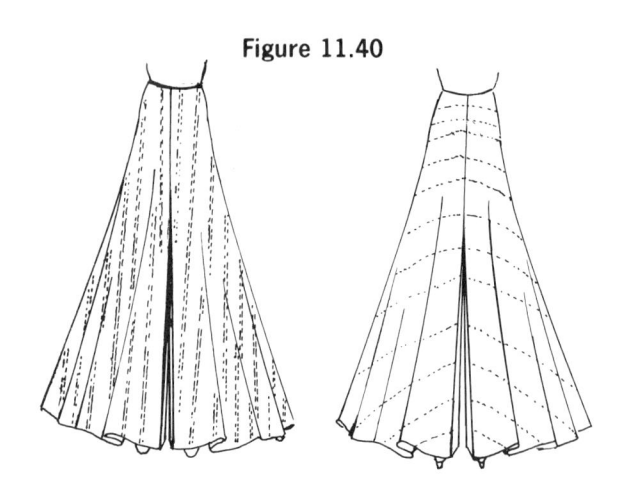

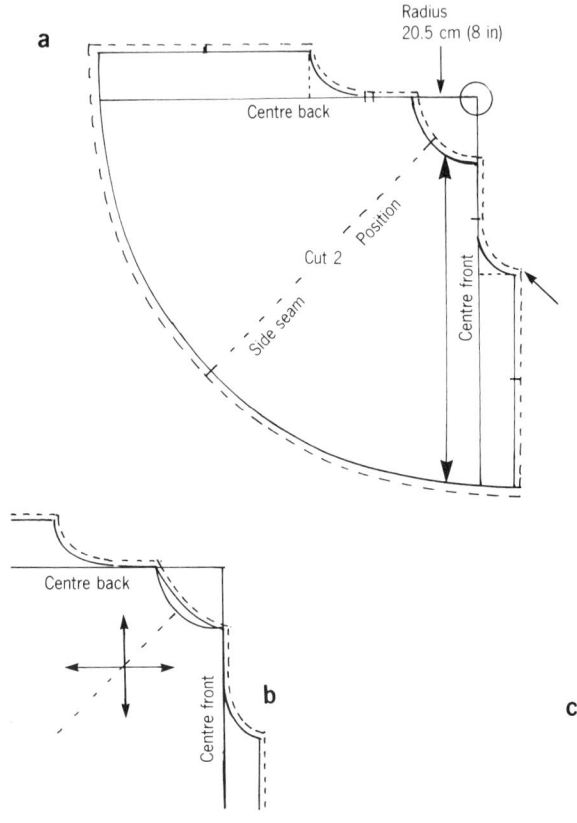

Figure 11.40 From point ○ square to left and down. Draw quarter circle for waist line with radius of 20.5 cm (8 in). Measure desired length from waist line; draft hem line. Lower crotch level to 33 cm (13 in) for loose fit. Add inside leg section as for standard culottes. Add balance marks, grain line and seam allowances.

b A shallower waist line will sometimes achieve a smoother fit with fulness more evenly distributed all around.

c Fabric of at least 140 cm (55 in) in width is required for half-circle culottes without side seams. Note grain line. CB is on weft grain and CF on warp. This can be reversed if wished. Side seam position can be placed on straight grain, but much wider fabric is required for this. A seam would, therefore, be much more appropriate.

d If width of fabric is less than 140 cm (55 in), in this instance 133 cm (52 in), part of inside leg pattern section is cut away and is cut out separately in fabric and then joined by a seam to the main body.

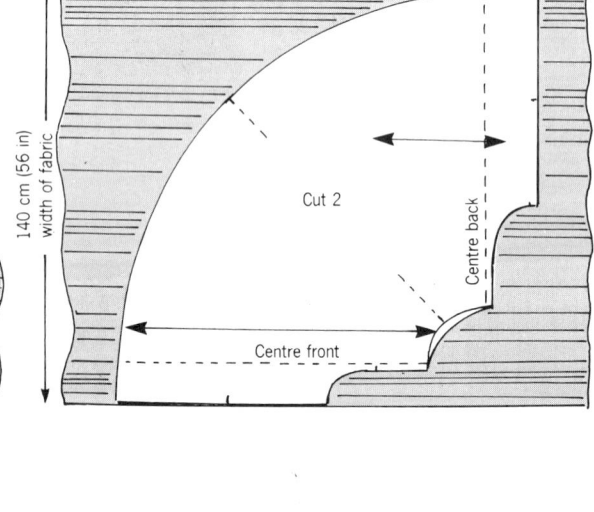

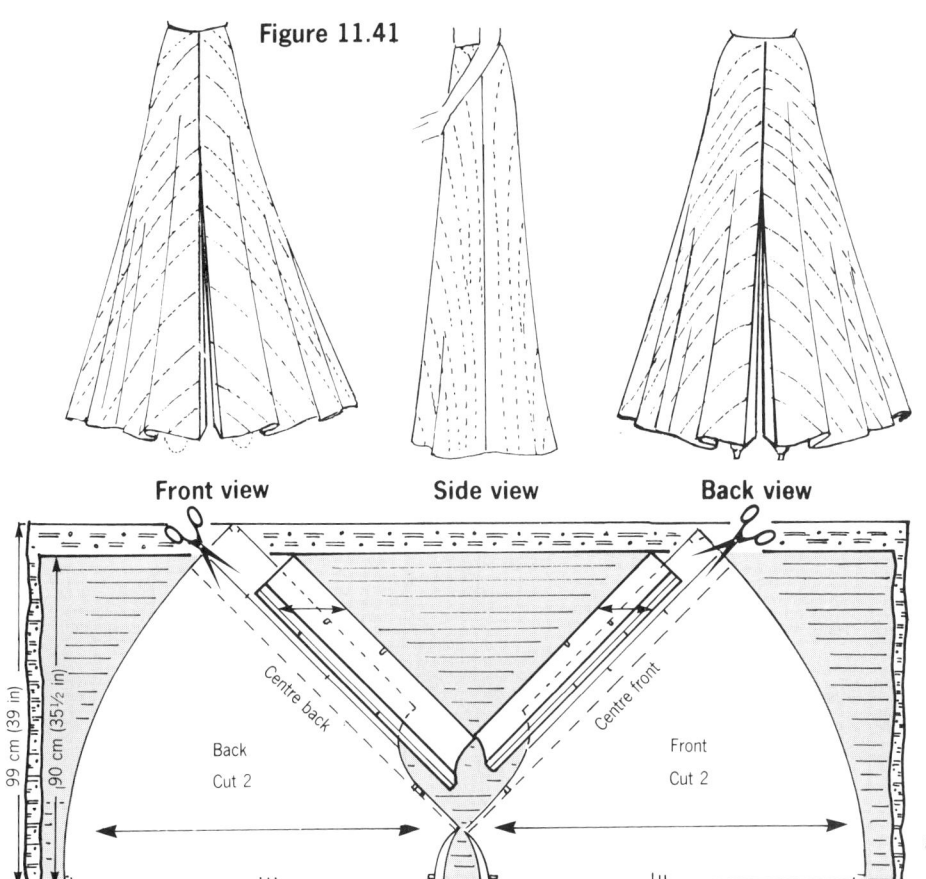

Culottes in narrower width fabric

Figure 11.41 The culottes shown are cut on a different grain from those in Figure 11.40. These culottes have side seams and can be cut from narrower width fabric. A further reduction in width is possible by cutting both inside leg sections separately.

Interesting effects with striped and checked fabrics can be achieved by placing the pattern on different grains of the material.

Four-gored half-circle culottes

Figure 11.42 For this style, the pattern is placed on the fabric with the straight grain running down the centre of back and front sections. The finished skirt hangs well and is evenly balanced all around. Mitred effects are obtained on all seams if striped or checked fabric is used.

a The lay shown is for two different widths of material. Compare also the length of the fabric.

12 Jackets

The dress foundation or hip block

Development of dress foundation or hip block, from waist block.

Measurements additional to waist block, size 12 (page 11)

Finished hip measurement is 2.5 cm (1 in) larger than bust measurement.

Waist to hip – 21.5 cm (8½ in) for all sizes.

The hip level can vary from approximately 18 cm (7 in) to 23 cm (9 in) below waist level; this is dependent on height and figure formation.

Figure 12.1 Lengthen CB, CF and straight side seam lines, and the centre lines of back and front darts of the waist block to desired hip level. Lower front hip line by 1.2 cm (½ in) as for waist block.

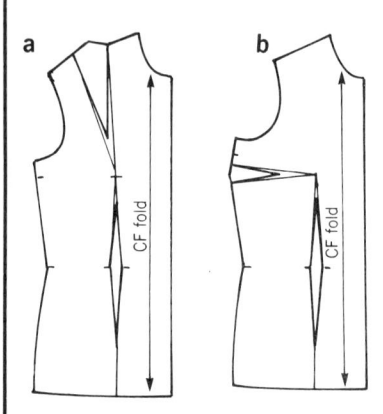

Figure 12.1

Reduce waist darts; shape side seam as shown.

When modelling the back hip block (Figure 2.20, page 26) it will have been noted that at hip level, the back side seam needed to curve slightly outward to follow the contours of that part of the body.

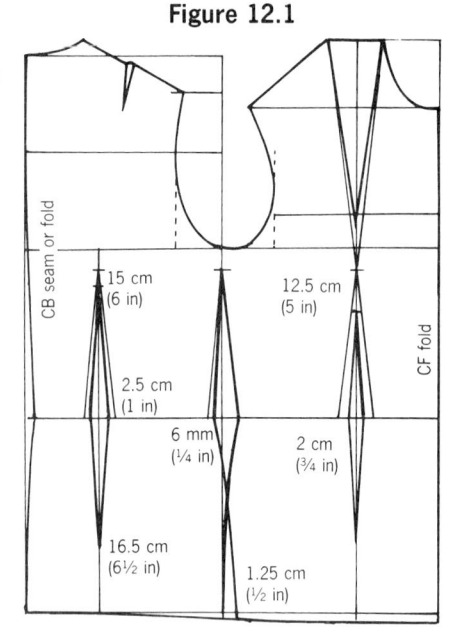

Trace back and front blocks onto new paper; place grain lines, balance marks and cutting instructions.

a and **b**. Move large neck dart to mid-shoulder or underarm as required.

Jacket block development

Edge-to-edge jacket

There are no hard and fast rules on what amounts of ease should be added or what specific measurements for adjustments should be applied to convert dress blocks into jacket blocks. Increases and adjustments are largely dependent on fashion, style and fabric, and on the intended function of the jacket.

A jacket worn over a light dress or blouse requires less overall increase than a jacket worn over a thick sweater. At a time when built-up square shoulders are in fashion, the shoulder line is raised and extended more than when rounded and natural shoulder contours are favoured.

Whether waists should be more or less tightly fitted is determined by the prevailing fashion silhouette and also by the function for which the jacket was designed.

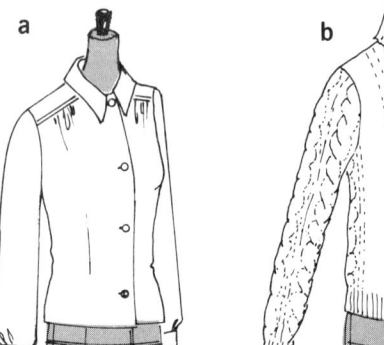

Figure 12.2

Figure 12.3 Outline back and front hip block (Figure 2.20). Lengthen according to full length measurement taken from nape of neck. Add 1.5 cm (⅝ in) at hip level for new CF line. Extend side seams by 1 cm (⅜ in) or according to bust measurement.

Jacket block size 12 – finished measurements
Comparison with dress hip block, Figure 12.1

	Jacket	Dress
Full length	65.0 cm (25½ in)	62.0 cm (24½ in)
Bust	99/102 cm (39/40 in)	97.0 cm (38 in)
Hips	106.0 cm (41¾ in)	104.0 cm (41 in)
Waist	89.0 cm (35 in)	85.0 cm (33½ in)
Across back	37.0 cm (14½ in)	35.5 cm (14 in)
Across chest	37.0 cm (14½ in)	35.5 cm (14 in)
Shoulder	13.0 cm (5⅛ in)	12.0 cm (4¾ in)
Armhole	48.25 cm (19 in)	42.0 cm (16½ in)

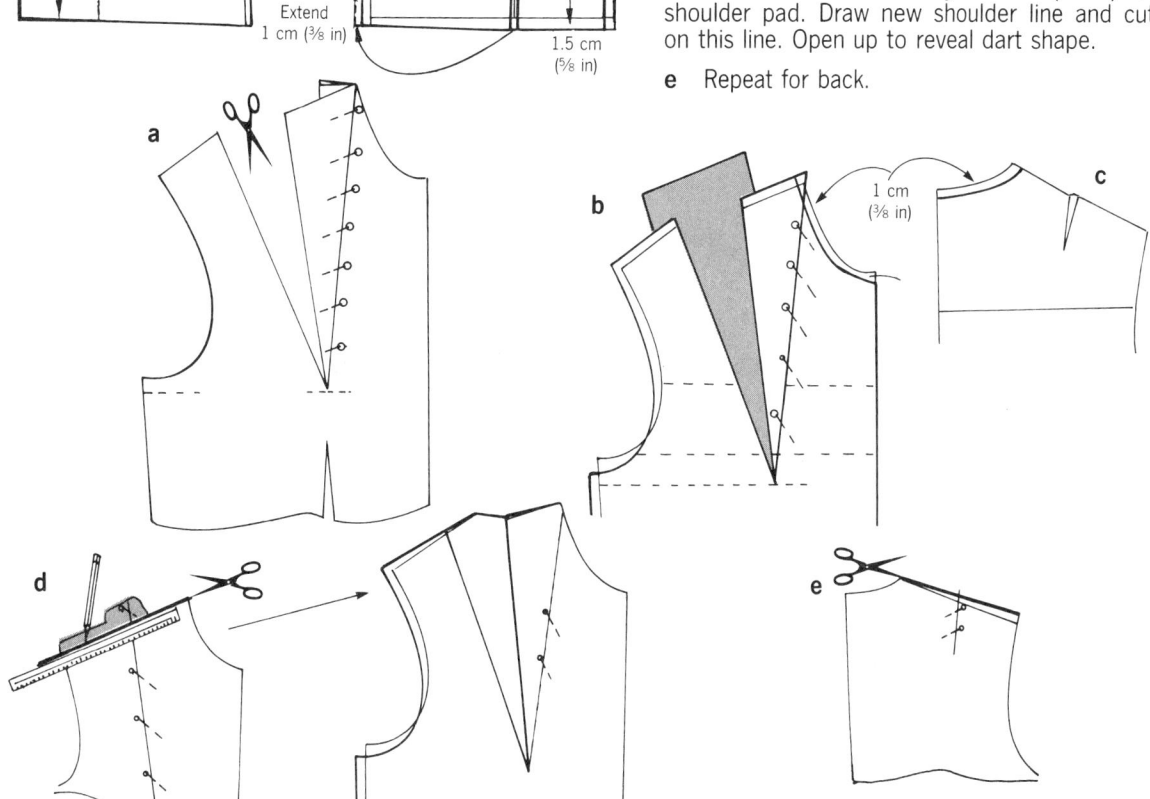

The jacket block and two-piece sleeve

Lower armhole by 1 cm (⅜ in).

Extend shoulder seams 1 cm (⅜ in).

Raise shoulder seams 1 cm (⅜ in).

Lengthen front waist dart to hemline as shown. Check hip measurement. Add amount taken out in lengthened dart to side seam if required.

Draw position of new shoulder dart in centre of front shoulder.

a Trace upper section of front onto new paper. Close dart; cut on new shoulder dart line to bust point.

b Stick paper behind open dart. Lower front neckline by 1 cm (⅜ in) and 1.5 cm (⅝ in).

c Lower back neckline as shown.

d Fold front shoulder dart, crease, pin. Raise shoulder line at armhole by 0.6 cm (¼ in) for shoulder pad. Draw new shoulder line and cut on this line. Open up to reveal dart shape.

e Repeat for back.

177

12
The jacket block and two-piece sleeve

d Foreshorten front shoulder dart (see Figure 2.14, page 21, and Figure 2.22 page 27.

f 'Marry' newly developed upper front section to remaining lower section. Recut back and front blocks, having added 3 cm (1½ in) seam allowances all around, except at neckline where 1 cm (⅜ in) is sufficient.

Cut out in a trial fabric of similar weight to the final garment fabric. Tack together for fitting. (Alternatively, the paper pattern can be pinned together and 'tried on'.)

g Pin a thick shoulder pad, which is the same size as the pad to be used in the making of the jacket, to the right shoulder of the garment-covered dress form or a person.

h Fit tacked half-jacket toile on to dress form. Allow toile to hang naturally and note in particular whether centre front edge hangs in line with centre front of dress form. Having drafted and cut CF edge 'off grain' (Figure 12.3) should have helped to ensure this.

If lower centre front edges hang away from CF of dress form, raise the shoulder-neck point. Observe the fit of the shoulder. There must be no sagging at the armhole. If sagging folds appear, take in the shoulder seam at the armhole end graduating it off towards the neckline or fit a thicker shoulder pad. Make adjustments to neckline, side seams and darts, if required. Mark all lines and intersections with soft pencil or felt-tipped pen.

i Unpin, true all lines and seam allowances. If necessary, cut a whole toile from the half-toile and refit. If satisfactory, transfer all marks from toile to pattern paper or card; develop back neck and front facings (see page 43).

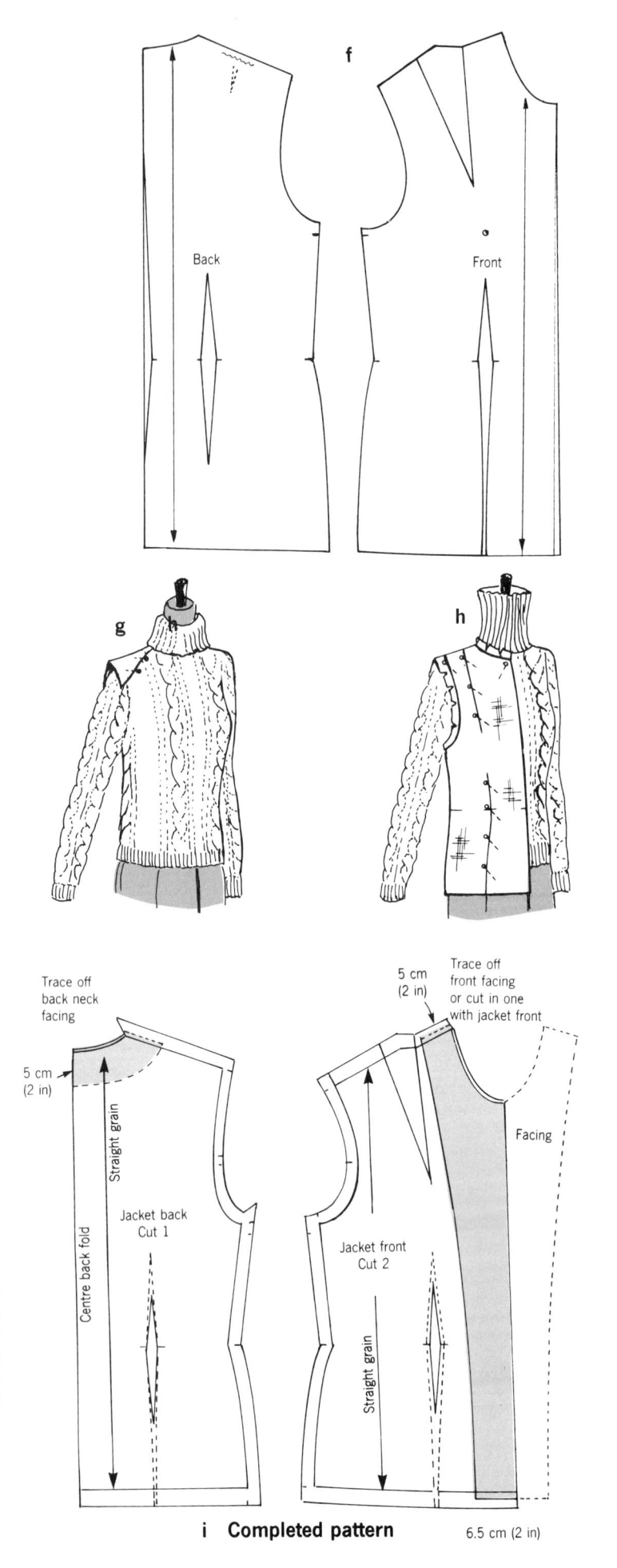

i Completed pattern

178

Blazer jacket with side body

Figure 12.4

Use edge-to-edge jacket block (Figure 12.3) without seam allowances to develop this jacket pattern.

Figure 12.4a Pivot the shoulder dart temporarily to an underarm position and outline. Allow 10 cm (4 in) excess paper to the right of CF and 9 cm (3½ in) above the shoulder-neck point.

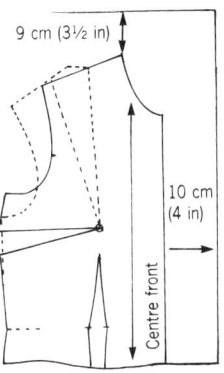

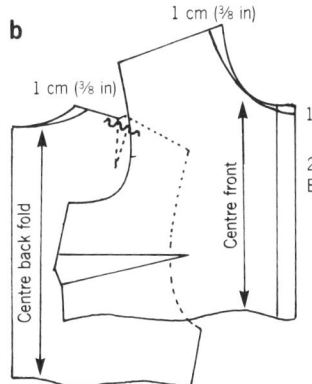

b Add 2.5 cm (1 in) button extension and reshape the neckline.

c Place back jacket pattern face downward with shoulder-neck points meeting at right angle. Determine break point according to design and draw break line.

d Fold paper under on break line. Crease and pin pattern paper (as yet incomplete) to dress form and outline with tape a number of possible collar and revers shapes as interpreted from your working sketch.

e Finally, draw the desired collar and lapel shape and trace through.

f Unfold paper and tentatively complete the collar at centre back.

g Straighten both collar and jacket necklines as shown. Place balance marks and cut the collar away from neck and lapel line.

h and **i** Develop top collar from undercollar by increasing top collar area from nothing at intersection with lapel to 3–6 mm (⅛–¼ in) all around outer edge, depending on thickness of fabric used.

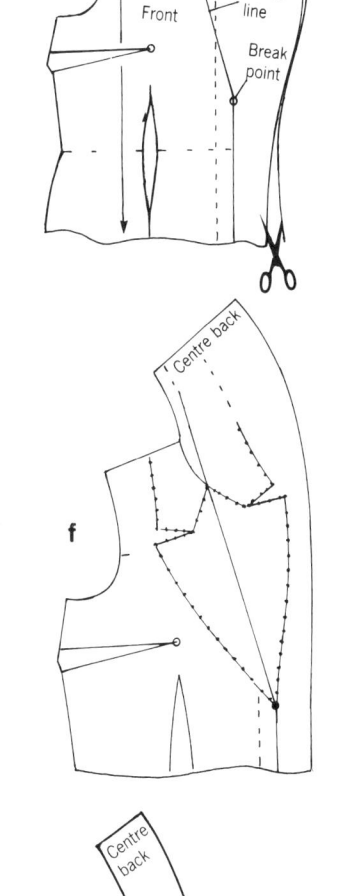

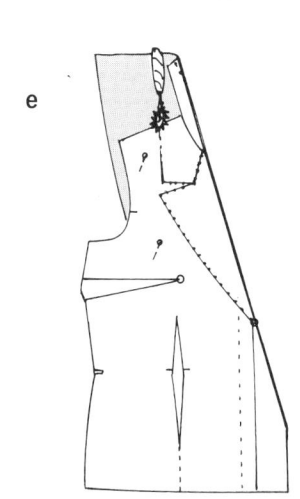

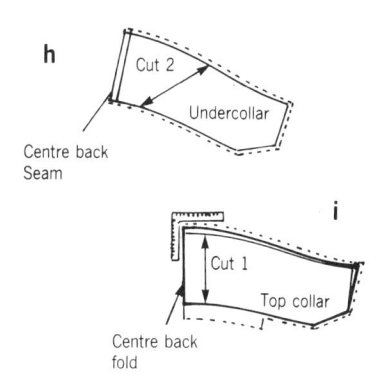

The jacket block and two-piece sleeve

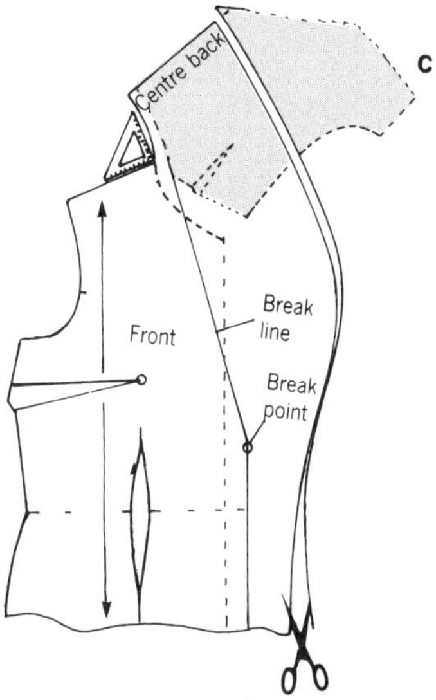

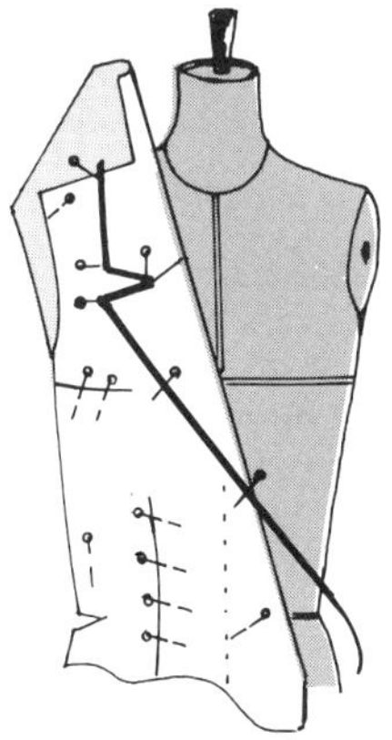

179

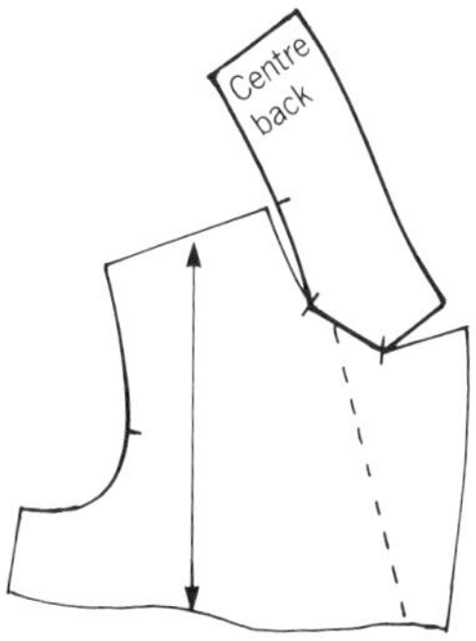

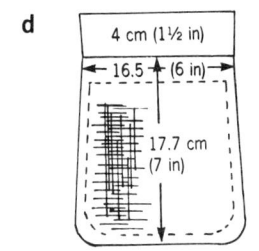

Figure 12.5

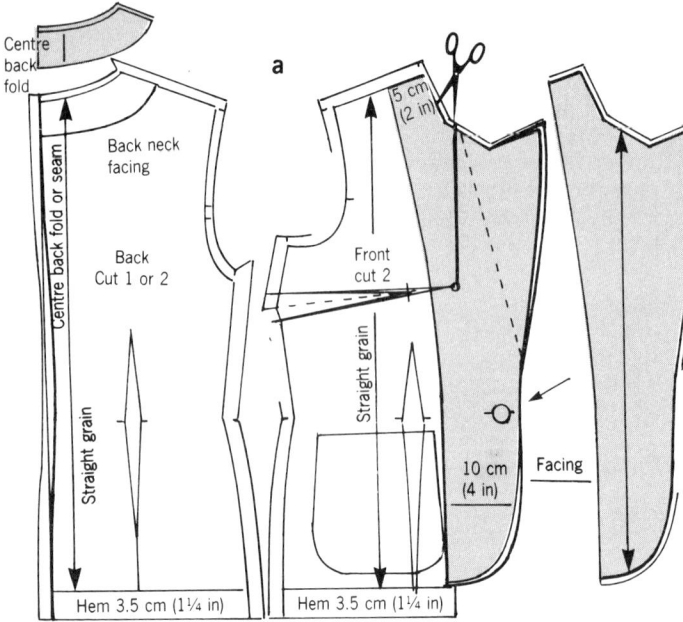

Figure 12.5a In the development of the front facing, the lapel area is increased from nothing to 3–6 mm (⅛–½ in) at lapel point, returning to nothing at break point. The facing area below this point is decreased by the same amount to cause the seam to roll slightly inward and be concealed.

Extend underarm dart by 5 cm (2 in); draw slash line from neckline to new 'bust point'. This is the new dart position.

b Close underarm dart; cut to new 'bust point'. Foreshorten neck dart to approximately 9–10 cm (3½–4 in). This dart should not be visible when the lapel is turned down. It provides bust shaping and is also a 'fish dart', improving the 'roll' of the collar and revers.

Place back and front side seams together (without seam allowances). Draw side body, 11.5 cm (4½ in) wide at armhole position and 15–16 cm (6–6½ in) at hemline, depending on length of jacket. The newly created seams now incorporate waist suppression which was previously taken out in the side seams and the back waist dart. This dart is now omitted.

Place balance marks; trace side body on to new paper. Straight grain runs through centre of side body. Trace pocket on to new paper (**d**).

Add seam allowances, grain lines and cutting instructions.

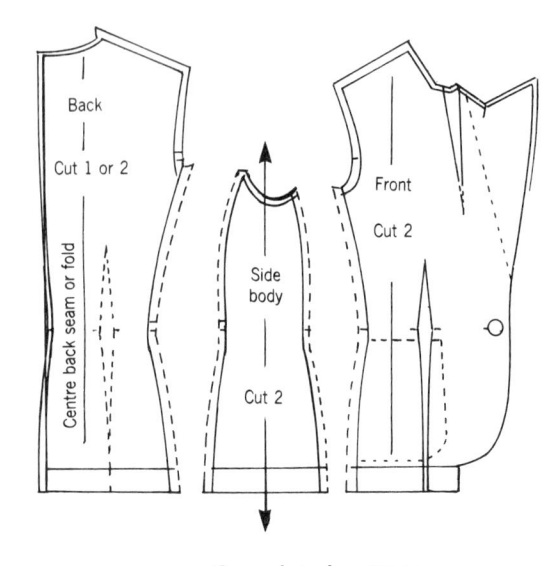

c Completed pattern

Two-piece sleeve for a jacket

Figure 12.6

This two-piece sleeve is developed from the dress sleeve block (page 15) and fits the jacket (Figure 12.5). Adjust and increase dress sleeve block measurements, see table.

	Dress cm	Dress in	Jacket cm	Jacket in
Armhole circumference	42.0	16½	48.25	19
Sleeve head circumference	44.5	17½	50–51	20
Underarm length	42.0	16½	41.43	16½
Upper arm girth	34.2	13½	35.5–37	14
Wrist girth	25.3	10	26–27	10½

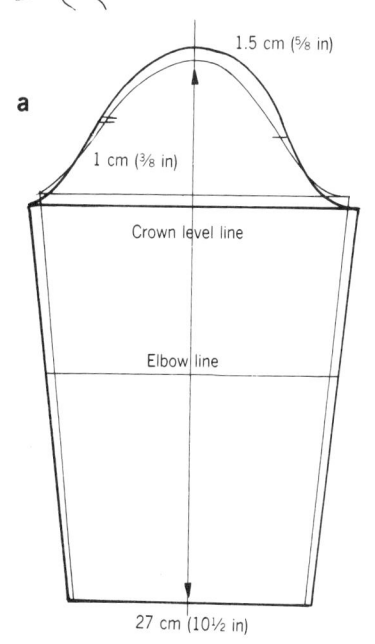

Figure 12.6a Outline dress sleeve block (page 15). Lower crown level line 1 cm (⅜ in). Extend to left and right to required measurement. Raise sleeve head 1.5 cm (⅝ in); increase wrist measurement to required amount. Cut out.

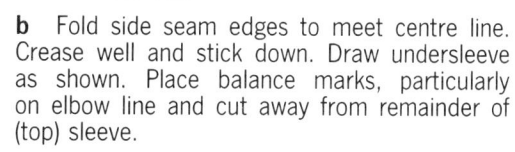

b Fold side seam edges to meet centre line. Crease well and stick down. Draw undersleeve as shown. Place balance marks, particularly on elbow line and cut away from remainder of (top) sleeve.

c Draw a vertical line. Align top sleeve to vertical line; outline upper section of sleeve to elbow line. Crossmark as shown. Place another crossmark 2 cm (¾ in) below elbow level mark. Pivot elbow line point down to meet lower crossmark and outline lower section of top sleeve. Draft optional wrist opening on outlined sleeve.

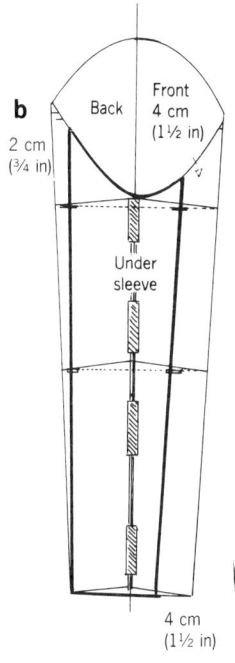

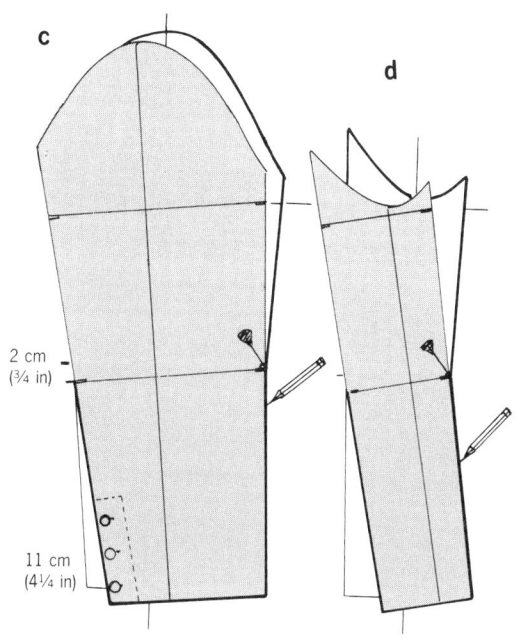

d Repeat this process for the undersleeve.

e Add seam and hem allowances, grown-on wrist opening facing and extension. Check balance marks and grain lines.

Cut out in a trial fabric, insert into jacket armhole and test sleeve for 'hang' and fit.

Make any adjustments, mark with soft pencil or felt-tipped pen and transfer to paper pattern.

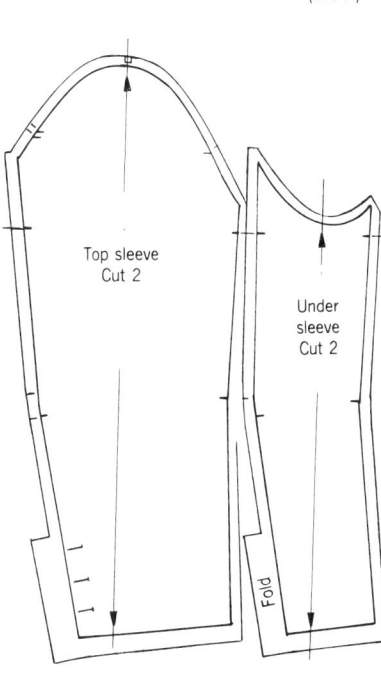

e Completed pattern

12 The jacket block and two-piece sleeve

13 Lingerie

Slips and cami-knickers

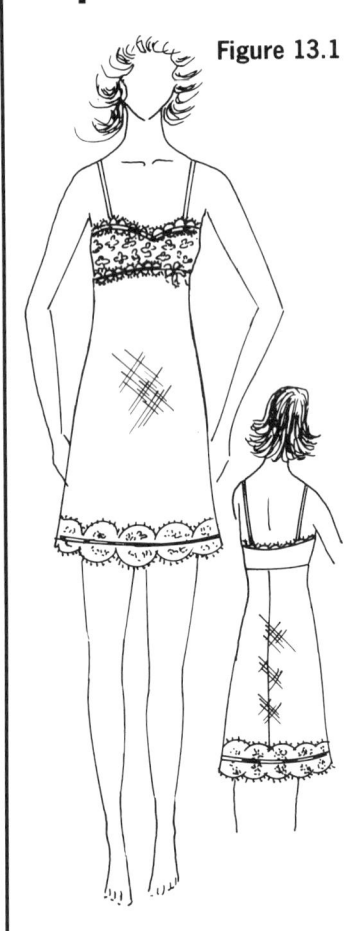

Figure 13.1 **Mini-slip**

This slip can be modelled straight on the figure without causing your model undue fatigue.

Use a fabric similar in weight to the slip material, or fine mull. The slip can be modelled in the material of the slip, which is an enjoyable experience but requires a little more fabric (see Chapter 6).

Figure 13.1a Pin centre front and centre back tape lines to a firmly fitting vest and panties. Tape style line under bust and continue to centre back. Pin. This serves as a guide for modelling the slip.

b The fabric illustrated is 90 cm (36 in) wide. Fold the fabric on the true bias as shown. With wider fabric, the weft edge, folded parallel to the warp edge, will not overlap as it does here.

Fold and refold the fabric, measure and re-measure until the measurement across, from the fold of the fabric, is a quarter of the body measurement plus a minimum of 5 cm (2 in) (see finished measurements, page 184).

Pin the layers of fabric together and cut out. Retain all the bias corners for cutting out the crossover bra-top, the back yoke and briefs. Repeat this procedure for the back of the slip. The back can be cut with or without a centre seam – see **i** which shows that the lay is more economical when a back seam is used.

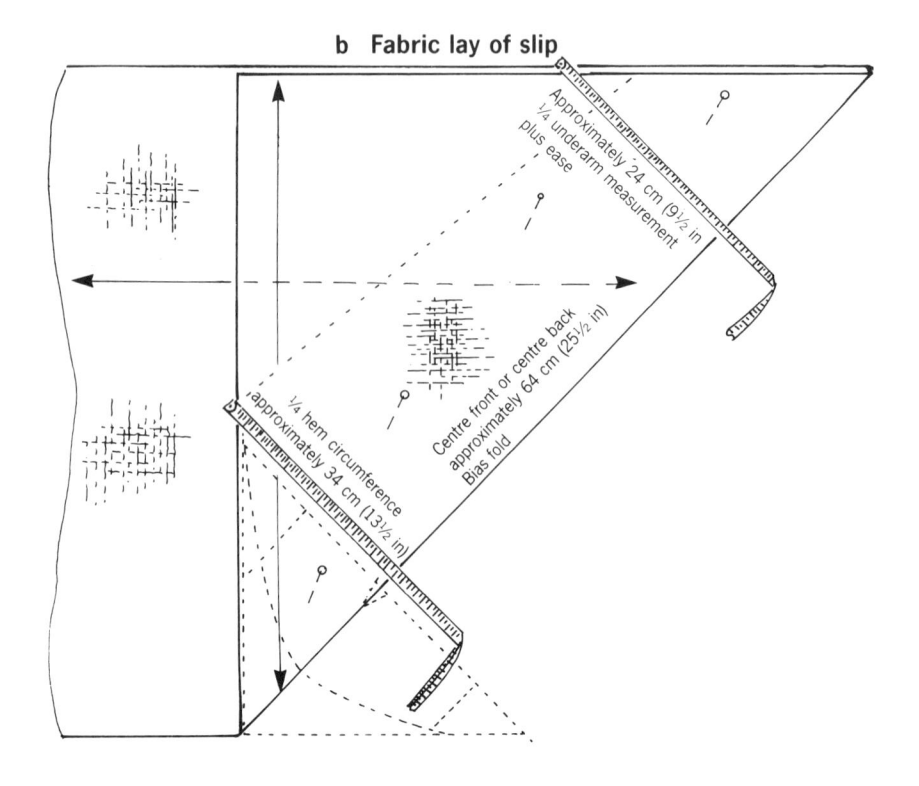

b Fabric lay of slip

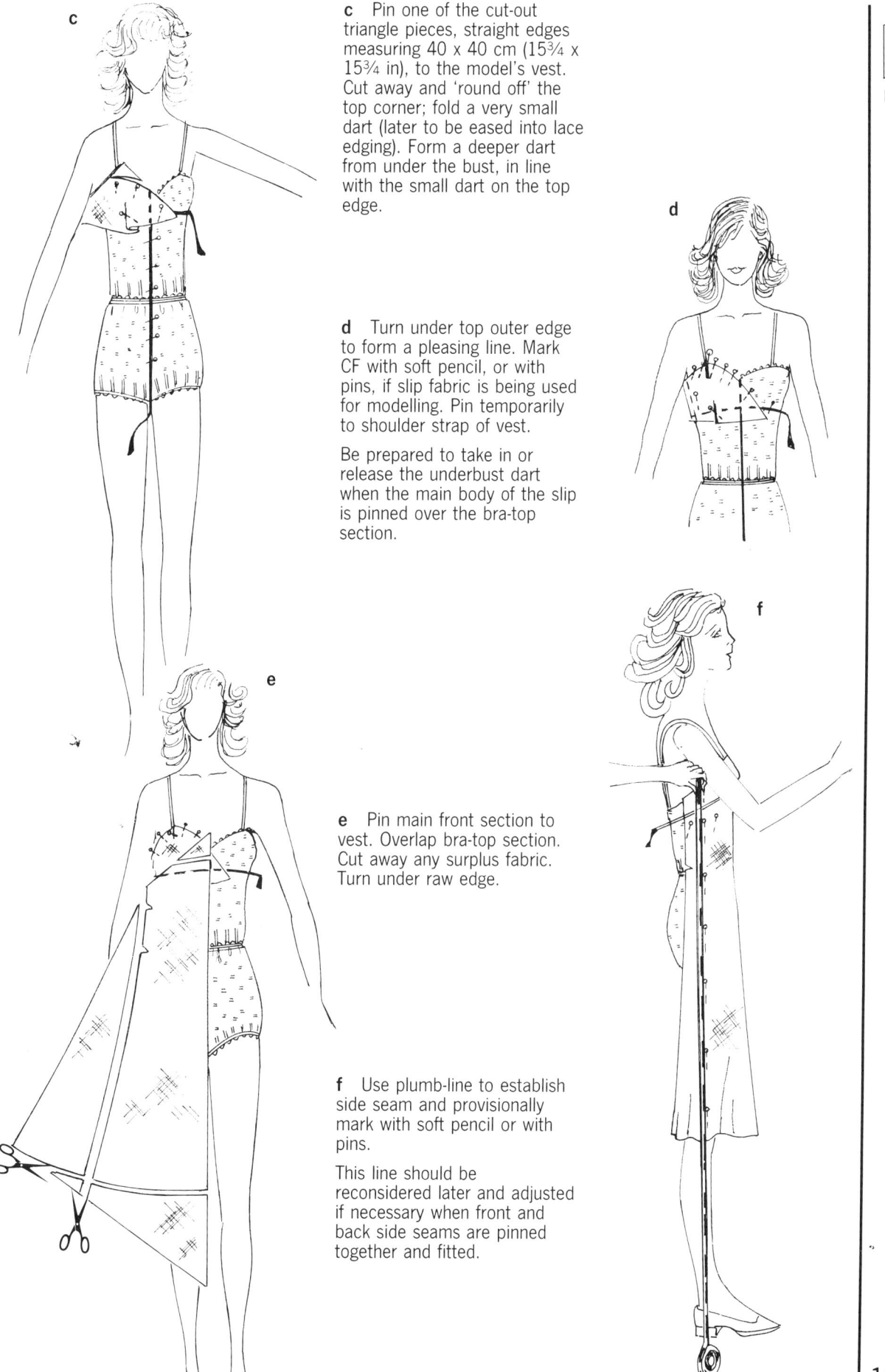

c Pin one of the cut-out triangle pieces, straight edges measuring 40 x 40 cm (15¾ x 15¾ in), to the model's vest. Cut away and 'round off' the top corner; fold a very small dart (later to be eased into lace edging). Form a deeper dart from under the bust, in line with the small dart on the top edge.

d Turn under top outer edge to form a pleasing line. Mark CF with soft pencil, or with pins, if slip fabric is being used for modelling. Pin temporarily to shoulder strap of vest.

Be prepared to take in or release the underbust dart when the main body of the slip is pinned over the bra-top section.

e Pin main front section to vest. Overlap bra-top section. Cut away any surplus fabric. Turn under raw edge.

f Use plumb-line to establish side seam and provisionally mark with soft pencil or with pins.

This line should be reconsidered later and adjusted if necessary when front and back side seams are pinned together and fitted.

13 Lingerie

183

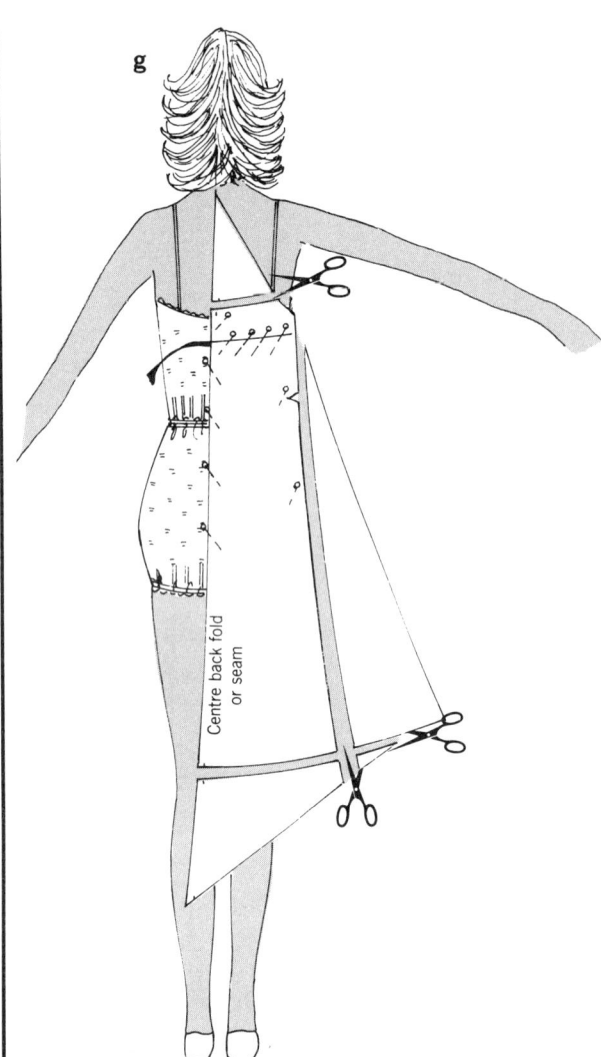

g Proceed with modelling back as for front. Pin side seams together with a slight inward curve at waist level but allow sufficient ease throughout for easy putting on and taking off the slip. A small side seam opening at waist level is necessary if a closer fit is desired.

Cut two temporary shoulder straps for use during fitting of slip. Narrow ribbon can be used for the finished garment.

Look critically at final result. Adjust fit where required, then mark all seam lines, balance marks and position and length of shoulder straps with soft pencil or pins. Remove garment from your model. True and transfer all markings to left side slip sections. Tack slip together and try on for fitting. Make final adjustments. Determine hem line. Transfer markings to pattern paper. Add grain lines and small seam allowances if seams are to be overlocked. For French seams allow larger turnings.

Size 12 – bias-cut mini-slip finished measurements based on British Standard Sizing

Bust	87 cm (34 in)
Hip	97 cm (38 in)
Underarm to hem	64 cm (25 in)
Hem circumference	122 cm (48 in)

h Lay plan showing where briefs can be fitted

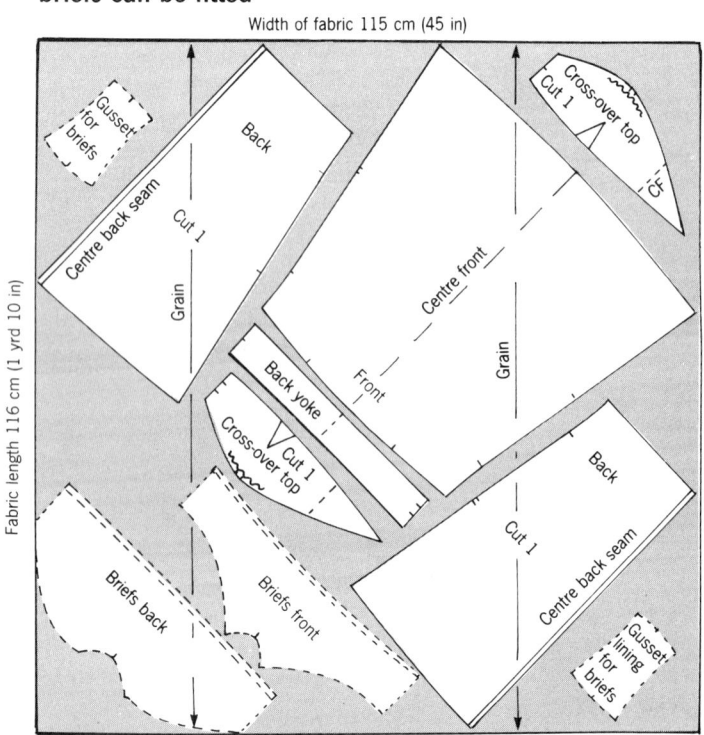

Cami-knickers developed from mini-slip

Figure 13.2

Figure 13.2a and **b** Outline back and front mini-slip. Raise hem line by 8 cm (3 in).

Add 10 cm (4 in) to side seams at hem line. Draw new side seam lines.

Draw style lines.

The gusset consists of two almost rectangular double fabric bands which button between the legs and are secured with the stitching of the hem. The back band is wider at the top and longer than the front band to ensure that the buttons are in a comfortable position. It is essential that the bands fit loosely. Lengthen bands if required.

Instead of the two-piece button-fastening, a one-piece band can be used.

Finished measurements – Size 12 based on British Standard Sizing

Bust	87 cm (34 in)
Hip	97 cm (38 in)
Length (shoulder to hem)	79 cm (31 in)
Hem circumference	160 cm (63 in)

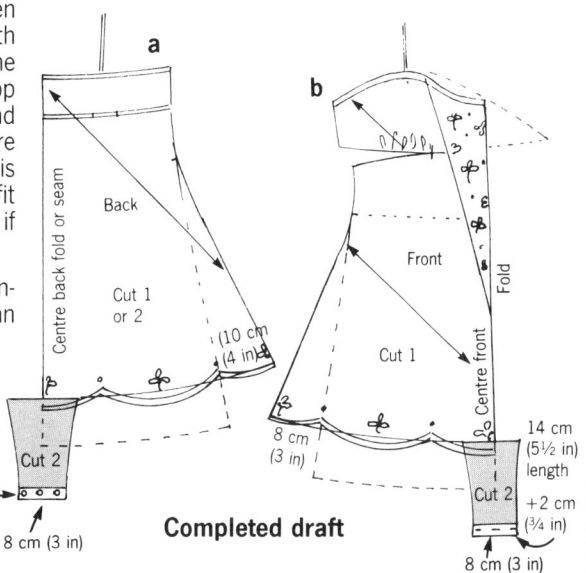

Completed draft

Camisoles, teddies and cropped T-shirt tops

Figure 13.3

Figure 13.3 Many lingerie styles can be easily developed by either the modelling or the flat cutting process (e.g. the basic mini-slip, Figure 13.5, the slip, Figure 13.15c and d, page 193 or for certain styles from the sleeveless bodice Figure 5.17a, page 64). Add less ease and tolerance for knitted fabrics.

13 Lingerie

185

Lingerie panties

Figure 13.4

Size 12

Figure 13.4c Draw large cross on pattern paper, vertical line 50 cm (19½ in) long and horizontal line 20 cm (8 in) down, the width of half finished, hip measurement. Place back and front straight skirt block against vertical line with hip line matching horizontal line. Mark points F and B. Outline.

d Draw crotch level line (body rise) 33 cm (13 in) down from the waist at right angle to CF and CB line.

Mark B^1 and F^1.

Lengthen horizontal line 10 cm (4 in) beyond CB line. Mark B^2.

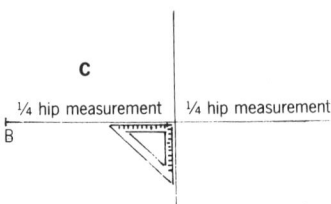

Finished measurements for lingerie panties, based on British Standard Size 12

Waist (elasticated)	64–98 cm (25–39 in)
Seat = hip + 1 cm	99 cm (39 in)
Body rise: Front	33 cm (13 in)
Back	38 cm (15 in)
Side length	33 cm (13 in)
Thigh circumference	50–53 cm (19½–21 in)

Lengthen 7.5 cm (3 in) beyond CF line. Mark F^2.

e On CF line, from crotch level line measure up 5 cm (2 in). Mark F^3. Measure down 2.5 cm (1 in). Mark F^4. On CB line, from crotch level line, measure up 6 cm (2½ in) and down 4 cm (1½ in). Mark B^3 and B^4. Connect B^2 to B^3 and F^2 to F^3.

Square out 6 cm (2½ in) from B^2 and 6 cm (2½ in) from F^2.

Draw dotted straight hem guide lines and outline shaped hem line as shown.

From CF and CB lines draw gusset seam lines 2 cm (¾ in) towards main body from B^4 and F^4. Connect to B^3 and F^3.

Raise CB line 5 cm (2 in) above original waist line to obtain longer crotch line at waist. Connect waistline as shown. The dotted vertical guide line can become the side seam for an elasticated waist if wished.

f Trace off gussets as shown or blend CB and CF crotch lines for panties with centre seams (Figure 13.4b).

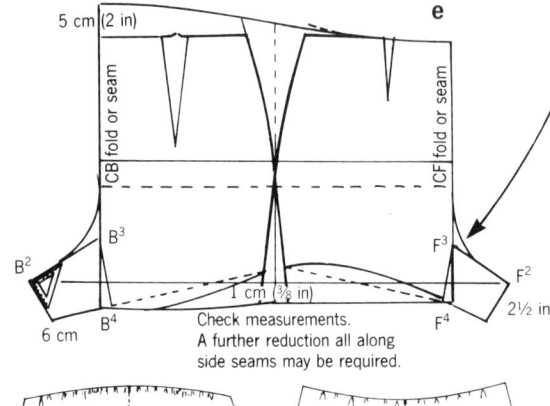

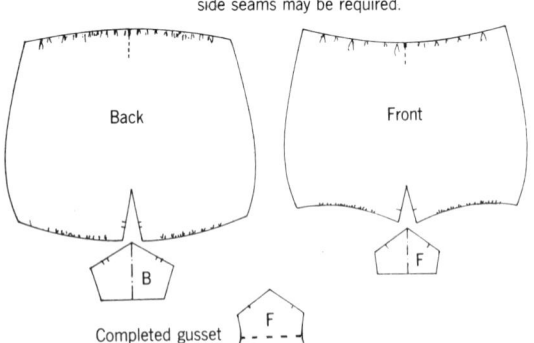

f Completed pattern

Panties and gusset styles

Figure 13.5 Note the different lengths of the side seams in each of the styles in relation to the leg circumference measurements, which are the same in a–d. The shape of the gussets is also affected.

Figure 13.5

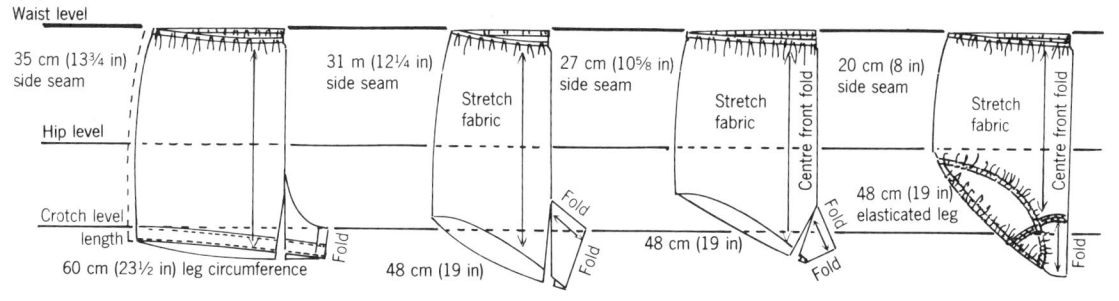

Waist level
35 cm (13¾ in) side seam
31 m (12¼ in) side seam — Stretch fabric
27 cm (10⅝ in) side seam — Stretch fabric — Centre front fold
20 cm (8 in) side seam — Stretch fabric — Centre front fold
Hip level
Crotch level length
60 cm (23½ in) leg circumference — Fold
48 cm (19 in) — Fold
48 cm (19 in) — Fold
48 cm (19 in) elasticated leg — Fold

French knickers slashing method

Figure 13.6

Use lingerie panties draft, Figure 13.4e for this development.

Figure 13.6a Lengthen side seam to 36 cm (14¼ in). Connect hem guide line to CF and CB points. Draw new lengthened and slightly flared, side seam line.

a
High hip line
Back   Front

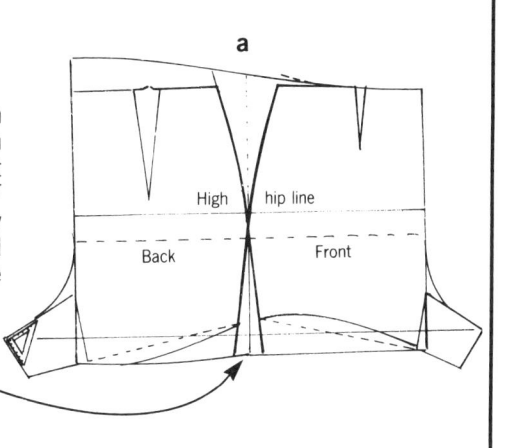

b

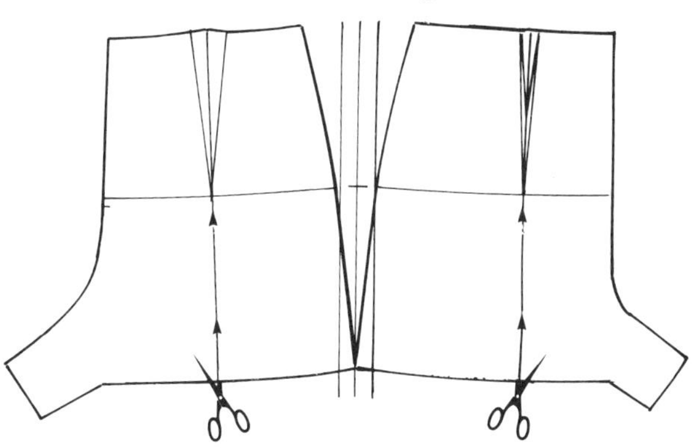

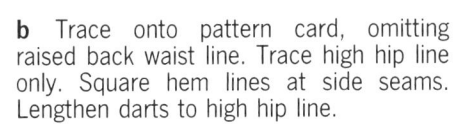

b Trace onto pattern card, omitting raised back waist line. Trace high hip line only. Square hem lines at side seams. Lengthen darts to high hip line.

Outline back and front patterns. Continue centre dart lines to hem as slashing lines.

c Cut from hem line to dart points. Close waist darts. True all lines. Reduce waist line according to waist measurement. These French knickers can be cut with or without side seams.

Add seam allowances, balance marks and grain line to ensure that the knickers are cut on the true bias grain.

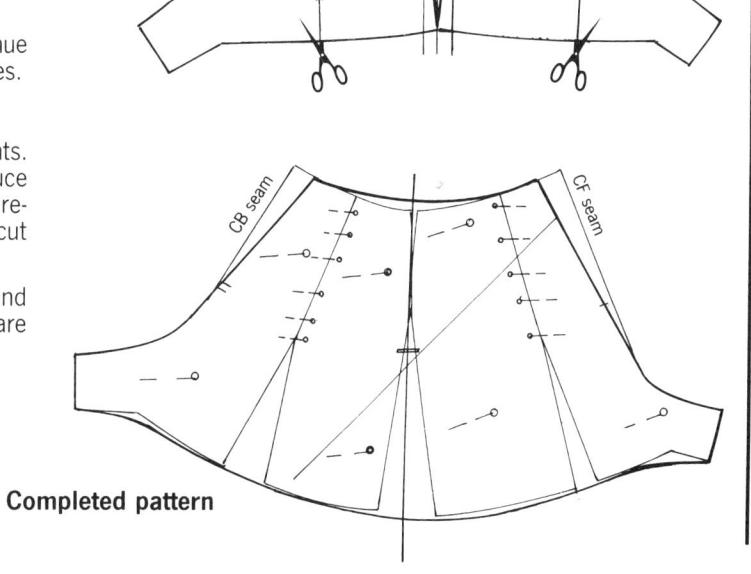

CB seam   CF seam

c Completed pattern

13 Lingerie

187

13 Lingerie

Figure 13.7

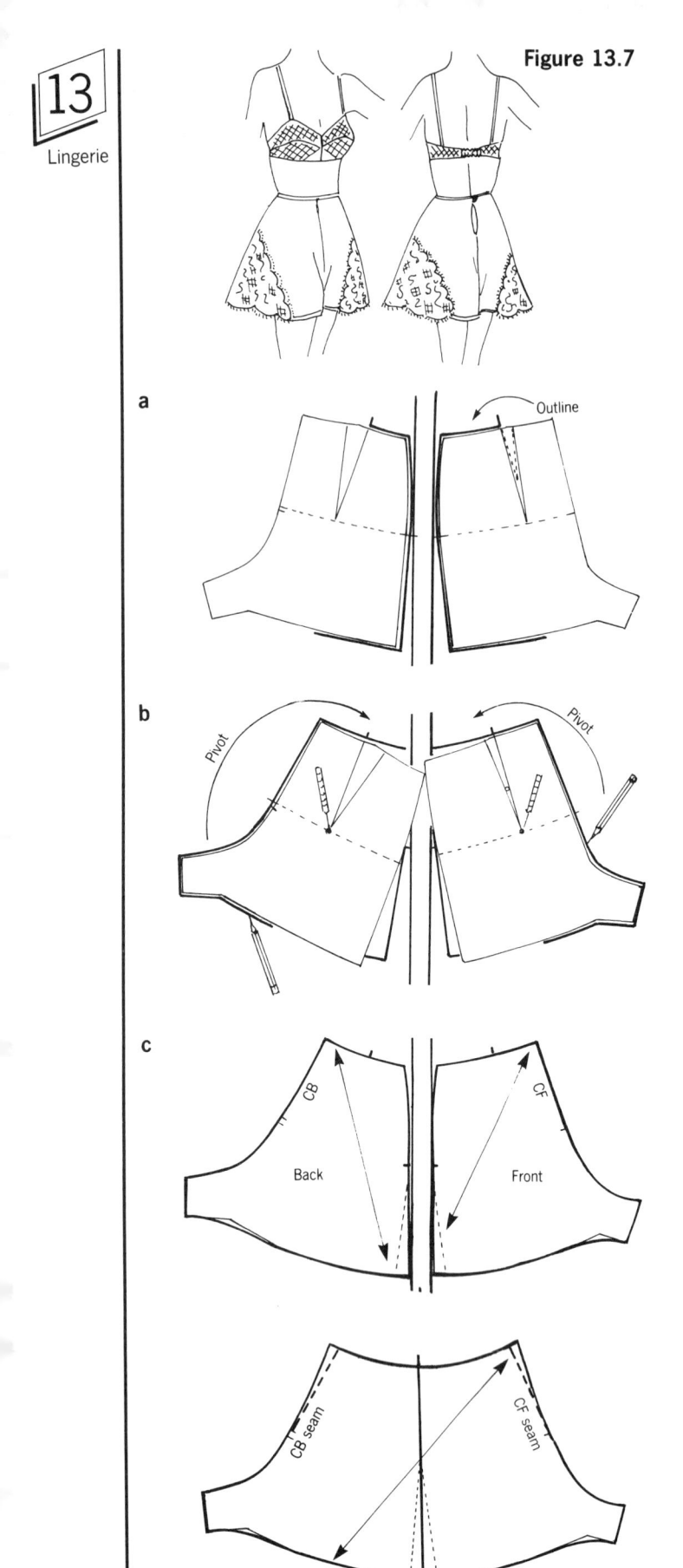

Pivoting method

Follow preliminary steps a and b of slashing method before continuing.

a

Figure 13.7a Draw two vertical lines 4.5 cm (1¾ in) apart. Place back and front side seams to lines as shown. Outline back and front sections to darts on waist line and to halfway on hem line as shown. Crossmark dart positions and balance marks on high hip line level.

b

b Close darts by pivoting patterns from dart points. Outline remaining CB and CF sections, including balance marks. Remove card. True all lines. Add additional flare to side seams at hem line.

c

This two-piece pattern with side seams can be used as it is (**c**) or placed together, cut in one piece.

d Reduce waistline if required.

Add seam allowances and grain lines to ensure a true bias grain.

d **Completed pattern**

Briefs, panties and trunks

In knitted stretch fabrics

The cut of these garments is influenced primarily by the function for which they are intended – whether they are loose-fitting or figure-hugging – and also by the fabrics selected. There are the knitted lingerie fabrics with a limited stretch/recovery ratio and at the other extreme the Lycra-type knitted stretch fabrics used for swimwear and corsetry which have a firm handle and a great stretch-recovery ratio. In between these extreme behavioural qualities lie a vast number of fabrics whose stretchability can be assessed only by testing the fabrics themselves and/or making trial garments from them. It is known that garments made from knitted fabrics require less ease tolerances than garments cut from straight woven fabrics – and more often their widths must be reduced to less than body measurement – but the exact amounts can be determined only by experiment and sample making.

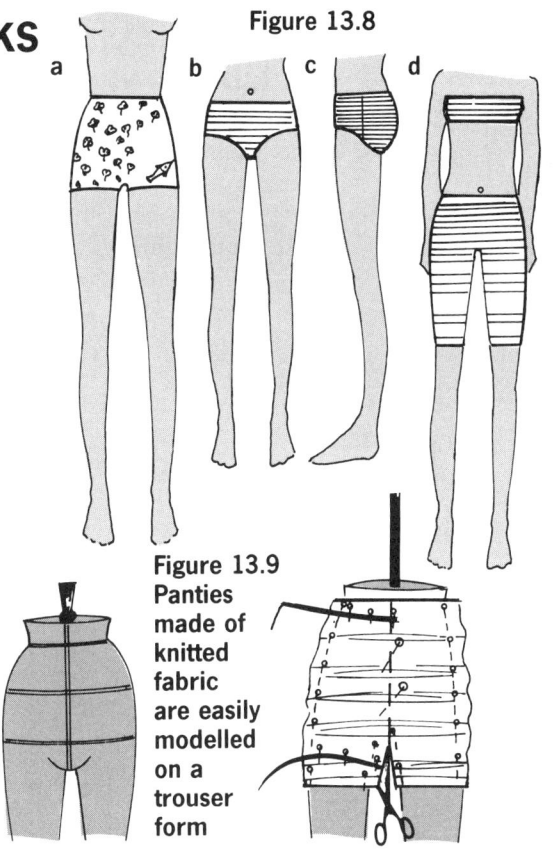

Figure 13.8

Figure 13.9 Panties made of knitted fabric are easily modelled on a trouser form

Short pants in knitted two-way stretch fabric

Figure 13.10 Length and girth measurements are reduced to less than body measurements. Test fabric beforehand. In this case 6 cm (2½ in) are subtracted from girth, and 2 cm (¾ in) from length of standard size 12 body measurements.

Finished measurements for two-way stretch pants, based on British Standard Size 12

Waist	62 cm (24½ in)
Seat (24 cm (9½ in) from waist equiv. to hip measurement	93 cm (36½ in)
Body rise	25.5 cm (10 in)
Side length	29 cm (11½ in)
Thigh	44–47 cm (17½–18½ in)

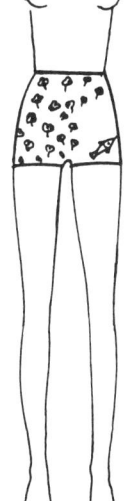

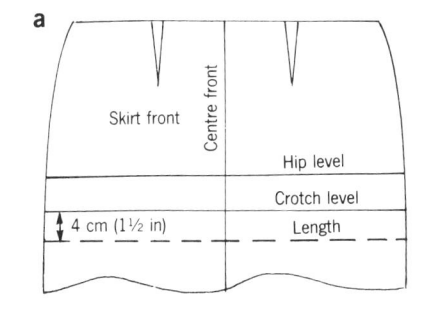

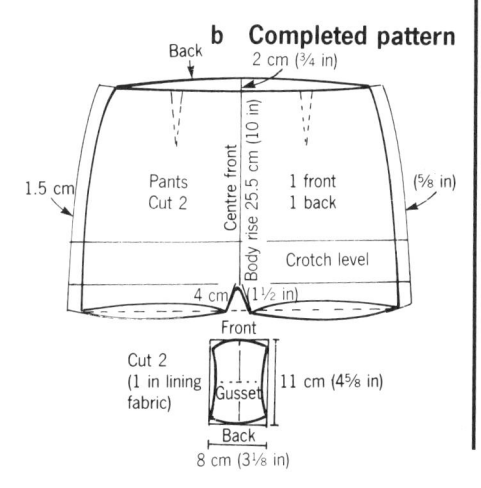

Figure 13.10a Use full front of straight skirt block (page 13). Draft to body measurements (see size chart) and outline. Mark body rise measurement on CF line and draw crotch level line.

b Reduce side seams by 1.5 cm (⅝ in). Shape leg lengths as shown (back length being 2 cm (¾ in) longer at its deepest point). Draft gusset 11 × 8 cm (4⅝ × 3⅛ in) as shown. Omit waist darts, take in side seams if required. Add seam allowances.

b Completed pattern

Hipster trunks in knitted stretch fabric – cut flat

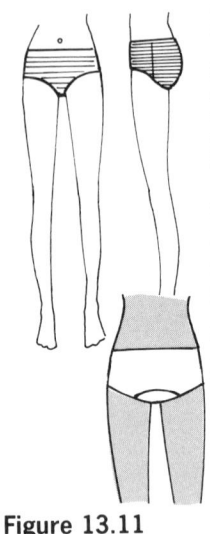

Proceed as for short pants Figure 13.10. These trunks have a gusset cut in one with the front resulting in only one gusset seam at lower back rather than two seams which is more frequent.

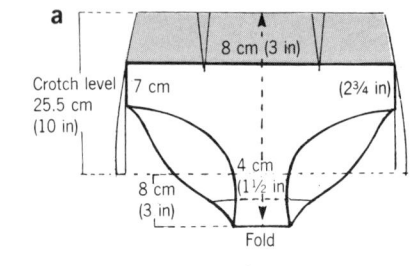

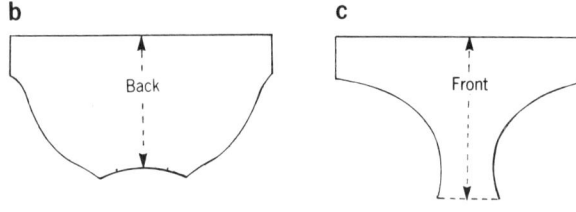

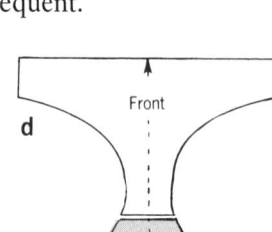

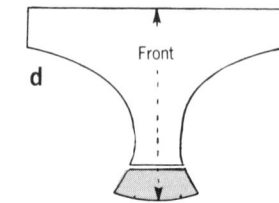

Figure 13.11

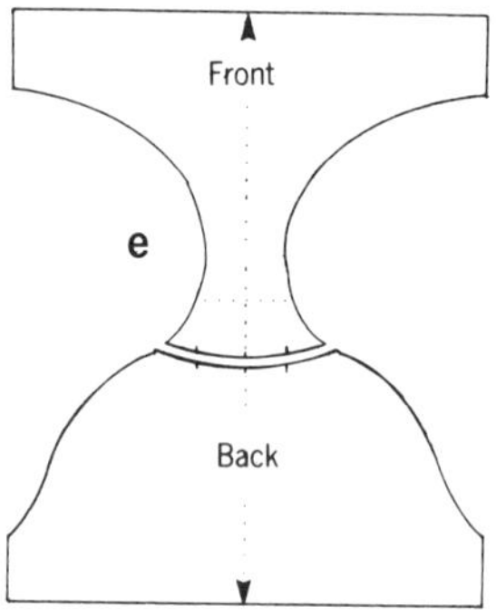

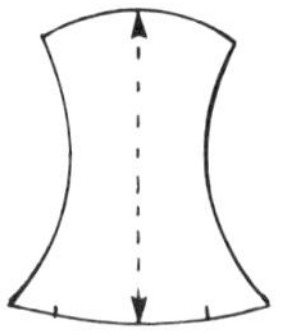

Figure 13.11a Lower waist level by desired amount. Shape front and back leg lengths according to design.

b Trace off back pattern to gusset seam.

c Trace off front pattern to where seam would normally be.

d Trace off back gusset section; add to front.

e These are whole patterns (not half) and must be folded on CF and CB and accurately trued. A gusset lining should be cut in appropriate fabric. Add seam allowances.

Model these trunks in Lycra fabric. Outline back and front style lines with tape on trouser form.

Figure 13.12

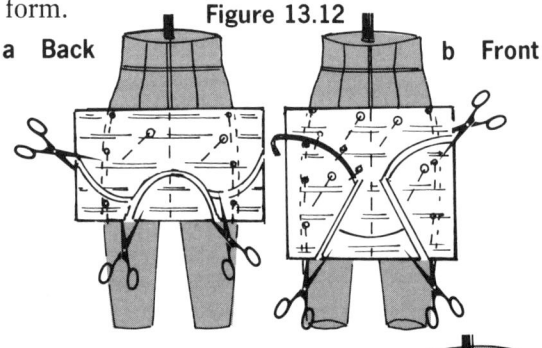

a Back   **b** Front

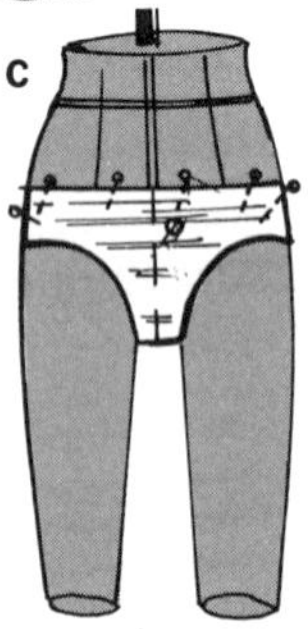

Figure 13.12a Cut rectangle of fabric 26 x 48 cm (10¼ x 19 in) wide. Chalk or tack centre line. Pin to back of trouser form, stretching fabric according to tightness required. Trim as shown.

b Cut rectangle of fabric 28 x 48 cm (11 in x 19 in) wide. Proceed as shown. Bring gusset section under crotch to back to cover semi-circle raw edge. Pin with raised seam. Also pin side seams, stretching fabric as for back. Turn under waist and leg edges according to sketch and styling tape. Mark one side of trunks with chalk or pins. Remove from form. Transfer markings to pattern paper. Pattern should resemble Figure 13.11e.

Bermuda stretch pants

Figure 13.13 Lower waist level and lengthen legs as shown **b**.

Note, the long gusset which is inserted in the inner leg seams and crotch.

Add seam turnings balance marks and grain lines.

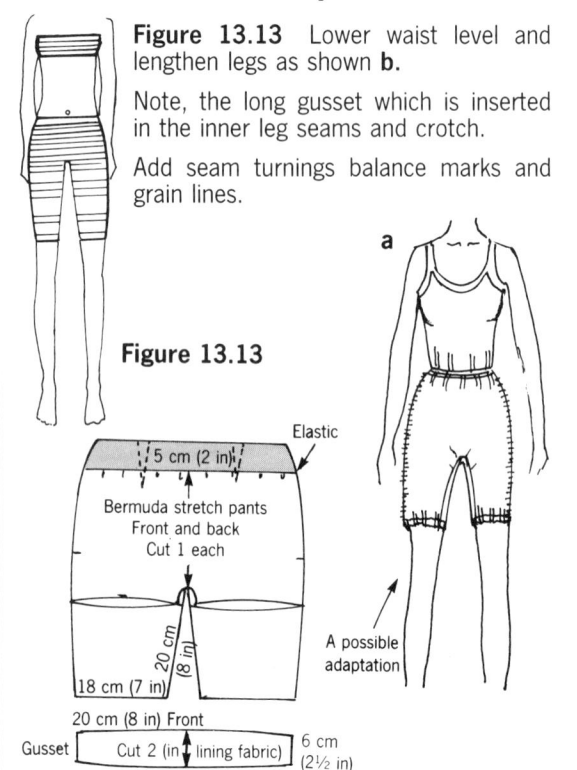

Figure 13.13

b Completed pattern

Cami-knickers based on the panties block

Figure 13.14 The construction of these cami-knickers is based on the combination of the basic mini-slip (Figure 13.1) and the basic panties block (Figure 13.4).

Figure 13.14 is cut with centre seams and 'grown-on' gusset and is less economical as regards fabric consumption than style **b** which has a separately cut gusset and no centre seams. Against this saving of fabric must be weighed the cost of greater skill and assembly time. In the end it is the consumer who determines which styles are in greater demand.

Size 12 cami-knickers – bias cut finished measurements based on British Standard Sizing

Bust	87 cm (34 in)
Hip	97 cm (38 in)
Length (shoulder to hem)	79 cm (31 in)
Crotch depth* (body rise)	36 cm (14¼ in)
Hem circumference (including gusset)	160 cm (63 in)

Figure 13.14

Outline mini-slip block, Figure 13.1h. Raise hem line by 8 cm (3in).

d and **e** Add 10 cm (4 in) flare to side seams at hem level. Draw new side seams to waist level.

Draw midriff style lines. Beginning at waist level, draw new CF and CB lines allowing 2 cm (¾ in) spring at hem line.

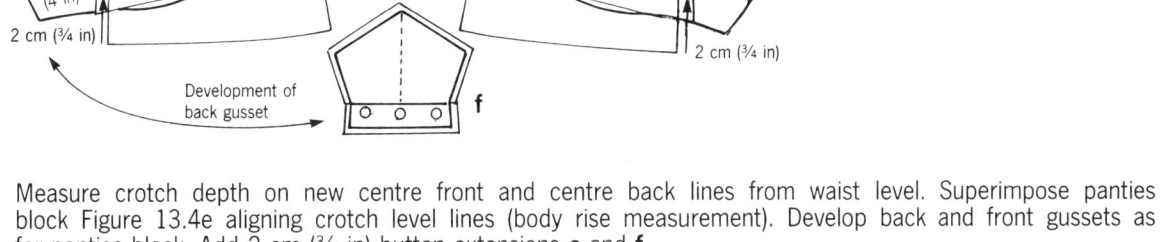

Measure crotch depth on new centre front and centre back lines from waist level. Superimpose panties block Figure 13.4e aligning crotch level lines (body rise measurement). Develop back and front gussets as for panties block. Add 2 cm (¾ in) button extensions **c** and **f**.

Complete draft, place balance marks, grain lines and shoulder strap position and trace all pattern parts onto pattern paper. Make up a toile to 'prove' the pattern and make any necessary adjustment to the pattern.

*Cami-knickers require an even lower crotch level than panties (compare with other lingerie body rise (crotch level) measurements) because of their one-piece construction and greater strain in the crotch area. The back gusset must be longer to ensure a comfortable button-fastening position.

Basic slip – cut flat

Figure 13.15

Draft developed from hip block.

The size chart plays an important part in this development as does a detailed knowledge of the ease and tolerance allowances incorporated in your particular hip block.

All size 12 blocks in this book are constructed to measure across:
Bust 97 cm (38 in)   Hip 102 cm (40 in)
Body measurements are   Bust 87 cm (34 in)   Hip 97 cm (38 in)
Ease and tolerance is   Bust 10 cm (4 in)   Hip 5 cm (2 in)

British Standard Institution Sizing suggest that no or very small tolerances be added to the body measurements for slips.

Size 12 slip – finished measurements based on British Standard Sizing

	Bias-cut woven and knitted	Straight cut woven
Bust	87 cm (34 in)	89 cm (35 in)
Hip	97 cm (38 in)	99 cm (39 in)
Underarm to hem	76–80 cm (30–31½ in)	
Hem circumference	127 x 132 cm (50 x 52 in) approx	
Length (from mid shoulder)	102 cm (40 in)	

Figure 13.15a Outline front hip block Figure 12.1a. Draw bust, waist and hip line 16.5 cm (6½ in) from waist as continuation from front block across paper.

b Align back hip block Figure 12.1. Outline. Establish length, measuring from centre of shoulder.

Increase shoulder dart by half its width. Connect to dart point. This reduction aims at achieving a closer fit around the top edge of the slip.

Reduce side seams as shown. Lengthen to hem. Measure resulting hem circumference and adjust angle of side seams according to desired circumference. Raise waist line 1 cm (⅜ in) as is customary for slips and camiknickers. Draw in waist darts.

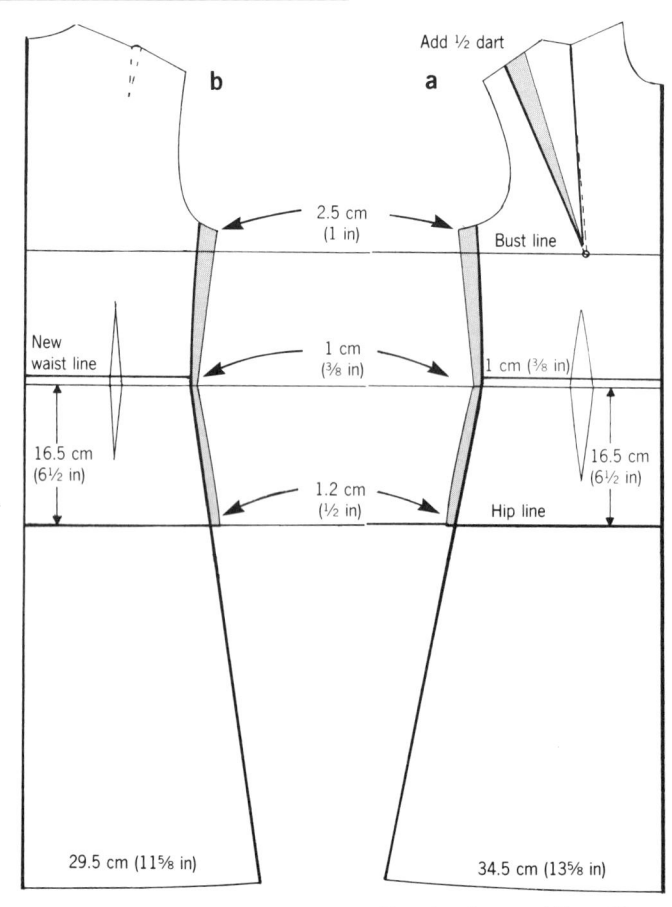

Hem circumference – 128 cm (50½ in)
Half hem – 64 cm (25¼ in)

c and **d** Trace slip foundation **a** and **b** onto new paper. Draw style lines as shown. Trace on to card. Perforate darts. Draw dotted lines through centre front and centre back darts parallel to CF and CB lines touching hem lines as shown. The darts (omitted for this style) and dotted lines will be required for the development of other styles, e.g. princess line.

Elastic lace edging around the top edge of the slip can replace the small bust dart if wished.

Use this basic slip also for the development of camisoles, cami-knickers and other body-fashion garments.

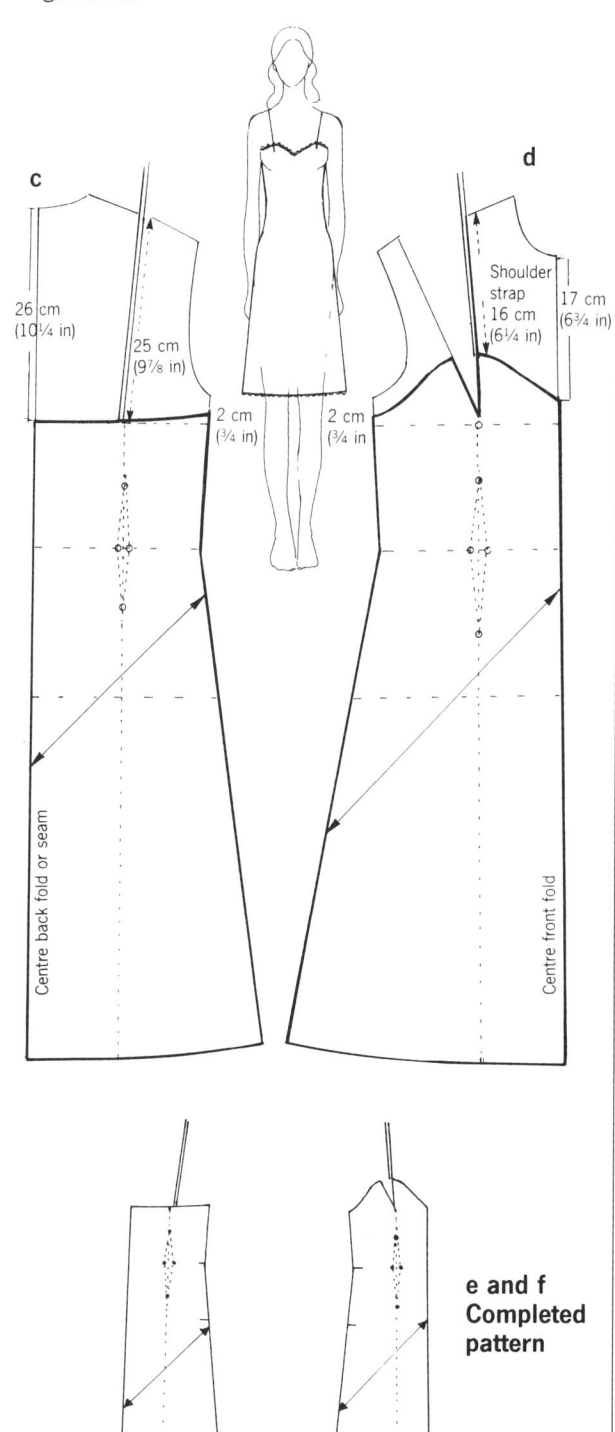

Basic cami-knickers cut flat

Figure 13.16

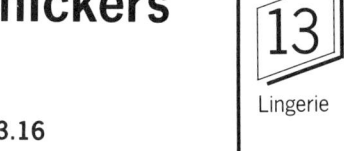

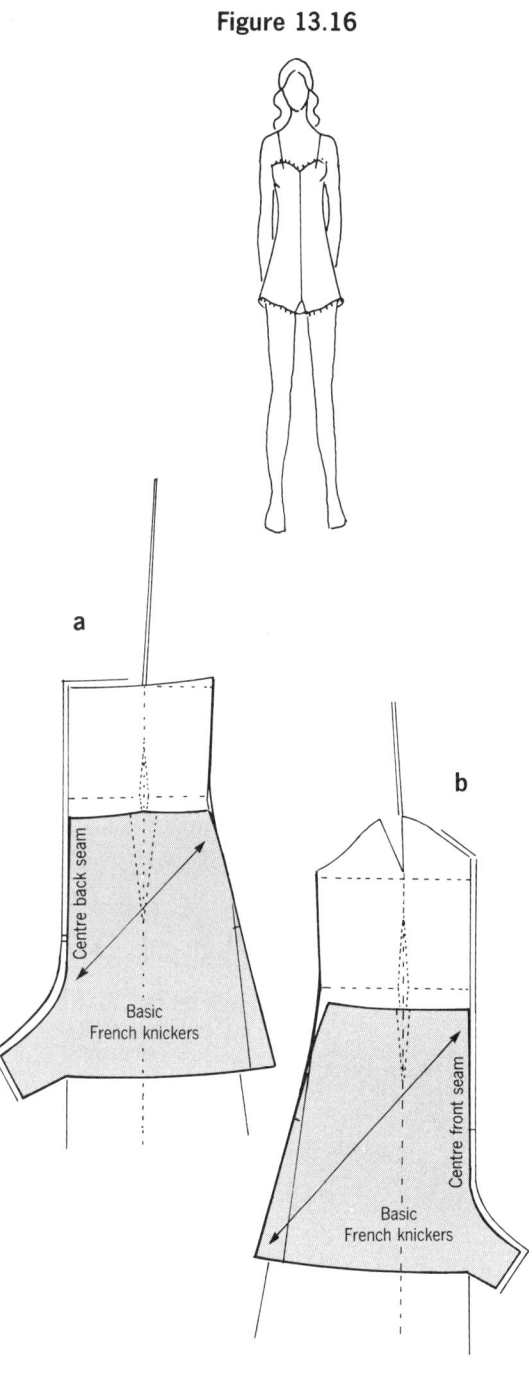

e and f Completed pattern

Figure 13.16 Cami-knickers are easily constructed by using the basic slip **e** and **f** above and superimposing the basic French knickers, Figure 13.7c, as shown. Darts are omitted. There is a centre front and centre back seam.

13 Lingerie

Princess line slip

Figure 13.17

Figure 13.17 This princess line slip is cut on the straight grain in woven fabric. Therefore more ease and tolerance must be added to the basic slip development, Figure 13.15 (see size chart, page 192).

The slip can, of course, be cut on the bias or in knit fabric.

The hem circumference is 134 cm (52¾ in).

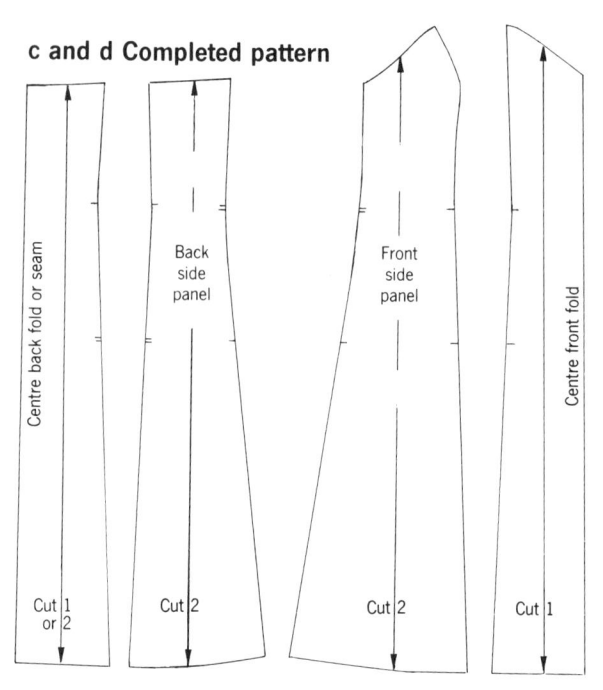

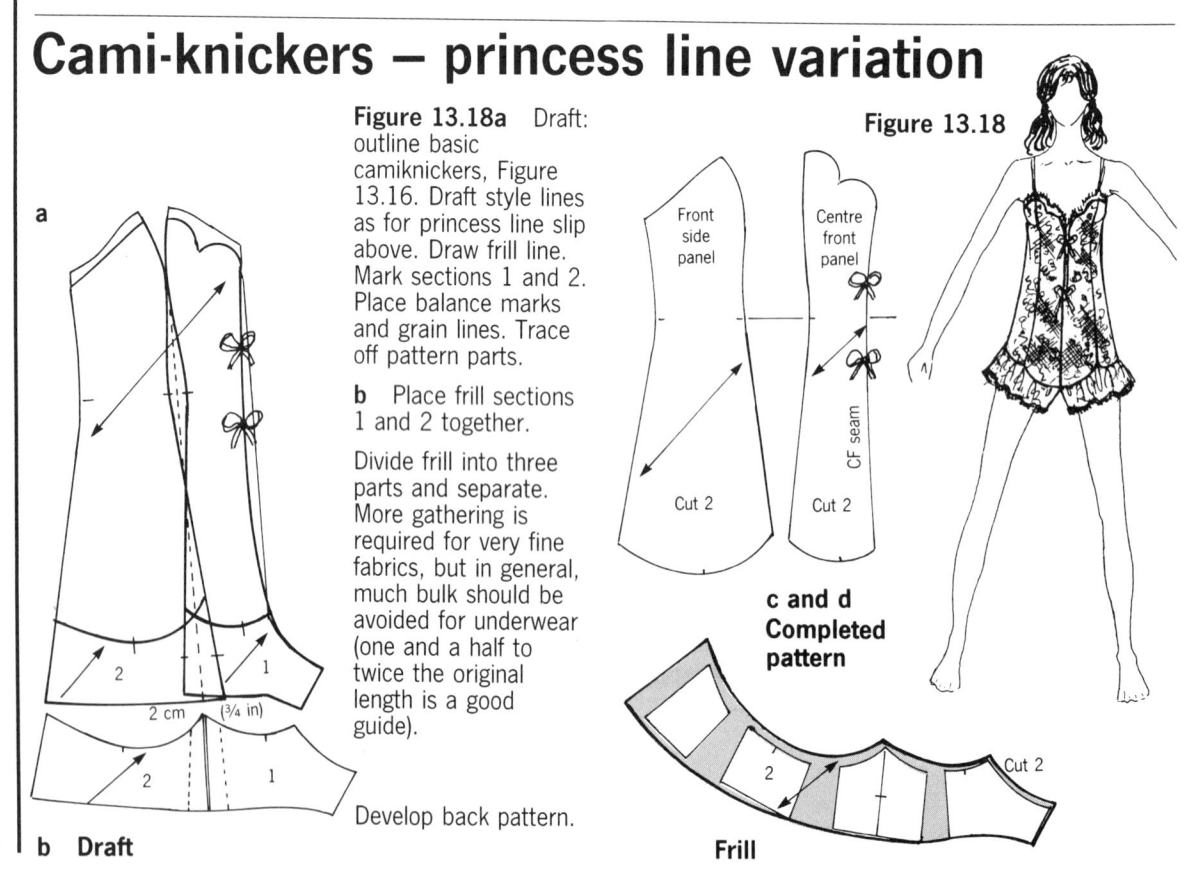

c and d Completed pattern

Reduce 1–3 cm (⅜–1⅛ in)

1.5 cm (⅝ in) 1.5 cm (⅜ in)

Centre back · Centre front

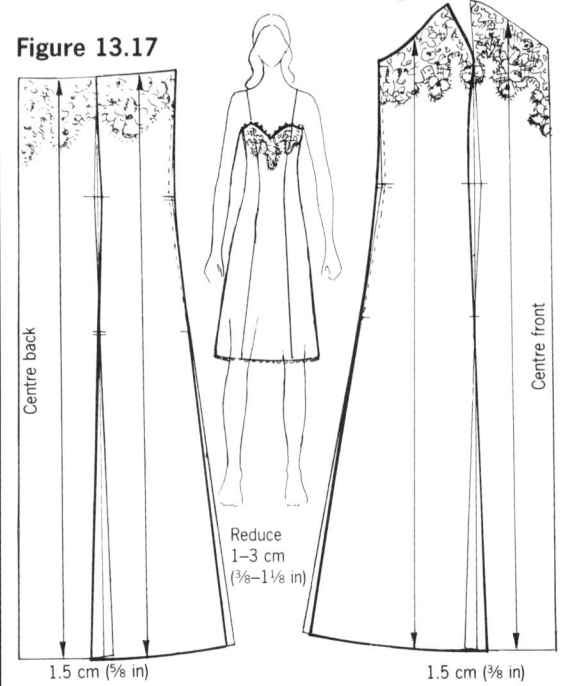

Back side panel — Cut 2
Centre back fold or seam — Cut 1 or 2
Front side panel — Cut 2
Centre front fold — Cut 1

a and **b** Outline basic slip, Figure 13.15e and f, including darts and vertical guide lines. Increase side seams according to bust and hip measurements on size chart (page 192). Proceed as for any other princess line draft (pages 54 and 55) and as shown. Place balance marks.

c and **d** Trace back and front panels onto new sheet of paper. Add seam allowances and cutting instructions.

Cami-knickers – princess line variation

Figure 13.18a Draft: outline basic camiknickers, Figure 13.16. Draft style lines as for princess line slip above. Draw frill line. Mark sections 1 and 2. Place balance marks and grain lines. Trace off pattern parts.

b Place frill sections 1 and 2 together.

Divide frill into three parts and separate. More gathering is required for very fine fabrics, but in general, much bulk should be avoided for underwear (one and a half to twice the original length is a good guide).

Develop back pattern.

Figure 13.18

Front side panel — Cut 2
Centre front panel — Cut 2 CF seam

c and d Completed pattern

Frill — Cut 2

2 cm (¾ in)

b Draft

Basic bra-slip

Figure 13.19

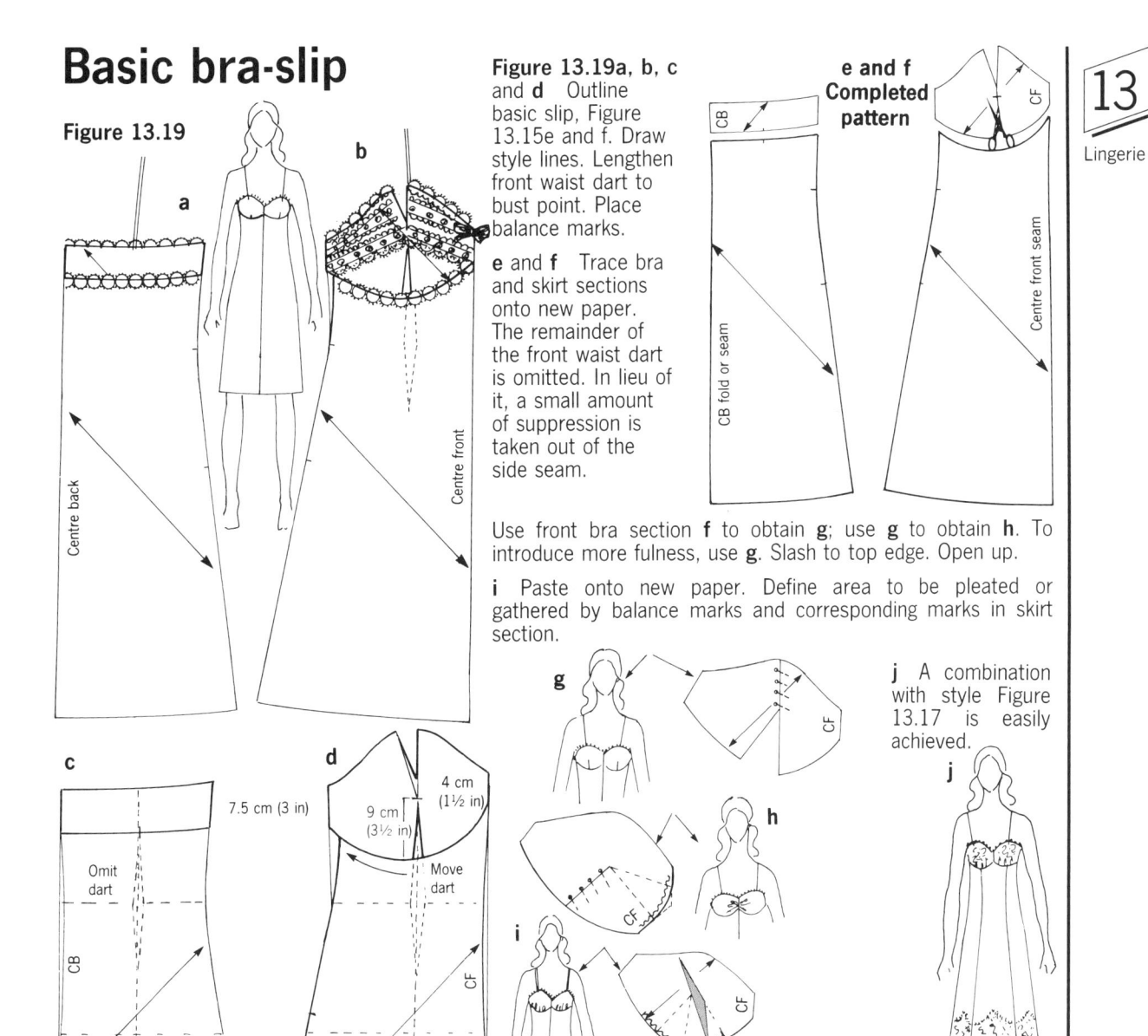

Figure 13.19a, b, c and d Outline basic slip, Figure 13.15e and f. Draw style lines. Lengthen front waist dart to bust point. Place balance marks.

e and f Trace bra and skirt sections onto new paper. The remainder of the front waist dart is omitted. In lieu of it, a small amount of suppression is taken out of the side seam.

e and f Completed pattern

Use front bra section **f** to obtain **g**; use **g** to obtain **h**. To introduce more fulness, use **g**. Slash to top edge. Open up.

i Paste onto new paper. Define area to be pleated or gathered by balance marks and corresponding marks in skirt section.

j A combination with style Figure 13.17 is easily achieved.

Cami-knickers (bra variation)

Figure 13.20

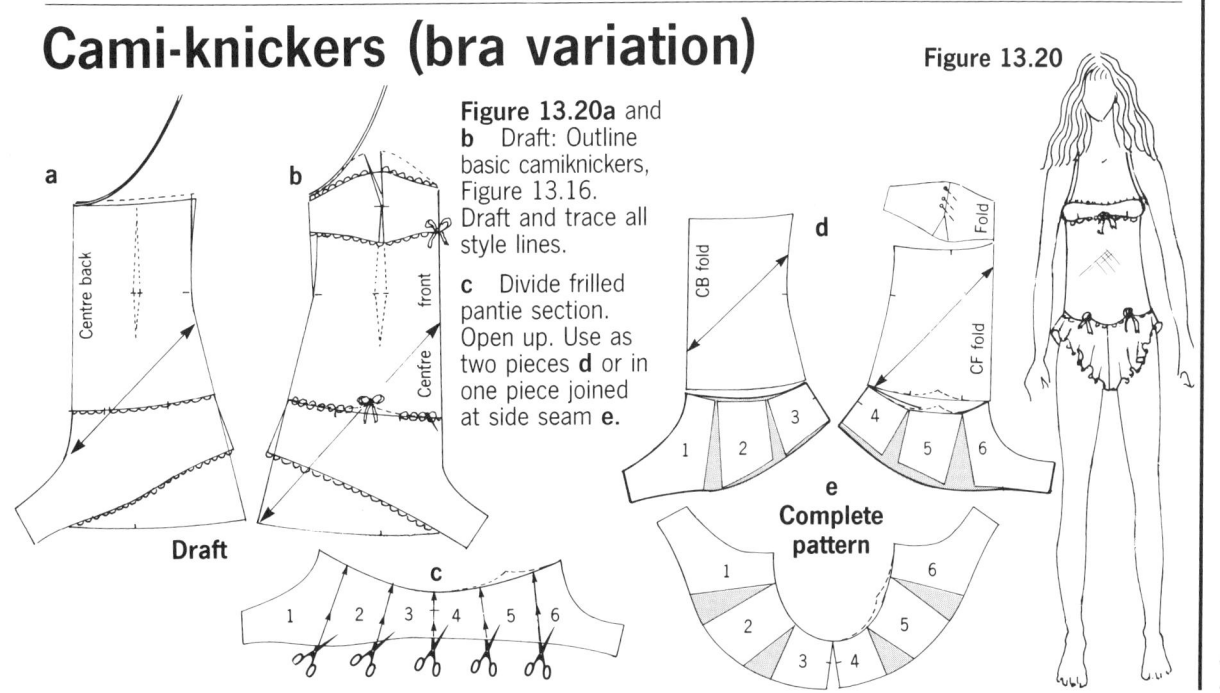

Figure 13.20a and b Draft: Outline basic camiknickers, Figure 13.16. Draft and trace all style lines.

c Divide frilled pantie section. Open up. Use as two pieces **d** or in one piece joined at side seam **e**.

e Complete pattern

195 | Lingerie

Brassieres

Basic brassiere draft

Figure 13.21a Draw horizontal bust guide line. Outline upper section of basic slip draft, Figure 13.15a and b. Further increase shoulder/bust dart as shown. Also double under bust dart and side seam suppressions. From bust point **B** measure up 10 cm (4 in) and down 9 cm (3⅛ in) at CF 2.5 cm (1 in) up and 3 cm (1¼ in) down; at side seam 4 cm (1½ in) up and 5 cm (2 in) down and at CB 2 cm (¾ in) up and down. Outline as shown.

b Close back dart and side seam. Move side seam 4 cm (1½ in) forward. Reshape back top edge for shoulder strap position.

Figure 13.21

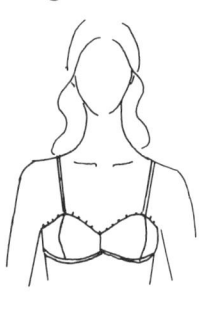

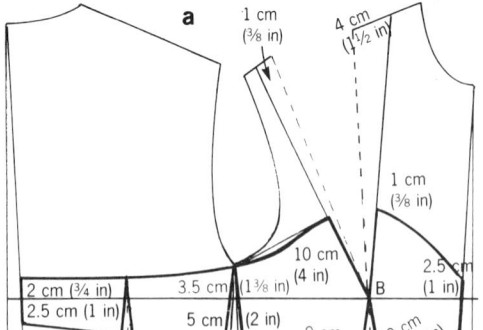

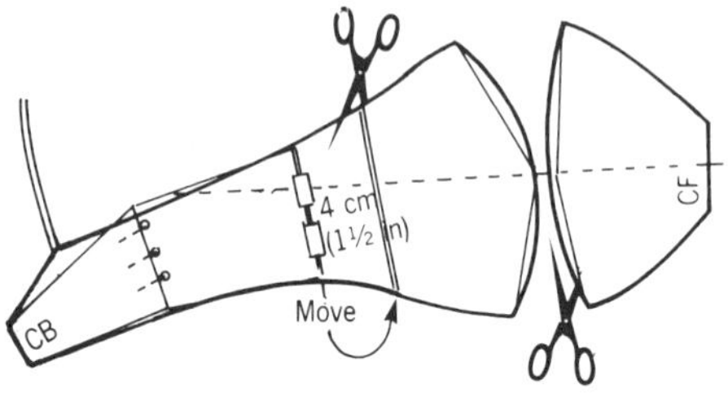

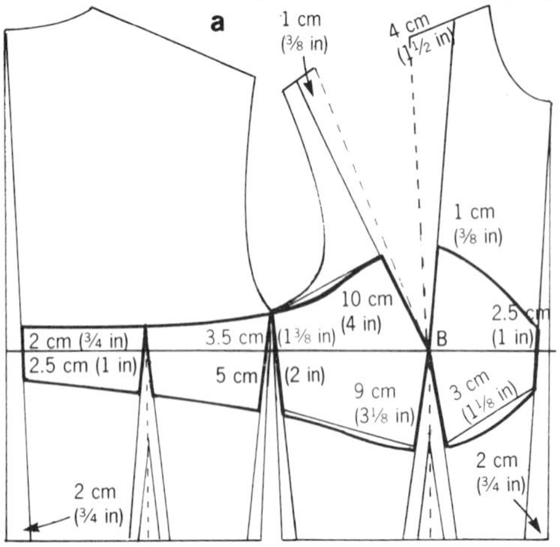

b Completed pattern

Figure 13.22

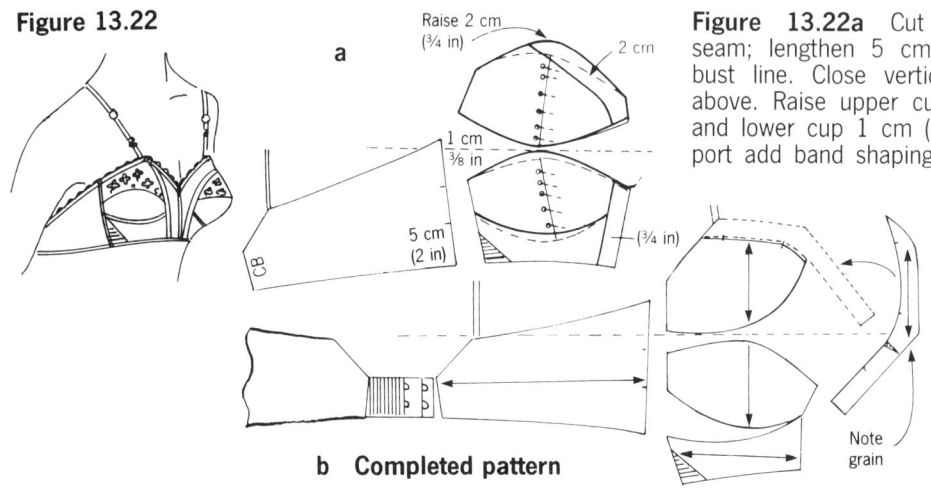

Figure 13.22a Cut through new side seam; lengthen 5 cm (2 in). Cut on cup bust line. Close vertical bust seam of **b** above. Raise upper cut edge 2 cm (¾ in) and lower cup 1 cm (⅜ in). For extra support add band shaping below cup matching length of new side seam. Draw 2 cm (¾ in) style line from top of upper cup, parallel to CF. Trace all parts and balance marks.

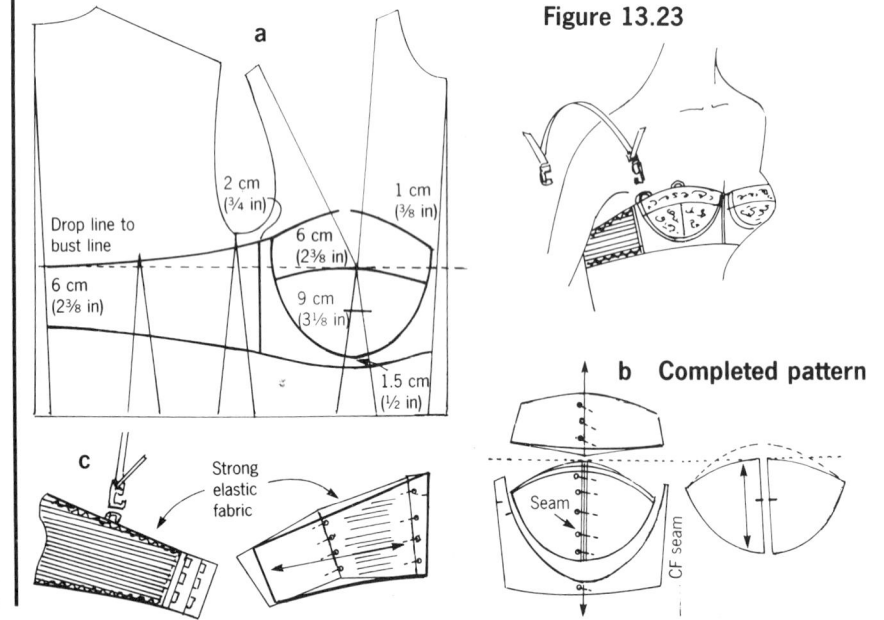

b Completed pattern

Figure 13.23

b Completed pattern

Wired cup strapless bra

The semi-circle cup wire measures 18 cm (7 in) across open top.

a Outline basic brassiere draft, Figure 13.21a. Draw style lines. Move side seam forward 2 cm (¾ in). Front upper edge is 6 cm (2⅜ in) from bust point. CB section is drafted below bust line.

b Raise lower cup an additional 2 cm (¾ in) for fuller bust if required. Add seam allowances to the quartered lower cup.

Shoulder straps are detachable (c).

Nightdress

Figure 13.24

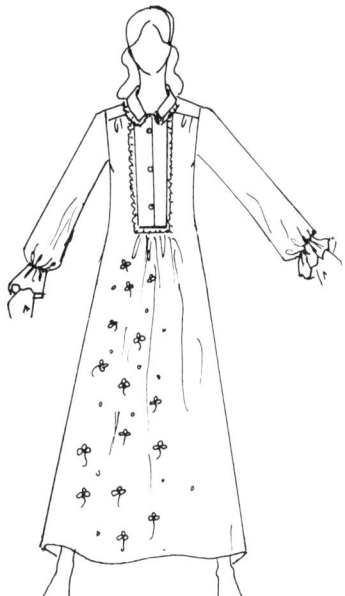

Finished measurements for nightdresses made in woven material
Based on British Standard Size 12, Bust 87 cm (34 in)

1	Bust	99–107 cm (39–42 in)
2	Hip	112–119.5 (44–47 in)
3	Neck circumference	37.6 (14¾ in)
4	Shoulder seam	14 cm (5½ in)
5	Armhole circumference	46–51 cm (18–20 in)
6	Sleeve – underarm length	43 cm (17 in)
7	Wrist stretched – elasticated	25–30 cm (10–12 in)
8	Hem circumference	from 145 cm (57 in)
9	Full length	132 cm (52 in)

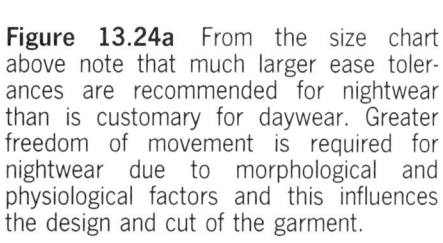

Figure 13.24a From the size chart above note that much larger ease tolerances are recommended for nightwear than is customary for daywear. Greater freedom of movement is required for nightwear due to morphological and physiological factors and this influences the design and cut of the garment.

Whether this nightdress is cut flat or modelled, larger tolerances around bust, hip, armhole and sleeve, based on the size chart, must be made.

Model this nightdress in calico, or in the garment fabric on the fold as shown here.

b Cut rectangle of double fabric on fold:

Full length 132 cm (52 in)

10 cm (4 in) allowance for hem and modelling equals 142 cm (56 in).

Width, ¼ hem: circumference 36.5 + 18 cm (14½ + 7 in) approximately for gathers, equals 54.5 cm (21½ in); plus 4 cm (1½ in) side seam and modelling allowance, equals 58.5 cm (23 in).

c Outline style lines in black tape on dress form. Lower neckline 1 cm (⅜ in).

The CF is marked with tailor's chalk and a small snip 13 cm (5⅛ in) away from folded or single long edge. Repeat for lower edge as shown. If calico is used, a line can be drawn between these two points.

d Pin rectangle of fabric with chalked and snipped CF to centre front of dress form. Pin at intervals as shown.

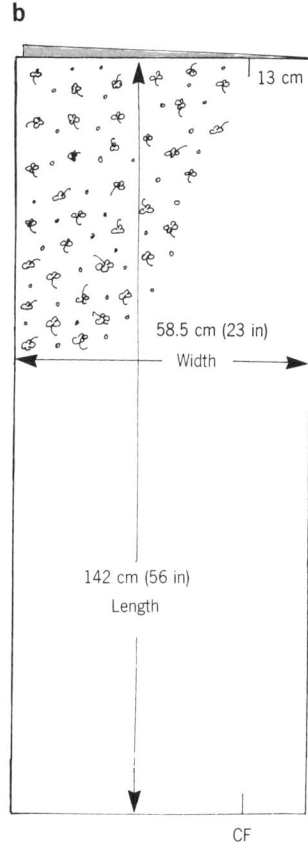

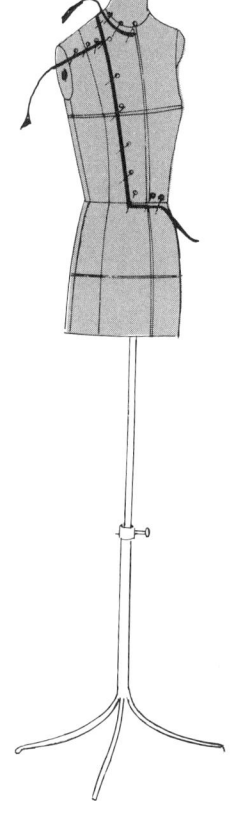

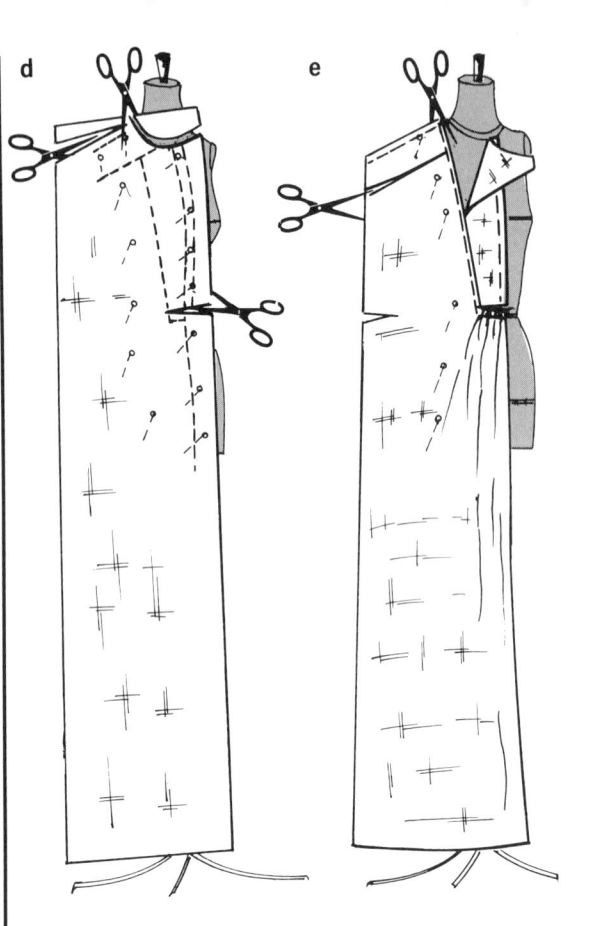

d (continued) Cut away surplus fabric at neck and shoulder lines leaving seam allowances. Mark all taped style lines which can be felt or seen through the fabric with tailor's chalk and pins.

Slash 1.5 cm (½ in) above taped waist style line from folded or single edge to within 1.5 cm (½ in) of vertical panel style line. Mark button stand by chalking and snipping 2 cm (¾ in) to right of CF mark. Repeat at waist level. Crease between these two points. Fold fabric (facing) under to wrong side.

e Gather skirt section until edge rests alongside button stand edge. Pin. Cut away centre front section to within 1.5 cm (½ in) of taped vertical panel style line. Retain for recutting later.

Cut away 'yoke fabric' 1.5 cm (½ in) above marked yoke style line.

f Gather lightly as shown.

Recut yoke from cut off 'yoke fabric' restoring the 1.5 cm (½ in) lost plus 1.5 cm (½ in) seam allowance. Turn seam turning under and pin over gathered section.

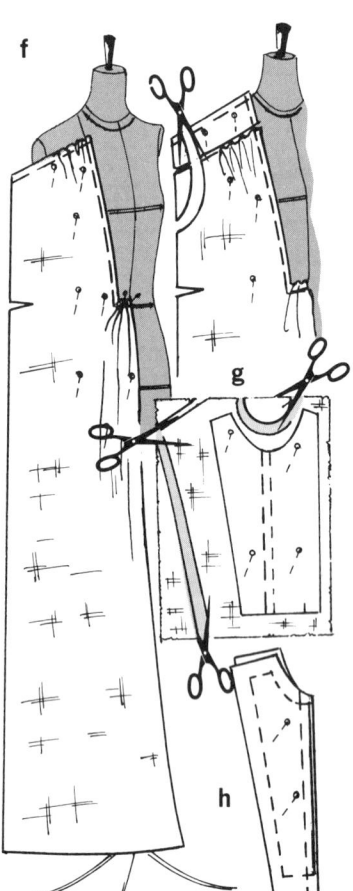

g Tear rectangle of fabric, length of cut away front section plus 4 cm (1½ in) above shoulder and below waist. Width: a little wider than cut away section. Pin section onto fabric rectangle. Cut out roughly.

h Fold facing under on button stand edge.

i Pin over cut panel line on dress form.

j For back of nightdress cut rectangle of double fabric on fold or single layer calico 142 x 47 cm (56 x 18½ in) wide. This allows for 6.5 cm (2½ in) gathering below 10 cm (4 in) deep yoke. Proceed as for front yoke **e** and **f**.

Compare bust and hip measurements with size chart. Modelled garment measurements should be larger due to the styling of gathers.

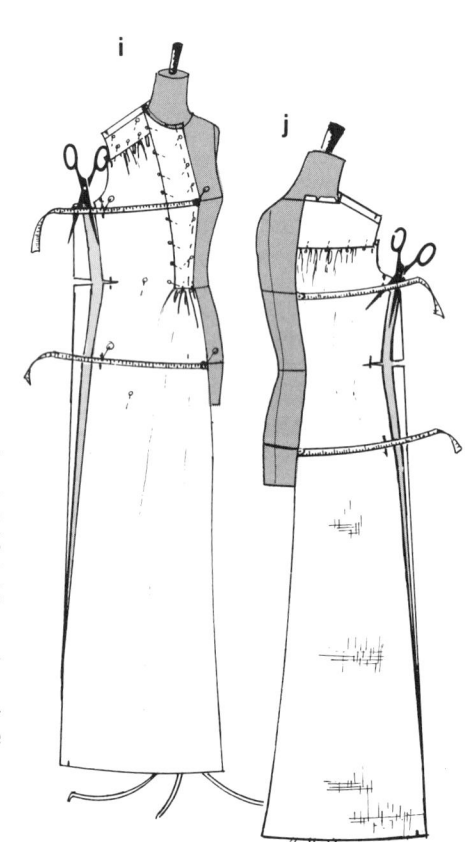

k Outline sleeve block, page 15.

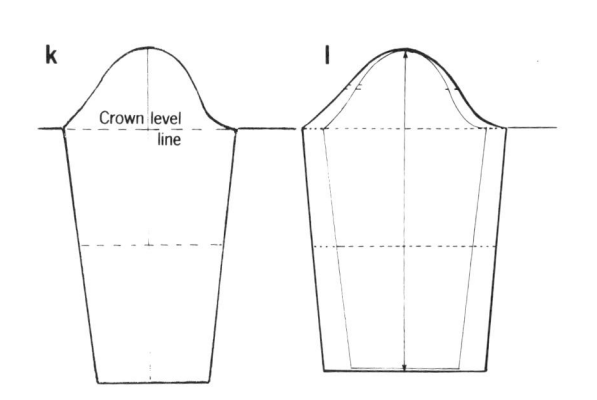

l Extend crown level line 2.5–4 cm (1–1½ in) each side. Widen wrist line to 30.5 km (12 in). Connect as shown. Use this new block for further development.

m Draw two horizontal parallel lines 2.5 cm (1 in) apart. Align sleeve crown level line with lower of parallel lines.

From centre sleeve pivoting point, pivot to left. Outline left half of sleeve head and part of underarm seam. Repeat for right half of sleeve. Connect sleeve seams to original wrist. Add flounce. Check armhole measurements. Transfer larger measurement to each side of sleeve if different from pivoted measurement.

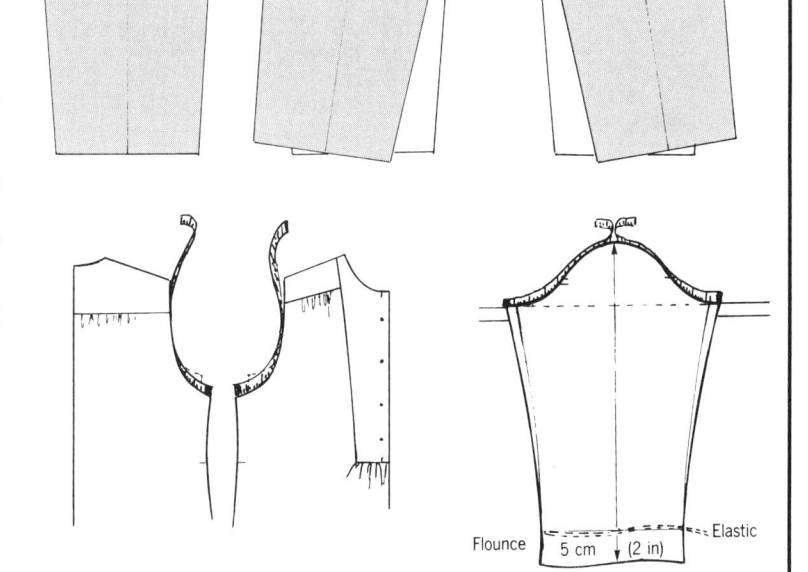

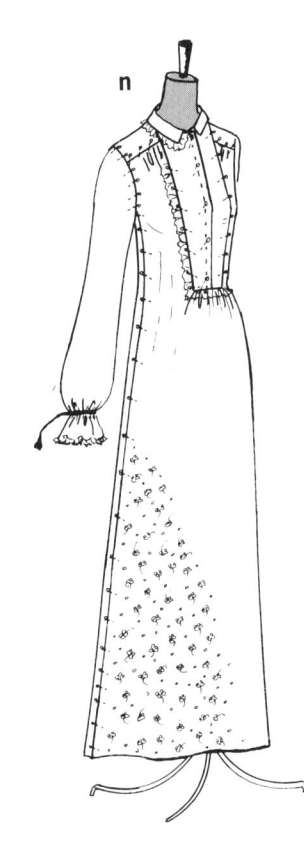

n Pin sleeve seams together (with lapped seam). Gather sleeve wrist with black tape. Pin onto garment armhole.

Model narrow collar based on Figure 5.27, page 68. Pin short piece of lace edging around collar point to judge collar length (the lace edging touches CF whereas the collar itself does not). Examine general appearance and fit for comfort of nightdress, on a live model if possible. Make any final adjustments.

Mark all seams and balance marks (with pins if the garment was modelled in garment fabric). Unpin. True all seam and style lines. Trace onto pattern paper. Complete pattern accurately with balance marks, grain lines, seam allowances and cutting instructions. Trim seam allowances on nightdress and check balance marks according to pattern before making up. Final pattern pieces should resemble Figure 13.25**m** and **n** cut flat.

Nightdress cut flat

Figure 13.25

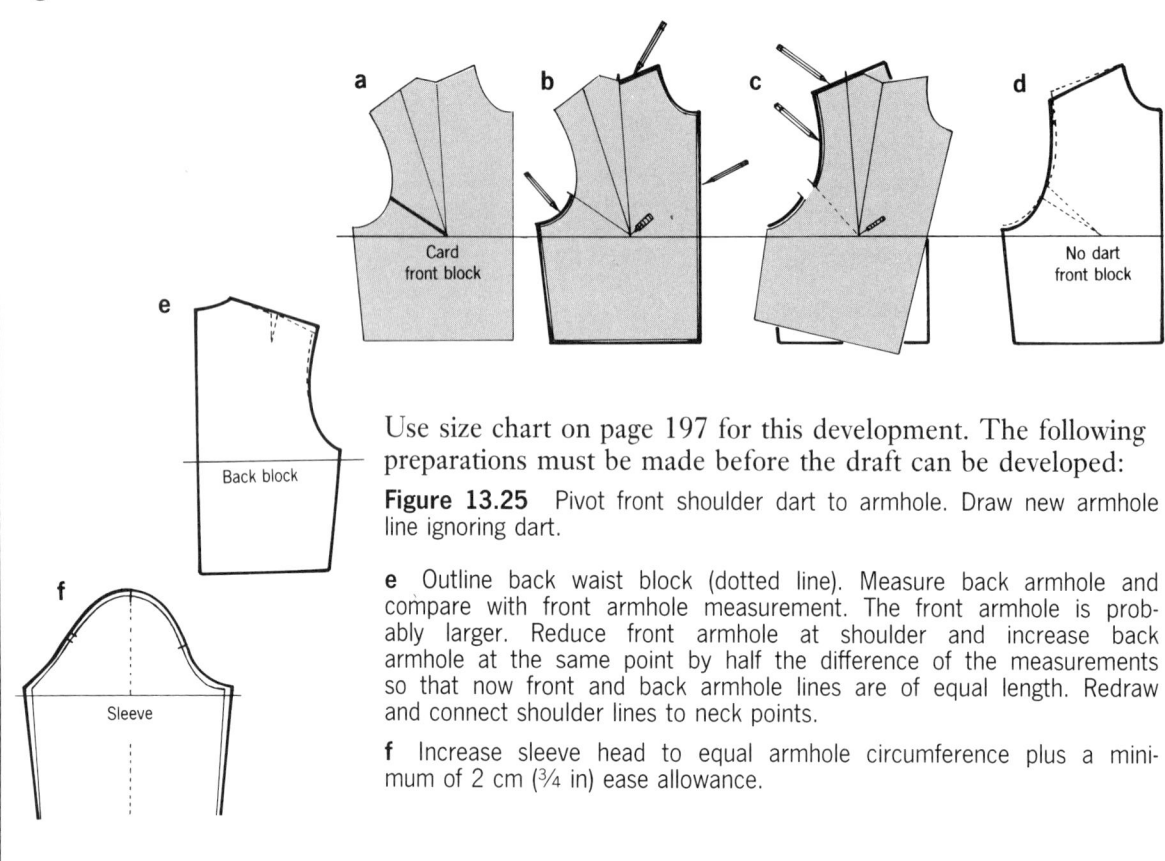

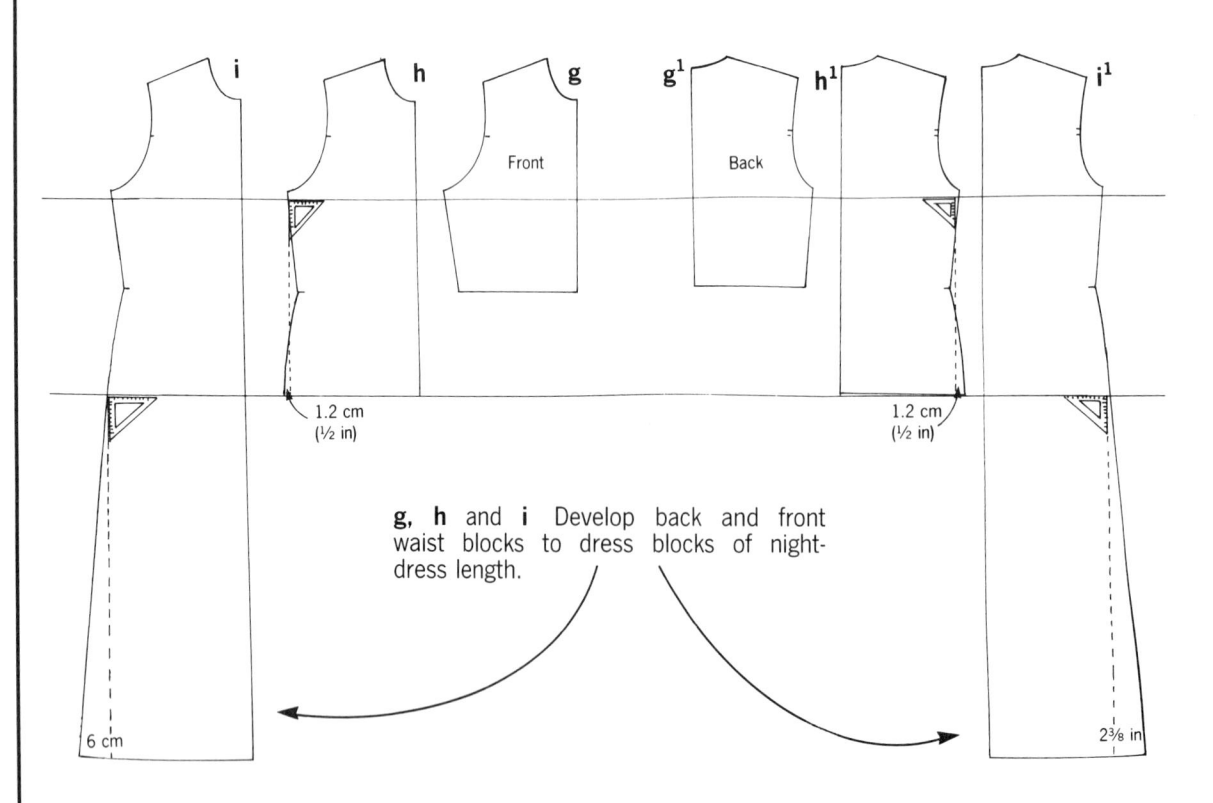

Use size chart on page 197 for this development. The following preparations must be made before the draft can be developed:

Figure 13.25 Pivot front shoulder dart to armhole. Draw new armhole line ignoring dart.

e Outline back waist block (dotted line). Measure back armhole and compare with front armhole measurement. The front armhole is probably larger. Reduce front armhole at shoulder and increase back armhole at the same point by half the difference of the measurements so that now front and back armhole lines are of equal length. Redraw and connect shoulder lines to neck points.

f Increase sleeve head to equal armhole circumference plus a minimum of 2 cm (¾ in) ease allowance.

g, h and **i** Develop back and front waist blocks to dress blocks of nightdress length.

Block bust	97 cm (38 in)
Nightdress bust	107 cm (42 in)
Block armhole	42 cm (16½ in)
Nightdress armhole	49 cm (19¼ in)
Block–hem circumference	130 cm (51 in)
Nightdress circumference	145 cm (57 in)

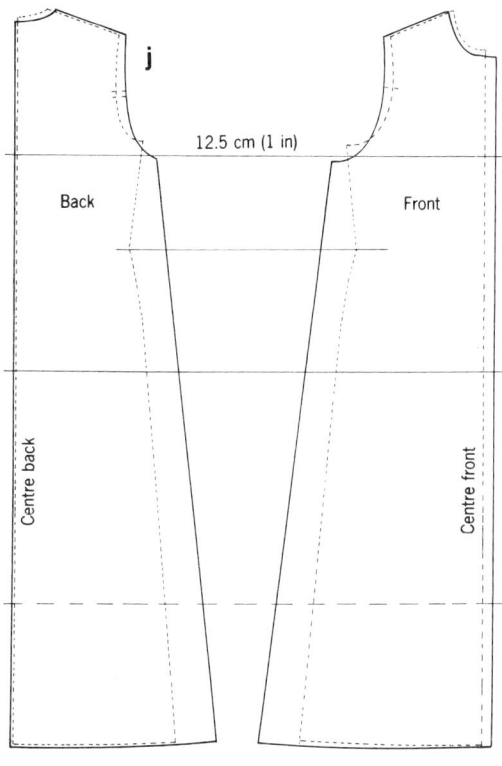

Lingerie

j Outline back and front long dress blocks. Lower neckline 1 cm (⅜ in). Lower armhole 2.5 cm (1 in). Extend side seams 2.5 cm (1 in) according to size chart. Extend shoulders 1 cm (⅜ in). Draw new armholes and side seams. Draw button stand 2 cm (¾ in) to right of CF and parallel to it.

k Draw back yoke style line approximately 10 cm (4 in) down from nape of neck. Extend CB 5 cm (2 in) below yoke line. Place balance mark for distribution of gathers.

l Draw front yoke and style line as shown. Extend 12 cm (4¾ in) to right of button stand for gathers. Draw slash line. Place balance marks on yoke line for positioning of gathers.

m Completed back pattern. Add seam allowances.

n Cut on slash line. Separate parts 5 cm (2 in) for gathers. Develop grown-on facing as shown. Add seam allowances to all pattern pieces.

Develop collar from either page 68 or page 72. The sleeve development is the same as for the modelled nightdress (Figure 13.24).

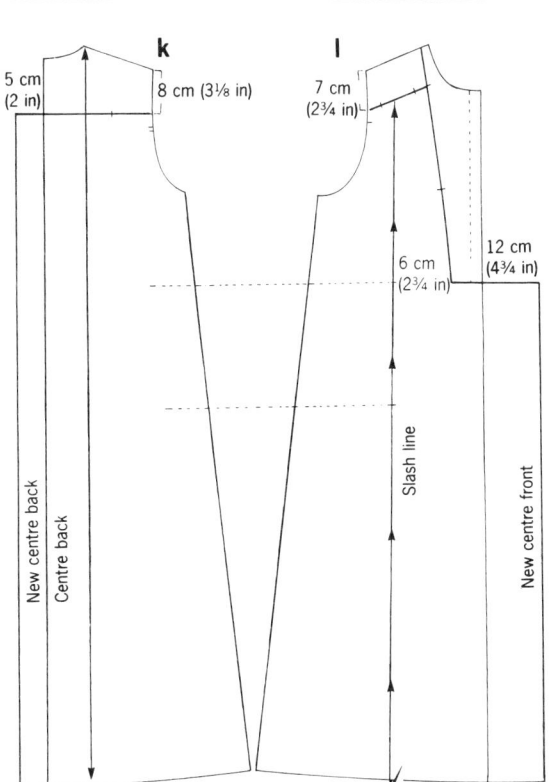

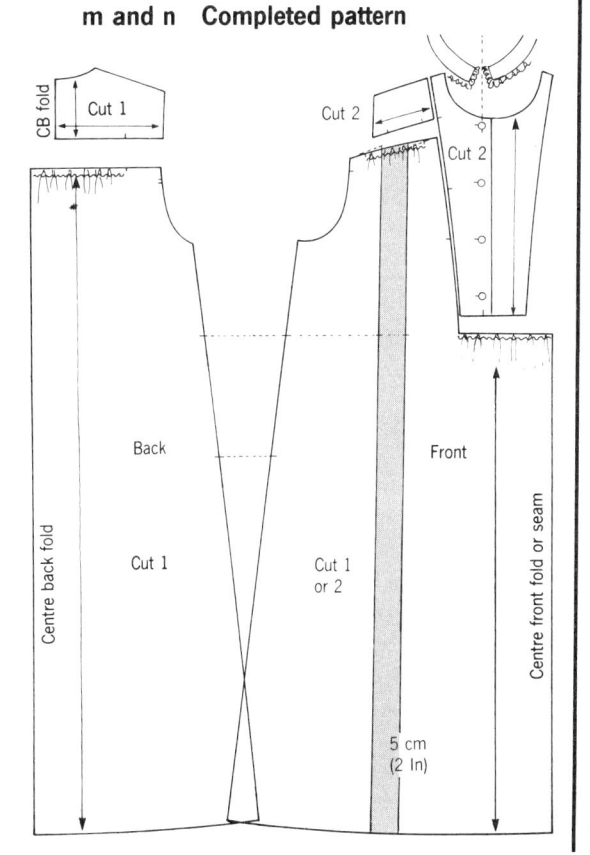

m and n Completed pattern

Pyjamas with bias piping

Figure 13.26 Finished measurement for pyjamas based on British Standard Size 12

Jacket		Trousers	
Bust	102 cm (40 in)	Seat 20.5 cm (8 in) from waist	107 cm (42 in)
Hip	107 cm (42 in)	Crutch level circumference	144 cm (56¾ in)
Neck	38 cm (15 in)	Waist stretched	97 cm (38¼ in)
Shoulder	14.5 cm (5¾ in)	Waist unstretched	63.5 cm (25 in)
Armhole	48.5 cm (19 in)	Front rise (seam)	49 cm (15⅜ in)
Sleeve underarm 1	43.5 cm (17 in)	Back rise (seam)	44 cm (17¼ in)
Upper arm circumference	40.5 cm (16 in)	Outside leg	104 cm (41 in)
Cuff at wrist	25.5 cm (10 in)	Inside leg	72 cm (28¼ in)
Full length	61 cm (24 in)	Ankle	36 cm (14¼ in)
Hem circumference	107 cm (42 ⅛ in)		

Pyjamas – size 12

Figure 13.26a Jacket draft: Outline hip blocks Figure 13.25h. Lower back and front necklines. Extend side seams 2.5 cm (1 in); Check bust measurement with size chart. Lower armhole 2 cm (¾ in). Add 2 cm (¾ in) button stand to right of CF and draft lapel shape and facing as shown. Equalise back and front armhole measurements (Figure 13.25d and e). Breast pocket overall size is 12 x 11 cm (4¾ x 4⅜ in). The decorative facing is 3 cm (1¼ in) wide. Hip pocket measures 15 x 14 cm (6 x 5½ in) overall, with facing 4.5 cm (1¾ in) wide. This pocket is lengthened by the width of the hem. Pockets are finished with contrasting colour bias piping sandwiched between pockets and double facings.

Sleeve

b Outline basic semi-fitted sleeve block Figure 1.12, page 15. Widen sleeve at underarm by amount that jacket side seams were extended. Follow size chart for underarm sleeve length and wrist circumference.

Collar

c Develop collar width and collar points to correspond with shape and width of lapel (See page 71 for development of top and under collars).

Contrasting bias piping is inserted between outer edge of collar, lapels and fronts.

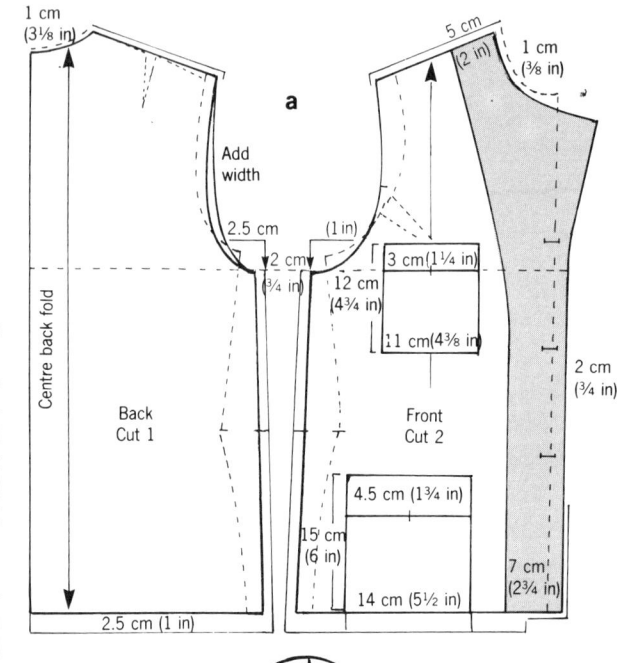

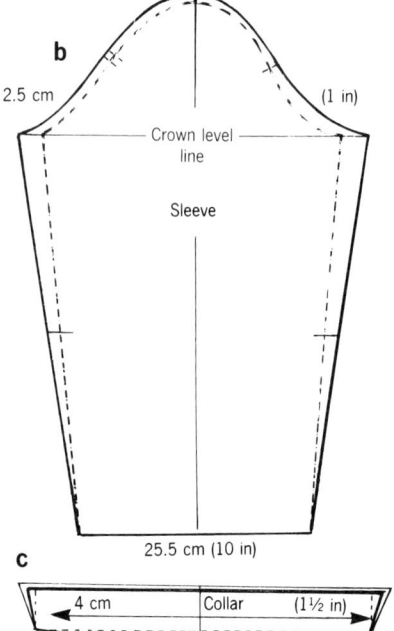

d Develop sleeve further. Raise sleeve seams at crown level line by amount that armhole was lowered (see pivoting method Figure 13.24m). Draw cuff line for 7 cm (2¾ in) wide cuff/facing. Place balance mark.

Pattern development

e Trace off sleeve cuff section and double for facing. Decorative piping is inserted between cuff and sleeve.

f Trace off pockets and pocket double facings.

g Trace off front facing.

h Trace off top and under collar.

Add grain lines, seam and hem allowances and button and buttonhole placings.

Trousers

i Draw long vertical line and line at right angles representing hip line. Place back and front panties block (Fig 13.14e, page 186) 2 cm (¾ in) away from vertical line, hip lines aligning (dotted line). Follow size chart for seat, crutch level circumference, waist, body rise, inside leg and ankle measurements.

Any body rise measurement which is longer than the panties' body rise measurement should be extended above the waist line.

Place balance marks and grain lines. Add seam and hem allowances including slot for elastic at waist line.

These trousers can be cut with or without side seams.

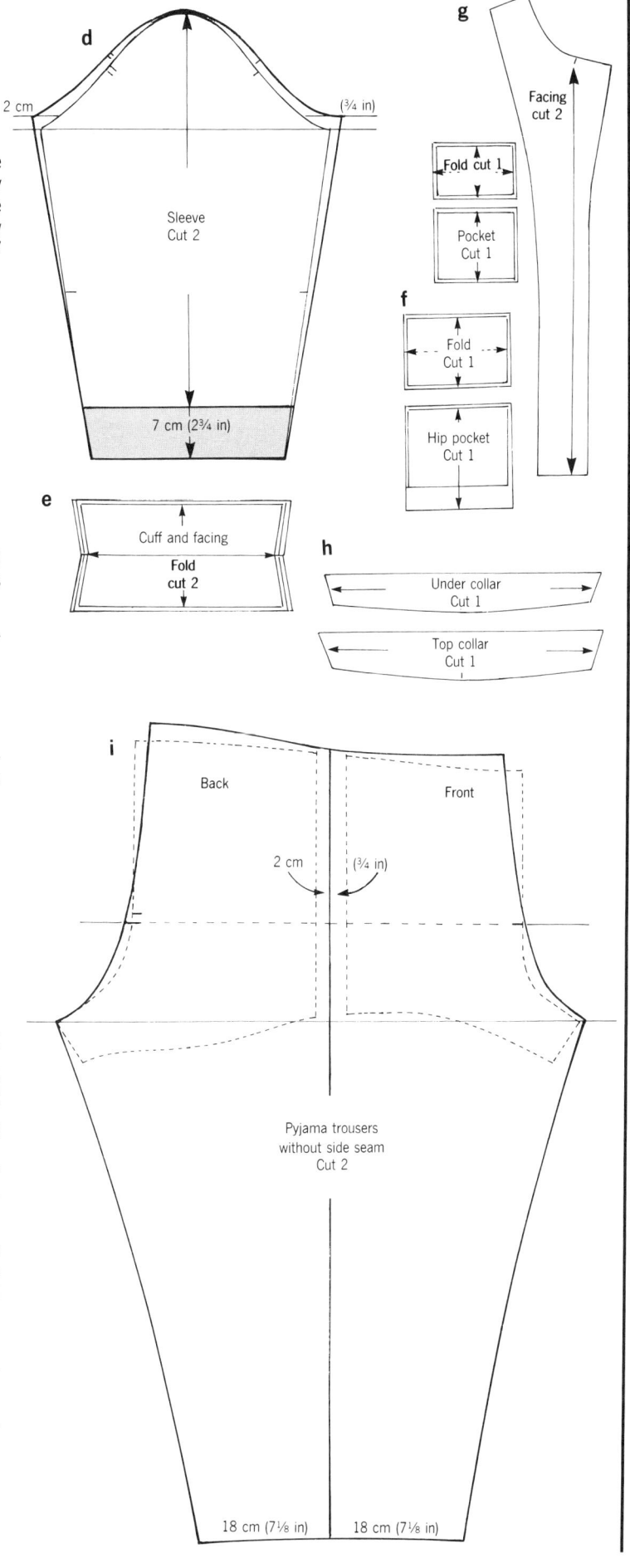

13 Lingerie

203

14 Maternity wear

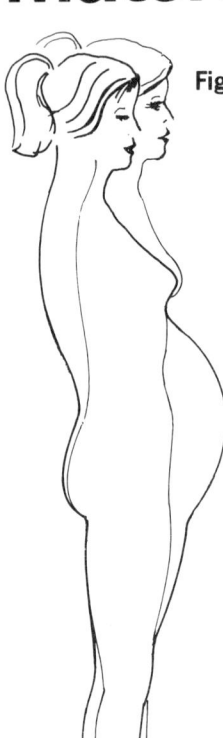

Figure 14.1

Abdominal expansion in pregnancy varies considerably. It is dependent on a number of physiological changes occurring throughout the nine months of pregnancy and these changes are further individually conditioned. On average, an increase of 18–26 cm (7–10 in) around the waist can be expected.

The **bust circumference** is expected to **increase 5–7 cm (2–3 in).**

Maternity garments are sized so that pregnant women can continue to wear their customary sizes, but patterns are based on the block patterns and dress forms that are one size larger than normal.

Figure 14.1a Garments must be cut wider, particularly in the centre front area, by at least the amount stated above, and cut longer in the front by 5–10 cm (2–4 in) due to abdominal expansion which tends to raise the front hem line of a garment.

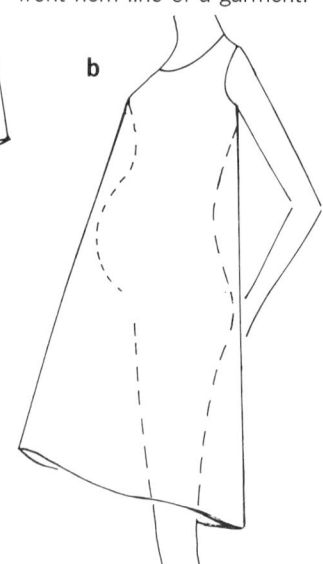

c–j A designer should consider the following points when designing maternity garments.

1 Divert attention away from the mid-section of the figure.

2 Aim at suspending fulness from the bust level to balance abdominal protrusion.

3 Emphasise rather than disguise any slim parts of the figure, for example, thigh region, legs and arms.

Method of padding a dress form

Figure 14.2

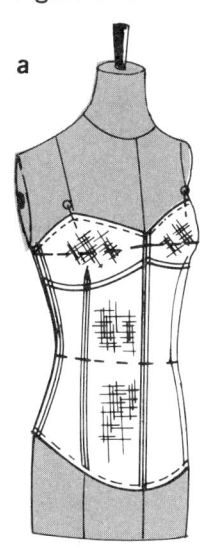

Figure 14.2 The dress form should be one size larger than the normal size.

a Model in firm cotton fabric, such as unbleached calico, one half of corset-type foundation to fit dress form. Cut bra section on bias of fabric. Shape princess line and CF seams. Add extension at CB for tape fastening. Mark bust and waist line with tailor's chalk.

b When satisfied with fit, mark all seams and underbust dart. Use modelled shapes to cut out other side of foundation. Sew up; press seams open. Pin foundation to dress form with raw edge seams facing outward.

For padding, keep ready plastic foam shoulder pads, to be used whole or sliced into wedge-shaped sections, and also washable polyester wadding. This type of wadding can cause skin irritation. It is wise, therefore, to wear gloves when working with the wadding.

c Pin, tack and sew four cut-to-shape foam pads to stomach area.

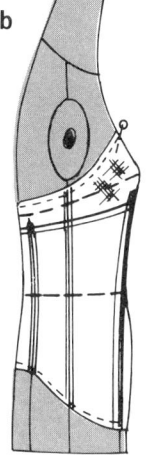

d Secure wedge-shaped foam pad slices to side seams, CB and princess line seams. Sew to foundation garment only and not to dress form! For this, a curved upholstery needle is very helpful.

e Now pin, tack and sew layers of washable wadding over foam pads and bust area as shown. Aim for a smooth graduated effect. Mark bust and waist line with chalk on each successive layer of wadding as you go along. Measure circumference from time to time as padding is added, until the desired increase has been achieved. Then, because the final calico covering tends to compress the wadding, add a little more padding as a precaution.

f Now model differently shaped outer cover over padding. Pin seams in harmony with new body shape, continuous with seams of dress form. Machine seams, attach tapes to CB, 'bag out' to neaten all edges and secure to dress form for further use.

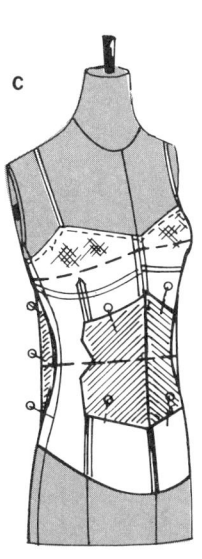

The author wishes to acknowledge the valuable suggestions made by Barrie H. Lancaster.

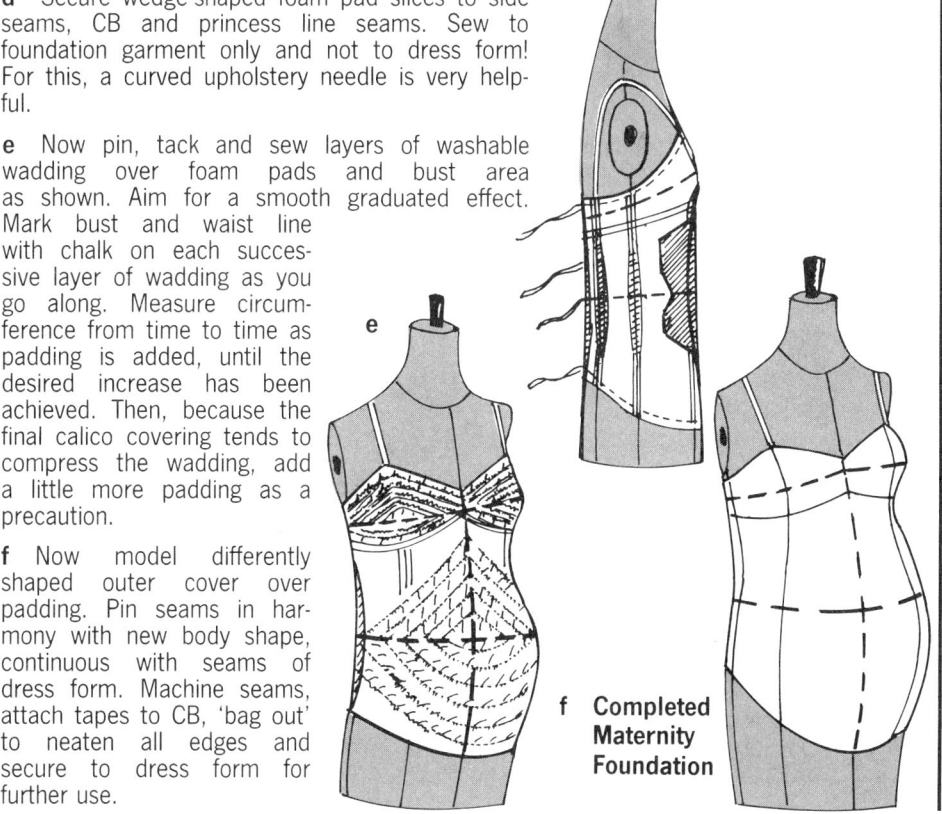

Modelling or flat cutting?

It is not essential to model maternity garments on a dress form. Changes in front length, and adjustments for ease and comfort can be made on the block patterns which are used to develop the desired styles.

However it is useful for the designer and cutter who is inexperienced in the designing and cutting of maternity garments, to model and see the toile of a planned garment on a padded dress form, or better still, on a pregnant figure. It enables the designer-cutter to note at once the effect, pleasing or otherwise, of the distribution of fulness on the figure and the most flattering placements of seams, yokes, pockets and buttons. Stripes, checks and other prominent fabric patterns can be indicated in pencil or felt-tipped pen or the toile material; the possible use of decorative trimmings can be assessed visually by experimenting until the designer is satisfied with the final look.

The knowledge and understanding acquired by working on a three-dimensional form can then be applied when constructing maternity wear patterns by the flat cutting method.

14
Maternity wear

f Completed Maternity Foundation

Development of the maternity dress block: 1

If a straighter side seam is preferred, use Development 2. In order to compare the fit and hang of the two blocks, cut each block in paper with seam allowances; pin together. Try on a padded dress form or a pregnant figure; note the difference. Then determine which of the blocks is more suitable for your design.

Figure 14.3 Use back and front hip blocks (page 176), but one size larger. Mark desired position of underarm dart on front hip block.

a and **b** Place front hip block on paper. Outline CF section from shoulder dart to underarm dart mark. Pivot block to right until shoulder dart and mark overlap. Outline.

c Remove block and complete underarm dart.

d Outline back hip block. Increase waist by 2 cm (¾ in); lengthen as shown.

e Outline front hip block. Repeat as for back. Draw slashing line 10 cm (4 in) below waist and cut.

f Open slash 6 cm (2¾ in). Outline and blend side seam from waist to hem line. Outline front.

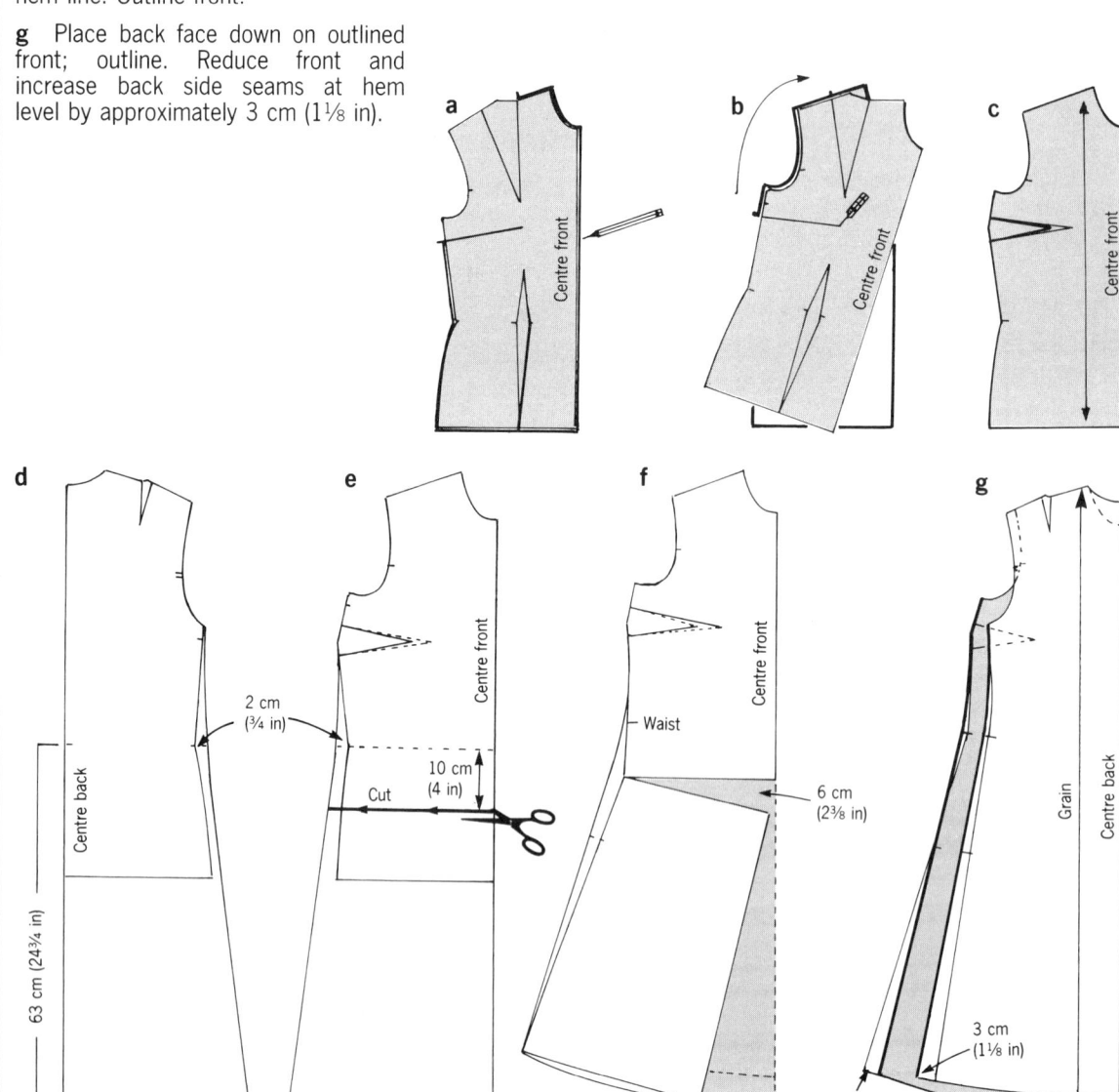

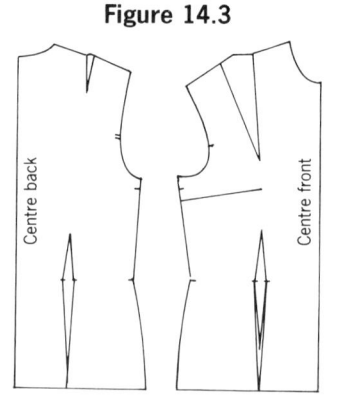

g Place back face down on outlined front; outline. Reduce front and increase back side seams at hem level by approximately 3 cm (1⅛ in).

Figure 14.3

Development of the maternity dress block: 2

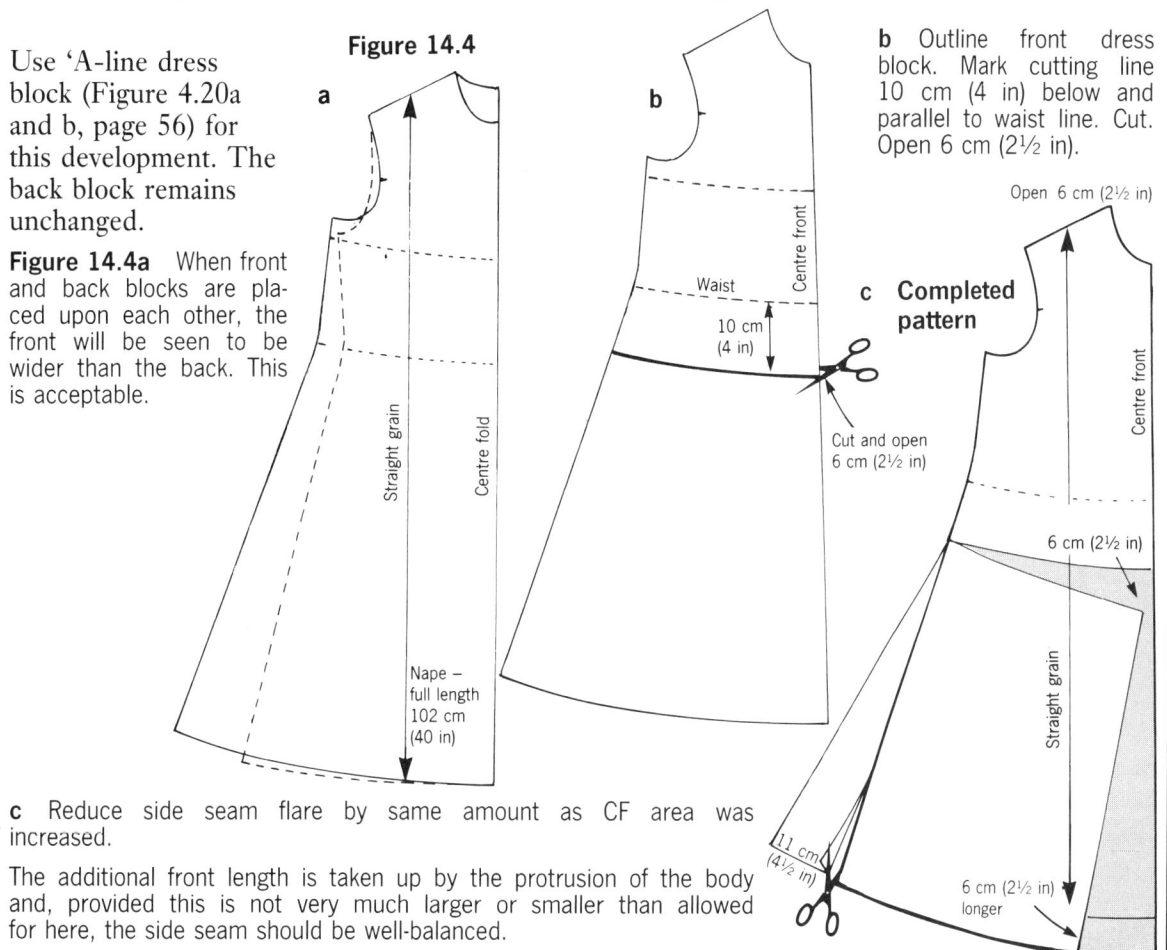

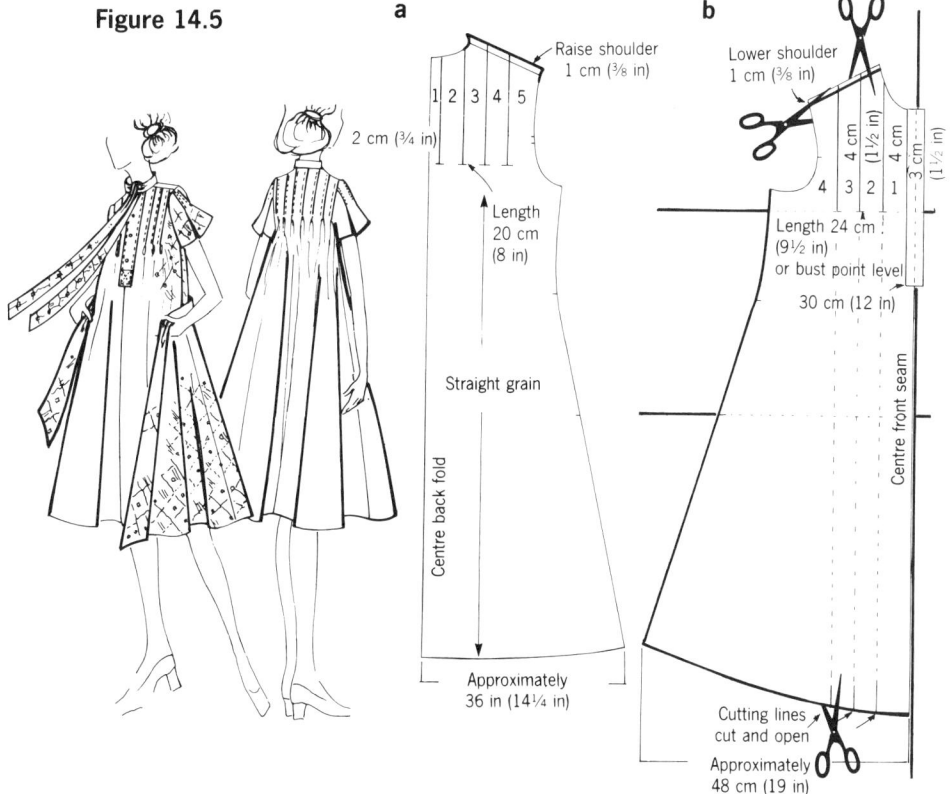

14 Maternity wear

Use 'A-line dress block (Figure 4.20a and b, page 56) for this development. The back block remains unchanged.

Figure 14.4a When front and back blocks are placed upon each other, the front will be seen to be wider than the back. This is acceptable.

Figure 14.4

a

b Outline front dress block. Mark cutting line 10 cm (4 in) below and parallel to waist line. Cut. Open 6 cm (2½ in).

c **Completed pattern**

c Reduce side seam flare by same amount as CF area was increased.

The additional front length is taken up by the protrusion of the body and, provided this is not very much larger or smaller than allowed for here, the side seam should be well-balanced.

Figure 14.5

Maternity dress

Figure 14.5a Outline front and back maternity dress blocks; move shoulder line forward by 1 cm (⅜ in). Divide bodice sections for pleat development. Draft tab opening.

b Draw long vertical line on pattern paper and two horizontal lines at right angles to it, representing bust and hip lines of blocks. Place blocks on to these lines. Cut on pleat lines; spread sections aligning with horizontal lines on paper.

207

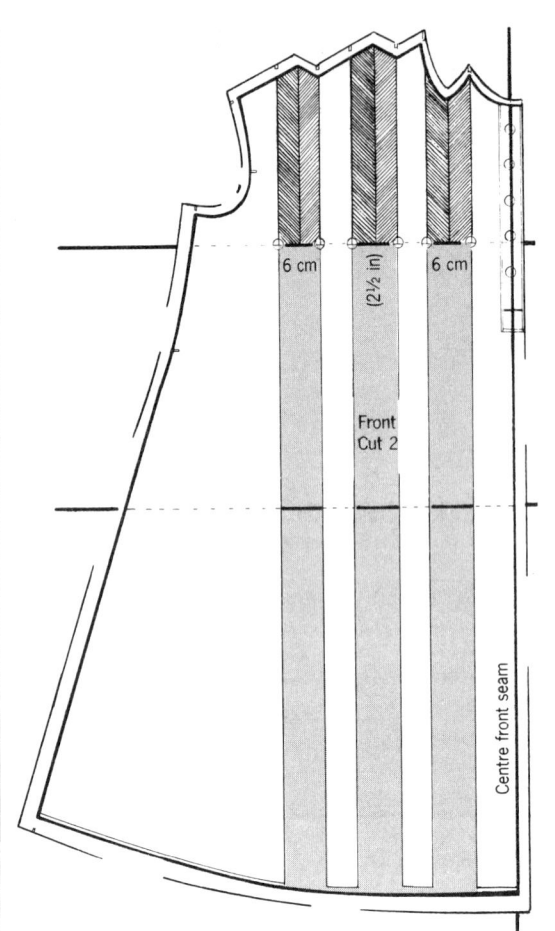

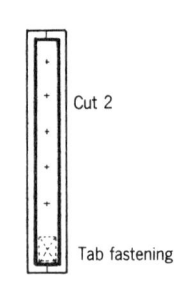

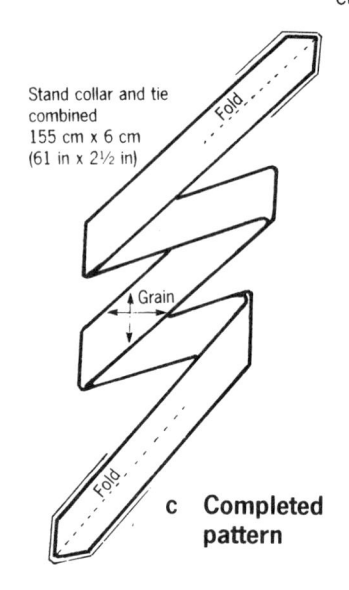

c Complete front pattern as shown, adding seam allowances, grain line and other relevant information. Develop back dress pattern in the same manner

For the tab fastening, cut two pieces, since one piece is applied as facing for the underside of the opening or cut on fold.

Cut 2
Tab fastening

Front Cut 2

Centre front seam

Stand collar and tie combined
155 cm x 6 cm
(61 in x 2½ in)

c Completed pattern

Alternative method of development

By using this alternative and quicker track-drafting method, the same final pattern (Figure 14.5c) can be obtained.

Figure 14.6 Draw three previously determined pleat lines (see Figure 14.4) and horizontal bust and hip lines on the maternity dress block (see also **b** below).

On pattern paper draw a horizontal line 30 cm (12 in) longer than length from shoulder to hem line. Square up two lines on block pattern representing bust and hip line positions.

b Place dress block on horizontal guide line. Align hip and bust lines. Outline neck and part of hem line to pleat line 1.

c Remove block pattern; draw pleat line 1. Leave 6 cm (2½ in) space for pleat allowance; draw pleat line 1^1.

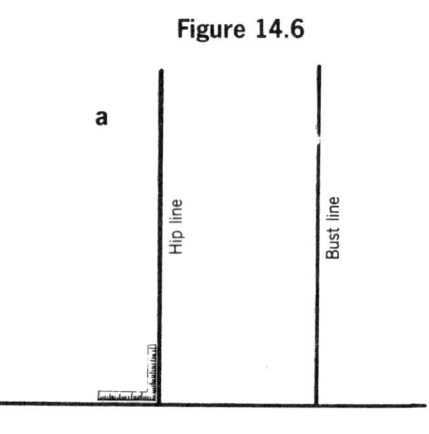

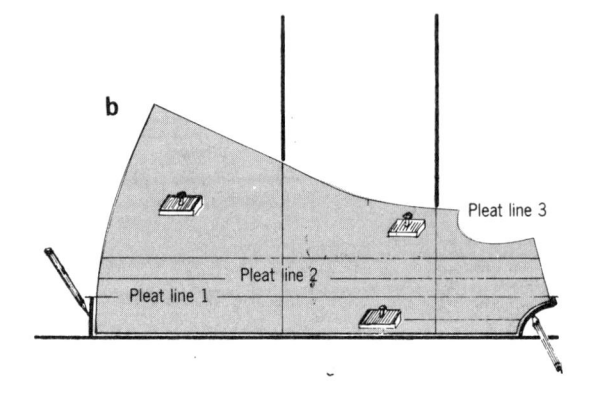

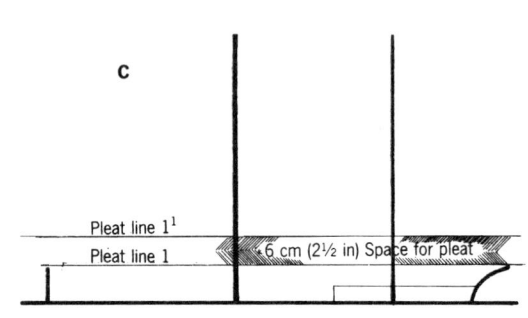

Figure 14.6

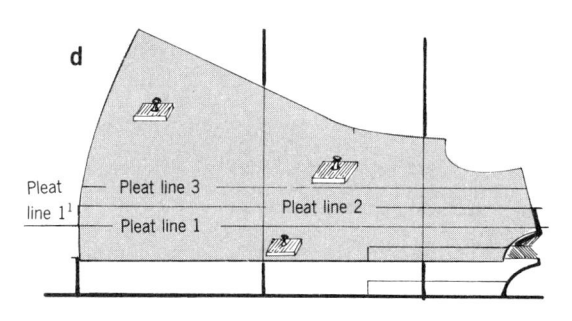

d Move dress block forward, aligning pleat line 1 with pleat line 1^1 on pattern paper. Outline as shown.

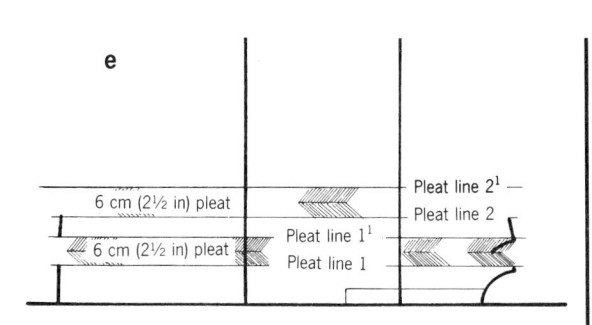

e Remove dress block and draw pleat line 2. Allow 6 cm (2½ in) for pleat, and draw pleat line 2.

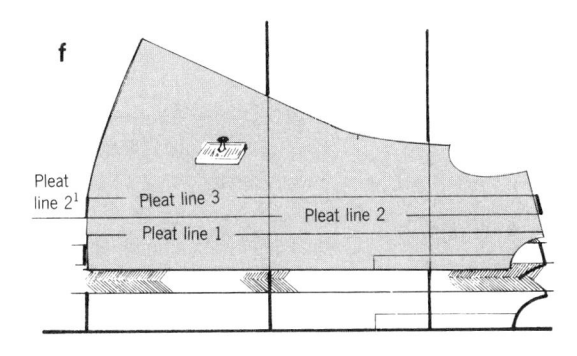

f Move dress block forward and align pleat line 2 with pleat line 2^1. Outline as shown.

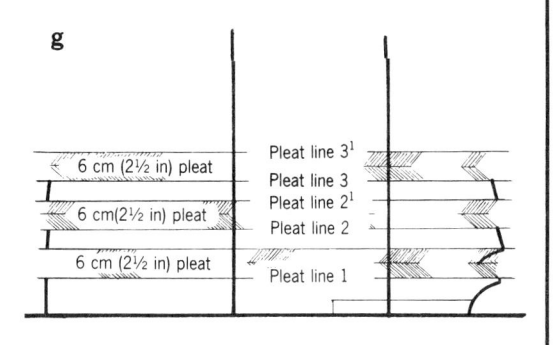

g Remove block and draw pleat line 3. Allow 6 cm (2½ in) for pleat and draw pleat line 3^1.

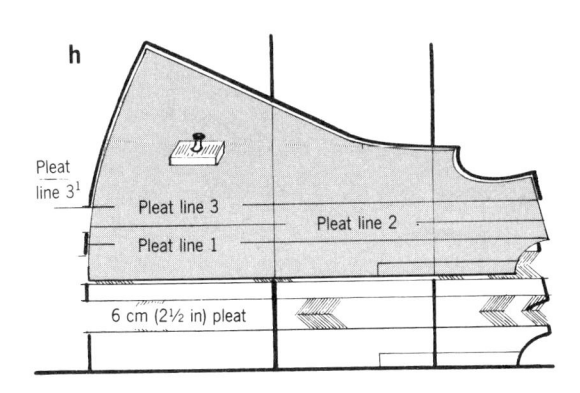

h Move dress block forward. Align pleat line 3 with pleat line 3^1. Outline as shown.

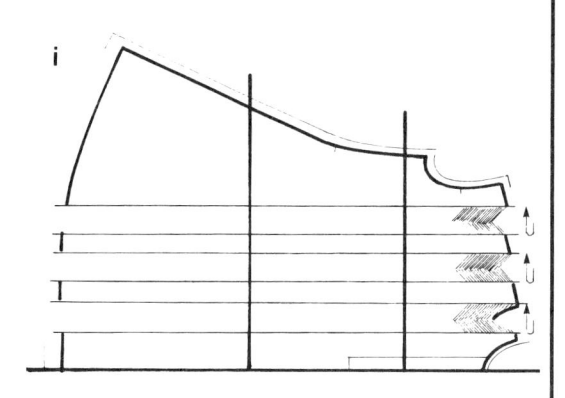

i Remove block and add seam turnings where possible.

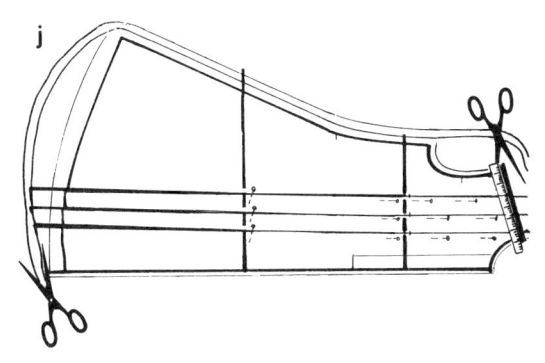

j Fold pleats and pin. Draw improved shoulder line. Add seam allowances and cut.

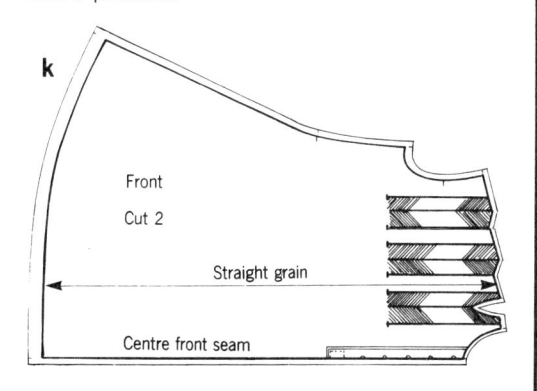

k Completed pattern

14 Maternity wear

209

Pleated sleeves for the maternity dress

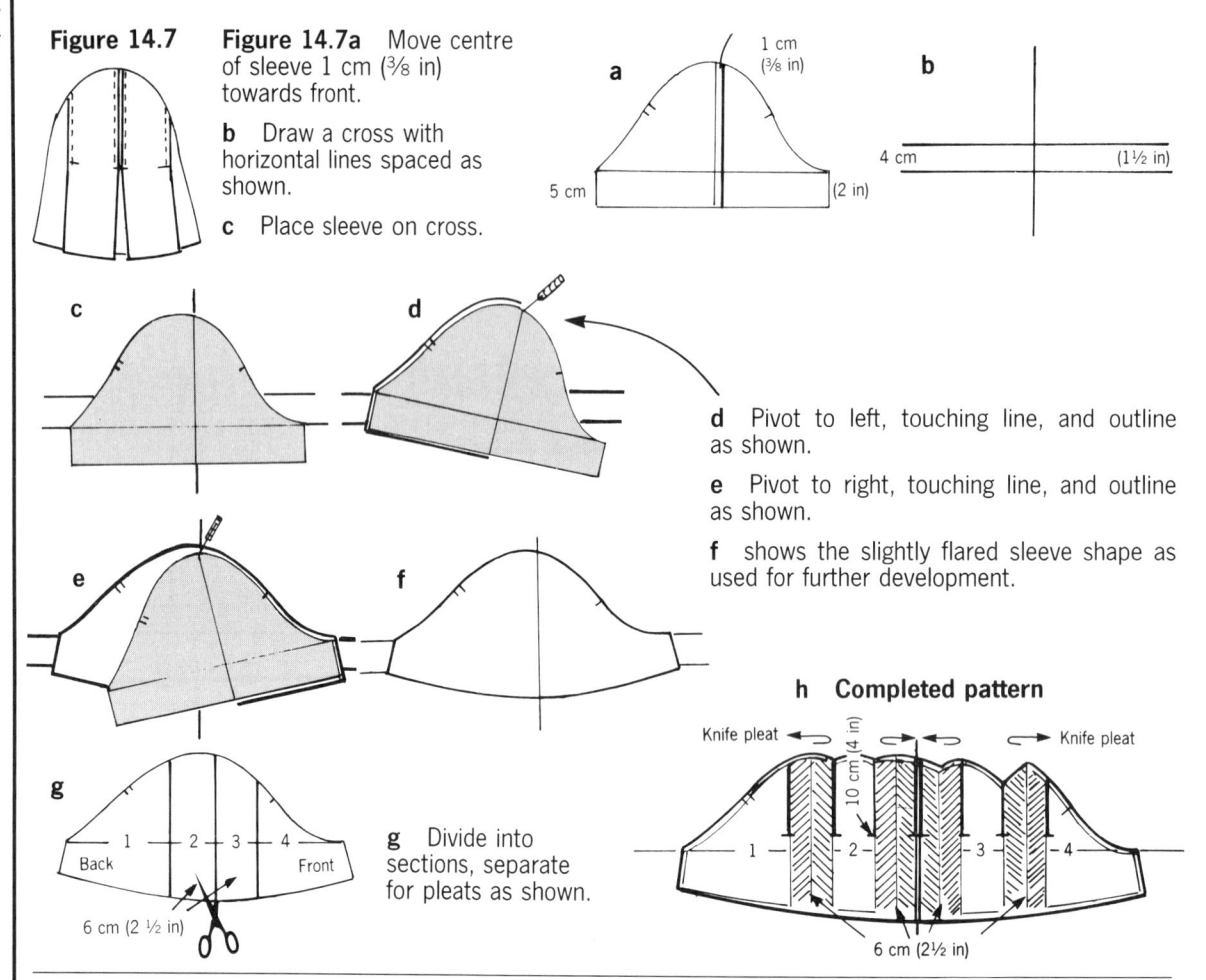

Figure 14.7

Figure 14.7a Move centre of sleeve 1 cm (⅜ in) towards front.

b Draw a cross with horizontal lines spaced as shown.

c Place sleeve on cross.

d Pivot to left, touching line, and outline as shown.

e Pivot to right, touching line, and outline as shown.

f shows the slightly flared sleeve shape as used for further development.

g Divide into sections, separate for pleats as shown.

h Completed pattern

Maternity smock

Figure 14.8

The maternity dress block (Figure 14.4a and c) is used in this development. The smock has shoulder pads and is worn over a blouse or sweater.

Figure 14.8a Outline maternity dress block. Lower back and front necklines. Raise shoulder-armhole points for shoulder pads; lower and enlarge armholes and allow more width across back and chest. Add more width at side seams from armholes to hem line as shown.

The amount of adjustment varies according to the thickness of the garments expected to be worn underneath the smock.

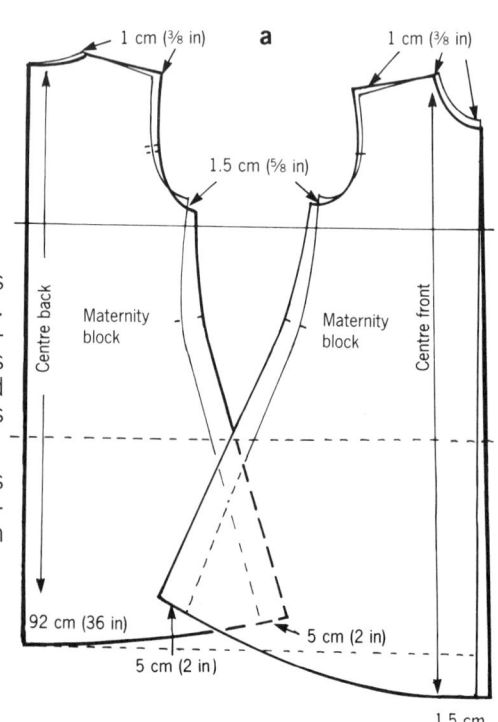

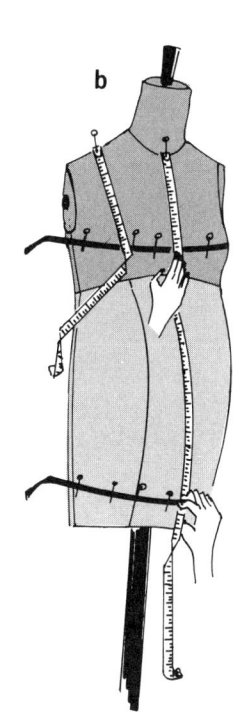

b Outline in black tape on padded dress form or pregnant figure, position of yoke and length of smock. Measure distances from centre shoulder and from pit of neck to desired yoke line and to full length.

c and **d** Transfer these measurements to outlined maternity blocks. Add 2.5 cm (1 in) button stand to centre front.

The position of balance marks on the yoke line ensures that gathers are distributed nearer the front of the garment than would be the case with a non-maternity garment.

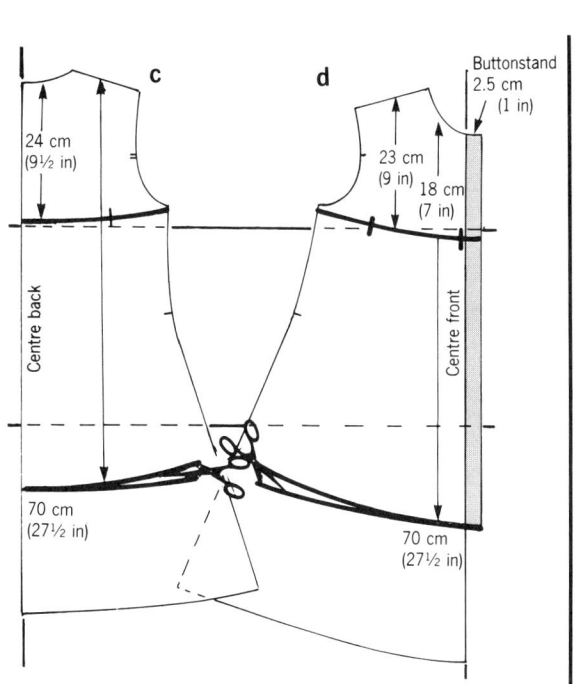

Developing the maternity smock

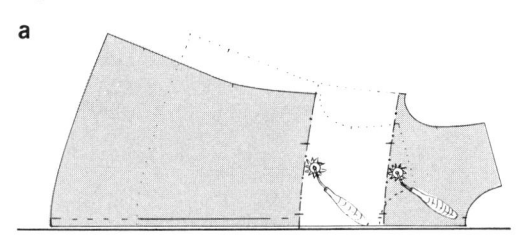

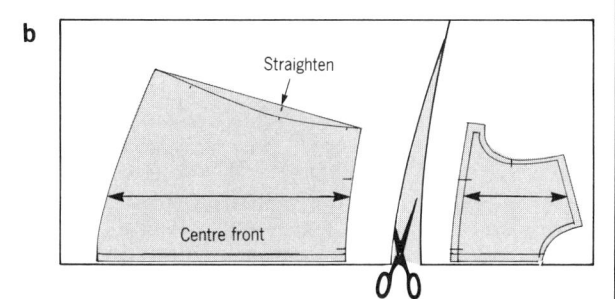

Figure 14.9

Figure 14.9a Place block on horizontal line. Outline yoke. Trace yoke line with tracing wheel. Slide pattern to left on horizontal line. Outline and trace remaining part of the pattern.

b Cut out yoke and lower pattern piece.

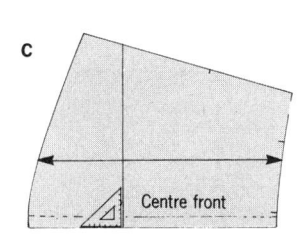

c and **d** On pattern and on pattern paper draw a line at right angle to CF. Place pattern on to paper, matching line on pattern with that on pattern paper.

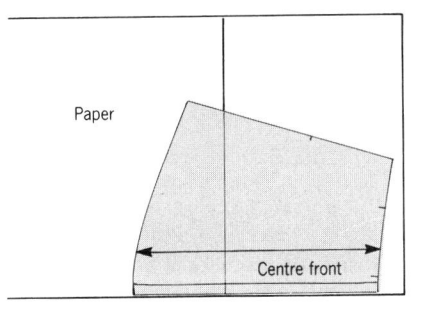

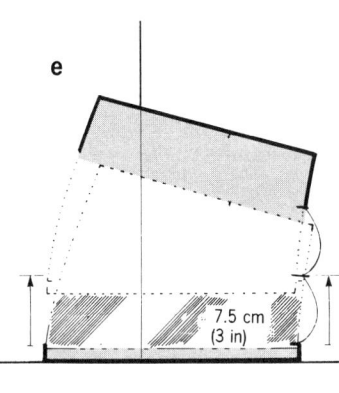

e Outline pattern to first balance mark. Crossmark. Also crossmark second gathering balance mark on pattern paper **before** sliding pattern forward to match first balance mark on pattern with second crossmark on pattern paper (this doubles the gathering area).

f Outline remaining side-section of pattern including crossmarking of second balance mark. Complete pattern as shown.

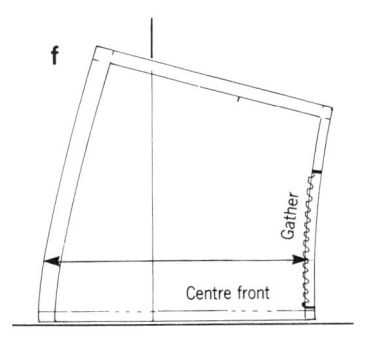

14 Maternity wear

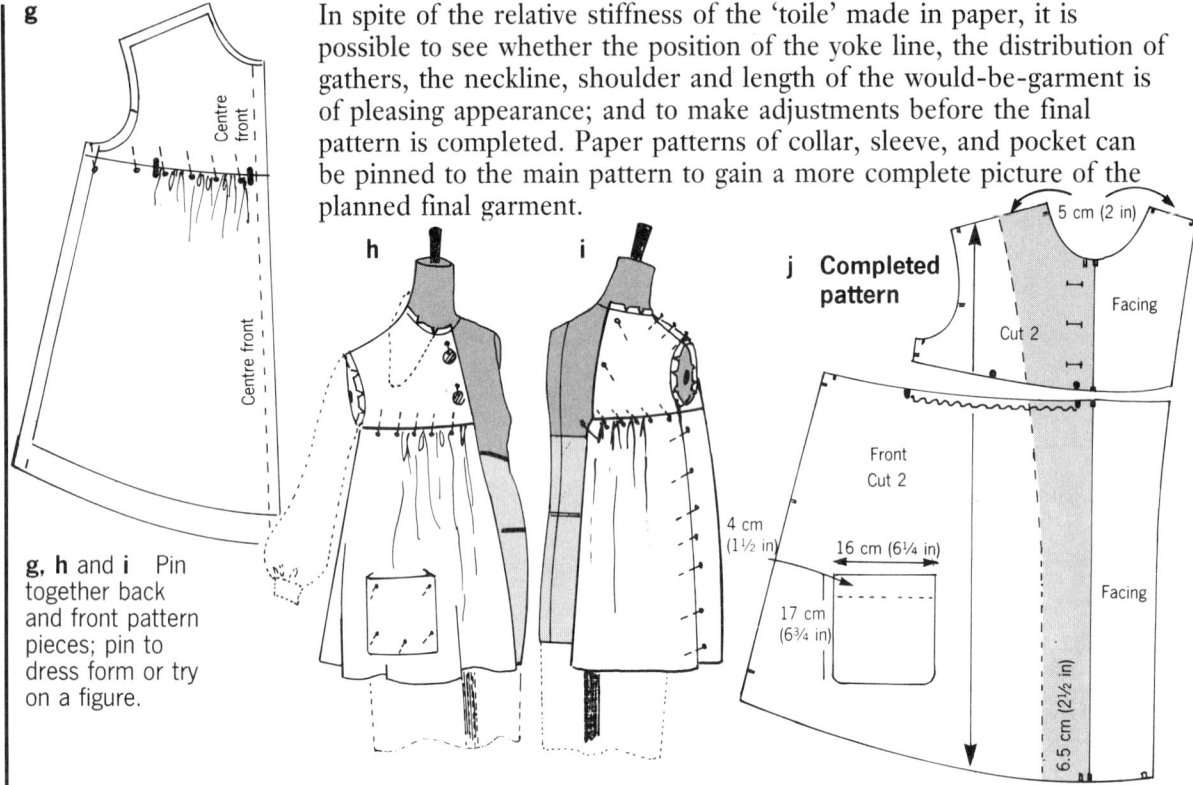

In spite of the relative stiffness of the 'toile' made in paper, it is possible to see whether the position of the yoke line, the distribution of gathers, the neckline, shoulder and length of the would-be-garment is of pleasing appearance; and to make adjustments before the final pattern is completed. Paper patterns of collar, sleeve, and pocket can be pinned to the main pattern to gain a more complete picture of the planned final garment.

g, h and **i** Pin together back and front pattern pieces; pin to dress form or try on a figure.

j Completed pattern

Soft collar

Figure 14.10

Figure 14.10a and **b** Neckline was lowered by 1 cm (3/8 in) (see Figure 14.8a).

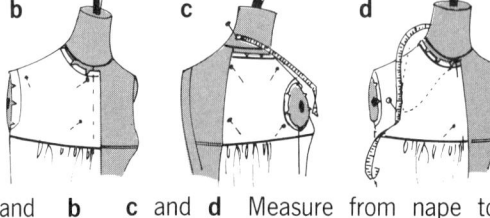

c and **d** Measure from nape to approximate position of desired collar point. Add 2 cm (3/4 in) to give a total of **35 cm (14 in) in length**.

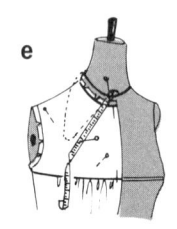

e Measure from pit of neck to approximate position of desired collar point, allowing for 'roll'. Add 2 cm (3/4 in) to give a total of **20 cm (8 in) in width**.

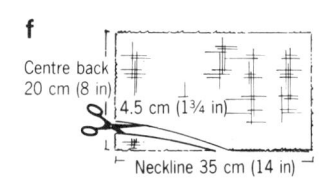

f Cut rectangle of modelling fabric. Mark left short side CB. Bottom long edge represents neckline. On CB line from neckline measure up 4.5 cm (1¾ in); cut away crescent-shaped piece of fabric to approximately half-way of fabric.

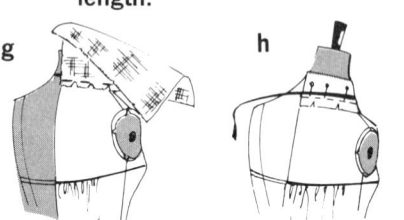

g and **h** Pin CB edge of modelling fabric to CB of garment neckline and dress form, arranging bulk of fabric above neckline. Pin and snip. Continue to front snipping edge where required and easing fabric over shoulder area. Fold collar fabric down occasionally to ensure a good roll and to prevent any tightness. CB of collar must remain in CB position and must not be pulled away from it.

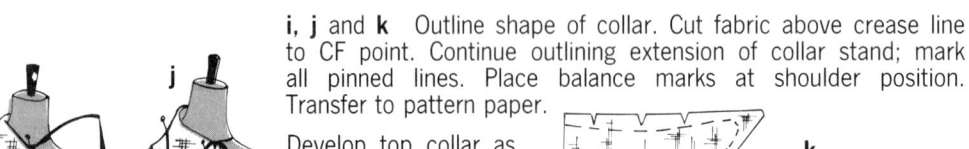

i, j and **k** Outline shape of collar. Cut fabric above crease line to CF point. Continue outlining extension of collar stand; mark all pinned lines. Place balance marks at shoulder position. Transfer to pattern paper.

Develop top collar as on page 71.

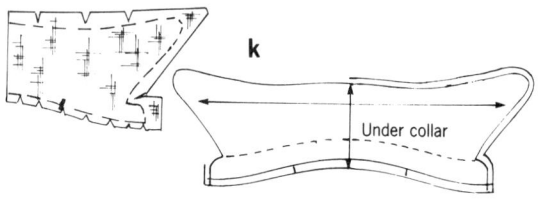

Sleeve for the maternity smock

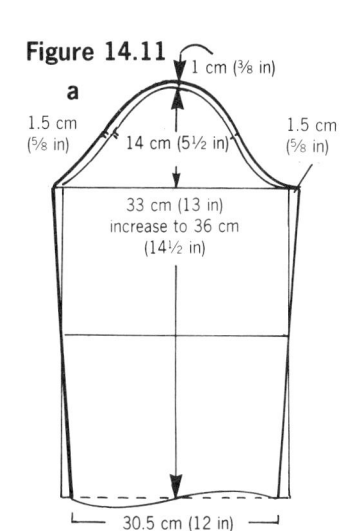

Figure 14.11

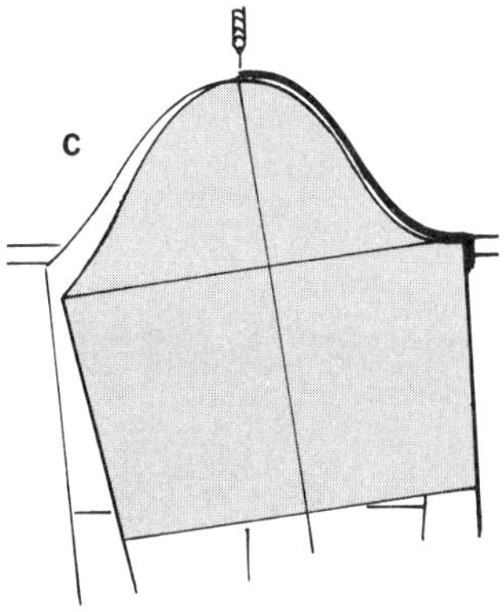

Figure 14.11a The sleeve block is adjusted to conform with the armhole of the maternity smock.

Outline straight sleeve block (Figure 7.9c, page 87).

Extend sleeve by 1.5 cm (⅝ in) at both underarm points.

Raise sleeve crown all around by 1 cm (⅜ in).

Narrow wrist line to 30.5 cm (12 in).

b Raise sleeve crown a further 1 cm (⅜ in) for shoulder pads. Shorten sleeve by 2 cm (¾ in) for a 4 cm (1½ in) deep cuff.

On pattern paper draw a horizontal line representing crown level line. Draw two short horizontal lines 1.5 cm (⅝ in) above and parallel to crown level line.

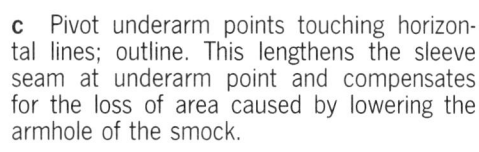

c Pivot underarm points touching horizontal lines; outline. This lengthens the sleeve seam at underarm point and compensates for the loss of area caused by lowering the armhole of the smock.

d Draw wrist opening half-way between sleeve seam and centre line and parallel to it.

Draft cuff.

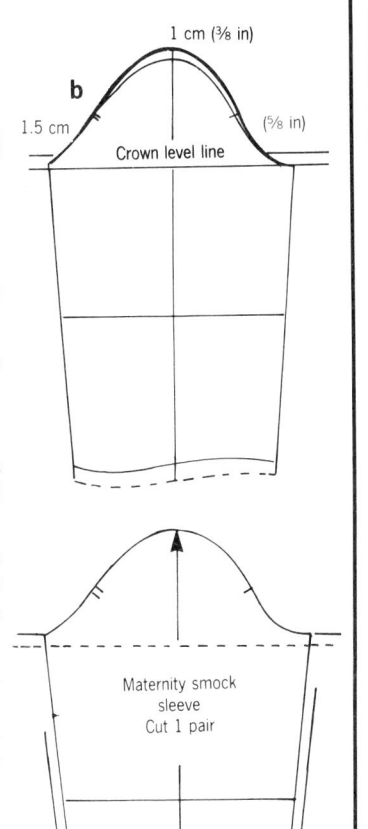

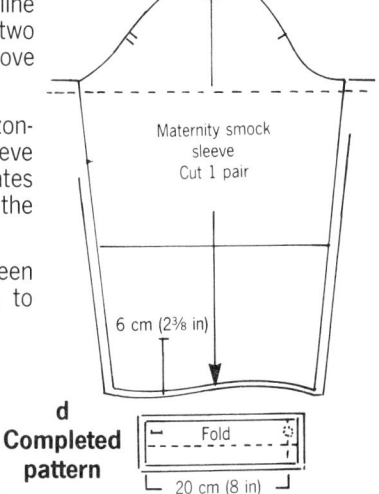

d Completed pattern

Raglan style maternity smock

Figure 14.12

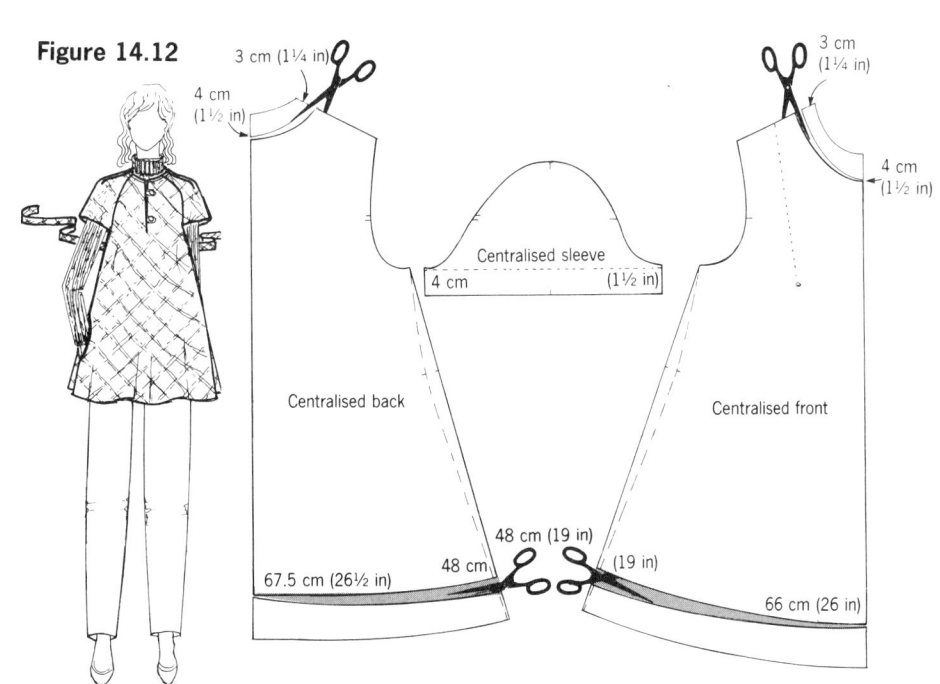

Figure 14.12 Centralise basic maternity smock (Figure 14.4). See instructions for centralising, page 94.

a Lower neckline; shorten hem line; straighten side seams as shown.

Centralise and shorten sleeve to 4 cm (1¾ in).

The pattern is now ready for further development.

a Centralised basic smock pattern

14 Maternity wear

b Draw vertical line 90 cm (35½ in) long. From top of vertical line draw two diagonal lines at an angle of 43°.

On vertical line measure down 31 cm (12¼ in) and draw short guide line.

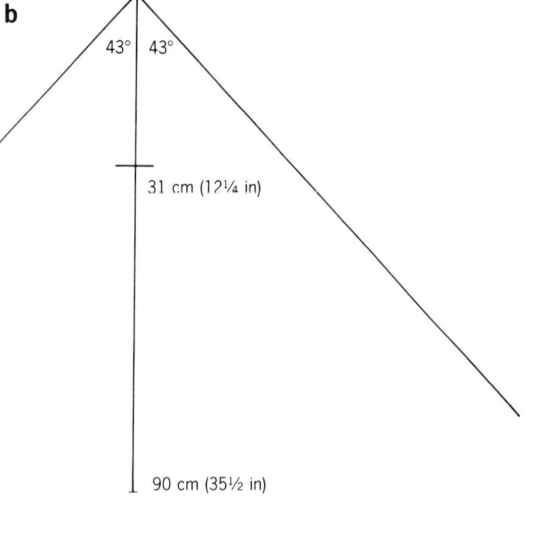

c Place centralised short sleeve pattern against short horizontal line.

The sleeve pattern may have to be moved up or down a little, in which case do not outline the pattern until it is proved to be positioned correctly.

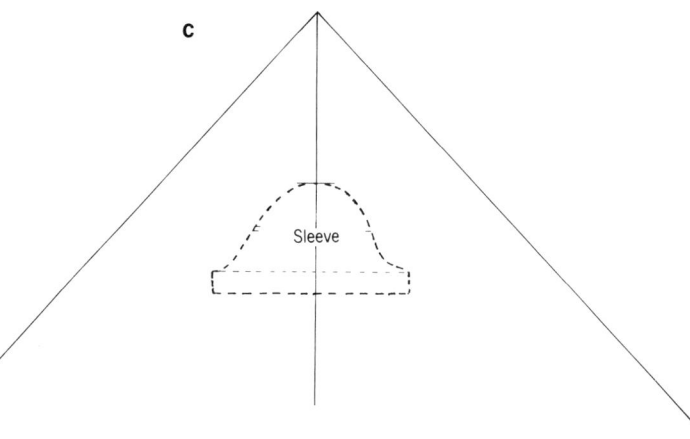

d Place centralised back and front smock patterns (**a**) to left and right diagonal lines. These lines represent centre back and centre front of the patterns.

The upper armholes should touch the upper left and right edges of the sleeve crown; sleeve balance marks should align, or almost align if possible.

The distance between shoulder-neck points can vary between 6 and 11 cm (2½ and 4½ in). Shoulder-armhole points will be some way above the short horizontal guide line. The reason for this variance can be traced to the difference in the shape of the armholes of patterns which are in common use in industry, colleges or commerce.

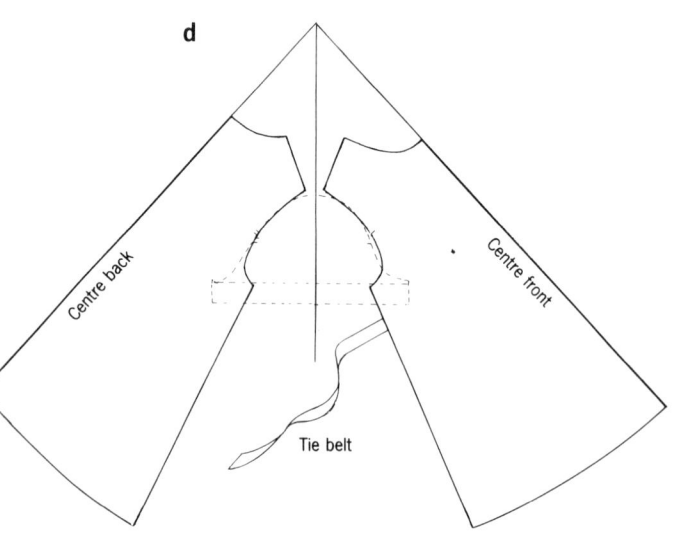

e Raglan draft

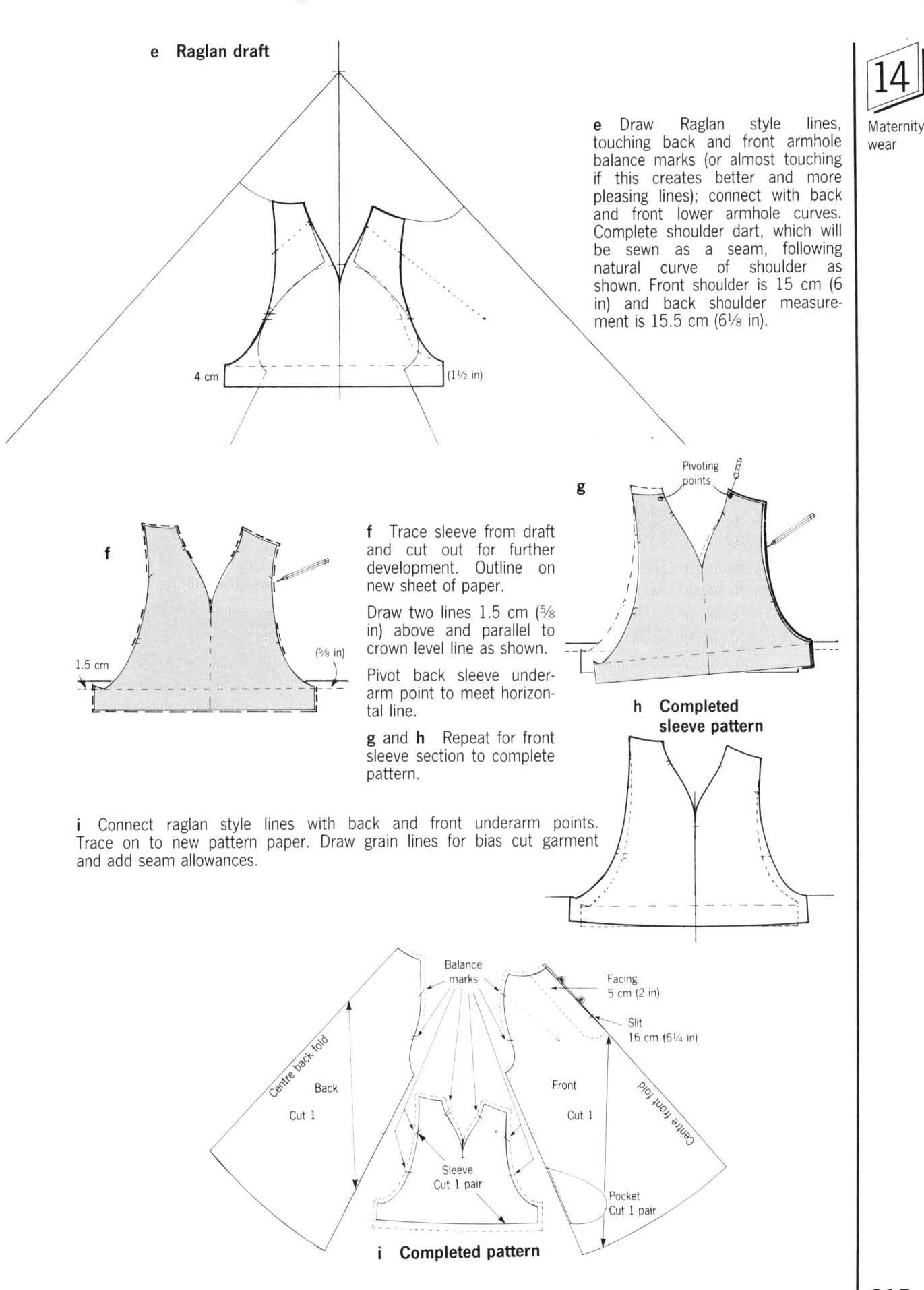

e Draw Raglan style lines, touching back and front armhole balance marks (or almost touching if this creates better and more pleasing lines); connect with back and front lower armhole curves. Complete shoulder dart, which will be sewn as a seam, following natural curve of shoulder as shown. Front shoulder is 15 cm (6 in) and back shoulder measurement is 15.5 cm (6⅛ in).

4 cm (1½ in)

14 Maternity wear

f Trace sleeve from draft and cut out for further development. Outline on new sheet of paper.

Draw two lines 1.5 cm (⅝ in) above and parallel to crown level line as shown.

Pivot back sleeve underarm point to meet horizontal line.

g and **h** Repeat for front sleeve section to complete pattern.

1.5 cm (⅝ in)

Pivoting points

h Completed sleeve pattern

i Connect raglan style lines with back and front underarm points. Trace on to new pattern paper. Draw grain lines for bias cut garment and add seam allowances.

Balance marks

Facing 5 cm (2 in)

Slit 16 cm (6¼ in)

Centre back fold

Back Cut 1

Centre front fold

Front Cut 1

Sleeve Cut 1 pair

Pocket Cut 1 pair

i Completed pattern

215

Waisted maternity garments

Figure 14.13 Waisted maternity garments, such as skirts and trousers, tend to cause constructional problems. This can be seen at once if one studies the contours of the pregnant figure. To begin with, the position of the waist line is difficult to define. If a tape were tied around the waist it would come to rest on line 1 yet lines 2 and 3 look more like possible waist lines. Further, the developing abdominal circumference in itself presents difficulties. The skirt or trousers must allow for expansion throughout the best part of six months and should also be as flattering to the figure as possible. Designers have produced garments with deep folds, gathers and wrapovers, which can be let out (Figure 14.14). This is satisfactory but it also increases the circumference below the hip level when the garment is let out, and makes the wearer look large where she would dearly love to present a relatively trim fit.

The nicest looking skirts and trousers are those that are cut to allow for expansion in the abdominal region, and taper to normal measurements below the hip level. Such garments are loosely fitted in general, and the waist front is gathered by a slotted-through adjustable elastic band (Figure 14.15). Other styles have insets of elasticised fabric (b) or have the abdominal section simply cut out altogether with a buttonholed elastic band slotted through the liberally cut waist for adjustment as required.

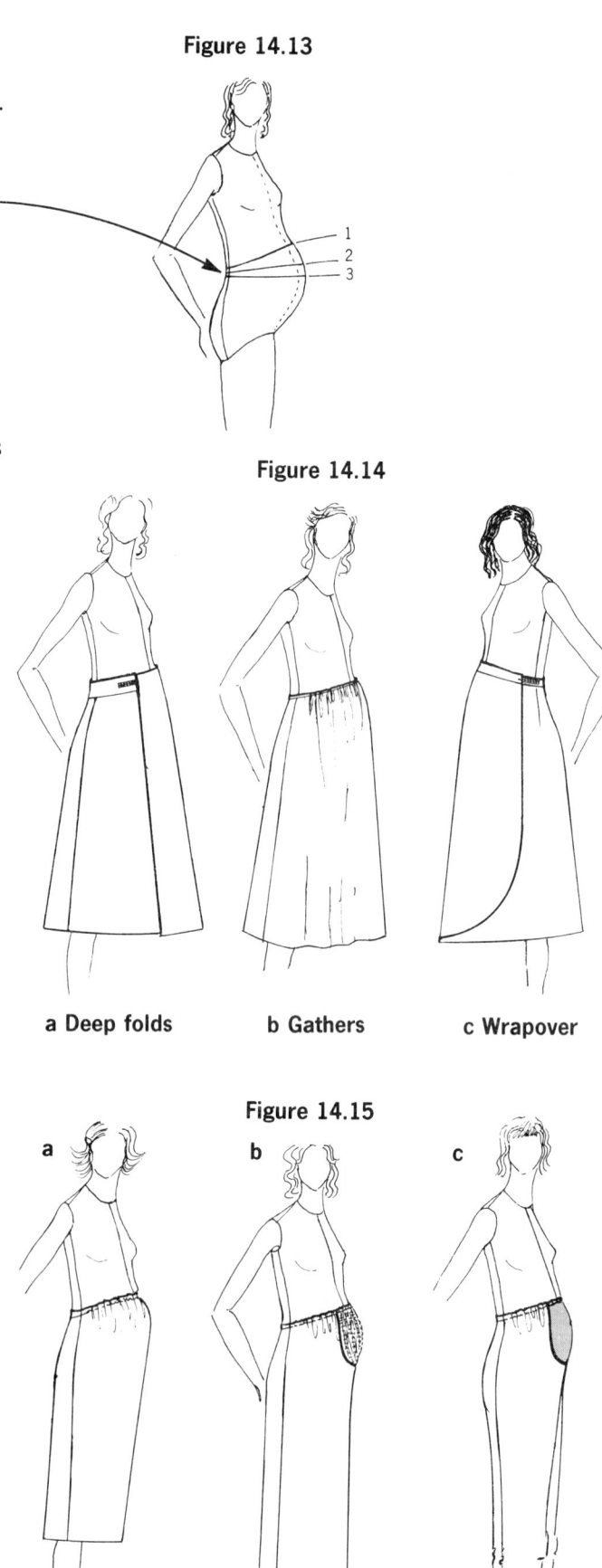

Figure 14.13

Figure 14.14

a Deep folds   b Gathers   c Wrapover

Figure 14.15

a   b   c

Maternity skirt with cascade drapery

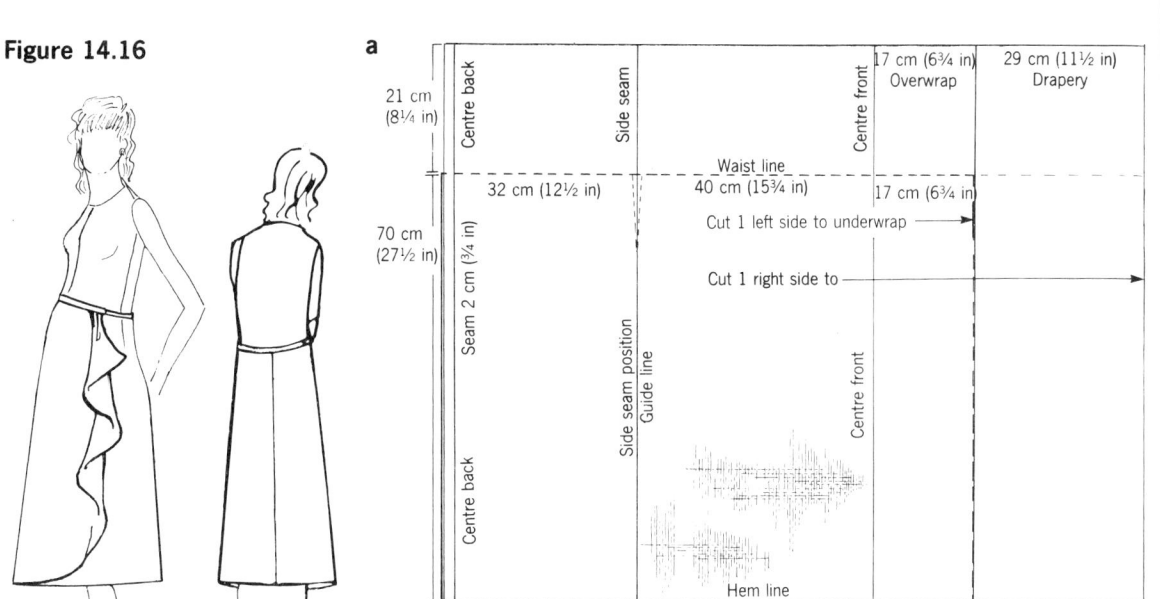

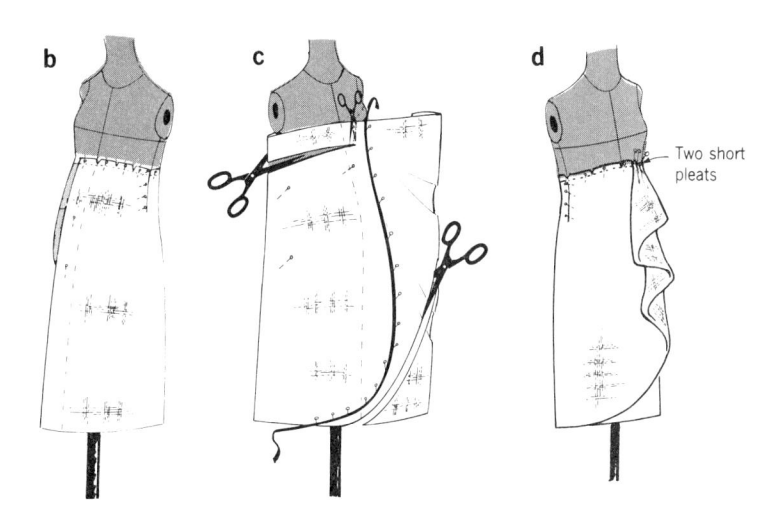

Figure 14.16

Figure 14.16a Cut out two pieces of mull, one to waist level for left side of skirt, the other to above waist level for right wrapover side of skirt and drapery.

b Pin mull representing left side to padded maternity dress form or pregnant figure, beginning at CB.

c Pin other piece of mull to centre back seam, wrap loosely over to left side, aligning centre front lines. Outline wrap and cut away all surplus fabric.

d Allow cascade drapery to drop; pin two short pleats. The drapery may require further reshaping to run gently in a curved line into the hem line.

Pin dart allowances as darts or, if preferred, as side seams, continuing to hem line, or elasticate with waistband.

e Mark toile. Remove from dress form; true all lines. Transfer to pattern paper. Add seam allowances. Fasten with Velcro.

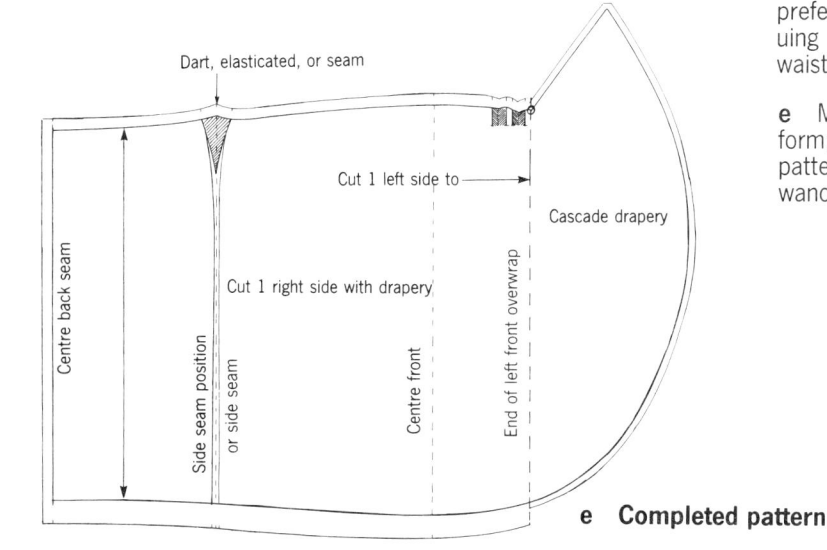

e Completed pattern

14 Maternity wear

Development of basic maternity skirt cut flat

Figure 14.17

All maternity patterns are developed from blocks one size larger than normal.

Figure 14.17a Outline back and front skirt blocks (page 13). Draw level **P** (Pivoting) line 33 cm (13 in) below waist line. All increases of measurements occur above level **P** line.

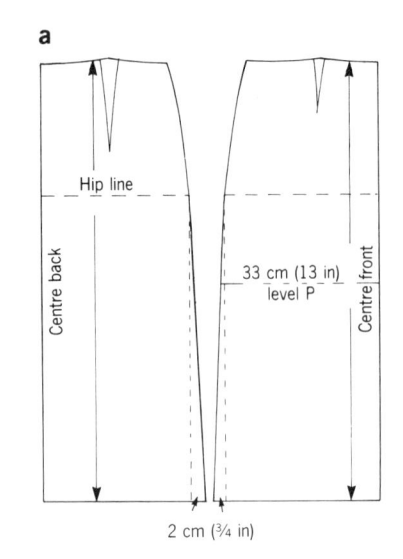

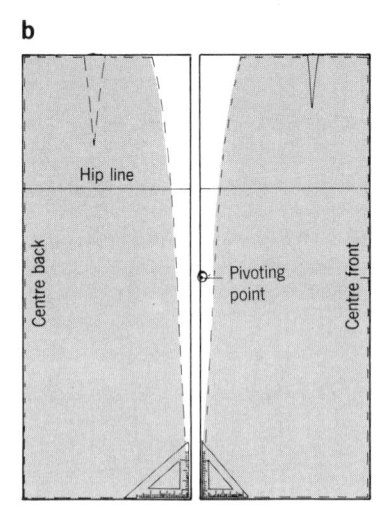

b Square up from hem lines. This creates two rectangles, one representing the front, the other the back skirt. Cut out in card. Mark pivoting point **P** on front rectangle. Use these card rectangles to develop the maternity skirt.

c Outline front rectangle. Extend waist line to left.

d Pivot card rectangle to marked point and outline.

e Completed front pattern is now ready for further development.

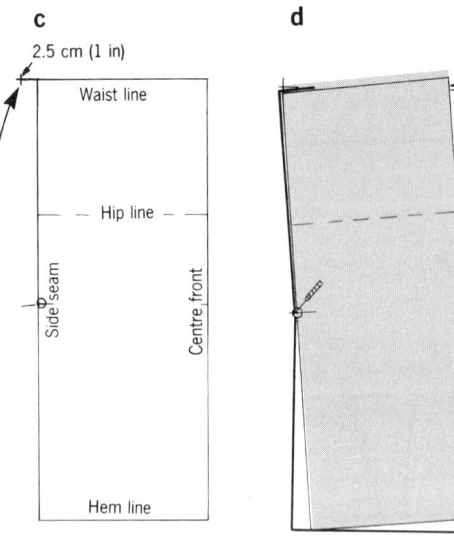

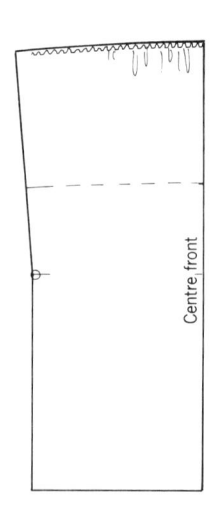

f Outline back rectangle. Reduce waist line at side seam to pivoting point level by same amount as that by which front waist line was increased – 2.5 cm (1 in). Back and front side seam angles are now the same. This forms the basis for further development.

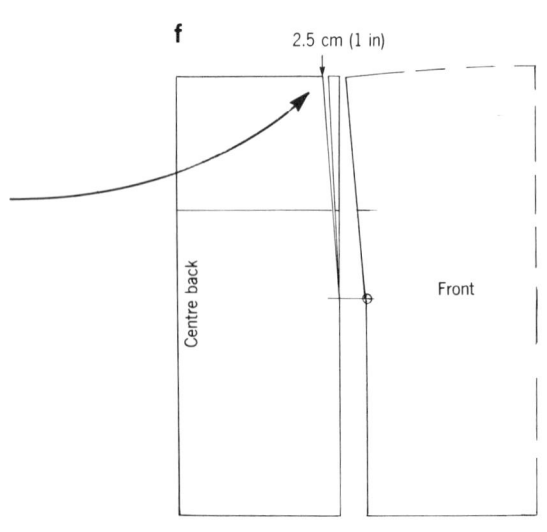

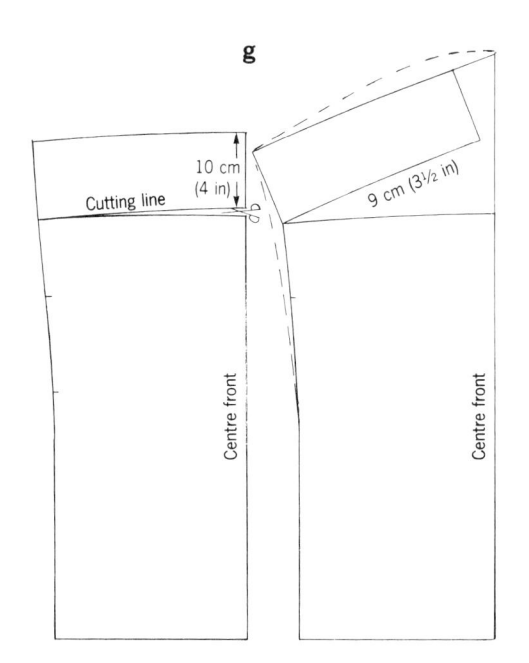

g Outline front skirt; draw cutting line 10 cm (4 in) below waist line. Cut to side seam line.

Open slash to 9 cm (3½ in). Extend CF line upwards. Extend waist line to meet CF line.

Place 'shaped' back rectangle (f) to drawn hem line; outline. Place front (g) on hem line next to back; outline. Complete as shown. Add seam allowances and cutting instructions.

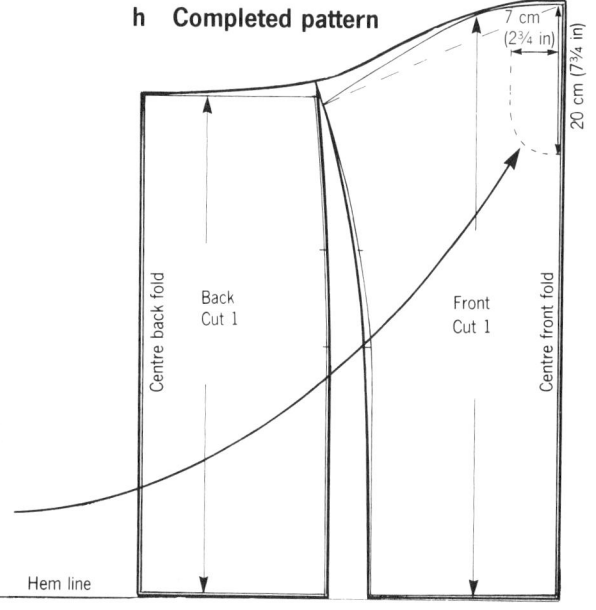

14 Maternity wear

h Completed pattern

Cut out in trial fabric nearest in weight to garment fabric and make any adjustments.

As an optional variation the centre front section can be cut out.

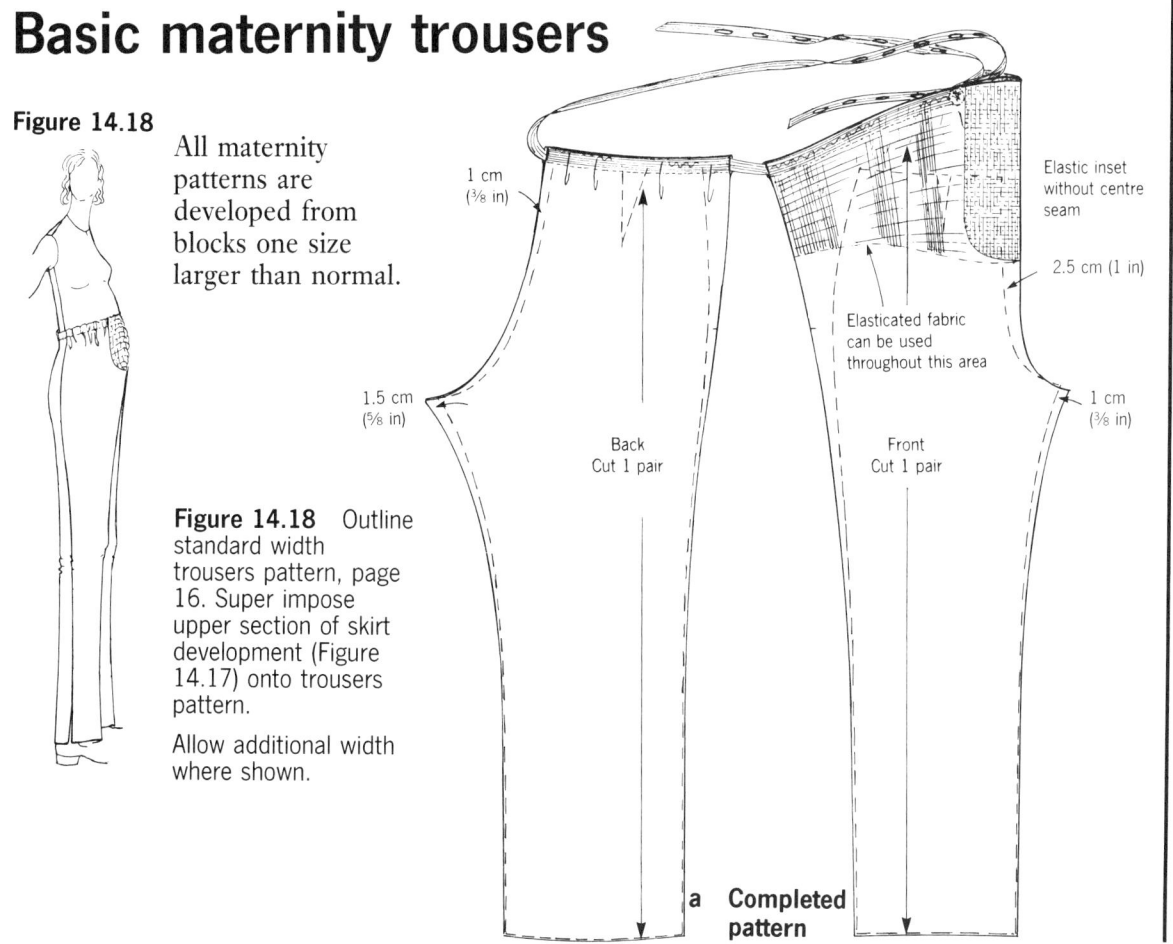

Basic maternity trousers

Figure 14.18

All maternity patterns are developed from blocks one size larger than normal.

Figure 14.18 Outline standard width trousers pattern, page 16. Super impose upper section of skirt development (Figure 14.17) onto trousers pattern.

Allow additional width where shown.

a Completed pattern

219

15 The technique of good fitting

A garment may be considered to fit well when centre front and centre back, shoulder, side and waist seams and armholes rest on the normal position on the figure without wrinkles, strain or sagging, when it allows freedom of movement and is neither too loose nor too tight in any particular part of the figure, when style lines rest in the intended position on the body, enhance the appearance of the garment and are consistent with fabric and fashion. Grain lines must be observed in order to achieve the right hang and balance of the garment.

The main factors affecting fitting

When fitting a garment, you should always be aware of the following interrelated main factors:

- The basic principles of fitting: grain, balance, ease
- Character of the garment
- Personality and age
- Figure types and defects
- Fashion and fabric.

The basic principles of fitting

Grain
This is probably the most important factor in fitting as it greatly affects the hang and balance, and indeed the whole aesthetic appearance of a garment. In general it can be said that the warp or lengthwise grain should run down the centre front and the centre back position on the figure and the weft grain should run across the bust, hip and upper arm lines at right angles to the warp.

There are, of course, exceptions to this rule. These are mainly connected with the design potential of a particular fabric when exploited as a fashion feature, e.g. stripes and checks. Another exception is bias cutting, when an entire garment (or sections of it) is cut on the bias to obtain a particular silhouette which may be in fashion at the time.

The grain on the right half of the garment must always be the same as that on the left half and any alterations carried out on the right side when fitting must be transferred to the left.

Balance
A well-balanced garment hangs evenly all round and ease and fulness of any kind is equally distributed unless the design demands otherwise. Any imbalance is particularly noticeable at the lower edges of skirts, jackets, bodices and sleeves where, often for no apparent reason, the hemline is raised in one place only and sticks out more than it should. There are several reasons for this: a wrong alignment of garment parts and incorrect matching of balance marks; careless laying up may be responsible for one section having been cut on the wrong grain or only slightly off grain, or part of the body may be over-prominent.

Ease
The amount of ease or tolerance allowed in a garment varies with the material used and the function for which it is intended, the personality and age of the

person and the fashion silhouette. On no account must the garment be too tight as wrinkles will appear and pull the garment out of shape. Too much tolerance all over, however, will result in a glaringly ill-fitting garment.

An average amount of ease is built-in in basic garment blocks, but this can be adjusted in accordance with the points made above.

Character of the garment

One should ask oneself what type of garment it is to be and what function it is to perform. The bodice of a formal evening dress will be fitted differently from that of a leisure or sports garment.

Personality and age

The fashion-conscious person who moves in equally fashion-conscious society will wish to express a different image from the more conservative person, and an older woman would tend to wish to conceal rather than emphasise her figure.

Figure types and defects

Many women do not conform exactly to the standard measurements used in the construction of basic patterns. There are often variations in, for example, posture, proportion of bust formation to shoulder construction, hollow back and others. These factors will be taken into account when fitting a garment.

Fashion and fabric

These factors are most important. Small details in the fitting of, for example, a more flared skirt against a straight one, a more fitted waist versus a loosely fitted shirt, or a square shoulder effect compared with a softly sloping one, contribute greatly towards obtaining a fashionable silhouette. The way of fitting is also influenced by the fabric of the garment, in the case of, say, taffeta or silk jersey.

Fitting in the wholesale sample room

Fitting is carried out in the wholesale trade to a greater or lesser degree, depending on the market for which the garment is produced. In general great reliance is placed on the 'perfect pattern' and therefore most fitting is directed towards perfecting the basic pattern in order to avoid remaking later.

When new blocks are developed they are made up in calico or mull and tried on a dress stand or sometimes on a model representing the figure type and measurements for which the company caters. This calico shape is then fitted and marked and the new lines are transferred to the new blocks.

Often a new sample is fitted on a dress form by the sample machinist during the making-up process or when it is completed. In both cases the garment, or parts of it, is machined up with a large stitch, checked and marked. When necessary, seams can quickly be ripped open and repinned on the fitted lines. Large seam turnings are allowed to make adjustments possible.

Although the blocks from which the dress pattern was developed may have been of excellent fit and construction, there are reasons why it is essential that fitting should be carried out:

a **Fabrics** vary greatly in thickness, structure and weight, and can be silky and clinging or coarse and bulky causing the pattern to require adjustment.

b The **block** may have built-in faults, e.g. shoulders too square, the fault of which would be magnified if a yoke without shoulder seams were to be developed from it.

c The designer may wish to emphasise a certain **fashion feature** which is not sufficiently apparent in the completed sample.

d **Necklines** often require adjustment, particularly low ones.

Generally, for reasons of time, one would aim at having as few fittings as possible in the wholesale sample room.

Fitting for couture and retail dressmaking

A minimum of three fittings is required. Large turnings are allowed when cutting out the garment. Garment sections are tacked together and each fitted in turn on the client. The bodice is fitted first, then the collar is pinned to the neckline and fitted. After this has been done the sleeve is pinned into the armhole and fitted and finally the skirt is attached in the same manner. Alterations are marked, usually with pins to avoid marking the material, and original tailor tacks or trace tacks are replaced by new trace tackings based on the fitting; the garment is then tacked up again and ready for the second fitting. The right side only is normally fitted unless the person, or the style, is not symmetrical. In second, third and possibly subsequent fittings, the question of trimmings and finishing details will be discussed and changes may be agreed upon should a particular design feature be found unsuitable.

Fitting a ready-made garment

The alterations must be minor ones and concerned with taking in seams, raising waist and shoulder lines, shortening hemlines, in fact reducing rather than enlarging the garment, as seam allowances will probably be small and no extra garment material is available. It is wise to consider these points before making the purchase.

The fitting of bodices

Figure 15.1

Allow 2.5 cm (1 in) seam turnings for shoulder and side seams and 1.5 cm (⅝ in) for all other seams. Tack as a lapped seam or machine darts, side and shoulder seams in a large stitch. Place a tacking line down centre front and centre back of bodice unless the design has centre seams or a centre front or centre back opening.

Process of fitting

Figure 15.1 Adjust the tacked or machined bodice on the figure so that the centre front and centre back lines rest on the corresponding centre front and centre back of the figure. Snip neckline, armhole and waist seam turnings. Ensure that the weft grain runs at a right angle to centre front across the bust line. This is the basic and most important factor of fitting. If the grain sags or is pulled out of position, this is a sure sign that all is not well with the fit of the garment.

Figure 15.2 Sloping shoulders: Examine shoulder and bust darts. If the bust darts appear in the correct position, direct your attention to the neck and shoulders. If surplus fabric is present and creases form near the armhole running towards the neck shoulder point, this indicates that the figure has sloping shoulders. Fit only the right side of the bodice. Pin a new shoulder seam which is deeper at the armhole point and tapers off to nothing at the neck point. The armhole at armpit level will probably have to be lowered to alleviate any tightness caused by the lower shoulder line at armhole point. A shoulder pad, or thicker shoulder pad, when in fashion, may rectify this fitting problem.

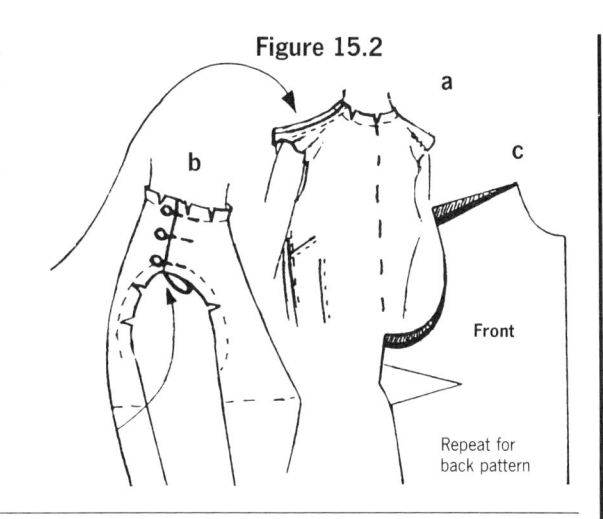

Figure 15.3 Square shoulders: The garment appears tight over the shoulders and loose at the neckline and creases appear at the neck, pulling from shoulder point at the armhole towards the neck in front, and often right across the upper part of the back. Open up part of the shoulder seam from armhole edge, let out some of the seam allowance and pin with a lapped seam tapering off to nothing at the neck point.

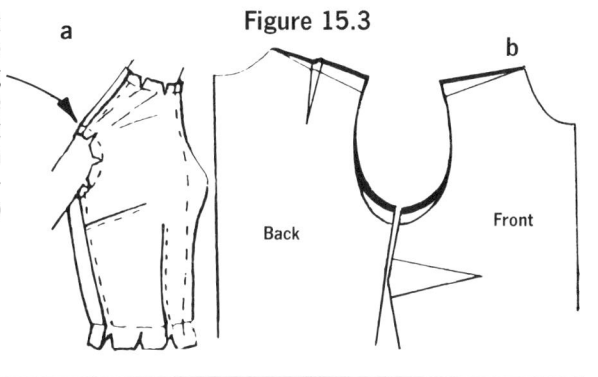

Bust darts

Figure 15.4 Bust darts should run towards the highest part of the bust. If this is not the case, fulness will appear where it is not needed. Open up the seam where the dart is situated and repin the dart in the new position.

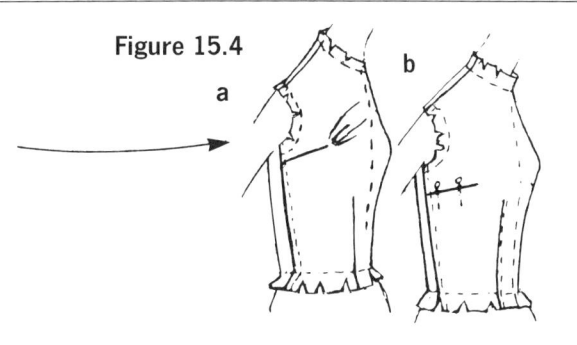

Figure 15.5 Bust dart not deep enough: If the bust is fuller than average, creases will appear across the bust. Increase the depth of the dart at its base and lengthen it a little. This will entail other changes: the affected seam will become shorter and, as in the case of **a** the waistline at the side seam will require reshaping (see arrows). A similar alteration is required for **b**, but this time at the waistline. At **c** the shoulder line is lengthened by the required amount.

Dart too deep for bust formation. The reverse alteration is required. Reduce the depth of the darts and shorten the respective seam turnings in accordance with back bodice seams.

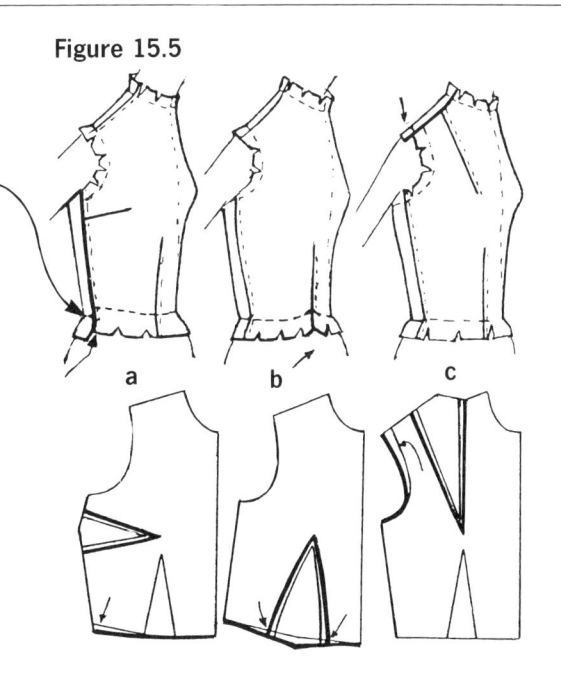

Figure 15.6 Round shoulders and prominent shoulder blades will cause creases from the most rounded part of the back to the side seams. The waistline, and possibly the neckline, will stand away from the figure **a**. Open the shoulder seam and pin in a small shoulder dart or deepen the existing one. Open the side seam and enlarge the waist dart. Let out the side seam at the waist line and repin. Lengthen the back shoulder line and mark the new armhole. A neckline dart is often used, depending on where the prominence is located (**c**).

Figure 15.7 If the bodice is **too tight** or **too loose**, all over or in parts. Simply let out or take in seams or darts where required.

If it is **too short** or **too long** reduce neck, shoulder and waist seam allowances to gain more length or increase these allowances where needed to achieve the opposite (Figure 15.7b).

For **badly placed seams** reposition seams on the right side of the garment and correct the new seam lines through to the left side (**a** and **c**)

All fitting is carried out on the right side of the garment and new fitting lines are corrected through to the left side.

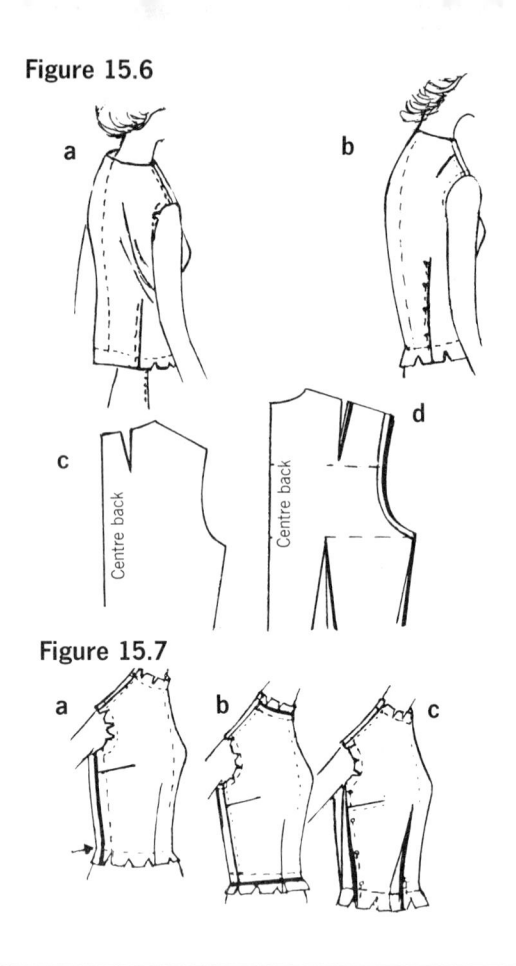

The fitting of sleeves

Figure 15.8a The armhole: When viewed from the side the armhole line should curve over the highest point of the shoulder bone and well under the arm. Viewed from the front the armhole line should appear parallel to the centre front and when seen from the back, parallel to the back. The average armhole circumference of a size 12 dress is 42 cm (16½ in).

b As a further guide, a measurement taken from shoulder point across armhole to underarm point is 14–15 cm (5½–6 in).

c The plain, set-in sleeve should hang straight on the arm with the warp grain running down the centre of the sleeve to elbow level and the weft grain at right angles to it. A small amount of ease is allowed around the outer edge of the sleeve crown at shoulder position but must never form actual gathers unless the design demands this feature. The sleeve should fit smoothly without diagonal or horizontal creases and must be comfortable when moving the arm. The underarm seam should hang in line with the thumb when the arm is held naturally at the side, and the elbow dart should be at elbow level. If the sleeve has a wrist dart, this should run in line with the little finger and should terminate at, or slightly below, the elbow point. The length of a long sleeve is very much a fashion feature and must be fitted accordingly. In general, it should cover the wrist knuckle.

Figure 15.9

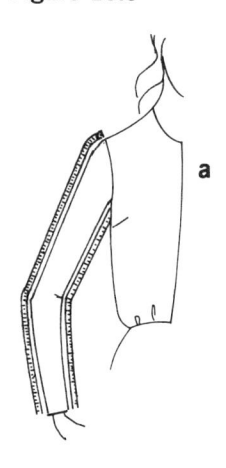

Figure 15.9 Preliminary preparations: Check your pattern and allow 2.5 cm (1 in) turnings for the underarm seams. Tack or machine with a large stitch the underarm seam of the right sleeve, place a gathering stitch around the crown edge of the sleeve and draw up slightly. Pin the sleeve into the previously fitted armhole when fitting.

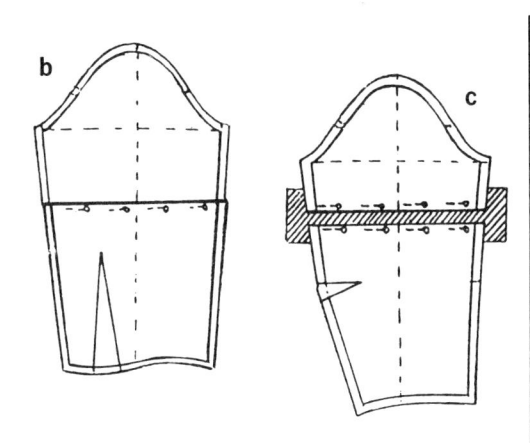

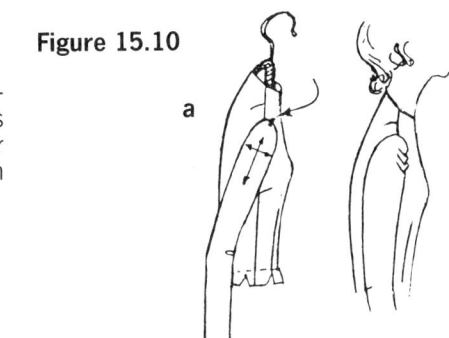

Figure 15.10 The hang of the sleeve: It is possible to see if the sleeve hangs well even before it is tried on the figure. In **a** the sleeve is pitched too far to the back and probably forms wrinkles **b**. Repitch the sleeve (see arrow, **a**).

Figure 15.10

Figure 15.11

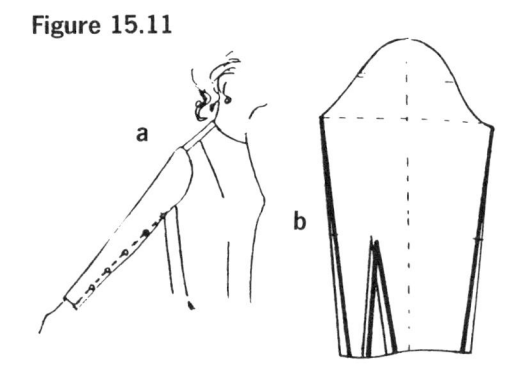

Figure 15.11a Sleeve too wide: Take in the underarm seam from nothing at armhole to the required amount at the wrist allowing sufficient ease for movement.

b The wrist dart may have to be moved slightly forward and made deeper or be converted to form a wrist opening for the hand to pass through easily.

Sleeve too tight: Reverse the alteration.

Figure 15.12 Sleeve too long or too short: Shorten to hem. Lengthen by letting down the hem allowance as far as possible or make a false hem if required. Reposition the elbow dart.

Figure 15.12

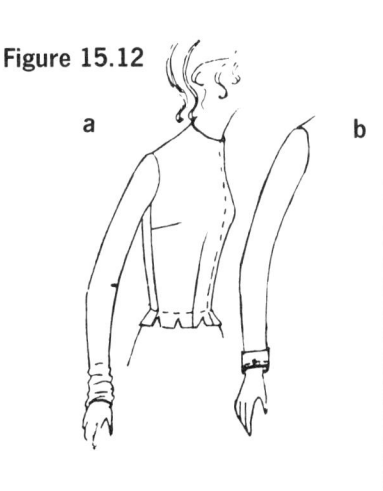

Figure 15.13

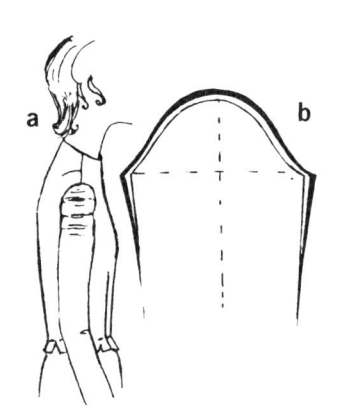

Figure 15.13 Tight horizontal creases across the sleeve crown: The sleeve crown is too narrow. Let out as much as is necessary.

15

The technique of good fitting

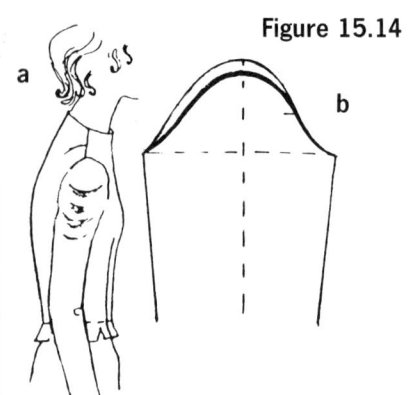

Figure 15.14 Loose folds in the sleeve crown: The sleeve crown is too high. Lower the crown by pinning a deeper seam allowance, particularly at the top shoulder point, until folds disappear.

Figure 15.15 Long diagonal creases pulling from shoulder point: towards front and back armhole. The depth of the sleeve crown is too short. Let out the seam allowance **b**. If wrinkles still persist, lower the armhole at underarm position. This will increase the depth of crown but will shorten the length of the sleeve somewhat (**c**).

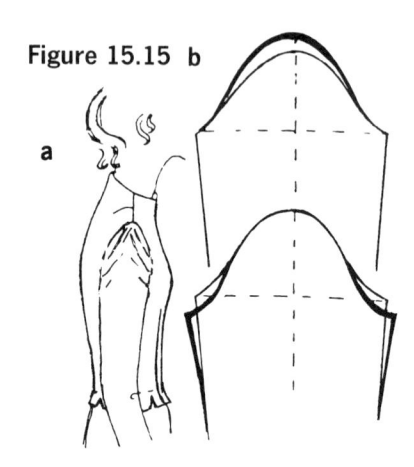

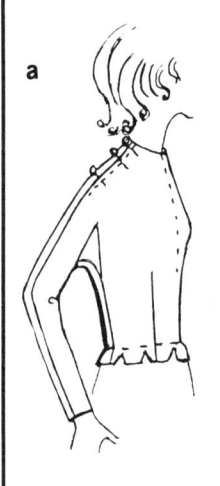

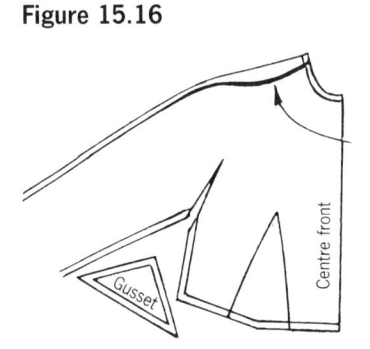

Figure 15.16 Kimono sleeves: These should not be overfitted. Fit closely to the wearer's shoulder contours.

Figure 15.17 Raglan sleeves: These should not be overfitted but sometimes require small alterations, particularly on narrow-shouldered figures. Slightly deepen darts and seams.

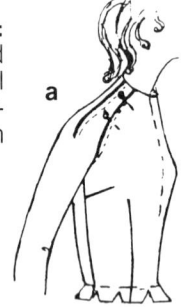

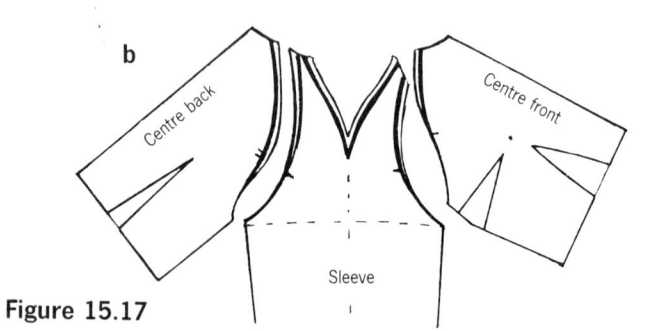

Figure 15.18 Large puff sleeves: These are the easiest sleeves to fit.

Fit right sleeve only, mark and transfer all new lines to the left sleeve.

The fitting of skirts

The fitting of skirts, in common with that of bodices, sleeves and garments in general, is governed by the same factors which must be considered carefully in order to obtain a perfect fit:

- The basic principles of fitting: grain, balance and ease
- The character of the garment
- Personality and age
- Figure types and defects
- Fashion and fabric.

Figure 15.19 Check the measurements of the pattern. Allow 2.5 cm (1 in) turnings on side seams and centre back seam if there is one. Add 6–7 cm (2½–2¾ in) hem allowance. Place a tacking line down centre front and centre back if there is no seam. Tack side seams together as a lapped seam or machine stitch in a large stitch. Leave an opening either in the left side seam or in the centre back seam. Pin a band around the waist on to which the skirt is pinned.

Look at the whole appearance of the skirt and consider the position of CF and CB grain lines, balance and ease as for the bodice.

Figure 15.19

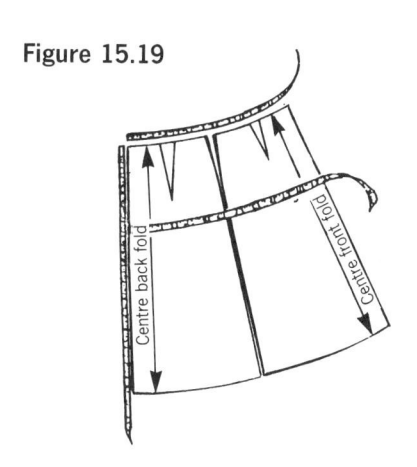

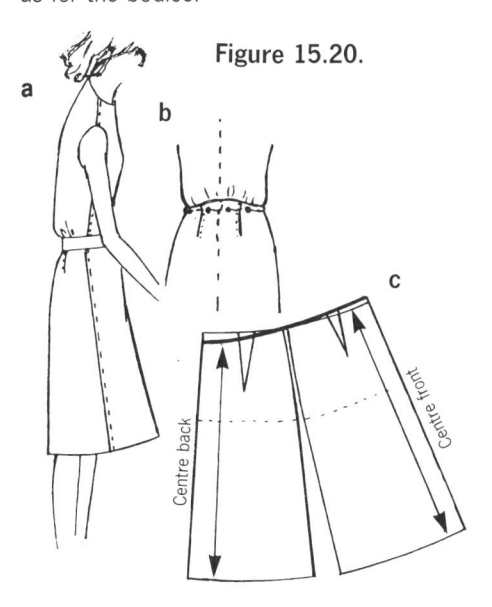

Figure 15.20.

Figure 15.20 Skirt swings forward and side seams hang forward as if pulled up at front waistline. Release some of the front waist seam allowance. Raise part of the back waist seam allowances pinning a horizontal dart across the waistline until a correct balance is achieved. Adjust the fitting of the waistline and darts to the pinned waist band and mark **c**.

Figure 15.21a Skirt swings towards the back: Reverse the alterations. Draw a new waistline as in **b**.

Figure 15.22a Hollow back: The skirt displays surplus folds at the back waistline. Pin as for **15.20b** until the weft grain is raised sufficiently and rests in the correct position on the figure. Lengthen and deepen the back waist darts if required.

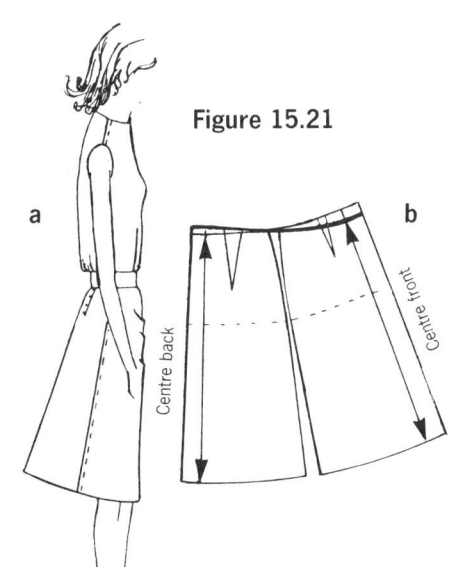

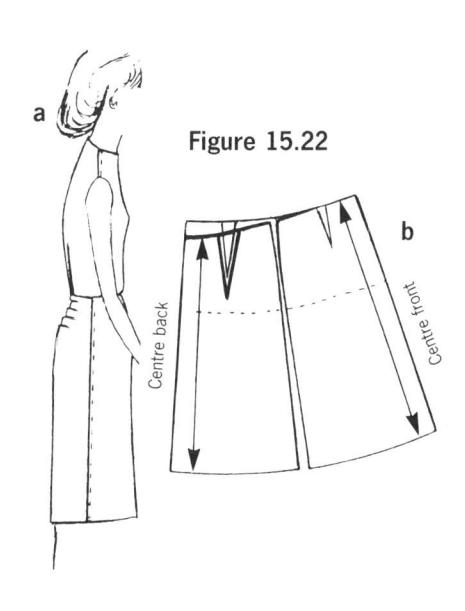

Figure 15.21

Figure 15.22

Figure 15.23 Circular skirts: Unless a definite backward sweep is desired as with certain long evening skirts, the flare in circular skirts is expected to be evenly balanced all around. In **a** the front lies almost flat and too much flare appears at the sides. Raise the centre front of the skirt, and possibly the centre back also, until an even balance is achieved. Pin and recut **b** and **c**.

Figure 15.24 Skirt swings to one side: and the CF tacking line does not rest in the centre of the body. This can be due to a larger hip formation on one side of the body. If this is not the case, the cause can be traced back to careless laying up of the pattern or badly folded or slightly twisted fabric resulting in the skirt having been cut 'off grain'. Experiment by raising that side of the skirt which demands adjustment and bring the straight grain to rest in the CF of the body, which should make the skirt hang evenly balanced all around. Pin to the waist band and mark the new lines. Open the darts and side seams, lay flat and inspect the fabric. If found to be 'off grain', stretch and steam press the fabric until warp and weft threads run at right angles to each other. Recut the skirt as in **b**.

Figure 15.25 Too wide or too tight: If the skirt is too wide, take in the side seams. Sometimes the darts have to be removed to harmonise with the new seams and the darts of the bodice if the garment is a dress.

Figure 15.26 illustrates tight wrinkle across the tummy and hips and a gaping side opening. This indicates that the skirt is too tight in this area. Let out the side seam where it seems tightest, but often, in order to obtain a good silhouette throughout, it is better to let out the whole length of the side seam right down to the hem. Alternatively, or in addition to this alteration, the waistline can be raised (lowered on the pattern) to allow more width at hip level. This will shorten the skirt slightly, but the large hem allowance should compensate for this. Mark all lines and transfer to the pattern.

Too long or too short: The skirt in question and the figure must be carefully considered. Often the simplest alteration is the best and it is sufficient to take up the hem in order to shorten a skirt. At other times, particularly if a degree of tightness across the hips is apparent, it is better to shorten the skirt by raising it from the waist. On other occasions still, when the skirt has a hip yoke for example, it may be advisable to shorten the skirt at that level or shorten the yoke.

In general, in order to lengthen a skirt, one would reverse the above alterations. However, the options available are limited by the hem and seam turnings that were allowed when the skirt was cut out. In this case a false hem may have to be added or the design changed to incorporate a hip yoke to provide extra length.

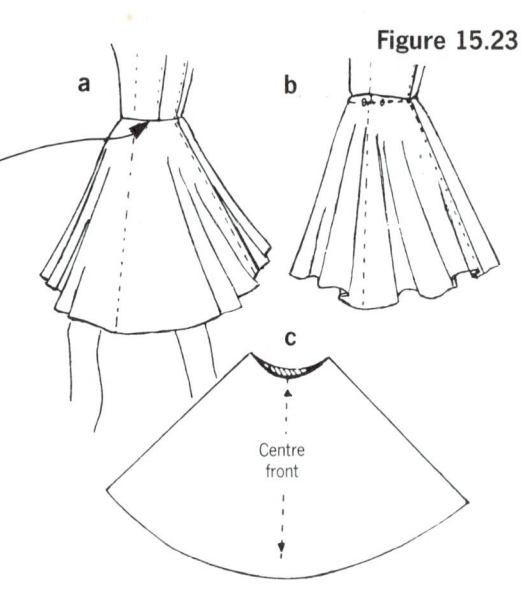

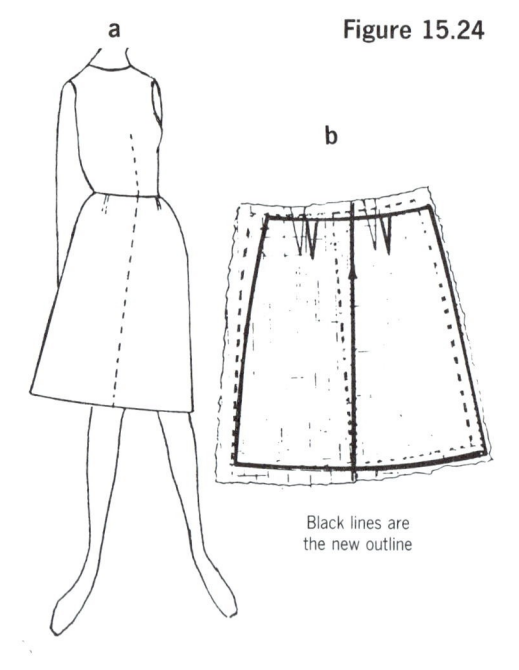

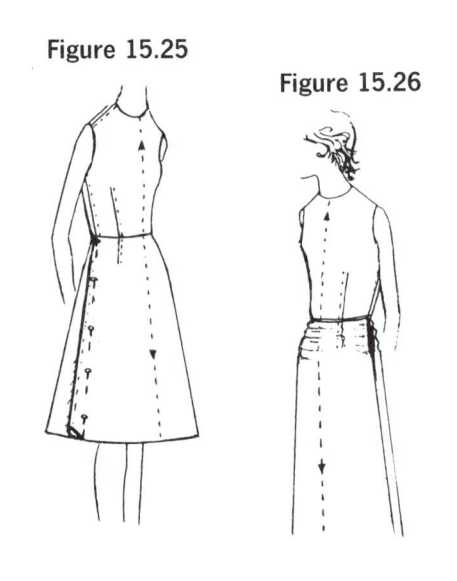

Figure 15.23

Figure 15.24

Black lines are the new outline

Figure 15.25

Figure 15.26

Index

Adaptations, trouser, 155–6
Adding collar stands, 73
A-line dress, 56
Age and personality, 220, 221
Allowances, ease, on all measurement charts and tables, *passim*
    seam, 6, 7
Armhole,
    circumference, 6, 7, 18
    dart, 29
    dress form, 18
    low, 47, 48, 49, 97–8, 199
    modelling, 20, 22, 24, 25
    raised and sleeveless, 64

Balance, 83, 220
    marks, 2, 3, 4, 14, 36, 37, *passim*
Basic blocks,
    drafting, 10–17
    skirts, 12–14
    sleeve, 15
    trouser, 16–17
    waist block, 10–11
Bateau neckline, 60
Bell sleeve, 89
Beachwear, 1 *see also* lingerie
Bermuda pants, stretch, 189
Bertha collar, 67
Bias cut, 1, 82–3
    cami-knickers, 185, 191, 193, 194, 195
    French knickers, 187–8
    sleeve, 86, 147
    slips, 182–4, 193, 195
Bishop sleeve, 87
Blazer jacket, 176–81
Block/foundation patterns, 21, 24, 26, 27, 176
    drafting basic, 10–17
    fifth scale, 2–5
    making of card, 36–7
Bloomers, 160
Blouse, 45, 46, 47
Bodices, 11, 21, 24, *passim*
    boned, 50–2
    fitting of, 222–3
    sleeveless, 64
Body rise, 6, 7, 16, 17, 153
    and crotch level, 160, 166, 170, 186, 189, 191, 202, 203
Boned bodices, 1, 50–2
Border prints, 80
Bra, 196
    brassiere with band, 196
    -slip, 195
    strapless, 196
    -style seaming, 58
    wired, 196
Break,
    line, 69, 75, 76, 77
    point, 69, 75, 76, 77
Bridal wear, 1, 136–50
Briefs, 189
British Standard Institution, measurement tables and charts, *passim*
Bust,
    formation, 52
    guide line, 19, 26
    line, 18, 27, 36, 37 *passim*
    measurements, 6, 7, 11
Buttons, 1,
    button holes, 43, 44
    button stands, 43, 44, 45, 46, 47, 48, 49, 117

Cami-knickers, 1, 185, 191, 193, 194, 195
Camisoles, 185
Cape, 67
    sleeve, 89
Capelet, flared, 67
Card patterns, 36–7
Cascade drapery, 1, 217
Centralising,
    shoulder and side seam, 93–4
    skirt, 94
Character of the garment, 220–1
Charts, size, 6, 7
    and tables, 11, 13, 15, 16, 47, 48 *passim*
Checks, 1, 82
Circle collar, 78
Circular,
    culottes, 174–5
    frill, 78
    godet, 108
    skirts, 120–3
    sleeve flounce, 1, 86
Circumference,
    armhole, 6, 7, 18, 47, 48, 49
    hem, 148, 184, 185
    trouser bottoms, 155, 156
Collars,
    Bertha, 67
    circle, 78
    convertible, 72, 202, 212
    flat, 65, 71, 74, 76
    grown-on, 69, 75, 76, 77
    jabot, 66
    and lapels, 62
    Mandarin, 70
    notched, 76, 77
    Peter Pan, 65, 71
    ring, 73
    and revers, 69, 77, 179
    roll, 68, 73, 167–8, 74 *passim*
    sailor, 66
    stand, 70
    standing wing, 70
    stands adding, 73
    tuxedo, 76
    two-piece notched, 69, 77, 179
    shirt, 49, 72
Couture and retail, fitting for, 222
Corselet, 50
Cowl drapery, 1, 124–35
    back, 131
    Doric chiton, 124
    halter, 131
    high, cum hood, 130
    low, 128
    modelling of, 126–7
    neckline on straight grain, 128, 129
    neckline variations, 131
    with shoulder pleats, 131
    in skirts, 135
    in sleeves, 133–4
    transfer of markings, 127
    underarm, 132
Crinoline underskirt, 150
Cropped T-shirt, 185
Crossed-over style, bodice, 32
Crotch level, *see* body rise
Cuffs, 47, 49
    flared, 86
    simulated, 86, 203
Culottes, 170–5
    circle, 175
    flared, 171–2
    with inverted pleat, 173
    various styles, 172
Curved and horizontal seams, 38, 39, 40, 42, 45, 46, 49, 81, 82
Cutting on the bias, *see* bias-cut

Darts, 20–37, *passim*
    armhole, 29
    in basic blocks, 11, 13, 14, 16, 17
    centre front, 28, 31
    fish, 77
    French, 31
    into gathers, 28, 34, 38, 39, 40, 41, 42, 45, 52, 58, 79
    guide line, 19
    moving of, by pivoting, 33–5
    shoulder, 21, 22, 23, 26, 27
    by slashing, 27–32, *passim*
    neck, 23, 25, 29
    in sleeves, 84, 85, 90, 101
    in skirts, 106–7, 123
    into pleats, 30, 32
Dartless,
    dress, 32
    shirt, 48–9
Defects and figure types, 220–1
Designer and designs, 1
Divided skirt, *see* culottes
Dolman sleeve, 84, 97–8
Double-breasted garment, 44
Drafting, basic blocks, 10–17
Drafts, *passim*
Drain-pipe trousers, 156
Drapery,
    cascade, 1, 217
    cowl, 1, 124–5
Draping versus modelling, vii
Dress, block, 26, 27, 32, 176
    A-line, 56
    no dart, 32
    with Peter Pan collar, 71

line, 54, 55
tions, 56, 57, 58, 59
1, 8
or modelling, 18
or maternity wear,
shoulder shirt, 48–9
Dungarees, 165–6

Edge-to-edge jacket, 176–8
Eight-gored skirt, 112
Empire waist, 57
Epaulet sleeve, 90
Equipment, 8, 9
Extension, button, *see* button stands

Fabric, 1
   bias, 82, 83
   checked or striped, 82
   and fashion, 220–1
   grain of, 28, 31, 82, 220
   knitted, 83
   for modelling, 9
Facings, 43, 44, 45, 180, *passim*
Fashion,
   and fabrics, 220–1
   silhouette, 1, 82, 84
Fifth scale block patterns, 2–5
Figure types and defects, 220–1
Final look, 1
Finished measurements, *see* charts
Fish dart, 77
Fitting,
   basic principles of, 220–1
   of bodices, 222–3
   for couture and retail, 222
   ready-made garments, 222
   of sleeves, 224–6
   of skirts, 227–8
   technique of, 220–7
   in the wholesale sample room, 221
Flared,
   culottes, 171, 172
   skirt, 109, 110
   sleeve, 87, 89
   trousers, 156
Flat collars, 65, 71, 74
   Bertha, 65
   capelet, 67
   jabot, 66
   Peter Pan, 65, 71
Flat pattern cutting, vii, 1, *passim*
   versus modelling, 204
   with modelling, 1
Flounces,
   in sleeves, 86, 145
   in skirts, 110
Fly-front opening, 44
   in trousers, 17, 159
Forms,
   dress, 1, 8, 18
   sleeve, 99
   skirt, 106
   swimwear, 51
   trousers, 151
Foundation patterns, *see* block patterns
French,
   dart, 31
   knickers, 187–8

Frills, 78, 112, 142
Full circle skirt, 122

Garment fabric, modelling in, 79–81
Gathers, from darts, *see* darts
   in skirts, 107, 108, 112, 113, 115–17
   in sleeves, 84, 87–9, 92, 100, 102–4
Godet, 108
Gored skirts,
   with pleat, 114
   eight, 112
   six, 111, 112
   twelve, 113
Grain, 19, *see* fabric, *passim*
   importance in fitting, 220
Grown-on collars, 69, 75, 76, 77
Gussets,
   kimono, 96, 105
   lingerie, 186, 187, 189, 190, 191

Half circle skirt, 120–2
Halter neckline, 64, 131
Head circumference, 130
Hip block/dress foundation, 26, 27, 37, 176
Hipster trunks, 190
Hoods, 62, 63, 130

Imperial size chart, 7
Important block patterns, 37
Industry, 1

Jabot, 78
   collar, 66
Jacket,
   blazer, 179–81
   collar, 179
   edge-to-edge, 176–8
Jeans, 158–9
Jodhpur breeches and trousers, 161–2
Jumpsuit, 163–4

Kimono,
   development, 84, 95–6, 105
   fifth scale blocks, 3
Knickers, French, 187–8

Lace, 146
Lapels, on V-neck, 62
Lay,
   paper, 9
   plan, 184
Leg-of-mutton sleeve, 103–4
Lingerie, 182–204
   brassieres, 196
   briefs, 189
   camisoles, 185
   cami-knickers, 1, 185, 191–5
   cropped T-shirt top, 185
   nightdress, 197–201
   panties, pants and trunks, 186, 189, 190
   pyjamas, 202–3
   slips, 182, 192–3, 194, 195
   teddies, 185
Lowered armhole development, 97–8, 199

Making card blocks, 36–7
Mandarin collar, 70
Marking tools, 9
Maternity wear, 1, 204–19
   dress, 207–9
   dress blocks, 206, 207
   sleeve, 210
   smock, 210–13
   Raglan style smock, 213–15
   skirts, 216–19
   trousers, 219
Measurement charts, *passim*
Metric size chart, 6
Midriff, 80, 81
Mini-slip, 182–4
Modelling, *passim*,
   versus draping, 1
   versus flat cutting, 204
   fabric, 9, 19
   in garment fabric, 79–81
   a synthesis, 11

Necklines,
   bateau, 60
   halter, 64
   raised, 62
   round, 60, 63, 64
   square, 61
   V-, 61, 62
Nightdress, including collar and sleeves, 197–201
No-dart,
   dress, 32
   nightdress, 200
   pyjamas, 202
   shirt, 48
Notched collar, 76, 77, 179

Oxford bags, 152, 155

Pads, shoulder, 84
Panties and pants, 186–90
Patternmaking methods, 1, 204
Peg-top skirt, 123
Pencil trousers, 152
Peter Pan collar, 65, 71
Pivoting of darts, 33–5
   skirts, 110
   sleeves, 85, 87, 88, 89, 98
Pleats, 30, 46
   in skirts, 114, 118–19, 173, 210
Pockets, 17, 59, 117, 159, 162, 165–6, 169, 173, 180
Princess line, 53, 54–8, 80, 81, 142, 146
Puff sleeve, 89
Pyjama, jacket and collar, 202
   size chart, 202
   sleeve, 202
   trousers, 203

Quarter circle skirt, 123

Raglan,
   sleeve, 91
   -style maternity smock, 213–15
   -type sleeve, 92
Raised, armhole, 64
   neckline, 62
Ready-made garments, 222
Retail and couture, fitting, 222

Revers and collar, 69, 77, 179–80
Ring collar, 73
Roll collars, 68, 73, 74
   principles of cutting, 68, 72
Round necklines, 60, 63, 64

Sailor collar, 66
Scale block patterns, fifth, 2–5
Set-in sleeves, 85–92
Shirts, 45–9
   band opening, 44
   sleeves, 47–9, 87, 100
Shoulder,
   centralising of, 93–4
   pads, 84
Silhouette, 1, 82, 84
   fashionable foundation, 50
   trouser, 152
Six-gored skirt, 111, 112
   with pleats, 114, 118–19
Size charts, 6, 7
Skirt blocks, drafting, 12–14
Skirts, 106–23
   button through with pockets in side seam, 117
   circle, 120–3
   fitting of, 227–8
   flared, 109–10
   form, 106
   gathered,
     centre front panel, 117
     side panel, 117
   gathered tiers, 108
   gathered waist, 107
   gathers and yoke, 113
   godet, 108
   gores, 111–13
   peg-top, 123
   with flounce, 110
   with frill, 112
   with pleats, 114, 118–19
   straight, 106–7, 123
   wrap-over, 118–19
Ski-suit, 166–9
Sleeve block, drafting, 15
Sleeves, 84–105
   bell, 89
   bias-cut, 86, 147
   cape, 89
   cowl, 133–4
   cuffs, flared, 86
   dolman, 84, 96, 97–8
   drop shoulder, 49, 92
   elbow fullness, 102
   epaulet, 90
   fitting of, 224–6
   flounce, 86
   frill, 142
   gathered crown, 88
   kimono, 95–6, 105
   leg-of-mutton, 103–4
   padded form, 99
   pleated, 210
   puff, 89
   Raglan, 91
   raglan-type, 92
   simulated, 86
   shirt, 47, 49, 87, 100, 199, 213
   with darts or pleats, 90
   with wrist dart, 85
Sleeveless bodice, 64

Slips,
   basic, 192
   bra-top, 195
   mini, 182–4
   princess line, 194
Smocks, maternity, 210–12, 213–15
Stand collars, 70
Strapless bodice, 50–2
Stretch properties and bias cutting, 82–3
Stripes, 1, 82
Sunray pleats, 122
Swimwear forms, 51

Tiered underskirt, 108
Top collar, 69, 71, 75–7, 179
Track drafting, 208–9
Trains, *see* wedding dresses
Transfer of markings, 1, 81
Trousers, 1, 151–69
   block, drafting, 16–17
   bloomers, 160
   development from skirt, 152–5
   dungarees, 165–6
   fifth scale blocks, 2
   fitting of, 157–8
   flared, 156
   jodhpurs, 161–2
   jeans, 158
   jumpsuit, 163
   maternity, 219
   measurements and tables, 6, 7, *passim*
   Oxford bags, 155, 157
   pyjama, 203
   silhouettes, 152
   ski-suit, 166–9
   standard width, 16, 155
   tapered, 156
   tracksuit, 160
Trouser form, 151
Tuxedo collar, 76
Trunks, 189–90
Twelve-gored skirt, 113
Two-piece,
   collar and revers, 69, 77, 179–80
   shirt collar, 49, 72
   sleeve, 181

Underarm cowl, 132
Under collar, 69, 71, 77, 179
Underskirts,
   wedding dress, 148, 149, 150

V-shaped necklines, 61, 62
Veil, 150
Victorian dress form, 1

Waistband, 111
Waist,
   blocks, 10–11, 19–25
   darts, 11, 21–5, *passim*
Warp, 19
   and lengthwise grain, 82
Wedding dresses, 1, 136–150
   bias stand collar, 145
   bias sleeve, 147
   close-fitting bodice, 146
   fabrics, 136
   history, 136
   joining lace, 146

   paintings, 136
   princess line, 142–4
   roll collar, 141
   sleeve,
     bias, 147
     with flounce, 145
     with frill, 142
   trains, 137, 138, 141
     in one with hem, 148
   underskirts, 148, 149, 150
   veil, 150
   Victorian and Edwardian, 137
   C. Willet Cunnington, 137
Weft, 19,
   crosswise grain, 82
Wholesale sample room, fitting for, 221
Wrap, 44
Wrap-over skirt, 118–19

Yokes, 42, 45, 46, 49
   in skirts, 113, 116, *passim*
   partial, 40, 41